THE GREEKS
AND
GREEK CIVILIZATION

Burckhardt's lecture notes: the start of his discussion of the *polis*
(cf. *Griechische Kulturgeschichte* (Darmstadt 1962) vol. I, p. 53, p. 37 in this translation).

THE GREEKS
AND
GREEK CIVILIZATION

JACOB BURCKHARDT

Translated by
SHEILA STERN

Edited, with an Introduction by
OSWYN MURRAY

St. Martin's Press ✠ New York

ISBN 0-312-19276-2

First published in Great Britain by HarperCollins*Publishers*

First U.S. Edition: October 1998

10 9 8 7 6 5 4 3 2 1

IN MEMORY OF

MOSES FINLEY (1912–1986)

J. P. STERN (1920–1991)

CONTENTS

PREFACE

In 1965 I published my first review; it was of an ignorant and badly chosen translation of selections from Jacob Burckhardt's lectures on Greek culture. Moses Finley wrote to congratulate me, and to reveal that he and Sheila Stern were preparing a quite different selection for publication. It was indeed Burckhardt who inaugurated for me twenty years of friendship with one of the three great historians of that age who dominated studies of the ancient world in the English language – Finley the American, Syme the New Zealander and Momigliano the Italian.

When Moses died in 1986, the half-completed translation had languished for many years. No trace of his own work on the project was found in his papers. But in 1989 I was delighted to receive a letter from Sheila Stern revealing that she had recently discovered her manuscript of the early sections, which she was retyping and wished to continue: would I be interested in reviving the long-delayed project, and taking over the task of editing the volume? Since I had just been rereading Burckhardt in the course of using his conception of the development of 'Greek man', I replied that nothing would give me greater pleasure than to help edit a version of that masterpiece. We revised and improved the selection that Moses had made, and began work on the translation in earnest. So it is that finally, on the centenary of Burckhardt's death, and also a hundred years after the first publication of his lectures (1898–1902), we present Burckhardt's ideas on Greek cultural history to readers of English. In this translation we have collaborated closely; but I am primarily responsible for the selection of material and for the introduction, while Sheila Stern is primarily responsible for the translation.

We would like to thank our publishers Stuart Proffitt and Toby Mundy for the enthusiasm with which they have welcomed and encouraged the project. We would also like to thank David McLintock for helping to revise the translation, and Anna Brown, John Sugden and Gideon Nisbet for their editorial work on the text and footnotes. We are also very grateful to Stephen Ryan for preparing the Index.

We dedicate our work to the memory of the two scholars who were in different ways closely connected with the preparation of this translation in its earlier days.

OSWYN MURRAY
8 August 1997

INTRODUCTION

OSWYN MURRAY

THE LIFETIME OF JACOB BURCKHARDT (1818–97) spans the great age of nineteenth-century historical writing. As a young man he had been taught in Berlin by the generation of scholars who rebelled against the Hegelian conception of history to create historical positivism; his teachers were the Greek historians August Boeckh and J. G. Droysen, and the great founder of modern historical studies and archival research, Leopold von Ranke (whose chair in Berlin he was subsequently offered in 1872). He was a contemporary of Charles Darwin, Karl Marx and Theodor Mommsen; he belonged (though as a Swiss in a characteristically oblique way) to the revolutionary 'generation of 1848', and the great watershed of nineteenth-century Europe. Among philosophers he admired most Schopenhauer, and was a friend and colleague of the young Nietzsche; other colleagues in Basle whom he admired included the anthropologist J. J. Bachofen,[1] the philologist Otto Ribbeck, his pupil and successor the art historian Heinrich Wölfflin, and the philosophical historian Wilhelm Dilthey. He was (as we shall see) less happy with the scholars of a younger generation like Wilamowitz, who tried to create a science of philology and elevate it above the history of the human spirit: it is symptomatic that Wilamowitz's first work was a violent attack on Nietzsche's 'philology of the future' (1872), which was defended by the young Rohde equally intemperately; while at the height of his powers after Burckhardt's death Wilamowitz could damn the present book with the magisterial comment mentioned below (p. xxxiv). Yet it is the *Greek Cultural History* which now appears to be the foundation of modern approaches to the Greek world; the mature Wilamowitz misunderstood Burckhardt just as the young Wilamowitz had misunderstood Nietzsche's *Birth of Tragedy*.

Life

Burckhardt was born in 1818 into a family which was a minor branch of one of the great burgher clans of Basle: the name of Burckhardt had been prominent in the city since the fifteenth century.[2] His father was a Protestant minister who had been much influenced by Schleiermacher's theology. Basle was a patrician city, conservative and increasingly prosperous, at the same time as being detached from the turbulence of European political events; Burckhardt belonged to its intelligentsia. He completed a degree in theology at Basle, but ceased to be religious, having become convinced by his youthful studies that the life of Christ was a myth. In 1839 he went to Berlin to study history under Ranke, Boeckh and Droysen; but his closest friend and greatest influence was Franz Kugler, the bohemian professor in the new subject of art history. In another friend, Gottfried Kinkel, he found one of the last of the great Romantics; he moved into the circle of Kinkel's mistress, the divorced Johanna Matthieux, and of Bettina von Arnim, who had once loved Goethe and who lived in Berlin with her sister, the widow of the great legal historian F. C. von Savigny. Burckhardt was Kinkel's best man at his wedding with Johanna in 1844; but he distanced himself from him during Kinkel's subsequent career as a revolutionary. Kinkel was condemned to death in 1848, and escaped with his wife's help to exile in London, where Johanna finally committed suicide.

Burckhardt was safely back in Basle in 1844, where he served for eighteen months as editor of the main conservative newspaper, the *Basler Zeitung*. He was already lecturing at the university on the history of painting, where he caused offence in religious circles by criticizing the dominant Nazarene School, a group of German religious painters in Rome who served as a model for the later pre-Raphaelites. In 1852 he resigned from the university and left for Italy, where he wrote the immensely popular *Cicerone* (1854), 'a guide to the enjoyment of art in Italy', which remained the standard guidebook to Renaissance Italian architecture, sculpture and art for three generations and went through seven editions during his lifetime. On the basis of this he was given a post at the Zürich Polytechnic. In 1858 he was appointed Professor of History at Basle, where he was required to lecture both at the university and at the high school; from 1874 he was also Professor of the History of Art. The first post he held until 1885, and the second until

1893. He was a conscientious and assiduous lecturer in both history and history of art, who taught as much as ten hours weekly, and also gave many lectures for the general public.

Burckhardt never married (although as a young man he was in love and wrote poetry to a girl whose parents disapproved); his youthful German friends drifted away, and in his thirties he confessed to being lonely beyond all expectations. He had a few close friends with whom he corresponded, and lived a regular and uneventful life in two rooms above a baker's shop, devoting himself to his lectures, his books and his travels.

Politically Burckhardt was a natural conservative, who disliked and despised the new industrialization and the development of the national state: he foresaw in the course of his own lifetime the coming of an age of 'terribles simplificateurs' and demagogues, who would control the masses and bring ruin to Europe. This pessimistic conservatism is characteristic of a reflective historian, who cultivated irony and distance from the enthusiasms of contemporary nationalist historians. In so far as he foresaw the development of industrial society towards the totalitarian popular regimes of National Socialism and Marxism, he was of course a prophet out of his time, standing against the tide of history. But he was not a political thinker; and these prejudices, however clear-sighted, are merely the regrets of a marginal observer over the decline of the patrician order to which his own family so clearly belonged. Hence his attack on the vice of reading newspapers and concerning oneself with the agitations of the present in the introduction to the present book.[3] It is not Burckhardt's political views or his pessimism in regard to the future which matter, but his conception of historical method; as he wrote already in 1846:

> But, my dear friend, Freedom and the State have lost nothing in me. States are not built with men like me; though as long as I live I mean to be kind and sympathetic to my neighbour; I mean to be a good private individual, an affectionate friend, a good spirit; I have some talent in that direction and mean to develop it. I can do nothing more with society as a whole; my attitude towards it is willy-nilly ironical; the details are my affair . . . we may all perish, but at least I want to discover the interest for which I am to perish, namely the ancient culture of Europe.[4]

So he developed the mask of a dilettante, immersed in his work and his few friends, and devoted to the study of European culture, by which he meant the artistic, literary and spiritual achievements of the past, placed in their context and explained as the result of the forces of history. History was the contemplation of the past: 'leisure, the mother of contemplation and of the inspiration that springs from it' (writing from London); 'Listen to the secret of things. The contemplative mood.' 'How is the collector of inscriptions to find time for contemplative work? Why, they don't even know their Thucydides! Don't bother about others.'[5]

Early Works

In the 1840s, while still a student, Burckhardt rebelled against the prevailing conception of history, 'the one-sidedness of the present that only wants to have a biassed history (*Tendenz-Geschichte*), just as it has a biassed poetry and a biassed art'.[6] 'For me the background is the chief consideration, and that is provided by cultural history, to which I intend to dedicate myself,' Burckhardt wrote in 1842.[7] From the start his conception of history was concerned, not with actions and events or the great men who appeared to have caused them, but with the cultural context in which such events occurred, a context which might explain the changes far more satisfactorily than by ascribing them to the actions of individuals or the workings of chance. How had Constantine converted the Roman Empire to Christianity, and what did that mean to contemporaries? This was the subject of his first book, *The Age of Constantine* (1852); it was translated into English a century later (1949),[8] and had an enormous effect on my generation of historians, who were in the process of discovering, for the first time in the Anglo-Saxon world since Gibbon, the inexhaustible fascination of late antiquity; for he taught us how to see the age as a cultural phenomenon, rather than in terms of its politics and power structures, or its governmental organization, as more recent historians had interpreted it.

In this book the arrangement is already around three thematic centres – politics, religion and culture. Politics in this period is a necessary evil, a defence against barbarian invasion and internal anarchy. Culture is in decline: literature is reduced to dependence on power (in panegyric) or religion; art is an adjunct of religion: 'the relevant myths were represented as symbolic husks of general ideas, and the separation between kernel and shell could in the long run only be injurious to art'.[9] Philosophy is a solitary pursuit, even if as Themistius said, 'the value of a philosopher's discourse is not diminished if it is delivered under a solitary plane tree with none but cicadas to hear'.[10] The Christian Church was already a powerful corporation. In this picture Constantine is simply a man of his age, almost irrelevant to the revolution in consciousness which he brought about; he belongs firmly in a world of mixed pagan and Christian beliefs, and his conversion simply ratified a formal division of equality between two cultures which already existed. The core of the argument lay in Burckhardt's portrayal of the dominance of religious modes of thought. Late antique paganism was an immensely complex set of rituals and beliefs trying to make sense of the spiritual world:

> Christianity was bound to conquer in the end because it provided answers which were incomparably simpler, and which were articulated in an impressive and convincing whole, to all the questions for which that period of ferment was so deeply concerned to find solutions.[11]

Burckhardt's most famous book, on which his reputation still rests, was *The Civilization of the Renaissance in Italy* (1860). Lord Acton, the founder of modern historical studies in Cambridge, described it as 'the most penetrating and subtle treatise on the history of civilization that exists in literature'.[12] It is indeed this book which still shapes and challenges all subsequent attempts to explain the central phenomenon in European history. Burckhardt set out to present an analysis of the new forces at work in the period, and how they interrelate. The first part treats of politics and warfare under the provocative heading, 'The State as a Work of Art'. That is to say, political life was no longer determined by traditional forms of government or by underlying forces revealed by the modern historian, but by the conscious knowledge of protagonists that there existed a science or art of government, which could be discovered either by experiment or by reflection. The catalogue of murder, treachery and tyranny which ensues shows the consequences of believing in the power of reason rather than tradition: it is a view of the history of events which places the new political science of Machiavelli at its centre; yet whatever its consequences in terms of anarchy and suffering, Burckhardt showed how politics had never before or since been conducted at such a high intellectual level by leaders with such practical and theoretical talents.

The second part describes 'The Development of the Individual'. This was a constant preoccupation of nineteenth-century post-Hegelian thought: how had the modern idea of the individual arisen from the tribal and religious stages of history? Burckhardt does not explain: he simply describes the forces which separated individuals from their communities, the creation of the ideal of 'the universal man' and the modern conception of fame, together with its antithesis, the modern idea of wit and satire:

> Man was conscious of himself only as a member of a race, people, party, family or corporation – only through some general category. In Italy this veil first melted into air; an *objective* treatment and consideration of the state and of all the things of this world became possible. The *subjective* side at the same time asserted itself with corresponding emphasis; man became a spiritual *individual,* and recognized himself as such.[13]

So Burckhardt establishes that 'it was not the revival of antiquity alone, but its union with the genius of the Italian people, which achieved the conquest of the western world'.[14] His third section concerns 'The Revival of Antiquity' and the education of this new man through contact with ancient literature and culture. The discovery of the New World is treated in a section which relates it to the inner exploration of the psyche, to the development of poetry and biography, and to descriptions of the external world, in 'The Discovery of the World and of Man'.

Under 'Society and Festivals', Burckhardt treats of how men and women actually lived in this new world, the principles of courtesy, good manners and outward refinement, styles of language and conversation, lovemaking, physical exercise and music, the equality of men and women within a masculine ideal of the courtier, and the development of a style of official popular festival, which was modelled on conceptions of ancient triumphs and bacchanals. Finally 'Morality and Religion' seeks to relate this new age to the medieval religious forces which it never wholly superseded, so that the last chapter concerns the mixture of ancient and modern superstition which led towards the inevitable disintegration of belief.

It is this work which marks the definitive establishment of a new form of history, which has come to be known in German as *Kulturgeschichte*, 'cultural history'.[15] Each theme is seen from an entirely new viewpoint, which is on the one hand descriptive and concerned with the details, and on the other corresponds to an underlying view of the basic elements which through their interrelation make up the idea of a culture. In this book Burckhardt was able to discard the determinism inherent in the philosophical problem of the meaning of history for the development of the human spirit, as Hegel had formulated it, while using contemporary philosophical concepts (such as the State, religion and the individual) to structure his description of reality. At the same time he avoided the trap of historical positivism, which consists in believing that the meaning of history is contained in a chain of cause and effect, and in the certification of the truth or falsehood of alleged events or facts. For Burckhardt the explanation of events lies not in their causes but in the interrelations between them, of which the idea of cause is only a partial and pseudo-scientific two-dimensional reflection. Societies are not linear series of events, but highly complex and interconnected systems, where a change in any element may provoke multiple effects elsewhere. Moreover what people believe and how they behave are far more important than whether their beliefs are true or useful: it is not the event which matters, but the perception of that event as a 'fact', which is neither true nor false, but simply believed.

It is a valid criticism of Burckhardt's view of culture that he concerned himself essentially with high culture, with the expression of values contained in the activities and beliefs of an educated elite. His concept of cultural history is therefore fundamentally different from that prevalent in modern universities, where 'cultural studies' means the investigation of popular culture and especially minority cultures. Even so the appropriation of the nineteenth-century term by this new modern discipline points to the fact that the tradition begun by Burckhardt opened the way to the study of gestures, customs and behaviour patterns, festivals and other forms of popular expression. Even if Burckhardt might not have relished it, he is in a sense also the father of this discipline, derived from a multicultural and egalitarian conception of society. But it is important to realize that the techniques, concepts and archival materials necessary to make this leap into the future were not available in Burckhardt's day; and that the great strength of his own reliance on the elite culture is that it was this culture which was self-conscious and fully realized, recorded in the literature and art of the period.

At one time the *Constantine* and the *Renaissance* had been intended to be the beginning and end of a great study of the development of European culture from antiquity to the start of the modern age.[16] But *The Civilization of the Renaissance* was the last book published by Burckhardt during his lifetime. Burckhardt came to believe that teaching was far more important: 'in my experience learned authorship is one of the most unhealthy, and mere teaching (however troublesome it may be and however detailed the studies and preparations need to be) one of the healthiest activities in the world'.[17] Behind this ironic withdrawal from the duty to publish, and his refusal to accept that teaching and writing are part of a continuous process of communicating ideas, lay a deeper distaste for the activities of his academic contemporaries, with their unreadable multiple volumes, their obsession with detail and facts, and the pompous arrogance of 'the *viri eruditissimi* in their professorial chairs' whom he refused to join in 1872, when he turned down the offer of Ranke's chair in Berlin. Heinrich von Sybel proclaimed the programme for the first number of the new historical journal *Historische Zeitschrift* in 1859: it was to be devoted to the true method of historical research, which was to be combined with a special place for modern history rather than older history and German history rather than the history of other peoples.[18] Increasingly Burckhardt could accept neither the political purpose nor the conceptual method of this new history. He no longer believed in the way positivist historicism was going, and could not bring himself to betray his vision of history as contemplation. The lecture hall in Basle was the one place where it was still possible for a professor to meditate on history rather than making political propaganda or writing boring books designed to kill the interest in his subject. As he said in conversation with his successor Heinrich Wölfflin:

> A teacher cannot hope to give much. But in the first place he can keep alive belief in the value of spiritual things. And secondly he can awaken the conviction that there is real happiness to be found in such things.[19]

Lectures on the Study of History

The notion of a philosophy of history expresses the reasonable idea that history has a meaning, and is not just a contingent set of random events without connection or explanation. Traditionally that meaning has been sought in the belief that the narration of history itself will reveal a general pattern or purpose in human events, rather than in the attempt to formulate explicitly general laws of history. After the decline of a Christian view of history as the realization of God's purpose in the human sphere, the eighteenth century developed the optimistic idea that history was the expression of progress, whether that progress might be seen as the will of God or as the gradual triumph of human reason. This 'Whig interpretation of history'[20] remains an unexplored assumption on the part of many historians, but was in part replaced by another more pessimistic and scientific conception of history, which became dominant in the nineteenth century – the Darwinian idea of historical progress as the survival of the fittest. In such a view we may commiserate with the victims of history, but must still recognize that history reflects a form of social evolution. Such are the comfortable if unspoken assumptions of an Anglo-Saxon world chiefly concerned with empirical and antiquarian investigations.

In his famous 'Lectures on the Philosophy of World History', delivered in Berlin on five occasions between 1822 and 1831, Hegel had formulated a theory of history as a universal process involving the gradual realization of the idea of spirit through a succession of phases of world history.[21] The dialectic of the spirit of nations had resulted in a gradual unfolding of the human spirit until (as Nietzsche wickedly put it) 'for Hegel the apex and culmination of the world process coincided with his own existence in Berlin'.[22]

The history of the world has also a geographical orientation, for it travels from East to West, in conformity with the course of the sun of self-consciousness. The East knows that *One* is free, the Greek and Roman world that *Some* are free, while the German world knows that *All* are free. History is therefore essentially the history of the development of the freedom of the human spirit. As a theory this corresponds to that held by many self-styled liberal historians today, especially in the United States, even if it is no longer expressed in such metaphysical terms. It is clearly intrinsically attractive; the problem lay in its detailed working out as historical narrative by Hegel. His lectures traced the course of human affairs from the ancient Near East through antiquity and the Middle Ages to the Reformation and the present day. Hegel was not a professional historian, and his exposition was both schematic and subordinated to the needs of his theory.

As the creators of the new historical science the founders of the German historical tradition possessed a self-conscious perception of its role, and a transcendental conception of the meaning of 'world history'. The figure of Hegel dominated the philosophy of history throughout the first half of the nineteenth century; it lies at the basis of Marxism, which finally replaced it as the most successful philosophical explanation of the meaning of historical events. Even for those historians who tried to see history as an empirical investigation in which general theories must be determined by the shape of the factual evidence, the belief that history had a spiritual meaning retained a continuing fascination.

At the other extreme the compilation of antiquarian handbooks of information without any theoretical interest was already well established as a typically German academic activity by the late eighteenth century. The early nineteenth century was also a period in which the critical study of history emerged as an academic discipline in Germany, and in which the systematic exploration of the past was developed.[23] Three schools of thought within this new empirical discipline can be discerned. The first was the realization that all historical narrative was built out of a succession of earlier accounts showing biases and preconceptions which needed to be discounted, before it was possible to arrive at a narration of the 'true facts'; this approach was primarily associated with the work of the classical historian B. G. Niebuhr (1776–1831), whose study of early Rome had a profound effect on European culture, and especially England.[24] This approach continued to be important throughout the nineteenth century; it resulted in an obsession with 'source criticism', the unfolding of the successive layers of distortion that enabled us to return to the original 'facts'. Inherent in this attitude was the assumption that all history (including that of the present day) was inherently liable to distortion through (especially political) bias; it therefore included in its claim to be interested in the truth and the methods of establishing the truth a contradictory admission that the activity of historians was affected by contemporary politics.

The second area of scientific history might seem at first sight more neutral. The discovery of the importance of archives and documentary evidence associated with the name of Leopold von Ranke (1795–1886) laid claim to producing an account of history 'as it really was'. Much of the organization of nineteenth-century historical scholarship was oriented around the collection and publication of archives in an apparently value-neutral way – private papers, official documents and reports, inscriptions, charters, medieval texts, coins, historical dictionaries of European languages. But this activity, though it could correct the bias of memoirs and past historians, was not in fact free of all bias; it failed to recognize, first that the choice of materials to collect was subject to the bias of the historical researcher, and secondly that the archives themselves had been created for a purpose, usually determined by earlier governments: they gave an official view of history, but not necessarily a true view. Nevertheless the school of Ranke established a permanent link between archival research and the writing of history.

The final important area of empirical research was the study of legal history. Lawyers had their archives ready made, and the legal approach is a powerful combination of the historical with the philosophical. The study of the historical origins of Germanic law in Roman law and ancient customs was closely connected with the attempt to create a new legal system based on historical principles, in opposition to the theoretical principles of the Napoleonic Code. The many political reforms of continental states were based on a conception of constitutional law and its relation to politics which made constitutional history one of the most important branches of historical research. From the great founders of German legal studies, K. F. Eichhorn and Savigny, to Theodor Mommsen's studies of Roman public and private law at the end of the nineteenth century, the importance of law as 'the expression of the life of the people' was recognized. But it is obvious that such approaches to history are bound up with the process of self-definition of the nation-state, and provide another example of the close relationship between historical research and contemporary political concerns.

The apparently empirical and positivist historical research proclaimed by the opponents of Hegel was therefore deeply affected by a conceptual framework which enabled historical studies to appear as the basis for the understanding of modern societies: history in the nineteenth-century age of historicism played the same role as sociology and anthropology today. It was therefore inconceivable that history should lack a meaning; in the age of historicism history provides the explanation, but history itself is in need of an explanation. Thus Hegel could be and was combined with the new 'science' of history, and this combination explains the dominance of historical studies in Germany in the age of historicism; for history replaced philosophy as the fundamental science of human nature and the explanation of all human society. The objections from historians to the Hegelian view of history were not therefore on philosophical grounds, but on grounds of the facts and the methods of their discipline. It was not until Nietzsche that the premises of historicism were fundamentally challenged; and Nietzsche's attack was itself inspired, or perhaps rather provoked, by the lectures of Jacob Burckhardt.

Three times between 1868 and 1873 Burckhardt gave a course of lectures 'On the Study of History'. The notes for these lectures (which Nietzsche heard in 1870) were edited as a literary text and published in 1905 by Burckhardt's nephew, Jacob Oeri. More recently, in 1982, my friend Peter Ganz published a scholarly edition of the original drafts, from which it is clear how carefully Oeri worked to create a composite original, incorporating Burckhardt's ideas into the creation of a single written text on the basis of the spoken versions. But Oeri made one significant change in the title: he called the work *Weltgeschichtliche Betrachtungen*; and this grand reference to 'World History' with its deep Hegelian connotations has distorted discussion of the text ever since (the English translation is called *Reflections on History*, which though strictly inaccurate reflects better the title that Burckhardt himself gave the lectures).[25]

Burckhardt as a young man knew of the Hegelian view of history,[26] but he arrived in Berlin at the time of the first historical reaction against the philosophy of history. He always claimed to be lacking in all philosophical interest, and it does indeed seem that he had never made a deep study of Hegel; as Ganz has shown, he did not possess a copy of Hegel's *Lectures on History*, and did not even borrow one from the university library until a mere three weeks before his first set of lectures on the subject in 1868;[27] even then his references in his notes suggest that he never got beyond the first hundred pages. In his own lectures Burckhardt insists correctly that he is not concerned with any Hegelian philosophy of history:

> The philosophy of history is a centaur, a contradiction in terms, for history coordinates, and hence is unphilosophical, while philosophy subordinates, and hence is unhistorical.[28]

His interest is different and his method less systematic:

> All the same, we are deeply indebted to the centaur, and it is a pleasure to come across him now and then on the fringe of the forest of historical study. Whatever his principles may have been, he has hewn vast vistas through the forest and lent spice to history . . .
>
> For that matter, every method is open to criticism, and none is universally valid. Every individual approaches this huge theme

of contemplation in his own way, which may be his spiritual way through life: he may then shape his method as that way leads him.[29]

Burckhardt's approach to the theory of history is clearly based on his earlier studies of Constantine and the Renaissance. It proposes three great 'powers' in historical human societies, which are not laws of history so much as principles around which the historian may group his attempts at historical explanation. These are the State, Religion and Culture. Each is essentially independent of the others; the first two, 'the expressions of political and metaphysical need, may claim authority over their particular peoples at any rate, and indeed over the world'. They are therefore constants. But culture is 'something essentially different':

> Culture is the sum of all that has *spontaneously* arisen for the advancement of material life and as an expression of spiritual and moral life – all social intercourse, technologies, arts, literatures and sciences. It is the realm of the variable, free, not necessarily universal, of all that cannot lay claim to compulsive authority.[30]

The formation of historical societies is a process of interaction between these three powers. Thus history cannot be reduced to a single explanation such as the political, but results from the complex interplay of competing powers. We might today perhaps quarrel with Burckhardt's choice of powers: for instance a modern theory would presumably wish to include 'the Economy'. But there is no doubt that Burckhardt's theory of history is, with Marxism, one of the two most important modern attempts to understand the historical process.

The theory owes nothing to Hegel; the first formulation of the idea of the three powers is found in Kierkegaard's notes of lectures on the method of academic study given by F. W. J. Schelling in Berlin in 1841, which Burckhardt may have attended.[31] But if the origin of the idea lies in his student years in Berlin, its detailed elaboration is original, and based on his own appreciation of the problems of writing cultural history, which takes as its focus the interplay between different spheres of human activity. For that reason the most important part of the working out of the theory is not the discussion of the individual powers in the first part of the lecture course, but the sections where he discusses the six types of reciprocal action between the three powers – culture determined by the state and religion, the state determined by religion and culture, and religion determined by the state and culture.

The weakness of such a theory of history is the weakness of all attempts to study history synchronically, rather than diachronically: if society is viewed as a unity composed of interdependent forces, this makes it difficult to understand the idea of change which is the focus of the traditional history of events, based on cause and effect and arranged as a chronological progression. Burckhardt addressed this problem in his final lectures. The first of these dealt with 'the crises of history' – that is to say change was viewed in terms of catastrophe or revolution, rather than development. The second group of lectures was entitled 'Individuals and the Community' or (on one occasion) 'the Great Men of History': here Burckhardt seems to suggest that the power of the individual great man can break through the static forces which hold cultures together: 'for great men are necessary to our life in order that the movement of history may periodically wrest itself free from antiquated forms of life and empty argument'.[32] It is of course these lectures which particularly attracted Nietzsche. From these attempts it is clear that Burckhardt understood only too well the problem that his theory was faced with; but he was I think ultimately unable to find a satisfactory solution. Although 'the essence of history is change', Burckhardt's view of the process scarcely went beyond a combination of external forces and internal degeneration:

> In nature, annihilation only comes about by the action of external causes, catastrophes of nature or climate, the overrunning of weaker species by bolder, of nobler by baser. In history, the way of annihilation is invariably prepared by inward degeneration, by decrease of life. Only then can a shock from outside put an end to the whole.[33]

Still, since the whole theoretical structure was seen as simply one especially productive way of approaching the 'contemplation' or writing of history, 'a mere device to enable us to cover the ground',[34] Burckhardt might well think that his analysis was adequate: it was Nietzsche, determined to use history for action, who would feel most clearly the unsatisfactory nature of these answers in relation to his own purposes.

Burckhardt and Nietzsche

Friedrich Nietzsche was appointed Professor of Classical Philology at the University of Basle in 1869 at the astonishingly early age of 24; Burckhardt was fifty, and had been teaching at the university since 1844, the year Nietzsche was born; he had been Professor of History since 1858.[35] From the start Nietzsche admired his older colleague enormously; in 1870 he wrote to a friend:

> Yesterday evening I had the pleasure which I would have liked you above all people to have shared, of hearing Jacob Burckhardt lecture. He gave a lecture without notes on Historical Greatness which lay entirely within the orbit of our thoughts and feelings. This very unusual middle-aged man does not, indeed, tend to falsify the truth, but to concealments, though on our confidential walks and talks he calls Schopenhauer 'Our Philosopher'. I am attending his weekly lectures at the University on the study of history, and believe I am the only one of his sixty hearers who understands his profound train of thought with all its strange circumlocutions and abrupt breaks wherever the subject fringes on the problematical. For the first time in my life I have enjoyed a lecture: and what is more, it is the sort of lecture I shall be able to give when I am older.[36]

In turn Burckhardt attended lectures of Nietzsche in 1872:

> He is still in debt to us for the last, from which we awaited some solutions to the questions and lamentations that he threw out in such a grand and bold style . . . He was quite delightful in places, and then again one heard a note of profound sadness, and I still don't see how the *auditores humanissimi* are to derive comfort or explanations from it. One thing was clear: a man of great gifts who possesses everything at first hand and passes it on.[37]

They had in common their love of Schopenhauer: 'The Philosopher's credit has risen again these last weeks. Living here is one of his faithful, with whom I converse from time to time, as far as I can express myself in his language' wrote Burckhardt about Nietzsche to a friend in 1870.[38]

On the personal level, Nietzsche always maintained his admiration for Burckhardt, 'our great teacher': even after he left Basle in 1879, and as late as 1887, he continued to send him copies of his books from *Untimely Essays* (1873–6) to *Human, All-too-Human* (1879), *The Gay Science* (1882), *Thus Spake Zarathustra* (1883), *Beyond Good and Evil* (1886) and *The Genealogy of Morals* (1887). But Burckhardt's letters of thanks reveal his increasing distance from Nietzsche's philosophy.[39] Nietzsche was oblivious of this change in the feelings of 'my honoured friend Jacob Burckhardt of Basle' to whom 'above all Basle owes its pre-eminence in the humanities' as he describes him in *Twilight of the Idols* in 1889.[40] Indeed Burckhardt was one of the recipients of his strange messages from Turin, written in late 1888 as he descended into insanity:

> To my most honoured Jacob Burckhardt.
> That was only a little joke, on account of which I overlook the tedium of having created a world. Now you are – thou art – our greatest teacher; for I, together with Ariadne, have only to be the golden balance of all things, we have in every part those who are above us . . .
>
> Dionysus

His last letter to Burckhardt began:

> Dear Professor,
> In the end I would rather be a professor at Basle than God; but I did not dare to press my private egoism so far as to abstain from the creation of the world.

It was this letter, arriving in early January 1889, which caused Burckhardt to consult Nietzsche's friend Franz Overbeck, who had the final responsibility of bringing Nietzsche back to Basle and committing him to medical care.

In old age Burckhardt liked to distance himself from the 'publicity stunt' that Nietzsche had become; in 1896 at the age of 78 he wrote:

> Moreover, since the philosophical vein is entirely wanting in me, I recognized from the time of his appointment here that my relations with him could not be of any help to him in this sense, and so they remained infrequent, though serious and friendly discussions. I never had any dealings with him in respect of

Gewaltmenschen, the power maniacs, and do not even know whether he clung to this idea at the time when I still saw him fairly often; from the time when his illnesses began I only saw him very rarely.[41]

But there is no doubt that in the early seventies the two men were very close. Both of them refer to the delight they experienced in finding someone who shared the same veneration for 'the Philosopher' as they both called Schopenhauer; each was profoundly affected by the same distaste for the growth of Prussian power and the cultural consequences of the triumph of Germany over France in 1870. And intellectually each influenced the other in a variety of ways.

At first impression it is the differences between the two which are most striking, to the extent that it becomes clear that each reacted against the other, and essentially found the other useful in the process of clarifying his own ideas. Nietzsche's belief in Burckhardt's agreement with him was of course unverifiable since the latter's views were expressed only in lectures, whereas his own were published. Thus he could claim that Burckhardt had accepted the great contrast between the Apollinian and Dionysian aspects of Greek culture:

> Whoever has investigated the Greeks, such as that profoundest student of their culture now living, Jacob Burckhardt of Basle, realizes at once the value of this line of approach: Burckhardt inserted a special section on the said phenomenon into his *Culture of the Greeks*.[42]

he wrote in *Twilight of the Idols*. But in fact, whatever may have led Nietzsche to believe this, there is little reference to Nietzsche's theories in the surviving manuscripts of Burckhardt's lectures on Greek culture, either in relation to Greek religion and Greek morals, or in relation to tragedy.[43] And indeed the whole argument of *The Birth of Tragedy*, with its attempt to relate ancient tragedy to the modern music of Wagner, can scarcely ever have appealed to Burckhardt, whose musical interests lay rather with Mozart and Verdi, and whose silence about Wagner hides a profound distaste for him.

Nietzsche had claimed that he was the only hearer to understand Burckhardt's lectures on the philosophy of history. In the 1870s Nietzsche was indeed struggling to free himself from the historical vision of his age. But his famous essay 'On the use and abuse of history for life', published independently in 1874 and two years later in *Untimely Essays*, is essentially a statement of rejection of all that Burckhardt had stood for in those lectures, even if at one point he refers to Burckhardt's description of the Italian Renaissance with approval.[44] The modern age is viewed as suffering from a surfeit of history, produced for entertainment, which leads to self-irony and cynicism; like the Roman from the imperial age, the modern human being

> continually has his historical artists prepare for him the festival of a world's fair. He has become a spectator who strolls about enjoying himself, and he has been reduced to a condition in which even great wars and great revolutions can scarcely change anything, even for a moment . . .
>
> Or is it necessary to have a race of eunuchs to stand guard over the great historical world-harem? Certainly pure objectivity is quite becoming in eunuchs. It almost seems as if the task is to watch over history so that nothing will ever come of it but stories – but certainly no events![45]

Although Burckhardt might have approved of Nietzsche's dismissal of objectivity, the main criticisms surely relate to Burckhardt's pose of the connoisseur and dilettante, writing and lecturing for the general public.

> Now picture to yourself the present-day historical virtuoso: is he the most just man of his age? It is true, he has cultivated in himself a sensibility so tender and sensitive that absolutely nothing human is alien to him; his lyre can echo in kindred tones the sounds of the most diverse ages and persons; he has become an echoing passivity whose resonance, in turn, has a resounding effect on other passivities of the same sort, until ultimately the air of an age is filled with the buzzing counterpoint of such tender and kindred echoes. Yet it seems to me that only the harmonics, as it were, of that original historical note remain audible: the harshness and power of the original can no longer be divined in the thin and shrill sound of the lyre strings. Moreover the original tone usually awakened deeds, difficulties, and terrors, whereas this pure tone just lulls us to sleep and turns us into gentle epicures. It is as though the Eroica symphony had been arranged for two flutes and were intended for the benefit of dreaming opium smokers.[46]

Burckhardt well understood that this was a criticism of himself, and replied to the gift of the book with a characteristic defence of 'amateurism':

> In the first place my poor head has never been capable of reflecting, even at a distance, as you are able to do, upon final causes, the aims and the desirability of history. As teacher and professor I can, however, maintain that I have never taught history for the sake of what goes under the pompous title of World History, but essentially as a propaedeutic study: my task has been to put people in possession of the scaffolding which is indispensable if their further studies of whatever kind were not to be aimless. I have done everything I possibly could to lead them on to personal possession of the past – in whatever shape or form – and at least not to sicken them of it; I wanted them to be capable of picking the fruits for themselves; I never dreamt of training scholars and disciples in the narrower sense, but only wanted to make every member of my audience feel and know that everyone may and must appropriate those aspects of the past which appeal to him personally, and that there might be happiness in so doing. I know perfectly well that such an aim may be criticized as fostering amateurism, but that does not trouble me overmuch.[47]

Indeed for Burckhardt amateurism was part of his historical ideal:

> The word 'amateur' owes its evil reputation to the arts. An artist must be a master or nothing, and must dedicate his life to his art, for the arts, of their very nature, demand perfection.
>
> In scholarship, on the other hand, a man can only be a master in one particular field, namely as a specialist, and in some field he *should* be a specialist. But if he is not to forfeit his capacity for taking a general view, or even his respect for general views, he should be an amateur at as many points as possible, privately at any rate, for the increase of his own knowledge and the enrichment of his possible standpoints. Otherwise he will remain ignorant in any field lying outside his own speciality, and perhaps, as a man, a barbarian.[48]

Nietzsche in fact had refused to accept the central conception of Burckhardt's lectures on history, though he borrowed his tripartite division: his own theory of history sees it as divided into three types, monumental (great men), antiquarian (facts) and critical (moral judgments). These categories are very crude and offer no great insight, except that his excessive emphasis on the first, which is concerned with history as the record of the actions of great men, shows that he already viewed history primarily as the arena for a display of the power of the *Übermensch* or the free spirit. Although Burckhardt had indeed tackled the problem of the Great Man in history, he saw history as concerned, not with individuals or facts or moral judgments, but with the three fundamental forces whose interaction shaped the development of civilizations. Nietzsche's own theory was concerned with the uses of history for his philosophy of revolutionary change in society; Burckhardt might set him thinking, but, from Nietzsche's point of view, he belonged in the historicist culture which must be destroyed.

What united them most was their common rejection of certain fundamental principles of historicism. They both dismissed the attitudes of the so-called professional scholars: while Nietzsche was provoking his colleagues and calling for a new philology related to the needs of a new vision of the world, Burckhardt was finding himself more and more at odds with the historical perception of the '*viri eruditissimi* in their professorial chairs'.[49] Burckhardt must have approved of Nietzsche's dismissal of objectivity and historical neutrality as historical ideals. And behind this lay a common rejection of the importance of facts and events in history. As Nietzsche wrote, 'The fact is always stupid and has at all times looked more like a calf than a god.'[50] At precisely the same time Burckhardt was writing to a friend during the preparation of his lectures on Greek culture, and in relation to current political events:

> To me, as a teacher of history, a very curious phenomenon has become clear: the sudden devaluation of all mere 'events' in the past. From now on in my lectures, I shall only emphasize cultural history, and retain nothing but the quite indispensable external scaffolding.[51]

At much the same time he wrote to a young historian:

> I further advise you simply to omit the refuse of mere facts – not from your labour – but certainly from the presentation. One really only needs to use such facts as are characteristic of an idea, or a vivid mark of a time. Our nervous strength and our eyesight are too precious to waste on the study of external facts of the past,

unless we are archivists, county historians or something of the sort.[52]

This rejection of the tyranny of factual history was elevated by Burckhardt into one of the most powerful methodological challenges that positivist historiography has faced. In the lectures on Greek culture Burckhardt developed a formal rejection of the cult of the event:

> One great advantage of studying cultural history is the certainty of the more important facts compared with those of history in the ordinary sense of narrated events – these are frequently uncertain, controversial, coloured, or, given the Greek talent for lying, entirely the invention of imagination or of self-interest. Cultural history by contrast possesses a primary degree of certainty, as it consists for the most part of material conveyed in an unintentional, disinterested or even involuntary way by sources and monuments; they betray their secrets unconsciously and even, paradoxically, through fictitious elaborations, quite apart from the material details they may set out to record and glorify, and are thus doubly instructive for the cultural historian.[53]

Cultural history deals with phenomena which are '*recurrent, constant, typical*'.[54] It does not matter whether the stories which it uses are true, as long as they are believed to be true. And even a forgery is an important piece of evidence for the period that perpetrated it, since it reveals more clearly than a genuine article the conceptions and beliefs about the past of the age that created it. This principle of unconscious revelation through representation derives ultimately from Schopenhauer's conception of the world as representation; and it is one of the most powerful tools in the modern historian's study of mentalities. As Burckhardt saw very clearly, it offers a solution to the sterile disputes of positivism as to whether a fact is true or false, and how such a proposition can be established: cultural history is primarily interested in beliefs and attitudes, rather than events – and falsehoods are therefore often more valuable than truths:

> Even where a reported act did not really occur, or not in the way it is said to have occurred, the attitude that assumes it to have occurred, and in that manner, retains its value by virtue of the typicality of the statement.

It is this common attitude to the unimportance of the truth of events compared to the significance of beliefs or statements about events that seems to me to unite Burckhardt and Nietzsche as the founders of relativist and 'post-modern' historiography.

Apart from the creative enthusiasm which resulted from their meetings, undoubtedly the most significant specific idea about the Greek world that Burckhardt and Nietzsche shared was the belief in the importance of the 'agonal' aspect of Greek and (in Nietzsche's case) modern culture. The realization that individual contest and the desire to be supreme lay at the centre of early Greek attitudes to the world is their joint discovery. Nietzsche seems to have realized the importance of the agon or contest, even before he arrived in Basle; but Burckhardt had already formulated it independently, and was busy working out in detail the consequences of this discovery for the understanding of every aspect of Greek culture.[55] This is indeed the most important of all Burckhardt's insights into the Greek mentality, and has proved continually fruitful in Greek history to the present day, where Greek ethical values are often seen as a conflict between competitive and cooperative virtues.[56] It can also be said that the unorthodoxy of each contributed to liberating the thought of the other about the Greeks in this great creative period for both of them. Thus Nietzsche's very critical approach to Socrates mirrors Burckhardt's equally critical but ironic version of the standard myth. And both men share in very different ways a hatred of the Greek city-state and of Athenian democracy as destructive forces.

Lectures on Greek Cultural History

It was in this climate that Burckhardt began the preparation of a new series of lectures on the history of Greek culture, which he was to call his *Lieblingskolleg* (favourite set of lectures).[57] Although (like Winckelmann, the great eighteenth-century creator of neo-classicism) Burckhardt had never visited Greece, he had of course been interested in the Greeks since his student days: while it is true that his Greece was a place of the mind, he did not idealize it; and he had studied the displays of Greek antiquities in the Vatican and London, as well as in many less important museums.

The earliest clear reference to the idea of such a series of lectures is in a letter to the philologist Otto Ribbeck in July 1864:

> Now or never I am going to read through Aristotle's *Politics* with my pen in my hand, besides on the heath stuffing Catullus together with your paper in my knapsack. I am still somewhat obsessed with that idea we talked about over a beer in the pub opposite the Baden station: somehow to roam through the Greeks in my strange and wayward fashion and see what emerges, not of course for a book, but only for a course of university lectures 'on the Greek spirit'. I imagine myself like La Fontaine's milkmaid, lecturing first very timidly one hour a week, then after more study for two hours and three hours to a small but serious audience. There seems to be much comparative eastern material from the Old Testament and the Zend-Avesta ... But you must not betray me, otherwise I shall feel embarrassed.[58]

What had started as 'an idea *inter pocula*' (in his cups)[59] slowly took on reality. The formal decision was taken in February 1869, the preliminary plan was established in January 1870. It was based on a systematic reading and rereading of the ancient sources; on his summer holidays in 1870 he was reading Pindar:

> Here and there, and despite all my admiration, the most disrespectful thoughts occur to me, and from time to time I catch sight of a lot of philistines, and Pindar with all his great pathos in pursuit. Pindar obviously had to deal from time to time with real thugs.[60]

In December 1871 he could say:

> My consolation is that I have gradually wrung a goodly portion of independent knowledge of antiquity directly from the sources, and that I shall be able to present by far the greater part of all I have to say as my own.[61]

By January 1872 the sketch of the final section was established. The lectures were given first in the winter semester of 1872, to an audience of 53 people; they were repeated in 1874, 1878 and 1885.

Initially Burckhardt had considered turning the lectures into a book; he revised the present first two volumes (essentially on politics and religion), but the second half was left in lecture form. In 1880 he was even approached by a publisher. When asked later, he denied that he had ever intended to write a book: 'the mistaken belief that I was to publish a history of Greek culture derives from a work of the unfortunate Professor Nietzsche, who now lives in a lunatic asylum. He mistook a lecture course that I used often to give for a book.'[62] To a close friend he explained:

> No, my friend, such a miserable stranger who stands outside the guild fraternity, would not dare to do it; I am a heretic and an ignoramus, and my dubious views would be severely handled by the *viri eruditissimi*. Oh yes, believe me. *Je connais ces gens*. In my old age I need peace.[63]

In his will he made provision for the destruction of his lectures:

> Since modern booksellers have the presumption to advertise in their catalogues the lecture-notes of dead professors, whereby immature and provisional drafts of opinions reach the public, the following notebooks shall be unconditionally destroyed:
>
> [these include lectures on ancient history]
>
> On the other hand there may be preserved as the personal property of Jacob Oeri of the history of Greek culture both the detailed plan of the whole and also the developed working out of the first half (pages in folio), on condition that no part of it is published.[64]

Burckhardt was right; when contrary to his wishes the lectures began finally to be published, the master of the guild, Ulrich von Wilamowitz-Moellendorff, thundered in 1899:

> I would hold it cowardice if I did not here assert that the *Griechische Kulturgeschichte* of Jacob Burckhardt ... does not exist for scholarship ..., that this book is incapable of saying anything either of Greek religion or of the Greek state which deserves a hearing, simply because it ignores what the scholarship of the last fifty years has achieved in relation to sources, facts, methods and approaches. The Greece of Burckhardt no more exists than does that of the classical aesthetes, which he could rightly have attacked fifty years ago.[65]

Others followed suit: 'a book by a clever dilettante for dilettantes' wrote Julius Beloch; 'these Greeks never existed' said Theodor Mommsen. But with the general reader it was an immediate success; Freud, on the threshold of the Oedipus complex, wrote to his colleague Fliess in January 1899, it 'is providing me with unexpected parallels'.[66]

Of course the experts were in a sense justified; even when the lectures had first been given, they were based on Burckhardt's private reading of texts, and on the handbooks of his youth; they did not take account of recent discoveries, notably of inscriptions and papyri. 'He built his knowledge of the Greeks on what *they* had written, not on what German professors had written about them in the last forty years.'[67] Twenty years later this product of the age of Nietzsche seemed doubly antiquated. How then has it emerged as the greatest work of nineteenth-century cultural history, and the most convincing portrait of the Greeks in the modern age? The answer to these questions lies on the one hand in its importance as an exemplification of the principles of Burckhardt's new methodology for cultural history, and on the other hand in the personal insights that the contemplative Burckhardt possessed into the nature of Greek culture.

The lectures on Greek cultural history are firmly based on the principles established in the lectures on the study of history. The material is organized around a structure of nine sections, the first eight of which are divided between the three powers of politics, religion and culture:

Volume I: 1. The Greeks and their myth
              2. State and nation

Volume II: 3. Religion and cult
              4. The enquiry into the future
              5. The general characteristics of Greek life

Volume III: 6. The fine arts
              7. Poetry and music
              8. Philosophy, science and rhetoric

Volume IV: 9. Greek man in his historical development

Thus the modern division in the first three volumes corresponds roughly to Burckhardt's intentional grouping of sections in relation to the three powers. The first section in volume I tackles the traditional problem of the historical value and meaning of Greek myth, with a refreshing combination of common sense and disregard for the wild theories that abounded (and still abound) in their study. The second section on politics deals with the nature of the *polis* and its development in history through kingship, aristocracy and tyranny, culminating in discussions of the two fully developed Greek cities, Sparta and democratic Athens. As in the *Renaissance*, the portrayal of the political sphere is of the State as a systematic 'work of art', essentially hostile to the other powers and to the development of the individual; Burckhardt finishes with a discussion of the origins of Greek political thought and political philosophy, and the conception of Greek unity and superiority over the world of the barbarians. The whole picture of the *polis* is both negative and ironic, expressing Burckhardt's dislike and fear of the political power and his recognition of the excessive importance that the Greeks attributed to the political life. 'Power is of its nature evil, whoever wields it';[68] the *polis* is an all-powerful instrument of compulsion, idealized as religion and as law, a presence from which there was no possibility of escape, a *città dolente* or city of suffering. Even culture could not set the individual free:

> Culture was to a high degree determined and dominated by the State, both in the positive and in the negative sense, since it demanded first and foremost of every man that he should be a citizen. Every individual felt that the *polis* lived in him. This supremacy of the *polis*, however, is fundamentally different from the supreme power of the modern State, which seeks only to keep its material hold on every individual, while the *polis* required of every man that he should serve it, and hence intervened in many concerns which are now left to individual and private judgment.[69]

That attitude makes his picture of Athenian democracy in particular essentially unsympathetic: the ability of the demagogues to manipulate the masses becomes the most dangerous and most tyrannical form of political power that can be imagined. The prevalence of malicious and arbitrary prosecution by individual sycophants in a system where the law was the expression of the will of the people led to a permanent situation, like that which had existed temporarily during the reign of terror in the French Revolution, where the power to impose confiscation of property, dishonour, removal of citizen rights, exile and death was absolute, and the individual had no rights at all against the will of the *demos*.

In this portrayal of Greek political life two points should be emphasized. The first is that it was Burckhardt who invented the modern conception of the *polis* as a specifically Greek form of social organization, and who set out to determine in what ways it was different from other types of 'city-state' organization.[70] Earlier discussions had either assumed comparability with other small-scale political systems, or failed to establish any difference at all between the ancient and the modern world. Burckhardt therefore stands at the beginning of all attempts to understand the individuality of Greek political life, whether or not we agree with his portrayal. A second clear break with previous historians is the way that Burckhardt ignored the importance of the great man. Pericles, Demosthenes, Philip, Alexander the Great are simply representatives of their age: in Burckhardt the great man disappears from history, to be replaced by the unseen movements of a culture as a whole. So despite his hostile attitude to the importance of politics in Greece, it was Burckhardt who first revealed the central importance of the political in Greek life, and who laid the foundation for modern attitudes to the study of Greek politics and political institutions.

In the second volume, on religion, he begins with the phenomenon of metamorphosis as grounded in the sense that all of the natural world is full of the divine, before discussing the Greek conception of their gods as a polytheistic system, and the special Greek phenomena of hero cult and oracle cult. Here his account, although interesting, lacks true insight: it is too much based on literary texts, rather than ritual, and is insufficiently concerned with the depth of real religious experiences as they were later described by Nietzsche's friend Erwin Rohde in his work *Psyche* of 1894, to mention only a book towards which Burckhardt would have been most sympathetic. But not without reason Burckhardt believed that 'the world of the Greeks and Romans was entirely secular', and Greek religion was subordinate to the other powers:

> The religions of that world were mainly determined by the State and Culture. They were State and Culture religions, the gods were State and Culture gods, while the State was not a theocracy; hence the absence of a priesthood in these religions.[71]

Personally indeed Burckhardt's irony and his lack of religious involvement created a distance between himself and the object of study, which is only occasionally relieved by flashes of real insight – as when he described Delphi, with its great buildings donated by victors from the booty of their wars, as 'above all the monumental museum of Greek hatred for Greeks, of mutually inflicted suffering immortalized in the loftiest works of art'.[72]

He ends the discussion of religion in section 5, with a fascinating and highly original account of 'the general characteristics of Greek life', which contradicts the traditional picture of the Hellenic ideal with a deliberately negative image of the Greeks, as a people for whom lying, treachery, cruelty and vengeance are essential aspects of a moral code which is divorced from religion and opposed to the basic beliefs of Christianity, and which is in no way compatible with modern views of morality in private or public life:

> Among the Greeks ... morality was practically independent of religion and in all probability more closely connected with the ideal of the State.[73]

There is here a close relationship with Nietzsche's view of the Greeks in *The Birth of Tragedy* and elsewhere; but whereas Nietzsche wanted to see the Greeks as models for a new cult of the amoral, Burckhardt seeks merely to establish that the Greek moral code was fundamentally different from ours, and that we should not therefore idealize the Greeks.

The section concludes with a description of the nature of Greek pessimism, the terrible burden of being Greek, their despair of life and their fascination with suicide. Here too there is a connection with Nietzsche's portrayal of the Greeks in *The Birth of Tragedy*. Both authors in fact took their starting point from Schopenhauer's famous conception of pessimism as a creative force in human culture, which in itself is a development of the Renaissance idea of melancholy and the melancholic man as genius. But Schopenhauer believed that it was Christianity, with its asceticism and doctrine of the meritorious nature of celibacy, which had asserted the denial of the will-to-live, and that it therefore lay at the origin of modern pessimism: earlier peoples (even the Jews, despite the temporary aberration of the doctrine of the Fall of Man) had been endowed with an incurable optimism.[74] This created a problem especially in relation to the development of Greek tragedy: was tragedy an expression of a pessimistic view of the world, and of the powerlessness of humanity in the face of the divine will, which was in itself unconcerned with human morality and human suffering – or could Greek tragedy be viewed as an optimistic vision of the human predicament, a form of higher 'cheerfulness'? It is the second view that is argued by Nietzsche in *The Birth of Tragedy*; for him Greek 'cheerfulness' is a fact, which resides in the Dionysian power of emotion to fuse with the Apollinian or rational aspect of tragedy, and assert life in the face of human disaster. It is primarily this paradox which has made Nietzsche's view that tragedy is a triumph of the human will so influential in the modern world.[75]

Burckhardt took the other way forward, by presenting the Greeks as themselves the creators and the sufferers in relation to Schopenhauer's vision of hopeless pessimism. As a view of tragedy this perhaps lacks the depths that the Nietzschean tradition has been able to achieve through the idea of tragedy as a form of reconciliation of opposites; but he grounded it, not in one literary genre, but in the whole Greek perception of the transitory nature of human happiness and of life itself. He saw that the real problem and the real achievement of the Greeks lay in their inability to accept the existence of an afterlife of any significance, which made the pleasures and pains of this life so powerful and so intolerably sweet even in suffering: he refers to

> ... the religion of the Greeks, who, with their clear insight into humanity and the limits of the individual, presupposed only a colourless world to come and spent little thought on it, leaving eschatology as a physical problem to the philosophers.[76]

It is easy to endure life if one regards it as simply a preparation for a future existence; the true tragedy lies in the realization that there is no future but the continuation of the present beyond individual sensation. So Christianity ceases to be the cause of pessimism, and the tragedy of the human predicament lies in the necessity of accepting the absoluteness of the here-and-now. For all the power of religion in the Greek world, Burckhardt's Greeks were the first to understand what it is to be human in the modern sense, and to live in the present without hope for the future. It is in this sense that the Greeks still provide us with a model of how to live, beyond morality and beyond hope. In this analysis Burckhardt developed the ideas of Schopenhauer into an explanation of the continuing power of Greek culture; for in his account of Greek morals he revealed what is the basis of the difference between ourselves and the Greeks, and in his account of Greek pessimism he showed why the Greeks nevertheless express the fundamental predicament of humanity in Western culture.

In volume III, on the arts in Greek culture, Burckhardt is at his most conventional: here if anywhere he is old-fashioned, unwilling to rethink the categories of the philological handbooks and the idealistic lectures of his youth, or to accept either new discoveries or the insights of Nietzsche into the relationship between ancient and modern art forms. The vision of *The Birth of Tragedy* is strangely absent, and Burckhardt remains bound in an aestheticizing appreciation of Greek literature and Greek art as timeless models, unrelated to the society that produced them. Despite the intelligence of his survey of Greek art, literature and science, it offers no permanent new insight, and makes us remember that one aim of his lecture course was simply 'to put people in possession of the scaffolding which is indispensable if their further studies of whatever kind were not to be aimless'.[77]

It is the fourth and longest volume, comprising a single section on 'Greek man in his historical development', which presents a major new departure in Burckhardt's method. It corresponds on the conceptual level to the problems he had tried to face in the second half of his lectures on the study of history – how to combine the three powers into a picture of the culture of a society as a whole, which would also be capable of explaining how such cultural units might change and develop over time. Burckhardt presents a series of portraits of 'Greek man' (or 'the Greek': in our translation in deference to modern sensibilities we have omitted to translate the concept *Mensch*, which of course in German has no specific connotation of gender). Five historically successive phases of Greek man are identified, the heroic, the colonial and agonal (as we might say, the archaic), the fifth century, the fourth century, and the Hellenistic. This series of portraits is a sustained and successful attempt to exemplify in detailed analysis those complex processes of interrelationship between the three powers which are described in the central sections of the lectures on the study of history.

The final problem of the lectures on the study of history had been how to explain the process of development from one period to another; in the lectures on Greek culture this is not addressed directly. Instead each separate portrait contains the elements which point forward to the next, as if to indicate the natural process of movement from one period to another. Perhaps the most important question that is raised by Burckhardt's presentation of his theory in action in relation to a historical society is how far this device in fact succeeds in solving the problem that his theory had identified. But in contrast to the various attempts which Burckhardt had explored in his earlier lectures, as in his other historical books he seems determined to avoid easy solutions: it is once again noticeable how he has refused to rely on the dynamic of the great man in order to move the historical process forward: for Burckhardt, Pericles and Alexander the Great explain nothing:

> When knowledge flows more freely, it is supremely desirable that
> the great man should be shown in conscious relationship to the

spirit, to the culture of his time; that an Alexander should have had an Aristotle as his tutor.[78]

Burckhardt's lectures on Greek culture are therefore important for two reasons. First in them Burckhardt used and exemplified the theoretical categories which he had developed for the study of cultural history. They constitute in fact the final expression of his attempt to found a new historical method, based on contemplation and understanding of the way in which cultural and social systems are composed. In an age in which the importance of cultural history has finally come to be recognized, in the study of the history of mentalities and the new trends in historical scholarship since Foucault, it is important to return to the work of the half-forgotten founder of this type of historical investigation, and consider what he has to teach us. For it was Burckhardt who overthrew positivism in history, and established the insignificance of the history of events in the face of the relativity of historical facts.

Secondly in the process of elaborating a new picture of Greek culture based on the insights which he had won in other periods of history, Burckhardt inevitably rethought the conventional categories of classical scholarship, just as Nietzsche did. And that, combined with his ironical and detached view of 'the glory that was Greece', enabled him to identify those leading aspects of Greek culture which remain at the centre of all modern studies of the Greeks. These are the primacy of the political 'power' in Greek life, which imposed a form of political rationality on Greek society such as has not existed in any other culture: Burckhardt did not of course invent the *polis*, but he uncovered its significance, and brought it to the centre of the discussion.[79] He also saw the fundamental importance of the agonal, competitive aspect of Greek life, especially in the archaic age, but continuing through the whole of Greek moral and social history. He identified the specific nature of Greek pessimism and its relation to the intensity of the Greek experience of life. And continually in detail he surprises us with the sharpness of his insight into specific aspects: it was for instance only after some years of working on the significance of Greek drinking customs that I recalled a series of brief paragraphs in this work, which together constitute the first serious analysis of the phenomenon of the *symposion*. In this and in so many other ways, Burckhardt will continue to surprise us: his work remains the first and the best modern account of Greek culture.

Principles of this Edition

In preparing this selection from the lectures of Burckhardt, we have borne in mind its origins as a set of lectures, not a book. The text we have used is that established by Burckhardt's nephew Jacob Oeri in his edition a hundred years ago (1898–1902). In the first two volumes it has the authority of a revised manuscript by Burckhardt himself; thereafter it is based on his notes for various courses, and the notes of his auditors; this is especially true of the fourth volume, where we are almost entirely dependent on the audience of the lectures, in the absence of an author's manuscript. Oeri was a highly conscientious classical scholar and a schoolmaster, who is described as rising daily about seven o'clock to retire to his summerhouse in the garden and work on his uncle's manuscripts until eleven, when he left for the town.[80]

Nevertheless, as Burckhardt said, lecture notes are like the underside of a carpet,[81] where the threads and the general patterns are visible, but the liveliness and the details of the original design are lost. A new scholarly edition of the lectures on Greek culture is in preparation in Basle at the Burckhardtarchiv, supported by the university and by the Swiss Science Council;[82] it will appear over the next decade. The principles on which they are working are the same as those followed by Peter Ganz for the lectures on the study of history – that is, to give exact transcripts of the variant versions in Burckhardt's notes and those of his listeners, rather than a composite and readable text. The end of the process will be to place us once again at the table in the summerhouse where Jacob Oeri worked, in possession of all the material that he had before him (and perhaps a little more), but faced with his same problem – how to reconstruct the actual set of lectures which his uncle gave on a series of occasions, with all their variety. And we shall lack that one essential ingredient, the insight into Burckhardt's mind that was possessed by his favourite nephew and literary executor, who had himself attended his uncle's lectures. For this reason we believe that the text of Jacob Oeri will not be replaced, however much our understanding of the lectures and of the development of Burckhardt's thought may be enriched.[83]

In selecting sections for translation we have tried to bring out the true originality of Burckhardt's vision of history, as I have described it above. In deference to the tolerance of modern readers and publishers, we thought it best to bear in mind Burckhardt's own words of advice to a young friend:

> And finally never go beyond one volume and remember the silent despair with which you and I regard some new three-volume monograph or biography, whose spiritual and intellectual contribution could have been put in four or five pages.[84]

For this reason we have selected only the most important sections from the first two volumes, and have chosen to present Burckhardt's thought in terms of his most original and final section, which fills the fourth volume.

In detail therefore we have taken from volume I the first eighty pages, comprising the introduction, the first section on the Greeks and their mythology, and the first part of the second section, the general characterization of the *polis*; with some regret we have omitted the rest of the political account, the long narrative of the historical development of the *polis* (including Sparta and Athens), and the sections on the origins of political thought and the conception of Greek unity.

From volume II we have omitted entirely the discussion of religion and cult, and included only section 5, on 'the general characteristics of Greek life'. The whole of volume III (on art and literature) has been left aside.

The core of this translation is the series of portraits of 'Greek man in his historical development' in volume IV, which is translated almost completely, omitting only Burckhardt's account of the age of colonization in the section on 'agonal and colonial man' (which is really only of antiquarian interest, since the picture has been radically transformed by archaeology in this century), and much of the section on Hellenistic man for similar reasons; we have also left out a few brief passages in the rest of the text, mostly compendious and repetitive lists of comparative material which add nothing to the argument. From the notes to the printed text we have selected Burckhardt's most interesting and characteristic observations, and essential references.

Envoi

One of Burckhardt's most delightful works is his last, prepared before his death, and left with instructions for posthumous publication. It is an essay on his favourite artist, Rubens, whom Burckhardt rightly saw as a supremely happy genius, who had lived a prosperous and successful life based on his ability to give pleasure to his contemporaries, and who had not mistaken worldly success for the secret of happiness, but had placed his family and his love for his wife above all public honours. Though he never married, Burckhardt himself was a private man, who was happiest with his small circle of relatives and friends and in his work as a teacher. He might understand the pessimism of the Greeks; but he too possessed the love of beauty, the wisdom and the happiness of his artistic hero. The *Rubens* is a work of old age and contentment; Burckhardt remained the ironical contemplative historian to the end, one of those who

> attain an Archimedian point outside events, and are able to 'over-come in the spirit'. Nor is the satisfaction of those who do so, perhaps, very great. They can hardly restrain a rueful feeling as they look back on all the rest, whom they have had to leave in bondage.[85]

And so, at the end of our labours we take leave of a lifelong friend and teacher, and hope that on the centenary of his death we have fulfilled in part the words of Burckhardt himself in his last letter to an old friend, written during his final illness:

> And now, goodbye, and continue to be well disposed to your old 'Cicerone'; our lives having crossed and recrossed so often and in such a friendly fashion; and after my death, take me just a little (not too much) under your care; it is said to be a meritorious work![86]

THE GREEKS

I

Introduction

THE SUBJECT OF this course of lectures is Greek cultural history. It should be understood at the outset that the course is and must always remain a tentative piece of work, and that the lecturer is and will remain a learner and a fellow student; and it must also be pointed out that he is not a classical scholar and begs to be forgiven any philological lapses.

The courses which seem most nearly related to the present one are those on Greek antiquities and on Greek history, and the dividing line between our task and theirs must first be drawn. 'Greek Antiquities', as presented in my youth by August Boeckh in his great series of lectures, began with a geographical and historical survey, established the general character of the Greek people, and went on to treat of the different aspects of their life; first the State in general in its main outlines, then a number of particularly important states with details of their political, administrative and legal institutions, then the alliances and hegemonies established between states. There followed the arts of war on land and at sea, and private life including weights and measures, trade, industry, agriculture, housekeeping (with food, clothing and dwellings), marriage, the structure of the family, slavery, education, burial and rites in honour of the dead. Next came religion, with the cults and festivals, and the arts (further study of these was left to specialists in the history of art), gymnastics, drama and music; finally there was a survey of the branches of learning cultivated by the Greeks. All this was treated by the antiquarian method, that is to say with a predetermined and constant degree of factual detail and completeness for each separate aspect of ancient life, as the groundwork for future specialized study; it was and still remains indispensable for the classicist, and also

3

requires a professional classicist and antiquarian to teach it, because only an expert is capable of making full use of the relatively slender material available.

I am not aware of the extent to which this course still exists as an academic one. It must have been largely superseded by the handbooks, notably the three-volume *Hellenische Altertumskunde* by C.F. Hermann and Wilhelm Wachsmuth. To ascertain what is the proper province of a handbook, and can scarcely form the subject of a course of lectures, we may glance at the list of contents of C.F. Hermann's *Privataltertümer*, consisting mostly of things that one would need to know for particular purposes, and which it is of the greatest value to have in organized book form. For our present course only a few paragraphs are relevant, and those in quite a different order. From all this material we need to select only what most strikingly illustrates Greek views of life.

But why, it may be asked, not study 'Greek History' and more especially political history, and deal with the general circumstances and forces digressively as they come up? – Because, apart from the fact that excellent histories of Greece already exist, the narration of events, let alone any critical discussion of them, would take up most of the allotted time, since nowadays a single investigation of a few external facts may well fill up a whole volume. In addition, the 'events' are exactly what it is easiest to learn from books, while our task is to establish vantage points from which to *view* the events. If, then, all that is most worth knowing about ancient Greece is to be conveyed in little more than sixty hours of lecture time[1] – and that to an audience which includes nonclassicists – the method of cultural history is the only practicable one.

The task, as I conceive it, is to treat the history of Greek habits of thought and mental attitudes, and to seek to establish the vital *forces*, both constructive and destructive, that were active in Greek life. It is not in the narrative mode, though indeed primarily through history (since they are part of universal history), that the Greeks must be studied in their essential peculiarities, those in which they differ from the ancient Orient and from the nations that came after them, and yet represent the great transition between the two. It is the history of the Greek mind or spirit that must be the aim of the whole study. The details, and even what are called events, can appear only as supporting testimony to the general, not for their own sake; for the factual knowledge we want relates to habits of thought, which are of course themselves also facts. The sources, when examined in this

4

sense, will speak to us in quite another way than they do to the mere researcher into antiquarian material.

In any case, all historical teaching in the universities has reached a point of crisis which may oblige everyone to hack out a path of their own. Historical interest has come to be very largely dependent on the general movement of Western thought, the general direction of our culture; the old categories and methods are no longer adequate either in books or lectures. This confers great freedom. Luckily it is not only the *concept* of cultural history that is in a state of flux, but also academic practice (as well as a few other things).

One great advantage of studying cultural history is the *certainty* of its more important facts, compared with those of history in the ordinary sense of narrated events: these are frequently uncertain, controversial, coloured, or, given the Greek talent for lying, entirely the invention of imagination or self-interest. Cultural history by contrast possesses a primary degree of certainty, as it consists for the most part of material conveyed in an unintentional, disinterested or even involuntary way by sources and monuments; they betray their secrets unconsciously and even, paradoxically, through fictitious elaborations, quite apart from the material details they may set out to record and glorify, and are thus doubly instructive for the cultural historian.

This kind of history aims at the inner core of bygone humanity, and at describing what manner of people these were, what they wished for, thought, perceived and were capable of. In the process it arrives at what is constant, and finally this constant comes to seem greater and more important than the ephemeral, and qualities greater and more instructive than actions; for actions are only particular expressions of the relevant inner capacity, which can always reproduce such acts. Desires and assumptions are, then, as important as events, the attitude as important as anything done; for at a given moment this attitude will be expressed in action:

The man whose inmost heart I have once probed
Is known to me in all his will and deeds.[2]

But even where a reported act did not really occur, or not in the way it is said to have occurred, the attitude that assumes it to have occurred, and in that manner, retains its value by virtue of the typicality of the statement; in the Greek tradition there are hosts of reports of this kind.

Perhaps indeed the constant that emerges from these typical statements is the truest 'real content' of antiquity, even more than the antiquities themselves. Through it we learn to know the *eternal* Greek, the whole structure instead of an individual factor.

'But in this way we lose sight of the *individuals*, not only the narration of separate facts! Cultural history would be nothing but a story without the great men whose biographies make up such a large part of Greek history!'

They will be given space enough; not, indeed, by telling their full life stories, but rather as illustration and witness to the things of the spirit. It is no disrespect to their fame that they should be cited only as incidental to a certain phenomenon; for they will be cited as its expression and its climax, as prime witnesses in this great review of evidence. True, the account of their careers will have to be sacrificed, but general facts, those of cultural history for instance, are surely to be seen as more important than the particular, the recurring more important than the unique.

It is a further advantage of cultural history that it can proceed by grouping things together and placing stresses according to the *proportional* importance of facts, and need not ride roughshod over all sense of proportion, which is often the failing of the antiquarian and the critical historian. This kind of history draws attention to those facts that can form a link with our own way of thinking, and awaken a genuine response, either by their affinity with us or by the contrast of their remoteness. The rubble of history is left on one side.

On the other hand it would be wrong to pass over in silence the difficulties of cultural history. The certainty of its facts is partly counterbalanced by the great illusions that threaten our researches in another respect. How are we to know what was constant and characteristic and what was not? Only long and varied reading can give assurance; in the meantime much will be overlooked that was of profound significance, and importance attributed to what was merely fortuitous. In the course of reading, every word the researcher happens upon may seem either insignificant or vitally interesting, and this will depend on current mood and state of alertness or fatigue, and especially on the degree of maturity that the research has arrived at. All this will adjust itself only after long reading of the various genres and types of Greek literature. Strenuous effort at this stage is precisely the wrong way to achieve the desired result; an attentive ear and a steady pace of work will succeed better.

Still it must be admitted that the wealth of material in some areas is overwhelming, and historians cannot avoid reproach for having been, until now, completely arbitrary in their choice of what to study. Furthermore, presentation of the facts in accordance with the methods of cultural history brings with it a very different set of problems from the conventional narration of events. Above all it is only possible to speak in a successive way, giving a gradually developing account, whereas the things themselves were in the main a great simultaneous whole. We are dealing with a gigantic continuum which might best be symbolized by the map of the stars; the attempt to trace it is continually confused, as the same single object appears now on the periphery and easily accessible, now more remote, and now in the very centre.

Anyone who has to present this material, like anyone studying it, must ask anxiously 'Where am I to start?' – and the answer is that you have to start somewhere.

In the first place, because things touch each other at all points, repetitions are unavoidable; for instance, the great myth that envelops all Greek thought, perception and feeling, the true spiritual Oceanus of this world, will have to be discussed in various contexts, and, moreover, in three principal connections under three different aspects, namely:

1) as a lasting power in Greek life

2) as related to the underlying Greek attitude to the world, and

3) as an image of a certain national epoch.

A large number of details will have to be accommodated as best they can; and in the many cases in which our study and our knowledge are insufficient, we shall arrive at a question rather than a conclusion. We shall also permit ourselves the occasional hypothesis, while making clear that we are doing so.

It will, in the end, be quite impossible to avoid a great deal of subjectivity in the selection of material. I lay no claim to be 'scientific' and have no method, at least none shared with other scholars. Given the same studies on which I have based my course, taking care in this subjective procedure to be guided by the relative importance of the material, another person would have made quite another selection, arranged it quite differently, and arrived at different conclusions; still more study might have yielded a more exact and a broader picture; and, with luck, I myself may hope to reshape this course in time to come. Meanwhile, let us be content with what seems attainable for us, and for the present moment, given the limited amount of time and the rather fortuitous character of our study.

It is important to be ready to jettison many things, everything in fact that does not bear a close relation to habits of thought and points of view, and first, however reluctantly, the critical examination of *beginnings* which would demand substantial comparative research into the origins of a number of other peoples besides the Greeks. We must forgo any discussion of what was proper to ordinary external life, of things common to other peoples at the same time and in similar climatic conditions, and concentrate on those features which provide an understanding of the specifically Greek mind.

This course also offers a particular academic prospect for nonclassicists; since the mere wholesale communication of antiquities is to be avoided, it makes classical studies immediately accessible. Any interested person can become a fellow researcher by reading the sources, which in this case are unusually open to the nonspecialist. 'Antiquities' demand an erudite, wide-ranging and comparative specialist study which governs one's entire life and aims at completeness, at least within certain areas, if it is to mean anything, while the discipline of cultural history as here understood can bring direct enrichment to any humanist; and if only for this reason it seems proper to pay respect to a shared humanistic education.

Any thorough study of a foreign literature in which there is an intellectual emphasis different from our own, or of any bygone and alien works of the mind, is an enrichment in the sense of the *tria corda* of Ennius: but this is especially true of Greek literature. Where in other literatures the form is unpleasing, the outer husk tightly closed and almost impenetrable, the manner so symbolical as to be hard to understand[3], in the case of the Greeks the expression given to the things of the mind has at least the merit of being more lucid than it is anywhere else – the thought and its dwelling are splendidly one; form and content correspond more perfectly than elsewhere. As for that content, it is the teacher's duty always to stress that every classical author of repute[4] is a source for the historian of culture. Thus Greek cultural history is a particularly clear and easily-scanned section of the history of mankind.

To take the narrative authors first: their lively and significant qualities are very often clearly seen to consist not in the event they tell of but in their manner of recording it, with the mental presuppositions determining that manner. No matter whether it really happened – they convey a knowledge of the Greeks and their perception of the external world as well as their inner habits of thought.

As to poetry and philosophy, highly-developed special disciplines deal with them in relation to their content, literary value and significance; seen from the point of view of cultural history they are the celebration of an incomparably gifted people of the past, a bygone and yet still living spiritual manifestation of the highest order.

This is why it is necessary to emphasize again and again the importance of reading the classical authors as 'sources' in the broadest and most liberal sense. In respect both of content and of form the fruits of this reading, if it is at all systematic, are available to everyone who makes the effort; what each reader lights upon will bring a personal relationship with each author.

It would certainly be an advantage not to be addicted to present-day literature, which appeals so much more directly to the nerves; above all not to the reading of newspapers. Whatever belongs to the present easily combines with our material self-interest; what belongs to the past is at least more likely to become associated with our spiritual nature, and to fuse with higher interests. Then our eyes may gradually quicken, and we may even learn to succeed in eliciting the secrets of the past. The fact that thousands have done this work before us cannot save us the effort. This kind of work is never 'finished with', never done once and for all. In any case each age has a new and different way of looking at the more remote periods of the past; for instance there might be a fact of the greatest significance reported by Thucydides which will only be recognized as such a hundred years from now.

It is not my intention to encourage students to undertake anything for the benefit of others, or to inspire specialized research in the usual literal sense, that is, the complete investigation or presentation of a single subject or set of subjects on which all one's powers must be concentrated; but rather to bring about a feeling of sympathy *for the whole*, an understanding of Hellenism in general. Erudition is served by modern historical and antiquarian writings: *we* are proposing a continuous lifelong process of education and enjoyment.

The manner in which the sources are to be read corresponds to this end; the more distinguished monuments – historians, poets and so on – each convey a total picture and are not merely to be quoted as documenting some special case, but read in their entirety. The interpreter will do well, though, to read the complete works of many second and third rank authors too, and not to rely on others who have read them before him. A monument is contemplated as a whole, and the literary sources are monuments; moreover the most important things are sometimes to be found in the most remote places.

It is perfectly in order to make use of the excellent translations and commentaries available. It is no disgrace to need some help with Thucydides, since Dionysius of Halicarnassus and Cicero both confess that they do not always understand him because of his difficult style; anyone who tries to read him without help will probably soon be discouraged and never get through him at all. What should impel us to read the *whole* of an author's work is the perception that only *we* can find what is of importance to *us*. No work of reference can possibly produce by means of excerpts that chemical reaction between a piece of information we have discovered for ourselves, and our own dim foreknowledge of it, that makes it our own intellectual property.

Everything we can gather from the Greek past can become a source. And not only what is written down. Every surviving fragment is of value, buildings and the visual arts most of all; and in literature not only history, poetry and philosophy but also political writings, oratory, letters, later anthologies and interpretations, which often transmit very ancient testimony. Picking and choosing is not the way to complete the detail of the great picture of antiquity. Even the forger, once recognized as such, can by his very forgery, with the purpose he intended it to serve, involuntarily provide very valuable information.

Naturally we shall prefer to return again and again to the great works of art, perhaps plundering the tragic dramatists for their historical wealth – myth in its fully matured form, at its highest and its most profound, great creative personalities and the presence of a style which is in itself an important event in cultural history. It is from repeated readings that most is to be gained. A first reading often involves too much of a struggle with difficulties of language and substance, and it is only later that the work may be looked at with more freedom and its form and content appreciated. There are certain authors, Hesiod for example, who provoke new questions and open new perspectives at every reading; Aeschylus' *Prometheus* reveals new features each time we come to it.

What is the relation of the present, especially of present-day German culture, to the Greeks?

From the time of Winckelmann and Lessing, and of Voss's translation of Homer, a feeling has grown up of the existence of a 'sacred marriage' (*hieros gamos*) between the spirit of Greece and the spirit of Germany, a special relationship and sympathy shared by no other Western people in modern times. Goethe and Schiller were classical in spirit.

Partly as a result, classical studies in schools and universities have gained a new lease of life and become more profound, and there is a general conviction that classical antiquity is the indispensable basis for all studies of whatever kind, in a deeper sense than had been supposed at any time since the Renaissance. Side by side with this there has been a tremendous general expansion of research into antiquity. The monuments of Egypt and Assyria, prehistoric remains in Europe, the re-creation of ethnography, researches into the origins of the human race and of language, comparative linguistics, have all demanded attention, and Greek studies have been crowded out.

In addition, specialization has set in to such an extent that even the least ramifications of the work demand a whole series of lifetimes of research as well as unconditional support from the State for institutes and collections.

Mommsen once wrote that in the grammar schools (*Gymnasien*) 'higher education prepares the child of the cultivated classes to be a Professor of Classical Studies'[5] – and the foremost instrument of education is, now as then, the Greek language. But after the school-leaving examination comes the familiar traditional process. Apart from the few who become classicists, the majority of students leave the classical authors severely alone. First, after three months or so, they forget the elaborate, painfully acquired metres of the tragic choruses, then, one after another, the verb forms, and finally the vocabulary – and many are glad to forget them. Life and study make other demands on them. A false relationship has grown up in this way between the grammar school and the true further development of the mind, which might well lead to catastrophe.

We, then, should be trying to do everything possible to preserve a living feeling for ancient Greece.

In conclusion:

We do not set out to glorify, and will not allow enthusiasm to colour our judgment. As Boeckh says 'The Greeks were less happy than most people suppose.' But the role of Greek intellectual life in world history, its position between East and West, must be made clear.

What they did and suffered, they appear to have done and suffered *freely*, and thus differently from all earlier races. They seem original, spontaneous and conscious, in circumstances in which all others were ruled by a more or less mindless necessity.

This is why in their creativeness and their potentialities they seem the representatives of genius on earth, with all the failings and sufferings that this entails. In the life of the mind they reached frontiers which the rest of mankind cannot permit themselves to fall short of, at least in their attempts to acknowledge and to profit, even where they are inferior to the Greeks in the capacity for achievement. It is for this reason that posterity needs to study the Greeks; if we ignore them we are simply accepting our own decline.

Their knowledge and their faculty of observation were extraordinary. By their study of the world the Greeks illuminate not only their own nature but that of all other ancient peoples; without them, and the philhellenic Romans, there would be no knowledge of past times, for all other nations attended to nothing but themselves, their own citadels, temples and gods.

All subsequent objective perception of the world is only elaboration on the framework the Greeks began. We see with the eyes of the Greeks and use their phrases when we speak.

It is self-evidently the special duty of the educated to perfect and complete, as well as they can, the picture of the continuity of the world and mankind from the beginning. This marks off conscious beings from the unconscious barbarian. The vision of both past and future is what distinguishes human beings from the animals; and for us the past may have its reproaches, and the future its anxieties, of which the animals know nothing.

So we shall always be in debt to the Greeks in the perception of the world, where they are close to us; and their admirers in the realm of creative ability, in which they are great, alien and remote from us. And it is because cultural history brings out this relation more clearly than the history of events that it must claim our preference.

II

The Greeks and their Mythology

Like the Germans, Slavs, Celts, Celtiberians and Italians, but in an even smaller area, it was as an influx of many different tribes, and probably by slow degrees, that the gifted people whom we call the Greeks came to settle in the lands that were to be their own. Perhaps one day, when the prehistoric remains have been investigated, we may have a more precise idea of the kind of inhabitants they found there. Strabo (7.7.1) and Pausanias (1.41.8) both offer the opinion that Hellas was once entirely or almost entirely inhabited by barbarians.

In time the Hellenes assumed the foremost place among the Greek races. All who could do so joined them and wished to belong to them, while some tribes of closely related origin, such as the Leleges, Carians, Dardanians, Dryopes, Caucones and Pelasgians were excluded as semi-barbarians. These peoples gradually split up into small groups or vanished completely, if only because no-one wanted to be counted as belonging to them any longer (Pausanias 4.34.6).

Perhaps all this is generally taken too seriously. Were the Hellenes an exceptionally active section of the nation, superior in physical, military and religious qualities as well? Or did their name gain pre-eminence only by chance? In the fifteenth century of our own era a group of allies in the Alpine foothills became known as the Swiss (Schweizer) only because, in a long war, the people of Schwyz had been in the forefront of the group. Had the Hellenes some reason not to reject those who sought to join them? Did they give themselves this name or was it given them by others? There seems to have been an earlier collective name, the Graeci, which was revived in Roman times. Was this no longer adequate? And why not? These are all questions to which we have no answer. All we know for certain is that in its earliest occurrences the name Hellas refers to two northern provinces, Thessalian Phthiotis and (according to Aristotle) the region around Dodona in Epirus; and that it was later extended first to the whole of Thessaly, then to everything north of the Isthmus at Corinth, and finally to the Peloponnese and the islands, till at last the name Hellenes applied to all nonbarbarians[1].

How the Hellenes proper then became subdivided into the well-known four tribes [Aeolians, Achaeans, Dorians, Ionians] is extremely obscure. The name of one, the Aeolians, was very probably used as a collective name for the whole nation, and another, the Achaeans, is of course so used by Homer; while the other two, Dorians and Ionians, were never anything but names for parts of the nation, though as time went on they acquired important connotations of contrasting customs, thought and language[2]. The celebrated genealogical table which tells us that Hellen's sons were Aeolus, Dorus, and Xuthus, and Xuthus's were Ion and Achaeus, is totally worthless and inconsistent; and this illustrates some particular difficulties of Greek ethnography.

In traditional accounts, early Greek times appear as a succession of migrations; one tribe drives out and supplants another until driven out in turn by a third, and this process may have lasted many hundreds of years. Not until the so-called Dorian migration of the eleventh century did the location and distribution of the Greek people begin to take on its final form, in a series of thrusts by which Thessalians, Boeotians, Dorians, Aetolians, Achaeans and Ionians, among others, acquired new homelands on both sides of the Aegean Sea, while new states were founded and a few old states disappeared. Often these migrations must have brought about a general upheaval. We see this clearly in the double or multiple names of so many places of which it was said that the earlier name was taken from the language of the gods. In one case, however, that of a famous island, the new name too is of divine origin. 'Once the eternal gods named this island Abantis, which Zeus now called Euboea, after a bull.'[3] Successive populations seem to have renamed the places for themselves.

It is certain that the legends about the earlier migrations, before the Dorian, contain a quantity of historical facts. These are related so fragmentarily, and chronologically so much at random, that they are hardly of any use in themselves; what is old, and what is oldest of all, are indistinguishable, and it is thus impossible to trace the movements of the peoples. Or the same expressions are used to describe both swift conquests and slow advances lasting for centuries. The wealth of genealogies of reigning houses seem, at first sight, informative about the migrations and destinies of peoples, but eventually we come to understand just what this kind of help is really worth.

For myth has swathed all this in its fine shimmering veil, embracing the terrestrial and the cosmic, religion and poetry, unconscious observation of the world, and experience distilled. The images that arose from it all were accepted as having a bearing upon the remotest times, but in a very free and flexible way. The wildest variations and contradictions, inevitable when the origins of the things recounted were so different, were not found at all disturbing. In addition, free invention was used to help out, particularly in genealogical matters. Authors of every period, even when they appear to lay claim to exactitude, always served an apprenticeship to myth, and saw everything in a mythical way; but apart from this they invented and elaborated in a manner completely alien to the modern world.

To a certain extent there was an awareness of this state of affairs. Tradition, originally the province of the rhapsodists and composers of theogonies, was later taken over by the so-called logographers, those collectors of regional and popular legends of whom Thucydides (1.21.1) says that they wrote more to give pleasure to their hearers than out of regard for the truth. Later we find in Strabo (8.3.9): 'The old writers recount many things that never happened, having grown up among the lies of the mythographers.' He says this in connection with Hecataeus of Miletus, perhaps the most important of the logographers; but Hecataeus himself had written, five hundred years before Strabo: 'The stories the Greeks tell are many and absurd.'[4] Ephorus, in the fourth century B.C., the first to venture on linking a general history of the Greeks with that of the rest of the world, had good reason to begin no earlier than the Dorian migration.

Here we must take account of a general assumption which coloured the whole Greek viewpoint. It is extremely probable that the Greeks came to their country from somewhere else, whether we suppose their previous habitation to have been in the Caucasus, in Asia Minor or in Europe; but it is certain that as a nation they had lost all awareness of this. The migrations which were still part of common knowledge were not thought to have originated outside the country but to have been movements within the Greek lands; the few recognized exceptions (Cadmus, Pelops, Danaus etc.) had to do only with royal houses, not whole peoples.[5] So while the whole nation considered itself an original autochthonous population, a few Greek communities also took a very special pride in the claim that they were still living on the very spot where long ago the human race itself had come into being with them. True, the words *autochthon, gegenes* (aboriginal, sprung from the soil) sometimes have only the negative sense that beyond a certain person nothing earlier is known, and may elsewhere be applied merely to the non-refugees who in mythical times were almost in the minority, since migrations, expulsions and flights from persecution were so much the rule. But there are many unquestioned sources to prove that in the main these epithets were taken literally and bestowed as a title of honour. A very early poet (Asius) sang of the first man and king of Arcadia: 'The dark earth allowed the godlike Pelasgus to come to life in the thickly wooded mountains, so that there might be a race of mortals on earth.'[6] On uninhabited Aegina Zeus answers the prayer of Aeacus by causing men to rise from the ground, or ants to turn into men. On Rhodes there once lived an autochthonous people under the ruling house of the Heliads.[7] In Attica there was true pride in autochthony, and here we also learn how it was symbolically expressed. Cecrops – according to the account of him as a native, not Egyptian-born – had a snake's body in place of his lower limbs.[8] The Greeks held many and various views as to the origin of the human race, but all agreed that mankind first arose in Greece and nowhere else. When credence was given to the later view that Prometheus had formed human beings out of a block of clay, then blocks of the same clay, which even had the odour of human flesh, were still to be seen at Panopeus in Phocis (Pausanias 10.4.3). On the other hand, if men were descended from the gods, then the Greeks possessed in their own country the birthplaces of these gods, their myths, the scenes of their battles with the giants, the famous natural cataclysms and finally the legend of the Flood, most of these localized in several different places. Linked with the legend of the Flood was that of the second Creation of Man through the agency of Deucalion and Pyrrha, safely established as having occurred in Greece.

It was in Greece itself, and before all other nations, that mankind was believed to have been given those aids to life which were particularly seen as the gifts of the gods. Thebes was the home of viticulture (Pausanias 9.38.3); pruning had been learned in Nauplia from the example of an ass, which ate the shoots and caused the vines to bear more fruit (Pausanias 2.38.3); but it was Attica which claimed to be the home of the more important plants. The field of Rharus near Eleusis, with the threshing floor and altar of his son Triptolemus, was the first sown field on earth. On the Acropolis in Athens there survived for many centuries the sacred olive tree, the gift of Pallas Athena; on the Sacred Way to Eleusis they would still point out the spot on which Demeter, after being hospitably received by Phytalus, thanked him by causing the first fig tree to grow; in the district of Acharnai, where Dionysus Kissos was worshipped, the first ivy grew, and even the bean was perhaps native to the country (Pausanias 1.31.6, 1.37, 2–5, 1.38.6).

Several inventions too were Greek in origin.[9] The Argo was the first ship to sail the seas; in Alesiai, near Sparta, Myles (the miller), son of the first ruler, Lelex, had the first mill (Pausanias 3.20.2), and the Athenians even boasted that it was they who had taught men to make fire (Plutarch, *Kimon* 10). In general, though, the Greeks easily accepted the idea that things redolent of human toil and of the banausic were borrowed from abroad – in strong contrast to the modern world, in which industrial inventions are thought to be the greatest achievement of the nations that lay claim to them, so that priorities of this kind lead to serious disputes.

Thus the Greeks conceded that Tyrsenus the Lydian had invented the trumpet, that the shield and helmet,[10] the war chariot and geometry had come to them from Egypt, the drapery of the statues of Pallas Athena from Libya, the alphabet from Phoenicia, the sundial and the division of the day into hours from Babylon.[11] They were quite content to be the centre of the world and to be able to show the 'navel of the Earth' on their own sacred soil in the temple at Delphi.[12]

To return to the migrations, then, the mythological expression is in some cases quite transparent. If the heiress to a throne is given in marriage to a foreign prince who has perhaps to prove himself by military conquest, or if the princess is got with child by Poseidon and her son comes to the throne later, it is easy to deduce a change of dynasty or of the ruling population, in the second instance by invasion from the sea. The kinship of two peoples is symbolized by a river flowing under the sea and coming up as a spring in another country. The famous example of the Peloponnesian Alpheus reappearing as the spring of Arethusa on the island of Ortygia (Syracuse) is not the only one, and Pausanias, who reports several (2.5.2) seems in no doubt that it is a physical possibility. Pride in the possession of excellent land, scorn for the less fortunate neighbouring people with a reputation for stupidity, may be expressed in legends of the region's having been acquired by successful deception. As late as the Dorian migration, the

Aetolians who joined it had managed to secure a better piece of land (Elis) than the Dorians acquired anywhere, and Cresphontes was supposed among the Dorians themselves to have won his fertile region of Messenia from the Spartans by trickery at dice. It was often believed that a duel between the opposing leaders had decided the ownership of a piece of land: 'They came out to fight in single combat in accordance with an old custom among the Hellenes' is the formula.[13] A popular touch is given to the story when the favourite weapon of one tribe wins the victory over that of the other. Pyraichmes the Aetolian and Degmenos the Epeian confronted each other, and Degmenos, a bowman, thought his long shot would easily beat the Aetolian, who was a hoplite, but he came with a sling and a sackful of stones. The sling had recently been invented by the Aetolians, and had a longer range than the bow; Degmenos fell, and the Aetolians kept the land and drove the Epeians away. The commonest way of expressing a claim to a parcel of land was to say that someone had received as a gift, or managed to acquire, a clod of earth from the land in question. Such legends however give little positive result if presented piecemeal in their chronological isolation.

The personification of a whole people in a hero is understandable enough, too, since the unsophisticated mind attributes every deed only to an individual. It is also easy to see the reason for the firm conviction that the people are named after their hero and not the other way round, and for the universal belief that each city was once founded, and must be called after its founder.[14] Closer investigation makes matters seem less simple, as not only a people, but localities too – a river, a mountain or a whole region – may appear in the genealogical tables as personalities.[15] Things become really complicated with the numerous cases of heroes' names which mean things that have somehow played a part in the destiny of the country, whether these are particular actions or occupations or ways of living. When we read that Teos was colonized by one Apoikos (the colonist) or that Paralos and Aigialeus (both meaning coast dwellers) populated Clazomenae and the coast of Sicyon, we tend to suppose that these are very late inventions. But even Herodotus (5.68) believes that the Aegialeans were called so after the hero Aegialeus, while in fact they and the hero undoubtedly took their names from the coast (*aigialos*). Everyone knows what the Greeks were like as etymologists, and this last case is easy to elucidate; so it is also when Pausanias (8.26.1) derives the name of Heraia in Arcadia from a founder Heraios, though it is quite obviously the city of Hera.

If only the many names of whatever origin were to some extent handed down in a serious attempt at genealogical order, we could take them as first-hand evidence of what was believed about race and the migrations. But besides the familiar figures of the heroic age, each with their characteristic adventures and exploits, whole troops of people are brought into the genealogies solely on the strength of their names. The conviction begins to grow that we are dealing with brazen fiction of a completely arbitrary nature, a total indifference to what actually happened. If, for example, in the case of Apollodorus we were prepared to accept the great genealogical tables of the first book as an actual excerpt, a vestige of epic poetry, he has still other genealogies, such as that of the royal house of Troy (3.12) the Tyndaridai (3.10) and so forth, in which the names – in part those of localities (districts, rivers or mountains) – are obviously grouped at random. They might just as well be arranged in a completely different order in the tables, up, down or sideways. The same is often true of Diodorus and of Pausanias, for instance in his great genealogy of Arcadia (8.3.1). To give another example, Conon and Parthenius, in recounting the myth of Pallene, introduce as human actors in the story a number of places on or near the well-known peninsula of the same name.[16] One look at such degrees of kinship is enough to show that we can give up any idea of discovering in them a true time sequence or actual blood relationships, or any chronological account of the founding of towns here named as if they were human beings. Even among the feuds referred to, we seldom feel inclined to recognize an ancient rivalry that really existed. Gaps in continuity are often stopped up with the most disreputable makeshift padding.

It may seem tempting to ascribe the enormous number of arbitrarily invented family trees to the idle scribblers of post-Alexandrian times, or even to much later forgers. Still, they had illustrious predecessors. In *Suppliants* (312 ff.) Aeschylus blithely improvises a family tree (taken over from him by Apollodorus) that goes like this: Epaphus is the son of Zeus and Io, and the father of Libye, whose son is Belus the father of Danaus and Aegyptus.[17] And in fact the classical epics were no more particular. In the *Iliad* a hero's name is often followed by a rapid account of his ancestry that sounds strikingly like an improvisation. This is why we remarked earlier that even the account of the relationship between Hellen and his sons is not to be taken seriously. In modern times genealogy is a laborious critical undertaking, while for the Greeks it was a diversion, and even mythical animals were not left out: there was a general conviction that the sow of Crommyon, slain by Theseus, was the mother of the Calydonian boar.[18]

Besides, not all ancient peoples resembled the Greeks in this. The genealogical table in the tenth chapter of Genesis, whether its contents are of Hebrew origin or, more probably, borrowed from a Phoenician source, is the result of the most earnest endeavour to collate everything there was to tell about the links between different peoples. How clear it is that Babel is the forerunner of Nineveh, that Sidon is of great antiquity compared with the tribes of the interior; the descendants of Abraham are treated favourably or critically according to their closer or remoter degrees of kinship – and what an impression of documentary exactitude it all makes! There is probably not a single superfluous name mentioned.

For the Greeks, though, quite apart from genealogy, the improvization and recitation of a multitude of names had a strong charm of its own. Cataloguing, which is nowadays, like genealogy, the object of serious and painstaking study, used to fill the epic and theogonic poets with pure delight. Once this lesson has been learned we shall not only ignore the family trees of Apollodorus but also perhaps cease to take the Catalogue of Ships in the second book of the *Iliad* too seriously. Yet for all this we cannot deny the probability that where old dynastic lists and genealogies survived, they occasionally contained the literal truth.

It is known that the later Greeks also sought to provide chronological support for their mythological past, and, as many of them believed themselves descended from gods and heroes, there may well have been a demand for a historical account of ancient times; but the genealogies, for what they were worth, were still available, and Hecataeus of Miletus believed himself to be descended from a god in the sixteenth generation (Herodotus 2.143). In Greece however there was no one caste traditionally charged with responsibility as chroniclers; writing long remained a rare accomplishment, and the official year was calculated variously and often inaccurately in different places. In these circumstances the information from which the reckoning by Olympiads (starting in 776 B.C.) was eventually worked out must have been far from reliable – even with the help of old lists of the Argive priestesses of Hera, the kings and archons of Athens, Sicyon, Argos and so on.[19] So people resorted to reckoning by generations, and it is no doubt by this heroic means that Herodotus arrived at his conclusion (2.145) that Dionysus lived 1600 years before his own time, Heracles 900, and Pan (here the son of Hermes and Penelope) 800. (He was calculating a generation as about thirty-three years (2.142) although he knew of a case (1.7) in which a sequence of twenty-two generations had yielded an average age of twenty-three.)[20] He found no difficulty in reconciling mythical acts of procreation with the average span of a generation, although they were often only a disguise for the relation of cause and effect, and in any case beyond any conceivable system of reckoning.[21] Another example, which shows the humorous possibilities of this subject, is provided by Isocrates in his *Busiris* (8.36 f.) where he floors an opponent with the chronological demonstration that Heracles cannot have killed Busiris since Heracles was four generations later than Perseus, Busiris more than two hundred years earlier. We know now that Heracles was a divine being while Busiris was simply a bogeyman of Greek fantasy. Isocrates nevertheless crushes his antagonist with the words 'But you have no regard for the truth, and repeat the blaspheming of the poets.' Again and again we must overcome the temptation to assume that a people as clever as the Greeks must have had something resembling a critical approach to the past. It is true that they were passionately attached to the particular and the local in their ideas of primeval times, but their antiquarian sense did not extend much beyond the mythical sphere.

It seems to have been from sources and methods like these that the so-called Parian Marble Chronicle was put together about the middle of the third century B.C. It was the work of a private scholar, and presents many mythical events and persons from Deucalion onwards, all complete with dates, such as Ares and Poseidon before the Areopagus, Cadmus in Thebes, the Danaids in Greece, Erichthon, Minos, Demeter and Triptolemus teaching agriculture etc. Not much later, Eratosthenes in his *Chronography* worked out the year of the capture of Troy, which he placed, as we know, in 1184 B.C., as well as a few other important dates down to the start of the dating by Olympiads. He too, in spite of his modest aim, can scarcely have avoided the division of time by generations, and others calculated the years from the fall of Troy quite differently.

Their only source of information about their antiquity was myth and its voice, the epic; the calamity, scientifically speaking, began later on, with the refusal to recognize this fact, and the insistence on treating Homer as a document, even when he was in conflict with some old piece of ethnographical information from elsewhere. These other sources must either be reconciled with him or be made to yield to his authority. Strabo, who is forever 'Homericizing', and tells us very little of the post-Homeric age until the Persian Wars, succeeds in one passage (9.5) in producing a grand confusion between the ancient ethnography of Thessaly derived from other sources and the reign of Achilles according to Homer. It is Strabo who makes us particularly aware how strong was the belief in Homer's exactitude, how every little town cherished the ambition to be mentioned in the *Iliad* as a 'well-founded citadel' and how, when it suited them, they would correct Homer until he provided the desired information. Those antiquarians who kept closest to Homer were then called *Homerikoteros* (more Homeric) as a title of honour. The problem of a large number of events which refused to be fitted into mythical times was coolly solved by attaching them to the official ending of that period, that is to the *Nostoi*, the legends of the heroes' wanderings after the conquest of Troy. Not only Odysseus and Diomedes, but also Menelaus, Calchas and the Trojans Aeneas and Antenor were believed to have gone wandering far and wide about the world, and could thus be credited with founding many towns. The very ancient dispersion of Greeks along the Italian and Asiatic coasts was undeniable, but it was myth that formed the great universal spiritual background of national life, and to have no part in it was, it seems, considered a misfortune. Thus Diomedes became the lord of the Adriatic, and Achilles lord of the Black Sea; and if all else failed then Heracles, 'lord of the West', must once have landed in the relevant spot.[22] So it was in such outlying lands that the cult of the heroes was particularly prevalent.

According to the poets, geography too seems to strive towards the condition of myth, although plenty of exact information was available. When the Black Sea had long been swarming with Greek colonies, quite close to the time of Herodotus and the masterly ethnography of Sicily in Thucydides (6.2.3), Aeschylus gives us in his *Prometheus* the most extraordinary fabulous geography, a perfect mythical dream world. The same charming fables that in Greece animated hill, dale and seacoast with their figures and stories also created the image of the people of the outside world, beginning with the Amazons, who, with Antiope, Hippolyta and Penthesilea, make such marvellous irruptions into the lives of the Hellenic heroes. It was to this magnificent or awe-inspiring fringe of their world that the Greeks clung longest.

However questionable their actual knowledge of ancient times may have been, myth was a powerful force dominating Greek life and hovering over it all like a wonderful vision, close at hand.[23] It illuminated the whole of the present for the Greeks, everywhere and until a very late date, as though it belonged to a quite recent past; and essentially it presented a sublime reflection of the perceptions and the life of the nation itself.

Other nations, too, have possessed a similar representation of themselves in the shape of their stories about gods and heroes. Whether the
relation of the Indians, Persians and Germanic races to their myth was
ever comparably intense is a question for experts in these fields. Possibly
the great dominating orthodoxies of the Orient and of Egypt, all resulting
from later developments, effectively sucked the lifeblood from more ancient
legends of gods and heroes, and reduced popular fantasy to the level of
fairy stories. In any case the Greeks enjoyed enormous advantages. They
were still in the first phase of their history; as yet they had no experience
of a great catastrophe overtaking an already developed culture – neither
migration, for the migrations we know of took place within the Greek
nation itself; nor invasion by another people, which might have led to a
break in the old way of life and obscured the memory of it; nor religious
crisis leading to a rigidifying of belief, an orthodoxy; nor, finally, any secular
enslavement. More positively, there was the remarkable good fortune that
Hellenic myth, having come into being in a wholly unsophisticated period,
yet survived in its full richness into a literate, indeed a highly literary age,
and was consequently recorded in astonishing completeness.

In Plato's *Timaeus* (22B) the aged Egyptian priest says to Solon: 'You
Hellenes are always children; there is no Hellene who is truly an old man
... you are all young in soul because you have no ancient lore, no old
learning, no age-old knowledge.' It is quite true that the Greeks, instead
of the bookish lore and erudite knowledge that bedevilled the Egyptians,
enjoyed a true empathy with their past that was almost without parallel.
Later, of course, when they too had become a learned nation, myth became
the subject of erudition and controversy and lived on as a kind of secondary
history. There were quarrels about the family connections of this or that
hero and who killed whom in battle, and the variants were compared; even
very late [Byzantine] scholiasts such as Eustathius, Tzetzes etc. were still
distinguishing better and lesser authorities. And the Romans, who took
over Greek myth as though it were a world they had received as a gift,
learned it all by heart in the sweat of their brows and loaded their poetry
with it. The Emperor Tiberius, half in earnest and half in mockery, pestered
his grammarians with pedantic questions such as 'Who was Hecuba's
mother?' 'What name did Achilles bear among the maidens of Scyros?' and
asked what song the sirens sang.[24] Tiberius could in fact have found a not
much younger contemporary who would not have been at a loss for an

answer; Ptolemy Hephaestion claimed to know five names that Achilles used on Scyros and the names of the teachers of Odysseus, Achilles, Patroclus and others, with much else of the same kind.[25] In very late times, indeed well into the Christian era, when the mythical figures no longer appeared on the stage and had almost ceased to be represented by painters and sculptors, these themes were still used in the erudite poems of Nonnus. Above all it was the rhetoricians of the schools who refused to give up this substratum of material. Comparisons would be drawn between the fame of Odysseus and that of Nestor; eulogies or condemnations of them would be delivered, speeches composed for and against mythical figures in court proceedings; pathetic declamations on crucial occasions were put into their mouths; we hear what Cassandra would have said when the wooden horse entered Troy, or Agamemnon at the moment of being murdered, Heracles as he prepared to ascend the funeral pyre, Menelaus at the news of his brother's death, and many similar things.[26]

The dominance of myth must have been much reinforced by the *polis* as the pattern of national life, and by the bards. Among the German-speaking peoples, as they settled down after the migrations, besides belief in the gods and various tribal stories, a dark saga of heroes may well have dominated mental life to a certain extent as an imaginary national history, and in this legend the chief figure was no doubt Dietrich von Bern. Here too, minstrels were very likely the principal means of spreading such legends, and may have been welcomed in noblemen's castles from very early times. Rural people, as these almost exclusively were, did not pass on such things with the elasticity of the urban population of the *poleis*, but contented themselves with the general imaginative stimulus provided by accounts of great men and fabulous happenings. The Greek audience consisted mostly of city dwellers with, undeniably, extraordinary gifts for the understanding and elaboration of what they heard, as well as with the will and the capacity to devote themselves to it continuously; such an audience gave an ideal reception to the art of the bards, without whom the dissemination of the legends which now became universally known in Greece would have been unthinkable. The local city myths attached to ancient temple cults might well have survived on their own. Without the minstrels, though, it is hard to imagine how the voyage of the Argonauts, the Calydonian hunt and the story of Oedipus, which have no historical basis, or hardly any, could have become accepted as historical events by all Greeks equally; and moreover have continued to arouse much greater interest, and for far longer, than anything that really took place, even much later. Thus the war against Troy, a common national experience of not too remote antiquity, was made to yield the foundation and solid basis for this whole world of imaginary figures. Compared with Theseus, Meleager, Pelops and the house of Atreus, all historical personalities were little known and regarded with indifference by the Greeks, and another factor in this indifference may have been that any given historical figure would belong to only one *polis* which was hated by all the rest. This would be equally true of most of the mythological personalities, and yet through epic poetry they became universally known.

Thereafter, for hundreds of years, throughout the time of the so-called 'epic cycle', the accumulated store was revised and elaborated; that is, wherever actual history might have established itself, it was thrust down and overcome by the proliferation of legend, or fiction, gradually filling up all the interstices through which historical accuracy might have taken a hold. Even such factual knowledge as did survive was envisaged and recounted exclusively in the spirit of myth; even what was really history was subjected to the laws of a tradition that long remained solely oral and poetic. A genuine genealogy may have been handed down only to be rendered suspect for critical purposes by being embroidered with fictitious genealogies, often the work of later local antiquaries. In the same way genuine ethnographic information is overlaid by the introduction of purely fabulous races such as the Centaurs and Lapiths, and every possible means is used to sustain the fabulous ethnography and geography.[27] Indeed the surprising thing is not so much that myth was capable of standing up to history, as that it could stand up to itself, that is that mythological tales were not constantly supplanted by other myths – in other words that a consensus was arrived at, with the bards joining on their narratives where a predecessor had started, or where he had left off.

Myth is the underlying given factor in Greek existence. The whole culture, in everything that was done, remained what it had always been, developing only slowly. The mythological or sacred origin of many outer forms of life was known, and was felt to be very near. The whole Greek nation believed themselves the rightful heirs and successors of the heroic age; wrongs suffered in prehistoric times were still being avenged much later.[28] Herodotus begins his account of the great battle between East and West with the rape of Io, and the Persian War becomes a continuation of the Trojan War. Later, indeed, (in 396 B.C.) when Agesilaus once more took up arms against the Persians, he went to Aulis on purpose to offer up a solemn sacrifice in imitation of Agamemnon, though his intention was severely frustrated by a surprise attack of Theban cavalry. Ancestral exploits in remote antiquity were employed as gambits in official negotiations. Thus, before the battle of Plataea, the Athenians argued very seriously that they had a better right than the Tegeans to wage the preliminary engagement on the grounds that they had formerly protected the Heraclids, vanquished the Amazons, given burial to the seven heroes who went out against Thebes, fought bravely in the Trojan War and, only as an afterthought, that they also won the battle of Marathon (Herodotus 9.27). Athenian funeral orations for the fallen made use of such themes over and over again as a matter of course; only Pericles, in his funeral oration, dared to leave out these mythical exploits and confined himself to the real powers of Athens then existing.

When the people of Megara voted honorary citizenship to Alexander the Great he laughed; but they said they had never before bestowed it on anyone except Heracles.[29] The Spartans too called upon Heracles as their ancestral hero and upon his sons, the Heraclids, both in war and in official decrees.[30] Traditional costumes and customs enjoyed effective protection through the emphasis on their mythical origins.[31]

How seriously such traditions were taken may be gathered from the fact that even in historic times a family still remained under a curse drawn down upon them by mythical forefathers. The great clan of the Agiads in Sparta, descended from the royal house of Labdacus in Thebes, suffered the deaths of all their offspring; in obedience to an oracle they built a sanctuary to the Erinyes of Laius and Oedipus, and then their children stopped dying.[32] Pindar offers to console Theron, tyrant of Acragas, who traced his descent from the same ill-fated family, with the reflection that what is done is done, justly or unjustly, and our mother Time herself cannot undo it, but by the blessing of Fortune we find help in forgetfulness (*Olympian Odes* 2.15). But where it was not a case of particular families a different view prevailed, and cities which were the scenes of the most appalling myths would not have given them up at any price.

The earliest history of Athens is especially instructive as showing the double flow of myth so clearly; on one hand it reaches down of its own accord into the present, while, on the other, historical development intrudes violently into myth. Attica had a heritage of ancient traditions; for example nearly all the seats of judgment in Athens were still associated with the legendary world, beginning with the Areopagus as the scene of Ares' conviction for the murder of Halirrhothius, and a large number of hereditary priesthoods boasted of their prehistoric origin.[33] Besides this, an ancient prehistory of the region survived, which was in part clearly a cultural myth, connected with the names of Cecrops, Amphictyon, Erichthonius, Pandion, Erechtheus, the Metionids and others. However, all this was interwoven with, and in a way rendered superfluous by, the figure of Theseus.

For Theseus is on one hand a genuine mythical hero of Panhellenic legend, and on the other a concept symbolizing the evolution of the Athenian state, quite late features of which were transposed to form elements of his life and his deeds. It is generally agreed that two of Plutarch's *Lives* are essentially condensations of the later experiences of whole peoples; these are the lives of Lycurgus and Theseus. But long before Plutarch, Xenophon had used the portrait of Lycurgus as a summation of Spartan evolution, while that of Theseus was the mirror of Athenian evolution as early as Thucydides (2.15), Isocrates and Aristotle. Theseus embarks on his political career by creating the preconditions for that very same state which according to other legends had already long existed. He destroys dangerous wild beasts and criminals. Then he assembles the population of Attica, who, living scattered in separate villages, have never till now met for counsel and have even fought among themselves. He unites them in one *polis* and institutes the solemn celebration of this new citizenship, the Panathenaea. But just as he was supposed earlier to have slain the bull of Marathon to ingratiate himself with the people, so he was now the first to woo the masses by abdicating as king.[34] While he is held captive in Hades another demagogue, an Erechtheid called Menestheus, leads a revolution, and Theseus returns to find everything changed and the *demos* completely spoilt; so he attempts to seize power again, gets into great difficulties, vainly engages in counterdemagogy and at last, angrily cursing – on a cursing spot which used to be pointed out to visitors – he goes off to Scyros, where Lycomedes hurls him from the clifftop. When in later times anyone asked the origin of an institution or a custom (even that of the two obols the souls of the dead had to pay the ferryman) the answer was likely to be 'Theseus decreed it so.'[35] The dance called Geranos, with its serpentine weavings, is a reminiscence of the windings of the Labyrinth, and was first danced by Theseus and Ariadne with the rescued youths and maidens after the Minotaur was slain. And in the same way, everywhere in Greece, everyday life was artistically linked with remote antiquity.

In later antiquity, too, there was a perception of a deeper, an ideal unity in the collective life of a city or a people. Plutarch's essay *Of the Delayed Vengeance of the Gods* is a collection of deeds from mythical times which were expiated or suffered for by descendants, some well into the writer's own day, and to some extent it is only additional evidence of the tendency to explain present-day phenomena by reference to the dim and distant past. But, somewhere in all this, Plutarch pronounces this weighty dictum: 'for a *polis* is one and indivisible!' – and all Greeks knew that the sins of the fathers shall be visited upon the children.[36]

Given the fixed intention of linking the present with the remotest past, it would be foolish to expect that any precise and detailed knowledge of that past could flourish. No criticism is capable of analysing into its component parts this whole, brought together by the youthful nation's powerful vision; and in fact this need cause us no anxiety. Not only mythical events, but some that were historical too, were transformed by long retelling until they took on a typical and characteristic resonance. Our recognition of this has its own value for our understanding of the Greeks.

Here, then, was a nation which vigorously defended its myth as the ideal basis of its existence, and tried at all costs to make connections between that myth and practical life. It was not only this that made history difficult; this people tolerated no historical drama on its stage and paid little attention to the historical epic, that is, the literary treatment of the relatively recent past.

This same people is now regarded as 'classical' in opposition to any kind of 'romanticism'. If, however, Romanticism can be equated with a continuous focusing on the relationship between things or points of view on one hand, and a poetic vision of the past on the other, then the Greeks had, in their myth, a tremendous Romanticism as the presupposition of their spiritual life. Can we say that the heroic sagas of the Germanic or Celtic peoples were anything like so powerful a force in the later Middle Ages?

There are few sites in our own Western Europe about which any reminiscences of our heroic sagas can be said to cling, and without the aid of learned antiquarians we would know almost nothing about the Untersberg, the Hörselberg, the Eckartsberg or the Wasgen Rock. Hauntings no doubt still occur in many places, but the legends told about them belong only to popular superstition, or show only slight links with our ancient myths of gods and heroes. In Greece it is quite different; the country was full of classical sites and well-preserved visible reminders either of general Hellenic mythology or of local myth.[37]

Besides, in every part of the country the local, often very elaborate, cult was always intent on making its origins as old and venerable as possible, and was celebrated in conjunction with the countless cults of local heroes, headed in each place by the supposed founder of the particular city. Everywhere, too, were signs of the polydaemonism that animated the whole landscape, even if it were only the love story of a stream and a sea nymph.

It was felt to be essential to know the spot on which each mythical incident had occurred, and Pausanias saw it as his duty to record the testimonies of local antiquaries on such points.[38] In Athens itself he can point out where Boreas abducted Oreithyia and Aegeus threw himself from the rock, where Silenus rested on his first visit to Dionysus, and so on through the whole city; on Salamis he knows the boulder on which Telamon was sitting as he gazed after his sons departing for Aulis and Troy. In Thebes, at Amphion's grave, the rough stones at the base were the very stones that had once followed the sound of Amphion's lyre. Orestes' memory lived on in a true Via Dolorosa between Megalopolis and Messene; at one place, it was said, he lost his reason, at another he bit off one of his fingers, here he was cured and there he cut off his hair after his recovery.[39] Pausanias finds it surprising, at Mount Cithaeron, that nobody knows the place where Pentheus went mad and where the infant Oedipus was exposed (9.2.3). Heracles, the Argonauts, Oedipus, Odysseus and Aeneas had turned up all over the country, and things of great or little importance were connected with their visits; the same Heracles who dug the pits at Pheneus in Arcadia had also uprooted the thistles in the gymnasium at Elis. For each and every striking natural phenomenon some mythical explanation was forthcoming; if the water of a spring had a bad smell, a centaur must have washed his wounds at it.[40] Other authors too give a wealth of such information; Strabo knows the spring at Corinth where Bellerophon captured Pegasus as he drank, and Aelian (3.1) traces the precise course of the sacred Pythian route from Delphi to the particular bay tree in the Vale of Tempe where Apollo was purified after slaying the Python. There were even some associations which retained a baneful influence. The Leucadian rock, from which in mythical times the lovesick Cephalus leapt into the sea, was later fatal to other unfortunates; each year the Leucadians hurled a criminal from it and then tried their best to save his life. No doubt the reason for this was to prevent the magic of the place, which was dreaded by the inhabitants, from breaking out in an epidemic of suicides, and yet as it were to ensure that the spell received its due victim.[41]

A natural consequence of this tendency to strong localization of myths was that the same myths were often given a home in different places, and especially those of the birth and upbringing of gods – which in turn, whatever the real reason for it, helped to multiply classical associations. Apart from the island of Delos (traditionally the birthplace of Apollo) there was in Boeotia, not far from Tegyra, a temple of Apollo near which the god was said to have been born.[42] A mountain near this place was called Delos, and 'Palm' and 'Olive tree' were the names of two powerful cold springs of sweet water behind the temple, which had also once been an oracle. Not far off was the Ptoon, where the goddess Leto was terrified by the apparition of the he-goat; and the place also linked the legend of the Python and of Tityos with that of the god's birth. Various places, too, were said to be the scene of the birth of Zeus and of Athena, the nurture of Hermes, the Battle of the Giants, the rape of Kore, the fetching up of Cerberus, the disappearance of Amphiaraus and other events. Later local antiquarians can hardly have been responsible for all this. It was rather that myth was omnipresent; the whole people thought in this way and were long confirmed in their belief by the epos.

History was quite another matter. Reminiscences of great deeds in historical times were virtually nonexistent, with the exception of a few battlefields where the offerings for the dead on the warriors' graves reminded people of what had happened there.[43] No-one gave a thought to the places where Solon, Pericles or Demosthenes had appeared on crucial occasions, yet everyone claimed precise knowledge about the sites of classical legend. It was just the same with the relics. True, there were certain historical relics, like the stringed instruments, writing tablets and stylus of Euripides, which the elder Dionysius bought from the heirs for one talent and offered up with suitable inscriptions in a temple of the Muses. Similar tokens may have found their way into the temples as offerings from famous men themselves, who wished to be commemorated in this way;[44] but in these same temples it was certainly the relics of mythical times that everyone wanted to see. The eighth chapter of the *Liber memorialis* of Ampelius, where the altar of Pergamon is mentioned, lists a whole mass of weapons, utensils, garments and other mementos from mythical times which could be seen in the temples of Greece, possibly even as late as the reign of Theodosius. Pausanias himself saw the spear of Achilles (3.3.6), Memnon's dagger (6.19.3), the sword of Pelops, the horn of Amalthea; but in one passage (9.41), making a great critical effort, he declares that, of a large number of surviving works of Hephaestus, only the Sceptre of Zeus in Chaeronea is really a work from the divine forge. Near the celebrated pine grove of Poseidon at Corinth could be seen the decayed but constantly restored Argo, the ship on which Jason and the Argonauts sailed. Magna Graecia (southern Italy) could also show such treasures – the arrows of Heracles in Apollo's temple at Thurii, the blacksmith's tools used to construct the Trojan horse in the temple of Athena at Metapontum.[45] In a temple of Athena in the territory of the Dauni (northern Apulia) they had the bronze axe and weapons of Diomedes, who seems to have held sway in those parts like a god; and in a temple of Artemis among the Peucetii (further south) was the bronze neckband which he had fastened on a stag. At least the Greeks did not convert such antiquities (except perhaps the Trojan statue of Athena called the Palladion) into *res fatales*, on whose magic the destiny of a state might depend, as the Romans did with the paraphernalia, imported partly from Greece, and kept in the temple of the Vestals. However even the Greeks had a superstition connected with the possession of the bones of heroes, sometimes because oracles had commanded them to be brought to a particular place, and anyway because of their reverence for graves. Apart from these considerations the wrath of a dead hero was to be feared if he were offended, and his blessing on the whole state might be hoped for if his remains were safely preserved. Not everything was sacred; many things were merely interesting souvenirs, as for instance the bones of giants and Amazons, and the hide of the Calydonian boar preserved in the temple of Athena Alea in Tegea – though his teeth had unfortunately been taken to Rome.

Rather more attractive, and still organically alive, were the ancient sacred trees.[46] Among these were the olive tree brought into being by Athena in the Erechtheum in Athens, and another bent by Heracles' strong hand near Epidaurus; at Troezen one that had sprung from his club, and another, carefully fenced, on Attic soil, from which he had taken a twig to plant in Olympia. Then there was what remained of the plane tree in the temple at Aulis, which had seen the departure of the Greeks for Troy, the plane tree Menelais near Caphyae in Arcadia and so on. Even some animals were believed to have survived from mythological into historical times. Thus a general of the Achaean League had had an ancestor nine generations back – that is about the fifth century B.C. – who was supposed to have seen at Lycosura [in Arcadia] a doe, weak with age and sacred to Despoina,[47] wearing round its neck a band inscribed with the words 'I was still a fawn when Agapenor lay before Troy.'[48]

But there was one way of being close to the mythical that must have seemed more desirable than any other. A widespread belief existed that gods and men were of the same race; but there were also many families and individuals who gloried in their descent from gods and heroes, and even claimed to be able to name the intervening generations, or at least to number them.[49] This kind of tradition was unknown to most other ancient peoples, and Hecataeus of Miletus [see p. 20 above], boasting to the priests of Thebes in Egypt that he was of divine descent sixteen generations earlier, received the reply that no man was descended from a god (Herodotus 2.143). But among the Greeks many heroes are themselves the sons of gods, not their remote descendants. Aeacus was the son of Zeus and father of Telamon and Peleus; thus Achilles and Ajax were grandsons of Zeus, and Achilles also the son of Thetis. Thinking of Hector, Agamemnon is struck by the curious fact that he is not the beloved son of a god or a goddess (*Iliad* X.50). Such royal houses as survived into historical times were also of the race of gods; not only were the Spartan kings descended from Heracles and thus from Zeus,[50] but so were the Macedonian Temenids – a fact Isocrates makes a great deal of in his *Letter to Philip* (33–34), as much for admonition as for glorification.[51] Aeacus' descendants, Achilles and Neoptolemus, were the recognized founding fathers of the Molossian royal house in Epirus; King Pyrrhus believed he was the twenty-first descendant of Achilles, and that it was therefore his duty to fight against the Romans, who were descended from the Trojans. The weapons he captured in battle from Antigonus Gonatas of Macedon, and which he dedicated as trophies in the temple, bore the inscription 'Now as in times past the men of the house of Aeacus are lancebearers.' But it was from Ajax and thus, through Telamon and Aeacus, from Zeus that the great Miltiades was sprung, and the historian Thucydides came of the same house.[52] The Blepsiads, and doubtless many other families on Aegina, were also of the house of Aeacus, as were, through Teucer's line, all the Cypriot kings down to Evagoras.[53] The Iamids and all their kin were descendants of Iamus, son of Apollo and grandson of Poseidon; and Pindar, whose task it was to glorify them and many other families of champion athletes, stressed their divine descent as often as he could.[54] In Athens the Peisistratids and Alcmaeonids were recognized as Neleids and therefore descended from Poseidon, whereas the Thymoetadoi were Theseids. Like all the Eteobutadai, the orator and financier Lycurgus came of the line of Erechtheus, the son of Gaia and Hephaestus.[55] In a dialogue perhaps not genuinely Platonic, but none the less very early, the first *Alcibiades* (121A), we hear Alcibiades claim his descent from Zeus through Eurysaces, and Socrates' ironic reply that he too is descended from Zeus through Daedalus and Hephaestus. The poet Epicharmus was somehow reckoned a descendant of Achilles;[56] the famous Hippocrates, according to his biographer Soranus, was a descendant of Heracles in the twentieth generation, and of Asclepius in the nineteenth – the latter fact was explicitly recorded in an Athenian decree honouring Hippocrates. Ammonius says that Aristotle was a descendant of Asclepius on both his mother's and his father's side. It was known of Epaminondas that he belonged to one of the families of the Spartoi, the Armed Men, who had sprung from the dragon's teeth sown by Cadmus, and this would have been verifiable if the descendants of the Spartoi really bore a birthmark in the shape of a spear, as some of them still did as late as Plutarch's time.[57] In conversation it was a charming compliment to be able to say to a person: 'You will be very fortunate in the afterlife, as you come of divine stock.'[58] In an age such as the fourth century B.C. when so many of the aristocracy had been killed in the civic wars, the survivors must have clung all the more obstinately to advantages of this kind. The comic writers seized upon the chance to satirize these monstrous pretensions, as Aristophanes does for instance in *Acharnians* where the citizen Twice-divine (*Amphitheos*), descended from Demeter and Triptolemus, calls upon these ancestors when he is threatened with the police.

Others could dispense with primeval antiquity altogether since they were believed to have been directly begotten by gods in what was historically speaking broad daylight. Great athletes were said to be the sons of marine deities, or of Heracles, and after their death, as a logical consequence, the rumour would spread that they had not died but had been mysteriously wafted away.[59] Plato's connections were especially glorious; for a start, both his parents were descended from Poseidon, but then he may not have been the son of Ariston, since Apollo was supposed to have visited the bed of his beautiful mother Perictione; this last story was spread by Plato's closest associates.[60] In the same way Alexander could do without his claim to descend from Heracles through the Temenids if he was the direct offspring of Zeus Ammon.[61] His successors, the *diadochoi*, to their credit, made very sparing use of personal deification and almost none of divine descent. Antigonus, when Hermodotus in his poems called him a son of Helios, replied with a coarse joke.[62] In Greece itself, however, the chief of the Achaean League, Aratus, was supposed, a whole century later, to be a direct descendant of Asclepius, and even under the Empire, in the reign of Maximinus Thrax, the sophist Apsines of Gadara was said to have been the child of Pan.[63]

A further, final testimony to the nearness of myth and the childlike quality of Greek mentality may be found in the theophanies of the historical period. The gods who so often in Homer made themselves visible, and who in the land of the Phaeacians frequently crossed the path of the solitary wanderer, or joined human beings at table for a feast, continue to appear here and there well into the days of late antiquity.

There is the famous story of Peisistratus and his Phye, about which Herodotus (1.60) expresses amazement. Writing in the enlightened fifth century, he finds it hard to believe how simple-minded people were a hundred years earlier, since as he says the Greeks stood out in comparison with barbarians by their shrewdness and freedom from superstition, and among them the Athenians were thought the wisest of all. A rumour spread among the rural population of the demes that Peisistratus was being led home by Athena; in the city too it was believed that the goddess had appeared, and people came to worship her and to welcome Peisistratus. When he took the beautiful wreath seller with him in his chariot, dressed in all the adornments of the goddess, he probably intended no deception; quite likely he thought his entry into the city would be easier if it seemed to be a festal procession, and his chief aim must have been to enter the Acropolis unhindered. But there were still crowds who could be persuaded by Phye's tall figure and her beauty that she was the goddess herself. It would not have been at all easy to create the illusion deliberately, because festal processions had accustomed everyone to seeing human beings dressed as deities, and it was usual for the priest or priestess at sacrifices to appear in the costume of the divinity who was being honoured.[64]

Something similar happened much later, in the time of the Achaean League (about 230 B.C.). The Aetolians, who had invaded Achaean Pellene, were terrified when they saw the priestess of Athena, for whom a feast was celebrated that day, coming towards them from the door of the temple helmeted and armoured like the goddess. They fled from what seemed a divine apparition, while the Pellenians knew the figure was human.[65]

For a long time it was still believed that minor nature divinities were seen or heard. Seamen, even in Pausanias' day, seem to have clung to periodic sightings of their sea daemon Glaucus and his predictions.[66] But Pan was an especially persistent survivor. He might appear between

Cithaeron and Helicon and sing a paean of Pindar's;[67] at the time of the battle of Marathon an Athenian messenger's meeting with Pan near Tegea was officially accepted, and a shrine to Pan founded as a result on the Acropolis, with sacrifices and games.[68] Theocritus' shepherds (1.16) feared Pan as a close presence, occasionally visible, and knew how he looked when his nostrils were dilated with anger. In the time of Tiberius his death was announced, and only recently has research uncovered the strange error that was involved;[69] a hundred and fifty years later the inhabitants of Maenalus thought they could hear Pan playing the reed pipe (Pausanias 8.36).

The private communion of a few favoured people with divinities never quite ceased. Euripides' *Hippolytus* is of course set in mythical times, but the poet may be drawing on an attitude that still survived in his own age when his hero says to Artemis: 'I am with you and speak to you and hear your voice, though I do not see your face.' Numa was not the only wise lawgiver who enjoyed the inspiration of the nymph Egeria; Athena gave Zaleucus every one of his laws and appeared in person on each occasion.[70] Even odder is the relationship of Sophocles to several gods. It is not so extraordinary that Heracles appeared to him in a dream, or that Dionysus concerned himself with the poet's burial in his family grave by sending dreams to other people; but Sophocles not only praised Asclepius in a paean, but entertained him in human form in his own house, which is why the Athenians later honoured the poet as a hero under the name Dexion (the hospitable) by erecting a shrine for him with an annual sacrifice.[71] He would have known how to behave when the god came to him, as there was a ritual for such occasions. Certainly it was known to the seamen who recognized Pythagoras as a god; they hastily put up an altar and laid upon it whatever fruits they had, and gifts from their cargo.[72]

How near the idea of theophany was to men is once shown in a comic way. Some drunken young men of Acragas felt the house going round and round, and thought they were on board ship in a storm, so they threw all the furniture into the street. When the *strategoi* (the police) arrived to restore order, the revellers took them for tritons, and promised to honour them in the future with divine observances in the same way as the other sea gods.[73]

If at a feast a sudden general silence fell, someone would say that Hermes was passing through the room.[74]

This, then, was the spiritual disposition of the Greek people; and on them the greatest destiny in the history of the world was to devolve. Caught in the toils of their mythical past, only slowly becoming capable of history in any true sense, attaining their full stature in imaginative poetry, they were destined in the course of time to be pioneers in the understanding of all nations, and in communicating this understanding to others; to conquer vast territories and peoples of the East, to make their culture that of a whole world, in which Rome and Asia came together, and to become, through Hellenism, the great leavening force of ancient times. At the same time they were to secure for us, through the survival of this culture, continuity in the development of the world; for it is only through the Greeks that different epochs, and our interest in them, are linked and strung together. Without them we would have no knowledge of early times, and what we *might* know without them, we would feel no desire to know. Besides this incalculable enrichment of thought processes, we have also inherited as an extra gift what remains of their creative achievement – art and poetry.

We see with their eyes and use their phrases when we speak.

Yet, of all civilized peoples, it was the Greeks who inflicted the bitterest and most deeply felt suffering upon themselves.

III

The *Polis*

This book is not generally concerned with the discussion of origins, but we need to consider some facts that long preceded the formation of any *polis*, and that bear on the life of the nation and its tribes.

The question as to where and how a nation begins is a difficult one, like all questions about beginnings. It can be said, though, that the social foundations of Greek life – family, honour and property rights – seem already to have existed in the pre-Hellenic period, at the latest when the Greeks and the Graeco-Italians still formed one nation. This social basis need not assume uniformity in this extended nationhood; but it must have been the creation (or the expression) of a *primal religion*, which assigned a central place to the cult of fathers and ancestors as well as that of hearth and home. It was this cult that held together the family, which we thus have to think of as being at least as much a religious union as a natural one. The cult of ancestry also determined monogamy, which was present in Greek life from the beginning, as is clear both from the formal ceremonies of marriage and from the severe penalties for adultery. Equally, the right of property in land stands in a causal relationship with veneration of the home and of graves. While the Tartars observed property rights only for the home, and the Germanic races made a new division of the land every year, the Graeco-Italians had individual rights in land from the earliest times, not, indeed, for persons, but for families. According to Diodorus (5.68) the hearth taught people housebuilding, and houses were originally separate; there were no party walls. The plot of land contained the family grave, and the plots were inalienable for this reason – not, for instance, merely to secure the ruling caste when victorious invaders divided land.

The right of inheritance was also linked to the law of succession which was determined by the cult of the dead. The son was the usual heir; originally, daughters did not inherit, but to ensure the sacrifices to the dead, legitimate daughters were betrothed to their nearest relative, and adoption was permitted, though not until citizenship of some kind was constituted by the State. The authority of the father must have been very wide-ranging. It seems certain that this authority, as well as the rights of property and inheritance, must have long predated the establishment of the *polis*, since it is a safe assumption that if the *polis* had already existed it would have decided these matters differently.

On the other hand, in the historical period the *genos*, i.e. the clan based on descent, was known only as an old tradition, and no longer existed anywhere in its primitive form. It was still remembered as the consciousness of shared ancestry and in the communal cult of graves, the grave being the only property held in common; but no-one in historical times experienced it as an everyday living reality. Even the relationship between the younger branches and the main family line is uncertain, and so is the modification of the clan community through the incorporation of slaves and paid workers. We are quite unable to imagine how clans were related to tribes, and can only hypothesize about this. Questions that remain unanswerable for us are whether families (*genos*) united into *phratriai* (brotherhoods), these into *phylai*, and *phylai* into ethnic groups (*ethnos*), or the other way round, with the *ethnos* as the primary unit dispersing into *phylai*, *phratriai* and families; that is, whether it was a case of subdivision or of merging.

Yet one venerable fragment of antiquity rises up from the political developments and vicissitudes of the Greeks as the jagged peak of an old mountain range towers above later alluvial deposits: the *phyle*. As often happens, the great changes which overtook the institution and its name have made it hard to understand what it originally was.

The population of the Doric states used to consist of three *phylai* or tribes: Pamphylians, Dymanes and Hylleis. Pamphylus and Dyman were the sons of King Aigimius and grandsons of Dorus, but Hyllus was the son of Heracles, who once came to the aid of Aigimius in the battle with the Lapiths; this third section must have been the most favoured, since the Heraclids sprang from it and led the Dorians in the celebrated migration in which they founded many states.

In Attica and probably in other Ionian states[1] there were four *phylai*:

Geleontes, Argadeis, Aigicoreis and Hopletes, whose eponymous heroes were the supposed sons of Ion – even if there was some difficulty about extracting a singular form for their names from the plural forms of the *phylai*-names.[2] Even in antiquity these names were thought indicative of different ways of life: roughly speaking, landowners, craftsmen, shepherds and a knightly aristocracy. But in the historical period, each *phyle* included aristocrats and ordinary citizens of every kind, while occupations or castes such as those mentioned, if they could be found in Greece at all, could not have been assimilable to equal rights in the State;[3] for the *phylai* became elective bodies, and under Solon's constitution each group of a hundred members sent a representative to the assembly. The names must have been very ancient, and gradually have lost their meaning – whatever that origin-ally was – until the people, who had used them for so many generations, had so far modified them that they again began to sound as if they had significance in themselves. In Doric usage the same no doubt happened with the name Pamphylians, which we must be careful not to translate as 'mixed population' (cf. 'Alemannic'). Whether, in the early period of tribal life, the *phylai* were distinguished by where they lived, it is impossible to tell; later, in any case, everyone lived together, and it was enough for individuals to know which *phyle* they belonged to. The names of the Athenians who fell at Marathon were arranged on the inscribed stone pillars of the great grave-mound according to their *phylai*, that is the new *phylai* which Cleisthenes had substituted for the old.

Are we, then, to say that the Dorians were first divided into three *phylai* and the Ionians into four? Or rather that the first were made up of three clans merging and the second of four? Perhaps it is better to avoid both expressions and recognize that the origin of these forms remains a mystery. A fiery melting process that we cannot comprehend brought a nation into being, which almost invariably chose this same form in its various states. Perhaps it is easiest to avoid error by borrowing from a mythical formula-tion: Clotho spins the vital thread of the Dorians from three strands, and that of the Ionians from four.

That the *phylai* were determined by descent rather than occupation is a conclusion we may come to partly because of examples of *phylai* being formed in later foundations by an artificial process. The ten *phylai* of Thurii consisted of the different tribes who came to live in this extremely mixed colony; after its upheavals, Cyrene sent for Demonax from Greece (before 530 B.C.) to restore order, and he created three *phylai* from the existing constituent parts of the population; the Therans, the Peloponnesians with the Cretans, and the people from other islands. Names used for the *phylai* of some other cities, where they have been preserved and differ from those mentioned, can tell us nothing certain about their origins because they derive from gods, heroes and localities.

It is possible that Rome, with its original three tribes, possessed a much older memory than it was aware of – that of the ancient cohabitation of the Greeks and Italians, whatever region they may have occupied. There is agreement about the names Ramnes, Tities and Luceres to the extent that, while tradition has it that they first belonged to the so-called Knights of Romulus, they were originally the names of the tribes. In Rome, it is true, a different legend was preferred, according to which these were three groups of peoples who came together only long after the foundation of the city – the Latins, Sabines and probably the Etruscans. But Dionysius of Halicarnassus, as a native Greek, rightly saw that all three tribes were original, and that the latecomers, Sabines and others, were subsequently distributed among the existing tribes. The third, Luceres, was as ancient as the two others; in remote times, perhaps long before the people were in Italy, the three merged together in one, and, as with the Dorians, two were equal and one different, either stronger or weaker than the others.

We may pass over the later new divisions of the *phylai*. When, in Attica, Cleisthenes made ten out of the four, it may have represented an urgently needed reform to even things up, possibly because the four old *phylai*, who were recognized by Solon as basic, had become very unequal in strength during the turbulent century between his time and that of Cleisthenes. Greek cities founded later reproduced this political form, including those of the *diadochoi*, and so did those founded by Hadrian with his passion for antiquity, such as Hadrianopolis and Antinoöpolis in Egypt. The various changes that occurred in the meaning of the word *phyle*, and how even purely regional divisions later came to be given this name, are proper to the study of 'Greek antiquities'. Institutions like these are truly Janus-faced; on the one side ancient events and the very beginnings of things, transplanted and preserved by descent, but on the other the basis of representation in states, altered many times and artificially recreated.

Even before the Greeks, the Phoenicians had founded *poleis*, city-states with constitutions; the powers of their monarchs were restricted by councils, whose members seem to have been the heads of privileged families. These cities were able to despatch colonists to found settlements freely modelled on their way of life at home. They were different from the old royal strongholds of the East, which for each nation represented the central point of the whole; different from the enormous military encampment of the Assyrian dynasties on the Tigris, or from Babylon, founded to be the common fortress of all possessions and all gods; different from the three alternating residences of the Achaemenids, or the huge markets of Oriental commerce, or the temple-cities of Egypt. They were already cities constituted by their citizenship. Extremely active, all of them fortified maritime cities, without a warrior caste or indeed any castes, the Phoenician *poleis* had successfully defended themselves in every way. Is it to be thought a slur on the honour of the Greeks if we presume that they learned from this model? It is now generally acknowledged that in very many respects Phoenician culture penetrated Greek life at an early stage, and it is possible that Thebes was originally a Phoenician city in what came to be Boeotian territory. In any case the Greeks must have been aware of the Phoenician coastal cities and their colonies.

For a long time, the Greeks themselves lived in a large number of smaller and greater tribes under chieftains who were called kings. In ancient times either the tribes or their kings must have founded strongholds and towns in various places, or have taken over some that already existed. Thucydides (1.7) believes these oldest settlements, both on the mainland and on the islands, were those lying far inland from the sea, because of piracy; for only the newer examples are on the sea, some on fortified peninsulas, following the establishment of the Greeks' own shipping. Mycenae and Tiryns are much more ancient than any of the *poleis*.

In the earliest period the great majority of the Greeks lived 'village-style' (*kata chomas*).[4] This is what Thucydides (1.10) calls 'the old manner of life in Hellas'.[5] Whether these communities were already politically organized, and how they were legally represented in the tribe, is not known, nor is the extent to which they were more closely linked with neighbouring communities by shared holy places, customs and military duties.[6] If they had fortresses in their district or tribe, these were probably used as refuges against attack by land or sea. The primitive Sicani in Sicily all lived in fortified places on the heights because of brigands, and yet are said to have 'lived village-style', though the word *poleis* is used by anticipation for these places.[7] In our own day, in Middle and Southern Italy, we can find many a so-called *castello*, resembling a fortified town, which is nothing but a safe haven for country dwellers at night and in troubled times. Until a late period, many Greek regions continued to live 'village-style', and remained so obscure that all knowledge óf their political system has been practically lost, because attention was centred on the *poleis* which developed afterwards.

A vigorous life force must have characterized the old Greek tribes more than other Aryans; the fierce vitality the nation later showed might be said to have been foreshadowed in the migrations, settlements and mergings of the old separate tribes, which must often have spent long periods on the move. Records on this subject are complex, confused and hardly sufficient to support any historical exactitude, but they are also extremely abundant. A wealth of detail is available even on the smallest scale; every tiny population has its legend of migration, while in Germanic history it is only the broad outlines that can be learned. By the seventh century our Alemannic populations seem to have lost all memory of the turbulent past they emerged from; their occupation of Roman soil left not one single trace in popular tradition, and hardly any in history; they were simply there. By contrast, Greek peoples show the strongest consciousness of ancestry and resettlement, always expressed in mythical form.

Personalization in the figures of founding heroes, their flights and new domains, the earnest incorporation of them in the general mythology, their graves and the cults connected with these, are a kind of security for the powerful vitality of the future *poleis*. But who were the people, within a group, who kept these memories alive amidst their daily labours? As always, they can only have been the bards who sang of the heroic legends [cf. p. 24]. Alongside them, and partly relying on their poetry collected from near and far, a more general genealogical and in fact also ethnographic kind of poem could arise, like the *Catalogue of Women* of Hesiod, the catalogue of ships in Homer, and similar 'epics'. Among the Germanic peoples, after the migrations, some dynasties such as the Nibelungs and Harelungs are glimpsed in the darkness, but all the rest centres on Dietrich of Bern, and he eludes all attempts to fix him anywhere on German soil. By Greek standards, a gigantic forest of dynasties ought to have flourished in Germany.

In these migration legends, the particular tribe is seen as free to use any and every means to defend its own existence; the children and children's children recount with triumphant mockery how this was done. One of the most authentic, and certainly derived from their own tradition, is the folk legend of the Aenians, a minor tribe which later lived in Thessaly.[8] Driven away long before by the Lapiths from the plain of Dotion (south of Ossa in Thessaly) they wandered about here and there; everywhere they found the area too small and their neighbours too hostile, but at last, at Cirrha on the Gulf of Corinth, in a great drought, they killed their king Oenoclus by stoning, as the god commanded. Then they made their way to the valley of the Inachos in Thessaly, inhabited by Inachians and Achaeans, and decided to stay there. An oracle advised that the land would be their own if it were willingly given them, so the Aenian Temon disguised himself as a beggar, and inveigled the Inachian king into giving him, as if in mockery, a clod of earth which he gleefully put in his knapsack.[9] Too late the Inachian elders saw through the trick and warned their king to seize him. Temon escaped by promising a hundred oxen to Apollo. A duel of the two kings was arranged; the Aenian demanded that the Inachian should chase off the dog he had brought with him; and while he was turning away to do this, the Aenian threw a stone (that oldest of weapons) which killed him. Thereupon the Aenians drove out the Inachians and the Achaeans, and worshipped the stone, offering sacrifices to it and covering it with the grease from the sacrificial animal.[10] From then on, when the hundred oxen were regularly offered up to Apollo, the descendants of Temon always received the 'beggar's meat' as it was called. The thoughts and feelings of the tribe in this legend would later be those of the *polis*, the later development and intensification of the tribe.

The *polis* was the definitive Greek form of the State; it was a small independent state controlling a certain area of land in which scarcely another fortified position and certainly no secondary independent citizenship were tolerated. This state was never thought of as having come into being gradually, but always suddenly, as the result of a momentary and deliberate decision. The Greek imagination was full of such instantaneous foundings of cities, and as from the beginning nothing happened of itself, the whole life of the *polis* was governed by necessity.

The small-state form was an invariable. Even when whole populations were expelled from their homes, they took with them on their wanderings the primary assumption that they had been dwellers in separate small states. The Achaeans, forced out of the southern Peloponnese, could certainly have formed a unified state in their new home in Achaea on the Gulf of Corinth, indeed it would have suited them well had it been in their nature; instead, in the twelve districts where Ionians had lived till then in villages, they founded the same number of *poleis*, and what they had in common amounted to little more than periodic sacrifices and festivals, probably at the Hamarion, in the grove of Zeus near Aegae.[11] And the Ionians, who had retreated before them and went, under Athenian leadership, to the west coast of Asia Minor, proceeded as a matter of course to set up a series of *poleis* numbering twelve as before.

As we shall see, the small state with a fortified town was very much aware that it needed to be limited in size and easily manageable. To control more extensive areas, in such a way that its individual settlements would not become centres of subversion, would have demanded either Spartan brutality or a quite exceptional natural disposition like that of the people of Attica. Attempts to form larger groups through alliances were only briefly successful, in time of war, but never in the long run. The hegemonies of Sparta and Athens were more and more hated the longer they went on, and the study of the *polis* will soon convince us that it was quite incapable of exercising even the minimal fairness towards weaker allies which would have served its own interest. The repeated attempts to make Boeotia a federal state were responsible for all the misfortunes of Boeotian history. Every alliance between Greeks seems characterized by the determination of the abler party to exploit and dominate. The traces of an early antiquity that was never fully understood, like the temple leagues or *amphictyoniai*, may safely be ignored in the period when the *polis* had come to full consciousness.

The feverish vital impulse which created the *polis* usually took the form of *synoecism*, the bringing of earlier village communities to settle together in a fortress town, if possible on the coast. The prevailing blend of piracy and commerce, features such as mountain foothills and bays, were perhaps the less essential influences; the chief consideration was to establish a strong political entity and to be prepared to resist neighbouring *poleis* in which the same process was at work. If the aim had been merely trade, material prosperity and so forth, the result would have been just a town or a city, but the *polis* was more than that.

However, the compulsive external incentive for its foundation was without doubt, in many cases, the movement known as the Dorian migration. The migrants themselves, as well as those who successfully resisted them, were seeking a system which would promise greater strength both in defence and attack, and be its own *raison d'être*. We have seen above how, for Achaea, the transition from village communities to urban life was explicitly connected with the Dorian migration; what we learn of that process from the accounts we have must have been repeated many times.

44

The period when people lived 'village-style' (*komedon*) or sometimes in districts of seven or eight villages, was certainly one of greater innocence, however unruly the tribes may have been; they had needed to defend themselves against brigands and pirates, but they lived as peasants, cultivating the land; now each *polis* confronted another, competing for existence and political power. And there is no doubt that in the earlier period cultivation had been much better attended to, for as the population withdrew to the cities the remoter parts of their agricultural land must have become neglected. *Synoecism* may have been the first phase of aridification in Greece.[12] The fact that Athenian citizens would go, in time of peace, to live on their estates all over Attica does not mean that the same was true elsewhere.

The process became the norm and was perpetuated. Whenever political power was to be concentrated, this drawing together of a population in a union of citizens took place, all having equal burdens, duties and rights, and within a locality usually already settled, but not previously fully fortified; however, it was not unusual for a completely new site to be chosen. The political imagination which developed later was fond of embroidering on the model of the most famous example, handed down from mythical times: this was the *synoecism* of the people of Attica achieved by Theseus.[13] In the twelve districts in which Cecrops had formerly settled all the inhabitants together for their safety, it was Theseus who first abolished all their separate *prytaneis* (councillors) and *archontes* (chief administrators) and allowed only one council (*bouleuterion*) and one *prytaneion* in Athens to serve everybody. They might go on living outside the city on their own land, but they were to have only one *polis*, with everyone working together; it could be passed on to posterity as a great and powerful one. This was the arrangement generally desired everywhere, and progression towards this final system of the *polis* was an inherent tendency in Greece as a whole. Without it the full development of Greek culture would not have been conceivable.

From the clearly recorded examples of the historical period, however, we learn of the sacrifices this *synoecism* might cost: violent resettlements of resisting populations or their extermination. What can only be guessed at is the misery of the many who complied, but were forced to leave their familiar villages, districts and small towns, or could continue to live in them and work the land only with much less security and prosperity. To be taken far away from the places where their forefathers were buried was itself a misfortune for the Greeks; they were obliged to give up the cult of the dead, or found it very hard to continue; in any case they missed the daily sight of their family graves. In the whole course of history there is hardly another such accumulation of bitter grief as in this Greek *polis*, where the people with the strongest sense of place, and reverence for it, were forced out of their own places by violent arbitrary decrees. These measures must usually have been carried out by powerful tyrannical minorities. In turbulent later times, the only way of escaping ruthless oppression must often have been to form a *polis*.

A telling symbol of the vitality of the *polis* and its struggle for birth is the story of the dragon's teeth sown by Cadmus. The Spartoi, a troop of armed men, sprang up where the teeth were planted, and when Cadmus threw a stone in their midst they fought until only five of them were left alive. From this remaining quintessence were descended the Cadmean families of what became Thebes. The idea of decreeing capital punishment for anyone who made fun of the city's defences was also typical. Underlying it was the thought that it is easy to jeer, and hard to give practical help, and that beginnings have to be made in a small way. It was because he failed to understand this that Toxeus was killed by his father Oeneus of Calydon for jumping over the trench, exactly as Romulus killed his brother for the same offence.

There are many tales of the founding of cities: Mantinea in the Peloponnese, mentioned in Homer, became a *polis* through the union of five rural communities – *demoi* as the local expression was, instead of *komai*. Tegea arose from nine communities, as did Heraea too, Aegion from seven or eight, Patras from seven, Dyme from eight. Elis was formed into a city, from many surrounding villages, only after the end of the Persian Wars.[14] During the Peloponnesian War, the Mytileneans wanted to force all the people of Lesbos to live in their city, but the Methymneans complained of the matter in Athens and the plan was abandoned.[15] In the year 408 Lindos, Ialysos and Cameiros voluntarily combined to found the fine city of Rhodes, which was to have a brilliant future; but the feelings of the majority who had to leave their ancient towns can only be imagined.[16] At the time of the Peloponnesian War, Perdiccas II of Macedonia persuaded the inhabitants of the peninsula Chalcidice to leave their coastal towns and settle in the city of Olynthos, which entailed deserting the Athenian hegemony.[17] The city of Argos was particularly infamous for its violent enforcement of *synoecism* on the pretext of defending itself against Sparta. Not only were Hysiae,

Orneae, Midea and other lesser places obliged to obey, but famous old cities like Mycenae and Tiryns were reduced to ruins, and if the inhabitants preferred to travel far away rather than become Argives this must have been because it was impossible to detain them. Against such an enemy as Sparta even Epaminondas had to resort to persuading a large number of Arcadian country towns to give up their identity and move to a 'great city', Megalopolis. The Trapezuntians refused, and those who were not slaughtered fled to the new Trapezus on the Black Sea. After the Battle of Mantinea many tried to leave Megalopolis again, but their fellow citizens, using extreme brutality and helped by the Athenians, forced them to return.[18] Some of the abandoned dwelling places were later left completely deserted, and some became 'villages' belonging to the Megalopolitans, that is, they still had a few residents, and their land was cultivated.[19]

Why were such cities not simply allowed to exist as country towns, perhaps sending elected representatives to the council of the *polis*? It was because they would never have remained compliant in the long run, but would have used all their energies to become independent and regain their status as *poleis*. Moreover, as we shall see, the mere delegation of representatives never satisfied the Greeks, because they would not tolerate any condition of things in which their popular assembly could not interfere at a moment's notice.

The entirely new city of Messene was perhaps the only one founded in a mood of completely undisputed enthusiasm, in 369 B.C. Epaminondas had no need, here, to bring in people expelled from their neighbouring lands; the new capital was built by Messenians who had fled long before to places all over the Greek world and were now reassembled in their native region. Those who had lost their homeland several generations or even centuries earlier, now regained it. In contrast, countless cities were founded by tyrants and powerful princes using the most brutal methods. The tyrants of Sicily, even the best of them, set about ruthlessly mixing the inhabitants of existing *poleis*, because they felt sure of being obeyed by them only when half or more of the population had been removed and replaced by strangers or mercenaries. Gelon, who in other ways was a good ruler, deported the upper classes of Camarina, Gela, Megara Hyblaea and other towns and concentrated them in Syracuse, while the common people were sold abroad as unwanted, since the *demos* was the least desirable element in the community. His brother Hieron transported the townspeople of Catana to Leontini, and settled five thousand Syracusans and the same number of

Peloponnesians within the deserted walls, partly to ensure that Catana, with its excellent defensive position,[20] would be permanently garrisoned, and partly to perpetuate his own name in a heroic cult, as founder of this fine *polis*, something Gelon had already achieved (Diodorus 11.49). So that it would be reckoned a new foundation, the city was given the name of Etna, but soon after Hieron's death, when his decrees were rescinded, it again took its old name, and is still known as Catania. The sole pretext the rulers gave was, always, that without these measures the cities would raise countertyrants against them and go over to the Carthaginians. King Mausolus, too, forcibly crammed together in his own Halicarnassus the people of six cities, that is three quarters of the eight Lelegian cities, whether they liked it or not.[21] In the history of the *diadochoi* the new foundations of towns in the East and in Egypt are given a great deal of attention, but since Asia Minor had long been Hellenized these must have involved violent deportations and mergings as well as the imposition of new names on cities that were old and famous. It is often maintained that only populations willing to move could be led in this fashion, but this does not stand up to the proof; more than once, when a new ruler allowed it, the people went away again.[22]

Of all the foundations of cities, the most likely to have been based on visible advantage to the population are those of Cassander of Macedonia. They may remind us of those of the thirteenth-century Counts of Zähring in Bavaria. Their purpose was to provide the safety of walled towns for their subjects, who were loyal and lived in freedom. Another parallel case of a decision by general consent, like the earlier Greek *synoecism*, occurred towards the end of the twelfth century, when Milan headed the Guelf party against the predominantly Ghibelline dynastic rulers, especially the Piedmontese, and prompted peasant communities to unite in constructing strongholds. At least this was the origin of Chivasso and Coni; then of Savigliano, built by peasants who had rejected the rule of the Marquisate of Saluzzo – though here Milanese help is not referred to; Alessandria, which had only just been created by the whole Lombard Alliance, assisted in building the new peasant-towns of Nizza di Monferrato, Fossano, and Montevico. Facing hostile Asti, between Tanaro and Stura, the town of Clarasco was being built, and many inhabitants of Alba were already moving there; indeed it seemed for a time as if Alba would consent to be demolished so as to be absorbed in Clarasco.[23] Many features of this period resemble those of life in ancient Greece. For instance the Emperor Frederick I, having conquered Milan, drove its people out of their city, which he was about to destroy, and directed them to four villages; in so doing he was following the example of antiquity, when it was called *dioikizein* (sending to separate districts); then too a victorious enemy would usually take revenge by dissolving a *polis* and forcing the inhabitants to return to their former village life. This was how King Agesipolis treated defeated Mantinea, and similarly the victors in the Holy War laid waste all the cities of Phocis except Abae, and sent their inhabitants away to live in the country.[24]

The making of a *polis* was the great, decisive experience in the whole existence of a population. Their way of life, even if they continued to cultivate the fields, became predominantly urban; formerly 'countrymen', they now lived side by side and became 'political', *polis*-beings. The importance of this experience was reflected in legends of the city's foundation, and of being saved from great dangers in the past. The city was conscious of its origin and gradual growth, of sacrifice and divine omens, all providing justification for its future. Even the drinking water, which was the very prerequisite of a foundation, perhaps the one pure spring in a large area round about, had had to be fought for and won from a sinister adversary; Cadmus slew the dragon of Ares, which guarded the spring at the site of Thebes. In many cities, on the agora, in the precincts of a temple or on some other notable spot, was the grave of someone who, in ancient, perhaps mythical times, had given his life, or hers, voluntarily or involuntarily, for the birth or the preservation of the city, usually because of an oracle. For whatever flourished on earth had to pay the dark powers their due. In Thespiae it was known that formerly a youth had been annually chosen by lot and given to a dragon which threatened the town (Pausanias 9.26.5). At the centre of the inner Cerameicos in Athens was the Leocorion, the area sacred to Leon's three daughters whom he offered up as a sacrifice when the Delphic oracle pronounced this the only way to save the city.[25] A monument in the Italian city of Croton recalled the following legend: Heracles, driving his cattle through Italy, had killed Croton as an enemy in the darkness, though he was only trying to help; Heracles, recognizing his mistake, promised to build round the gravestone a city that would bear his name.[26] If it was not a monument, the remembrance might be linked with a spring. At Haliartos in Boeotia the river Lophis flowed from the blood of a boy who had beaten his own father to death, because in a time of total drought the Pythia commanded him to kill the first living thing he met (Pausanias 9.33.3). Once, at Celaenae in Phrygia, the ground opened and swallowed up many houses and people. The oracle said they must throw the most precious thing they had into the abyss; when gold and silver proved useless, the heir to the Phrygian King leapt in on horseback, and the crack closed up again.[27] In some cases animals showed more mercy than men and gods. An expedition sailing out to found Lesbos was told by an oracle that when they were passing the cliff of Mesogeion they must throw a bull into the sea as a sacrifice to Poseidon, and a living girl as a gift to Amphitrite and the Nereids. The girl was chosen by lot from the daughters of the seven leaders, and, richly bejewelled, was lowered into the water; but her lover jumped in after her and embraced her, and both were rescued by dolphins.[28] There are some examples of the foundation of a city being secured when the bones of someone who had died in mythical times were brought to the spot, for instance at the formal foundation of Amphipolis by the Athenians under Hagnon, when he secretly sent men to the field of Troy and had the remains of Rhesus fetched from his grave-mound (Polyaenus 6.53); or human sacrifice might be replaced by more innocent procedures, the so-called *telesmai*, or burial of mysterious objects. The precedent was the lock of Medea's hair which Athena gave to Cepheus for the foundation of the city of Tegea to ensure its impregnability (Pausanias 8.47.4). However, the horrible old rites were repeated even in later centuries when the foundation was to be a very solemn one. Seleucus, in other ways perhaps the noblest of Alexander's *diadochoi*, initiated the building of his great cities in Syria by sacrificing innocent maidens, and then put up bronze statues to them, by which the murdered girl was transfigured into the *Tyche* or fortune of the city, with her own cult in perpetuity.[29] In Laodiceia the unfortunate child was one Agave, and in Antioch on the Orontes the name of the one chosen has come down to us. She was immortalized in the famous bronze *Tyche* of which the little marble copy is now in the Vatican; in the centre of the planned city, at sunrise on the preordained day, the high priest sacrificed the beautiful Aimathe. On this occasion we are not told that the deed was urged by oracular decree, just that the destiny of the city was to be magically protected as a precaution.

In the agora there were also less fearful monuments to the dead: in Thurii the great Herodotus was buried in the agora,[30] and indeed later a perfect forest of statues of the famous, and of altars, rendered many squares in Greek cities almost impassable, but the monument to the sad memory of a sacrificial victim was seldom lacking.[31] Among other peoples a similar legend is sometimes connected with the building of a castle; when the Serbs composed the impressive song of the foundation of Skadar, they may well have been influenced by a Greek tradition.[32]

In truth this single human sacrifice seems a symbol of the many greater sacrifices demanded by the institution of nearly every *polis*, of the abandonment of the cultivated fields in a wide region, of the destruction or brutality inflicted on smaller inhabited places for the sake of the new settlement. It is no wonder that the life process of such a *polis* is characterized by violence.

We would know much more of these things but for the destruction of all the relevant sources apart from a few scattered fragments. A special branch of narrative in poetry and prose was devoted to the history or mythology of city-foundations; exalted names like that of Mimnermus of Smyrna, Cadmus of Miletus, and Xenophanes of Colophon are among the tellers of such local legends, and the last named also recounted the bold wanderings of the fleeing Phocians up to the founding of Elea (Diogenes Laertius 9.20). These are the true beginnings of what later became Greek historiography.

The external features by which a *polis* was distinguished from the village, and from the cities of other peoples, become plain from a negative description. Pausanias (10.4.1) says: 'Panopeus is a city of the Phocians, if one can speak of a city where there is no official building, no gymnasium, no theatre, no agora and no water running together to a fountain.' In fact the Panopeans lived in caves over a stream in a ravine. The 'official building' means primarily the house where the council daily sat, that is the *prytaneion*: 'the symbol of a city, for the villages have no such thing'. There would also have been the magistrates' court and the chamber for the greater council, the *bouleuterion*, where one existed. At a later date the gymnasium was found wherever Greek culture spread; the theatres however were not universal until the time when the political power of the State was in decline.[33] Particularly in the complete overview they gave of the city population, and as the scene of the popular assembly, they were of immense value, and must have astonished any non-Greek. But the true focus of a *polis* was the agora, the public square.

In small old-fashioned cities this was all-important; here were the *prytaneion*, the *bouleuterion*, the court of justice and one or more temples; it was also used for public meetings and games. But even in towns where other, grander arrangements existed for these purposes, the agora was the chief vital organ of the city. 'Marketplace' is a very inadequate translation, and every nation which had towns must certainly have had marketplaces. 'Agora' by contrast comes from the verb *ageirein* to assemble, and indeed often means the assembly without reference to the place; Aristotle helps us to a clear distinction (*Politics* 7.10 f.). He thinks there should be an agora of free citizens, where nothing is on sale and where no workman or peasant may come unless summoned by the authorities; and another separate agora for the needs of buying and selling. Even the Achaean camp before Troy had its agora with altars to the gods, where justice was meted out.[34] In seaports the square must have been near the harbour, at least it was so among the Phaeacians, whose whole existence was arranged in the best possible way (*Odyssey* VIII.4). Here, in full view of the ships, surrounded by as many temples, civic buildings, monuments, shops and money-changers' stalls as there was room for, the Greeks could occupy themselves with *agorazein*, that activity no northerner can render in a single word. Dictionaries give: 'go about on the marketplace, shopping, chatting, consulting etc.', but can never convey the delightful leisurely mixture of doing business, conversing, standing and strolling about together. It is enough to know that the morning hours were generally described by it: the time when everybody is in the agora. Naturally it was only to be thoroughly enjoyed on the square of one's hometown, and those Persians who pursued Democedes home to Croton after he had given them the slip found him there very easily, *agorazonta* – 'being in the agora' – (Herodotus 3.137). Even in barbarian lands the Greeks were recognized by this habit; the Samian Syloson promenaded at Memphis in his scarlet cloak (Herodotus 3.139), and barbarians who had become fond of Greek customs liked to frequent the agora in Greek cities. Skyles, king of Scythia, whenever he brought his army to the city of Olbia on the Borysthenes (in southern Russia), would leave his troops outside the walls, change his Scythian dress for the Greek tunic, and enjoy a walk in the agora with no bodyguard or retinue – until his Hellenic tastes proved unlucky for him (Herodotus 4.78).

When an urban proletariat developed in the cities, it was inevitably centred on the public square, and, thinking of the many activities in the Greek agora, Cyrus the Elder is said to have told a Spartan messenger: 'I am not afraid of a people who have a place in the middle of their cities where they meet to deceive each other with false oaths.'[35] In an institution of national life, such as the agora, there is an inextricable mixture of great and small, good and bad; but from the point of view of history it is certain that the intellectual development of the Greeks cannot be imagined without conversation, and that this is true of them to a greater extent than it is of other nations; the agora and the symposium were the two vital settings for conversation.

If it could be said of any people that they were greater than their dwelling place, then it was true of the Greeks. The living *polis*, the community of citizens, was very much more than all its walls, harbours and splendid edifices.[36] Aristotle says that man is by nature a *polis*-being. In an eloquent passage in Book 7 of *Politics* he then compares the Greek with the two kinds of barbarians, the northern savage and the civilized Asiatic, and acknowledges the best qualities of each – the valour of the one and the intelligence of the other – as attributes of the Greek, who is therefore not only capable of being free, and of developing the best political institutions, but also – as soon as he is able to form a state – fit to rule over all other peoples.

Above all, the *polis* existed before there was any theory about it. Odysseus encounters nations everywhere who already have a *polis*; the Laestrygonians have their Telepylos, even the Cimmerians have theirs, enveloped in mist and gloom (*Odyssey* XI.14). The founding of cities became a continuous process in Greece itself and in hundreds of places on barbarian shores. But the underlying desire was that each Greek race should have a *polis* of its own, and thus Bias could advise the Ionian citizens threatened by Persian power to emigrate to Sardinia and found an Ionian city there. Herodotus (1.170) says that if they had followed this advice they would have been the most fortunate of the Greeks. Even in comedy the theme is taken up, and Peisthetaerus' most important task is to impress on the birds that there is to be only one Bird-*polis* (Aristophanes, *Birds* 550).

The notion of the rights of man did not exist anywhere in antiquity, not even in Aristotle. The *polis*, for him, is a community only of the free; the metics and the numerous slaves are not citizens, and whether, apart from that, they are human beings is not discussed (*Politics* 3.4). The demands that are made upon the citizen are in fact, as will be seen, not for all and sundry, and it would be impossible to make them applicable to everybody. Those living outside may, if they can defend and assert themselves, live like the Cyclops, without an agora and without laws, each man ruling over his own family (*Odyssey* IX.112); in the *polis* things are different.

Quality is the most important consideration here, and quantity must, it is felt, be subject to limitations. Children born misshapen or deformed should not, according to Aristotle, be reared, and this is comprehensible when we think what an unhappy existence a cripple had among the Greeks (*Politics* 7.14.10). To limit the population, however (Aristotle continues) it is preferable not to practise exposure but to abort the child before it has independent life and consciousness; the dividing line between the permissible and the criminal is where life and consciousness begin. As is well known, though, large numbers of children always were exposed if only because their parents could not or would not support them.

The measure of population which a *polis* should contain is given in the word *autarkeia*, 'what is sufficient to itself'. To our understanding this is a very obscure expression, but it was easily grasped by the Greeks. An area of land capable of yielding the essential supplies, commerce and industry to provide for all other needs in moderation, and a hoplite army at least as strong as that of the nearest, usually hostile, *polis* – these were the elements of 'sufficiency'. Aristotle is as clear as could be wished on this; an overpopulated *polis* cannot really go on living according to the laws (*Politics* 7.4). It is the number of those who are fully citizens that makes a city great, not a preponderance of artisans with a small number of hoplites. Beauty consists, here as elsewhere, in moderation and proportion. A ship a handspan long is not a ship, nor is one that measures two furlongs. A city with too few people is not self-sufficient; one that has too many can of course suffice for its own needs, but more as a mass than as a city, for it can have no true constitution, no *politeia*. What general could lead such a mass? What herald could serve, unless he were [Homer's] Stentor? To administer justice and to allot the offices to the deserving, the citizens must all know each other and each man's quality. Ideally the city should be as large as the needs of life dictate, while still remaining manageable. And it seems that a city of 10,000 adult citizens was considered to approximate to the desirable size;[37] Heraclea Trachinia [in central Greece] had this number, and so did Catana [in Sicily] on its refoundation under the name of Etna. Then there was the popular assembly of the Ten Thousand in Arcadia, and, since even the utopias of the philosophers can throw so much light on the Greek state and Greek customs, we may mention that according to Hippodamus of Miletus the ideal state was to contain the same number.[38]

What the *polis* was, desired, was capable of or might be permitted, can best be deduced from its historical behaviour. All the city-republics of Western Europe in the Middle Ages, though they often strongly remind us of the *polis*, were fundamentally different; they were separate parts of previously existing larger realms and had broken away to become more or less independent. Even among the Italian city-states, only Venice possessed that absolute degree of autonomy that the *polis* enjoyed. Besides, the Church was a common bond, above and beyond all cities and kingdoms, and that was completely absent in Greece. But apart from these differences the *polis* in itself was a creation of quite another kind; it is as though, this one time in history, there emerged, fully developed in strength and single-mindedness, a will which had been waiting impatiently for its day on earth.

In modern times (philosophical and other idealistic programmes aside) it is essentially the single individual who postulates the State in the way he needs it. He demands of it only the security in which he will be able to develop his own powers; and in return he is willing to offer it carefully calculated sacrifices, but his sense of gratitude is in inverse proportion to the extent to which the State concerns itself with the rest of his activities. The Greek *polis*, by contrast, starts from the whole, which is conceived of as chronologically prior to the part, whether the individual household or the individual person. An inner logic allows us to add that this whole will also survive the part. It is not only the general taking precedence over the particular, but also the eternal over the momentary and the transient. Not only on the battlefield and in emergencies was the individual expected to give all that he had and was; it was equally so at all times, for he owed everything to the whole; and, in the first place, that security of his very existence which was enjoyed only by the citizen, and then only within his own city or as far as its influence reached. The *polis* was a higher product of Nature; it had come into being to make life possible, but continued to exist in order that life might be lived properly, happily, nobly and, as far as might be, in accordance with the standard of excellence. Anyone who had a part in ruling and being ruled was a citizen; the 'ruling' was more precisely defined as sharing in the judicial and other public offices. Only the citizen realized all his capacities and virtues in and for the State; the whole spirit of the Greeks and their culture was closely bound up with the *polis*, and, in the golden age, by far the highest achievements in poetry and the arts belonged to public life, not to the realm of private pleasures.

The expression of all this is often sublime, and we find it in the poets of the golden age and sometimes in the philosophers and orators of the fourth century, who no longer record these ideas as actuality, but as an ideal.

A man's native city (*patris*) was therefore not just the homeland where he felt happiest or for which he would be homesick, not just the city in which he took pride despite its shortcomings, but a higher, divinely powerful being.[39] Above all it was death in battle that he owed the city, and if he died thus he was only repaying 'the cost of his nurture'.[40] Even Homer gives the Trojans, especially Hector, the most ardent expressions of patriotism, and the lyric poets sound the same note in the few fragments of their work that survive. Aeschylus is the most authoritative witness of all. His *Seven Against Thebes*, a tragedy 'filled with the spirit of the war-god', combines, in the speeches of Eteocles, the most exalted view of the citizen's duty to sacrifice himself for his native soil with the ardour of the king and the defender. In his own epitaph the poet speaks not of his poetry but of his valour: 'let the grove of Marathon tell of it, and the long-haired Mede, who has encountered it'.[41]

However, the great deeds really belonged not to the individual but to the native city; it was the city, not Miltiades or Themistocles, that was victorious at Marathon and Salamis, and Demosthenes [in the next century] considers it a symptom of decadence that many have begun to say 'Timotheus took Corcyra' or 'Chabrias defeated the enemy at Naxos'. Even the most meritorious citizen always owed more to his native city than the city did to him.[42] Pythagoras taught that anyone who has been treated unjustly by his native city should confront her as he would his mother in a similar case.

Apart from the duty to fight for victory without thought of self, there is in the great poets an ecstatic sentiment that is brought to the motherland like an offering. In particular, the Greek way of thinking permits of prayers for the prosperity of an individual city; Christianity could not do so, since as a world religion it must be mindful of mankind as a whole. In *Suppliants*, the magnificent choral ode of the Danaids (624 ff.) heaps every conceivable blessing in profusion on hospitable Argos, but Aeschylus reserves the best of all for his native city in the last great chorus of *Eumenides* with its interjections by Athena. Only in one text of the ancient world are such notes sounded with greater power; Aeschylus voices wishes and prayers, but Isaiah in his vision of the New Jerusalem (chapter 60) is both prophesying and seeing the fulfilment of his prophecy.

The *polis* was, further, an educative force; not only 'the best of nurses, who when you were at play on the soft earth faithfully nourished and cherished you and found no care too tedious' – but continuing to educate the citizen throughout his life. She kept no school, though she promoted the traditional instruction in music and gymnastics. We need not detail here the many opportunities for spiritual development available to all citizens in the choral odes at the festivals, in the splendid cult rituals, buildings and works of art, and in the drama and recitations by the poets. It was the very fact of living in the *polis*, the ruling and being ruled, which was valued as a continuous education. In the better times the *polis* gave her people very strong guidance through the honours she could confer on individuals, until here too abuses set in, and wiser men preferred to forgo their claim to crowns, heralds' proclamations and so forth. In sum, the whole previous history of a famous city seemed one of the strongest encouragements to excellence: nowhere but in Athens, says Xenophon (*Memorabilia* 3.5.3), could men tell so many glorious stories of the deeds of their ancestors, and many citizens, first inspired by this, then sought to dedicate themselves to virtue and to become strong.

So the *polis*, with its vitality much more developed than that of the Phoenician city-republic, was a creation unique in the history of the world. It was the expression of a common will of the most extraordinary vigour and capability; indeed the *polis* succeeded in rising above mere village life thanks only to its deeds, the power it exercised, its passion. This was why the strictest criteria were needed for the definition of a full citizen, who after all was to form a part of this power. These *poleis* underwent quite a different order of good and bad fortune from the cities of other peoples and other epochs, and even in the liveliest of the mediaeval republics, such an intensity of living and suffering was only occasionally attained.

Hence too their violence. Externally the *polis* was in general isolated, despite all treaties and alliances, and was frequently competing with its nearest neighbours for its very life. In time of war, martial laws were in force with all their terrors.

Internally, the *polis* was implacable towards any individual who ceased to be totally absorbed in it. Its sanctions, often put into practice, were death, loss of civic rights, and exile. And we must bear in mind that there was no appeal to any external tribunal, except when cases were referred to be heard in the courts of Athens from cities in her empire. The *polis* was completely inescapable, for any desire to escape entailed the loss of all personal security. The absence of individual freedom went hand in hand with the omnipotence of the State in every context. Religion, the sacral calendar, the myths – all these were nationalized, so that the State was at the same time a church, empowered to try charges of impiety, and against this dual power the individual was totally helpless. His body was in bond for military service in Athens and Sparta till the end of his life, in Rome until his forty-sixth year; and his possessions were entirely in the power of the city, which could even determine the value of many of them. In short, there could be no guarantees of life or property that ran counter to the *polis* and its interests. Although this enslavement of the individual to the State existed under all constitutions, it must have been at its most oppressive under democracy, where the most villainous men, ridden by ambition, identified themselves with the *polis* and its interests and could therefore interpret in their own way the maxim *salus reipublicae suprema lex esto* ('let the safety of the Republic be the highest law'). Thus the *polis* got the maximum price for the small amount of security it afforded.

Yet since, in good times, all that was highest and noblest in the life of the Greeks was centred upon the *polis*, then fundamentally the *polis* was their religion. The worship of the gods found its strongest support against alien religions, philosophies and other undermining forces in its importance for the particular city, which had to maintain this worship exactly and in full, and the main cults were mainly the direct concern of the State. So while the *polis* was itself a religion, it contained the rest of religion within itself as well, and the communal nature of the sacrifices and festivals formed a very strong bond among the citizens, quite apart from the laws, the constitution and the public life they shared.

> Because all this is offered by the State and only by the State, it is perfectly clear why the Greek needs no church, why, in order to show piety in his own way, he need only be a good citizen; why there is no question of hierarchic rivalries, why the highest cult official in Athens, the *archon basileus*, is a State official, and why, finally, it is an offence not only against the duties of a citizen, but also against loyalty to the faith, to worship the gods in any rites but those recognized by the State.[43]

When the *polis* began to decline, the cult of the gods no longer sufficed, not even that of the 'gods (and heroes) who protect the city', and the *polis* deified itself as Tyche (Fortune) with her crown of walls. This transition becomes very clear in some lines of Pindar's. Tyche is one of the personifications of Moira, or Fate, and it is in this general character that Pindar addresses her, asking her favour for one particular city: 'I beg you, daughter of Zeus the Deliverer, to protect strong Himera, Tyche our saviour! At sea you command the swift ships, and on land the fierce battling armies and the wise counsels of the agora.'[44] But the cult of the single city, idealized as Tyche, had probably begun in various places by the fifth century, with special temples and sometimes a colossal statue. The usual earlier representations of Tyche, like that set up by Bupalos for the Smyrnians, showed her with her wand and cornucopia;[45] now her attributes were the crown of walls and some feature of the particular city. Some superb figures were made for the purpose, for instance the row of bronzes Pausanias speaks of (1.18.6) fronting the columns of Hadrian's Olympieion in Athens, representing the *Tychai* of the Athenian colonies.

Later on Tyche herself was not enough, when the democracies who had taken power in most cities rubbed salt in the wounds of their defeated opponents by idealizing themselves as Demos. This, too, often took the form of colossal statues, like the one in the agora at Sparta,[46] which must have been put up at the lowest point in the fortunes of the city. As this Demos was usually shown in the likeness of the so-called 'good daimon', it could become the object of a real cult. The point of all these deifications could only be the certainty of continuing prosperity; there is no record of the way people viewed such statues when everything lay in ruins.

There was also another sense and another form in which the *polis* regarded itself as an ideal whole, and that was in its *nomos*, a word used to embrace the laws and with them the constitution. *Nomos* is the higher objective power, supreme over all individual existence or will, not satisfied merely to protect the citizen in return for taxes and military service, as in modern times, but aspiring to be the very soul of the whole *polis*. Law and the constitution are hymned in the most sublime phrases as the invention and gift of the gods, as the city's personality, as the guardians and preservers of all virtue. They are the 'rulers of the cities', and Demaratus the Spartan seeks to explain to Xerxes that his people fear King Law (*despotes nomos*) more than the Persians fear their Great King.[47] The officials in particular are, as Plato puts it, to be the slaves of the law. The lawgiver therefore appeared as a superhuman being, and the glory of Lycurgus, Solon, Zaleucus and Charondas sheds a reflected light on much later men, so that for instance, as late as about 400 B.C. the Syracusan law reformer Diocles received heroic honours and even a temple after his death (Diodorus 13.35).

Above all, *nomos* must not pander to the transitory interests and caprices of the individual or of those who happen to be in the majority. It was strongly felt, at least in theory, that old laws should be retained; indeed, customs and manners which were even older than laws, and had perhaps been in force from the very foundation of a city, were recognized as having a vigour of which the laws were only the outward expression.[48] And even inadequate laws, as long as they were strictly observed, seemed a better guarantee of stability than change would be.[49] Alcibiades said as much in the conclusion of his great speech in favour of the expedition to Sicily.[50] In certain states boys had to learn the laws by heart, set to a tune or cadence, not just to fix them in the memory but to ensure that they became unalterable.[51] (The Greek word *nomos* has the double meaning of law and of melody.)

None the less we learn from old sources, not merely late anecdotes, that even Solon, when he left the country for ten years after completing his legislative programme, had to bind the Athenians by solemn vows to alter nothing in his laws while he was away.[52] Soon afterwards they underwent a severe political crisis and finally [after nearly a century] changed his constitution into a fully democratic one. It was much the same story in many other Greek *poleis*; and even most of the colonies, in spite of all the initial lawgiving, had a restless, even stormy history. In its full development, democracy had a passion for revision; the letter of the constitution might be loudly praised and honoured while at the same time being altered and completely undermined by the endless promotion of popular decrees (*psephismata*). That was the state of affairs in which, in Aristotle's words (*Politics* 4.4.3) it was not the law, but the masses (*plethos*) who ruled.

For, as we shall see, the Greek idea of the State, with its total subordination of the individual to the general, had at the same time developed a strong tendency to encourage individuality. These tremendous individual forces ought in theory to have evolved entirely in the general interest, to have become its most vital expression; freedom and subordination ought to have been harmoniously fused into a unity. But in fact the Greek idea of freedom is qualified from the start, because, as we have said, the *polis* was inescapable; the individual could not even take refuge in religion, since this too belonged to the State, and in any case there was no assurance that the gods were kind and merciful. The highly gifted, obliged to stay on and endure, strove to gain power in the State. Individuals and parties ruled in the name of the *polis*. Whatever party happened to be in power behaved exactly as though it were the whole *polis* and had the right to exert its full authority.

In antiquity, anyone who believed he had the right to rule, or who merely wished to rule, at once resorted to extreme measures against his opponents and rivals, even to annihilating them. Occasionally in some unemphatic words of the poets this way of thinking slips out as the normal one. One need only study the speeches of the tutor in Euripides' *Ion*, where he urges Creusa to murder Xuthus and Ion.[53] Would it be possible, we wonder, for a criminal character in any modern drama to express himself so candidly in the name of power and authority? All political punishments in these city-states (some of them, it is true, for very serious offences) have the quality of revenge and of extermination. We shall see examples of punishment visited not only on the children of those exiled or executed but on their ancestors as well, when the family tombs were laid waste.[54] The Greeks thought they saw a clear alternative; either we destroy these people or they destroy us – and they acted accordingly with ruthless logic. The characteristic feature of this terrorism was its solemnity. The fact that tyrannicides, if they survived their deed, might receive the highest honours and be commemorated after death with monuments and rites, is too well known to give us pause. But one consequence was that obscure cutthroats were named as benefactors of society, granted citizenship, publicly crowned at the great Dionysian festival and so forth, because they happened to have murdered a man later found to have been a rogue and a traitor, like Phrynichus at Athens in 411 B.C., while their accomplices would at least have their names inscribed on the memorial column and be rewarded in other ways.[55] The intention of the ruling party here was by no means just to intimidate and humiliate its remaining enemies, but chiefly to make their own triumph as striking as possible. Those who did the deed were honoured irrespective of their motives or their personal qualities.

Because the *polis* was the highest of all things for the Hellenes, in fact their religion, the struggles that surrounded it had all the horror of religious wars, and any break with the *polis* would cut off the individual from all normal conditions of life. Civil war was bewailed as the worst of all wars, the most appalling and most godless, loathsome to gods and men,[56] but this insight did not bring peace. In many cities the existing constitution, whatever it may have been, was the orthodoxy, and was defended by all the methods of terrorism. For generations, no-one dared to say openly that the fiction of the duties of citizenship as paramount had overstretched what human nature could bear, but there was no way of preventing the growth of secret, inner disaffection among intellectuals, and as time went on some came forward to declare it openly and defiantly. Philosophical ethics followed, gave up its earlier identification with the State and became the ethics of humanity in general. In the school of Epicurus, the *polis* is stripped of all its feverish divinization to become a mutual contract of security among all its members. The real *poleis*, however, convulsed as they were, continued on the path of violence. One thing they could not do was to surrender their autonomy to another city, a larger federal state or a ruler. Later the *polis* was to struggle for survival at any price amid terrible sufferings. 'A single wicked man,' says Isocrates (8.120) 'may die before retribution overtakes him; but cities, since they cannot die, must suffer the vengeance of men and gods.'

IV

The General Characteristics of Greek Life

To discern the truth about general attitudes to life in a bygone culture, even one that is well documented, involves accepting many reservations and restrictions. The only really appropriate evidence is what can be shown to correspond to the views and the understanding of the majority, if not all, of the people – primarily popular literature; in the case of Greece, this means, first and foremost, epic poetry and Attic drama. The Greek spirit ranged so widely and explored so deeply that an enormous variety of different attitudes are expressed, all no doubt essentially Greek and often bearing witness to remarkable intellectual capacity, but not each representing the whole, and often starkly contradicting each other. These opinions were explicitly formulated and claimed the status of coherent doctrine, while popular opinion expressed itself randomly and unsystematically. The concept of a 'view of life', though, is a very wide one, and to narrow it down does violence to it. It includes, first, attitudes to the gods (their powers and their will) and to the invisible world; then the whole area of morality must be examined, that is the individual struggle against egoism and the passions, to the extent that this effort is accepted as right; further, human desires, and the hierarchy of objects of desire – what is called the 'forms' of life's pleasures; the final consideration must be the general attitude to the value of a life that is subject to so many limitations. The relationship between these various phenomena is the subject of some excellent surveys, among which Nägelsbach's study of theology after Homer is still pre-eminent;[1] I shall therefore confine myself to some additional evidence and marginal comments, and devote closer attention only to the last-mentioned part of the subject.

The gods and what they meant to the Greeks have already been discussed.[2] Despite the efforts of philosophers, Greek religion remained polytheistic, if only for fear of incurring divine wrath if particular gods were neglected; also the most powerful force of all, the *polis*, had made this part of life its own, and cult was associated with every aspect of popular entertainment. This divine world and its mythology seemed to have been secured for ever by matchless visual art. Yet the gods lacked sanctity, that is, the quality they needed to become models for human morality, and the fear that they inspired fell short of reverence. Religion completely lacked the element of instruction and there was no priestly caste. Fear of the supernatural was felt obscurely, often strongly, but irregularly, and more by anxious individuals than by the people as a whole.

Thus the *polis* alone was the moral educator of the Greeks. The quality to be developed in its citizens, that virtue that corresponded to the *polis* itself, was called excellence (*arete*).[3] No stress is ever laid, in Greek discussions of motives, on a purely humane concern for the happiness or suffering of others, and it must be assumed that in practice this was part of the concept of duty to the members of the *polis*. However, not everyone was regarded as a citizen in the full sense; women and children were excluded, not to speak of metics and slaves, and yet they were expected to have moral standards of their own. Besides this, from the time when such expectations originated, the *polis*, despite its devotion to the common good, had developed in such a way that mutual aggression, and feuding among the citizens themselves, both provoked and excused the strongest passions. The first historical image of the realities of state and justice in the earliest times, in Hesiod's *Works and Days*, shows a world full of unrighteousness, and the poet inspires belief despite his personal tone. At the same time he was, as no priest could have been, the first and most revered teacher of his people, and it would have been to their advantage had they paid more attention to his views.

The ethical theories of the philosophers are themselves important evidence for an understanding of the Greek mind, and to some extent became an element in general culture and in daily discourse, though they were obviously of minor influence among the mass of the people and for the conduct of life. Philosophical ethics certainly took one of its principal points of departure from a genuinely popular ideal which predated it – that of moderation or *sophrosyne*. This is a note sounded throughout Greek ethics in the form of a continual admonition to seek the mean (*meson*) between two extremes; but originally it is the natural outcome, for the more reflective Greeks, of the contemplation of the gods, the order of the world and a belief in destiny. Every people accumulates a mass of similar convictions, whose guardians are those who have gained some experience of life. For the Greeks, *sophrosyne* was the negative pole, the curb, just as *kalokagathia* was the positive pole, the spur. How far *sophrosyne* actually ruled life could be determined only by comparing a number of test cases with others from non-Greek peoples; as a guiding, living force it can be most readily demonstrated from Greek art and poetry. It is also included among the Platonic cardinal virtues,[4] which are an unsatisfactory assemblage of moral, intellectual and temperamental qualities.[5] Moderation in all things, and especially in reponse to the changes of fortune, is praised as an essentially Hellenic virtue in the conversation of Solon with Croesus – though not as it is reported by Herodotus; it is not found before Plutarch's account.[6]

The fact that a nation praises its own quality of moderation can be viewed in two ways. In the first place it is creditable to have at least proclaimed such an ideal; but on closer scrutiny it rather suggests a kind of national awareness that this is how they *ought* to feel and behave, a taste for the good rather than the strength to act accordingly. The Greek tendency to pride and boasting must make us cautious, and not too ready to take the Athenians at their own valuation. Still, it was no small achievement that the more enlightened Greeks at least recognized the voice of conscience, the 'unwritten law', as a rule of conduct.

Inevitably the whole ethics of the age of philosophy, literature and rhetoric is put in the shade for posterity, that is for later Western culture, by the Homeric world, so noble and, despite all its passion and violence, so pure. In that age, sensibility was not yet fragmented by reflection, and morals not analysed out of existence; beside its goodness and delicacy of feeling, Greece in its later full development appears spiritually coarse and blunted, for all its intellectual refinement. All that was best in this later period can be traced to the survival of Homer and to his representation of the figures of myth. Without him even Aeschylus and Sophocles could not have achieved the sublimity of their finest creations. But the significance of tragedy for the history of morals is another question. The following observations on some dominant elements in the Greek character must be confined to their links with religion and the *polis* in reality rather than in literature.

Revenge has special features among the Greeks. Human beings in general, and indeed the higher animals too, commonly take revenge for injury, and the Greek gods were excessively vengeful. Among Homer's characters there was still room for anger to be turned aside by appeal and entreaty;[7] later the poet Alcaeus is supposed to have pronounced that forgiveness is better than revenge.[8] Most often, though, the Greek conscience, notably acquiescent in matters of power, domination or pleasure, was just as reckless in regard to vengeance, and set no restraint on the victories of egoism. A particular class of cases may demand to be judged differently – those in which acts of vengeance arose from hatred felt by whole parties, so that the individual could feel himself and his actions approved and sanctioned by a large group. For instance the enemy whom Theognis[9] has in mind, when advising that he should first be flattered and then, once he is off his guard, relentlessly destroyed, is certainly one of the opposing party in Megara who were oppressing and exploiting the people. The same is true of the vengeful actions of rulers, which they may have believed to be required by the interests of their house and their official duty, not merely of their own persons, in order to stamp out permanently some form of resistance. But there too some moderation had to be observed for fear of arousing the resentment of the gods, who were thought to have a prior claim in great acts of vengeance. The Princess Pheretime of Cyrene, who committed a frightful atrocity against the people of Barca, was eaten alive by worms: 'for excessive vengeance draws down the jealousy of the gods on mortals'.[10] These are the words of Herodotus; yet he seems fully to approve the sophisticated revenge taken by Hermotimus of Pedasus on the man who had castrated him and sold him into slavery, despite the cruel deceit it involved.[11] The unconditional right to revenge is often asserted. It is not uncommon to find it admitted as a motive before the courts, and it was permissible to express wholehearted hatred in public. During the time of the thirty tyrants a man on his deathbed made his family solemnly swear to take vengeance on his denouncer.[12]

In tragedy, too, revenge is recognized as a justifiable motive and reflects no discredit on sympathetic characters, allowing us to assume that the poet and the spectators were in agreement. Of course revenge was largely inherent in the myths on which plots were based, but the personal approval of the poet is often clearly apparent in his tone. The only explicit reservation, put into the mouth of a wholly sympathetic character, is that a father should not revenge himself on his son[13] – so Oedipus and Polynices. But the whole conduct of the hero in *Oedipus at Colonus*, so favourably portrayed by the poet, deserves close examination; his departure from this world corresponds to that of a mediaeval saint, whose tomb would similarly become a sacred spot for the locality and the region. The Christian resignation of such a suffering hero, as it would appear in the relevant legend, makes a striking contrast with the blind King of Thebes. The most secular modern version of such a story would scarcely represent its hero dying as Oedipus does without a single hint of remorse or reconciliation.

In Euripides above all it is clear that the unashamed passion for revenge of several principal characters spoke straight to the heart of his audience. Hecuba, who, as the myth relates, was turned into a dog after her death, is apparently, in the play, punished for her terrible revenge on Polymestor; yet her most passionate speeches seem to have found a distinct echo in the Athenians who heard them. To Agamemnon's question (754) 'What would you ask of me? Freedom? That I can easily grant', she replies: 'No! If I can take my revenge on cowards (*kakois*) I will remain a slave my whole life long.' It cannot surprise us that the chorus in *Bacchae* (868 ff., 889 ff.) should be reckless in the passion for revenge as they are in every respect; but we hardly need such examples since in another passage Euripides makes the prevailing attitude so abundantly plain in his presentation of characters who are ideal, that is to say the poet's own favourites. In his *Orestes* (1100 ff., 1132, 1163 ff.) Orestes, Pylades and Electra, expecting to be put to death at any moment, plan to take vengeance on Menelaus by murdering Helen (though they have no more reason to hate her than any other Greek has) after which they will seize and threaten Hermione as a hostage and set fire to the palace of Argos. Plainly it never occurred to Euripides that he might thus be showing them as morally flawed. How splendid, Orestes says, if we could kill, but save our own lives (*ktanousi mè thanousin*)! Just before this, all three have been uttering exalted sentiments. Revelations like this make it unnecessary to wonder at the insistence on retribution in the real life of Greece, whether it is that of individuals or of whole groups. Phocion in his prison cell, before drinking the hemlock, tells his son not to preserve the memory of the injustice he has suffered from the Athenians,[14] which may be the command of a noble heart, or simply a prudent warning. In a remarkable fourth-century text, gratitude is closely linked with vengeance as a counterbalancing virtue;[15] 'As it is just to take revenge on those who have injured us, so too it is fitting to return good to our benefactors.' A grievance unavenged can only be consistent with honour when it is visited on mankind by the gods; Niobe is the *mater dolorosa* of myth.[16]

Even if philosophy failed to speak out explicitly against vengeance,[17] its influence, especially that of the Stoa, must have worked in that direction by prescribing the avoidance of passion in general. Despite the multiplicity of states bitterly hostile to each other, Stoicism preached a great world society of peaceful intentions, and was bold enough, at least in the private life of some of its later practitioners, to approach the ideal of love for enemies.[18] All the same, some Stoics were apt to lose their self-control on the subject of Epicurus and his school.

It was the Greeks' attitude to another important feature of human egoism, *the right to falsehood*, which early drew down on them the Roman saying about *Graeca fides* – 'Greek faith'. It would be idle to attempt a statistical comparison of lying and deception in different nations down to the present day with its incidence among the ancient Greeks, yet the following factual examples lead to the inescapable conclusion that they richly deserved their reputation. There had been no lack of admonition; Pythagoras said that telling the truth and doing good (*aletheuein kai euergetein*) were the finest gifts of the gods, and came nearest to their own ways.

We may readily admit that a young nation full of imaginative power may be as little able as a gifted child to distinguish, in storytelling, between reality and dreams. A narrator whose fantasies became too vivid might be interrupted by a hearer with the words 'and then I woke up'.[19]

Untruths in Greek historical accounts[20] are certainly matched by totally one-sided falsifications of history by modern authors, and appending a distinguished old name to a new piece of writing was more innocent then than it would be now. But in the conduct of daily life, in small matters or great, truth and lying are another matter.

Truth would appear to have been well protected by the perpetual solemn swearing of oaths, and perhaps no other people can show as many ancient customs concerning oaths as the Greeks. For them the god named Oath (*Horkos*) had his own myth. He was the son of Eris, and his was the fifth day of each month, when the Erinyes went about avenging perjury.[21] It is noteworthy that in important cases the ceremony was made even more striking, as if an ordinary oath were not enough. In Syracuse there was a so-called 'great oath' in the sanctuary of the Thesmophorai;[22] in Sparta, and probably elsewhere, by a special offering at the altar of Zeus Herkeios, (Zeus of the farm), a family could force one of its members to confess the whole truth.[23] Anyone swearing a false oath in the crypt of the Adyton at

Corinth, where Palaemon was mysteriously present, could be sure he would not escape punishment.[24] Competitors at Olympia had their conscience sharpened by the oath in the *bouleuterion* before a statue of Zeus with thunderbolts in both hands – 'of all likenesses of Zeus the most effective in impressing the heedless sinner'; on the bronze plate at its base were verses intended to terrify perjurers.[25] When peasants in the country were found to have grown too casual towards their 'simple' rural deities, anyone who wished to obtain a secure oath from the village people would take them into town, because the gods within the walls were still 'real' and vigilant.[26] In the *Iliad*, it is true, Zeus was a master of perjury, while gods and goddesses, even on occasions of only moderate importance, had been obliged to swear the terrible oath on the Styx if they were to be believed at all;[27] yet Homer still influenced the Greeks. It was customary for anyone giving his word at a crucial moment to offer to perish with all his children if he were untrue to his oath, and Lysias paid Peison a talent for such an oath; later on he had to pay him more, although he knew him to be 'a man without respect for gods or men'.[28] It is hard enough to invent a safe oath when there are no heavenly gods, harder still to extract one from a man without a conscience.

There is no need to depend on the verdict of other nations or epochs for information about Greek practice with regard to oaths. For example, it was believed that young Persians were trained to tell the truth as an indispensable part of their education, and Cyrus in old age was characterized by his reply to a Greek messenger: 'I do not fear people who have a place in the middle of their city where they meet in order to deceive each other with false oaths.' But the writer who tells this story is Herodotus.[29] In later times many considered the swearing of oaths simply as a means to an end, and thus a matter of indifference, especially in political dealings. When Theognis (399) warns that 'oaths ruinous to men should be avoided', he probably means only within the circle of close acquaintances, having previously given the advice 'to deal honourably among friends'. Among the symptoms of the total moral decay which overtook the Greek nation during the Peloponnesian War, Thucydides (3.82) notes the worthlessness of oaths of reconciliation, saying that these were only honoured as long as it was unavoidable and expedient to do so. At about the same time Lysander said: 'Children can be deceived with dice, men with oaths.'

There can be no denying that where the motive was success, or achieving their own ends, or power, or pleasure, the Greeks permitted themselves, or considered comprehensible in others, behaviour that has been condemned, at least publicly, by other nations – those, that is, who have possessed religions which still influenced them, or who were disposed by temperament to disapprove of such actions. If in modern times false oaths are commonly sworn in the law courts, it is done with a sense of guilt, and is not supported by public opinion. In the Greek world, tragedy, for instance, can show deceptions practised, even by sympathetic characters, in a way that would not be tolerated today; and Aristophanes actually rebukes Euripides for making a distinction, in a scene of perjury, between the tongue that swears and the will that protests.[30] It is true that the Chorus in *Medea* laments with great feeling (439) that oaths have lost all value, and that shame no longer dwells in Hellas but has taken flight to the skies. There was to be much more such talk of virtues flying off for ever.

The Romans, apt to speak of the Greeks as habitually breaking their word, had certainly become distinctly pharisaical in the final days of the Republic; and yet the remarks Cicero made in a courtroom oration can hardly be set aside: 'I grant the Hellenic race in general their authors, their wealth of art, the delicacy and power of their eloquence, and much else that they would claim as their own, but scrupulousness and truthfulness in giving evidence were never much cultivated in their nation, and they fail to understand the importance of these things ... A Greek witness coming forward with malicious intent gives no thought to the words of the oath, only to the damage he can do. Being refuted or confounded is what he fears as shameful and tries to stave off, he is indifferent to everything else ... To people of this kind the oath is a joke, and giving evidence a game; the way you (Romans) think is quite obscure to them; praise, reward, favour and subsequent congratulations all depend on brazen lying.'[31] It is bad enough that it was possible, a century earlier, for a very shrewd Greek to write as follows of the abuse of official positions almost universal among his compatriots: 'the public administrators, when they are entrusted with as little as one talent, do not act honestly even if there are ten signatories, ten seals and twenty witnesses against them, while Roman military leaders and ambassadors remain true to their oath however large the sums involved. Among the Greeks, it is seldom that a man keeps his hands off state funds – with the Romans the contrary is the exception.'[32] Polybius, in deploring these facts, connects them with the decline of faith in gods and the underworld, and speaks of his age as sadly vicious in general, but in fact embezzlement of public money went back a very long way. Even Themistocles had not only spent an enormous amount on his political career in Athens, but had saved up for it in advance on a grand scale. He often spoke of his dread of the speaker's platform, and the reason for it was certainly not merely the knowledge of Athenian fickleness.

As a last document of Greek deceitfulness the *Stratagems* of Polyaenus may be cited, though its late date may diminish its value.[33] However this author, a veteran soldier of Macedonian origin, has left an account of Greek untrustworthiness which deserves to be read in full; it is collected from sources old and new, by no means all relating to military situations. The way of the world may not have changed much, least of all in war, and there is no reason to assume that Polyaenus approves of all he has to tell. In any case the general impression is that the Greeks were completely indifferent as to the means they used to win success against every type of opponent.[34]

However often the Greeks listed the principal motives of human conduct, their reckoning never failed to give its due place to the *love of honour* (*timé*). Thucydides puts it in the first rank alongside fear and utility,[35] while Isocrates subordinates it to pleasure and profit.[36]

Greek life offered conditions more favourable to the pursuit of honour than those found at other times and among other nations. First there was the fact that the public nature of activity in the *polis* gave the opportunity and leisure to know and be known by other people; secondly there existed a remarkable openness in expressing one's own personality, and in discussing the circumstances of others in conversation with them, which seems to have been thought compatible with good manners. Socrates' conversation with the aged Cephalus, at the beginning of Plato's *Republic*, gives an idea of this, as do Xenophon's *Symposium* and other accounts of social intercourse in the upper classes. Besides, the widespread custom of agonal competition, ranging from public appearances at the games to every kind of achievement and self-assertion, excluded the social inhibition which today, as a rule, hardly permits any competition except in business affairs, and otherwise restricts the individual to the negative aspects of the feeling for honour. That is, people now try to avoid anything that is disapproved of, and to obtain respect while shunning notoriety; where the modern aggressively competitive type goes beyond this, it is for the sake of rank and wealth, not for fame, and self-advertisement primarily serves the same purpose.

In contrast, the aim of the talented Greek, since Homer, was 'always to be the first and outshine the rest', and from the same early period the wish for fame after death was also often expressed – not the chief preoccupation of the modern age, even for those in high places. It would have suited the *polis* very well to adapt this individual *philotimia* to its own service, but the impulse found other outlets. The man of outstanding personality displayed himself to his contemporaries without diffidence, flaunting signs of power, often resorting to wholehearted self-praise; the Greeks were inclined to be very indulgent to energy of character, as long as they did not personally suffer from it or find themselves put too much in the shade. All these matters deserve to be seen in a wider context, but here we will consider only the general antagonism that the distinguished man had to contend with.

'Envy is mourning over another's superiority, delight in his misfortune (*Schadenfreude*) is pleasure at what disadvantages him'[37] – this definition of things that are as old as mankind may be the right way to describe the universal grounds of that antagonism. But envy as we know it today, which can never be avowed, but must conceal itself behind any available mask, usually operates behind the victim's back, while the Greek's envy broke out at the first opportunity in open attacks and in mockery.

Right from the outset, the Greeks thoroughly understood *kertomein*, the ache in the heart that words can inflict. It is particularly associated with mockery of unsuccessful attempts and actions; Homer tells of the victor's jeering and the pain it gives to the vanquished; the reader hears the full accumulated bitterness of Odysseus in his justifiable vengeance on the blinded Cyclops,[38] and the venomous mischief-making of Thersites. In the post-Homeric age, with the iambics of Archilochus, verbal abuse (*loidoria*) became an artistic genre, and people were convinced that the victims of Archilochus, like those of Hipponax, had been driven to kill themselves. Both these poets had to await the appreciation of modern literary historians; in antiquity they enjoyed little respect, though they were admired for their vigour of expression. Satirical poetry occurs in all the literatures known to us, and in the modern period as early as the Provençal school, but the fame and influence of these two poets was perhaps possible only in Greece. The dissemination of satirical verses was a ploy of vengeance and ill will in later times too. At the beginning of the Peloponnesian War, 'many people sang songs and malicious epigrams'[39] about Pericles, and the oldest hate-epigrams (*skoptika*) in the *Anthology* go back to that period. There was as yet no press, but its function was anticipated by gossip in the agora and probably at banquets too, and those determined to remain anonymous could scrawl their slanders on the walls of public buildings.[40] Caricature, also drawn on walls, had its uses too, and as for caricature in sculpture, it was almost the origin of Greek portraiture. About the middle of the sixth century, the sculptors Bupalos and Athenis persecuted the poet Hipponax with likenesses of this kind, which led to his taking revenge in iambic verses, and thus, it was supposed, to their suicides. Their approximate contemporary, the sage Cleobulus of Lindos,[41] warned against making fun of the victims of satire because of the bitter enmity aroused.

Mention of Pericles has already brought this account into the fifth century, which saw the full development, for the Athenians in particular, of good things and bad, of democracy and also of comedy. In the rest of Greece there may have been similar appearances of striking individuals and of spirited antagonism between enemies, but it is only for Athens that fairly complete documentary evidence exists.

The real dangers surrounding the citizen who made himself in any way conspicuous were so great that mere social sensitivity must have retreated into insignificance. A permanent terrorism was exercised by the combination of the sycophants, the orators and the constant threat of public prosecution, especially for peculation and incompetence, as well as the ever present risk of being accused of *asebeia* (impiety). A certain hardening of the nerves must have resulted from all this; not all accusations were successful, and anyone with influential contacts could not only defend himself but make counteraccusations; still, with the perpetual assemblies and trials there must always have been something going on to command attention and keep passions at a high pitch.

But beside this political activity, comedy was growing in importance, and by no means restricted itself to the social and private imperfections of individual Athenians. On the contrary its preferred theme was the state and its officials, and the fact that this was permitted remains astonishing despite attempts to explain it. Granted that the origin of comedy was a festive celebration of Dionysus, who himself 'loved to laugh'[42], and that joking and mockery were a feature of all Dionysian festivals – this is still insufficient reason for comedy having been able to make fun of state institutions and authorities, as it did for a whole century. Aristophanes' *Wasps* alone heaped lasting ignominy on the popular courts of Athens. Elsewhere the council, that is the *prytaneis* in office at the time, had corruption and even cuckoldry thrown in their faces; in *Knights*, the Demos appears incarnate as a person of very limited intelligence – until, later in the play (1121, 1141) the audience is given to understand that he was only pretending to be so stupid. Attacks like these admittedly name no names, nor do the curses hurled at the whole of Athens. More extraordinary are the wholesale attacks on named individuals carried out by Aristophanes, whose tone is said to be quite decent (*semnoteron*) compared with the bitter and scandalous abuse of Cratinus and Eupolis,[43] whose comedies have not survived. Aristophanes was indeed not the creator of his literary form, but developed its style to the point of complete mastery; later satire in poetry and prose drew upon him much more than upon the iambic poets, and Lucian himself is still rich in Aristophanic turns and expressions.

In most cases the poet no doubt achieved his purpose of causing *kertomein* or heartache, even if many people were hardened and the very worst had lost all shame.[44] Learned scholiasts of the past have ensured that a great deal of the satire is comprehensible to posterity. Those who were its named victims, or actually attacked by means of recognizable masks, either were, or were supposed to be, embezzlers of property, cowards, usurers, robbers, contractors,[45] sycophants and so on.[46] Towards the end of *Frogs*, when Aeschylus is returning to the upper world, Pluto gives him a number of ropes for people whom he names, one of them a tragic poet, as well as for the 'exactors' (*poristai*) in general; these, it seems, were appointed by the State to administer new taxes. Aristophanes' treatment of his literary colleagues is celebrated; the family of Euripides, for instance, assuming they wished to retain any respect, would certainly have to go to law if such things were said of them at the present day. Aesthetic objections to poetic works were habitually interwoven with the most personal insults, for example the things that are said to Agathon in many passages of *Thesmophoriazusae*. It may not surprise us that the ancient Greeks jeered at the physically deformed, but even so it was despicable. *Birds* alone attacks a good fifty Athenians by name, though the poet purposely omits the many accused in the hearings over the mutilations of the Herms, which were then going on. Entire choruses, for instance in *Acharnians* (V. 836–59) are solely intended to express venom against a number of people.

It might be said in defence of comedy that it was performing the function of a nonexistent police authority or even of justice itself, though this would have been taking on a fearful responsibility in a very frivolous way; it can also be said that comedy usually waged war on demagogy, and that, with his great campaign against Cleon, Aristophanes drew down vengeance on himself. But this will hardly do as the basis for the moral transfiguration of Aristophanes in some modern views of him. In general he was safe enough, since the *demos* was not unwilling to laugh at its own leaders and at those who thought themselves superior to the 'poor and common people' they came from;[47] still the usual victims of his scorn were 'rich or highborn or influential'. Besides, Aristophanes assured himself of unfailing popularity by his constant advocacy of peace, even at moments in the Peloponnesian War when peace would have been possible only at an intolerable price. *Lysistrata* for example dates from the year 411, when a powerful Spartan army was occupying Attic territory in Deceleia. Aristophanes' satire on Lamachus is an attack on one of the most brilliant and unselfishly devoted of all the military leaders.

Ultimately comedy gave way to the temptation to use the charge of *asebeia* against individuals; it was one of the most dangerous accusations of all. In his *Clouds* Aristophanes introduced Socrates on the stage in a manner that was to become world-famous: it was wonderfully funny but totally reckless. According to the accepted legend, Socrates himself sat laughing with the rest of the audience;[48] all the same, the poet, in the vanity of his inventive wit, must have blinded himself to the fact that he was arousing in the undiscerning spectators one of those mass prejudices which are never to be eradicated, and will always be handed down to later generations. It is true that twenty-four years were to pass before the trial and execution of Socrates, but without *Clouds* the cause and motive of those events would have been almost entirely absent.[49]

Subsequently, what is called Middle Comedy abandoned personal masks but still continued the wholesale denunciation of individuals, as the surviving fragments in Athenaeus show. Among others, the philosophers of various schools were now victimized by name, also notorious gluttons, and all those who were supposed to have taken money in the Harpalus affair. It is evidence of the pitiful poverty that overtook the genre that a certain Philippides, who was known for his leanness, occurs in no fewer than three of these later comic writers, and that it was not beneath them to invent a verb – *philippidousthai* – derived from his name.[50]

All these theatrical goings-on were still, as we have said, less important than the constant political and judicial perils the citizen had to live with; indeed mockery, which was public and sometimes admirably stylish, could be a means of betterment for the noble-natured. But to judge accurately we would need to find out how many worthy people secretly determined on silence and renunciation. The turning away from the state, and the acceptance of poverty, are clear at this time; but no-one can know the extent to which spontaneity was destroyed, and with it the precondition of cultivated social life and of poetry.

All in all, old and middle comedy are just the exceptional and official utterances of a satirical energy which prevailed in Athens the whole year through, if only because the steadying influence of regular work had been replaced by a perpetual concern with public matters, that is with other people. The spirit of mockery, whether gentle or harsh, seems to have dominated all intercourse.[51]

The reader who turns to the orators of the fourth century encounters the wildest personal attacks, but may be even more astonished by the meekness with which the authorities and the people put up with them, as long as no names were mentioned. As with the audience at the comedy, it was professional colleagues who had the thickest skins. The clients of Lysias complain of thefts from state funds by unnamed men who are evidently sitting in court, but who know that nothing will happen to them. The sycophants, certainly present, repeatedly have it said to their face that they are vile and disreputable; they seem not to have felt its application to them.

This hardening against mockery and direct attack did have its limits, and was often only assumed, hiding profound chagrin and hatred: 'Socrates, mocked in a comedy, sat and laughed; but Poliagros hanged himself.'[52]

Alexis, a poet of Middle Comedy, puts this complaint into the mouth of one character: 'All this social life, and the many symposia every day, have the effect of refining mockery, but it gives far more pain than pleasure; it begins with malicious gossip, then comes a reply in kind; slander follows, then fighting and drunken rage.'[53] Others give similar warnings.[54] To be laughed at not only in private, but, much worse, in life's aims and ambitions, has always driven people to desperation. Euripides allows his Medea to justify her terrible purposes and actions by her need to forestall mockery or get her own back on those who had laughed at her.[55] Sometimes perhaps a mere smile, or irony at the wrong moment, is more exasperating than outright laughter, because it asserts superiority as a matter of course. When Socrates went about among the crowds, his ironical way of speaking must have been the reason for his being answered with blows, kicks and hair-pulling, to which we are told he would also reply with a joke; but most of the people laughed at him contemptuously.[56]

76

Always and everywhere, to be rebuked in the presence of others has been felt to be particularly humiliating. A pupil of Pythagoras, to whom he had spoken somewhat sharply in front of the rest, went away and hanged himself, after which Pythagoras never uttered so much as an encouraging comment within hearing of anyone else.[57] Socrates, in contrast, betrayed his smug thoughtlessness in such things when he asked his judges: 'Why did so many seek me out for so long? They enjoy listening when I am questioning others, who think themselves clever but are not, because it is very amusing.'[58] No doubt it was, but not for the sacrificial victim.

As time went on, lack of sensitivity became a philosophical virtue, especially in the Cynics and Stoics, and could be learned by training. This weakens the effect of anecdotes told of Cleanthes, Arcesilaus and others on the subject. The cynic Crates applied the oddest form of training in this hardening process: he would scold whores and stand listening to their replies.[59] Better still, the man attacked might get the onlookers on his own side by a clever retort or a witticism, and some of the answers Diogenes gave are of this kind. However when the philosophers' sectarian hatred set them quarrelling, their impassivity often broke down, and (at least in their writings) ridicule no longer satisfied them; they tried to ruin each other by evil slanders. The Attic orators, too, would revile their opponents as well as all their followers and friends in the most personal terms, not forgetting their forefathers – for whom no-one can be held responsible – and the details of all this are better passed over in silence.[60] There was great reluctance to engage in lawsuits for slander, quite understandably in the general state of Athenian justice; and Lysias reports one of his clients as saying: 'Even if an enemy had accused me of murder, I would consider it a trifle, because I believe only illiberal and litigious men go to law over verbal insults.'[61]

Greek behaviour suggests that physical assault was borne more patiently than it is today,[62] and that being proved inferior to someone else in strength and brutality did not then determine a person's worth and reputation.[63] A man who had raised his stick was addressed in words which are as typical of the time as they are unthinkable today: 'Hit me if you like, but listen to me!' It hardly matters whether they were spoken by Themistocles, or someone else, to Eurybiades or to Adeimantus.[64] The ill-treatment Socrates calmly tolerated has already been spoken of, and there are similar stories about Diogenes, but other cases contrast even more strikingly with modern behaviour. After the performance of *Knights*, Cleon had Aristophanes beaten up (by the guards at the theatre, it seems). Two years later the dramatist explained to his audience in a parabasis to *Wasps* (1284 ff.) that he had been much to blame for mocking Cleon's sufferings at the time, and had even expected some such trick from the victim of his unkindness. Either Aristophanes had an extraordinary passion for keeping his name before the public, or else the Athenians were not sorry he should get an occasional whipping, though they could still respect him in his way and their own.[65]

It was of course open to anyone to go to law in cases of physical assault, but it was also possible to settle out of court. Demosthenes chose this method twice, when Meidias slapped his face in the theatre and when he was wounded by Demomeles. On the morality of such settlements, the orator's later biographers are the only source; his malign adversary Aeschines naturally seized the opportunity to say that Demosthenes had found a way to make an income out of his face.[66] In all these matters it is important to remember the framework in which they took place, that of the completely unscrupulous *polis* which for centuries made use of agents such as the sycophants. It is instructive, too, to observe how the declarations of *atimia* (loss of civil rights) operated; loudly proclaimed by the *polis* with the most solemn curses, they were often reversed for reasons of expediency, the emotion that had been whipped up being quietly suppressed.[67] In these circumstances, physical violence among citizens was bound to be judged in a different way from our own.

Alongside this peculiar hardening of feeling, and almost as an aspect of it, though a positive one, there was a certain tolerance, a capacity for listening to opponents which is far more difficult for leading parties today. Amidst all the noise of Athens and other democratic cities, beside the ruthless pushiness of the ambitious, there was still a degree of objectivity in judgment, an admiration for talent, which made it possible for men to distinguish themselves if they felt they had the right and the energy to do so. To such people, and even to the less gifted, an astounding tolerance was extended. No assembly of our own time would be likely to listen with patience even to a popular address like Cleon's;[68] what was heard from other orators and from the comic dramatists would now be prevented as incitement to disorder, or cause immediate violent reactions, and in any case the authorities would feel compelled to suppress or punish such utterances in the name of peace and the law. In Athens though, at least in the fifth and fourth centuries, no orator seems to have been dragged from the rostrum or obliged to withdraw by stonethrowing or a beating, though private vengeance was not unknown. As long as its vital principle was not attacked, the *demos* left the individual representatives of its power to get on as best they could; these men were not invulnerable, not protected by that power in a general immunity, and if they had to be thrown to the wolves, others could be found to take their place.

Some reports, supposed to relate to a very early time, from the Italian cities of Greater Greece when the great lawgivers Zaleucus and Charondas were active there, give a picture of a society whose members were less hardened and shameless, and let themselves be guided by the impulse called *aidos* (honour, modesty, kindness, discretion).[69] We are given to understand that sycophants convicted then had to go about garlanded with tamarisk, so that many killed themselves for shame; that those who had deserted in battle or evaded military service were not, as elsewhere, liable to the death penalty, but had to sit for three days in women's clothing on the public squares; that women were allowed only one maidservant to accompany them 'except when they were drunk', and could not leave the town at night 'unless for immoral purposes', nor wear embroidered dresses 'except for the harlots'. However, this whole report is easily recognized as a late invention, perhaps dating from the beginning of the Empire; in the real Greek *polis* there was never a time when people could be controlled by the power of symbolism or irony. None the less, such texts had their influence, however long delayed; during the French Revolution, St Just, for instance, who never hesitated to sacrifice his political victims on the guillotine, declared that ordinary murderers would be sufficiently punished by being forced to go about veiled in black; but he did not carry this private fantasy into effect.

Greek opinion constantly praises the virtue of *aidos* (sense of shame), and it is especially commended to the young, surrounded as they were by so many examples of its opposite. Among the people of developed nations there is always a dual ethic: the real one, embodying the better features of national life, and the postulated ethic chiefly represented by the philosophers. The second too may have some meaning for the nation, but only as defining areas in which the pangs of conscience can be expected to make themselves felt. Democritus took the view that *aidos* should develop of itself from education in grammar, music and the agon.[70] A saving grace was that it had existed long before, in Homer, in the form of the noblest delicacy of feeling, and the Greeks could be sure that their ancestors, listening to the poet's song, must have had a moral understanding of what was finest and most admirable in human behaviour. This certainly had its effect on the best of them; the others went with the current of life in the form it had taken, mainly under the influence of the *polis*.

It would be hopeless to attempt to draw up a balance sheet for and against the Greeks in the narrower moral sense and from the point of view of another nation and culture. The Greek reply to Roman moralizing at their expense might have been that they needed no gladiatorial combats to give them an appetite or to win votes. One might assemble a good many such debit and credit accounts between the two peoples, based, for instance, on the pleasures of life, behaviour within the family, the treatment of slaves, the passion for inflicting total destruction on enemies or rivals, and so on. On the debit side would appear the many accusations the Greeks made against each other; they were the only people in the ancient world who possessed the gift of comparison between nations, and we have already made use of some of these judgments. Herodotus, we have seen, sometimes read his compatriots a lesson, and composed a dialogue between Xerxes and Achaemenes (7.236 ff.) with the intention of forcing the Greek *polis* to confront the deep malevolent envy between its citizens and its practical effects, making an exception only of 'the virtuous few'. It is well known how vigorous this envy could become in the later development of the *polis*, and the subject gives me occasion to express a personal wish. It seems to me that a comparison both of quantity and quality might be made between examples of chicanery in the courtroom speeches of Athenian lawyers, and similar cases coming before the courts in modern times. The combined efforts of a classical scholar and a forensic specialist might result in some conclusive judgment. It would then become clear whether it has been possible in any other period of world history for the diabolical delight in ruining others to be so openly voiced as it was among the Greeks, chiefly through the encouragement and protection given to sycophancy, as can be learned from the surviving speeches of lawyers from Antiphon right down to Demosthenes and Hyperides. It is certain that if courts of law should again come into being, anywhere in the world, which tolerated plaintiffs and witnesses of the kind described in those proceedings, similar practices would again become common.

The further consequences the *polis* had for the life of its citizens, whom it had first so exalted, and later made prosperous on such dubious terms, are not relevant in this context, nor is the sad decline which the nation was to undergo in its homeland, while, in the East, the Greek spirit was finding important new regions to inhabit. One thing is certain: that the disposition, will and destiny of the Greeks form an integral whole, that their fate was not the work of chance, and that their withering and decay was the outcome of the political and social life they led. It is distressing to think of the beauty and greatness which only the Greeks could have achieved, and which never came into being because of this.

Yet we cannot help being drawn to the melancholy appeal of the couplet in which an ordinary Greek of average moral feeling, courageously looking into his own heart, sums up his character: 'at least I have never betrayed a true and worthy friend, and there is nothing slavish in my soul'[71].

On the Greek doctrine of the '*highest good*', the *succession* or '*identification*' of the blessings of life, only a few points will be added here. Three phases of consciousness can be clearly distinguished: that of Homer and Hesiod, that of the time of the nation's greatness, and lastly that attained by the reflections of the philosophers. Yet in the daily life of later periods the echoes of the earliest phase can still be found, where the old poets and the viewpoint of myth continue to prevail. If we know anything of these matters it is because the Greeks openly dared to hope that worldly wisdom and apathy should not entirely suppress all man's deeper aspirations.

Prayers to the gods would be by far the best source, if they had been preserved in clearer form. Words which have a spontaneous beauty are used, for instance, in Homer, when Nestor calls after Athena, as she vanishes: 'Look favourably on me, goddess, and grant me noble fame, to me, to my sons and to my virtuous wife.'[72] 'Noble fame' (*kleos esthlon*) was always the first desire of true Greeks, and these words of Nestor's, including his wife and children too, show that it was not confined to victory in war or in the games, but involves the whole of an honoured existence. Other supremely desirable gifts are incidentally revealed in Homer; the 'gift of sleep'[73] for instance, may be received, and is really a gift that might be longed for. Another object of wishes was a painless death in old age, not preceded by illness; on the legendary island of Syrie, we are told, Apollo and Artemis come with their silver bows and put old people to death.[74] In post-Homeric but still early times, a series of blessings is spoken in the *Hymn to Aphrodite* (103) by Anchises, after he has recognized his beloved as the goddess and promised her an altar; he prays to her for fame surpassing the other Trojans, for a healthy son, and for prosperity and happiness in a long life. Hesiod's account, in *Works and Days* (226 ff.) of blissful existence

81

in the city of the just, has its place here too, for it is a catalogue of heartfelt wishes. In poetry, such a list may not always indicate an order of importance, as the demands of metre will have influenced it.

A genuine order of importance is found, though, in a document from the historical period, a poem of Solon's:[75] first *olbos*, then reputation, the love and honour of friends, and lastly the ability to terrify and harm one's enemies. *Olbos* presents a difficulty, since no single word translates it; it is an expression that comes down from early antiquity and has a mythical glamour, conveying prosperity of every kind. Later, *olbos* is clearly distinguished from mere wealth: 'If a man flourishes and has many possessions in his house, but is without noble ambition, I would not call him *olbios* but only a comfortable guardian of treasures.'[76]

Pindar's list of life's chief blessings, at the end of the first Pythian ode, is shorter than Solon's: to live happily is the most desirable thing, a noble reputation the next; anyone who attains and keeps both, says Pindar, is the possessor of the most splendid crown.[77]

In all these definitions of desiderata, the implicit assumption of personal moral worth and nobility of character is fundamental, and explicit wishes for these attributes are also to be found, often combined in the most matter-of-fact way with material possessions. According to Theognis (V. 255, cf. 147) to be just is the finest of all,[78] the best is health, the most delightful, to succeed in obtaining what one loves – and here it is uncertain whether he means actual love or simply the realization of wishes in general. Somebody inscribed this wish almost word for word on a wall in the propylaea of the Latoon at Delphi;[79] the whole list is found again in Sophocles,[80] almost as if copied from Theognis. Usually, however, a Greek did not wish for moral qualities in himself, but believed he already had them; and indeed it was inadvisable to ask the gods for a moral disposition when everyone knew what the morality of the gods was like. Such an idea could only have occurred to the later Stoics with their totally new conception of divinity; but our present concern is with wishes that arose from the Greek temperament, not with moral views based on reflection. Something different again from wishing and entreating is the habit, from Socrates' time onwards, of praising virtue, seen as the central element of which all other good qualities – plentifully listed – are the expression, and as the prerequisite of all happiness.[81]

High reputation among compatriots or mankind in general, ranging from respect to honour and fame even in posterity, is gradually less and less emphasized and ultimately disappears from the list, although in life the passion for fame still prevails.[82] Instead, health and wealth move to the fore, and the god of Delphi once offered the choice only between these two. This was in the remarkable legend of the foundation of Syracuse and Croton: Archias prefers wealth and founds Syracuse, later to be so important; Myscellos chooses for himself and his future city 'to be healthy', and Croton then becomes the home of athletic excellence and of a robust strain of inhabitants. In complete contrast, the Birds in the comedy (729), in exchange for being worshipped as gods, promise men both advantages combined, and for this Aristophanes coins the expression 'health of riches', *plouthugieia*, one of the best of his many hybrid words. The other benefits the Birds promise for succeeding generations – peace, everlasting youth, laughter, dances, festivals, and hens that give milk – are of course a comic catalogue. Earlier (604 ff.) Peisthetairos has cheekily suggested that being rich might count in itself as a great claim to good health, and that those in financial difficulties would be sure to feel ill.

The Greeks well knew that health was the prerequisite for all other kinds of good fortune, and the fine scholium of Ariphron bears early witness to this.[83] That of Simonides is of only slightly later date: 'To be healthy is the best of all things for mortals, the second best is a noble character, the third is wealth obtained without dishonour, the fourth, to spend one's youth with dear friends.' A comic writer of the fourth century, commenting on these famous words, allowed health the first place but wanted noble character placed after wealth, since a noble person who is hungry can be terrifying.[84] Philemon wishes first for health, then general wellbeing, thirdly a light heart, and last, not to owe money to anyone.[85]

Greek elegy often turns to praising life's specific blessings, above all those the poet longs for or regrets; at symposia the subject came up naturally, and the same theme is often heard when the elegy becomes gnomic or epigrammatic, or takes on the character of poetic epistle. All these modes are to be found in Theognis, corresponding to varying moods; a fine example (933) runs: 'Energy (*arete*) and noble character are rarely combined in the same person; happy the man who has both, he is honoured by everyone, young and old make way for him; in old age he is still among the first citizens, his place undisputed in private and in public life.'

Wealth, as has been said, was once among the preconditions of happiness that were the objects of naive desire;[86] but as time went on many complained that wealth had become too important, and anyway was usually in the wrong hands. Theognis in particular is always lamenting poverty and the helplessness it brings, while riches (699) give their owner precedence over the wise, the intelligent, the eloquent and the fleet of foot.[87] Euripides goes further: anything said by a rich man is considered wise, but a poor man, even if he speaks well, is laughed at; people would rather betroth their child to a bad rich man than to a good poor one.[88] For most people, though they still paid lip service to 'excellence', gradually came to rate it, and even noble birth, as less important than the pleasure and power that riches could bring. Yet the rich man was surrounded by enemies and dangers that threatened and soured the enjoyment his possessions gave him, besides which he was under an obligation to display his wealth openly. In Euripides, the rich miser, who lives austerely, is thought capable of treating his friends as enemies and even of stealing from temples.[89] A century later, Alexis insists that the rich man should live in splendour and display the gifts he has from the gods as a sign of his gratitude:[90] if he is secretive and pretends to have no more than others, the gods will think him ungrateful and probably take away what they have given him.[91] It is important to remember how many distinguished men of the middle and later periods in Greece voluntarily chose poverty, partly because the only occupation open to them would have been considered beneath them, and also because for them the dangers of wealth outweighed its benefits.

Finally the cheerful enjoyment of pleasure (*hedone, terpole*) was also reckoned among the blessings of life, though how this was to be understood and in what measure depends upon the speaker, and Solon, as is well known, admits a wide range of such pleasures. We shall return to this in connection with the protests against pessimism; here it is enough to refer to the twelfth book of Athenaeus, with its striking quotations from Simonides and Pindar in praise of enjoyment. Only a few poor fragments survive from Pindar's rival Bacchylides, but one of them gives a glimpse of a more spiritual attitude: 'There is only one condition and one way for mortals to find happiness, and that is to renounce the passions: those who hanker after a thousand things will be heavy-hearted day and night, worrying over what is to come, and still find their efforts are all in vain.[92]

The philosophers and their ethical reflections, always in praise of virtue and the virtues as the desiderata, have so far been passed over in this account; but they also give attention to the wishes of ordinary people. Of most interest in this respect is Plato, who gives two great lists in their order of importance. The first reckons up the blessings of human life, beginning with the virtues;[93] the others are health, beauty, strength in running and in all physical exercise, then riches, but only in combination with intelligence (*phronesis*). Another speaker adds: acute senses, especially sight and hearing, then high rank to ensure freedom of action, and, after the full enjoyment of all this, 'to become immortal as soon as possible' – but all these blessings are reserved for the just and holy. The other catalogue, a location not of blessings, but of human values in nine categories, corresponds not to prevailing Greek attitudes but to Plato's own, which is what makes it important.[94] Occasionally the philosophers commented on or revised popular wishes: Antisthenes admitted pleasure as a blessing, but only if it left no remorse;[95] Menedemus, when he was told that the highest good was fulfilment of desire, said it was a better thing to desire only what was seemly.[96] Aristotle makes the nice distinction between external good fortune (*eutuchia*) and that inner happiness (*eudaimonia*) which is independent of fate (*tuche*).[97] Much later the virtuous Plutarch predictably lays stress on the conditional and unreliable nature of all earthly possessions in order to support his doctrine of culture and education as the infallible means to attain virtue and happiness. Noble birth, he says, is a fine thing, but credit for it is only due to past generations; wealth is respected, but a matter of chance and precarious too, exposed to wicked enemies and often in the hands of the basest men; fame is sublime but not immutable; beauty envied but of brief duration; health precious but uncertain; physical strength valuable but vulnerable to age and illness, and puny compared to that of bulls, elephants and lions; of all we have, only culture is immortal and godlike.[98]

Lucian's remarkable document of free fantasy wishes entitled *The Ship* is of only slightly later date.[99] Timolaus, the cleverest of the speakers, wishes he had those magic rings, particularly the one that confers eternal strength, health and invulnerability; others would bring him the gifts of invisibility, giant strength, the power to fly, and so on, and best of all to be universally loved, as well as youth perpetually renewed for a thousand years. Cultural history cannot afford to neglect statements of this kind from long distant worlds of the imagination; they are dreams coloured by the age and the nation that cherished them.

The constant thought accompanying all discussions of earthly blessings, their desirability or drawbacks, is one that demands the last word: is life itself desirable for its own sake? It is notable that Aristotle gave an affirmative answer.[100]

Certain nations have been preoccupied with the idea of the value of existence, and with establishing generally accepted views on this subject. Others have shown much less inclination and ability to concern themselves with it, or perhaps these faculties have remained latent, without finding literary expression; or, again, a powerful religion may have pre-empted this entire area of thought.

Since the great flowering of German humanism in the eighteenth century, the position of the ancient Greeks in this respect was thought to have been settled. The glory of their heroism in war and of their political achievements, their art and poetry, the beauty of their country and climate, all caused them to be considered fortunate, and Schiller's poem 'The Gods of Greece' conveys all these assumptions in an image which still retains its magic. At the very least, those who lived in the age of Pericles were believed to have enjoyed rapturous happiness from one year's end to the next. This must be one of the most tremendous historical falsifications that have ever occurred, and the more innocent and single-minded its proponents, the more irresistible it was. They were deaf to the loud united protest of the whole of recorded literature from myth onwards, and they were wilfully blind as well to Greek national life in particular, attending only to its attractive aspects and usually cutting short their survey at the battle of Chaeronea, just as if the next two hundred years, in which the nation was led to the brink of physical annihilation – mainly by its own actions – were not the continuation of what had gone before.

What is to be said here addresses only the general Greek estimation of human existence; no parallels will be drawn with the thought of other peoples, not even with the fundamental pessimism of the Persian Book of Kings, a legend in which the most heroic and virtuous regularly end by falling into evil ways. The Greeks, inclined as they were to believe in character as immutable, do not represent human beings as becoming worse than they were to start with, but as unhappy in any case, with or without divine intervention.

We have already tried to give an idea of how these divinities seemed to the Greeks; from their beginnings as very terrifying figures they became givers of gifts, but exercised only limited control over the world and human life, since they had to share their power with fate. Also the gods were not always happy, if only because they suffered from envy; and this envy they visited on outstanding human beings, especially the heroes of myth.

The hero who dies performing great deeds is a theme in the legends of many nations, and the Burgundians in Attila's train are a notable example. The ruler who forces his daughter's suitors to duel with him to the death (*gambroktonos*) also figures repeatedly in folklore, and there are of course other recurrent themes. What distinguishes the Greek use of them is the rich and detailed celebration of a great race or dynasty whose history is precisely known, which did not die out but came to a violent end, as well as the reverence felt by posterity, and even by the poet's contemporaries, for the race with which they compare themselves. Thus the Greeks thought that most of the last great generation of heroes fell in the Trojan War, or on their way home and afterwards,[101] but, even long before, a dark fate had already haunted the deeds and sufferings of the older heroes. The myths about them are filled with this awareness of destiny from the beginning, and where epic gives voice to motives and reflections the mood is uniformly pessimistic. It was on this foundation that tragedy was to develop its structures of crime, curse and mourning into high art.

Nowadays we are often told that many of the legends are based on mere natural phenomena, mainly astronomic and meteoric. Bellerophon's madness and misfortune signify apparent disturbances in the courses of the sun and moon, or the story of Phaedra and Hippolytus refers to the sea in which the morning star goes down. But even if such interpretations were irresistible, the elaboration of these terrible human stories from such origins would only be the more strikingly and peculiarly characteristic of the Greeks. Who but they, listening to the nightingale's plaint, would have associated it with the behaviour of three other birds to form the horrifying myth of Philomela, Procne, Tereus and Itys? The will to seek out darkness must have been strong indeed; and the way in which grimness is ingeniously intensified by the tragic poets, as they transform heroic myths into fictions, reveals that this tendency became stronger still with the rise of Hellenic culture. Our interest here is not in anatomizing the legends into their primary elements, but, precisely, in the drift of the amplification they received.

Even the earliest movements of populations, dimly remembered, are personified in the guise of heroes who have committed murder and gone off to a distant region where a heroic ruler takes them in, absolves them, confers gifts on them and perhaps makes them his heirs.[102] Fugitives of this kind are stock figures at every royal court. Elsewhere the deed is associated with a blood feud, and demanded of the suitor by the injured family as the condition of his betrothal. This seems trivial beside the passionate personal vengeance taken to the extremes of horror, as in the feasts of Thyestes.[103] Besides the fury of retribution, envy stalks heroes and gods alike in myth. At the storming of Troy, Heracles draws his sword against his companion Telamon, simply for having been the first to enter the town. Daedalus, myth's first artist, is a terrifying character, and the oldest example of a legend common to all nations – that of the master who murders his apprentice for envy of his talent.[104] The enigmatic artist-race of the islands, the Telchines, are also known for their envious malice. Often, too, myth brings down terrible misery on the envious as well as their victims. This vice begins to flourish early in men's souls, and twin brothers like Proetus and Acrisius, among others, are at odds even in their mother's womb, and grow up to fight for mastery. No sooner have the Spartoi sprung from the scattered teeth of the Theban dragon than a stone thrown by Cadmus sets them fighting and destroying each other till only five are left, who then, with the quintessential strength of all the rest, become the founders of the Theban people. A whole series of women in myth are terrifying creatures, either because, like Eriphyle, their greed for possessions and jewellery devastates the region, or because when crossed in love they take a frightful revenge, and in Ephyra, the Corinth of myth, the poison left by Medea lies ready for their purposes. The late Roman writer Hyginus compiled, or simply translated,[105] a comprehensive catalogue: the fathers who killed their daughters, the mothers who killed their sons, the marital murders, suicides, murders of relatives and so on, with three examples of those whose own children were served up for them to feast on.

But the doom that fate and the gods determine is by far the most common, and to this category belong the figures and stories which are most typical of myth. In Homer the death of 'many' Achaean heroes is the will of Zeus as well as of fate, and Achilles accuses Zeus in so many words.[106] At first Zeus delays Patroclus' death at Hector's hands so that Patroclus can kill as many Trojans as possible; Apollo thereupon does all he can to harm Patroclus without actually killing him, and although he is wounded by Hector's spear the dying warrior groans: 'I am slain by the Fates and the son of Leto!' Post-Homeric myth (as is evident in the *Cypria*) is not content with the extinction of the heroic race: there are just too many people in the world. So the earth goddess appears before Zeus to beg him to relieve her of the burdening mass of human beings; the god organizes the Theban War, which disposed of a good many, and then the Trojan War, which was supposed to complete the process satisfactorily. In Euripides, Apollo particularly emphasizes that the gods have sent Helen and the war over her 'so that they might liberate the earth from the impudence of countless throngs of mortals.'[107] Achilles himself was created so that his strength might destroy men, and his spear – an ashplant from Pelion – had been given to his father Peleus by Cheiron long before, 'to stamp out heroes'.[108] The two agents of destruction [Achilles and Helen] are later transfigured into divine likeness and enthroned on the island of Leuce, where they bring the winged child Euphorion into the world.[109]

This generally pessimistic background sets off the even more sombre destinies of the most celebrated heroes of myth. 'They did not live to be old after a life free of care and danger,' says Simonides,[110] but this anyway would not have been heroic, and the legends tell of many far worse terrors.

By far the most important of these figures is Prometheus. Aeschylus' noble story was merely an expression of what all Greeks knew about Prometheus: his generous gifts to mankind and his sufferings were enough to nurture a deep rebellious grievance against the gods and fate. In the midst of the most brilliant sacrifices and festivals the image of the bound captive on the mountain must sometimes have come to remind people of what they could expect from the gods. However the story was told, the gods were always seen as having begrudged mankind the gift of fire, that precondition of all culture and wellbeing. Whether the man who brought it to them was a primeval fire god, or a Titan, whether in opposing Zeus who intended to destroy them he had proved the saviour or even the father of mankind, were matters of opinion, but the main outline did not vary.

Heracles is a figure whose original meaning, much disputed, is of little importance; the suggestion that has been made, that Hera's enmity and the whole relationship between Zeus and Hera are to be explained in terms of meteors, had no significance for Greeks of the historical period. For them, the mighty hero Heracles developed increasingly (and especially among the later Greeks) into the conqueror and benefactor of the whole world,[111] but he was seen in popular belief much more as patiently performing menial drudgery. Elements in the figure of Heracles that may have been borrowed from the Lydian Sandon and the Phoenician Melkart were all transformed into sufferings by the inevitable pessimism of the Greeks. His service under Eurystheus, for whom the twelve labours were performed (regardless of whether they symbolize the sun's journey through the Zodiac) is not a divine trial and purification, ordained indeed by the Pythia, but a piece of trickery by fate; in later writers, such as Apollodorus, the despicable master contrives to reject some of the labours on the grounds that Heracles accomplished them with helpers or for wages.[112] Hera intervenes to inflict madness on Heracles, so that he kills his own children; his arrows also cause the deaths of the good centaurs that he loves, and finally on his funeral pyre on Mount Oeta he has to bequeath his bow to whoever does him the service of lighting the fire. This character was presented to the Greeks in many different lights, often indeed as a comic figure, since clever people naturally took it for granted that a hero who showed so much humility must have been halfwitted. Such was the gratitude of the intelligent.

In the myths and folktales of many nations, heroes are exposed to terrible dangers and vainly threatened by cunning and deceit. Perseus overcomes all this by means of the magic he can command, and is last heard of as a ruler in the Peloponnese. In contrast, Bellerophon, though a radiant hero like Perseus, victorious over dreadful monsters and whole tribes, goes mad and incurs the hatred of all the gods; 'presumptuously' he tries to storm the dwelling of Zeus on his winged horse, but is cast down and smashed to pieces like Phaethon. If this madness, like that of Heracles, is really to be understood as symbolizing irregularities in the behaviour of the sun, the question still remains as to why it was only the Greeks who spun these terrifying stories from such material.

Another motif frequent in Greek myth and largely peculiar to it is that the most splendid creatures die young. The attitude of Greeks in the historical time towards youth and age will be discussed later, and with it the open envy of early death. This feeling is certainly prevalent in myth, and in the cases of Hippolytus and Androgeus, for instance, we do not need the interpretation that they symbolize the morning star sinking into the sea or paling before the rising sun; popular imagination and dirges are full of *divine* beings who died early and violently, such as Linus, Hyacinthus, Hylas, Bormus, Cinyras, Adonis and so on. If it is true that the short heroic life of Achilles (*minunthadios, panaorios*) was originally meant to correspond to a forest torrent flinging itself into the sea, no obvious trace of this remains. The epic poets concentrated all that was finest into one young life and wove its melancholy destiny through it from the beginning with compelling sympathy. Achilles is so wonderful because he will die young, and that he will die young is because he is so wonderful. No matter whether he was first a nature divinity; independently of this, his apotheosis after being mortally wounded by Paris's arrow, and his union with Helen on the island of Leuce, must have come about because the Greek imagination had lavished so much of its best upon him. Many of the less glorious dead were worshipped as heroes; Achilleia were erected in many places to the son of Thetis.

In contrast to the figure of the hero who dies young, Odysseus exemplifies the mighty sufferer and survivor, the Greek as mature man. Other nations have invented tales in which a series of perilous adventures are heaped indiscriminately upon their heroes, who emerge at the end alive and happy; in the *Odyssey* things are different. Homer passes over the whole of the early life of Odysseus with his selfish wiles and acts of violence, and starts with the famous return from Troy. One by one the companions perish, not always because of their own guilt; the disaster in the land of the Laestrygonians is not caused by any individual's action; Scylla's victims are blameless, and the companions deal with Polyphemus more shrewdly than their leader; but their general fate represents that of the vast majority of mortals. Odysseus himself declines from his status as a king and military leader and becomes a solitary castaway. The suspense of his longing for home and family is immensely drawn out by his visit to the underworld and his dallying with Calypso, till ultimately the gods are obliged to show mercy to this man who has remained so impressive and so strong – but only to him. After the death of the suitors the hero still has some duties to perform, but then a peaceful old age ruling over contented subjects is predicted. This version however is only in the *Odyssey*;[113] other legends have later lively adventures in store for him and his family, some, indeed, discreditable.[114]

The wanderings and contests of Odysseus are only the best-known among the stories about the return of the heroes (*nostoi*). Greek imagination set out to show the vanity of a great victorious campaign, and, so it might be said, of everything that the world considers glorious, in the story of the dark destinies of most of those who returned. Ajax, son of Telamon, dies by his own hand even before the Greeks leave Troy; Ajax the son of Oïleus is killed on a cliff by Poseidon's trident. Others die when Nauplius, father of Palamedes who was treacherously murdered, lures their ships on to the steep cliffs of Euboea with fiery signal-torches, and later legend tells us that it was this same Nauplius who led the wives of the absent heroes astray into adultery, Clytemnestra above all. Diomedes, too, returning to Argos, finds his Aigialeia the mistress of a son of Sthenelus. In danger of assassination, he flees to the altar of Hera and then to Italy, where he becomes the divinity of the Adriatic and Tarentine Sea and in effect begins a new life.

Otherwise the usual outcome for the younger Greeks is a violent death, like that of Neoptolemus at Delphi; one, Nestor, is fated to grow old in his official role so that he can recount the deeds of an earlier generation to the young. The general impression that the legends of the return made on the listener is that he should regard those who fell at Troy as the luckier of the heroes.

In myth generally, it is fate and the jealousy of the gods that determines the heroes' destinies, and fate hardly seems to condescend to catching the hero out in any matter of moral blame. It might be expected that blame should be of the kind incurred in relation to human beings, and thus comprehensible to people of all times and all nations, not merely, for instance, the offence of omitting a sacrifice due to a divinity; yet this is often what causes a terrible end to overtake even the man who has committed really blameworthy actions. The emphasis is not on the justice of fate but on its inevitability, and thus oracular prophecy provides the Greek imagination with an incomparable source of themes. Information given about the future is only partial, and this brings about the downfall of the questioner; Oedipus, warned by Delphi that he will commit parricide and incest, flees Corinth and his supposed parents, only to plunge into catastrophe. The hero of myth scrupulously directs his whole life according to an obscure saying of the gods, but all in vain; the predestined infants (Paris, Oedipus among others) left to die of exposure, are rescued and afterwards fulfil what was predicted for them. But where the child fated by an oracle to kill his father is not exposed and they take every precaution to avoid each other, fate finds a way to bring about the parricide, as in the horrible story of Catreus and Althaemenes.[115]

A prophecy of misfortune takes another turn in the legend of the Seven against Thebes and their journey. One of their leaders, who is also a famous seer, knows that their cause is opposed by the will of Zeus, and all know it through him; premonitions of death and a series of ill omens[116] accompany them on their way, and Adrastus alone returns, a grief-stricken mourner for the rest of his days. On the journey they are the guests of the King of Nemea just after his child has died of a snakebite; the Seven bury the child, and Amphiaraus says it is a sign of their own end, so they call the boy Archemorus, the one who leads to death. Can there be an expedition such as this in the heroic legends of any other people? Hector's foreboding has a far deeper ring: 'The day will come when sacred Ilium shall fade away'[117] – for he is not the leader of a band of adventurers, but the staunch defender of his native city, and continues to defend her in the knowledge that his cause is lost.

The fact that this homeland of Hector's was till then a place of supreme happiness ensures that its destruction shows all the more clearly and poignantly the fragility of earthly things menaced by fate. All the splendour and divine favour that a ruling house could hope for had been enjoyed in abundance by the sons of Dardanus; fame, riches and material delights were theirs until the Achaeans arrived – but the outcome for most of these victors has already been told. The destinies of Trojans as well as Greeks reveal the true Greek assessment of the value of earthly things, but the gods, with their vacillating and treacherous interventions, only act as agents of a more powerful common will: the favoured races were to cease to exist. Even on the Greek side, dark premonitions had been felt; Odysseus had pretended to be an imbecile in the hope of escaping the war, and Thetis had hidden her son among the women of Scyros, but all in vain.

Truly man is inwardly formed by the Fates for suffering, and must be able to grapple with the most terrible pain; accordingly 'the gods prepare a full measure of misery for his life'.[118] At times the gods themselves are struck by the thought that they are foolish to take sides in the dealings of these wretched mortals who grow like the leaves on the trees and vanish again.[119] 'Nothing on earth is so miserable as man!' says Zeus, 'of all that breathes and creeps on its surface.'[120] He speaks these words to the immortal horses of Achilles who are weeping for the death of Patroclus, and pities them, who never grow old, for having been given to the mortal Peleus; the god and these animals understand each other and can converse about human destinies.[121]

It is well known that two vessels of destiny stand at the threshold of the house of Zeus.[122] No-one receives his share from the good vessel alone; the proportion is such that many have their fate allotted only from the bad one. Pindar later makes this more precise: for each good thing the gods bestow two evils on mortals.[123] Before predicting good fortune to anyone, it is therefore wise to utter a caution against the common earthly fate. Alcinous knows that his Phaeacians in their magic ships can only bring the stranger safe home: 'from then on he will suffer whatever the implacable sisters have spun into the thread they made when his mother bore him'.[124]

When the gods wished to revel on Olympus, the Muses would sing to the music of the lyre about mankind, and how they are doomed to live helpless in their suffering knowing no remedy for death and old age.[125] There is no need to repeat here how often and how fearfully divine jealousy inflicted abject misery on mortals, and how even the simplest domestic happiness and goodwill among men proved intolerable to the gods. But it is important to keep in mind the behaviour they were considered capable of, despite all the praises to their glory. Phineus, the ruler of the Hellespont, has committed a crime, and Zeus offers him the choice between death and blindness; he chooses the latter, but this angers Helios, because Phineus has decided to look on him no more, so he sends the Harpies to persecute him. Poseidon promises three wishes to Theseus, who demands and is granted first the liberation of his friend Pirithous from Hades, secondly his own safe return from the labyrinth, and last, cruelly, the death of his son Hippolytus, which he has wished for, tricked by the calumnies of Phaedra and Oenone.[126]

The imagination that plays with such attitudes and beliefs likes to build up a picture of a golden age when people were happier than they are now. There is a longing for escape at any price, not asking whether cruel gods existed then too. All nations have similar dream pictures, down to the trivial Land of Cockaigne.[127] The real conditions of individual life seem all the worse by comparison; but Greek consciousness, as it is displayed in Hesiod's account of the five ages of man, probably exceeds anything in other literatures in its total pessimism and despair of both present and future.[128] As early as Homer there began the celebration of distant peoples who lived justly and happily, which came to be a great feature of mythical geography and later invaded real geography as well;[129] it seemed as if the outermost boundaries of the world must harbour the wellbeing that had quite disappeared from the centre: 'happiness is where you are not'.

One small observation must be included here. Since life is as it is, it was permissible among the Greeks, even from the time of the epic, to refer frankly to the approaching death of old people – Penelope's web is the shroud for her father-in-law Laertes.[130] Well into the historical period, Pindar gave no offence when he arranged for Theron, the ruler of Akragas, to hear a song of his about Theron's death as an event soon to be expected.[131] To anticipate with another instance, the Stoic Zeno was a model of virtue for so many years that the Athenians marked their respect in his lifetime, by decreeing him a golden crown and a memorial stone at state expense.[132] It is interesting to reflect how supposed good manners have conspired to make such a thing quite impossible and unmentionable in the modern world. In the first place this must imply that our world can find no fault with itself and looks forward to its own perpetuation, and secondly – though this is not likely to be openly stressed – that someone's death is too great a loss to be contemplated. The Greeks, unlike ourselves, were as naive in this regard as they were in their wishes.

Finally, disaster in Greek myth has a very peculiar ideal purpose. The gods, Alcinous says, have ordained the destruction of Troy and doomed mankind to ruin so that all this should be a *song for future generations*.[133] The same thought, transferred to another species, is behind the words of Hermes to the tortoise as he is killing it: 'in life you move laboriously, but when you are dead you will make beautiful music'.[134]

At all events the epic poets knew that their mythical forerunners, the bards of primeval times, had paid for their gift with their lives or their wellbeing. Orpheus was torn to pieces by the Maenads, Thamyris blinded and deprived of his gift of song by the Muses after he competed with them and lost.

From this prehistory of Greek pessimism, derived from myth and epic, we turn now to Greek thought in the historical period. Here again, all parallels with the Near and Far East and with Egypt will be avoided, as well as any consideration of the possibility of intellectual contacts between these peoples and the Greeks. This is not to be a generalized discussion but a collation of facts with statements. No conclusions will be sought as to mankind's capacity to judge happiness and unhappiness in themselves and their fellow beings, even their compatriots; the ordinary criterion will be observed, that what is perceived as happiness or unhappiness is really so for each person, and it follows that the Greeks must be allowed to speak for themselves.[135]

The important characteristic of the Greek people was that they felt their sufferings intensely and with full awareness. In contrast to the resigned acceptance of the human condition in Eastern cultures, and to any contemplative quietism, the Greeks were exposed and vulnerable to physical and mental afflictions. Nations, in their beginnings, have only a collective consciousness of life which may even last into fairly advanced phases of civilization, but the Greeks had become individuals earlier than others, and experienced the glory as well as the pain of this condition. Even in the epic, the fathers of Achilles and of Glaucus sent their sons to fight at Troy with the admonition 'Always to be the first and strive to outdo the others';

what awaits the heroes is not only combat with the enemy but also the jealousy of their comrades – between the leaders, indeed, mortal enmity. The next age was that in which the whole Hellenic world was driven and preoccupied by the competitions and the fame of the victors, at home as much as at the great festival gatherings, while the much more numerous unsuccessful competitors certainly experienced a far greater sum of misery than the sum of happiness that the winners enjoyed. It is a fair question whether the pride of the agonal victors, like that of Greeks of all periods who achieved some success, was not too dependent on the opinion of others, and whether Greeks in general did not tend to live too much for the eyes of spectators. In any case this was how it was. The next development was that of competing individual powers in the *polis*, that is to say the democratized *polis*, and here we must confront the real Athens of Pericles, not its traditional idealized image; the best way to study it would be to start with Pericles himself and the events of his later life. From that time on, as far as can be learned from the historiographers and orators of the fifth and fourth centuries, the control of public affairs was in disreputable hands, while political life was so to speak the only life permitted, with constant spying and denunciations on capital charges; it would be wrong to forget the uncounted number of those who suffered, and to ignore their existence because they were forced to remain silent. The palpable facts are clear, and above all the flight from the State of so many able persons who are known to have embraced poverty and renounced the possibility of family life. Yet all were Greeks, that is naturally disposed to seek personal distinction, and some of them people of the very finest abilities, who did not lightly give up their activities and their desires. This state, too, in which and for which its citizens suffered so much, this be-all and end-all was exposed, if defeated by external enemies, not only to plundering and humiliation but, according to Greek military law, to destruction – the execution of the men, the enslavement of women and children, so that of countless Greek cities nothing but a heap of ruins remained. For those who experienced it, the transition from a life they had lived in its utmost intensity to this total annihilation must have entailed appalling human misery and rage. This must be borne in mind in considering all the partisan struggles and upheavals which reduced the nation, materially speaking, to a shadow, until it collapsed into the hands of the Romans.

There is no doubt that many privileged human beings were able to enjoy all the forms of happiness the mind can confer, whether as sublime art and poetry, thought or speculation, and also to convey these things, as a reflection of their own lives, to all the others who were capable of understanding them.[136] There had always been an element of optimism in this area of Greek life, that is, artists, poets and thinkers had always found it rewarding to offer their splendid creations to the Greek world, whatever its condition. However sombre their personal view of life, their energy was always ready to bring to light the great free images of their inner selves. At times, thought rose to a height of joyful aspiration over Attica and all Greece in contemplation of the universe. As Anaxagoras says: 'it is better to be born than not to be born, for the sake of observing the heavens and the cosmos'. Diogenes proclaimed a similar intellectual optimism: 'for the noble-minded every day is a celebration, the whole cosmos a shrine we enter from the moment of birth, with its sun, moon and stars, streams of fresh water and the plants and animals the earth bears; our life is the initiation into these mysteries, and should be tranquil and full of joy, but most of us desecrate it by constant complaints, gloom and anxiety'.[137] What this leaves out of account is that the world consists not only of responses to nature, but also the impressions of human life, which surround each of us and prove the chief source of care. Long before the time of Diogenes this had been expressed by Aesop, if these remarkable verses are his: 'How is anyone to escape you, life, unless he die? Your pain is thousandfold, and it is not easy to flee from it or to bear it; the loveliness nature gives you is blissful – earth, sea, stars, the courses of the moon and sun, but all the rest is only fear and suffering, and if some lucky chance comes to us, a nemesis is sure to follow.'[138] It would have been strange if the Greeks had failed to be enraptured by the beauty of nature, but they felt and thought more of the terrors of human life.

In what follows, it will be possible to describe the variety of philosophical views only incidentally, where the opinions do not depend solely on particular systems, but clearly correspond to some aspect of popular consciousness. To reach correct judgments about representative Greek attitudes, the ideas of the philosophers are not a helpful criterion; their value lies elsewhere, and for the present purpose demands only a rapid survey. Socrates was explicitly optimistic, and his belief in good, creative and redemptive gods is a barely veiled monotheism.[139] Plato, where he follows Pythagoras, is a pessimist, but in his Utopias obviously speaks as an optimist; and the *Phaedo* teaches how the agreeable (*hedu*) and the saddening (*luperon*) influence each other. The hedonics of Aristippus suggest the question whether this doctrine of pleasure in the present moment is not best explained by total despair for the *polis*, a state of mind that might well prefer deliberate forgetfulness of past and future.[140] Hegesias of Cyrene, many of whose hearers are said to have committed suicide, seems to have gone as far as possible in painting a gloomy picture of human life. The doctrine of the Cynics may express itself as optimism or as pessimism, but the Stoa is fundamentally pessimistic, despite its talk of 'the best of all worlds' and its teleology. In the case of Epicureanism much depends on whether the shunning of contact with society (*lathe biosas*) is interpreted as pessimistic or not. We shall have to rely on the traditions of popular consciousness.

Hope, the companion of Greek and all other human life from its beginnings, is judged, on reflection, to be a deluding influence. Yet the Aeschylean Prometheus, in implanting hope as a blind instinct in mankind, can at least be said to have put an end to their perpetual contemplation of approaching death.[141]

The whole phenomenon of Greek pessimism is the more remarkable for the contrast it presents with the decidedly optimistic cast of the Greek temperament, fundamentally creative, sensuous, outgoing and also – superficially – inclined to value and make the best of the passing moment. This has nothing to do with public entertainment and the joyful mood at festivals, which even a nation given to melancholy may be capable of for short periods; it never occurred to the Greeks to praise life as such, let alone for the sake of these pleasures, nor to thank the gods for it as a gift. How much their existence brought them in the way of happy moods or passions fulfilled may be guessed at but never measured. It is most likely that the symposium and its customs were a means of warding off pessimism, and it gives rise to the calls for merrymaking which sound sometimes poetic and beautiful, sometimes merely frivolous.[142] *Zethi!* – live! (i.e. rouse yourself to enjoyment!) was the cry, combined perhaps with a word or two about the brevity of youth and the fragility of happiness.[143] A coarser injunction to pleasure: *ede! bibe! lude!* (eat, drink and be merry), was more commonly used in fictional epitaphs for oriental rulers such as Ninus and Sardanapalus; but even an Attic comic writer praises noisy jollity.[144] With time a special style of jocularity developed, and would deserve a place in a study of Greek sociability; Philistion, a comic writer contemporary with Socrates, wrote poetry which mingled 'the lamentable life of man with laughter', and is said to have died of a fit of laughing.[145] It hardly needs to be said that this kind of thing is a feeble substitute for a genuinely cheerful attitude to life; still, the Greeks felt no need to have a model mummy carried around among the guests to encourage drinking and good humour as the Egyptians did[146] – and even in Egypt this custom was confined to the rich, as ordinary people there were perfectly able to enjoy themselves without being spurred on in this way.

Apart from festive enjoyment there are also recommendations to live '*eikei*', i.e. 'taking it as it comes', free of care, and not to bother with hopes or fears.[147] Perhaps the more fortunate people really lived in this way.

It is much more in poetry and in prose, though, that Greek pessimism shows itself as a fact of ordinary life, and this not at all as the outcome of reflection, still less with the complex rational foundation it has acquired in the nineteenth century, but proclaimed to the world in brief harsh statements as a matter of mood and attitude. It is impossible to know how many people prudently chose to behave as if they personally were contented or at least indifferent, but there was some satisfaction to be derived from joining in the general chorus of complaint. What this conveys is a vigorous denunciation of life; mankind is born to sorrow, and not to be born, or to die early, is the best. 'We are doomed to suffer, and the wise are those who bear what fate sends in the noblest way.'[148] Single words (*merimnai, phrontides*) indicate that a great amount of unhappiness stems from the human temperament itself, from its useless, niggling, tormenting preoccupation with the threat of possible dangers, and especially with the future; even in the midst of expected pleasure people feared some intervention between the cup and the lip;[149] but the subject never seems to have been treated with psychological thoroughness.[150] We have to content ourselves with the allusions of legend; the general vague apprehension of misfortune, and the vain wish to placate the dark powers by a bitter sacrifice, is most beautifully illustrated by the story of Polycrates and his ring.[151] In an earlier version, the ring may have been a talisman; the dearest possession a Greek could sacrifice was a splendid artefact.

Pessimism takes little account of the gods because they were not the creators of the world and the human race;[152] in the fate of mankind the old predominant view of 'destiny', *Moira*, retains its hold. Again, the lament that the good are unlucky and the bad lucky, so frequent in other contexts, is only cautiously expressed here, since the bad too must fall victim to the common fate. But one complaint heard among others is that life is embittered by the spectacle of the wicked enjoying good fortune.[153]

A further aspect of this is that the Greeks' poor opinion of the great majority of their fellow beings, and of their compatriots in particular, is part of their pessimism, or at least interwoven with it from early times. Athena herself, in the figure of Mentor, says that the generation which follows on the idealized one of myth will be inferior: 'few sons are the equal of their fathers, most are inferior and seldom is one better than his father'.[154] In Hesiod's description of the just and happy city, in *Works and Days*, all that can be expected is that children do not turn out worse than their parents; but the general picture of post-heroic humanity, sketched in the same poem as the doctrine of the five generations of mankind, progresses downwards from golden tranquil happiness to the profoundest darkness of misery (cf. especially 173–200). In later ages there is unanimity in the most varied sources, including the Seven Sages: most people are worthless, and Bias, who takes this as his motto, drew the conclusion that those we are fond of should be loved as if we may one day have to hate them.[155] Any careful inquirer, says Sophocles, always finds out the wickedness of people.[156] The same lament is more solemnly and feelingly expressed: one virtue after another is said to have abandoned the world, vanished from men's sight, flown away up to the gods. Hesiod bewails this in respect of shame and modesty;[157] Theognis (v. 1137, cf. 647) of loyalty, moderation and the Graces; Euripides of shame;[158] lastly Aratus, in the era of the *diadochoi*, says the same of Astraea, an embodiment of *Dike* (Justice).[159] The Alexandrian poet transferred the goddess to the zodiac, where she was to occupy the place of Virgo, and Roman poetry adopted the fancy from him. Ovid ends his picture of the terrible last age of the world with the famous lines:

> *Victa iacet pietas, et Virgo caede madentes*
> *Ultima caelestum terras Astraea reliquit.*[160]
> Vanquished lies Piety, and last the Virgin Astraea
> Departs to heaven from the Earth that reeks with slaughter.

When they heard such verses, sung perhaps by the chorus in a tragedy or in some other noble poetic form, people must have felt edified in a mournful way and resigned themselves to the inevitable, each perhaps regretting that others were so bad. If a person wished to take this perception to the point of full-blown misanthropy and to be publicly acknowledged as an eccentric, as Timon of Athens did just at the period of the great tragic writers,[161] that was his own affair; only he had to resign himself to being the butt of every anecdote that had ever been invented or related about misanthropes.

This world of wickedness was by no means ready for repentance, and if change had been intended, the gods would have had to make a start with themselves. Ascesis and rejection of the world – that is authentic religious pessimism – made no headway, while the Pythagorean and Orphic influence did not last; we cannot judge whether the fear of punishment after death may have improved personal morality. A saying of Democritus has a bearing on this: 'all human beings, feeling that evil rules their existence, languish all their lives in confusion and fear; what is more, they indulge in false imaginings of what follows after death'.[162] Cynicism, though, was not at all ascetic in the sense of trying to detach men from the world; its aim was only to help the individual, still living in the midst of the world, to reject its mastery over his will.

It is impossible to avoid some repetition in speaking of the Greek lament over human misery, insistent and all-pervasive as it is; the same thought is expressed now simply, now more elaborately, mingled with all kinds of circumstances and notions. An example to begin with is the awareness of the negative quality of happiness and the positive character of pain, already clearly established in the fourth century; 'whatever gives pleasure, superficial as it is, has wings and always some flavour of suffering, but pain comes undiluted and whole and enduring'.[163] Or happiness is completely left out of the reckoning: 'There is,' says Sophocles 'no-one without suffering; the happy are those who have least of it.'[164] The world and life are considered not only petty, but bad and evil.

To the Greek way of thinking, the obligation to work, life as toil, was itself a form of suffering, and is probably the age-old root cause of pessimism. Even in Homer, Zeus imposed toil (*ponein*) on mankind as a heavy curse at their birth, as Agamemnon acknowledges when he and Menelaus have to go about summoning their men individually for a nocturnal task.[165] In Hesiod's *Works and Days* the gods in general are to blame for having concealed men's sustenance from them: 'but for this, you could earn enough for a whole year by one day's work, and be at leisure; you could hang up your steering oar over the chimney piece and there would be an end of all this labour with oxen and mules'.[166] But Zeus hid the means of nourishment in his anger when Prometheus deceived him; for after men were deprived of fire, which they had already possessed, Prometheus brought it back to them in a hollow reed, and in retribution Zeus sent a punishment for all future generations, one they would at first consider a blessing. This was the creation of Pandora, that is of woman herself, to be supported by man in perpetuity, 'a woe to the industrious earner', for till then people had lived 'without ills, sickness and painful drudgery'. The national hatred of all that was banausic, all toiling for subsistence, grew in proportion to the necessity for it. To keep slaves for labour was only possible for those who could buy them; but any dependent position, even if it could bring gain and pleasure, was a bitter thing to the free Greek, and the attitude of the *polis* ensured hourly reminders of the low status of honest work.

Disagreeable necessities are sometimes listed in detail, for instance in the epigram of Poseidippus,[167] and in the pseudo-Platonic dialogue *Axiochus*, already referred to, where Socrates recounts them as occurring in an oration by Prodicus.[168] This is a very instructive description of essentially Athenian life seen from the dark side and from the cradle onwards, but associated with particular trades – for instance the miseries of the seaman, the countryman and so on – which were in part a matter of choice and not necessarily linked with human destiny in general; the most important statements concern that destiny itself.

Central to all that we know of ordinary people in Greece is the unique testimony Herodotus gives as to the wretchedness of life; what he has to say is untouched by philosophical reflection or rhetoric, but owes its maturity to the observation of humanity in distant countries as well as his own. It is hard to imagine a modern historian of whatever nationality feeling moved to speak of this, even if the occasion presented itself; Herodotus seeks such occasions and actually goes out of his way to invent them, for instance in connection with his belief in the jealousy of the gods. Above all he teaches the mutability of fortune, the rule of 'circularity in earthly things' (as Croesus says to Cyrus in the land of the Massagetae) alternating to prevent the same people being happy all the time. The famous conversation between Croesus and Solon (I.30 ff.) is not entirely the invention of Herodotus; earlier Greeks had dramatized the views of a Lydian king on mortal happiness, and the later Valerius Maximus (7.1) certainly repeats an older account of this. In this text, it is not Croesus but Gyges who asks whether another man exists who is as happy as he is, and he puts the question not to a Greek sage but to the Pythian Apollo, who then, instead of several men, names only one, a poor but contented Arcadian, old Aglaos of Psophis. Croesus' later life was very eventful; his splendid wealth and then his fall must have provided plenty of material for Greek discussions, probably in dialogue form. Everything in Herodotus is informative; in Solon's story,

Tellos' great good fortune in life consists of two points, one that he was lucky enough to fall in battle for his country, the other that no member of his family died before him. It is in connection with the Argive brothers that we are told an early death 'is best for mankind'; Solon argues that, as in a normal life of seventy years there are 26,250 days, no two of which offer exactly the same experiences, it would only be possible to speak of happiness if the outcome of all these fluctuations could be known in advance; but for man everything is chance; many are only shown the good life (*olbos*) by the gods and then ruthlessly destroyed. The exchange between Xerxes and Artabanus (7.45 ff.) goes much deeper. The King, seeing his armies and fleets at Abydos, weeps for the brevity of human life, and his wise uncle replies: 'There are worse things in the course of our life; brief as it is, no man is so fortunate that he does not often feel it would be better to die than to live on; with its many ills and sufferings our short life seems long, and is so wearisome that death is a much desired refuge for mankind.' Some military counsel follows, but in Chapter 50 Xerxes opposes this opinion with a general energetic defence: those who reflect on everything are incapable of action; better to risk all and bear the average of failures, than to fear everything and suffer nothing. Elsewhere, and rather enigmatically, in the middle of a report on the dealings between Argos and Persia (7.152) Herodotus remarks: 'This I know, that if all men were to make a great heap of the ills each has to suffer, intending to exchange their own for others, a good look at what the rest have to put up with would end with everyone gladly taking home what he brought.' Valerius Maximus (7.2) attributes the same dictum to Solon himself; he also tells the story of his taking a sorrowing friend up on the Acropolis and pointing to the roofs of the whole city of Athens with the words: 'Think how much grief has lived and lives and will live here, long ago and at present and in the future, and do not complain of your own misery!' Solon's pessimism is more directly conveyed in one of his own distichs: 'Not one mortal is happy; everyone under the sun is unhappy.'[169] And Solon was one of the seven wise men of Greece.

There is a wide range of such tirades against life as not worth living, dating from various periods.[170] The sophist Antiphon finds it intolerable that phrases are made about life as wonderful and sublime; he calls it petty, feeble, fleeting and shot through with great misery. Aristotle maintained that life was desirable in itself; yet these cruel words of his have been handed down: 'What is man? A monument of frailty, prey to the moment, the plaything of fate, an image of reversals (of fortune), sometimes more plagued by envy, sometimes by unlucky chances; the rest is slime and bile.'[171] 'The animals are much happier and in truth cleverer than men; the ass we abuse so much is at least not to blame for its own ills,' says Menander, and Philemon agrees with him; the animals only bear what nature imposes on them and need make no judgments and no decisions, while we men in our intolerable life have invented laws, and are slaves to opinion and to our ancestors and descendants: we perpetually find new pretexts for being unhappy. Elsewhere the same poet says: 'storms are not only met with at sea, but even when you are walking under porticos in the street, and at home in the house too; seafarers are rewarded after the gale with a favourable wind, or get safe into harbour, while I suffer storms not just for a day, but all my life long, and suffering always has the upper hand'. The doctrine that the gods envy human talent was an old one, and Sotades later complains that the gifted endure special misfortune and come to a bad end, while the peculiar malice of fate balances great qualities with great disadvantages; he concludes: 'A single day without pain is a blessing, for what are we indeed? And of what stuff are we made? Consider what life is, what you come from and what you are, and what you will become at last.'

Unfortunately only a few scattered traces remain of the whole genre of poems consecrated to laments for the dead (*threnoi*). One beautiful fragment from Simonides, however, shows that they did contain complaints of life, whose brevity was mourned in spite of all its cares.[172] These choral songs performed at burials were only the last lingering echo, in a much refined artistic form, of the deafening, wild keenings of the early Greeks. It is possible that complaints about the misery of existence occurred in those too, along with praise of the dead and grief for them.

This selection of harsh accusations against life is not yet complete. According to Pindar life is 'only the dream of a shadow';[173] 'time hangs treacherously over mankind and rolls life's tide away with it'.[174] Sophocles says that man is nothing but a breath and a shadow.[175] In his *Ajax* (125) Odysseus mourns the hero's dreadful fate, inflicted by Athena as a boastful proof of divine power, as if it were his own: 'for I see that all of us, all who live, are no more than phantoms and flimsy shadows'. But in a famous chorus of the old men at Colonus, Sophocles, who was the friend of Herodotus, gives a much broader range to the complaint of life:

Not to be born is best, when all is reckoned,
But when a man has seen the light of day
The next best thing by far is to go back
Where he came from, and as quick as he can.
Once youth is past, with all its follies,
Every affliction comes on him,
Envy, confrontation, conflict, battle, blood,
And last of all, old age lies in wait to besiege him,
Humiliated, cantankerous,
Friendless, sick and weak,
Worst evil of all.[176]

It would be an error to believe that Sophocles was the first to declare that not to be born is better than to be born. Several tragedies of Euripides, in which the same expression (*me phunai*)[177] occurs, may well be older than *Oedipus at Colonus*. Indeed, at some uncertain date, Homer was supposed to have replied to the question what was best for mankind: 'above all, not to be born, or else to pass through Hades' gate as soon as may be'.[178] In that enigmatic mythical dialogue between Midas and his captive Silenus, originally from a lost work of Aristotle's, but used in Plutarch's *Consolation to Apollonius* (Chapter 27), the King of Phrygia asks the demigod what is best for man and most to be desired. After long silence and insistent urging the answer comes: 'Frail offspring of toil and misery, why force me to tell you what it is better not to know? For there is least grief in life if each is ignorant of his misfortune; but the best thing for all mankind is not to be born, and the next best is to die as soon as possible after birth.' Plutarch himself adds: 'One might go on with countless examples of the same kind, but there is no need to make a long list.' In other nations it is very rarely, and only in extreme anguish, that anyone is said to have cursed the day they were born.

There are many anecdotes, amounting almost to an anthology of Greek pessimism, to confirm that not to be is better than to be, and that being able to die is a grace from the gods given as the reward of noble deeds. Among these are the stories of Cleobis and Biton, the sons of the Argive priestess of Hera; of Trophonius and Agamedes, who built the temple at Delphi, and so on. Events of this kind continued to occur. Delegates to the sacrifices who travelled from Thebes to the Ammonium in Libya prayed that the great Pindar might be granted 'what is best in human destiny for one beloved (of the gods)', and he died the same year, already very old, though normally it was an early death that was asked for.[179] The reason for thinking it a blessing was either that life was full of misfortune, or – a shade of feeling more frequently admitted to – that a person who had been fairly lucky up to a certain point feared vexation and unhappiness in the future. As we shall see, people sometimes died of their own free will merely because of doubts as to what awaited them, and if anything can prove that life was by no means the thing most highly prized this must be it. It goes without saying that the love of life was inborn in the Greeks as in other nations, and that most of them, like everyone else, feared death, but this fear was openly derided, and the opposite feeling often prevailed. As for the notion that the age of Pericles was one of uninterrupted rejoicing, it is useful to hear what Pericles himself says in his funeral oration;[180] the habitual mood, from his account, is earnest and gloomy (*luperon*) and needs to be dispersed by the daily diversions of competitive games, sacrifices and pleasant domestic arrangements. One hundred years later, Hyperides consoled the fellow citizens and relatives of those who fell in the Lamian War with these words: 'Dying may be equivalent to not being born, but our dead are now free from sickness, sorrow and all the other ills that besiege the living.'[181] No statesman of modern times in a comparable situation could possibly express such a view.

As well as statements of this kind, which might be considered subjective responses to a single occasion, there is the testimony of poets; pessimism in the writers of tragedies could be thought to be governed by myth, but the elegiac poets, with full freedom of choice, show the same cast of thought. Theognis is clearly completely under its sway; for him too (425) not to be born (*me phunai*) is far the best, and next, to die as soon as possible. Further on (1013) we hear him praising the enviable lot of those who can at least die before the worst of trials, such as betrayal by their friends. In a remarkable fragmentary elegy (1137) he lays the blame not on human life itself, but rather on Greek life of his time; this starts with the lament already mentioned [p. 100 above] on the flight of loyalty, moderation and the Graces. There is no longer any reliance on oaths, no humility before the gods; the race of the pious has died out; law has ceased to prevail; and yet, so long as a man's life lasts and he sees the light of the sun, he should honour the gods. Here follows the praise of hope – otherwise quite uncharacteristic of the Greeks – and the injunction to offer up sacrifices to hope not only as to all the gods, but first and last.

Old age occupies a very special place in the complaints about mortality. It is true that many famous Greeks lived to a great age in robust health, and in the dialogue between Socrates and Cephalus at the beginning of Plato's *Republic* Cephalus says that age has few terrors for old men of culture and of even temper. This and a few other statements of opinion form Stobaeus' little anthology of sayings in praise of old age, but most of them are from the dramatists, in whose works, depending on the speaker, it was obligatory to refer occasionally to old age as venerable.[182] In all neutral contexts old age is bewailed loudly and unrestrainedly, and this is frequently so in drama too. Two elements can be distinguished here; fear of old age itself because of the sufferings it brings, and the fact that the Greeks of the later period evidently felt little respect for the old; and secondly the exceedingly high value placed on youth. Sophocles, in that chorus in *Oedipus at Colonus*, might warn of the dangerous folly and horrible experiences that belong to youth, but by far the majority of plays glorify youth in lines that suggest the voices of mature men looking back to a lost paradise. What it comes to is that youth is the only real time of life for the Greeks, and all the rest a very dubious prolongation.

No other nation bargained in the Greek way over the boundaries of this precious time of youth, seeking to extend them as far as possible. The first stage was the *pais* (boy), then *meirakion* (young person), then *neaniskos* (a youth), before the name of *aner* (a man) was admitted to, then came *presbytes* (older man) and at last *geron* (old man).[183] For *aner*, man, there was also a pleasanter expression, *akmazon*, a man in the prime of life; Aristotle extends this, as applied to the physical aspect, to the period from the thirtieth to the thirty-fifth years, and, for the powers of the intellect, right up to the age of forty-nine.[184] It should be observed here that as early as the Peloponnesian War those who were going grey thought fit to dye their hair,[185] and that Agathocles, later on, took to wearing a myrtle wreath to conceal his baldness.[186]

From its very beginnings with Mimnermus, elegy was the champion of youth as the only part of life worth living. The poet of Colophon admits that he would be glad to attain his sixtieth year if it were possible to avoid illness and serious anxieties, but the end of youth was also the end of all its joys, and youth was only a brief space, only as long as a dream; and after that, he says, it would be best to die. For what comes after it are domestic upheavals, poverty, waiting in vain for the birth of children, illness – it is enough: no man exists without Zeus sending him many sufferings.[187]

Semonides of Amorgos first describes the hopes of youth, believing that tomorrow or next year happiness will come, but instead age comes prematurely, or death from illness, in war, at sea or by suicide.[188] In Theognis (vv. 1007, 1017, 1069, 1131) the glorious bloom of youth goes hand in hand with noble striving; he is moved at the sight of this grace and beauty, because it should last longer and in fact passes like a dream; people are foolish to mourn the dead and not rather the disappearance of youth.

Where elegy leaves off, tragedy takes up the theme; the parents of the youthful dead are reminded of what their children might have had to go through.. 'Cease your weeping, look about you at all the unhappiness everywhere and console yourselves with the thought of all the mortals languishing in chains, of the many who must live into old age deprived of their children, or who are reduced to nothing after being prosperous and influential; these are the things that you should be contemplating.'[189] At a later period Lucian sums up all that the subject suggests in the ironical speech of a dead son to his father, and the conclusion is typical of him. 'All this time,' says the corpse, 'I have been wanting to burst out laughing at what you are saying and doing; I am only prevented by the cloth and the wool you have tied round my jaw.'[190]

Almost all these complaints mingle the praise of youth with Greek lamentation over old age, and many more could be added.[191] Anyone not inclined to be persuaded by the words of poets should read Aristotle's horrifying comparison between youth and age. It is not just concerned with the difference between the two periods of life, but with the human qualities of young and old – the first chiefly good-natured, the latter shown in the darkest colours; all their experience has left them without hope, and they see the present as mainly bad, the future as still worse.[192] It was usual to speak disrespectfully of the old, to call them Chronos, Iapetos or Tithonos,[193] but nowhere are they treated as harshly as this. Sophocles says of the old: 'Their intelligence is extinguished, they do useless things and worry about nothing!'[194] In Euripides it is an old man himself who says: 'We old ones are no better than a throng of phantoms, and go about like images of dreams; our brains are gone, however perceptive we think ourselves.'[195] And long before this, in a Homeric hymn, Aphrodite says: 'even the gods hate old age.'[196]

In the dialogue with Socrates already quoted, the aged Cephalus tells of the complaints usually heard among his contemporaries. Mostly they bemoan their incapacity for the pleasures of youth such as love affairs, banquets and so on, and declare that all those things were life and their present existence does not merit the name; some also complain of being treated contemptuously by their families. Cephalus however disagrees, and says that age, rid of stormy passions, is a state of 'peace and freedom', and points out that Sophocles, with whom he has discussed this, was glad to have 'escaped from a wild and savage master'. But old men too could be haunted by the love of life, and the aged Epicharmus, sitting in the *leschê* with his old gentlemen, and hearing one say he would be content with five years more, while another thought three or four would be 'enough', boldly replied that arguments of this kind were foolish: 'all of us are declining as fate wills, and it is high time we went our way before we fall victim to yet another senile trouble'.[197] People were surprised when the very old showed any wish to go on living, and Gorgias, when a hundred years old, was obliged to answer an impertinent remark of this kind by saying that his age was not yet giving him grounds for complaint.[198]

It cannot surprise us, given the evaluation of life suggested by the foregoing, that logical arguments should occasionally be voiced against the begetting of children. Besides common human sentiment, the Greeks had special reasons for being attached to the family: the wish to leave children to perform the funeral rites, and also the need to ensure that their house was not orphaned and defenceless. Euripides' Orestes (62 ff.) begs Menelaus to save his life, not for himself, but in the name of the dead Agamemnon whose house would otherwise stand orphaned. Once the *polis* was acknowledged as the chief purpose of Greek life, the birth of citizens was essential to it. But Thales declared that his reason for not marrying was that he loved children too much,[199] and Democritus advised against marriage on various grounds, not only those of philosophical independence; he recommended adoption instead, because in this way people could choose their children.[200]

A related subject is the exposure and murder of children.[201] A manifestation of the paternal authority so despotic among the Greeks and even more among the Romans, this fate inflicted on the newborn really originated in the father's convenience, so that he could avoid the expense of a large family.[202] Myth tells of so many doomed infants exposed and yet saved as to suggest that predictions or bad omens later led to some children really being exposed or killed. But there is a strong probability that the widespread pessimistic view of life made it easier to decide on exposure or murder, that is that a form of compassion was involved. It was a consequence of the same conviction that did so much to encourage suicide.

The recognition of a child who had been exposed at birth (*anagnorisis*) is a device occurring so frequently in later comedy as to be certain proof that the exposure of infants was common even among the well-to-do. In Terence's *Heautontimorumenos*, based on Menander (626 ff.), a husband and wife reproach each other with such a proceeding in plain words; the man wished to kill their child if it turned out to be a girl, but the mother gave it away to be exposed; evidently a situation that was perfectly familiar to the audience. Much later, in the pastoral novel of Longus, the motif is used quite as a matter of course.

Legislation to forbid or try to restrict the custom is referred to as exceptional. Thus in Thebes it was illegal to expose a child or to 'throw it out into a deserted place';[203] poor people could present the child to the authorities, to be handed over to anyone who would pay even a small amount for it.[204] The child would then be brought up as a slave, and its servitude was considered to pay for its upbringing, but it is not recorded what happened when nobody made an offer. In Ephesus exposure was tolerated only in times of severe famine.[205] Dionysius of Halicarnassus has this to say of very early Rome – and whether he was right or not is unimportant – he is intending to give his Greeks a lesson, as he often did: 'One of the ways in which Romulus made his city populous was by his edict that all male offspring should be reared and all the first-born daughters too, but above all that no child was to be killed before its third birthday, except if it were maimed or born deformed; and even then it might be exposed only after being shown to five neighbours who gave their consent.'

Before the time of Mahomet the early Arabs had also killed most of their girl children, and since the nomads were so often threatened with famine they may have been influenced by the fact that the girls would be sure to suffer worst. There is little doubt that it was the custom of most ancient peoples to kill malformed children at birth. In the case of the Greeks, though, this was the probable fate of every child except the first-born; and if it seems strange that for centuries practically no mention was made of this,[206] it must be remembered how little reason there would have been for any writers whose work survives, e.g. of the Hellenistic period, to deal with this matter. Then, in the early years of the Empire, in a report of Plutarch's, a harsh light is thrown on the whole of the past: 'The poor do not rear their children because they fear their lives may be intolerably miserable, enslaved, uneducated, deprived of any share of beauty; to them, poverty is the worst of all evils, and they cannot bring themselves to hand on this terrible disease to their children.'[207] The question is how widely this is meant to apply; certainly not only to the poor of Chaeronea or of Boeotia, more likely to those of Greece as a whole, and it is possible the practice was widespread in the lands of the Roman Empire of the period. Whatever the truth, this is yet again the clearest expression of pessimism, even if only among a particular class.

Within the family, once it existed, lurked the sorrow of parting, the threat of death.[208] The nurse in Euripides' *Hippolytus* (253 ff.) feels that human relationships should always be only loose attachments, to save each from having to suffer the fullness of grief for both, and though she says this in the context of her affection for Phaedra, it surely characterizes an emotion that was the source of pain within blood relationships as well. Phaedra too has her feelings about mortal destinies (377): 'in the long nights' she puzzles not over the 'If', but the 'Why' of universal unhappiness, and finds the answer partly in human beings themselves.

Great men, though, when their sons died before them, even by violence, would say only: 'I knew my child was mortal.' This is reported, in exactly the same words, of Anaxagoras, Pericles, Xenophon, Demosthenes, King Antigonus and others, and even if it is an anecdote transferred from one to another, it would still indicate a widely held and generally accepted attitude. Usually this is explained simply as strength of mind, but these were thinking men, so convinced that life was worthless that they were glad their sons had the happiness of ceasing to be. The laments for the dead, especially wild and insistent in the early period, are not a sign of grief for the sake of the dead, but express the sorrow and loss of the survivors. Semonides of Amorgos says: 'If we had any sense, we would not give more than one day to thinking about a person who has died.'[209] On the island of Chios, of which we shall have more to say, the men did not mourn at all, neither cutting their hair nor wearing special clothes; only a mother whose son died young would mourn for a year.[210]

The prospect of life's hazards must have made it easier to face an early death than it is nowadays; people understandably preferred to die before they lost their health or their possessions,[211] and it was perhaps in this frame of mind that many ended their own lives. It was a splendid fate to die in the moment of great good fortune, because the resultant envy, whether that of gods or men, was instantly stifled. Polycrite, the heroine of Naxos, having successfully defended her hometown against the Milesians, was greeted with the most tremendous acclaim as she stood in the gateway; her joy was too much for her and she sank down dead. Another account has it that she was suffocated under the garlands and ribbons that were heaped on her. She was buried on the very spot, and the place is known as 'the tomb of envy', for the possibility of it was laid to rest with Polycrite.[212]

Apart from their own pessimism, the Greeks believed that the same sentiments existed among many barbarian peoples. We shall not concern ourselves with the suppositions of Oriental nations that suffering reflects a divine error in creating the world. From the far north and west, among the Cimbrians, the Celtiberians and others, the Greeks knew of a delight in slaughter, rejoicing in the approach of death, and mourning only those who died in their beds. Herodotus (5.4.5) tells of nearer neighbours: the Trausoi of Thrace weep over the newborn and celebrate the burial of their dead as liberated and happy; when a man dies among the Thracians north of Creston, his best-loved wife is selected and killed on the grave by one of her relatives amid songs of praise.[213] It is to be noted that this was not for the sake of the dead man's rights, in which case one of his relatives would have been the executioner, but rather a favour granted to the wife. Some very savage tribes in the Caucasus were believed to behave according to the verses in Euripides' *Cresphontes*, weeping over the newborn for the sufferings that awaited them, while the dead, freed from all ills, were carried out of their houses to joyful celebrations of their happiness.[214]

It is uncertain whether the Greeks openly or tacitly counted the Romans as barbarians. It was a long time before the Romans came out with a view on the value or worthlessness of life, and when they started to discuss the matter they were already halfway to being Greeks. At the beginning of his *Jugurtha* Sallust makes a conventional protest against the bewailing of human weakness and the brevity of life, the power of Fate, and so on, which at least shows that such complaints were commonly heard.[215]

In Greek fable there is one case where even animals are assumed to take a very poor view of life in general.[216] The hares are depressed at being so weak and cowardly and only good at running away, and they decide to go and drown themselves in a stretch of water; but a lot of frogs jump in first, to get away from them, and the hares, seeing that there are creatures even weaker than themselves, change their minds and go on living.

The low value put on life by a whole gifted nation was a reason to look death in the face. Here we approach the question of suicide among the

Greeks. The subject has often been dealt with, and only the essential points need to be discussed, together with a few neglected aspects.

The thought of what came after death was inescapable. A variety of opinions existed about the hereafter, and everyone was free to choose his own; pious zeal in the matter of sacrifices did not preclude the Homeric belief in a melancholy undifferentiated world of shadows. Many, however, believed in rewards and punishments, and some sinners lived in profound apprehension. A few important statements throw light on the multiplicity of these views.

Democritus was above such anxieties and held that the fear of an afterlife, 'this invented edifice of myth', was a self-imposed burden, simply part of the rest of human misery.[217] It is not known whether he expected total nothingness, but many certainly did so. Here is the evidence of an epitaph, with the deceased as speaker: 'It was not my fault that I was conceived by my parents, and now I go sadly to Hades . . . I was nothing, and I shall be nothing as before. The human race is nothing and again nothing. Friend, let the goblet sparkle for me once more and give me the drink to cure sorrow – pour the wine on my grave!'[218]

Euripides, as so often, echoes the views and sayings current around him. In several places, and as it seems with great feeling, he uses the daring words: 'Who can tell if (earthly) life is not really death, and death life?'[219] – for which he is twice mocked by Aristophanes in *Frogs*. Assuming that the Athenians had any idea what this dictum meant when they heard it declaimed from the stage, it follows that many of them must not only have ceased to set any value on their much-praised Athenian existence, but looked forward with hope to another world. Again, the Nurse in *Hippolytus* (V. 159 ff.) has a speech that foreshadows Hamlet's best-known monologue; after some of the familiar remarks on the general misery of life, she goes on to say that the condition which might perhaps be more desirable than this life is hidden from us by an encircling cloudy darkness, and all we have is our unhappy love for this world that shines out on earth, while the other life is unknown and the underworld untried, and we are misled by our imaginings.[220]

Hopes of the afterlife may have been positive, dubious or shadowy, but in any case there is no evidence at all as to whether people feared they would be punished for taking their own lives. Did the majority expect nothingness? and does the frequency of suicide go to prove this? What it certainly does prove is how few notable or famous people shared the

Pythagorean and Orphic belief in the transmigration of souls, for suicide was totally irreconcilable with metempsychosis. Nägelsbach comments: 'I have absolutely no evidence as to whether suicide was popularly regarded as a sin *against the gods*.'[221] Not surprising, since life was not in their gift.

The same distinguished scholar lists the chief motives for suicide both in myth and in historical cases, and C.F. Hermann may be consulted on the attitude of the *polis*.[222] The official reaction was as crass as the way in which severe punishment was generally used by the *polis*; having rendered life intolerable for countless citizens, including many of the best, and made emigration practically impossible, it punished suicide with *atimia*, refusal of burial, cutting off the right hand of the corpse and other kinds of disgrace. Its fury in these cases was no less than it was against those who managed to preserve their fortune instead of submitting to be robbed of it by the State, either piecemeal or by confiscation. However there were two *poleis* where an attempt was made to create a legal form of suicide once it had become an established practice.

Immediately off the hilly coast of Attica lies the island of Chios, whose capital was then Iulis, and it should have been easy for the Athenians to leave an accurate record of customs there.[223] Instead, the surviving accounts are contradictory, the one constant feature being that old people (those in their sixties, it is said) died voluntarily and together, and that this was regulated by law. Explanations for the practice include the poor diet the island afforded, or perhaps one particular occurrence of famine when, besieged by the Athenians, the inhabitants had agreed that the old people should take their own lives. The custom is said to have arisen then, but still as a free choice, merely sanctioned by the law. In fact the common decision is also described as a free one, taken by old people when they felt they were of no use in their community and might be nearing senility. The act itself, when they drank hemlock or poppy juice together, was made into a graceful kind of festival at which everyone was crowned with wreaths.[224] Morality on the island is said to have been very strict, and the islanders remained healthy into old age in the natural course; so without waiting to be overtaken by illness or other physical accidents a group of old people would determine on the day for their shared death. As we have already mentioned, mourning for the dead was not much observed on Chios.

It is not one of these communal festivals, but the voluntary death of a single old woman of Chios that is described by Valerius Maximus, who witnessed it during the reign of Tiberius, while travelling in Greece with Sextus Pompeius, the great-grandson of Pompey the Great. His report throws light on the whole subject of suicide among the Greeks. A respected citizeness, over ninety years of age, had given public notice of her intention to take hemlock, and expressed the wish that her death might be honoured (*clarior*) by the presence of Sextus Pompeius; he came to her and tried to dissuade her by an eloquent address. Lying half-raised on her couch, which was beautifully arranged for the occasion, she first thanked him for taking the trouble to urge her to live, as well as for coming to look on at her death; she said she had always been fortunate, and did not want to risk future misery by merely clinging to life. She advised her two daughters and several grandchildren to live in harmony, and distributed her possessions among them, giving the sacred objects of her household and her jewels to her elder daughter; then she bravely grasped the beaker, poured a libation to Hermes while calling on him to bring her gently to a pleasant place in the underworld, and drank off the poison in one eager draught. She described how her limbs were gradually stiffening, and as death slowly neared her heart she asked her daughters to close her eyes. Even the Romans were moved to tears at her death.

Valerius Maximus is also the chief source of information about the attitude of the city of Massalia to voluntary deaths. Apparently the old Phocaean spirit had still not quite vanished under the Romans, and made it possible to regulate suicide more strictly there than on Chios. In the solemn atmosphere of Massalia, natural deaths were not greeted with mourning or loud laments; a sacrifice in the house and a feast for the relatives were thought sufficient, for life was not highly valued. Yet those who chose to leave it were not permitted to do so as a matter of course; they had to give their reasons to the Council of Six Hundred, and then the city would provide them with the hemlock which killed swiftly. Unhappiness was accepted as a reason, and so was long and perfect happiness, for people might well want to die before it ended. No doubt a number of suicides took place without permission being sought, but at least in this place there was a publicly recognized custom to appeal to.

As elsewhere, it was recognized in Greece from ancient times that true greatness might consist in enduring the most terrible situations. One of the most powerful utterances of Odysseus is his cry 'Bear this, too, my heart, you have suffered worse things!' – and when, while he sleeps, his companions have caused catastrophe by opening the wind bag of Aeolus, he still has the strength to ponder whether to let himself be submerged in the sea, or to live on: 'I suffered and stood firm.' He wraps himself in his cloak and lies down on the deck of the ship.[225] Yet Heracles, the greatest of all the heroes who suffered, ended his own pain on the pyre of Oeta; this was the Greek understanding of the myth, even if it is true that it originally signified the end of the solar year.

There is a huge gulf between such a death and the slight provocations on which later Greeks ended their lives. Pessimism was so widespread that a passing mood of severe depression or a chance caprice of the imagination was enough to decide them. When people died as it were with forethought, from anxiety lest their previous good fortune should let them down, they must have cherished the idea long before; but otherwise there were plenty of reasons to act on the spur of the moment, even if it were only a financial loss which would force them to change their habits. The story was told of three aristocratic Athenians, impoverished by extravagance, who toasted each other in hemlock and departed from life 'as if leaving a banquet'.[226] Very different were those who took their own lives after the death of someone they loved; Plato's *Phaedo* makes it clear that this commonly happened in the joyful anticipation of reunion in Hades.[227] Indeed a hasty reading of the *Phaedo* itself could produce the same result; a certain Cleombrotus in Ambracia killed himself by jumping from the city wall, because what he gathered from the book was that it is better for the soul to be separated from the body.[228]

In modern times suicides in particular places have sometimes spread as though by infection, so it should cause no surprise if the same thing happened in Greek cities. An epidemic of this kind once afflicted the girls of Miletus, and was attributed to a morbid influence in the air; all of a sudden they longed for death, and many strangled themselves. The pleas and tears of their parents and friends had no effect, and they evaded the closest surveillance, until a clever man suggested a public edict stating that those who died in this way must be carried naked through the agora; this put an end to the problem.[229]

Mention may be made here of the Leucadian rock, from which unhappy lovers used to leap into the sea.[230] Where on the steep island of Leucas the cliff was situated, and how high the drop was to the water, is not recorded. Some drowned, and others, who survived, are said to have found they were cured of their passion, so that the lovers' leap seems to have been in the nature of a question put to Fate. A certain Makes of Buthrotos is supposed to have made the experiment successfully four times. The inhabitants of the city of Leucas, who no doubt found the custom unacceptable, took to celebrating an annual feast of Apollo by hurling over the cliff a criminal reserved for the purpose; however he was hung about with live birds to diminish the force of his fall. Down below a number of small boats waited to rescue him, after which he was deported from the region.

Among the serious reasons for suicide generally admitted without argument in antiquity, including the Roman period, was any incurable illness.[231] The prolongation of life for such an invalid by medical skill was openly disapproved of, and an extract from Plato on the subject is worth quoting:

> Sickly people should not go on living, or at least not have children. Asclepius taught the art of healing for those who can be helped in temporary illness, but he never undertook the carefully regulated bleeding and dressing of bodies that are inwardly diseased, only to prolong a miserable existence, and to produce children who in all probability will beget others equally afflicted. Such patients, he believed, ought not to be treated 'since they can be of no use to themselves, or the state ... even if it were a person as rich as Midas'.[232]

A similar argument in Euripides concludes with this forthright proposal:[233] if people in this condition are of no use in the world, they should depart from it, and not stand in the way of those who are younger.[234]

Extreme old age was also held to be sufficient reason for the decision to die, especially if illness or mental debility threatened; this may best be discussed in connection with the deaths of philosophers.

Again, everywhere in the world there must be sympathy, or at least not blame, for the practice followed by Greeks defeated in war, who had not died defending their city walls; if they had time, they all took their own lives together after first killing their wives and children. This behaviour was perfectly appropriate and even generally admired, given that these Greek *poleis*, so often held up as a model, all shared a rule of war by which the defeated men were massacred and the women and children all sold into slavery. 'I tell you one thing only; do not allow yourself to be taken alive into servitude, as long as you can still choose to die free,' says Euripides,[235] and the ancient writers are unanimous in the view that slavery is worse than death. If the victor can do as he likes without restraint of any kind, suicide is the indisputable right of the vanquished, and we cannot attach a moral stigma to their last desperate means of saving themselves; to do so would be siding with the chance possessors of a detestable power.

There was one famous model for behaviour in extremity, dating back to semimythical times, which was universally known as 'Phocian despair'.[236] When the Thessalians had invaded their land, the Phocians, before marching out to battle, collected their wives and children at one site with their most precious possessions, and got the women's assent to their plan; wood was piled up all around and thirty trusted guards appointed, who, on the news of defeat, were to kill everybody and set fire to the place. It did not come to this, as the Phocians were victorious, and the memory was kept alive by a great commemoration festival in honour of Artemis, which was regularly celebrated in Hyampolis. But it taught others how such a situation was to be faced. When Trinacria, the last Sikeliot city, was defending itself against the Syracusans, and the fighting men had all been killed, the old people committed suicide to escape the misery of surrender; the victors dragged away the rest of the population into slavery, destroyed the town and sent the best of the loot to Delphi[237]. Events like these were commonplace, and other ancient peoples did the same when their 'cities' were threatened with ultimate ruin. The half-barbarian city of Isaura could only expect the worst from Perdiccas, one of Alexander's successors, because in the Great King's lifetime a satrap of his had been assassinated there. One night, after most of the defenders had been killed by the Macedonian army, the whole city agreed on a course of action: the women, children and old people were locked in the houses, which were set alight, and all usable objects were thrown into the flames. To the enemy's astonishment fighting continued to rage in the breach until Perdiccas was forced to retreat, and then the last defenders, still unconquered, leapt into the still burning houses and 'buried themselves with their own'.[238] The people of Saguntum, as is well known, perished in a similar way in 218 B.C. when Hannibal took their city; the survivors of Zacynthos escaped the Carthaginians by burning themselves alive. Soon after, in 200 B.C., the Hellenic world in turmoil saw another example of what a Greek community was capable of, when Abydos on the Hellespont was attacked by Philip V of Macedon.[239] The last part of this detailed and horrifying account tells how the men guarding the women and children, instead of killing their charges when nearly all the defenders were dead or wounded, sent to ask Philip for a truce; but while he was occupying the city the remaining men of Abydos carried out their intention, stabbed the women and children and themselves, or threw them into the flames, strangled them, or drowned them in the water tanks; finally the last of them leapt from the roofs to their death. To survive would have seemed to them a betrayal of those who had died for the city. Without hesitation, whole families together hurried to their deaths. The king was seized with horror, but had to confess that the guilt was entirely his own, for at the outset of the siege he had refused the citizens' offer to come out 'each with nothing but the garment they wore', and had demanded unconditional surrender from a city which was useless to him.

For prominent families, those of princes or tyrants defeated and overthrown, there was no choice but mass suicide, since all their members faced certain slaughter by the most horrible means. Even if their conquerors were more merciful, some rulers' families might prefer not to go on living. Prince Nicocles of Paphos had a secret alliance with Antigonus against Ptolemy Lagi, who was already overlord of Cyprus, and who sent two emissaries to murder Nicocles. They obtained troops from the Egyptian commander of the island, surrounded Nicocles in his castle and informed him that he must die. After briefly attempting self-justification he killed himself, and his wife killed her unmarried daughters and persuaded Nicocles' sisters to die too, although Ptolemy had promised safe conduct for all the women of the house. When the castle was filled with sudden death and wailing, the prince's brothers locked the doors, set fire to the building and committed suicide.[240] In modern times all except Nicocles would have settled for a life pension.

Still later (after 78 B.C.) a Pamphylian pirate chieftain named Zeniketos burned himself and his whole household to death in his fortress, which dominated the rocky coast of Taurus, when Servilius Isauricus was about to overwhelm him with a Roman squadron.[241] Mithridates, who may just be reckoned still to belong to the Hellenic world, met a different end in 64 B.C., in the palace of Panticapaeum, when his last remaining soldiers had gone over to his son Pharnaces; first he poisoned his women and his other sons, with or without their consent, and drained the poison himself. This having no effect, he was killed either by a loyal Celt obeying his order or else by the invading army of Pharnaces.[242]

In Cleopatra's palace at Alexandria, in 31 B.C., the queen and Mark Antony were surrounded not by a family but by a whole court prepared to die together.[243] Their set (*synodos*) had till then been known as 'the Order of Companions of the Peerless Life' (*amimetobioi*); after the return from Actium the name was altered to that of 'those who will die together' (*synapothanoumenoi*) – or the Suicide Club. The queen herself collected every variety of poison and tried them out on criminals to find which were the most painless; the bite of an adder proved the most suitable, since other rapid poisons were too painful and the painless too slow-acting. It is not known how many other members of the society were faithful to their oaths in these astonishing events, but it is certain that only a few faithful ladies-in-waiting died with Cleopatra.

From the earliest times it was an article of faith that Greek women must take their own lives rather than fall into the hands of ruthless enemies, and even Christian theologians have defended the suicide of those threatened with rape. The preferred method was strangulation or actual hanging; Queen Olympias offered her stepdaughter Eurydice hemlock, the sword and the rope, and Eurydice chose the last,[244] though Euripides' Helen says hanging is ignoble and not even fit for slaves, but thinks stabbing has style.[245] It seems that the daughters of influential families were prepared by precise instruction in this matter, usually by their mothers. In the third century B.C., at the fall of a tyrant of Elis, his wife hanged herself, and his two daughters were granted the privilege of committing suicide without being raped. The elder took off her sash, wound it about her neck, kissed the younger and told her to watch, and imitate her action carefully; but the younger pleaded to be allowed to die first, so her sister showed her how to put the noose round her neck. When she was sure the younger girl was dead, the elder covered her body and asked only for decent burial for herself. Even the 'enemies of tyranny' wept as they looked on at these deaths.[246]

At about the same time, but in a very different sphere of life, there was a long drawn out rebellion of the Chian slaves, led by one Drimacus. Growing old, and with a high price on his head, he asked his lover to decapitate him and claim the money, which the man did.

The Greeks were no strangers to complex arguments as to the point at which great peril, usually political in origin, conferred the right or even imposed the duty to commit suicide. It may be cowardly to remain alive, and equally so to die.

Wherever 'dishonour', in the widest sense, might threaten, the general sentiment naturally approved of suicide. Twice in Euripides' *Helen* (830 and 981) Menelaus explains, in eloquent words that must have impressed themselves on his hearers, the method he would use, in case of need, to kill first his wife and then himself on the tomb of Proteus. This does not of course occur – it is just that the poet seizes the opportunity to arouse emotion – but 'to be in love with life' (*philopsychia*) is a reproach, and one that the Greek would defend himself personally against, as the tragic dramatist avoids it for his heroic characters. 'Only a coward or a fool,' says Sophocles 'will cling to life in misfortune.'[247] Servants and slaves are often accused of 'loving life', a low trait which distinguishes them from free men.[248] Agathocles pacified a savage revolt in his camp in Africa by threatening the soldiers, his 'comrades', with his suicide, saying it was not his way to submit to an outrage from mere cowardice and love of life[249] – and at once they let him lead them to victory, while the Carthaginians were expecting them to desert.

Nice distinctions were made over the right to suicide, and once at least are expressed by a notable head of state. Cleomenes, the last king of Sparta, defeated with his whole Greek alliance at Sellasia by the Achaean League in 222 B.C., told a companion who was urging him to suicide that it was justifiable not as a way out but only as a political action.[250] He said he did not live or die for himself alone; if there were no hope left for his country, then it was time to die. He evidently wanted to preserve himself for a possible improvement in the Hellenic cause, for he set off at once for Egypt. Some time later, under Ptolemy Philopator, when all hope of this was gone, the glorious end came in Alexandria for Cleomenes and all his followers in their public suicide, and the promise he had given at home was fulfilled – to act, in life or death, as was best for Sparta. They did not fall in captivity, as he had said, 'like fatted sacrificial animals', and the desire for dignity in death was satisfied. A peculiar sense of style marked this deed even to the end; Cleomenes ordered his lover, Panteus, to go among them all and give the *coup de grâce* to anyone still alive; when he had also done this last service for his king, whose facial muscles were still moving, Panteus embraced him and then stabbed himself.

Half a century later, King Perseus of Macedon survived his defeat by the Romans, walked in the triumphal procession and lived out his days in Roman hands. His appalling reputation makes it hard to credit him with the patriotic purpose Cleomenes had in living on, and his contemporaries certainly accused him of vulgar love of life. Indeed Aemilius Paulus, the victorious general, scornfully reproached him with it when Perseus begged not to be exhibited in the triumph.[251] It is also in connection with this war against Perseus that Polybius gives his view on the justification of voluntary death for those in public life. Part of Epirus had allied itself with Perseus at the insistence of three men, who killed themselves honourably (*gennaios*) when the catastrophe came. They deserved praise, Polybius says, because they were not simply throwing themselves away; they recognized that they had allowed themselves to be put into a position unworthy of their previous careers. On the other hand it was right for those in Achaea, Thessaly and so on, who were not definitely compromised, to submit to investigation and follow up every chance of being cleared, for it was just as much a proof of an unworthy attitude (*agennaios*) to commit suicide prematurely, without a bad conscience, from mere terror of political opponents or the injustice of the powerful, as it was to yield too much to the love of life. Again, taking quite another view of a different case, Polybius has nothing but contempt for Perseus' two chief adherents on Rhodes, whose guilt was proved beyond doubt and who were an embarrassment to their native island, and who yet had not the courage to make their exit from the world (*ekpodon*) but hesitated, from love of life, when all hope was gone; they, he feels, had forfeited every remnant of sympathy and respect from posterity.[252]

Two decades later, in 146 B.C., after the general defeat of the Greeks by the Roman armies in the last Achaean War, despair turned to madness and caused countless suicides;[253] everywhere people plunged into the reservoirs or threw themselves from cliffs, so that it was heartrending even for the conquerors, who intended no harm to most of them.

We need give only a brief account of the suicides of some philosophers, as the subject has often been discussed. The reports are unreliable, as there were seldom eyewitnesses, and those perhaps unwilling to testify precisely; some, like the various legends of the death of Heraclitus, are clearly invented.

Believers in the doctrine of metempsychosis were forbidden to end their own lives, and this alone discredits the story of Empedocles leaping into the crater of Etna. Pythagoreanism taught that souls are condemned to inhabit bodies as a punishment; suicide cannot liberate them from the 'cycle of generation'; one who fails to endure the body till freed by the gods incurs still more misery, and that is why the believers waited patiently for death in old age.[254] Apart from these, philosophers claimed the same freedom to die that they had in life, and voluntary death gradually became part of their systems of thought. Xenophon emphasizes that Socrates virtually committed suicide by his refusal to flee, given the calculated ruthlessness of his judges.[255] Democritus, when almost a hundred years old, determined to starve to death, but the women of the household begged him to delay for a few days because the Thesmophoria, the women's festival, was imminent, so he kept himself alive by taking a little honey. As a rule philosophers chose to die only when they were close to being helpless, or incurably ill. Aristotle was opposed to suicide, and there is convincing testimony that his death at Chalcis was from natural causes, although he took the most sombre view of life and especially of old age. We have only anecdotes as to the behaviour of the Cynics, though they sound typical enough. Diogenes brings a dagger to the ailing Antisthenes, who, when he does not immediately stab himself, is accused of 'loving life'.[256] Once Diogenes himself became very ill, and someone advised him to end his life, but was given this reply: 'It is right for people to go on living if they know how to behave in life and what they should say; you, for instance, could perfectly well die.' However Diogenes died by deliberately holding his breath when he reached the age of ninety.[257]

We have already mentioned Hegesias the Cyrenaic and his profoundly pessimistic doctrine, which is said to have driven many of his hearers to suicide. The chief document for this has not survived; it was a conversation between a man who was starving himself to death and the friends who wanted to keep him alive. Menedemus, founder of the school of Eretria, died at the age of seventy-four, at the court of Antigonus Gonatas, by starving himself for a week, because the king had refused his request to free his native city (or grant it democracy).[258]

Epicurus taught that intolerable pain justified leaving life as if leaving the theatre; he himself died aged seventy-two after a two-week illness was diagnosed as incurable. He lay in a bath of hot water and drank undiluted wine; at the end he spoke about all the joy that philosophical discussions had brought him, and asked his friends to be mindful of his teaching. The Stoa permitted suicide for a wide range of reasons, and in any kind of suffering considered it a duty. Zeno, the founder of the school, strangled himself in old age when injured in a fall;[259] Cleanthes died by starving himself at eighty, and well into the imperial period a number of Stoics, or the stoically inclined, chose to end their own lives.[260] Marcus Aurelius thought death desirable in general, chiefly for the sake of the people who attended on him, and whom he treated kindly.[261] He reserved the ultimate right to suicide in a general way: 'We may quit life when people do not allow us to live as if death were near in any case; if there is smoke in the room, I go outside, but if nothing drives me out I am willing to stay.'[262]

Notable scholars who ended their own lives included Eratosthenes, in 195 B.C. when he was eighty and going blind, and Aristarchus at seventy-two in Cyprus, because he had dropsy; both starved themselves.[263] Polemon of Laodicea on the Lycos, a rhetorician and sophist at Smyrna in the second century A.D., lay down in his grave and died by the same means when he had terrible gout, telling his grieving family: 'Give me another body and I will go on holding forth!'[264]

The last famous philosophic suicide was that of the Cynic Peregrinus Proteus, who burned himself to death on a pyre during the festival at Olympia in 168 A.D. With this act, the Hellenic love of fame, which had already gone hopelessly astray in all its other aspirations, stage-managed its own end with every possible kind of advance publicity as an apotheosis in the style of Heracles.[265] True, it happened in a century that was filled with lamentations over all-pervading wickedness and was used to hearing expressions of contempt (in Lucian) for the whole world, for the gods and for mankind.[266] It was high time for another society to arise beside the old: one that would display, in a thousand martyrdoms, an equally strong willingness to die, but, in life, would have a new and sublime aim.

GREEK
CIVILIZATION

I

Introductory Remarks

WE MIGHT EXPECT that it would be representational art that would tell us most about the physique of the Greeks. But this hope can be only partly fulfilled; art does not show an average, but the exceptional, selected and arranged on ideal principles; it is proof only of what was considered admirable and splendid, and of how people would have liked to look. Even so, art provides strong evidence that the Greeks were beautiful. A nation of ugly people would not have been able to produce this beauty merely by longing for it, and what passed for beauty must often have been seen in reality. Apart from the grave-finds, which will help to establish a norm of skeletal structure, we must rely chiefly on literary testimony, and since the Greeks' opinion of their own beauty can hardly count as evidence, we are forced to wait for outsiders to give their views. A document of this kind does exist, though it is of late date (the beginning of the fifth century A.D.); it is an important passage of the *Physiognomica* of Adamantius and was discovered by O. Müller.[1] Here a baptized Jew is speaking of the Hellenes as a race already considered remarkable. Apart from some general observations he says they were 'just sufficiently (*autarkos*) tall, sturdy, pale-complexioned, with well-formed hands and feet, a medium-sized head, strong neck, fine brown softly-waving hair, square-faced (*prosopon tetragonon*, that is not oval but with fairly strong cheekbones), the lips delicate, the nose straight, the eyes lustrous and expressive, (*ophthalmous hugrous, charpous, gorgous*): they have the most beautiful eyes of any people in the world'.

This very interesting statement is the only one of its kind; all others only provide partial information. Either they report that within the nation certain tribes, the Ionians for instance, were considered specially hand-some,[2] or they list elements of beauty, that is the individual features of an ideal canon, and those as exceptional, not as average and typical,[3] or else they relate these elements to changes in time, noting a decline in beauty, as for instance when Cicero observes that when he stayed in Athens there were hardly any beautiful youths there.[4] Aristotle's views on beauty are important. In a quite unexpected place, the *Politics* (5.7) he asserts, with the same logic he applies to the state, that various types are equally valid: for the nose, as well as the most beautiful straight shape, one somewhat incurving, and the eagle type, can also be beautiful, if the divergence is not too pronounced. In his opinion beauty is also in part acquired, so that one can speak of a double beauty, in that, for instance, the competitors at the pentathlon are built for speed as well as strength; and beauty differs from one time of life to another – the old man may possess it as well as the youth and the man in his prime.[5] Obviously, independent of theory, beauty has always been admired in a variety of forms.[6]

Not only were the Greeks most strongly affected by beauty, but they universally and frankly expressed their conviction of its value, in sharp contrast to the moderns, who do their best to see it from the ethical viewpoint as a very fragile gift. In the first place no shyness hindered people from openly praying for beauty. An example is the Spartan child, later the wife of Demaratus, who because of her ugliness was daily carried by her nurse to the temple of Helen at Therapne; there the nurse stood before the statue of the most beautiful of women and implored that the child's ugliness might be taken away. One day a female figure appeared, stroked the child's head and promised that she should be the most beautiful of all Spartan women, and she at once became so.[7] It was also possible for beauty to be rewarded with semidivine honours after death; indeed beauty in itself made enemies think of a man as a demigod, and to believe that they should do penance for having killed him. Thus the Segestans (who were only half Greek) built a heroon and brought offerings to Philip of Croton, an Olympic victor and the finest-looking Hellene of his time, after he fell in battle fighting them and the Carthaginians (about 510).[8] Or it might happen that a warrior charging down on the enemy in all his youthful beauty would be spared because they recognized something superhuman in him. In such cases national prejudice was set aside, as we learn from the fact that the Persian general Masistius, killed in skirmishing before the battle of Plataea, was carried about the field because all the Greeks wanted to see his beautiful corpse.[9] Even Xerxes himself was acknowledged by reason of his beauty as worthiest among all his myriads of men to be the leader.[10] To our own thinking it is particularly striking that a person can praise his own beauty without diffidence; in Xenophon's *Symposium* (4.10 f.) Critobulus says plainly and in detail how much value he places on it, and adds that he would not exchange it for the power of the Persian king. The first wish made for sons who are to rule is that their appearance should match their destiny; the essential is that physique should have its own claim to high rank.[11]

The Greeks must surely have perceived the inner man in his exterior and made assumptions about physiognomy which turned into convictions. These are the basis of the science of physiognomics as we know it from Aristotle.[12] The link between beauty and spiritual nobility was a matter of the firmest belief.

A small detail which shows how much the Greeks differed from us is their habit of anointing the whole body, which we should find intolerable. Their outward appearance was very much enhanced by the exquisitely simple design of the clothes they wore. Even the poor man's cloak, hired by the day for half an obol from the fuller, was certainly as becoming as the rich man's, if it was worn with grace.[13]

The fact that the Greeks enjoyed *good health* needs to be mentioned here. Many of them lived to be so old that we can be sure this is no delusion. Also notable in famous Greeks is the absence of infirmity in old age. Even Homer's Nestor makes no concessions to age;[14] but a large number of celebrated poets and philosophers lived a very long time, and as with some great Italian artists, their most important work was often done in their last years. Sophocles wrote his *Philoctetes* and *Oedipus at Colonus* in old age, and so did Euripides his *Bacchae*, and they are the same poets who bewail age and paint it in the darkest colours; but it affected them as little as it did some of the philosophers presented by Lucian in his *Long Lives*.[15] In any case the Greeks as a race must have possessed a wonderful vigour, which made possible the most extraordinary feats with no fear, for instance, of catching cold. When Odysseus and Diomedes return covered in sweat from a night voyage they jump straight into the sea, and Nestor (the old man) with Machaon (the field surgeon) coming back heated from battle, at once expose themselves to the wind on the shore, to the horror of all present-day victims of rheumatism.[16] We may well ask whether the ancients ever noticed a draught.

It is true that the race was forcibly kept up to the mark by methods we could not use today, chiefly the result of the conviction that only the healthy deserved to live.[17] The Greeks, like the Romans, had a deep fear of anything abnormal. The birth of the deformed or handicapped was not only a misfortune for the family, as it still is, but was terrifying for the whole city, indeed for the nation, and meant that the gods had to be placated. So it was out of the question to bring up a crippled child; the lame or crooked were wise to make themselves inconspicuous, or they might fall into the hands of an Aristophanes.[18]

We need to give brief attention to the *names* of the Greeks.[19] Where the Romans named a person first after their clan (*gens*) and secondly after the branch of it to which they belonged, the Greeks simply had their own name, particularized only by that of their father and of the deme. Unlike the Roman, Greek names were thus individual. In Athens, as we know, the child usually received its name on the tenth day of its life, when a feast took place (cf. Aristophanes' *Birds* 494). The first son was usually called after the paternal, the second after the maternal grandfather, the third after his father; so for example Euripides, son of Mnesarchos and son-in-law of Mnesilochos, had three sons named Mnesarchides, Mnesilochos and Euripides;[20] but names of other relatives and friends, especially guests, were also given, and a name was often newly coined, and agreed on as the free invention of the father, or even of the mother.

We are reminded of the Greek facility in creating enormous numbers of names for mythical figures. Even the old Germanic peoples had some success in this; but the Greek poets took real delight in parading a wealth of names which would not be available in any modern language. Every divine or human being is named even if they are a member of a group of a dozen, or of forty or fifty, and even if no other particulars are known of them – for instance the many half-divine beings we encounter in Hesiod.[21] In part these are simply abstract nouns such as Nike (victory), Cratos (force), Zelos (rivalry), Bia (compulsion), while others, the names of things etymologically transformed into persons, hover, as both adjectives and appellatives, between abstraction and personal name. The fifty names of the Nereids are simply plucked out of the air by Hesiod.[22] For the most part they bear some relation to marine life and the sea, weather, coasts etc., while the names of the daughters of Oceanus and Thetis, forty-one in number, are on the whole less easily interpreted and seem to be assembled from various realms of life.[23] But Hesiod also knows the individual names of the Moirai, the Horai, Charites and Muses, even of the Harpies. Homer too can not only tell the names of Penelope's suitors but has a quantity of names for all the Phaeacians, with connotations of the sea and seafaring. The invention of names in the *Battle of Frogs and Mice* seems mere child's play, and from poetry, where, especially in hexameters, the name runs easily along in the verse, this joy in name-giving is transferred to the mythographers. Pausanias, following the great bards, gives a catalogue of the suitors of Hippodameia who were killed by Oenomaus and buried by Pelops (6.21.7); Apollodorus can name the fifty Danaids and their fifty suitors, all of whom, except for one couple, died without doing anything at all; he knows the fifty sons Heracles begot with the Thestiadai, the fifty sons of Lycaon who were almost all immediately struck by lightning, and those of Priam, also fifty in number, and gives the detailed genealogy of the Aeolidai; Diodorus too gives a quantity of names of Amazons (4.16), and Hyginus those of the Tyrrhenian pirates who were changed into dolphins by Dionysus (*Fabulae* 134). The artist Polygnotus, too, arbitrarily invented a complete set of names for his figures in the *leschê* [of Cnidos] at Delphi.[24] This is a matter that seems to us a weary labour, but was pure pleasure for the Greeks.

Other peoples also had significant names, for instance the Persians, whose names were supposed to refer to their fine physique and their love of splendour.[25] But the Greek name usually held more meaning. Apart from the fact that, in naming, bad omens had to be avoided and good omens invoked,[26] the Greek name derived active power from its verbal or adjectival element. The name-givers were tireless in inventing these compounds, drawing upon a profusion of heroes, persons and things of every kind; some are very beautiful.[27] Periodically, of course, fashion played a part. For instance at the time of the aristocratic *hippotrophia* (keeping purebred horses) names that included *hippos* were popular; Aristophanes makes fun of this in the well-known passage in *The Clouds* (60 ff.), where his Strepsiades tells how he wanted to name his baby son for his paternal grandfather Pheidonides 'the thrifty', but the aristocratic mother was intent on a name such as Xanthippos, Charippos or Callippides, and so they agreed at last on Pheidippides ('spare the horses'). With full-blown democracy come the many names reminiscent of popular assembly and the popular speech, ending in -agoras: Aristagoras, Diagoras, Athenagoras among others, and in -demos, as Charidemos, Nicodemos and Demosthenes. We must note the special case of the ambitious tendentious names, often geographical, given to their children by Themistocles and Cimon. Themistocles' were called Archeptolis, Mnesiptolema, Italia, Sybaris, Nicomache, Asia; Cimon's sons were Lacedaemonius, Eleius, and Thessalus.[28] The daughters of Adeimantus, the Corinthian admiral, were given names alluding to victory in battle – Acrothinion, Nausinike, Alexibia. Ambition can also be seen in the elder Dionysius naming two daughters Sophrosyne and Arete; Pyrrhus had a Nereis, Neoptolemus, king of the Molossians, an Olympias and a Troas;[29] and in the frequent use of names such as Achilles.[30]

It was in bad taste to give slaves famous names, like the man Lysias mentions (*fragment* 67) who called his Musaeus and Hesiod;[31] slaves' names were generally short and simple for the practical purpose of calling them, sometimes after their native place such as Lydos, Syros, Iapyx,[32] or just the names common in those places, so that a Phrygian would be Manes or Midas, a Paphlagonian Tibios.[33] More elegant and affectionate names occur for girls at the courts of the *diadochoi* (Panariste, Mania and Gethosyne).[34] Probably simpler names were used for women than for men.

Animals also had an inexhaustible variety of names – in *Cynegeticus*, Xenophon gives a selection of forty-seven dogs' names, all disyllabic for calling easily. Pausanias records the names of horses belonging to Olympic competitors from historic times, and also those of the steeds of Marmax and Adrastus.[35] Myth, indeed, is rich in this respect as in others. Not only do we learn from Homer the names of Hector's four horses – Xanthos, Podargos, Aithon and Lampos (*Iliad* VIII.185) – but also, from different sources, those of Poseidon, the Dioscuri, Phoebus and Eos. The snakes that killed the sons of Laocoon were Porkes and Chariboia,[36] Geryon's dog that Heracles slew was Orthos;[37] four of Actaeon's hounds are named – perhaps it is surprising that we are not told the names of all fifty.[38] Finally, an old epitaph on the warrior Hippaimon also gives the names of his horse Podargos, his dog Lethargos and his servant Babes.[39]

Names also proliferated in the invention of two or more for the same place, probably after the arrival of new settlers, the older name thought of as the one used by the gods. Thus the same island was called Parthenia, Anthemos, and Melamphyllos, while Rhodes and Samos had three and Euboea four other names.[40] On the other hand, Larissa is found as the name of several towns,[41] and there is a marked scarcity of names for rivers, with four or five occurrences of Asopos, Acheloos and Cephissos.[42]

Introductory Remarks

The subject of the *natural gifts* of the Greeks as opposed to the barbarians is a difficult one. Just as the mingling of races that produced the Hellenic people must remain mysterious, it will never be possible to judge how far the *Phoenicians* were their forerunners. We can never know whether, in the Phoenician *poleis*, there was any stirring of the spirit of *individuality* which inevitably comes of living in a free city. By contrast with all the rest of the ancient East, the Greeks are like pure spirit as opposed to the material, or pure free spirit compared with the spirit racially or despotically enslaved. While the *poleis* brought a wealth of new focal points in life, the *number and variety* of the states and cults created freedom of the mind. Combined with the feeling of community and social cohesion, there was from an early time something higher and more positive – the study and recognition of otherness, the appreciation of what was different, and this was soon extended beyond the limits of the nation itself; it was accepted as a mission for humanity. In Genesis (2.19) Jehovah brought all the beasts of the field and the birds of the air to man, to see what he would call them, and whatsoever he called them was their name. The Greeks, though, are *meropes* (namers or contemplators of parts) in quite another sense. While the whole Jewish imagination revolved around its centre, the theocratic State, the Greek gift for seeing, and for the figurative, created beauty on all the margins of things. The individual certainly stood firmly on the ground of his own *polis*, and was more a part of it than was the case elsewhere. But because, at the same time, the Hellenic temperament had awoken to the need for transcending this *polis*, a powerful sense of citizenship coexisted with the first general awareness of unity with the whole of the world. This was reinforced by the Greeks' great creativity in poetry and art. From an early stage, the endless variety of human beings seemed to them fascinating and worthy of celebration; even in Homer, delight in the shifting surfaces of things, as well as the emotions that sway the soul, are already perfectly evoked. From the very beginning, poetry became the ideal image of the world, and the figurative arts created the most splendid forms in the realm of the visible.

The question remains as to whether the Greeks were not somewhat lacking in *gentleness*. Subjective lyrical poetry would have been of value to us here, but theirs has not survived; we have only fragments, and sometimes they are powerful, as are also aspects of the epic, elegy and epigram. But this is overshadowed by the consequences of the *polis*, in its terrible squandering of humanity and the annihilation the Greeks visited on each other.

We can only regret what has been lost. But this should not prevent us from learning what we can from this richly endowed nation. There is much more to admire than to debate.

II

The Heroic Age

IN EVALUATING different civilizations, we tend nowadays to think in terms of 'progress' and of 'inventions', a method of accounting by which the Greeks come off very badly. The Egyptians and the Babylonians had been industrious peoples thousands of years earlier, and had the most remarkable achievements to their credit in technology, engineering and chemistry, before *they* ever started on their barefaced borrowing and stealing. 'The Greeks did not leave behind a single practical invention worth speaking of,' says Hellwald, 'and even in the realm of thought and creativity they completely failed to throw off the powerful influences of the Near East.'[1]

One might answer Hellwald by saying that what they did was merely to put their imprint on everything they touched. As for progress, there are two things to be said. First, it is obviously an error to think that intellectual progress must necessarily be preceded by the material enrichment and refinement of life, on the premiss that barbarism can only disappear when poverty is overcome. In certain favoured races, even when the culture is materially primitive, and in the absence of that 'comfort' which Hellwald prizes so highly and is at such pains to distinguish from 'luxury', we see the most perfect and abundant beauty in all that relates to the inner life of the people.[2] What, for example, can surpass the story of Nausicaa in spiritual beauty and delicacy? Similarly, material wealth and refinement of living conditions are no guarantee against barbarism. The social classes that have benefited from this kind of progress are often, under a veneer of luxury, crude and vulgar in the extreme, and those whom it has left untouched even more so. Besides, progress brings with it the exploitation and exhaustion of the earth's surface, as well as the increase and consequent proletarianization of the urban population, in short, everything that leads inevitably to decline, to the condition in which the world casts about for 'refreshment' from the as yet untapped powers of Nature, that is, for a new 'primitiveness' – or barbarism.

As we do not intend to depict the Greeks in their external, material aspect we can, happily, omit discussion of the material tradition which they inherited from the Near East. They themselves did not generally begrudge other nations their inventions and discoveries, even if occasionally their pride led them to feel that it would have been a fine thing to have achieved something of the kind.[3] In mythology the progress of civilization is personified, among others, in Prometheus, who brought fire to mankind so that they no longer had to eat raw flesh.

We shall not be dealing with origins at all, least of all with the hypothetical original state of all mankind, though Lucretius gives a picture of it well worth reading (*On the Nature of Things*, Book V), probably drawn from the teaching of Epicurus. Nor shall we speak of prehistoric man, of the troglodytes and the lake dwellers of Macedonia, or of the supposed successive waves of Indo-Germanic immigrants arriving by way of Phrygia, or indeed of the ill-fated Pelasgians. Also, as it is only in myth that the heroes have come down to us *alive*, and as archaeological research may produce new evidence at any time, we are not concerned with who actually reigned and who served in ancient Ilion, Orchomenos, Tiryns or Mycenae,[4] and shall refer only briefly to the fame of the Greeks beyond their borders at a time before their myth came into being at home.

Heroic myth separates this world of remote antiquity from that of history, sometimes only as a thin veil, sometimes as a solid dense curtain; from beyond it we may see a faint gleam or hear the clash of arms and the stamping of horses, distant cries and the rhythmic stroke of oars; the sounds, the gleam of past happenings that can no longer penetrate to us as actual historical facts. And it is scarcely even to be regretted that they cannot; those old pirates might well be glad that we can know so little about them for certain; the knowledge would probably not be very edifying. Only the curtain transforms the factual, the transitory, into the immortal.

We shall also leave out the legendary migrations and the earliest mythical conquests of cities. We have already discussed as much of the migration legends as we need to do ('The Greeks and their Mythology' above); as to the conquests, the tales of Heracles taking various cities originate in various periods and circumstances. In any case, cities such as Athens and Thebes took pride in having gone through an immense number of experiences before the beginning of recorded history, and one may wonder if in all the world there can have been another city with such fateful antecedents as Thebes.[5]

To end this list of exclusions, we shall also omit any account of the characteristics of the various Greek *peoples*, despite the ancient emphasis on the differences between them in the founding of colonies and still later in the Peloponnesian War, or such remarks as that in Thucydides (1.124.1) where the Corinthians say: 'We must help the Potidaeans, as they are Dorians besieged by Ionians.' In later times, at least, these differences are evoked only as special pleading.

The nation known to the world as the Greeks had at different periods of its existence a most unusually varied distribution, so that one must constantly take note of the considerable changes in their geographical horizon. Thus, even for mythology, we are obliged to deal with the locales of the pre-Trojan and Trojan generations and of the return of the heroes, but we may ignore the ancient notion that the landscape itself was also on the move; the Hellespont, the Euripus and the Straits of Messina were all supposed to have cut a way between previously connected landmasses, Lesbos to have been a fragment of Mount Ida, Ossa of Mount Olympus and so forth.

Foremost among the regions of legend were of course the Peloponnese and the western islands, with Hellas and Thessaly, but Aetolia and even Epirus were also celebrated. A considerable coastal stretch of Macedonia and Thrace was assumed to be Greek; Perithous and Ixion reigned in Gyrton, in Perrhaebian Magnesia at the foot of Olympus; the peninsula of Pallene was the home of the giants slain by Heracles; Asteropaeus, son of Pelegon, was a native of what was later Macedonia; Abdera was named for Abderus, who was devoured by the horses of Diomedes; Samothrace was the home of Iasion and Dardanus, as well as of Orpheus, who came from the Thrace of epic, or Pieria, and once lived in the village of Pimpleia, near Dion.

Then the northwestern corner of Asia Minor, with Lesbos, is famous in mythology. The *Iliad* reveals an intimate acquaintance with the whole district about Mount Ida; in the courts there, Homer's predecessors may have sung their songs.[6] The voyage of the Argonauts to Colchis was also given a place in heroic myth, and to the south, myth takes in Pergamum in Mysia (the scene of the later legend of Auge and Telephus) and extends to Mount Sipylos, the home of Tantalus, Pelops and Niobe. On the other hand, in spite of the fact that Homer lived and sang there, the whole of Ionia seems cut off, like Caria, from the central mythology, although its coastal region was not without its own religious myths. The Ionians must somehow have lacked the necessary powers, or else missed the right moment, to incorporate themselves into the mainstream of myth; for this reason we cannot quite accept the view put forward by Curtius, among others, that they were originally Greek before the Dorian migration. Rhodes, however, was the seat since remote times of the Telchines from Crete, with its sanctuary of Athena at Lindos founded by the Danaids. Lycia is quite unexpectedly famous in mythology, with its ancient cult of Apollo, its legends of Leto, who found shelter there with her children, and the myth of Bellerophon and the Chimaera.[7] A number of islands are also celebrated in myth; Crete is among the most important. As for the places founded on the coast of Pamphylia, in Cilicia and on Cyprus, we cannot hope to trace the process by which they were or became Greek. Besides those that declare themselves post-heroic since they claim links with the warriors returning from Troy, there is occasionally one which tries to show an older connection.[8] And when myth reaches out to Phoenicia and to Egypt (Andromeda, Busiris, Proteus) it is no more than a beautiful fable.

In the West, as with the south coast of Asia Minor, the question is whether myth is very ancient or merely a reflection of later colonization; but in general it is quite evident that myth only arrived with the colonists. We are thinking of the followers of Iolaus in Sardinia (Diodorus 5.15); all the places where Heracles is rumoured to have been, as far as the Pillars that bear his name;[9] the stories of the fugitive Trojans, such as Antenor, the founder of Patavium [Padua],[10] Aeneas, who touched Sicily and got as far as Latium,[11] the Trojan Elymians in Sicily;[12] and the return of the Achaean heroes, particularly Diomedes, whose dominion over the Adriatic was symbolized by the *insulae Diomedeae* [now the Isole Tremiti] and who was still worshipped as a god by the Veneti in Strabo's time.[13] The West was also provided with a king, Latinus, who had daughters in readiness for any new arrivals, e.g. Laurina for Locros.[14] There were also Phaethon on the Eridanos, the Pelasgians who came from Thessaly to found Caere-Agylla (Cerveteri), Nestor from Pisa [in Elis] as founder of Pisa in Italy, Jason on Elba and the Argonauts in Istria, Evander on the Palatine, Polites the companion of Odysseus at Temesa, the founding by Philoctetes of Petelia in Lucania and of Crimissa, the localization of Homer's Aeolos on the islands of Lipari and many others.[15]

Everywhere there was a dual process. On the one hand the Greeks came with lovingly preserved legends of the travels of their intrepid compatriots; on the other, wherever Greek civilization penetrated, the other nations received their mythology as a wonderful invention and wished to be linked with it themselves. But it is no longer possible to determine the relative importance of the Greeks' urge to expansion and the eagerness of the other peoples to meet them halfway.

What is certain is that everything local was envisaged mythologically, and it was at the ends of the earth that poetry felt most at home. The half-fabulous or entirely fabulous races, the Lapiths, Centaurs, Pygmies and so on already formed a frieze that challenged and improved on reality, framing the life of the heroic Greeks. Add to this the land of the Hyperboreans with its mysterious landscape so wonderfully described by Sophocles, and the journey of Helios bearing the golden cup over the ocean that Stesichorus sings of, and we glimpse a great mythical world in which Earth and Sky are seen in a mighty, fabulous relationship. Beyond the Ocean dwell the Gorgons, on the farthest limits, with Night, where the voices of the Hesperides resound, and at the ends of the earth, beyond these voices, stands Atlas, holding up the sky on his head and his tireless hands.[16] Ocean surrounds Earth with the sea, flowing back on itself; from it all waters spring – sea, rivers and fountains, and this must have been explained by the idea of a subterranean flux; the sun rises and sets in the sea, and the stars, like the gods, bathe in it. Both good and terrible things are found by the sea; the Ethiopians, the Cimmerians, Elysium, the groves of Persephone, and again, as we have said, the Gorgons, and the waters of the Styx are a tithe of its flow. Here too are the Islands of the Blessed, they too, as Pindar says, cooled by the breezes of Ocean.[17]

The regions of Dante's nether world can be surveyed and mapped; these cannot, least of all the Tartarus of Hesiod's *Theogony* (721–819). A bronze anvil would fall from Earth for nine days and nine nights before reaching it; the domain itself is surrounded by a brazen wall, and Night flows about its shoulders; above grow the roots of Earth and the Sea – we may think of them as a vaulted roof – and in misty darkness the Titans sit there captive. There too are the sources (that is, the origin) and the ends of Earth, and also of Tartarus itself, of the Sea and of the starry Heaven; they are described as fearful, mouldering, a horror to the gods themselves. This place, an enormous abyss, is perpetually swept by a terrible storm-wind coming from all sides at once, and there stands the dreadful House of Night; outside it stands Atlas, supporting the vault of the sky, where (evidently at a gate of Tartarus) Night and Day, swiftly changing, greet each other as, one coming, the other going, they cross the great threshold.

A word is needed about the degree to which Greek myth was elaborated and the many forms in which it was handed down. These forms, as the Greeks knew them, were various; epic poetry that far surpasses any other in the world, a great series of cyclical epics, a wealth of dramas, religious rituals cast in dramatic form, superb visual art and, lastly, the work of anthologists, of commentators on the poets and so on. No theological systems had affected myth, and no tendentious interpretation – at least none that left any traces – nor had it ever been intentionally restricted or mutilated.

Obscurity still hides the origins of the myths of gods and heroes and their elaboration into connected sagas. True, many of the elements and basic features are found among other Aryan peoples; but it is through connections and motivations peculiar to it that Greek myth becomes a great reflection of the national spirit. This was most probably the work of the bards, for the people, left to themselves, would have been content with separate images and stories. The fact that, for all the freedom of narrative variants, there could yet be a consensus and a shared familiarity with heroic myth is best explained by the existence of a mythical tradition in schools of bards, which spread far and wide through their wanderings.[18]

Turning to the subject of the temperament and behaviour of the hero, one point immediately strikes us;[19] the fundamental principle of Greek life has already been established, and remains valid for later times:

'Always to be the best and to outdo the others'.[20]

But this does not imply the hero's being an ideal of humanity. All his actions and his passions go to extremes; what is ideal in him lies in the beauty and freshness he embodies. He is not haunted by nobility of soul, aspirations to dignity or moral perfection; he represents the wholly unspoiled, spontaneous egoism of human nature, unrepentant but great-hearted and benign. Thus the poet is able to base his rich edifice on a strong foundation. There is in Homer a certain chivalric courtesy, but no trace of the dissembling that is the consequence of social life.[21] The tragic dramatists followed this example in portraying to the best of their ability a naïve world, even intensifying and deepening this aspect, for instance in Sophocles' *Ajax.*

Even his misdeeds do not detract from the ideal qualities of the hero, any more than Zeus is diminished by sending a dream to deceive Agamemnon. These are not just peccadillos: Heracles treacherously hurls Iphitus from the clifftop, Odysseus and Diomedes ruthlessly murder Dolon after guaranteeing his life, and Peleus and Telamon, the sons of Aeacus, kill their half-brother Phocus out of pure envy because he has distinguished himself in the games. But in general the most terrible deeds do not proceed from great wickedness or cruelty. It is not a question of guilt personally incurred, but rather that certain *categories* of acts carry a curse, doubtless because they could entail the vengeance of particular divinities. The pollution is therefore expiable precisely because the guilt is not very great and the deed is the consequence of pardonable passion or mere ill-luck, or is perhaps actually just and praiseworthy.[22] For this purpose there exists the ceremony of purification (*katharsis*), usually performed by a hero, which must follow *every* killing. Apollo is in need of it after killing the dragon Python; Theseus goes to be purified by the Phytalides at the altar of Zeus Meilichius, when he has slain the brigands and criminals (one of whom, named Sinis, is indeed his blood relation through [his maternal grandfather] Pittheus); and even Coroebus is purified at Delphi after killing the spectre *Poinê* [Punishment].[23]

One main aspect of the heroic character is embodied in Homer's Odysseus, the other, just as clearly, in Achilles. This hero is presented to us in his striving for the superhuman, in the excess of his passion and in his insatiable hatred of the Greeks, for whose downfall, with the exception of himself and Patroclus, he longs; and then again in his deep grieving for his dead friend and in his terrible and total vengeance on Hector, which draws down on him the strong condemnation of Apollo and of Zeus himself.[24] With all his faults he has greatness of soul; he knows he is doomed to a brief life, and how soon his death must follow upon Hector's, but in contrast to Hector's melancholy, Achilles faces his death with sublime tranquillity. Finally his full nobility is displayed at the funeral games for Patroclus and in the encounter with Priam. The process of his divine transcendence, for which we are prepared by various indications throughout the poem,[25] reaches its completion here; but even in these last speeches, when full emotional sympathy has been established between him and Priam, he still warns the king, who has merely expressed impatience, not to anger him, since otherwise he fears he may yet kill him.

This primal ferocity of the heroes reminds us of the Serbian Marko Kraljevic, who is feared even when asleep. It shows itself in the vanquished as well, when, for example, Priam in his grief for Hector covers himself with dirt and rolls on the ground, and then, still lamenting, bitterly upbraids his surviving sons (which at the same time makes clear the enormous distance that separates Hector from the other sons of Priam and all the Trojans); or when Hecuba desires to sink her teeth into Achilles' body and devour his liver. Heracles too has his fair share of ferocity. When he takes Troy, for instance, he draws his sword on Telamon, who has been first through the breach, because he cannot allow another to be before him in prowess, and he is only restrained from a violent deed by typical quick thinking on Telamon's part.[26]

What the hero most wishes for is perpetual youth, and the immortality of the gods; Hector expresses it once in battle (*Iliad* VII.538), though there are also a few heroes who are old *ex officio*, like Nestor in Homer and Tiresias in the Theban legend, who are honoured precisely because of their age.

As far as character is concerned, the main stress is on heredity and breeding. Quite apart from the customary divine descent, the women and their parentage are also treated as very important by the poet, though at the same time we detect the bitterly pessimistic view that sons are usually less than their fathers. Isocrates remains within the general spirit of myth when he makes Paris reflect, on Aphrodite's offer, that all other gifts of fortune are soon lost, but noble birth is constant, so that in choosing Helen he is providing for his posterity, while the gifts of the other two goddesses would only last the space of his own lifetime (*Helen* 44). The conviction that *fortes creantur fortibus et bonis* (the strong are begotten by the strong and the good) still prevails in the succeeding agonal age, and the occurrence of unsuitable marriages causes the greatest grief to Theognis (183 ff.).[27] There is a corresponding belief in character as innate, incorruptible in the good, incorrigible in the wicked. Thus the child's upbringing by tutors and nurses is only of secondary importance, though it is sometimes highly valued as a factor in the making of a great man; not only Achilles but Jason too are counted among the pupils of Chiron, the personified ideal of the teacher in mythology.[28]

The greatness of the hero is primarily revealed in battle, most strikingly of all when Ajax decides to dispense with the help of the gods, and when Diomedes pursuing Aeneas is not to be intimidated even by Apollo; only after rushing upon him four times 'like a daimon' does he at last turn back when the god calls to him in a terrible voice: 'Be warned and yield! Gods and men are not of one race!' (*Iliad* V.440–2).[29] In fact it is in battle, or in the camp, or in the besieged city that all the endless variations of the heroic type are revealed, set off only by a few contrasting figures such as Thersites. The hero is dear for his own sake to the heart of the poet, as he is to the genuine chronicler; we may think of Froissart, who leaves us perpetually in doubt whether he is on the side of the French or the English. No discernible partisanship is displayed by the poet, least of all on the side of success; in fact for most of those returning from Troy, victory turns to ashes in the mouth.[30] For this epic joy in events the main thing is that the battle should rage furiously, and recurrent lines signalize this, such as:

> Then there rose up together the heroes' laments and shouts of
>   triumph.
> Men killed and were killed, and the ground ran with blood.[31]

The most remarkable instance of poetic objectivity occurs at the end of the fourth book of the *Iliad*, where Apollo is urging the Trojans on and Athena the Greeks, and where, by the introduction of an impartial observer, the scene is brought to an admirable close. If Homer does anywhere show a preference for the Greeks over the Trojans, it is perhaps in the opening of the third book, during the march into battle, where the Trojans array themselves amid shouting and uproar, like the cranes for their encounter with the pygmies by the ocean, while the Greeks advance in silence, full of courage and determined to stand or fall together. Homer gives particularly splendid images of armies forming in battle order, and also of the onrush of individual heroes; Diomedes is likened to a lion bursting into the sheep-fold after the shepherd has managed to inflict only a glancing blow on him (*Iliad* V.134).

The technical precision, too, with which Homer describes battles, blows, weapons and wounds is extraordinary. Certain famous weapons take on magical qualities in the myth and become *res fatales*, like the bow of Heracles in the hands of Philoctetes. The bow of Pandarus is very lovingly depicted (IV.105); that of Odysseus positively becomes a living creature. Another example of this realism is the account in the eighth book of the warrior's predicament when his charioteer is struck down and he has to take the reins himself (VIII.124 ff.).

Cunning is perfectly permissible, and even deceit; Odysseus is the incarnation of it, and will use it even against a comrade such as Philoctetes, so long as the main objective is served. In earlier years Odysseus had intended to obtain poison for his arrows, but he only succeeded much later, because the man he first asked feared the gods. Thus one may have a bad conscience about an action and do it none the less.

Compared with the later politicization of a Heracles or a Theseus, these heroes have as yet no true relation to their state; their semidivine nature and their authority are still unquestioned, and if ever they are driven from power this is not done by their peoples but by rival heirs or by enemies. It is true that even in the *Iliad* the community of the camp sometimes seems disunited,[32] and the *Odyssey* portrays the political condition of Ithaca, if still purely as poetry. It was the tragic dramatists who first showed a strong inclination to inject the political conditions of their own day into the states of the past. Thus Aeschylus has a popular assembly meeting in the *Suppliants*, and a political note is often heard in the *Agamemnon*, for instance (849) when the king is quick to play the doctor for his subjects and to use fire or the knife for healing purposes; or when Clytemnestra (883) pretends to have sent the boy Orestes away to Strophius as a precaution in case the raging anarchy of the people should bring to an end the wise counsel of the kingdom. Euripides uses politics as often as it suits him; one example is the popular assembly, with its voting and resolutions, described by the messenger in *Orestes*.

The gods have it in their power to bestow glory upon the heroes and even to lend a radiance to their persons, so that on occasion a glimpse of the supernatural is seen in them, and Odysseus at certain moments appears divine. Fame after death is also an heroic ambition. Hector thinks of those who will sail through the Hellespont in time to come, and see the monument set up to the man he is to vanquish, so that the victor's fame will be preserved. The Greek who successfully spies on the Trojans is promised the reward of towering fame among all men, and before a battle they reflect that whatever happens the vanquished will enhance the glory of the victor.[33] Always, the greatest events are bound to be sung of by later generations.

When the Homeric heroes revile each other they do it with a totally unselfcritical abandon quite appalling to hear. Achilles, having obeyed Athena's entreaty and sheathed his sword, abuses Agamemnon in a torrent of words. There is no well-bred dignified swallowing down of the epithets that rise to the hero's lips at the moment when he is longing to be at his adversary's throat.[34] Even in the jeering at the fallen there is no trace of magnanimity; Patroclus is particularly savage in his taunt to Hector's charioteer 'who would have made a splendid diver'.[35] But if the heroes are easily stirred to anger they are none the less good-humoured, not needlessly quarrelsome, and can be on the best of terms again immediately after exchanging hot words. Paris, mocked by Hector as a coward and for the gifts he has had from Aphrodite, admits the charge, but says he should not be blamed for the divine bounty, which is not to be despised; the gods themselves have bestowed it and no-one could win it by his own will.[36] Again, after Helen has bitterly scolded him for being beaten by Menelaus, Paris answers that he will win another day because there are gods on the Trojan side as well, and anyway it is time they went to bed (*Iliad* III.437–46); we must recognize this as a deliberate comic effect.

These heroes also weep like children, not only in great reunion scenes like that between Odysseus and Telemachus, where it is entirely appropriate, but, for instance, in anger too, as Achilles does until Thetis (his mother) rises from the sea to caress him, asking, as if he were a spoilt boy, 'Child, why do you weep? What grief has entered your heart? Tell it me and do not hide it in your mind, so that we both may know it.' In this heroic age there is still a satisfaction in tears, or rather in weeping one's fill. Penelope satisfies her heart with weeping on the eve of the decision, before entreating Artemis for death.[37] But when it has gone on long enough mourning is stilled; Menelaus in his palace often remembers the dead, and sometimes he soothes his heart with wailing, sometimes in silence: 'man soon has his fill of chill lamentation'. And when he has mourned with Helen, Telemachus and Peisistratus for lost Odysseus, Peisistratus points out that it is not pleasant to grieve after supper; tomorrow will be another day for it; and Menelaus agrees, saying: 'Let us leave off weeping and think of the feast again.'[38]

Another naïveté is that the heroes may lose courage. Even the greatest take to their heels when Zeus thunders; Odysseus is deaf to Diomedes calling him to help Nestor who is in danger, and he flees like the rest to the hollow ships (*Iliad* VIII.78–98); Agamemnon twice counsels raising the siege and sailing for home, though indeed he is sharply rebuked both times, first by Diomedes and later by Odysseus (*Iliad* IX.16–49 and XIV.64–102).

Most naïve of all is the unselfconscious expression of wishes and desires by the heroes. Odysseus among the Phaeacians, though he is deeply grieved, openly confesses his hunger, the most shameless of needs; and then he pleads with them to send him home the next day, mentioning, as the objects of his longing, not his wife and son but his estate, his servants and his high-vaulted house (*Odyssey* VII.207–25). Later, having astounded the Phaeacians with the first part of his narrative, he seizes the opportunity to ask them to fit him out with a rich provision of gifts, since it will be far better for him to return home with full hands.[39] But it is Nausicaa who represents the highest and most endearing instance of the naïve when she not only admires Odysseus after he is washed and dressed, but innocently says she wishes to have a husband like him; and Alcinous too wishes for such a son-in-law – 'one, as you are, of one mind with me. To him I would give my household and all I have.' (*Odyssey* VI.239–45; VII.311–15) There is as yet no law of poetry to forbid the expression of wishes that are not to be fulfilled.

Earlier in this work [p. 107 above] we have noted that the approaching death of old people may be openly referred to; this freedom (apart from the fact that the Moira comes neither sooner nor later than she wishes) arises from there being as yet no optimistic hypocrisy about longevity. Absence of hypocrisy is also at the root of the self-praise which was compatible with the noblest delicacy of feeling. Not only is it possible for Odysseus to say openly (*Odyssey* VIII.215 ff.) what a bowman he is, 'far the best of all who now eat bread in the world', except for Philoctetes, – though he will not compare himself with those of earlier times such as Heracles and Eurytus – but in general no-one need pretend from modesty to being less than the best.

Love of truth is quite often praised,[40] but in practice it was never, perhaps, a typically Greek virtue. To balance this we may recall the *purity* not so much of manners, judged by so-called moral standards, but rather that of the poet's presentation. Nausicaa bathes with her maidens, but there is no description of how she looked when she was bathing.[41]

Although the age is by no means a golden one, and in spite of the predominance of evil and ill fortune, still the heroic existence is pervaded by the ideal. Other nations will always envy one whose normal picture of the imagined past resembled the world of Homer. It is, of course, a 'non-utilitarian' world, in which, characteristically, apart from poetic similes, the peasant never appears except as the guardian of movable property, as a shepherd, and once indeed, in the case of Laertes, as a gardener.

On the other hand splendid figures like Eumaeus and Eurycleia are highly idealized. For everything in this world is noble and high-bred; serving and menial tasks appear only in relation to the heroes, and reflect their radiant existence.

So it is that the men of that time are credited with greater physical strength than 'the mortals that live now', and that posterity imagines them as of gigantic size.[42] But we may particularly note how, throughout Homer, persons and things belonging to the heroes are distinguished by what are known as ornamental epithets. Sacredness is transferred not only to kings, as in 'the holy strength of Alcinous', but the swineherd is 'divine', the servants 'proud', the very horses and sheep are praised for their fine coats. Even individuals who are disapproved of, even the wicked, are bathed in the golden light of the great age, as later the wicked characters in tragedy are. It is true that myth has a few villains of its own, such as Salmoneus and Capaneus, and some ruthless men, like Sinis, Procrustes and particularly Nauplius. The last named presents a strange combination of knowledge, commercial experience, wickedness and vengefulness, making himself useful to those wishing to sell their daughters overseas, or, by false signal fires, causing the shipwreck of heroes returning from Troy.[43] Thersites too is in strong contrast with the prevailing idealization. Penelope's suitors, though, have their share in the ideal splendour; although they are all slaughtered, they are yet godlike; Odysseus did not return from his wanderings to kill a pack of oafs.[44]

Life is pleasant and comfortable at the courts of Nestor and Menelaus in the *Odyssey*.[45] A man who, like Nestor, has received from Zeus the gift of noble wellbeing (*olbos*)[46] at birth and at his marriage, will lead a comfortable old age in his own quarters, and his sons are wise and the finest of spearmen (*Odyssey* IV.207 ff.). There is frequent reference to material wellbeing; we learn that the food prepared for the kings is better (*Odyssey* III.480), and the same words are always used to describe the procedure for sacrifices.[47] Only the noblest wine is reverently spoken of, for instance the wine kept for Odysseus' return, and that supreme wine of Ismaros which is given to him by Maron, the only surviving priest of Apollo. Of this wine it is said that not one of the servants and maids of the house knew of it, only Maron, his wife and a single housekeeper; and that one goblet of it mixed with twenty parts of water was enough to send up a fragrance from the mixing bowl so sweet, so unearthly, that it would pain a man not to be offered any.[48] If to the delights of the table were added that of the minstrel, who sang for the guests as they sat in order of rank, then this was considered the perfect fulfilment of the heart's desire.[49]

The Phaeacians are an exception. Their way of life is presented as a good deal more exalted and splendid; the total picture is obviously more fabulous than that of the courts of Pylos and Sparta. The Phaeacians, near to the gods and dear to them, live far off over the sea, on the edge of the world, unvisited by other mortals. Their days are spent in perpetual feasting, song and dance. The climate of their island resembles that of the Canaries and the Azores; whatever the season, the west wind blows perpetually, and flowers bloom while fruit ripens. In the palace of Alcinous everything is of precious metal; golden hounds, 'undying and ageless', keep watch before it, and youths of gold (animated statues) stand within as torchbearers. Alcinous himself has his throne in the hall, where the queen too sits by the hearth surrounded by her maids and spinning purple wool, and there he sits and drinks 'like an immortal'. The noblemen about him are 'sceptre-bearing kings', the people obey him as a god, and the queen Arete, too, is honoured more highly than any wife on earth and herself settles disputes among the men. The best thing about these people, who spend their days in pleasure, is that in their ships, which are swift as a thought or a wing, steering straight for the right place without helm or helmsman even in fog, they come to the rescue of stormbound sailors. From time immemorial, gods have made their appearance among the Phaeacians when great sacrifices are offered up to them, and have sat and feasted with them. Even if they meet a wanderer alone, the gods do not conceal themselves from him, for the Phaeacians are as near to them 'as the Cyclopes and the wild races of the Giants'. The peculiar divine favour they enjoy lies in the casual way they mingle with the gods and in their fabulous seamanship.[50] This happy existence, however, is menaced by Poseidon.[51]

Elsewhere on the margins of the world, too, there is a special degree of good fortune, as on the island of Syrie, where hunger and sickness are unknown, and where, when people are very old, they are shot dead by the arrows of Artemis and Apollo.[52] To return once more to the Phaeacians, we must mention the expression of noblest hospitality by Alcinous, who says that the stranger and the suppliant are as welcome as brothers to the man of feeling (*Odyssey* VIII.546–7). The Phaeacians also provide the best example of the level of politeness at these courts – the hospitality offered to the noble guest before they ask his name. Note how, though they are anxious to know his identity, the revelation is deferred by the poet to achieve the maximum suspense: 'our guest, I know not who he is,' says Alcinous, presenting Odysseus to his courtiers.[53]

In this world of heroes there is occasionally a protest against the banausic, though Hesiod shows no hostility to it. Euryalus the Phaeacian unfavourably compares the merchant seafarer, whose eyes are fixed on his wares and his miserly gains, with the man skilled in competitive games (*Odyssey* VIII.159–64). Certainly there could be no stronger contrast than that between the banausic way of life and one where the great issue is whether a man dies and brings fame to his opponent, or conquers and wins fame for himself. At the same time a man's ability to turn his hand to anything does not derogate from the heroic ideal. Laertes is a gardener, Achilles carves the meat for his guests, Odysseus builds his raft with his own hands and takes pride in even more trivial things: 'In the skill of service,' he says to Eumaeus 'no mortal can compete with me, in building a fire properly, splitting firewood, carving and roasting and pouring wine' (*Odyssey* XV.321–4). Nor does going out to wash the clothes diminish the nobility of the king's daughter; Nausicaa casually asks her father for the waggon, explaining that she has to see to the washing for him and her five brothers, three of whom are still unmarried and always wanting clean linen for the dancing.

The later myth gave credit for all 'inventions' to Palamedes – and predictably he incurs misfortune as a result; depending on the event he is held responsible for good or evil.[54] Beside him we may set the mythical artists and inventors, Daedalus, Trophonius and Agamedes, the Dactyles and the Telchines, as well as the great seafarers – Tiphys, helmsman of the Argo and inventor of the helm, the far-seeing Lynceus who could see the reefs under the water and was the first to hail a distant coast,[55] and Phereclus, shipbuilder to Paris.[56] The greatest symbolic embodiments of seafaring are of course Odysseus and the Argonauts. Those who remained at home believed all that the sailors told them, and those who had travelled themselves added more detail to the fabulous geography. They must have been the most wonderful liars the world has ever seen; the yarn-spinning travellers of the Hellenistic age are prosaic in comparison.

A border of lighthearted comedy surrounds the ideal world of the heroes. We have in mind all the tales of satyrs and such individual figures as the great thief Autolycus, grandfather of Odysseus, who, when he lived on Mount Parnassus, was blamed for breaking into neighbouring houses, and chose as his confederate Sisyphus, who was just as bad.[57] Then there were the Cercopes, two brothers, who raised hell far and wide until they crossed the path of Heracles, who had them strung up from a beam head downwards. In this painful situation they began to laugh so much at some light remark that Heracles could not help laughing too and let them go.

It is notable that for all the naïve and often positively criminal greed for possessions, there are no legends about *treasure* as such, for instance gold buried or in mines (apart from the stories of a supposed crypt in Delphi). The legends speak only of individual precious objects which also have magical properties, some of them made by Hephaestus and thus of divine workmanship, for instance the Golden Fleece, the necklace of Harmonia or the sceptre of Zeus.[58] Cupidity is aroused by such things as these and not by treasure in a general way. And this though the Greeks knew well enough from the example of the Phoenicians what mining was, and though they were familiar on their own territory with the remarkable buildings, believed to be treasuries, at Mycenae, Orchomenos and elsewhere. It is interesting to compare all this with Northern Europe, where popular imagination has always been preoccupied with buried hoards, caverns in mountains and so on.[59]

Apart from the heroes there are the representatives of the professions, the specialists. In the ideal world they constitute an exception, almost an interruption, but they are essential to the motivation of myth. One example might be the doctor; but Homer's Machaon is no ordinary army surgeon, he is a prince and a ruler, specially marked out only by his knowledge of healing. As for the teacher, we would refer to what has been said of Chiron [p. 142 above]. Here we will concentrate on the bard. His art is so much revered that Achilles himself is a bard;[60] in fact the whole world of the heroes with its mythology exists only for the sake of the poet. Alcinous, noticing that Odysseus sheds tears when Demodocus sings of the fall of Troy, asks the reason for his emotion and tells him that this fate was decreed by the gods, and Troy's ruin ordained so that future generations should also find matter for poetry in it (*Odyssey* VIII.579 ff.). The bard is the virtuous and reliable man par excellence. When Agamemnon went to Troy he appointed a bard to protect and watch over his queen. Aegisthus bore him off to a desert island, killed him there and left his body to the birds, and only when she was abandoned by this higher moral power did Clytemnestra succumb to her seducer (*Odyssey* III.267–72). In the eighth book of the *Odyssey* Demodocus is splendidly introduced (61 ff.) and appears no less than three times – with the song of the quarrel between

Odysseus and Achilles, that of Ares and Aphrodite, and that of the Trojan horse. The Muse herself has taught him the outline of the narrative (480 f.) and the inspiration comes to him from a god (499). In Ithaca, Telemachus loudly defends the bard Phemius when his mother tries to stop him singing of the return of the heroes. It is Zeus who inspires inventive singers with songs, but the singer is not to be blamed for singing precisely *this* song, for people love the newest stories best (*Odyssey* I.325–523). In this age the bard, as the narrator of myth, delights the aristocratic company of the armed camp, while in the next the aristocratic symposium brings the elegy into being.

Poetry may also sing its own praises. Eumaeus compares the story which Odysseus has been recounting to him for three whole days to the spellbinding of a bard, who has learned honeyed words from the gods, and whose hearers would wish him to continue his song for ever; and Alcinous too declares that he tells his story as well as a bard (*Odyssey* XVII.513–20, XI.368). In fact, whenever the hero is praised for his speaking, it is the poet who is praising himself at the same time, as when he causes his hearers to fall silent and linger spellbound in the shadowy rooms. Phemius defends the singer's art magnificently when at the end he begs Odysseus to spare his life: 'To you yourself it will be a grief to have killed the poet who sings to gods and to men. I did not learn from others; it was a god who implanted songs of all kinds in my heart, and I think I sing to you as if before a god' (*Odyssey* XXII.345–9). The bard has his part to play not only on joyful but also on sorrowful occasions, as we see when he appears beside the body of Hector in Priam's palace (*Iliad* XXIV.720); and in Hesiod's celebration of him he is said to bring consolation to the afflicted (*Theogony* 94–103).

The status of hero is also bestowed on the herald, even if he is the servant of an individual – for instance Mulius, the Dulichian herald, who mixes and pours out the wine for the suitors and is called a servant of Amphinomus (*Odyssey* XVIII.423 ff.). The minstrels and the heralds at these courts must have known each other intimately and both at times have acted as jesters. At the killing of the suitors Telemachus intercedes not only for the bard but also for the herald Medon, and Homer seems to lay a malicious comic stress on him; Medon creeps out from under a chair, casting off an ox-hide he has covered himself with, and clasps Telemachus' knees, whereupon he is pardoned by the 'smiling' Odysseus (XXII.354 ff.) Clearly the poet intends to establish a distinction between bards and mere heralds.[61] Besides, the herald – like the seer and the charioteer – is also entitled to be heroically honoured by posterity.[62] They used to show the site of Talthybius' grave in two places, at Sparta and in the agora at Aegium in Achaea (Pausanias 7.24.1); in both these places offerings were made to him, and his anger was moved against Sparta as well as Athens at the murder of the heralds of Darius who had come demanding earth and water [as a sign of submission] (Pausanias 3.12.6).

While the seer, the doctor, the carpenter and the bard are welcome, the beggar's arrival is not (*Odyssey* XVII.382). Clearly he is a familiar figure in the heroic age, otherwise the contrast between the wicked and the good beggars in the persons of Irus and Odysseus could not be presented with such perfect realism and ease. No doubt the poet feels sympathetic to the good one because his own condition so often verged on the beggar's, and so he shows Odysseus in this disguise with evident liking and most exquisitely. Note the words in which Odysseus (XVII.281 ff.) expresses his resignation at the immediate prospect of ill-treatment; how he accepts the gift of food (352 ff.), quotes the fact that a beggar may not feel shame (578 ff.), and how, after Antinous has thrown a stool at him 'because he is hungry', he is ready with a beggar's curse which will strike Antinous if there are any Erinyes to protect beggars (470 ff.). There is great realism in the curse of Melanthius against beggars (217 ff.) and also in the threats exchanged at the beginning of the Eighteenth Book by the two beggars, which would lead to a brawl but for the suitors arranging the fistfight, the only duel appropriate to beggars, which ends with the terrible final lesson to Irus. Nausicaa treats such people kindly (VI.207 ff.) and says that strangers and beggars are sent by Zeus, and that even a small gift is welcome to them. A friendly attitude to them can also be seen in the beautiful song known as *Eiresione*, in which a beggar profits from a betrothal party to pick up something for himself. Hesiod on the other hand has not nearly as much feeling for them; he notes that they are as prone to envy each other as the members of other classes (*Works and Days* 25 f.).

The women of myth are wonderfully presented in Homer; Nausicaa, Penelope, and the less important Arete, Anticleia and Eurycleia are much nobler than his goddesses. It is extraordinary how the later Greeks completely lacked any such figures, apart from the few, like Antigone and Iphigenia in Aulis, who may be regarded as handed down from myth. Nausicaa, as she is introduced in the Sixth Book of the *Odyssey*, is enchantingly graceful and innocent, indescribably touching. Homer himself evidently has no idea how she must affect the reader when she openly admires

Odysseus after he has been properly tended and dressed. She wishes to have a bridegroom like him (259 ff.) and then instructs him in the way he should behave to avoid gossip, and to win her mother Arete's good opinion (255 ff.).[63] Her mother appears beside her, the equal of her husband Alcinous in dignity and status, so that the suppliant visitor must first address her, the queen who can arrange and order everything. The combination of grace and strength is most apparent in Penelope, though the poet does not spare her some sharp remarks from her son. Right from the start, he firmly claims the men's precedence in speaking, especially for himself as the head of the household (I.356 ff.). She is surprised, then encourages him and goes away; but upstairs she weeps until Athena wraps her in sleep. The same thing is repeated when she commands that Odysseus should draw the bow; Telemachus asserts his sole right to decide about this, and, using the same words, sends her to the maids in the upper chamber, and again she obeys in astonishment and weeps (XXI.344 ff.). As well as the other women, there is the mournful ghost of Anticleia, Odysseus' mother, and last the archetypal faithful nurse, the venerable Eurycleia.[64]

Homer's Helen, quite unlike the other women, is a radiant figure, essentially passive, but of irresistible grace. She is in fact the innocent victim of Aphrodite, and her love for Paris is inflicted on her as a fate (*Ate*) by the goddess. Because she accepted that she had to submit to her destiny, she is able to weave into her tapestry the battles fought over her by the Trojans and the Greeks (*Iliad* III.126 ff.). She heaps terrible reproaches on the goddess (*ibid.* 399 ff.), who, she feels, has misused her as a means of pleasing her favourite; then Aphrodite at once leads her into Paris' palace in reconciliation. When Telemachus visits Sparta, Helen appears in her dazzling beauty, quite unlike Penelope, and when she laments over all that has happened because of her – 'when you Greeks came to besiege Troy for my sake, shameless as I am' – her words are so frank as to seem almost defiant (*Odyssey* IV.120 ff.). She has no qualms, either, about telling Menelaus and Telemachus amusing incidents from the time of the siege; but she also knows a remedy to help grief, and in the end is even visited by the spirit of prophecy (*Odyssey* XV.172 ff.). In the *Odyssey* it becomes apparent that she was formerly a goddess, as Nausicaa and Penelope were not.[65]

Chryseis and Briseis in the *Iliad* are merely objects; but it should be noted that when Agamemnon gives Briseis back, he is obliged to swear that he has not touched her.[66] In the account of mythical women in the underworld (*Odyssey* XI.225 ff.), besides the generally brilliant consorts of gods and the famous beauties, only *one* appears who is very unfortunate – Epikaste (Jocasta), and Phaedra is among others who are just mentioned by name; only Eriphyle is described with abhorrence. It was in tragedy that the terrifying aspect of women was first developed and motivated, with the creation of the heartless Medea and the Phaedra type;[67] but it already existed in the tales of myth, and the true moment of the break with the older attitude is to be found in the same underworld episode of the *Odyssey* (XI.433 f.) when Agamemnon says that Clytemnestra had brought shame on all future women, even those admirably skilled in women's arts. Agamemnon goes on to warn in general against putting complete trust in any woman, even if Penelope is different from others and better, and advises Odysseus to take the precaution of arriving incognito in Ithaca, since women are no longer to be relied upon; and indeed Odysseus puts his wife to a severe test. Athena herself gives Penelope a good character in theory, but it is far below her true deserts (XV.20 ff.); the goddess treats Telemachus to a sermon made up of crass platitudes as if there could be no argument about them: women are fickle, they slavishly follow a new lover, forgetting the children of their first marriage, and so forth.[68]

The Greeks lacked two types of the feminine; one is that of Semiramis, the great goddess-queen in whom Aphrodite might have been an element, just as Mylitta-Astarte was; Helen does not come up to this. Perhaps, if the Greeks had been united as a nation, they might have had such a figure. Secondly, there is no woman hero as the saviour of her people, no Miriam, Jael, Deborah, Judith or Esther.[69] Indeed, despite Medea, Clytemnestra, Eriphyle and others there is no example of a terrifying female ruler – no Jezebel or Athalia – and this is because even the men are heroes rather than kings. Instead, the Greeks have their *viragos*, Atalanta and Hippodameia; they invent the character of the Amazon, and later that of the traitress, typified by Tarpeia.

Later, mythical animals also gave the impression of extraordinary strength, apart from those which were monsters. Pausanias, telling of the Cretan bull, says: 'Long ago, men felt more fear of animals, such as the Nemean lion, the Parnassian, Calydonian and Erymanthean boars, and the sow of Crommyon, for it was said that the earth had given birth to some of them, while others were sacred to gods, and yet others were set loose on mankind as a punishment.'[70]

As a whole, the world of the heroes was one of such brilliance that people could cherish the idea that some of them, especially those who had fought at Troy, had not really died, but been taken by Zeus to live in the Islands of the Blessed, on the margins of the world. This idea is expressed in *Works and Days* (166 ff.); but here, the heroes are succeeded by the fifth generation of man, and with it the most extreme declaration of the arguments of Greek pessimism, so that in spite of all the violence and suffering they had endured, the heroic forerunners retreat by comparison into a golden cloud. Although mythical, these figures, for us, are historical in the most important sense; they show us the changing phases of the inner life of the Greeks, of which we would otherwise know nothing.

Homer's own people are distinguished from the heroes by the fact that the two Homeric poems bear clear traces of the civilization in which they came into being;[71] again and again Homer sets off his contemporaries (*hoioi nun brotoi eisin* – men as they are) against the heroes, and always as inferior to them. His own time is characterized above all by the existence of the *Iliad* and the *Odyssey* themselves; the bard too, as we have come to know him, must have been the poet's contemporary.[72] Furthermore, the manner of fighting the poet describes must be that of his own time; it would be impossible otherwise to account for the precision of his description of the Greek camp, or of the act of taking aim, finding the mark or missing it, and of weapons and wounds. Even at this early date, less respect is shown for mere bowmanship than for throwing the lance; the wounded Diomedes scorns Paris as a mere archer;[73] shooting an arrow does not count as single combat (*antibion*). The weapons of self-defence, too, certainly belong to the poet's own time; two headpieces, worn by Diomedes and Odysseus on their very characteristic nocturnal reconnaissance, must originally have been 'caps of darkness' conferring invisibility; in Homer they have become helmets made out of the heads of a bull and a boar.[74] Most telling of all, the agon held at the funeral games for Patroclus sets the stamp of the period on the poem – it is that of the agon. Hesiod personally took part in a musical agon at Chalcis and won a tripod there.

The images in the *Iliad* deliberately transport us into a world other than that of myth. Here we are offered hunting and other scenes from the life of animals, phases of weather and of the sea, rural activities and botanical observations; but nowhere any urban occupations, and it is all seen and heard through the eyes and ears of shepherds and country people. There are wonderfully vivid descriptions, for instance, of the dogs in the farmyard becoming restless when a powerful beast, with hunters and hounds in pursuit, goes crashing through the woods far off (X.183 ff.), and great realism in the poet's accounts of the lion attacking the flock (X.485 f. and particularly XI.172 ff.). There is a fine picture, too, of the jackals dismembering the stag wounded by the hunter, and being frightened off by the lion. Among the images from peasant life are ploughing with mules, which are better suited to the work than oxen (X.351 f.), then the reapers closing in on each other from two directions (XI.67 ff.), the hungry wood-cutter in the forest (XI.86 ff.) and the shepherd with his load of wool; only the woman spinning wool to sell, and weighing it out, suggests an urban setting (*ibid.* 433 ff.).[75] Once, too, an image is drawn from military life, when the fire that streams from the head of Achilles, as he goes out to seek revenge, is compared with the signal fires of an island-town under siege.

Among these earliest realistic images offered by epic poetry, those that fill out our picture of post-mythical life in the greatest detail are the descriptions of the two shields, one in the eighteenth Book of the *Iliad* (478–608), and the shield of Heracles in the poem after Hesiod; the second, although it can hardly have been composed very long before 600 B.C., is relevant here because its viewpoint is still that of the older period. First, then, the shield of Achilles with its miraculous workmanship. At its centre are the earth, the sea and the stars, then, arranged round them in concentric bands, come: first the city at peace with wedding processions and the lawcourt in session in the agora;[76] then the city under siege, the rearguard action outside, the battle developing as the flocks are ravaged, the war-gods and the Kerai taking possession of their spoils; then the tilled fields and the reaping, the vineyard with the grape harvest, song and dance, the cattle attacked by lions and the sheep grazing in the rocky valley; finally the splendidly wrought double ring of dancers and acrobats. This whole 'world' picture, in which the happiest features of popular life have been idealized, is encircled by Oceanus.

Hesiod's treatment ('The Shield of Heracles', 139–320) gives a much more distinct impression of supreme craftsmanship, both in the introduction and in the various images; the hovering figure of Perseus, separate from the main subject, is shown as especially masterly (216 ff.). The centre represents a fearsome dragon, and the surrounding bands are: first, battle scenes with no special theme, the twelve serpents' heads, fights between boars and lions, a battle between Lapiths and Centaurs with Ares and Athena, the gods with Apollo playing the lyre and the Muses singing, a seaport with dolphins and a fisherman,[77] and Pegasus pursued by Gorgons:

then the besieged city, evidently imitated from Homer, but much more dramatically agitated than his; the Kerai too are depicted in much more detail here.[78] Then comes the happy city with the wedding procession, dancing, singing, a feast, and the townspeople going to and fro outside the walls; we are shown the horse-breaking, ploughing, harvesting, gathering the grapes (this too in greater detail than in Homer), boxing and wrestling, hare-chasing, and, as evidence of the relatively late date of the composition, a fairly broadly sketched chariot race, with a tripod as the prize. Clearly, the period is already that of the agon.

What is completely absent from these descriptions is any form of trading. On the other hand, agriculture and rural life – in Homer – are shown in a noble and cheerful light, and the general note is of enjoyment; the shepherds play reed pipes; at the end of the furrow a man serves wine to the ploughmen; the king, with his staff of authority, stands still, happily watching the reapers, while beneath the oak tree the heralds are already slaughtering the ox for the banquet; the grape harvest and the dancing are most beautifully rendered, while in Hesiod the first is much more coolly described, and the dancing suggested in a few words (280 ff.). Not many nations have left such admirably natural descriptions of their lives. It is true that Egyptian scenes of the kind have been found in the tombs of Beni-Hassan: sowing and ploughing are shown in progress on the land belonging to the royal persons who are buried there; but everything seems precisely preordained. In Homer, it all seems as if it were happening by choice; instead of exactness, Greek life appears to us full of joy and freedom.

Thus these shields are simple, typical representations of an existence that still remained ideal, the dreams of the poet's contemporaries, turned into works of art.

A very different existence from that of Homeric man emerges from the teachings of Hesiod's *Works and Days*, quite apart from its sombre prologue. It seems extraordinary that there should ever have existed a people who responded to this gnomic lore and created a poetic tradition from it. We might ask how far the Dorian migration and its consequences may have been responsible for making life more violent and gloomy, and certainly the clear-cut development of the *polis* came later; but Homer lived later too, and seems completely untouched by this gloom. What is certain is that in the *Works and Days* we hear the voice of a writer whose father fled 'not from riches and substance but from evil poverty', from Aeolian Cyme [in Asia Minor] to the poor village of Ascra on Mount Helicon with its unpleasant climate (637 ff.). It is a primeval voice from a time when work was already a curse, but not yet called *banausia*; when it was honoured as the only salvation, and when the ploughman in his strength and freedom (441 ff.), the day labourer and the hired woman (602 f.) still had their place beside the unfree *demos*.

Alongside the heroes and their descendants we are here shown a people of peasant stock, longing only for just judges and glorifying *justice* in every way, mythically and directly.[79] They do so, of course, because in the aristocratic period justice was perverted by the 'bribe-devouring' judges, members of the great property-owning class, and Greek intrigue and corruption had increased correspondingly. Property is the main thing in Hesiod's world (cf. 686); but only honourable gain is praised, and praised loudly (298 ff.). Good neighbours are supremely important, more so even than relatives (342 ff.). Kinsmen are in fact not wholly to be relied on; even in making a contract with a brother it is recommended that a witness should be called in, as if in jest (371).[80] Families should be small; the countryman is urged to have only one or two children – a policy which Plutarch later felt called upon to interpret as favourably as possible. Here too, long before Plato, is a warning against sea voyages; it is the good fortune of the citizens of a law-abiding town not to have to travel in ships (236 f.); at the same time, though, the poet includes all kinds of instructions on the subject for the occasion that may arise, in his seasonal rules for the household and husbandry. The hostelry (*lesche*) and the smithy are the general meeting place in a village or a small place like Ascra, which has not the status of a *polis*; the industrious are earnestly warned not to be led into idle ways there (493). Towards the end there follow some general rules for life and conduct, and popular superstitions, mixed in with an almanac to assist in the choice of days on which to perform or abstain from certain activities. All this gnomic lore is thoroughly homely and rustic, and it speaks highly for the country people of Boeotia that such a picture of their life and duties should have been preserved. There are charming sketches of the girl well wrapped up in severe winter weather (519 ff.), and of the harvest supper (528 ff.).

Finally we must add a word on a very important aspect of primitive Greece – piracy. Wherever there are coasts and islands, piracy appears early in history among all the peoples of the world, and has still not been stamped out. Even among our civilized nations, a short period of turbulence and anarchy would certainly bring pirates back to terrorize the seas. The inhabitants of rugged coasts, where the fishing is poor, are naturally tempted to make forays into prosperous agricultural territory to seize crops, livestock and even human beings. This was the practice of the Cilicians and others in the last centuries of the Roman Republic, and of the Normans in the early Middle Ages. The Greek archipelago seemed formed by nature for the purpose of piracy. The starving robbed those who had work, and for this reason people preferred to live inland from the coast and fortify their dwellings. According to Thucydides, most ancient cities were situated at a distance from the coast and each possessed its harbour-town (many of these are listed by Pausanias). In mythology, the model of the pirate is Odysseus; indeed from beginning to end of the *Odyssey*, piracy is an under-lying assumption, and even at that time robbers amassed riches in order to cut a figure in the world. There are also in myth some 'sons of Poseidon', pirate captains, who remain in the region they came to ravage, marry the daughter of a local ruler, and become Greek princes; often a *polis* is then counted as their foundation, just as happened in mediaeval times with the Normans. Later, even in the age of the developed *polis*, opposition factions were frequently driven to piracy, just as in the late Middle Ages one or another exiled Genoese party would seize some of the fortresses on the Riviera and sally out to harass the shipping of their native city.

III

The Agonal Age

THE TIME WE SHALL DESCRIBE as the period of the agon extends from the end of the Dorian migration almost to the end of the sixth century B.C.; it might well be called the Middle Ages of Greek history. The division is arbitrary, like all divisions, but will prove useful to us; we are obliged to organize our material and select categories as best we can.

This period is generally characterized first by the alternating domination of the *polis* by aristocracy and tyranny; secondly, along with the firm belief in breeding, by the peculiar ideal of *kalokagathia*, the unity of nobility, wealth and excellence as the distinguishing mark of the Greeks, heralded by Pindar. The nobility reigned everywhere, even in the states that were not transformed by the Dorian migration. The right of the overlords was founded on superior blood, greater landed wealth, skill in arms, and knowledge of the sacrifices and the laws. The *banausic*, that is tilling the soil, crafts, shopkeeping, commerce and the like, was despised. The only occupation fit for a nobleman was the practice of arms or work for the games or the state, not work concerned with the necessities of life. Masses yearning to be free were encouraged to emigrate to the colonies where they became aristocrats in their turn.

This nobility was neither a scattered rural squirearchy (*Junkertum*) nor a military caste (*Rittertum*); it was more nearly comparable to the patriarchate in mediaeval cities, particularly the Italian – a social group living together in the city and taking an energetic part in its administration, while at the same time constituting its society; the ethos of the agon would have sufficed to unite such a group even in the absence of other factors. Tyranny, because of its utilitarianism, was inimical to the agon. Sparta too, with its austere Doricism, where the practice crystallized in a special way, stood apart from the rest of Greece; for here there existed no true society, but a conquering people ruling harshly, directing all their gymnastic and other activities to the practical aim of reinforcing their supremacy. Throughout the rest of Greece things were quite different; the nobility were open-handed and pleasure-loving, chiefly concerned with maintaining fine horses and chariots, and this atmosphere was so marked and so pervasive that even a few tyrants (for instance Cleisthenes of Sicyon) found it necessary to lay claim to noble excellence and to imitate the agon, though of course these are only exceptions that prove the rule.

Education in this society combined two aspects. One was the festivals, splendid ritual sacrifices, choruses and the dance, all linked with religion, which in its extension as myth was the starting point and root of all culture. The other was gymnastics; this was not the cause but the consequence of the agon, since personal competitiveness was no longer to be satisfied by training directed simply towards military efficiency. The aim was now to develop the body to the highest perfection of beauty, a purpose for which each individual had to submit to a methodical discipline just as severe as training in the arts, denying himself any personal manifestations of 'genius'. Gymnastics, with all that belonged to it, was able to draw on the general conviction of the value of training, a conviction so powerful that the state had no need to take active measures (apart from building the gymnasia).

This way of life left a strong and lasting imprint on Greek attitudes in general. Contempt for the banausic could never again be banished from the Greek mind and took root in the literature, despite some warnings, e.g. that of Phocylides[1]. Ordinary people could hold this conviction even if they were not particularly wealthy; they might resemble Xenophon who, in his deliberate return to the patriarchal ideal, is described as 'an excellent man in other respects too, and especially a lover of horses and hunting, experienced in warfare, pious and fond of sacrifices and skilled in inter-preting omens' (that is, halfway to being a seer)[2]. Even at a relatively late date, outspoken praise of *kalokagathia* was possible in Athens: in a passage in Aristophanes' *Frogs* (718–37) the image of the old silver coinage, which was then yielding to bronze, is used for the well-born, virtuous, noble, just and excellent citizen, educated in the *palaistra*, in choruses and with music – though this is recognizably the kind of image which is only used when what is described is on the wane. In earlier times there had been complaints of the decline of the true agon, chiefly in Ionia and the western colonies;

but one needs to know in each individual case how far luxury was really linked with decadence and declining energy, for often what we hear is clearly only the envious gossip of one city about another.

An important difference between that age and our own consists in their having (somewhat as the French still do) more respect for quality than for size of population. Besides, when full democracy emerged, it consisted in reality of an aristocratic minority as opposed to the metics and the slaves. It is only in modern times that men earn as much money as possible to support the maximum number of children, no matter what the privation and drudgery involved and however the quality of the population may suffer in the process; we have already spoken of the means, ruthless as they were, that the Greeks adopted to limit numbers. In any case, this society was a splendid one to contemplate; the poet of the Homeric hymn to Apollo can say of the Ionians (151–5) as they appeared at the festival of Delos: 'He who meets them all assembled would say that they are immortal and ageless, he would see how graceful they all are and would rejoice in his heart when he saw the men, and the women finely clad, and the swift ships and their many riches.' Then follows special praise for the maidens of Delos and their song, which set the seal of perfection on this magnificent existence.

This brings us to the agon. While on the one hand the *polis* was the driving force in the rise and development of the individual, the agon was a motive power known to no other people – the general leavening element that, given the essential condition of freedom, proved capable of working upon the will and the potentialities of every individual. In this respect the Greeks stood alone. Even in primitive or barbarian peoples, competitive activities may often develop to a certain point independently of warfare; wrestling games, riding skills and so forth are practised, but always only within the given tribe and the given social stratum. In the Asiatic cultures, despotism and the caste system were almost completely opposed to such activities. By Greek custom every Greek could participate in certain sports which could not possibly have been open to every Egyptian. Within the privileged class in Egypt, anything resembling the agon would probably have been totally excluded, partly by the equality or the hierarchy imposed by despotism, and partly by the undesirability of competing in the presence of the lower castes. Ambition, in the individual Egyptian, would be confined to the hope of an honour from his king for official or military services. Even now the eastern custom is not to compete among equals but rather to have mock fights performed as a spectacle by slaves or paid entertainers. Only small free aristocracies could allow the expression of the will to self-distinction among equals before judges, who were elected or fairly chosen in some other way, and then only in a nation like the Greeks; the Romans, who differed from them chiefly in their dislike of anything 'useless', would never have developed this practice.

In the heroic world the agon was not fully developed, if we think of it as excluding practical usefulness. The hero usually accomplished his great tasks on lonely journeys; his adventure was not yet seeking to compete with other adventures.[3] But there was a dawning of the competitive spirit, perhaps, in the communal enterprises of a number of heroes, and also in divine myth, for instance when Cecrops has to arbitrate between Athena and Poseidon, or Paris between the three goddesses; and in later times the birth of the agon was of course retrospectively transferred to the world of myth and was assigned its particular forebears in the mythical age of gods and men. Thus the victory of Polydeuces over Amycus the Bebrycian was accounted one of the most notable incidents in the history of Greek gymnastics, and it was with the discus that Apollo killed Hyacinthus. Heracles and Theseus were the greatest wrestlers, and while the Olympic games owed their foundation to Heracles, Theseus on his return from Crete founded an agon on Delos in honour of Apollo.

All the various manifestations of the agon were part of the familiar world for Homer, and he displays a highly developed expertise on the subject. His standpoint, naturally, was that of his own time, and in this he resembles the authors of the *Nibelungenlied* and other epics of the twelfth and thirteenth centuries, who transferred mediaeval customs such as tournaments into the legendary periods they described. Epic poets have never had any hesitation in allowing reflections of the present to play like this upon the past. The island of Scheria [in Homer] is particularly rich in this source of pleasure, joy and excitement. At Alcinous' suggestion the youths compete in turn in racing, jumping and wrestling, in throwing the discus and boxing (*Odyssey* VIII.97 ff.). Then the sight of Odysseus with his splendid physique arouses their desire to see him perform as well, and Laodamas, addressing him, pronounces that the greatest fame of mortal men is in their hands and feet. Odysseus at first refuses the invitation and is challenged in an insulting manner; in the end he makes a tremendous throw with the discus and then takes part in all the other sports including archery and javelin-throwing, with the single exception of the foot race.

Then Alcinous conciliates him by conceding the inferiority of the Phaeacians in boxing and wrestling, and commands that they should begin the dancing, for which selected judges are in readiness. The most ancient description of a boxing match conducted according to rules and under supervision also occurs in the *Odyssey*; this is the beggars' duel between Odysseus and Irus, which starts as a brawl but becomes a match on the intervention of the suitors (*Odyssey* XVIII.1 ff.). In this case there is also a prize – a haggis is offered – and the spectators solemnly promise to remain impartial; the fight ends for Irus with the terrible and carefully calculated blows of Odysseus.

The urge 'always to be the first and outdo all the others' is often fulfilled in the games told of in the *Iliad*, and particularly in the chariot race. Agamemnon has no higher praise for splendid horses than to call them 'prizewinning racehorses' (*Iliad* IX.124). The funeral games for Patroclus (Book XXIII) are naturally the occasion of the most elaborate kinds of agon, and the chariot race is the first event of the day; this race is here described in greater technical detail than anywhere else in the whole of Greek literature except perhaps for the account of the Pythian games in Sophocles' *Electra*. Patroclus' funeral is the occasion for nearly every kind of contest customary in later times, and there are exact descriptions of the various incidents and the breathless suspense of the onlookers, only as it were in an early stage of development; boxing, wrestling, racing, throwing the roughcast iron plates and shooting with bow and arrows at a captive dove. A hand to hand spear-fight is also on the programme, the first wound to be decisive; but as soon as Diomedes and Ajax have begun, the Achaeans fear for Ajax and bid the warriors abandon the match and share the prize. Achilles, too, in order to prevent a fatal outcome, puts a stop to the final javelin-throwing and instead distributes the prizes among the entrants[4]. The prizes offered by Achilles are however not wreaths – which would be considered sufficient in the time of the true agon – but a great quantity of objects, some very costly; treasures in precious metals, beautiful utensils, animals and slave-girls; there are even consolation prizes for the losers, as many as five for the foot race.

How, and by precisely what association of ideas, the gymnastic agon came to be held at important funerals, is an interesting question. We may think of customs among other nations where, on the death of some great man, his followers fought to the death beside his body, and of the mortal gladiatorial combats the Etruscans held at great funerals. Perhaps the custom is most easily explained by the idea that whenever and wherever many Greeks assembled, an agon took place almost as a matter of course, and, further, that the family of the dead man were bound to offer prizes for contests just to ensure that the burial would be well attended.

To return to Homer, the agon in his poems is never more than an innocent first step compared with its later development. Although in the *Iliad* all varieties of sporting contests exist, they do not as yet determine and permeate the life of the heroes; at Troy they have other things to think about. Special myths are linked with each famous figure, and those who had no other fame are sufficiently occupied with the real battles, where they perish in great numbers. Men engaged in war have no need of jousting. The Phaeacians would have had more free time for the true agon; but among them it was more of an amusing diversion, and as we have seen they admit to Odysseus that they are not distinguished in boxing (the only sport that was taken seriously on Scheria). Thus the agon was as yet an occasional rather than a regular occurrence, and it was not until the period of the agon that the whole of life was directed to this activity, and only then that the victors became great celebrities.

The cultivation of the Muses too was practised as an agon in early times. On the shield of Heracles there was a likeness of the Muses singing and dancing; Hesiod travelled by sea to Chalcis for the funeral of Amphidamas, and for his prizewinning hymn he was awarded a bronze tripod which he dedicated to the Muses on Helicon (*Works and Days* 650 ff.) – a triumph later giving rise to the legend of a contest between Homer and Hesiod. In Hesiod we find the agon manifested in civic and rural life, that is to say, a kind of competitiveness that formed a parallel to the aristocratic and ideal form of the agon. This is associated with his doctrine of the good and the bad *Eris* (strife), to be found at the beginning of *Works and Days*. The good *Eris* was the first to be born (while the bad was only a variant form fostering war and conflict) and Hesiod seems to find her not only in human life but also in elemental Nature, for Cronos had placed her among the very roots of the earth. It is the good *Eris* who awakens even the indolent and unskilled to industry; seeing others rich, they too bestir themselves to plough and plant and order their houses, so that neighbour vies with neighbour in striving for wealth.

Thus after the decline of heroic kingship all higher life among the Greeks, active as well as spiritual, took on the character of the agon. Here excellence (*arete*) and natural superiority were displayed, and victory in the agon, that is noble victory without enmity, appears to have been the ancient expression of the peaceful victory of an individual. Many different aspects of life came to bear the marks of this form of competitiveness. We see it in the conversations and round-songs of the guests in the symposium, in philosophy and legal procedure, down to cock- and quail-fighting or the gargantuan feats of eating. In Aristophanes' *Knights*, the behaviour of the Paphlagonian and the sausage seller still retains the exact form of an agon, and the same is true in *Frogs* of the contest between Aeschylus and Euripides in Hades, with its ceremonial preliminaries. The way that life on all levels was influenced by the agon and by gymnastics is most clearly illustrated by Herodotus' account of the wooing of Agariste (VI.126). Cleisthenes of Sicyon announced at the Olympic games, where he had just won the victory in the four-horse chariot race, that he invited applicants for his daughter's hand. The wooing, itself an agon, is a kind of mirror image of the mythical wooing of Hippodamia, daughter of Oenomaus. Thirteen suitors came forward, all personally outstanding and of high birth; two were from southern Italy, one Epidamnian, one Aetolian, one Argive, two Arcadians, one from Elis, two Athenians and one each from Euboea, Thessaly and Molossus [in Epirus]. Cleisthenes had a stadium and a palaestra prepared for them, kept them with him for a year and tested their courage, temperament, upbringing and character; he accompanied the suitors to the gymnasium and observed their behaviour at feasts. How the victory fell at last to Megacles the Athenian we shall discuss later [p. 205 below].

While the agon soon gained ground and indeed became the paramount feature of life, gymnastics were both an alternative and, as we have seen, an offshoot of the agon. The one is unthinkable without the other, although the gymnastic art too was credited to mythical inventors and founders; in any case, without the agon, gymnastics could never have become such a distinctive feature of the Hellenes' life. Competitive games were instituted everywhere, even in the smallest communities; the full development of the individual depended on his constantly measuring himself against others in exercises devoid of any direct practical use.

It must, then, have become usual for freemen's sons to be handed over to the teacher of gymnastics, and to receive their entire education from him, apart from the instruction given by the lyre player and the grammarian. Only the fairly wealthy, however, could spend their whole life in this way, and only those of completely independent means could make the gymnasium a conditioning factor of their lives. Thus gymnastics was in itself a popular activity, but in its advanced stages an aristocratic one, especially when combined with the practice of the agon and all that it entailed. The gymnasium was the chief social centre of Greek life. We can hardly date its origin earlier than the seventh century, and the full development of its equipment certainly came later, though in Plato's description it has all the special areas mentioned anywhere thereafter. The palaestrae were simple structures of a more modest character, often in fact merely private institutions, whereas the gymnasia always belonged to the State, which took a hand in this branch of education because it had an immense amount to gain from the regular training of the ephebes (the young men between eighteen and twenty years of age).

There were gymnasia even in the most insignificant towns, and this continued into late times. Among the gymnasia in Athens were the Lyceum, the Academy, and also Cynosarges for the sons of mixed parentage. The basic function of the gymnasia was the training of the ephebes, but in Athens also of boys, who were admitted to all the exercises, and of athletes. Reading Xenophon, Plato, Aristophanes and others one has the impression that nobody was excluded. It was in Athens that the greatest variety of gymnastics was practised; Athenians were victors in every kind of contest, and their athletes and trainers were recognized as the best. The five principal events, the so-called Pentathlon, were the foot race, jumping, wrestling, discus- and javelin-throwing, and as optional additions also boxing and the *pankration*, a combination of boxing and wrestling. In some cities these exercises formed a single whole. Important shows put on by the Athenian ephebes were the torch-races at the Promethaia and the Hephaistaia, and in all cities there were locally organized public events. The trainers, sometimes former Olympic victors, were certainly very influential men; Melesias, whom Pindar praises, had as many as thirty victors among his pupils (*Olympian* VIII.71). The citizens appointed by the State as gymnasiarchs also had great power; their office permitted them to dismiss sophists, rhetoricians and philosophers from the gymnasium if they became convinced that the doctrines they taught exerted a bad influence on young people. Certainly in Athens about the time of the Peloponnesian War the gymnasiarchy, an expensive *leitourgia*, was a means of attaining popularity.

These gymnastic exercises proliferated astonishingly and with endless refinements. There were cities in which the practice of them was actually a condition of citizenship. In the city of Pellene in Achaea for instance we learn that the old gymnasium served for the exercises of the ephebes, and that no-one could be admitted to citizenship until he had completed the full course. In Sparta, above all, the whole of gymnastics, as laid down there, was a compulsory part of state education.

As well as this athletic training there was the agon with horses. Because chariot fighting was the noblest form of combat in Homer's war of the heroes, the chariot race was very early ranked highest of all competitions in time of peace. Not till the aristocratic period was it identified with horse breeding, that is with the class of the nobility, and it then became the foremost agon. Chariot racing was much less suited than the other sports to be adequately celebrated in the confines of the individual *polis*. It was altogether the nature of the agon to transcend territorial boundaries, because its interest diminished if the same individuals were always involved; but chariot racing in particular, as the province of a wealthy minority, demanded more generally accessible festive locations. As soon as competition was introduced with entrants from other places on neutral ground or at some holy site, the Panhellenic agon developed, and very quickly – perhaps not by explicit agreement – more places of competition, with wider participation, came into being, and were soon provided with their foundation myths. The establishment of these Panhellenic sites, which yet remained exclusively Hellenic, was a very important element in the growth and self-consciousness of Hellenic nationalism; it was uniquely decisive in breaking down enmity between tribes, and remained the most powerful obstacle to fragmentation into mutually hostile *poleis*. It was the agon alone which united the whole nation as both participants and spectators; those who cut themselves off from it, like the Aetolians, the Acarnanians and the Epirots, forfeited to a greater or lesser extent the right to be counted among the Hellenes.

One ancient site of chariot racing must have been the Grove of Poseidon at Onchestos in Boeotia, mentioned (1.230 ff.) in the Homeric Hymn to Apollo. When, in the same hymn, (1.243 ff.) Telphusa tries to scare Apollo off from her own region by alluding to the noise of chariots and horses, it is probable that chariot *racing* is meant, not merely the traffic around a spring. Again, it was possible to hold a splendid popular festival on Delos combined with a magnificent agon in boxing, dance and song in honour of Apollo, whose cult was flourishing at the time; but what prevented Delos from becoming or remaining a general site for the agon was probably the fact that it was unsuitable, as an island, for this noblest form of competition.

At other great assembly points which were established later, such as the Panionion or the temple of Hera Lacinia at Croton, contests were certainly held without these places becoming famous for the agon, let alone attracting pilgrims.

Olympia must have been the first to take on a Panhellenic character, and the myth of Oenomaus and Pelops must be only the reflection of this development. The Pythian games at Delphi were old too, but at first consisted only of a musical agon and then gradually came to include gymnastic and all-round equestrian events, as those at Olympia did, in rivalry with the other festival sites. The Isthmus had a name for chariot racing from the most ancient times and was certainly a site at which very early games were held in honour of Palaemon Melicertes. The Nemean games may well have become generally accepted at a time when Olympia was not accessible to all Greeks or not sufficiently neutral. All four festivals were considered Panhellenic, and all claimed heroic origins, and if it were proved a hundred times over that, for instance, the Nemean games had begun at such and such a date, they were still supposed to have been founded by the Seven against Thebes, because the Greeks saw everything through the eyes of myth. The extraordinary thing is that different sections of the nation not only competed together at these famous sites but also mingled with each other, so that during the truce that reigned for their duration even the citizens of warring *poleis* could meet in peace. About Olympia in particular there was a special sacredness for the whole nation, and the games there, which had been largely Peloponnesian at the start, slowly became the unique revelation of Greek unity in the true sense of the word, whether of those living in the motherland or in the colonies. Indeed the national importance of Olympia found yet another special expression in the fact that the overall reckoning of time was linked to the winners in the foot race there, thus providing an easy solution to a problem that would surely perplex the modern world.[5]

Elsewhere too, Greece was filled with festivals, open to people of other communities as well as to citizens, which might equally have been called Panhellenic. Anyone who had enough money for the journeys, the offerings, the fees to pay a Pindar or a Simonides could spend the whole year in such occupations, and if he were often a victor could earn fame among men; everywhere the local contests at festivals were innumerable. This made it possible for the great athletic celebrities to keep in training, like the wrestler Polydamas, the boxer Euthymus, the famous Milon of Croton and the incomparable Theagenes. Their names were household words, and the whole of Greece knew anecdotes and fables about them. Theagenes' career for instance had begun with his carrying home the statue of a god that he had won; he competed in every sport and everywhere; his crowns numbered 1,400 according to Pausanias, and at least 1,200 according to Plutarch (*Moralia* 811 d-f) though it is true this author adds that most of them were trivial.

The association between the agon and the aristocratic made it possible for individual families to cherish a tradition of competing and winning. Such families of champions were Pindar's best customers, and it is from him that we learn of them; he is our indispensable informant on the competitive spirit, though we must bear in mind that his clients will have been among the last aristocrats to take part, and that here as in other things we only become acquainted with a phenomenon in its last stages, for soon afterwards democracy was to make the agon dangerous or impossible for this class. However Pindar brings before us, for example, the Oligaithidai of Corinth, with a long catalogue of the successes achieved by members of this family and the many places where they occurred (*Olympian* XIII.45 ff.). He often writes too of the Aeakidai of Aegina; once he alludes to the way in which champions come up in alternate generations of the same family (*Nemean* VI, Introduction). Pausanias too mentions athletic dynasties of the same kind, such as that of Alkaenetos of Lepros and especially the Diagoridai of Rhodes, who were descended from Aristomenes of Messene, and who took part in the emotional occasion at Olympia when the father was carried round by his victorious sons while the Greeks cheered and pelted him with flowers (Pausanias 6.7.3 ff.). Such families were of course of aristocratic or Spartan inclinations. A son of Diagoras, Dorieus, a victor in many contests, took his own ship to fight for Sparta in the Peloponnesian War. Taken prisoner and brought into the popular assembly in Athens, this famous champion was released unharmed by the Athenians when they saw him a captive, although there was much resentment against him.

At the equestrian contests which, as mentioned above, were held with the athletic games from an early date (at Olympia from the twenty-fifth Olympiad) there was four-horse chariot racing, with simple horse racing soon added, then chariot races with a team of mules or a single mare – both of which varieties were later abandoned – then with a pair of full-grown stallions and later with young horses. The horse breeders (with their horsy names: Phainippus, Hipponicus, Hippocleides and so forth) coolly laid claim to fame alongside the athletes, though they did not need to ride or drive themselves and indeed often sent their animals from great distances. For since the Greeks, with their passion for spectacle, demanded this splendid and most exciting sport, the rich and often princely owners of the horses could have their own way and insist on being crowned for an achievement which should have been credited to the charioteer alone. A man who drove his own chariot had the privilege, if he won, of having a 'Castor hymn' dedicated to him (Pindar, *Isthmian* I, Introduction); and Pindar also insists (*Pythian* V.32 ff.) that Arcesilaus of Cyrene owes formal thanks to his brother-in-law Carrhotos for driving in his place at the Pythian games.

As the whole thing depended on chariots and horses, victories with the four-horse chariot could be renounced in someone else's favour, as Cimon the Elder, then in exile from Athens, did for his half-brother Miltiades and again for Peisistratus, who in return allowed him to come home.[6] One might ask whether the public were informed of the victory being transferred to another person, or whether they did not even know who owned the team in the first place. Probably they often had the wool pulled over their eyes in connection with these games, as we can see from the bewildering and dazzling effect that Alcibiades was able to produce.

Only rich men or rulers could afford the luxury of keeping horses for public entertainment, and sometimes envy took its revenge on the four-horse champions by inventing stories about the scandalous origin of their wealth. Thus the rich Athenian Alcmaeon is said to have made the most unscrupulous use of Croesus' permission to help himself from his treasury (Herodotus 6.125). Even Herodotus in his day knew only two examples of people who had won the four-horse races three times. Cyrene is named as a city well known for the local passion for horse breeding (ibid 6.103). The Spartans, after the Persian Wars, are said to have gone in for it more wholeheartedly than all others, no doubt as a result of the decline in population and the accumulation of inherited wealth in fewer hands.[7] This continued for a time until, early in the fourth century, Agesilaus made an end of the practice by a brilliant stroke. In order to prove to his Spartans that horse breeding was only a matter of wealth and not of skill, and thus cure their taste for it, he sent a four-horse chariot to Olympia in the name of his sister Cynisca; this seems to have had the desired effect. A victory at Olympia with charioteers and horses was a high point in life even in late times, as we know from the report about King Philip of Macedon who got the news of Parmenion's victory in Illyria at the same time that he learned of the birth of his heir Alexander; he was equally delighted by a third message saying that a horse of his had come in first (Plutarch, *Alexander* 3).

Of course this sport was immensely dangerous. Chariot driving was extremely hazardous to life and limb. Pausanias speaks of frequent serious injuries at the hippodrome of Cirrha (10.37.4), and Pindar tells us that in a race there forty fell, though Carrhotos was unhurt (*Pythian* V.65). Even if forty is an approximate figure it still indicates a great risk of falls and dangerous injuries, and the impression is reinforced by the wonderful narrative of the Tutor about the death of Orestes in Sophocles' *Electra* (677 ff.). Not for nothing were sacrifices offered up in fear and trembling in the hippodrome at Olympia to the object which resembled a circular altar and was known as Tarahippos (the horse-shy) 'where the horses shy and the chariots are wrecked and the drivers are often hurt'; the purpose of it was to placate an ancient malevolent hero (Pausanias 6.20.81).

In the boxing and the *pankration* (combining boxing with wrestling) men were brutally battered, and sometimes permanently disfigured. Pindar blithely writes of the victor's glory as the remedy for painful blows (*Nemean* III.27); it is well known that the statues of pankratiasts are recognizable by their cauliflower ears, which became a positive touchstone of art. Teeth were also knocked out, and not everyone to whom this happened had the presence of mind, like Eurydamas of Cyrene, to swallow them before his opponent could notice. In wrestling it was permissible to break an antagonist's fingers, and two who were notorious for it were rewarded with statues in Olympia. Deaths were a not uncommon result of throttling or of powerful blows to the abdomen. Such cases were treated with leniency by the umpires, who knew that at critical moments it was hard to assign responsibility, and usually the offender was allowed to go free while the victim might be crowned even in death, and, as the euphemistic expression went, sent to the land of the blessed.[8] Sometimes men died on the spot simply as a consequence of overexertion. This happened to one from Croton even as he was stepping up before the official judges, and to a Spartan victor in the Pentathlon at Olympia while he was still wearing his laurels. The famous runner Ladas became ill after his win there, was carried nearly to Sparta and died at the roadside. Later satirists made capital out of these things, and Lucian says in an epigram (21); 'At Olympia I still had one ear, in

Plataea one eye, and at Pytho they bore me away lifeless'; but the Greeks would have it so and would not be contented with less.

The victor's reward originally took the form of valuable prizes, as we know from Homer, and only later of crowns, objects of the greatest pride. At Olympia the crown was of wild olive, at Nemea of ivy, at the Isthmus of pine and at Pytho of bay. At the musical agon it seems to have been customary from early times also to give as prizes bronze tripods, which were not retained but dedicated to the god. At minor places, prizes of lesser value were probably given, such as the warm *chlamys* won by a poet who defeated Pindar in Pellene. But the true motive for the contest was victory itself, and this, especially at Olympia, was considered the highest thing on earth; for it assured the champion he had attained the aim of all Greeks, that is to be admired in his lifetime and praised at his death. Above all, when a victor's son was also victorious, the father could tell himself that though he might not climb to the bronze heaven he had achieved the most magnificent destiny on earth, and could descend to Hades in that knowledge (Pindar, *Pythian* X.41 f.)

Some parents had early premonitions of their sons' victories. A mother dreamt, for instance, that the child in her arms was crowned; the boy was of course brought up to the agon and won the boys' race at Olympia. In Artemidorus' dream book we not only find the dreams of people who hope to compete themselves or to accompany their sons to Olympia, but it emerges generally that the imagination is dominated by the agon and its various events. Or it happens that the wish gives rise to a miracle, so that a father living on Aegina has a vision of his son's victory at Olympia on the day it occurs. In Pindar we hear the echo of the rejoicing that breaks out in the home of a victor whose family were entirely devoted to the agon. Not only does the victor inspire his grandfather with the vigour to defy age and, in his joy, forget that he must soon go down to Hades (Pindar, *Olympian* VIII.92 f.) but all victors dwell on the fact that a deceased father or uncle will hear the news. Such a triumph belonged not only to the individual but with him to his whole clan and indeed to his whole native town. Its inhabitants quaked and trembled together over the coming defeat or victory, and a suspense that silenced the rest of life and all its affairs must, in ancient times, have been bound up with this experience. The honours paid to the victor prove how overwhelming it was. On his return, his entry was surrounded with every kind of pomp, amid sacrifices and crowds of people. Thucydides (4.121) can find no more fitting comparison

for the welcome that greeted Brasidas, the liberator of Scione, than that
'they adorned him with ribbons and ran to meet him as if he were an
athlete'. More lasting distinctions followed, such as precedence at festivals
and leadership in battle: the Spartan kings for instance were accompanied
by the Olympic champions as their guard of honour; in Athens too, notably,
the victors had dining rights in the Prytaneion. No city wished to attract
a curse such as that visited on the Achaeans by the victor Oebotas whom
they failed to honour, to the effect that never again should one of them
win at Olympia – a curse which could only be annulled at a later date with
the help of Delphi and by the institution of a heroic cult for Oebotas. We
must not forget what things were like for the defeated competitor returning
home, of whom Pindar says that he crept in miserably through unfrequen-
ted back alleys and was obliged to remain silent in disgrace when others
spoke.[9]

The cities did their best to encourage the agon. Some set up prizes for
their victors, no doubt to make the long and expensive preparation more
acceptable to them by the prospect of a reward. Thus in Athens a law of
Solon's decreed 500 drachmae for an Olympic champion, 100 for a winner
at the Isthmian games and others in proportion. Perhaps Solon had political
reasons for caring about the Olympic victories of his citizens – who might
otherwise have been too shrewd to take the trouble to compete elsewhere
– and thus thought it well to give some slight support to an enthusiasm
that was already diminishing. The special chariot, built at public expense
and maintained in Argos, was obviously intended to make it easier for any
skilled horse breeder to compete at Olympia. A city might even build a
stoa for a famous wrestler and pankratiast to practise in, as Aegion did for
Straton who had won both events at Olympia on the same day.

The honours even outlasted life itself and sometimes turned into a
heroic cult for the particular champion. The smallest town would at least
erect a monument to its Olympic victor. The people of Achaea gave a
public funeral as the reward of valour to a man victorious on several
occasions (it is true he had been killed in the Lamian War) according to the
inscription on his statue by Lysippus. In the case of the famous four-horse
champion Cimon of Athens, Herodotus (6.103) knows not only the site of
his grave but also that his thrice-victorious horses are buried over the way
from it.

Cities that had been destroyed, or had lost their former status and
independence through synoecism, still retained vitality through the memory

of individual victors at the games. Some contestants were commonly still spoken of centuries later. But if a city had been defeated in the person of its champion it might happen that the defeats were denied many years afterwards, as the Thessalians denied those of Polydamas; if they were believed, mere lies might bring the success that had been hoped for. Stranger still were the usurped victories. An Olympic champion was bribed to name himself after a city other than his own, and thus a Caulonian of southern Italy had himself announced as a Syracusan after Dionysius' agents had failed to bribe a Milesian. It was as early as the fifth century that the elder Hieron persuaded a certain Astylus from Croton to claim Syracuse as his home when he won for the second and third times, after which the Crotoniates turned Astylus' house into a prison and removed his statue from the temple of Hera Lacinia.

We must not omit the dark side of the athletic career. No true happiness could result from the concentration of the whole of life on a few seconds of terrible tension; the suspense must have meant anticlimax, or profound anxiety about the future, for those involved. In their lifetime enmity and envy were naturally their lot and could continue after death – hence the nocturnal whipping inflicted on the statue of the famous Theagenes. The emergence of younger men forced the aging athlete into a retirement which must have been sorrowful, unless he had the good sense to carry on as a trainer and thus, perhaps through the fame of a pupil, to live on in popular memory. It was intolerable to contemplate the decay of one's own strength. The pankratiast Timanthes in his retirement would daily test himself by drawing an enormous bow; out of practice after a journey, he found it was no longer in his power, so he lit a pyre and burnt himself alive, obviously to imitate the death of Heracles. Others took to bad ways even in their prime, and it would be interesting to count up the Olympic champions who came to a sad end. Either their very successes were evidence of an extraordinary competitiveness, or else their mood after victory demanded stimulants. Or an Olympic victor might become a political agitator like Cylon, who met his death in Athens in the struggle for the tyrant's throne; the Olympic victor Philip of Croton, the most handsome Greek of his day, was a man of boundless ambition and behaved accordingly. Giant strength in itself seems a predisposition to misanthropy even in cases where contests are not alluded to. Thus we learn of the Aetolian Titormus, brother of one of Agariste's suitors and greater in strength than any other Greek, that he shunned mankind and went to live in the remotest regions of Aetolia. The famous boxer Nicodorus of Mantinea presents a rare case, becoming in old age a much revered lawgiver to his native city; it is true he was helped in this by Diagoras of Melos. The most favourable outcome for a victor was to go on to distinguish himself in war, like the Pythian champion Phayllus of Croton, who took part in the battle of Salamis with his own ship, or like Milo, who is said to have fought in the great battle of the Crotoniates against the Sybarites wearing his six Olympic crowns with a lion's skin and wielding a club.

In some cases, though, the athlete was so venerated that he was credited with divine lineage and a supernatural death. The wrestler Hipposthenes in Sparta is said to have had a temple built for him where, in recognition of his prophecies, he received the same honours as Poseidon. It may be supposed that the Spartans were merging the wrestler's identity with that of the god (whose epiclesis may have been 'Hipposthenes') and that they were convinced of this by a seer. Euthymus of Epizephyrean Locri, reputed a son of the local river Caicinos, is also said to have lived to a great age and not to have died but to have 'departed from mankind in another fashion' (Pausanias 6.6.3 f.). Theagenes of Thasos was called the son of the priest of Heracles there, but was really begotten by Heracles who had taken on the priest's semblance. Of his death too the expression 'departed from mankind' was used, and the Thasians were in the habit of sacrificing as to a god before his statue (the same that was whipped by an enemy) not before it had suffered the strange fate of being sunk in the sea and hauled up again by the intercession of the Pythia (Pausanias 6.11.2 f.) After the mysterious disappearance of Cleomedes of Astypalaea, a command came from Delphi that he should be honoured as the last of the heroes.

I shall now consider the festival at Olympia, though without digressing to speak of the enormous number of antiquities preserved there. Judging by the immense quantity of dedications found buried in the soil, the site was certainly that of an ancient cult. While it is probable that an oracle existed here from early times, the games, re-established in the year 776, may not be very ancient, and their foundation by Heracles and so forth is no doubt only a reflection of the image they presented in the historical period.[10] If we try to imagine what Olympia was like during the festival, we have to guard against the notion of a *town* putting up the shutters and forgetting everyday concerns for a while to celebrate with anonymous hordes from elsewhere in feasting and drunkenness. There was no massing of booths and stalls as at our modern fairs or carnivals; on the contrary, it was a place where great privations were willingly undergone. For a start, the geographical situation was hardly convenient for those from the whole eastern side of the Greek world. Nor was the place well equipped; people were crowded together and slept in the open or in tents – only the Iamidai had houses; by day they suffered the full heat of the sun and often extreme thirst, for the water of the river Alpheus seems to have been scarcely fit to drink.[11] All this was made up for by the tremendous mood of exaltation which prevailed there. A huge five-day festival was celebrated, always at the full moon. Pindar's eleventh Olympian Ode is intended to depict not the festival as it was but its first mythical foundation. However he takes his colours from reality and tells us how, after the separate contests are done with, the lovely light of the mild moon shines down and the whole area resounds with songs in praise of the victors (lines 90 ff). Before this peaceful conclusion went an experience of tension exceeding anything we know from our modern race meetings, amidst a crowd of spectators all violently excited and showing great expertise in the detail of the various competitions.[12] What is more, the setting was a magnificent site filled with works of art; before and after the contests an enormous number of rituals and sacrifices occupied everyone's attention. The underlying solemnity of the affair was expressed in the elaborate appointment of officials; everyone knew that the Hellanodikai had spent the previous ten months being instructed in all their duties by the Nomophylakes in the house at Elis devoted to this purpose. This training must have been indispensable if the authorities were to stand fast against pressure from the defeated competitors.[13]

We may mention here that the Olympic festival, in common probably with all important competitions, was confined to men, with the female sex rigorously excluded. No doubt the reason for this was the fear that women might respond overenthusiastically to qualities other than gymnastic excellence. Young women were allowed to watch only the foot race in the stadium, and the priestess of Demeter Chamyne had her official seat at that event.[14]

Apart from the competitors, splendidly equipped festival delegations brought offerings of animals and gifts from states and individuals; choirs of every kind, especially boys' choirs, came to accompany the ritual sacrifices with their songs.[15] People streamed in from the whole of Greece and the colonies; all dialects, all interests and friendships met there, so that the size and geographical spread of the Greek nation was on display. It was represented as a whole, not only as countless separate *poleis*, and it was freely and spontaneously held together in its shared intensity by the contests, in which not merely individuals were competing but also, it was felt, the *poleis* from which they came.

In this place, neutral since it was distant from the most powerful and ambitious Greek cities, the leaders of Greek intellectual life appeared. It is doubtful now whether Herodotus read aloud from his history; but, between the races, performers such as Cleomenes would come on and recite the invocations of Empedocles, entrusted to him by the author because a very powerful voice was needed in order to be heard at this site (Diogenes Laertius 8.63). Here too we find, as we might expect, the official orators, Gorgias and his like, with their flowing cloaks, making fine speeches on the unity of the Hellenes and the struggle against the barbarians, or calling for the overthrow of Dionysius of Sicily;[16] and finally the philosophers, right down to that Cynic Peregrinus Proteus, who represents the end point of self-glorification at Olympia, for the tired world of antiquity never recovered from his leap into the fire. Even later scholarship was still preoccupied with Olympia; in the time of Hadrian, Phlegon of Tralles was writing his *Olympiads*, and Philostratus in his *Gymnasticus* seizes every opportunity to refer to what went on there.

Delphi might have developed into a strong rival to Olympia, as the Delphic agon, originally almost wholly musical, with gymnastic games for boys, gradually progressed to include all kinds of athletics and also chariot racing. But it seems that Olympia's real competitor was Athens. 'Other festive meetings occur at long intervals and are soon over; but our city is a festive gathering for visitors the whole year round,' says Isocrates, not without justification, in his *Panegyric* 46. The Panathenaea became a festival almost as comprehensive as the Panhellenic games, and second only to them in splendour. For the same kind of prizes, that is for crowns, and vessels filled with oil from the sacred olive trees, men competed here as at Olympia in all the athletic, equestrian and ultimately artistic events; from Pericles' time the Odeon served for these last. In Roman times gladiatorial spectacles may have rivalled Olympia too. They first flourished at Corinth, and were to have been introduced in Athens, but this was averted by the pleas of Demonax.[17]

But it was Olympia that remained unique as the site of general Greek *publicity* and in this respect was not to be supplanted by Delphi, whose own superior position was based on quite different things. To make something known to all Greeks it was essential to appear in person at Olympia or to set up an inscribed monument there. While in our time statues and sculptures are kept to adorn their city of origin, the Greeks, whether individuals, corporations, cities or alliances, sent such things to the great festival site or had them made there to order, and we learn from Pausanias that the aim of 'fame among all the Greeks' was thus really achieved for centuries afterwards. Apart from the statues of athletes, there were at Olympia numerous statues of political and military celebrities. They may well have existed in their own cities too, and yet this was felt not to be enough.

This brings us to the matter of monuments devoted to the agon as such. The moment was bound to arrive when the Greeks demanded that the sculptor's art, already splendidly developed, should immortalize fame won at the agon, for them the true and almost the only kind of fame; 'you *must* be able to do it' they might have said, addressing their artists. The principal task (to ignore equestrian victors for the moment) was to represent the athlete, the wrestler, pankratiast, discus thrower and runner. Their monuments could not take the form of the grave marker, the heroon or the like; allusion and symbolism in the message of a monument were inappropriate here. Nor was the champion, apart from exceptional cases, depicted in relief on a stele or part of a building. Primarily he was an isolated naked figure and meant to be seen in such a way that the spectator should recognize him as a gymnastic or artistic victor; a human life, even in its fleeting instant of winning, was to be rendered immortal. The question arises to what extent, and sometimes if at all, the *head* is to be thought of as a portrait. Perhaps the sculptor did not invariably see the victor, and had to make do with basic information about his age. Yet the statues were to be personal, and it may be said that portraiture, which in this case *begins*, by and large, with the whole, necessarily naked figure, never again had such an origin anywhere in the world. The athlete forms an artistic genre before there is any such thing as a statuary of statesmen or warriors, to say nothing of poets.[18]

At Olympia itself the two earliest statues of athletes (winners at the 59th and 61st Olympiads) were of wood, one in fig wood and the other in cypress (Pausanias 6.18.5). Soon the sculpture of athletes, determined by the active posture of the figures, their suitability for open-air display and so forth, was felt to demand casting in bronze, and by encouraging this technique it came to have great influence on the whole art of sculpture. In Athens the statue of Cylon was of bronze. Pausanias found this honour surprising since Cylon had aspired to the tyranny, and explained it by his having been the handsomest of men and winner of the double race at Olympia as well as son-in-law to Theagenes of Megara (Pausanias 1.28.1). It is true this statue may have dated from a later time than Cylon's own, for it was not unknown for victors to be honoured retrospectively: thus at the 80th Olympiad a victor of the sixth was commemorated by his countrymen the Achaeans because the Delphic Apollo had commanded it (Pausanias 6.3.4). The statues were erected sometimes by the victors themselves, sometimes by their admirers or relatives; it might be their native city who arranged it either at the festival site or at home,[19] or again the authority in charge of the games.[20] In any case the honour of having a statue was enormously prized and awaited with impatience. The Cyrenean Eubotas, who was informed of his Olympic victory before it occurred 'by the Libyan oracle', had his statue made in anticipation, and, having no doubt brought it along, was able to set it up on the very same day that he was proclaimed the winner (Pausanias 6.8.2). Milon of Croton is even said to have carried his own statue into the Altis (Pausanias 6.14.2). In the third century it happened that a winner in the foot race at Olympia was awarded three statues for three victories. As a punishment for later bad behaviour a victor's statue might be destroyed.[21] One grateful victor persuaded the Eleans to have his wrestling instructor's statue set up beside his own.[22]

Chariots and horses also began to be commemorated. In earlier times horses were given a magnificent burial: Miltiades interred his in the Cerameicus, and the Laconian Evagoras also did the thing in style;[23] the chariot was simply sent, as it was, to be dedicated at Olympia. As time went on, from the 66th Olympiad onward (Pausanias 6.10.2) a great many chariots were set up in sculpture with their wealthy owners, alongside the charioteer and grooms, equestrian groups and single horses (Pausanias 6.13.5, 6).[24] For a while these sculptures seem to have attracted lively interest at Olympia, Delphi and other places, which must have been of benefit for the training of real horses. But athletic training must once more have become, and long remained, the principal subject of sculpture.[25] At Elateia, even down to Pausanias' day, they still had beside the road the bronze statue of 'Mnesibubos the runner', a man who had been killed fighting off an attack on the town by brigands. But he had probably been awarded the statue in his lifetime for having won the ordinary foot race and the double race with shield at the 235th Olympics (Pausanias 10.34.2). It was inevitable that the agon, personified, should be given its own artistic representation along with the contestants. Pausanias saw it in the temple of Hera at Olympia, in the company of Asclepius, Hygeia and Ares (*ibid* 5.20.1).

The Greek agon, then, became known far and wide partly by way of the colonies and even among the barbarians. It is true that when Pausanias says (6.32.1) that statues of Hermes, Heracles and Theseus (*sic*) were customary in gymnasia and palaestrae in many barbarian places he no doubt refers to the lands of the *diadochoi*, where such things were introduced along with the theatre.[26] But what are we to make of gifts presented to Olympia by barbarian princes, or of the fact that the imagination of a foreign people of half-Greek culture, such as the Etruscans, appears to have been preoccupied with the idea of the Greek agon as the height of fashion? We know this from the vases found in Etruscan and Southern Italian graves, a disproportionate number of which are painted with gymnastic scenes; since they illustrate the whole activity of the palaestra, they are, for us, an essential complement to the athletic sculpture. Many of the vases bear the inscription 'from the games in Athens' and thus they appear to be the kind of Greek prize that could be carried home to Etruria, whereas the crowns given at the Panhellenic contests were, as we know, not to be taken away. Of course there is no question of their all having been won by Etruscans. But this people, who bought gladiators for the enjoyment of fighting as a spectacle, evidently delighted in paintings of the Greek or anyway non-Italian agon – we need not ask what curious notions of the agon may have developed in the barbarian mind – and the Panathenaia were so famous that they wanted to be reminded of them by the inscriptions. Whether the vases were actually brought from Greece, or whether, as Gerhard concluded, they were the products of gifted Greek ceramic artists in Vulci supplying all the surrounding regions of Etruria with pottery, they remain the strongest evidence of an intoxication with the idea of the agon. Through them, the fame of Athens abroad was further increased, a phenomenon we shall examine later.

To conclude this account I turn briefly to the artistic agon. Mention has already been made of the rhapsodes' appearance at the festivals; Hesiod's victory at Chalcis typifies this early phase for us.[27] Among the Panhellenic games Delphi was the most important for music and poetry. I have said that the Pythian games seem to have originated entirely in the poetic agon, and here the hymn to the god was performed by *kitharodoi* with lyre accompaniment; there were also flute players, *aulodoi* – though their music was soon excluded as too melancholy (Pausanias 10.7.2 f.) – and, from the eighth set of games, non-singing lyre players. In ancient times it was a matter of life and death to succeed or fail in this, and the judges carried out their task with great seriousness;[28] later, as everywhere else in Greece, the old practice may well have given way to musical virtuosity and the exhibition of individual talent.

In conclusion, the wider significance of the artistic agon must be considered. In the whole ancient world the Greeks stand alone by the fact that the agon took possession of the cult and drew the artistic elements of religion into its own sphere, so that to a great extent the art of poetry develops under the determining influence of the agon.[29] In drama, it seems, tragedy as well as comedy were competitive almost from the beginnings; this is equally true of all the festival choirs, which in Athens for instance were organized competitively by the tribes, that is, imposed as an expense on the wealthier citizens according to a rota, so that the *choregia* became one of the most important civic duties.[30] This custom took on such proportions that Plato complains in all seriousness of the quantity of rival choirs who appear on every religious occasion and produce an incongruously mournful effect (Plato, *Laws* 800 c.). Institutions of this kind involved the formal appointment of judges whose expertise and honour were beyond question.[31] Without them the partisan enthusiasm of the people might turn to frenzy, as we learn from the story of a lyre player murdered in Sybaris.[32] Such cases show the dark side of the agon; the feverish preoccupation with it went beyond all bounds; to the fanatics, opinions different from their own were blasphemy, and it seemed to them a virtuous act to do away with a performer who was not up to standard.

All this led to the whole of Greek life being dominated by the habit of competition. Performers on the lyre, the cithar and the flute are judged as a matter of course at each public appearance; everywhere there are victors and losers.[33] The shepherds in Theocritus cannot hold their singing competition when there is no judge at hand. 'If only Lycopas the cowherd were here!' sighs one of the singers, and the other replies, 'I don't need him! But if you agree we will call Morson the woodman who is over there cutting heather' (Theocritus, *Idylls* V.62). Both then ask this man to judge them fairly.[34] Even the dialogue as a form of philosophical discourse became an agon; there was an oratorical agon like the one organized by Artemisia in praise of Mausolus, in which the speakers were Isocrates, Theodectes of

Phaselis and Theopompus. Dilettantism made an agon of every judicial trial so that 'agon' became the standard technical term for 'trial'. We must not forget the agon of visual art, or at least of painting: one on Samos between Parrhasius and a rival, the subject being the duel of Ajax and Odysseus, and one at the Pythian games between Panaenus and Timagoras of Chalcis.

Probably it was not until the athletic and artistic agon had completely pervaded Greek life that education began to take full account of them, not that each pupil trained to compete at the sacred games-sites, but to the extent of giving adequate attention to the agon as it dominated daily life. This was the aim even of the grammar teachers, the citharists and the instructors in gymnastics, the indispensable first tutors for anyone, in Athens or elsewhere, who wanted to be educated; the boys were constantly winning and losing, constantly being awarded crowns.[35] The idea of political *ephebeia* had been combined with that of a particular gymnastic preparation,[36] and this traditional attitude was perpetuated until Roman times. Various gods, too, Hermes, Apollo and Heracles, began to preside over this activity. In art they came to be used as the physical models to which everyone aspired, and the myth of Heracles developed more and more towards representing him not as a victor in the agon – though this element too is to be found in the later elaboration of Olympic myth – but rather as a constant defender of the wellbeing of individual regions or of humanity as a whole, who had earned his divine status by valour. After all, the whole of Greek art is interwoven with the symbolic crowning of the victor at the agon.

Daily life from childhood on, the agora, conversation, war and so forth played their part in educating each boy for the agon. The existence that resulted from all this was of a kind never known before or since anywhere on earth – all of it saturated and dominated by the agon, and all based on the principle that anything might be achieved by education, that is by a principle which left as little space as possible for the family and home influences.[37] If we look at the role of competition in our own world we are instantly struck by the chief difference, which is that the Greek agon always had the entire population as its audience and witness; while today – whether in the case of performance in person or, as with pictures and books, a silent offering – it is the audience or the public that decides, purchasing or not purchasing, paying an entrance fee or staying away. But mostly our modern form of competition is determined by quite different aims. If in schools some degree of competitiveness exists, usually slight apart from a few unusually ambitious types, the 'longing for fame' in adult life has been replaced by something very remote from it, which is business competition. Men of today are far more likely to want to win financial success than rapid recognition of their talents, and they know perfectly well why the success they seek is of a material kind; life requires it. As for education, the Greek *paideusis*, aiming almost exclusively at future achievement, has been replaced by our higher schooling, aiming at knowledge that is to be 'thorough yet many-sided'. Among the Greeks the feverish striving for hollow fame (*kenodoxia*) was seen by a later generation, retrospectively, as a motive even in mythical figures. Salmoneus and others behaved as if they were gods; Trophonius is among those who, according to a rationalizing version of their myth, were said to have hurled themselves into clefts in the earth so it should be believed they had been 'carried up' out of the world. In sum we may well believe that the Greeks sought the value of life too much in the opinions of others, and the agon declined until it came to consist in men staking everything to win the favour of the crowd.

The *status of work* among the Greeks is a subject that requires a brief comparison with the ancient East. In the early civilizations, ideas about the relative dignity of various activities seem to have been established with their very origins. A ruling caste of priests and warriors had appropriated power, war, hunting and good living, and left everything else to the rest of the population, whether or not they were divided into castes according to different inherited occupations. Manufacture, whether mechanical, chemical or craftwork, had no doubt reached a high degree of perfection, but was certainly despised as toil and seen as an inherited fate; agricultural work was nothing but slavery if only because of the heat of the climate. The nobility in the European Middle Ages evolved similar attitudes of complete contempt for work and commerce; but alongside this there gradually arose a middle class, not only working but holding work in high honour.

Between these two worlds the Greek world stands apart, since here the *middle classes* themselves held most work in scorn, though unable to dispense with its products. The simple explanation that the Greeks had slaves for work is not enough; for they despised most free work too. Nor can the blame for this be shifted to the climate, which is not so extreme that field work and freedom were mutually exclusive.

For the evaluation of work, the period and the circumstances in which a nation evolves its ideal of existence are the most important consideration. In modern Europe, that ideal derives principally from the mediaeval burgher class, which slowly became not only superior to the nobility in wealth, but also its equal in education, though indeed this was a different kind of education from that of the nobility. In contrast, the Greeks had their image of the heroic period, that is of a non-utilitarian world, and never rid themselves of it. Their relationship to the world of the heroes, comprising only battles, dynastic tragedies and divine interventions, was immeasurably closer than the relationship of the mediaeval citizen to the world of Germanic legend. But while the heroic age, at least in its decline, in Hesiod's *Works and Days*, still acknowledges a conception of peasant life as honourable, and even esteems a certain kind of trade, the agonal age that followed was bound to encourage an increasingly exclusive attitude of contempt for physical work. The members of the ruling class by right of birth were no longer a small minority; instead there came into being a large urban aristocracy, living chiefly on income from property, whose aim in life, and ideal, was combat – not so much in the military sense as in that of equals pitted against each other. The whole nation was convinced that this was the highest thing on earth. The outlay needed was modest, so that large numbers of people were able to participate, and those who could not admired and envied those who could. Many sites for competition thus developed, and many types of contest, and gymnastics as the preparation for them, became the chief purpose of education. However this way of life was incompatible with any economic activity; the agon occupied the whole of existence.

At the same time slavery certainly increased. But this was not the decisive factor; often the only workers were peasants who had no rights, only the obligation to pay a tithe, and who were in fact serfs; in Sparta the ruling caste had no subjects but these. Even if the farmer or manual worker was a slave-owner, his own labour was no more highly respected on account of that. All that can be said is that the extension of slavery intensified an attitude that already prevailed. It was the viewpoint of this aristocratic period that remained influential down to later times in Greece, and particularly in the fully developed democratic state.

Sparta was the most completely antibanausic state of all. The Hellenic ideal realized in the Spartan way of life was the diametrical opposite of any kind of earning; it was the possession of the greatest imaginable 'wealth

185

of leisure', which Plutarch calls one of the most splendid and fortunate of all gifts. Here the whole edifice of the State was founded on the presence of a subject race forced to work, and it was a source of pride that no Spartan did anything except in the service of the *polis*.[38] But elsewhere too, at least in theory, citizenship posited zeal in the service of the state (*arete*) as the goal of human life; only those who had this quality were worthy to be citizens. Aristotle held that *banausia* was opposed to education (*paideia*), and was democratic and part of poverty and low birth; while education, combined with nobility and wealth, typified the oligarch.[39] Not only does he banish from education the true *banausia*, hard physical work, but he even wants the liberal arts pursued in moderation. Too much effort to master them perfectly, he says, leads to one-sidedness.[40] The aim is evidently the harmonious combination of all qualities with none predominating; if at all possible the Greek desired to be a whole man, and could be one if he devoted himself entirely to public life, gymnastics and noble culture – something that in our day would demand quite extraordinary enterprise and good fortune. But all specialization makes a man only a part, and thus banausic, however indispensable that specialization might be for the common good, and however sublime the gifts required. One may ask how far human nature could tolerate the realization of ideals such as these. Even in later times the Greeks never woke up to the fact that they had a large number of 'false citizens' whose utterly banausic activities counted among the merits of the *polis*.

Set against all this, obviously, was the necessity of earning money and the ease with which it could be done; the Greeks had a natural capacity, in fact a positive vocation, as sailors, colonists and merchants. The Phoenicians, with their apparently unique bent for overseas trade, had provided the example; after that it was inevitable that the attraction of movable property, and the early recognition that money was power, should lead to an exception being made in favour of commerce, even in the Hellenic world. Where wit and intelligence counted for so much as they did in travel and trafficking abroad, it was not likely the Greeks would be left behind. Trade and shipbuilding became the chief sources of wealth, and though the colonies were first intended as *poleis*, most were not viable without commerce; as soon as they were well established, commerce held its own as an occupation in full parity with the dignity of landowning. The colonial attitude, highly commercial, naturally reacted on the motherland. This does not imply that flourishing trade went together with democratic constitutions. The trading *poleis* tended rather to be timocracies, and in Ionia and Italy the great merchants and shipowners were often the rulers, just as in mediaeval Western Europe the leading guildsmen would be either of equal dignity with the city fathers or simply the same people. Despite its predominantly mercantile rather than agonal ethos,[41] this ruling class – in the Ionian cities for instance – was, by virtue of its adventurous voyaging, a continuation of the ancient heroic tradition, and as strongly idealistic as any aristocracy, as we see from its poetry and philosophy, large and splendid temples and lavish offerings.[42] One result of successful trade was, no doubt, that these states fell prey to luxurious habits. In this the Ionians must have come under strong influence from the Lydians; but perhaps some things only seemed luxurious by contrast with the general Greek sobriety in dress and diet.[43] The defeat of the Ionians by the kings of Lydia was caused more by internal turmoil than by soft living.

There are some special instances of anti-commercial edicts; in Sparta full citizens were forbidden to engage in trade, and Epidamnos dealt with the Illyrian hinterland exclusively through the annual appointment of a respected citizen as the official 'vendor' because contact with the barbarians tended to make the citizens aggressive and discontented – but these are of little weight compared with the broad overriding interests.[44] In Athens especially, trade had long been exempt from the slur of *banausia*, and Solon's example proves that even the aristocrats went on business trips. Plutarch, at pains to provide a noble explanation for Solon's deciding to travel in this way, remarks that such journeys bring experience of barbarians, friendship with kings and the knowledge of many things.[45] In his constitution, Solon certainly founded his system of graduated citizens' rights entirely on landownership, but at the same time his legislation acknowledged work as honourable. For him the whole question was pre-empted by the massive migration to the city, for the poor soil of Attica could not feed an idle population (Plutarch, *Solon* 22). This was why he decreed a certain status for skilled crafts, required his citizens not only to be active themselves but to bring up their sons to a craft, admitted foreigners to citizenship when they came to Athens with their whole families to follow a trade (Plutarch, *Solon* 24), and made it an offence to jeer at certain occupations.[46] Thus even though a prejudice persisted against manual work, and common opinion in Athens remained antibanausic, the principle was established that 'it was no disgrace to confess to poverty; disgrace was failing to escape from it by work'.[47] It is said that when Solon discussed the project of 'cancelling debts' with his friends, they hurried out and borrowed a lot of money which they spent on fine houses and landed property; this gives an idea of the Athenian tendency to speculation, even at this early date.[48] As time went on, barter and trading in every conceivable article became indispensable for Athens;[49] the city was one great emporium, increasingly so with the immense development of financial and money-lending business, manufacture employing huge numbers of slaves, and the Attic silver-mining industry. Without the very considerable income which could only be produced by trading and commerce, the Athenians would never have sustained their state expenditure. Solon's successor Peisistratus was also a ruler with utilitarian views, and resembled some other tyrants who set their faces against the antibanausic attitude, demanding that everyone should work, and actually seeking to destroy the agon.

As for agriculture, the first point to make is that the absolute *necessity* of work weighs heavily on a nation at an early stage of its history, in this respect quite unlike our own late civilization in the West. Hence Hesiod's complaint that the gods have hidden the means of life from mankind (*Works and Days* 42 ff.). Yet the same poet declares that peasant life is under special divine protection, is very honourable and has its own agon: 'When men compete in ploughing, planting and domestic order it is a sign of the benign *Eris* (strife); and work is no disgrace, but idleness is' (*ibid* 311 ff.). Agriculture was never quite deprived of its ancient letters patent. Even when the landowner had all the real work done by slaves, he had to be present, for otherwise his harvest would suffer. Thus the Spartans, and particularly Spartan women, were obliged to supervise their toiling helots in person; and from this, inevitably, there developed a similarity of living conditions for masters, slaves and free workers. This was no disqualification for full citizenship, and there was a particularly strong consciousness of the noble link between agriculture and courage in war; Euripides can still speak of 'those who till their own land' as the only true guardians of their country.[50] The day labourer (*thes*) was really regarded as inferior, and was scarcely better treated than a slave, just because he was compelled by circumstances to work, and perhaps the derogatory opinions about agriculture in fact apply to this class, not to the farmers. One frivolous little country town perhaps represents the unworthy exception; the Thespians are said to have considered it a disgrace to learn a trade or engage in farming.[51]

Some authors show clearly enough that agriculture had many attractions for the Greeks; in Xenophon's account, Socrates ranks it with war as an occupation worthy of a citizen, and goes on to explain how no other produces more splendid first fruits for the gods or richer festivals, how none is liked so much by slaves or is pleasanter for women and children.[52] But then we have Plato making use of the same Socrates to force the farmers down among the manual workers, excluded from leadership in his ideal state, and this at a time when the real Athenian state would have had good reason to thank the gods if the farmers had still kept a leading role in politics. It is a puzzle to know how the interpretation can have changed so much. Possibly Plato was thinking more of the general view of things, as actual field work was almost entirely done by slaves. It had certainly long been considered more distinguished to live only on income from land, to spend the time in horse breeding, hunting, philosophy and so on, and at most to combine these activities with the personal overseeing of one's estates. For Aristotle the right to citizenship is essentially linked with bearing arms, so of necessity he must rank the peasants somewhat higher than other manual workers. Yet, in those parts of the *Politics* where he expresses his ideal of the state, he reckons them with the masses, who are an indispensable element in the *polis*, but have no say compared with the counsellors and warriors, and whose members may not appear uninvited in the free popular assembly.[53] Evidently their occupation comes under the general heading of the banausic, defined as embracing all those things which would render the freeman physically, morally or intellectually unfit to practise the duties of a citizen, since all daily labour robs the mind of leisure and lofty aspirations.[54] Admittedly when he addresses himself to the real state of things rather than to his ideal, Aristotle himself says that if democracy *must* be, then an agricultural *demos* is the best.[55] Thus he concedes that the peasants are not quite negligible, and they might have amounted to something in reality; the great theorists ought to have had second and indeed third thoughts before they assigned them to the lowest place.

While the status of field workers declines steadily from Hesiod onwards, shepherds must have come in for a far more favourable judgment, otherwise they could hardly have become an important theme of bucolic poetry in the third century. Since their hard work was not seen or not recognized, while that of the peasants and slaves toiling in the fields was always conspicuous, the shepherds seem not to have been reckoned banausic, but were supposed to be living a life of uninterrupted leisure. Thus it was possible for the idealized figure of Daphnis to come into being at an early date, and Apollo, too, was a shepherd, but never a peasant; the herdsman and the god are noble idlers. Whether the shepherd was a slave or not is of little relevance here, because even if a slave he appeared to come and go freely without any strict control by overseers.

The general view of craftsmen and artisans was much less rosy, though in reality there was an extensive and lucrative craft industry, capable of producing skilled work of fine design. In their low esteem for these occupations the Greeks were at one with their contemporaries in antiquity.[56] But there is a great difference; in the advanced Oriental states, the caste system dispensed with the need to distinguish between manual workers and others, and in less advanced civilizations the demand for such crafts was slight, in so far as it existed at all apart from the work of the women and slaves of the house. Among the Greeks, consumer demand was great, and yet a generally contemptuous attitude prevailed, based on theory and with occasional practical consequences. The source of this contempt was a double one; working for money was looked down upon as illiberal (*aneleutheros*), and secondly, sedentary work performed in the shade and tending to deform the body was despised as 'banausic' in the narrower sense.[57] Thus in Athens, in spite of Solon's opinion that no-one should be reproached for the work he does, the public standing of the *banausoi* was low, as may be seen from the derisive listing of different kinds of craftsmen which Aristophanes permits himself.[58] The philosophers go much further; they are all agreed that manual workers represent an inferior species of men. Socrates himself really despised them, though he was always loitering in their shops, and to take one example, mortally offended Anytus, who then held high office, by advising him not to put his son to his own trade as a dyer.[59] Xenophon reports Socrates as saying that banausic occupations were harmful to the body because of the sitting position, the hours spent indoors and the heat of the furnace, and that through the softening of the body the mind too was weakened.[60] He thought this would show itself most clearly in case of enemy attack; if the fieldworkers and the craftsmen were asked separately whether the land should be fought for, or abandoned for the defence of the city walls alone, the peasants would all vote for defending the land while the others, because of their training, would want to sit still and not risk exertions and dangers. In his *polis* Plato keeps the craftsmen as well as the peasants remote from political activity, and represses them as underlings who yet have to pay taxes.[61] For Aristotle the paramount question is that of the right to citizenship, which is the real meaning of his *arete*; for him the true disqualification is working for wages.[62] Fundamentally he considers the *banausos* equivalent to the slave, except that the servitude of the first is limited and of the second unlimited, being determined by nature.[63] In his view all of them should be excluded from the *polis* as having no excellence. The extremes to which contempt could go, even for the most important services, if they were specialized and somehow involved practicalities, and how narrowly the bounds of liberal activity were drawn, can be seen most clearly in Plato's *Gorgias*, in the figure of Callicles.[64] Socrates reproaches him with despising the military master engineer and his science too, although the engineer's skill in defending whole cities equals that of the general, and his skill with fine phrases that of the orators themselves; Callicles is unwilling to give his daughter to this man's son or to take his daughter to wife. This may be compared with the important discussion in Plutarch where, in connection with Archimedes, the view is expressed that it is an actual disgrace for mathematics to lend itself to ends of practical importance.[65] Archimedes himself considers this to be banausic and Hieron has had to compel him to undertake this work.

It was certainly the case that a man could be an honoured citizen if he were a wealthy manufacturing capitalist employing trained slaves, while himself perhaps lacking precise knowledge and running his business by means of specialized overseers.[66] Thus Sophocles' father made weapons, like the father of Demosthenes, and Isocrates' father manufactured flutes. It is very characteristic that in the biographies of the sons there is invariably some debate as to whether such a man could really nevertheless rise to high rank. Had the fathers engaged in the work themselves, it was thought that the son of Sophilus[67] could not have become a general beside Pericles and Thucydides, nor could the son of Theodorus have been awarded the honour of a statue at Olympia. Thus in many towns these trades were chiefly left to those classes of the population who by reason of being unfree, or strangers, were not qualified for or called to civic activity. We find in Athens and other democracies that as time went on these occupations tended more and more to pass from the hands of citizens into those of the metics, who therefore came flooding into commercial centres from the furthest parts of Greece and the neighbouring countries. Many of the metics in Attica may have been Lydians, Phrygians, Syrians and Jews. Themistocles was the first to offer financial incentives to this class in order to attract them in numbers, though the metic was not allowed to own land, was subject to torture like the slaves, and could be sold as a slave if he failed to pay his taxes. Aristotle explicitly records that some *banausoi* were also citizens, but mentions too that banausic tasks had always been chiefly performed by slaves or foreigners (*Politics* 3.3). The overriding fact was that a banausic class was quite indispensable if only for the manufacture of weapons, the more so with the growing use of scientifically constructed catapults and so on; but also for every form of metalwork, which necessarily involved the despised furnace and anvil.[68] Thus it was that despite the old Athenian dictum about 'Landowning for citizens, manual work for the metics,'[69] a large number of immigrants who lived only by the skill of their hands were admitted directly to full citizenship in the time of Themistocles and even as early as that of Solon (Plutarch, *Solon* 24).

For a modest person like Antisthenes it was perfectly easy to make ends meet by banausic work. In his opinion no kind of work was too lowly to bring him in a living.[70] But others found it positive misery to be a *banausos*. In the pseudo-Platonic *Axiochus* the first speaker is one of these, bewailing that he is forced to work from daybreak to nightfall, and is still hardly able to earn a living; all his waking hours are filled with complaining and worrying.[71] However the penpushers chose to regard the lot of the *banausoi*, it is a certainty that in Athens, from Pericles' death onwards, craftsmen and manual workers rose from the lower orders of citizens to play a part in the *polis*, though lacking a liberal education in music and athletics. From that time onward they had their say in the popular assemblies and held office, and since they made no pretence of being better than the masses, it was much easier for them to deal with the populace than it was for the aristocrats.[72]

By chance the whole of representational art fell into the general category of *banausia*. To us latecomers, the art and poetry of the Greeks seem incontestably the highest and most marvellous of their achievements, and we naturally suppose the Greeks to have taken the same exalted view of art and artists. When we imagine the temples of their golden age, the dazzling statuary groups on the pediments, the halls full of monuments, the fine sacred paintings, we feel sure that the creators of such splendours must have been venerated almost as supernatural beings, that only to approach them must have been thought a privilege, and that it was an incomparable spiritual joy to learn something of their emotional world. The reality was quite different. The sculptors themselves were subject to the harshest antibanausic prejudices, and no sublimity of soul could redeem them from the fact that they earned their livelihood, and that they wielded the chisel or stood at the anvil.

In earlier centuries, that is the seventh and sixth, when the first notable master artists appeared, they were surrounded by an aura reflected from the holy places they adorned; oracles protected them, and they were still allowed to place their own likenesses beside or near their sacred works. Later masters were no longer religiously venerated in this way. Even in the *Iliad*, unfortunately, the artist among the gods was not only lame from his fall, but also depicted as physically deformed in the very way that was considered typical of the *banausos*; Hephaestus is a broad-chested giant with powerful shoulders, but with lame and feeble legs.[73]

As we have seen, the artists were regarded with the same contempt that was the lot of all who devoted their lives to a particular task, a speciality; the musicians and many poets were in the same case. It may sound very grand when the Greeks are praised as the people among whom, as far as possible, everyone cultivated his gifts, and lived in the pursuit of wholeness and not for one thing only; but we in posterity are bound to feel we owe more to some of their one-sided specialists than to those who hardly knew what to do with themselves for sheer harmonious *kalokagathia*, and most of all in the conditions of the real *polis* as it was after the Peloponnesian War, when they could scarcely find an appropriate role in which to make use of their 'excellence'. When this stage had been reached it might have been better to accord specialists the status they deserved.

It is true that the coherent statements of this attitude which survive belong to the period of the Roman Empire; but we cannot fail to recognize in Plutarch and Lucian the echo of an old Attic way of thinking for which these authors are so often our indispensable sources. The tone they use is, as we shall see, one in which ancient, widespread and universally accepted convictions are usually uttered. In the *Life of Pericles*, Plutarch prepares us at the outset for the fact that one might love the work of art and scorn the artist: 'We love scents and purple dyes, but regard the perfumer and the dyer as unfree and banausic.' This is said in reference to the over-thorough and as it were professional study of music, and reinforced with anecdotes from the fourth century. One tells how Antisthenes said of Ismenias: 'Must be a wretched fellow, or he couldn't play the flute so wonderfully!'; another how Philip of Macedon at a banquet reacted to his son's accomplished performance on the lyre by snarling at him: 'Aren't you ashamed to play so well?' This is followed by the notorious statement (c. 2):

'No youth of good birth, gazing on the Zeus at Olympia or the Hera of Argos, has ever wished to be Pheidias or Polycleitus, nor, when he was enjoying their poetry, to be Anacreon, Philemon, or Archilochus; even if the work gives pleasure, it does not necessarily follow that the master is worthy of emulation.'[74] Elsewhere Plutarch reveals yet another disadvantage artists are under:[75] 'Alcamenes and Nesiotes and Ictinus and all these *banausoi* and manual workers have forsworn oratory.'[76] It was indeed impossible for a master of plastic form to have the time and leisure to learn that art which in the decline of Greece was the precondition of all public achievement; quite conceivably the great artists on their side secretly felt a hearty contempt for that majority of orators and sycophants who used eloquence for unworthy ends.[77]

Many who held a low opinion of creative artists none the less desired the public honour of statues for themselves. The pretentious King Agesilaus on his deathbed goes so far as to disclaim any such wish: 'If I have achieved anything worthy it will be my monument; if not, I shall get no good from statues, which are anyway the work of lowly *banausoi*.'[78] So the whole of antiquity had to do without a portrait of King Agesilaus, though we get quite tired of the way he turns up at every crossroads of Greek history for decades on end.

Even at a time of flourishing and well-established connoisseurship in art, and when the highest prices were paid for antiques, writers treat art itself only as a craft.[79] In Lucian's *Dream* the whole attitude is expressed in a coherent way (c. 8–18). He had been bound apprentice to an uncle who was no more than a worthy stonemason and maker of herms, but 'Techne' appears to him in a dream and encourages him to higher things: 'Do not be ashamed because your body is shrunken and your clothing soiled, for Pheidias began in this way and yet created the Zeus, and Polycleitus made the Hera; Myron became famous and Praxiteles was admired, and now they are venerated like gods. Would you not also like to become celebrated among men so that your father is envied for begetting you?' However, 'Techne' could only say this with stammering and mistakes in speech, and then comes the vision and the advice of 'Paideia', that is of literary and rhetorical culture, which was then thought immeasurably superior to art: 'If you too are to be only a stonemason, you will always be a mere physical worker, unknown to fame, narrow in mind, little esteemed by friend or foe, one among the multitude; you will bow to the mighty and have to flatter those who can speak; you will live like a hare, the victim of the stronger. Even if you were to become a Pheidias or a Polycleitus and create miraculous works, of course everyone would praise your art, but nobody with any sense would wish to be in your shoes; for whatever your mastery you would still be considered a *banausos*, a manual labourer, one who must live by his work. Socrates, who was trained as a sculptor, abandoned that career to join me as soon as he was old enough to know better.' Paideia goes on to describe the two ways of life. On one hand is the man of eloquence and fine appearance, who is awarded praise, prizes, influence, office and fame, and is envied for his intelligence; on the other the unhappy creature in a dirty apron, slavelike, with his lever, chisel and drill, crouching in a corner over his work, bowed down and busy with trivialities, held down in every sense; with no hope of standing upright, or of a manly free decision – condemned to constant care that the statues turn out harmonious and well formed, but not able to care to become harmonious and noble himself, and therefore counting for less than the stones he carves.

Lucian paid heed; he became a travelling orator and later delivered this account of his dream to his countrymen in Samosata. He concluded by saying; 'And now I am at the very least no less famous than a sculptor!' Not much to boast of in the decadent state of art under the Antonines, and it was a very good thing he was not obliged to carve any statues of the gods. But the feeling for art that had been awakened in him has given us much important information and some vivid observation of the world of art in ancient times.

The contempt for artists characteristic of the most brilliant age in Greece was perhaps fortunate for art itself. Art was able to continue creating splendid works in perfect spontaneity as though the Peloponnesian War and the threat to the rest of life in Greece had not existed; art alone remained outside the general crisis, and sustained the ideality of the figures of the gods, while philosophy abandoned them and middle comedy dragged them down into its burlesque mire. There was another misfortune which art escaped only through the general scorn of artists: while tragedy, regarded as 'the ideal profession', attracted a swarm of amateurs, the 'thousand boys' mocked by Aristophanes, the visual arts were shunned by the dilettante, and only a strong inner vocation could have caused anyone to become a sculptor. For those sublime *banausoi* their preoccupation with gods and heroes no doubt gave deep joy and satisfaction, making up for the social stigma they met with from their 'harmoniously' developed countrymen.

On the other hand, when the magnificence of his work brought an artist fame and reputation in spite of prejudice, the Greek vice of envy could ruin him.[80] Pheidias died of poison in prison, and Menon, who denounced him, and whom he had brilliantly repudiated, received exemption from taxation as a reward, while the *strategoi* were required by popular demand to protect Menon's valuable person – a form of recognition which in fact the *polis* offered to other informers too.

A peculiar advantage that the great masters of sculpture had enjoyed from an early period, and one which seems a compensation for the disrespect shown to their profession, was that they were sent for to carry out important commissions in places far from their homes. Even if they had the status of metics for the time they spent in the foreign city, still that city had paid art the homage of calling in a non-citizen, perhaps one from a politically hostile state, although local talent would usually have been available. In the temple of Tyche at Thebes, where the goddess is shown carrying the infant Pluto on her arm, the head and hands were by Xenophon the Athenian, and the rest by the Theban artist Callistonicus.[81] A stronger motive than any antibanausic prejudice or dislike of employing a foreigner was the agon, that great fundamental force in all Greek life, acting here in the rivalry between cities, each determined to have a statue no less perfect than those which could be seen elsewhere. And as well as the artist the perfect stone was often transported too, so that Pentelic and Parian marble was cut and used for building in Boeotia, Arcadia and Phocis.[82] From mythical times builders too were at home everywhere they were needed, and Trophonius and Agamedes 'when they were grown, became famous by building temples for gods and kings' palaces for men'.[83]

To come back to the contempt in which artists were held, how did it happen that an exception was made for painters, who were not reckoned as *banausoi*? The fact is beyond doubt, if only because of the way the more successful painters dressed. Zeuxis appeared at Olympia in a robe which had his name in golden letters woven into the pattern. Parrhasius went further, wearing purple and gold with a garland of gold; he praised himself in verse as a child of Apollo, as the first among Greek artists, as the one who had attained the limits of art.[84] Besides, there were likenesses of painters, while the features of Polycleitus, Scopas and Praxiteles were not preserved, since of course statues of *banausoi* were not allowed to be displayed at places like Olympia; and Pheidias, apart from the charge of treason, was also accused of impiety for having smuggled his own portrait and that of

Pericles into the frieze of the Battle with the Amazons, on the shield of Athena in the Parthenon.[85] The reason for the painters' higher social position can only have been the general belief that their work was much less strenuous, and above all did not involve the fire and the anvil; their situation is similar to that of the shepherds in relation to the labourers in the fields [see p. 189 above]. Besides this they did their best to escape *banausia* by other means: as soon as they got enough money together they began to work for nothing, or to make gifts of their paintings – or, if they did not, it was later firmly stated that they had. Plutarch tells us even of Polygnotus that he was not one of the *banausoi*, and his works in the *stoa* were painted not for gain but in love and reverence for Athens (*Cimon* 4); he was rewarded with Athenian citizenship and, by order of the rulers of Delphi, in return for his paintings there, the right of being entertained at public expense in all Greek cities. Zeuxis (according to Pliny) gave his works away in later life, on the grounds that they were literally invaluable – his Alcmene to the Agrigentians, his Pan to King Archelaus. The fact that he charged an entrance fee for seeing his Helena did not make him a *banausos*, since this involved no physical labour and served to establish his fame. It was not accepting money that was banausic, but the need to earn.[86]

In time it even became possible to bring in drawing lessons as part of the education of freeborn boys.[87] This honour could never have been accorded to modelling or moulding.

The kind of work that incurred the most complete contempt was petty trading (*kapeleia*); the term denotes not only all purchases of raw materials and retail sales, but every transaction in which a price is asked for any kind of service, as for instance catering,[88] and of course all moneylending by bankers and moneychangers. Plato, in *Laws* (11.9b ff.) acknowledges that this class is absolutely indispensable, but explains that the individuals who compose it are contemptible because of their boundless greed and rapacity, which give them a bad name. He introduces the pedlars and innkeepers at an inn on a remote country road where the travellers are 'taken in' in both senses and plundered like enemies captured in war. Aristotle states that petty trading and barter deserve their bad reputation, for profit in these dealings is not right and proper but the consequence of cheating others (*Politics* 1.3). Usury above all is justly loathed, he says, for treating money not in its true function as a means of exchange but in order to accumulate it through interest.[89] Aristotle also scornfully lumps the market traders (*agoraioi*) together with the *banausoi* and day labourers; in his view, because they are always hanging about in the market and throughout the town, these people tend to come to the fore in popular assemblies, for which they certainly possessed the necessary vocal ability (*ibid.* 6.2).

What determined these judgments was evidently in part that these people tended to be dishonest, and in part the fact that they lacked ability for any other occupation. The special distaste felt for moneylenders may also be explained by the high rates of interest then charged, which amounted to usury; ten per cent was expected between friends, but rates of twenty-five, or indeed thirty-six, i.e. three per cent a month, were not uncommon and seem to have caused no remark.[90] In a vicious circle, the more they were despised the more despicably they behaved; anyone who had sunk so low was not fastidious about anything, and they were beyond improvement. Those who complained of being badly served might have told themselves that their own behaviour towards the trading class was such that no respectable person would have cared to take on these occupations. The outcome, and the darker aspect of this attitude, was that by the sixth century many people were not prepared to work for any price, and that, in total opposition to the true character of the Greeks, flatterers and parasites multiplied. The only way out, that is the asceticism of the (genuine) Cynics, was not attractive to most people in an age when expectations had become high.

It must be a source of perpetual astonishment to the modern northern temperament that, as far as we can see, these people lived without earning and apparently without any income. Where did they get the money even to buy their slaves? The whole of modern Europe, it seems to us, would soon be dying of hunger given such a way of life. The explanation is in the first place that moderation and frugality in all things were the general rule, though on occasion everyone gladly joined in drinking and feasting, and expected the really rich, such as Callias and his kin, to show their wealth. One habit that was absent was that of eating and drinking from pure boredom and apathy. They did not suffer from northern boredom and were not listless.

Life itself, and the spectacle it offered, counted for something – and still does in the south, here and there. Since there was no pressing hurry about anything, people could give themselves up to the particular scene, and to the wise and witty comments on it that some of the bystanders would make. Those who wanted a change from the agora and the Cerameicus went to Piraeus to look at the ships. Thus, even in the Roman period, all four of the speakers in Lucian's *Ship* have gone down to the Piraeus to see the free spectacle of an extraordinarily large ship which has anchored there, one of those which ferried corn from Egypt to Italy; the crowd of onlookers is so great that one of the friends gets lost in it.[91]

In all ages wealth was loved, and loved with passion; but not to the point where people would be easily tempted to earn it by any exertion considered vulgar. In theory if not in practice, what was valued in life would be sought in successful competition with others, but not in industrial competition. Even today there are certain limits on the activities a so-called 'cultivated' person is prepared to envisage; even one who has only completed a secondary-school education will not consent to be a road mender. But these limits are now enormously expanded; hard manual work does not exclude the kind of 'cultivation' which roughly corresponds to the Greek *kalokagathia*, and in our view, artistic pursuits ennoble the physical effort they entail. It was different in the time of Socrates, in whose circle the aristocratic *kalokagathia* had been replaced by the philosophical; he names leisure (*argia*) as the sister of freedom.

Among the other social changes noticeable in this period, the situation of women demands attention. They were excluded not only from the symposia, but from what was by far the most important aspect of Greek life, that is the agon [see p. 177 above]; they were not even allowed to look on at this highest activity; offering the victory at their feet, as in chivalry, was the last thing anyone would have thought of. But the agons were not only exhibitions of gymnastic skill but also of youth and beauty, and these were the guarantee of future civic greatness. In antiquity a connection was soon perceived between the agon and the occurrence of homosexual love, not yet apparent in Homeric times,[92] but more and more a constant feature of Greek life from the period of the agon; it seems indeed positively innate in the Greek spirit, and takes on an ideal aspect. A contributing factor must be the admiration of man for youth and of boy for man, which the agon encouraged; in gymnasia the statue of Eros was to be seen between Hermes and Heracles; in war too the relationship was held to be of value.[93] Still the matter has a darker and more mysterious side; for instance it assumes a special quality that varies with the region (Crete, Sparta, Elis, Boeotia), that is it has gained the status of a general custom.[94] The only governments which proscribed homosexuality and also gymnastics seem to have been those of the tyrants, who feared that conspiracies might arise in these circles;[95] in other states there was generally no penalty. Athens only punished rape, and forebade male prostitutes to appear in public; disgrace set in only where violence or venality were involved.[96]

At the same time, marital and extramarital relations with women went on with no perceptible diminution. Marriage was just as important for the *polis* as ever before, for it was only from true marriage that the true citizen could be born, but all the heart seems to have gone out of it; frivolous and jeering remarks about women become more and more frequent.[97]

Even the shade of Agamemnon in the *Odyssey* has some bitter things to say; but the two versions of the Pandora story, which were probably not interpolated in the Hesiodic epics until this period, provide a clear case of the same attitude symbolized in mythical form.[98] That of Theognis has it that all women are descended from Pandora, and the image of the drones in the beehive is used for them. In *Works and Days* Pandora's mission is presented still more circumstantially as the vengeance of Zeus on mankind because Prometheus had brought them fire; the name Pandora first occurs here, and is explained by this creation of Hephaestus having been endowed with gifts by all the gods 'for a curse on industrious men'. We also have an iambic poem from the seventh century by Semonides of Amorgos; it is a contemplative work, extremely harsh in tone, dating of course from a time when iambics were habitually used for unsparing attacks. A century later Phocylides still echoes the bitter verdict on women.[99]

Not only in heroic myth, but also in popular legend and in the tales of the founding of cities far and wide – those later used for instance by Parthenius as material for short novels – all trace of feminine gentleness is excluded; the dominant traits are heartless rapacity and violence. Here we see kings' daughters hellbent on the satisfaction of their lust, making all the advances (often very shamelessly), and in the course of time sending off their sons to the father with some secret sign by which he will be recognized. A particular archetype becomes widespread; we might call it the Tarpeia plot.[100] This is where the woman, in love with an enemy, commits the worst crime then possible, which is betrayal of the *polis*, her own city. The story of the founding of Lesbos includes the account, handed on by Parthenius, of Peisidike, princess of Methymna. From the walls of her city, which is bravely resisting a siege led by Achilles, Peisidike sees him and falls in love with him. She sends her nurse with a message to promise him the city's surrender on condition that he marries her. The traitress draws the bolts of the gate and looks on while her parents are murdered and the women dragged away to the ships; but her deed disgusts

Achilles and she is stoned to death by his men.[101] Generally speaking the stories tend to demonstrate the conviction that terrible events are women's doing. Denunciations which result in the man's death play an important part here; it could be said that just as in the Middle Ages the rule was a romantic idealization of the female as an angel, here it is a romantically ruthless image of implacability. And where these legends and foundation myths left off, tragedy later continued in the same vein.

While poetry and legend mainly give this sombre picture of the female personality, the Greek attitude towards women varied from one place to another. Their status was lowest in Ionia (where Lydian influence was perhaps the explanation for the restrictions on their lives) and in Athens. Here women were confined to the house, and their education was limited to what was necessary for domestic matters; this must have been the result of the exceptional development of the *polis*, which privileged public affairs. Other communities had other attitudes. The Peloponnese presents a varied picture; in Corinth, with its extensive prostitution, women were little respected, while in Lacedaemon, where the Spartan women had to look after the farms, their status was of course higher. There the girls were actually brought up to the agon, and were allowed to compete in sports, probably not with the sole aim of ensuring their fitness to bear children. Similarly in Elis; on the banks of the Alpheus (perhaps in Arcadia) a beauty contest for women was held at the celebrations of the Eleusinian Demeter, and the contestants were given the title of gold bearers (*chrysophoroi*);[102] there were also competitions in the moral virtues and in housekeeping skills.[103] Aeolian communities come out particularly well in their attitude to women. There is an epitaph of Simonides of Chios on a powerful huntress of Boeotian Thessaly called Lycas, 'whose bones still make the wild beasts tremble'; such a model could not have existed in Ionia but might still be accepted in Boeotia (Bergk, *frag.* 130). In Aeolian communities, there are women poets as well as men; at the end of the sixth or beginning of the fifth century the young Pindar encountered Myrtis and Corinna as his rivals at the public agon and was once beaten to the prize by Corinna. Lesbos, a hundred years earlier, was the home of the lyric poet Sappho and her friends Damophila and Erinna, among whom, even if they composed no choral odes, some rivalry must naturally have arisen, not very different from the relationship in the musical agon;[104] beauty contests were also held on Lesbos and Tenedos.

Wherever women were oppressed the hetaerae predictably gained in importance. Women who were bought and sold had been available in large numbers from time immemorial; the rise of slavery meant that they passed rapidly from hand to hand, and slave girls were frequently presented to temples. Corinth was widely famed for its rapacious temple prostitutes, and in fact their trade was taxed as an important branch of industry. In Athens too there were public institutions of this kind, originally founded by Solon, who built a temple to Aphrodite Pandemos from the proceeds. The important question for us is who was the first individual woman to become famous in this profession, and as far as we know (since we cannot tell how early the fame of, for instance, various Milesian women began) this was probably Rhodopis, whether or not Herodotus[105] is right in what he says of her or, as Athenaeus maintains,[106] he has confused her with Doricha of Naucratis. Perhaps no single detail about Rhodopis is safely established. A native of Thrace, she is said to have been a fellow slave with Aesop, who flourished about 580; still a slave, she was brought to Naucratis in Egypt to practise her trade and then purchased and freed by Charaxus, the brother of Sappho. As a freedwoman she amassed so much wealth that the Greek imagination credited her with having built the pyramids of Mycerinus. Rich and independent, she conceived the great ambition of leaving a monument to herself in Greece. She dedicated a tithe of her earnings in the form of a large bundle of iron roasting-spits for whole oxen, and instead of offering them at some temple of Aphrodite she sent them to Delphi, where they were still to be found in the time of Herodotus, behind the altar of the Chians, opposite the temple.[107] After Rhodopis had achieved her aim of becoming so famous that her name was known to everyone in Greece, it was the turn of Archedike, also from Naucratis, where as Herodotus tells us the hetaerae were very talented. She too was praised in poetry (*aoidimos*) and was famed everywhere; but the 'club-gossip' was less concerned with her than with Rhodopis, that is she was less highly rated by connoisseurs[108] – here Herodotus no doubt conveys a distinct nuance of public interest. Others who achieved fame were Leaina, the mistress of Harmodius, and Nanno, the flute-girl of Mimnermus. It is clear that the reputations of these hetaerae rested on their wit and conversation; women who were merely physically attractive were too common to become famous. Perhaps even in those days Greek men found in the hetaerae a compensation for the intelligent society that they neither expected nor found in marriage.

The social life of the time had changed since the heroic period, and was no longer confined to royal courts and military encampments; wherever people gathered together in the Greek world it formed a great part of their enjoyment of life. The symposium was the basis of social life from early times, but it was a very different institution from one stage of Greek development to another. The brusque, sober conviviality of the Spartans at their *syssitia*, with its artificial insistence on moderation and ridicule of others, was capable of any amount of laconism but not of spontaneity, nor of poetry. This was the principal lack in Spartan culture; the *syssition* was not a symposium, and like everything else in Sparta it essentially lacked freedom. By contrast, it was the *free* Hellenic custom to have all kinds of parties on no particular pretext, quite apart from those of a public nature, which might be banquets on political or religious occasions, and family feasts like weddings, celebrations of the naming of a child or of a victory at the agon and so on. The *eranos* (or communal picnic) is very ancient too, occurring in Homer and in Hesiod, and clearly represents an additional degree of freedom;[109] for whether those invited paid their contribution in money (as was often done later) or brought it with them in a basket, they incurred no obligation to anyone in either case.[110] The *eranos* made it possible for anyone, not only the rich, to offer hospitality, and so represented a form of equality. But even when someone sent invitations to a symposium in his own house, there was no order of precedence by rank (at least in pre-Roman times) and although, as a rule, the invitation was sent early enough for the guests to dress appropriately,[111] it was all so informal that they were free to bring others who were not invited.[112] This is conceivable only if the whole point of the thing was the conversation, outweighing all other enjoyments.

The procedure at the symposium was a simple one. In Plutarch's *Banquet of the Seven Wise Men*, for instance, a late re-creation of the customs of a very distant age, the dining tables are removed at the end of the meal and crowns are handed to the guests. Then wine, undiluted, is poured as a libation, and the flute-girl plays briefly; when she has left the company, drinking and conversation begin at the newly arranged tables.[113] Wine is the high point of the feast, and is spoken of, even in the *Odyssey*, with a reverence that has no parallel in our age [cf. p. 147 above]; it was usually very much diluted with water, either because it was very strong[114] or because the Greeks seldom drank, and were quickly affected, and the feasts were supposed to go on for many hours.[115] Zaleucus in his laws is said to have forbidden the use of unmixed wine on pain of death. Beer was only good enough for Egyptians, brandy did not as yet exist. It was the charming custom to drink wearing crowns, for the symposium took place in honour of a god. This religious element required the guests to be crowned, and Apollo's laurel or the ivy of Bacchus symbolized a lofty shared dedication.[116] In the earlier period it was usual to sit at table, allegedly because the gods were believed to be present;[117] but in the time of the agon it became normal to recline, which had the advantage that, since all present lay facing towards the middle, conversation was general.[118]

The symposium, then, was the source of a kind of conversation whose importance to the Greeks is clear from the delight with which they speak of it. Long before, Hesiod had said in his *Melampodia*: 'The sweetest thing of all is the delight of conversation at table and at splendid feasts, when eating is over' (Athenaeus 2.13). There is similar praise in the sympotic elegy as we know it from surviving poems by Theognis and Xenophanes, and in figurative art too. The oldest works of art (vase paintings, grave decorations, the reliefs of Assos) show banquets as their favourite subjects, and even if they are sometimes meant to be the banquets of the dead, these are only the sublime reflection of those on earth. What did they talk about? We only know that it was universally believed that the symposium was the greatest of all pleasures. Wit, humour, argument, malice and affection all had their place.[119] 'In winter-time,' says Xenophanes, 'men should lie on soft couches near the fire on the hearth, having eaten well, drinking sweet wine and nibbling dried peas, and talking together: "Who are you and where do you come from? How old are you, good friend? How old were you when the Mede came to our land?" (i.e. Harpagus, the messenger of Cyrus).'[120] We are free to imagine how the pleasant evening would go on. It is certain the symposium was also the home of political discussion; the state and all its affairs were talked over by people of exceptional wit and sense.[121] Those of opposing parties are hardly likely to have been invited together; perhaps this may have been the origin of the institution of the *hetaireia*.[122] [see p. 275 below]. It was a matter of good form to show tact and tolerance to those who could not go on drinking, or could not keep awake – this is clear from an important passage in Theognis;[123] at the same time we must remember that in society a general frankness was accepted which would now be thought extremely indiscreet.[124] Besides conversations on the agora, those at the symposia represent a second aspect of a specifically Greek style of life, and how much they were treasured can be seen from the lament used of someone who died: 'For him there is no more feasting and no more music.'[125]

I return to the irresistible story that Herodotus tells of the wooing of Agariste, daughter of Cleisthenes,[126] because it allows us to make a number of deductions about social life in Athens. Agariste had eleven suitors, among whom the two Athenians, Hippocleides son of Tisandrus, and Megacles son of Alcmaeon, had made the best impression after lengthy inquiries; of the two, Hippocleides was preferred both on personal grounds and because he was descended from the Corinthian Cypselids. On the day of the decision, when there was competition at the banquet in music and in conversation, Hippocleides was easily ahead of the rest until he went too far and fell out of favour with Cleisthenes. He not only danced the Emmeleia but got up on a table to perform other Attic and Spartan dances, and at last actually stood on his head and waved his feet in the air. This was too much for the tyrant, who called out: 'Son of Tisandrus, you have danced away your wedding!' and received the reply: 'Hippocleides doesn't care.' In this case the Athenian aristocrat had of course exceeded the bounds of noble dignity, which allowed the display of gymnastic and musical skills, but only in restricted forms. In Athens it was the aim to amuse oneself and other people and to go in for everything that was found entertaining. The Athenian who knew Spartan and Attic dances, and could even dance like a tumbler, while in other places only the local dances were known, is a prototype of the later Athenian versatility. Even if he did forfeit a good match by showing off, the Athenian could take it lightly, not only out of frivolity but because, in living life to the full, he was sure to find many other ways to console himself. In the end, though, it was to an Athenian that Cleisthenes gave his daughter in marriage.[127]

Athens in that age deserves to be dwelt on a little longer. Plutarch's account of developments there in the seventh and sixth centuries, though it may be distorted and tendentious, gives a better idea of the inner life of the people than we have of any other nation; consciousness and reason do not exist elsewhere to the same degree.[128] When Solon, to take one example, finds the golden mean (*meson*) between the various predominating interests, he reveals a profound and many-sided social culture. A glance at his poems shows an extraordinarily lucid reflective power directed to every aspect of the world.[129] All in all, he not only makes by far the most outstanding impression of all the Seven Sages, with Thales the nearest to equalling him, but in his special consciousness as an Athenian he seems the incarnation of his city's finest qualities.[130]

To complete the outline of Athenian society, the assumptions which underlie the dialogue between Solon and Croesus in Herodotus (1.30 ff.) are very telling. The patriarch Tellus is an authentically Attic figure, who even had the good fortune to die in battle while leading the Athenians to victory; while the Argive story of Cleobis and Biton exhibits more the far-ranging general nature of the Herodotean world-view. Other important elements are the religious awe which caused the people to see visions after the murder of Cylon's followers, and led to the summoning of Epimenides (Plutarch, *Solon* 12); and, in a different way, what is said of the early Athenian love of jewellery and of high living in the Ionian style.[131] The Panathenaia, which must already have been famous even in Italy [see p. 181 above] were, after 566, no longer limited to chariot racing, but now included a gymnastic agon, while the Eleusinian games had grown to the point where all Hellas revered them and everyone wanted to visit them. Peisistratus and his sons demonstrated their ambition to make Athens a rich trading city; it is clear they also aimed at intellectual supremacy, at a time when the Ionian cities were already falling to the Lydian and Persian kings. There is evidence of this in the collection and editing of the poems of Homer, though opinions differ on who was responsible, most sources naming Peisistratus or Hipparchus, while Diogenes Laertius gives the credit to Solon. Books are also said to have been available for public use – that is, a very early public library was set up, which tells us, first, that there was already a need for a repository of written documents, and secondly that a public existed who wanted to read, to which Peisistratus responded.[132] It is characteristic in quite another way that after Daedalus not one Athenian artist can be named with certainty until the end of the Peisistratid period, a fact that cannot be entirely explained by the destruction of Athens in the Persian War. Even if nothing were known of them but their names, the Athenian love of fame would not have allowed those names to be forgotten.

In this period, *celebrities* gradually begin to appear; people, that is, whose names were known all over the Greek world, and who began to put the victors at the agon in the shade. These were first the tyrants, then poets and artists and later, particularly, the founders of weird cults, and the Seven Sages. Most of them have been mentioned in other connections; they were characteristic of a time when mere weight of numbers was not yet the dominant factor, and when powerful individuality was still felt to be important. A most remarkable aspect, and one that should not be taken for granted, is the increasing fame of artists' names; it can only be explained by the rise of individualism and individual celebrity. It can always be assumed that if the artist's name was known he had inscribed it, or indeed added his own portrait to a dedication or statue; thus when Theodorus of Samos, who cut the jewel for the ring of Polycrates, is referred to as the first gem-cutter 'whose name has come down to us', this surely means that he himself took care it should do so, though gem-cutting had probably been practised for half a millennium or more. The reputation of sages usually coincides with and results from a shortage of influential priests. Among the Greeks there were first those fantastic intermediary figures, purifiers and miracle-workers, referred to above as the founders of strange cults, and Epimenides certainly had a great vogue in Athens. Although what we know of the Seven Wise Men is chronologically confusing, it is a fact that about 600 B.C. certain revered figures became famous as Wise Men.[133] It is not clear how early and on what authority their sayings (*apophthegmata*) were composed, but they were believed by the Greeks to have been often uttered or repeated at some gathering by these wise men. It is not possible to establish by what consensus they were accepted by the temple at Delphi nor in what social sphere these seven reputations arose – to start with they were all of widely varying types. But to be called 'a Sage' (*sophos*) the man must have been directly designated by the god in an age when the Delphic oracle was consulted on all matters, and the accompanying words indicated that no-one was wiser, or that this was the wisest of men.[134] These sages were given splendid burials by their native cities; in the case of Bias, the people of Priene dedicated a sanctuary to him, the so-called Teutameion, and paid him heroic honours.[135]

Now *individuality* as such emerged, and it was this development that made the Greeks a nation different from any other. At the same period, when personal fame selected individuals from the mass, it was soon possible for one of them to triumph over another without any victory in the agon or similar formal advantage. Wit and sardonic malice began to exert an influence they had never previously had. Mockery was nothing new; abusive speeches at festivals, especially the Dionysia, but also at the Eleusinia, were an ancient ritual, and even in myth the maid Iambe jeers at the mourning Demeter. But now the Greeks discovered that verbal abuse, which obviously had always existed, was capable of a *style*, and developed it in poetry and in the sociable frame of the symposium. Archilochus is a key figure here, with his 'impartial abuse of friend and foe', and his elaboration of the iambic metre to its full power for his slanders. In person he was unpleasant and unfortunate in every way and himself laid claim to the worst possible character; and Hipponax, whose own ugliness embittered him, seems to have had a very similar temperament (Aelian, *Varia Historia* 10.13). But besides these principal satirists, who achieved a name through their enormous gift for bitterness, more noble natures also went in for direct abuse, as witness Alcaeus' attacks on Pittacus. The epigram took a long time to emerge as the regular vehicle of wit, though there is one biting epigram by Alcaeus;[136] those of Simonides are all sepulchral, monumental and dedicatory, with the exception of the last, and are also rather more jests than witticisms.

It was in this period that the figure of Margites was elaborated, though the version in which it later existed was supposed to be the work of the same Pigres to whom a most charming parody is attributed – the *Battle of the Frogs and Mice*. The character of Margites was used in a collection of sketches and anecdotes, probably built up gradually from jokes exchanged at symposia and so on. The hero is no ordinary bumpkin, but one who interferes in everything and thus draws attention to himself. He is a rich mother's darling who has received some education, but is incompetent at everything and misunderstands all the many things he knows about. So he is a proverbial ass, ignorant of the simplest matters and literally unable to count beyond five; the Greek love of smutty humour makes him ridiculous by combining foolishness with sexual situations. It is out of the question that this should be a parody of Homer, and the fact that it was seriously taken to be Homeric gives us an idea of the quality of Greek criticism. Fictions of this kind arose in a phase of national development when people thought themselves immensely clever and wanted a butt for their feeling of superiority.[137]

In Sparta, Laconism became the fashion; it was really only a way of expressing truths in the most concise form, but naturally tended towards wit; the give and take of teasing mockery at the Spartan *syssitia* was a sort of training for it.[138] The derisive jokes made in some *poleis* about other towns belong to this period too.[139]

The seventh and sixth centuries also saw the blossoming of the so-called animal-fable (*ainos, muthos, logos*). It was a kind of story that had certainly been long current among the Greeks, and some fables are of proven antiquity, like the one told in Hesiod's *Works and Days* (202 ff.) of the 'Hawk and the Nightingale'. Not only have some by Archilochus and Stesichorus survived from this period, but Aesop, whose historical existence is a certainty, seems to have flourished about 580, so the age was one of gifted

and active fabulists. It is worth asking why this was so; for the choice of
fables and parables to convey general truths and observations can no longer
have answered a need by the time we are speaking of. It had long been the
case, certainly as early as Hesiod, that all direct reflection was from life;
the Greeks simply seemed to be late in taking to the fable, while among
the Arabs, for instance, Lokman 'the Wise' passed for a contemporary of
Solomon.[140] I am inclined to believe that the question can be answered by
reference to the great increase in the slave population at that time; and
Aesop, historical personage though he was, would be the living symbol of
this fact. What I imagine is that the foreign slave in a Greek household, as
soon as he could speak a little stumbling Greek, would tell the children
simple and primitive versions of the fables that had long existed in his
oriental or Libyan homeland. They must have made a strong impression
on Greek hearers, for the wisdom of these stories was common to all
peoples. Perhaps they revealed a quite unknown world beside the myths
of gods and heroes; the Greeks took pleasure in it and increased the value
of this treasury they had been given, as a truly wealthy nation becomes
richer by accepting what they can from others and developing it further.

Aesop himself is identified sometimes as a Thracian, sometimes a Phrygian or an Ethiopian. He is said to have been a fellow slave of Rhodopis on
Samos, to have served Croesus and finally to have been hurled into an
abyss by the people of Delphi. The Greeks did not think of him as the only
teller of fables; late writers on rhetoric such as Hermogenes, Aphthonius,
and Theon mention Cypriot, Egyptian, and Sybaritic fables besides his,[141]
and distinguish, too, those of other lands from which most slaves came to
Greece – Phrygia, Caria, Cilicia and Libya.[142] However, not all the fables
known to the Greeks were taken from the general stock; some were specifically Greek, including a few composed for a particular time and place with
didactic intent, like the one Stesichorus himself made use of, when he
warned the Himerans against Phalaris with his story of the horse which
consented to be ridden by men in order to get its revenge on the stag. The
speakers in fables are not only animals, but people with animals or just
people, sometimes also trees and plants;[143] in one, a dish berates a woman
for dropping it.[144] In fact gnomic wisdom, moral attitudes, political topi-
cality, humour and wit assume any form desired.

Apart from the pleasure they gave to grown-ups,[145] the fables were
meant to introduce children to a knowledge of the way of the world.[146]
Nothing, alas, survives of the delightful tales the slaves must have told

them, because the classical spirit rejected such things. For there undoubtedly were children's stories, simply told to amuse, not meant to impart a lesson, alongside the didactic fables.[147] For instance, the mother of Cleobulus the Wise is said to have made up a story about the moon for his little brother. The moon asked her mother to weave a little dress to fit her because she felt so cold; but her mother replied: 'How can I make it to fit? – today you are at the full, soon you'll be a half-moon and after that just a sickle.'

The great flowering of fable coincides with the beginnings of the Ionian school, which, though essentially concerned with enquiry into nature, also prepared the way for philosophical reflection. Political and sociopolitical argument came early, in the sixth century, with Solon and then Theognis, while moral consciousness appears in its full maturity in the great lyric poets of the eighth to the sixth centuries; in their work we find a sweetness of emotion that was not later surpassed. But while poetry had thus already reached some of its full splendour and was quietly developing in many new directions, visual art had not yet broken out of its shell or learned to give expression to the human soul. When Sappho saw Aphrodite enthroned in glory and her immortal smiling countenance, the smile she saw must have been different from the rigid one that sculpture depicted in her time. Still, it was a great advantage for the visual arts that their first task, before ever they came to represent the power of the spirit, was to show physical vitality in the form of the athletes' statues. So the difficult beginnings were already overcome before they faced the challenge of spiritual beauty and the inner forces – a kind of good fortune that the art of later periods had to seek by roundabout ways.[148]

We shall deal briefly with the state of religion in the period. The era of the agon was also the time when *Delphi* flourished most. Herodotus often reports visits to the place by barbarians and Greeks, whether for predictions of the near future, instruction on religion, or advice on the foundation of colonies. The authorities at Delphi were the medium of a peculiar compromise between inspiration and reflection.[149] As for their national function, we must note that nobody was *obliged* to go to Delphi; even consultation on colonial questions was a *free* custom; Delphi was a power which was only valid to the extent that was desired, but prized as a repository of information, as the centre of Greek knowledge about the world. *How* the pronouncements were arrived at was something people in that age (perhaps deliberately) refrained from worrying about; the very strong belief in the existence of the oracle allowed no doubt to arise, and as it was generally accepted that Delphi gave good advice, there was no reason to make difficulties.

At this time there was a marked revival of the cult of Dionysus, with its immense celebrations and mysteries, though almost no firm dates can be given for this.[150] At least the festivals in honour of this god, if not the temple rites, must now have overtaken all others in size and splendour; his cult would not otherwise have occasioned the huge ceremonies, for instance in Athens, which led to the birth of drama; though in fact the drama is a subordination of the Dionysian impulse to the discipline of a formal principle that might very well be called Apollinian. Dionysus even finds his way, as Iacchus, into the Eleusinian mysteries, although it might be thought that Koré would have sufficed for their symbolic needs;[151] most likely the decision was taken to regulate and assimilate this element, which it was impossible to exclude. There was no escaping Dionysus, and in the guise of his Thyiads he pursued Apollo to the very summit of Parnassus.

A group of Apollonian men form a contrast to this Dionysian movement; they were eccentric holy men, such as Epimenides, Abaris and Aristeas, whose counterparts were in turn the Dionysian followers of Orpheus. A remarkable stage of transition seems to be personified in these forerunners of philosophy. It was, as we have said, in Ionia that the beginnings of true *philosophy* soon developed, as did full *individualism*. The question is how far Thales, Bias and others became self-aware, and to what extent this beginning was already combined with rejection of belief in the gods, myth and Homer. Certainly these men left the gods out of their statements about the world; but they did not as yet withdraw from the State, as Heraclitus withdrew from Ephesus a hundred years later.

Finally, the importance of Pythagoras must be acknowledged. It was with good reason that he abandoned Ionia and Greece itself for southern Italy, the scene of his work and influence.[152] We must regret that Herodotus left not even half a page about him, only a single enigmatic remark; but one thing seems certain: he inspired thousands of followers to share an active communal life.[153] For instance the tradition that his disciples shared all property in common cannot have been merely invented by those of a later time, even if, as with the Early Christians, this was only an experiment tried once. It was not universal popular communism that was attempted, but mutual help and sharing among the initiates,[154] as the true expression of the sincerest loyalty.[155] A communal life came into being, and it is entirely credible that these friends built a huge auditorium in Croton. It is probable that a powerful personality full of conviction, like this 'long-haired man from Samos', must have made an immense impression on the inhabitants of these towns of Greater Greece, talented, and longing for education, who felt that they were suffocating in their own prosperity. The single element of his doctrine that was likely to have popular appeal was that of the transmigration of souls; it must have been the source of great excitement. His inner strength was the religious and ethical system he based on this belief; with a breadth of learning that was extraordinary for the time, an outstanding gift for communication and a striking personality, he felt he could be all things to all men, and his status in both spiritual and worldly respects must have been that of a prince.[156]

We do not know whether he intended to counteract the Dionysian excess then raging throughout the Greek world, and that later became notorious in southern Italy as the cult of Liber and Libera and of Bacchanalian orgies; the women followers of Pythagoras at a later time still practised simplicity and purity. At least in *one* way he was at odds with the current attitude, for his warning to everybody was 'to beware ambition and love of fame, which cause the worst envy, and to avoid going among crowds'[157] – as much as to say: 'Away with the agon, or it will dominate the whole of life!'

In contrast and in opposition to him was the whole of the *polis* as it developed in Greater Greece. Inevitably it became jealous, since all his adherents, but particularly the inner core of disciples, dissociated themselves from their fellow citizens by proclaiming the ascetic way of life against colonial affluence, rather as Savonarola's followers did from the rest of the Florentines. We should also remember the mysterious symbolical utterance of the Pythagoreans, and think of the natural contrast between the spiritually potent leader and the great mass of the people, even if in each town this mass only consisted of the thousand wealthiest, to understand the hatred of the unconverted, which brought about the fall of the sect in Croton and Metapontum. Yet Pythagoreanism lived on. As late as the fourth century it found expression in the conspiracy of Damon and Pythias against Dionysius the Younger.[158]

The condition of Greece in general, when we look back on it, gives the impression of being still restricted in a way that worked for its happiness, but this is only because our information is scanty. In reality there was already a great deal of freedom; but in this period the spoken word, the gossip, is not preserved for us as it will be later, and so the time seems one in which creative action predominates. For instance, we still know little or nothing of the political thinking of the Greeks; but in actual fact we can see hundreds of real colonies, that is of *poleis*, coming to birth. The discussion of rights must certainly have entailed mature political argument, and timocracy as the most widespread system did not come into being overnight. It was the period of the so-called lawgivers, the authors of constitutions, known to us in almost every case only by a few lines of what they wrote. Solon, the one we know most about, was still strong enough to declare ownership of land the basis of the right to citizenship, and in this he was probably already swimming against the current.

The most enviable feature of the age, though, was the rarity of wars among the Hellenes. Apart from the expansion of Sparta into Messene, Arcadia and Argolis and perhaps the fighting in Euboea, a few raids in the name of the Delphic Apollo and some fierce battles in Ionia, there were hardly any wars to speak of; restless elements were absorbed by colonization, and the Greeks were not yet preying on each other. Synoecisms, carried out by force with the aim of accumulating power, were still in the future; so were the city-hegemonies, like Thebes, which would encourage the destruction of those who resisted them, and the annihilation of cities by a stronger *polis* in order to clear their own neighbourhood of Spartan allies, as Argos, after the Persian Wars, annihilated Mycenae and Tiryns. This time, though, was infinitely rich in beauty: the visual arts were preparing for greatness, and poetry was already splendidly mature.

IV

The Fifth Century

THE FIFTH CENTURY began brilliantly for the Greeks, but ended sadly. Geographically it was the time of the greatest expansion of the Hellenic world before Alexander. The colonies were almost all still flourishing; not till well into the second half of the century, from the 430s onward, did the cities of southern Italy begin to suffer from the inroads of the Lucanians and the Bruttians. This was counterbalanced by the retaking of Ionia from the Persians; we do not know how far they had affected Greek influence on life there. For the Greeks, the extension of their culture was a source of pride.

The most important factor was the effect on national consciousness of the battles of Marathon, Salamis, Himera, Plataea and Mycale, in which the Greeks were victorious over a world-monarchy and the powerful trading republics of the Phoenicians.

The rise of world-monarchies capable of crushing even the most efficient of single states tends to occur when a society which has developed strong institutions at an early date organizes itself at some major turning point as a military state under a powerful dynasty, or with the help of religion, and overruns neighbouring peoples who may be more or less civilized than itself. National and regal pride then demands the heaping up of treasures in a palace,[1] the herding of hundreds of thousands of slaves for building work, and the exemption of the ruling people from taxation. Since conquest has defined their identity, it is impossible for the invaders to remain idle; they go on to subdue other vigorous primitive peoples, not for plunder but to force them to serve in their armies, as Cyrus did the Massagetae and Darius the Scythians, in order to make further conquests possible; seafaring peoples must also be defeated for the sake of seizing their fleets. The internal organization of such powers is rudimentary; in essence the world-monarchy remains barbaric, that is to say its culture is arrested at the stage in which it came into being. It must contend with continual resistance and be always reconquering its foreign possessions, such as Egypt; but it is still evil and dangerous even in decline; despotic government with its brutal methods and contempt for morality is its permanent feature.

The specific dangers that confronted the Greeks in their struggle with this form of power were of several kinds. First, some Greeks had already been defeated and had to provide levies to fight their compatriots. Then there were high-ranking Greek refugees living at the Persian court; the exiled King Demaratus of Sparta, for instance, won favour with Xerxes by helping to persuade Darius that he should succeed to the throne. In Greece every kind of bribery was offered to individuals, and Greek exiles were welcomed and richly rewarded. Finally, desperate cities and parties in Greece joined Persia, like Cleisthenes and his followers when they were threatened by Sparta; in 490 the herald of Darius was immediately offered earth and water by the Aeginetans, because they wanted to make war on Athens with Persian help (Herodotus 5.73, 6.49). While all these signals were being sent out to Persia, the Persian administration in Ionia was ingratiating itself there; Mardonius, who had been given command by land and sea after the ill-fated Ionian revolt, tried clemency. Taxes were not increased, and the discredited tyrants were replaced by the granting of democracies to the cities, a masterstroke which shows how well the Persian governor knew the Greeks. The land enjoyed the usual advantages of Persia's subjects, law and order were secured, and prosperity could be expected to return to Ionia.

In these conditions the Persian Wars began. We must wish that even one non-Athenian account of them had survived, one not distorted by self-glorification. As it is, we have to make do with history that has been tidied up, rearranged and embellished with legends, and view the events with this reservation in mind.[2] The war began in 490 with the expedition of Datis and Artaphernes and their defeat at Marathon, which only postponed the encounter; ten years later a great avalanche of men, reputed to number 1,700,000, marched against Greece.[3] It was a senseless and ill-organized horde; the various tribes retained their preferred national weapons and their native leaders, though these were not considered officers but slaves, since the nominal commanders were all Achaemenids, connected by birth or marriage to the king. With more decisiveness or more insight the Persian monarchy might have sent perhaps a tenth of the number of troops, trained together and properly prepared to fight Greeks. It was only after Salamis that Mardonius was allowed to select the men he wanted and lead a rational campaign with, it seems, 300,000 men. Yet at Plataea the battle depended on the Persians; the other national contingents fled without striking a blow as soon as they saw the Persians scatter.

An interesting question is what would have happened if Xerxes had won; he had not hesitated to lay waste the Babylonian temple of Belus and kill the priests. In spite of Mardonius, who wanted to become satrap of Hellas, he would probably have depopulated the country, deporting the Greeks to the interior of his kingdom[4] as the Eretrians had been deported after the campaign of Datis; indeed he would have had no alternative if he wished to avoid continually having to renew his struggle with these tough city-states. In the kingdom itself the cult of Ahura-Mazda would have swept everything before it. This religion was expounded in detail in the inscription of Behistun; Ahura-Mazda had been thoroughly exploited by the Persian king to ensure the submission of all nations to the ruler under the god's protection. No other religion of antiquity was so perfectly adapted to foster the arrogance of perpetual self-righteousness and omnipotence as this version of Zoroastrianism;[5] perhaps victory over the Hellenes would have allowed this delusion to erupt into complete madness. The polytheistic Greeks, till now pragmatically good or bad, and not yet trained in hypocrisy, might have been forced to sell out in their Mesopotamian exile.

After this danger had happily been averted, the inevitable followed, with the liberation of the cities of Asia Minor, which had been first under Lydian and then Persian control. Certainly political life there never amounted to much, and as the relations between Heraclitus and his fellow citizens of Ephesus suggest, was not very fortunate; despite the cultural level of the population these must have been weak democracies. Still, the liberation was achieved by the united Hellenes, and heightened the strong Panhellenic sentiment of the time. The new relationship of Greece and Sicily with the rest of the world demanded new rules. In the aftermath of decisive victories, then as now, the damage done to the nation was quickly revealed. It was *after* the Persian wars that Argos destroyed Mycenae and Tiryns 'in order to defend herself against Sparta' and soon afterwards Athens attacked Aegina; and it was then that first the tyrants and later the people contended with the native populations of Sicily for hegemony, not to mention the disappearance of old cities such as Plataea in the Peloponnesian War. In this latter war, victory very clearly contributed to national misfortune. It was fought over Athenian hegemony, which broadly speaking was the prize and goal of victory; but in the course of it, in an agreement over financial support, Sparta handed over to the Persians, who had earlier been so resoundingly defeated, all the lands and cities the king's ancestors had formerly possessed.

To introduce the general discussion of Hellenic life at this period, we must first give a sketch of the city whose new prominence forms the one main difference from the sixth century, the Greece of Greece, as Athens is described by her great historian.[6] The region itself and its products are boasted of. 'Our air here is a perfect mixture, with no extremes of either heat or cold. The charms of our country allow us to attract the most beautiful products of Hellas and Asia,' says Euripides in a fragment of his *Erechtheus*,[7] and in *Medea* too there is a marvellous description of the sons of Erechtheus always moving about with grace and ease under their radiant sky, and the goddess Cypris drawing up waves from the beautiful River Cephisos and breathing them out as mild, gently caressing breezes.[8] With its light but fruitful soil the land produced better honey, wheat and figs than the whole of the rest of the world;[9] the quarries of Hymettos and Pentelicon yielded superb marble, and the silver mines of Laurion, where in Strabo's time only the slag heaps remained to be worked, must still, in the fifth century, have been productive.

All this praise of the land is very much undercut by a passage in Plato's *Critias* (111) where Attica is described as a deforested and calcinated region – like Provence and much of Italy today – in which, certainly, superb fruit can be cultivated, but no respectable tree can flourish. In mythical times Attica suffered fewer changes of population than other areas, and even Thucydides himself explains this (I. 2) by the fact that the shallowness of the topsoil was not attractive to hungry invaders; Boeotia and Thessaly were much more fertile, and Sparta superior in natural wealth, as long as Messenia was part of it.[10] When the chorus in *Oedipus at Colonus* sing wonderful praises of their region, it is probably only a favoured corner of Attica that is referred to.

From a well-known speech by Lysias we learn that the Peloponnesian War left a wilderness where formerly dense olive groves had stood (Lysias 7, *On the olive stump*); but even apart from the effects of war, Attic farming as Lysias depicts it had its disadvantages, for he speaks of the land having changed owners and tenants far too often.[11] The state was insecure in a country so quarrelsome, and occupying such an artificial political position, which was yet – despite the field of Rharus and the legend of Triptolemus – incapable of producing anything like enough corn for its half-million inhabitants, all dependent for the bread they ate on crops grown abroad, anywhere between Egypt and southern Russia. In this respect the self-sufficiency (*autarkeia*) of Athens had an ominous breach in it; Boeckh calculates that between 800,000 and one million *medimnai* of imported corn were required, and any maritime war could cause famine, since one of the most important functions of the fleet was to secure these imports. To obtain Russian corn and salted fish alone meant keeping some garrisons on the Thracian Chersonese and on the Bosphorus to safeguard the Black Sea route.[12] After Aegospotami, when communications with these regions were cut, Athens ran short of everything, and especially of food (Diodorus 13.107).

The corn trade was protected by strict laws. It was decreed that no Athenian or metic could invest in a ship unless it was to bring grain or other goods to Athens as return cargo;[13] a citizen returning to Athens by sea was expected to transport grain with him, a custom also observed by metics and foreigners to gain favour.[14] Moreover, no citizen or metic was permitted to transport grain elsewhere;[15] they could be denounced for exporting it abroad, and one consequence of this was that Attic shipowners completely gave up carrying grain. Retail trade by dealers was also ruinously restricted and penalized; they were only allowed to make one obol per *medimnos*. But the wholesalers were evidently not subject to control, so they often made a ring with the vendors and drove prices up by means of panic rumours (Lysias 22.14). The *sitophylakes*, inspectors appointed annually by lot, were as liable as other Athenian officials to join the conspiracy. It was easy, too, for sycophants to denounce innocent people as grain-profiteers;[16] contraventions were subject to the unreasonably harsh penalty of death.

We know, however, that *sitophylakes*, although they were full citizens, were often executed for having been outwitted by cunning dealers, and so were dealers, even if they could produce testimony to their innocence (Lysias 22.16.18). All this severity was futile; the *polis*, determined to keep the upper hand, had only run itself into an impasse, for the point was reached where neither the wholesalers nor the dealers were Athenians. The former were obviously nearly always foreigners; they were not subject to the law and had to be treated with the greatest deference, though this was in sharp contrast to the general Athenian practice.[17] The dealers were usually metics, who readily took on the business which citizens disdained; they were of course liable to be accused any day in matters of life and death, but the profits were so great as to make the risk worthwhile. However loudly the *polis* proclaimed its dislike of this hostile clique, and however many death penalties it exacted, it was helpless to do away with this highly undesirable dependence on non-Athenians; and the reason was that the *polis* itself was making the corn trade impossible by ridiculous and impractical laws.

To do justice to Athenian life, we must first come to terms with the exaggerated rhetoric that persists throughout its history. What were the things the Athenians were so conceited about?

The first question is how they acquired the fixed idea of a quite peculiar Attic piety. 'Nowhere else in the world have I found piety like yours, nor the gentleness of your way of thinking and the avoidance of lying,' says Oedipus to Theseus in Sophocles.[18] It is amazing that this could be heard without a blush towards the end of the Peloponnesian War, when sycophants and corrupt witnesses were everywhere. In Athens people believed themselves to be the priestly nation to whom, at a time of universal famine, Apollo had entrusted the mission of taking vows on behalf of all the Greeks and barbarians. It was also generally accepted that there was a special Athenian nobility and sobriety of character,[19] involving outstanding hospitality, particularly towards refugees; and finally, though the Greeks otherwise laid no great claim to inventiveness, Attica was traditionally credited with the inventions of civilization to an extent positively insulting to all other nations and the rest of the Greeks. According to this tradition, it was the Athenians who first taught the human race how to sow crops and use spring water;[20] not only were they the first to grow olives and figs, but they invented law and justice, the agon and physical exercise, and the harnessing of horses to carts.[21] In later times this was all made easy for the Athenians: the whole Hellenic world sang their praises in a way that can only be compared with the nonsense that is nowadays talked about Paris. They were praised for having been the first to raise an altar of mercy, to impart a civilized way of life to the Hellenes, and to draw up laws that put an end to a life of savagery and injustice, the first to save refugees and to show to all men the right treatment of suppliants for protection; and lastly they were praised because Athens was the common centre of education for all humanity;[22] the Pythian god was said once to have named the city the hearth and the *prytaneion* of the Hellenes.[23]

This brings us to the subject of Attic myth. Only in Athens and, to some extent, in Thebes was there a kind of continuous legend interweaving the history of an ancient political evolution with a strong tradition of culture, both expressed in the myth of an earlier period.[24] The very nature of this myth shows that it is a special case; it has numerous points of contact with Greek myth in general – for instance Theseus is its principal hero; but it has a separate and very ancient existence.[25] It seems as though a number of names which were partly traditional, partly symbolic, had been organized into a chronological sequence alternating between genealogy and politics. As time went on, the writers of tragedy acquired great influence on this tradition,[26] and, like them, the orators also possessed a whole stock of references tending to the idealized structuring of the Athenian past, while in the demes there were all kinds of surviving local legends at variance with the rest of the myth.[27]

In the mythical stories of Actaeus, Cecrops, Cranaus, Erichthonius, Pandion etc. down to Theseus there is a strange blending of nature myths, political views and religious ideas. We cannot venture to attempt the dating of the different elements. The legends are connected with places, the Acropolis, the Areopagus, the Pnyx, and those of Celeus and Triptolemus with Eleusis too; the main one concerns the struggle of Poseidon and Pallas for the Acropolis, which was settled by the testimony of Cecrops; it is either an old allegory or an even older nature myth. Enemy attacks are recorded; clashes with Carians, Boeotians, Pelasgians, Amazons – the last named supposed to have camped on the Areopagus – all ended with Athenian victories. Then, when Theseus has been overthrown by the usurper Menestheus, the city appears as a participant in the Trojan War, represented first by Theseus himself, and after his fall by his sons Acamas and Demophon; the Athenians are famed as 'experienced in war', and liberate the aged Aithra, Theseus' mother. But little else is recorded of them, indeed all the passages in the *Iliad* and the *Odyssey* where Theseus and his sons are mentioned may well be later interpolations.[28] As early as the second century B.C., the spiteful Daphidas, who hated Homer and mocked Delphi, maintains that the Athenians did not fight in the Trojan War at all;[29] so they must have distorted Hellenic myth to attach themselves to it. In any case the impression remains that they earned no great glory at Troy, and were later dogged by the story of their quarrel with Homer himself; they were believed to have fined him fifty drachmas because they thought he was mad.[30]

Whatever may have happened in the Trojan War, it is a fact that as a result of the Doric migration the colonization of Ionia was led by Athens.[31] The house of Theseus appears to have been ousted by the Neleids, who were expelled from the Peloponnese by the Heraclids; the succeeding kings were Melanthus and his son Codrus. The sons of Codrus, legitimate and illegitimate, led the countless fugitives to the Cyclades and the coast of Asia Minor,[32] and at this critical time Athens by its outstanding vigour and ability placed itself at the head of an enormous colonial undertaking, the real existence of which cannot be in doubt; one proof of it is the feeling of piety towards Athens which the Ionian cities retained. It was of a dual nature; on the one hand the population prided itself on autochthony, based on the notion that Attica had always been inhabited by the same race, since with its poor soil it was not attractive to invaders, and on the other hand it was known that powerful settlers who were driven from elsewhere in Hellas had taken refuge in Athens and become citizens, making the region populous to the point of overcrowding, so that colonists had to be sent out to Ionia. This belief in a mingling of autochthony and hospitality, first expressed by Thucydides[33] and once more giving Athens the status of an exception in the whole of Greece, remained prevalent and was later very much amplified and glorified by the epideictic orators.[34]

The hospitality of Athens (which may not always have been entirely voluntary) is also reflected in general Hellenic myth, which itself visits Athens for this purpose. Not only must the Thracians under Eumolpus and the Amazons under Hippolyta have entered the country with hostile intentions;[35] the Heraclids too seek help from Athens against Eurystheus, and the war by which he tried to force her to hand them over is the first the city has to wage against Peloponnesians.[36] Lapiths, Minyans and Cadmeans come to live there at different times; after the defeat of the Seven against Thebes, Theseus responds to the pleas of Adrastus by forcing the Thebans in a successful battle to give up their corpses, and buries them at Eleusis;[37] everybody, it seems, has spent time in Attica. The reconciliation at the end of Greek myths may also be transferred to Athens. Here Oedipus finds peace, after the whole unhappy clan of the Labdacids have come from Thebes to plead his cause, as it were, before the old men of Colonus and King Theseus; in Euripides, Theseus welcomes Heracles himself after the murder of his children. It is the tribunal of the Areopagus that acquits Orestes;[38] the Athenian passion for fame even insisted that in the litigation which preceded the first war between Messenia and Sparta, the Messenians had asked for arbitration from the same court.[39]

As for the tone of Attic myth, it is fair to point out that its humanity gave some grounds for pride compared with the stories of Oedipus, the Atreidae, Medea and so forth. Isocrates, who stresses this, observes that in Athens, even in mythical times, dynasties of four or five generations regularly ran their course without horrible family bloodshed (*Panathenaicus* 121 ff.). This moral superiority reaches its high point in Theseus, whom the orators credit with the introduction of democracy, which was to be considered the model of lawful government ever after. The other Greeks are said to have learned from Athens what constitutions and what wars would make Hellas great, and even Lycurgus is held to have picked up useful political and military hints from the city. It is the absurd fiction of Euripides that Theseus, besides being a heroic king, was also the founder of the principles of democracy and of liberalism.[40]

While the Eupatrids ruled, and throughout the seventh century, Athens seems not to have been marked out from the other Greek populations. But from the sixth century there gradually began that unique political development in which all transitions took place without any terrible revolutions and reactions. The legislation of Solon, above all, represented the victory of reflection and mildness, and then came the tyranny of the Peisistratids, the most enlightened and efficient of all tyrannies, just as the succeeding evolution of democracy under Cleisthenes seems the most peaceful and leisurely; after the expulsion of the tyrants the initiative in all Greek matters remained with Athens.

All this is proof of the most impressive political gifts. At the same time, Athens took the lead among all the Hellenes in education, art and social manners, whereas up to this period the Hellenic spirit and its fruits had been more evenly distributed among the various races, and was strongest in the Asiatic Ionians. The impetus for this was given by Attica's central situation and its happy blend of rural and business activity; but here too the deciding factor was the inborn gift, greater here than anywhere else in the world. It was as if, for centuries past, nature had stored up all its forces to expend them here, and the society of Athens gave it a position similar to that of Florence in the Renaissance, the only parallel in history. That is, one city had the will and the potential that were wished for by a whole people, just as in one child the specific gifts of a whole family emerge most fully. From that time the whole of free Hellas was coloured and determined by Athens; every Hellene recognized this city as the primary expression of Greek civilization.[41]

As a result of the free rein given to energies, including the aberrant, Athens wore itself out in the political sense fairly quickly; but its cultural position was secured, and it continued to be the spiritual capital of the Hellenes when the agonal sites and the Delphic oracle had lost their central importance, just as it also saved itself materially and was able to live out its time with dignity under the Romans.

We have plenty of descriptions of the manners and customs of the Athenians; they and posterity have provided more information about them than about any other Greeks. The funeral orations of fallen warriors are a chief source for this. When the Carthaginians lost many men they used simply to hang black cloths over the city walls;[42] in Athens the custom was to arrange a public burial and to let an orator praise the dead and their native city. Like others, this custom was transferred to mythical times: Menestheus was supposed to have spoken the funeral oration for Ajax at Troy. Nothing is known of this practice historically until the beginnings of rhetoric, for which it provided uplifting themes. We shall come later to the account Thucydides gives of the funeral oration of Pericles; in antiquity a memorial speech by Gorgias was also known, though its author, as a non-Athenian, cannot possibly have delivered it himself, but it must have served as a useful model for such occasions. The oration of Lysias for those killed in the Corinthian War (hardly a resounding victory) may have been written by Lysias or by someone else, or it may have been made up as a scholastic exercise; but it shows Athenian vanity at its most fulsome, with its opening declaration that the whole of time would not suffice for the composition of a speech that would do justice to the deeds of the fallen. This speech, listing the Amazons, the Seven against Thebes, the Heraclids and the Persian Wars, all to the glory of Athens, makes use of a set pattern of mythical and historical achievements which was probably a creed for every Athenian. Herodotus must have been equally familiar with it, since he describes the Athenians before the battle of Plataea formally boasting of the protection of the Heraclids, of their victory over the Amazons, of the burial of the Seven and of the battle of Marathon (9.27). The same exploits recur in the speech in praise of the fallen at Chaeronea, which was attributed to Demosthenes; that its true date was much later is evident from its scope and perspective, which views this battle as marking the end of freedom for Greater Greece. The composition of funeral orations for the fallen must certainly have been a favourite task for pupils and dabblers in rhetoric, for the beginner would naturally choose the most solemn theme available. In the pseudo-Platonic *Menexenos* the author puts the formula for such orations into the mouth of Aspasia, probably intending this as a mockery of the whole practice. By the fourth century, when the armies were no longer recruited from citizens, it was a custom that made little sense in any case. If citizens were among the fallen, however, the funeral oration still had some point. Demosthenes did deliver one, not preserved, on those who died at Chaeronea, and that of Hypereides, on those killed in the Lamian War, has been rediscovered. This orator, possibly following the example of Pericles, recounts no myths or mythical exploits, but praises the deeds of Leosthenes and those who fell with him. They are to be greeted in Hades by the heroes of the Trojan War, by Themistocles and the Athenian tyrannicides, though they are said somehow to have outdone all these. They have sacrificed their lives so that Athenians and Greeks can live in freedom, and are credited with achievements that came only after their deaths, but for which they laid the groundwork. They are called fortunate, and the bereaved consoled, in the same terms Pericles used; the orator believes Leosthenes' victory has averted the enslavement by Macedonia which afterwards became a bitter reality. At times an orator, speaking on other themes after a recent war, will fall easily and mechanically into the obituary mode. Thus Lycurgus, in his accusation against Leocrates, cannot let the occasion pass without praising the dead of Chaeronea.[43]

In the winter of the first year of the Peloponnesian War Pericles delivered the funeral oration recorded by Thucydides (2.35 ff.); it shows how the image of Athens was transfigured at that time. It is obviously intended for a nation in critical mood, not yet receptive to facile enthusiasm; anyone with a big official speech to make ought to read it beforehand. Above all, Pericles avoids all reference to myth, and, while praising the dead, confines himself to celebrating the vital and dynamic qualities of their generation, taking a very broad view. It is hard even for us to resist the optimism with which this is done, but on close inspection it comes to seem rather dubious.

Pericles praises the constitution based on equality, by which privilege in the state depended entirely on merit – standing at his side was Cleon, overshadowing him more and more. He praises the tranquil private life, recreation of the mind through agons, rituals and pleasant home surroundings; the relaxed existence, free from constant military training, which yet produced men with as much courage as those who perpetually drove themselves to the limit (i.e. the Spartans). At the time when he spoke of this relaxed existence Pericles was harassed by continual lawsuits, Aspasia was being prosecuted on criminal charges, and it was only with difficulty that he could save Anaxagoras from execution. He also praises the Athenian love of beauty without extravagance[44] – easily said when the allies paid the taxes which made magnificent buildings possible. He praises the way in which tradesmen took part in politics – again we think of Cleon, who was a tanner. He describes how the Athenians win friends by giving, not by taking, and not calculating an immediate return but trusting in others' generosity; how their state is an education for all Greece, Athens unique in excelling its reputation, the only state whose enemies are not dishonoured by defeat, and whose subjects do not feel humiliated by servitude – though Thucydides himself tells how Athens was detested by its subjects. It is not difficult to refute Thucydides out of his own mouth, but all this is expressed with great brilliance, as if a matter of course; then comes the declaration: 'We shall be admired now and in the future, we need no Homer, everywhere land and sea are the background for our courage; in this way we have erected immortal monuments to the good as well as the evil that we can bring about.' – And then follows the phrase: 'and for such a city these men have died'. As has been said, it is hard to resist this optimism, which was punished so soon by terrible catastrophes: the genius of the presentation is incomparable. It must be admitted that this helps us to a better knowledge of the Athenians. Human beings are not simply what they are, but also what they set up for themselves as ideals, and even if they can never come up to those ideals, the mere will to do so defines something of their nature.

The second speech of Pericles which Thucydides records is also of great interest (2.60 ff.). In this, at a time when their region was occupied by the Spartans, and the olive groves largely destroyed, he shows the Athenians that it is impossible to turn back, and urges the need for noble ambition. The little realm of Attica now laid waste, he tells them, was only a garden plot and a minor pleasure conferred by their wealth beside their real power; they were not in a position to choose to renounce the hegemony, the greatest Hellas had ever known; though it was by now a reign of force, they could not survive autonomously without it; and only those who preferred to be envied for the greatness of their aims were judging rightly. Again, the fact that this could be said to the Athenians gives their measure.

Thucydides gives another excellent characterization of the Athenians in Cleon's address urging severe punishment for the renegade Mytilenians (3.37 ff.). Rough and harsh though he is described elsewhere, Cleon comes out impressively here. He speaks to his compatriots in his own way and is not afraid to upbraid and reproach them most tellingly as slaves of the extraordinary who despise the mundane, each wanting to be an orator or at least a heckler, quick to anticipate what is proposed, but reluctant to foresee the consequences of things. Finally he insinuates that, if they show mercy in this case, they will have to give up ruling and settle down to a quiet life with no more adventures; after what Pericles had said it is doubtful whether they still had this option.

Lastly, Thucydides is also the source for statements made about the Athenians by their enemies, for instance the Corinthians (1.70 f.) They said that the Athenians loved progress, were quick to make decisions and execute them, not used to hesitation, keen on foreign adventures; they pursued an advantage as far as possible, and sacrificed their bodies to the State as recklessly as if they were not their own. Plans not carried out they counted as losses; every gain seemed to them trivial compared to what was left to do, and after any failure they would hope for something new.[45] Whatever the toil and danger, their energy was undiminished throughout their lives; they never paused to enjoy what they had, and pleasure for them meant getting on with the immediate task; they were born to give themselves no peace and allow none to others. This Corinthian view of the Athenians does much in itself to explain the Sicilian expedition.

In all these orations what emerges is the passionate common will that drove these people on. Their true stimulus was their eternal discontent with something not attempted or not thoroughly carried out. Since passion was the impetus, they were not always in control of their decisions, but could sometimes achieve the incredible. It was, after all, astonishing that the Greeks could pursue the Persians into every harbour of the Eastern Mediterranean; conclude an alliance with Egypt which, led by Inaros, had deserted the Persians;[46] then overrun most of Memphis and, even when finally defeated and forced to burn their own ships, succeed in getting safe passage out of Egypt. Immense energy and enterprise is reflected in the surviving inscription listing the fallen in one year of the Egyptian War (458), beginning: 'These men of the Erechtheian *phyle* fell in the war on

Cyprus, in Egypt, in Phoenicia, at Halieis, on Aegina, and at Megara, all in the same year.'[47] It must be remembered, though, that the Athenian hegemony in its prime demanded great sacrifices from the rest of Greece, even from a famous *polis* like Aegina, when it stood in the way of Athens and refused to be part of the hegemony. Aegina was flourishing then and full of pride; it was rich and had many triremes, and also important works of art;[48] but the enmity with Athens was long-standing, and it is hard to judge the rights and wrongs of it. In 457 the Athenians came, ravaged the island, exacted tribute from the town, and later expelled the inhabitants, replacing them with settlers from Attica. The Aeginetans were, however, given land in Thyreatis by the Spartans, and then returned to their homeland by Lysander in 404.

Even before the humiliation of the Aeginetans, Athens won a victory at Oenophyta in Boeotia, and went on to devastate the coasts. In 455 Tolmides ravaged Cythera and the shores of the Peloponnese, and burned the Lacedaemonian arsenals there; he took the towns of Cephallenia and overran Naupactos, where he settled the Messenians who had deserted from Sparta. In the year 453, then, the Athenian hegemony was at its height.[49] After the victory Pericles won near Sicyon, even though he could not take the city, he laid the region waste and plundered the Acarnanian coast; the Corinthian Sea was all more or less in the power of Athens. But after Cimon's death on Cyprus and the truce with the Persians, which was to prove a lasting peace, the hegemony began to falter. In 447 Athens was defeated at Coroneia, and lost her influence in Boeotia and the other regions of Central Greece, then Megara deserted, and Euboea, intending to do the same, had to be harshly disciplined by Pericles. The thirty years' peace agreed with Sparta in 445 secured the general Athenian alliance, but was soon followed by the quarrel between Samos and Miletus, in which Athens favoured Miletus, and then by the war with Samos waged by Pericles (440–439), ending with the walls of Samos being razed to the ground and the introduction of a democracy on the island.[50] Here too a great danger was averted; but all these incidents, for those who could think ahead, foreshadowed more important events, and though, as Diodorus says, peace and prosperity prevailed all over the world about 440 B.C. (12.26), there was no guarantee that this would endure for long.

In Athens itself at the same period the democratization of the citizenship was completed, with the three salary grades for war service, justice and popular assemblies, the full development of sycophancy, state trials and so on. All this was supposed to be compatible with the far-flung hegemony over all those disadvantaged Greek compatriots, a form of rule which has been successfully exercised in the history of the world only by aristocratic republics – Venice, Genoa (divided, it is true, but aristocratically divided), the States General of the Netherlands – and then chiefly over subjects who were foreigners. The allies were very imprudently antagonized by confiscations and by being forced to take their lawsuits to Athens, and many must have left the areas of the hegemony to escape oppression at home, and gone to Thurii, which Pericles had founded in 445 to replace the former Sybaris.[51] If a *polis* tried to break away from this rule by armed resistance, the last resort for Athens was, at best, to crush the uprising and settle colonists in the territory, or at worst to destroy the city and set up minor democracies in the ruins. It is not surprising that Sparta's popularity increased by comparison. So Athens drifted on towards the Peloponnesian War. It was her task and her duty to transmit a splendid inheritance to the world, and infinite gain or loss for mankind depended on the existence or disappearance of her culture; the recklessness of Athenian policies and the irreversible conditions they led to must be instructive even to us at the present day.[52]

The Athenians themselves paid a heavy price for the existence of Athens. The fullest account of what it cost to be an exemplary Athenian is given by Antiphon in one of his tetralogies (1.2.12). The model citizen is one whose income has been often severely taxed, who has often served as a trierarch, provided handsome *choregiai*, contributed to funds for many friends in need, stood bail for large sums, earned his fortune by work, not by lawsuits, borne his share of offerings, and loyally served the city. It is a wonder that anything was left after all these taxes, trierarchies, *choregiai*, subscriptions, guarantees and offerings (i.e. entertainments).[53] In addition to being exploited in this way, the citizens were plagued by their city in many others; worst of all was political harassment in the never-ending state prosecutions, the associated growth of sycophancy, which must have made life almost intolerable, and constant recourse to the law in general. This was the inveterate custom of the Greeks. In the *Iliad*, the very shield of Achilles shows a scene of litigation, and the treatment of it is as remarkable as its presence (*Iliad* XVIII.497 ff.). In all the Greek cities the practice continued through the time of the aristocracy. It was interrupted only during the tyrannies, partly as a reform, but in the democracies lawsuits again became a continual and very unhealthy preoccupation. In that period it is documented only in Athens.[54] Apart from a few villains intent on revenge or extortion, a spirit of feverish litigation encouraged by idleness was aroused in many citizens by court proceedings, the glamour of public speaking and so on, and formed a parallel to political sycophancy. Several of the lawsuits recorded, not only by Lysias but earlier by Antiphon, are evidently of this kind.[55] A general statement in a speech for the defence may run: 'Nowadays the totally innocent are in no less danger from intriguers than those who have committed evil deeds' (e.g. Lysias 5.2).

The example of the *sitophylakes* has shown how hastily officials were condemned to death [p. 218 above]. On one occasion, blinded by suspicion, the Athenians executed all but one of the administrators of the state treasury, and the last was already in the hands of the Eleven when the truth came to light;[56] one can hardly help feeling that the Athenians were the kind of people who always think they are being robbed. The fact is that the *demos* was indeed often deceived and cheated by those in charge of public affairs, and at the same time was kept in a constant state of angry mistrust of its authorities, as well as being greedy for sensation. At a time of crisis and passionate feeling, such as that of the Sicilian expedition, nervous excitement intensified, and during the trials connected with the mutilation of the herms, and with the mysteries, Athens showed unmistakable signs of the megalomania that responds to the slightest resistance with outbreaks of complete lunacy. The informers declared at once that the attacks on the herms were not the work of a small group but were aimed at bringing down the democracy; the *demos* trembled, and for once came near wanting to use torture on citizens. It was then the rule that the guilty who turned state evidence on fellow offenders were acquitted, but if they were not believed, they were sentenced to death.[57]

Plutarch's Nicias, because of his wealth, lives his whole life with the feeling of being under siege (*Nicias* 4f.) His extremely retiring habits were no protection against importunity; petitioners and clients were constantly in and out of his house; to those who could do him harm he gave no less than to the deserving, and so was ridiculed by the comic writers for his fear of sycophants. When we are told that he saw how the *demos* sometimes made use of talent and oratorical skill, but was so suspicious of outstanding ability that such men were deliberately kept down and denied respect and proper pride, we recall that in the fifth century Athens had already exhausted its best powers. Pheidias died in a dungeon, Pericles of the plague, but no doubt of grief too; Nicias himself preferred to end his days in Sicily.

By the time Alcibiades was living in Asia Minor people could be heard to say in the streets: 'There isn't a man left in the city' (Aristophanes, *Lysistrata* 524).

We can well imagine the state of mind not only of intriguers but of true politicians too, when besides all this the wild joker Aristophanes and the other comic writers were always pushing caricature of situations and personalities to grotesque limits. The general view of things was saturated with contempt and mockery, overflowing with the electric force of scandal-mongering which could discharge itself at any moment; Aristophanes makes this so clear that it seems to us almost childish when scholars try to distinguish, in the reports of Stesimbrotus of Thasos (or Plutarch), between what is, or is not, mere gossip. If this looks like a considerable restriction on the supposed happiness of these times, how must thinking people have felt when Athens, ignoring the warnings of the war from 431 to 421, was led by Alcibiades towards the great disaster? The later blind belief in the splendour of life in Athens is at odds with, for instance, the numerous desertions to King Archelaus, despite his evil reputation. As well as non-Athenians such as Choerilus of Samos and Zeuxis, even Euripides and Agathon took refuge with him; Agathon, it is said, remained permanently in Macedonia *with many others* and lived happily at the royal court.[58]

Fifth-century Athens appeared in a rosy glow even to those living in the following century, who praised the past age in the awareness of their miserable present. Among the orators, Isocrates is inconsistent on this subject. Sometimes he glorifies the Athens of the past, sometimes he makes different judgments, dating the decline, for instance, from as early as the hegemony, and declaring that when Pericles took power the State was already in a deluded though still tolerable condition (Isocrates, *Peace* 126). But Demosthenes transfigures the past in the third Olynthiac Oration (3.35):

> Those men, without being flattered and toadied to by the orators as you are now, ruled for forty-five years over all the submissive Hellenes, brought more than 10,000 talents to the treasury of the Acropolis, kept the King of Macedonia in subjection, as Hellenes should keep barbarians, showed such personal valour by land and sea that they could set up many fine monuments of victories, and, alone among mortals, left fame that is beyond the reach of envy ... For the state they created buildings and temples of such beauty

and grandeur that they can never be surpassed; yet in private life they were so modest and so faithful to the spirit of the democracy that even Miltiades and Aristides, as you can still see, had houses no better than their neighbours'. For they did not use the state to enrich themselves; every one of them believed his duty was to increase the wealth that belonged to all.

Of course 'the orators who never flattered' show the operation of a pious imagination as much as 'the submissive allies'; the speaker could not give a critically exact picture of the past condition of things, but his nostalgia itself makes his testimony important to us.[59]

In the fifth century, the Athenian people had become the centre of all Hellas. They were known for producing the best and the worst of everything, just as the soil of Attica gave the best honey and the most deadly hemlock.[60] More than that, they were the general focus of attention, so that the words of one Cydias, recorded by Aristotle, might be applied to this earlier time: 'All the other Hellenes are ranged round about the Athenians not only to hear, but also to see for themselves what they decide.'[61] The Athenians were also the most many-sided of the Greeks, in some ways representing the whole of Greece. 'The other Hellenes have their particular speech, customs and costumes; in Athens all these things are a mixture of Greek and barbarian' – to quote the document on the Athenian State.[62] Even in external matters it was only the Athenian who really observed the doings and the speech of the other Hellenes and could imitate them individually. Just as Hippocleides knew not only the Attic dances but the Laconian and others too,[63] Aristophanes uses all dialects in his comedies. Alcibiades takes on all the colours of the rainbow; in Ionia he carouses worse than any Ionian, practises athletic sports in Thebes, in Thessaly is a better horse-breaker and rider than the Aleuadae, outdoes the Spartans in Sparta in strength and austerity, and, when he goes to Thrace, proves that he can drink more undiluted wine than the native sons, which was not a common boast. That the same man directed foreign policy in Sparta and then under Tissaphernes suggests his temperament must have been very much like that of Themistocles.

Athens was the great marketplace for the products of the whole world, as Critias lists them in an elegy, even down to birds of exotic plumage.[64] In peacetime it was a delight to be there, at least for those who were not persecuted by the sycophants. Aristophanes in *Peace* (529 ff.) gives a description, filled with nostalgic longing, of all the good things that are to be seen, with their fragrances, melodies and shimmering colours: the joy of autumn, feasting, the Dionysia, flute-playing, songs of the grape harvest (the comic poets), poems of Sophocles, fieldfares, verses of Euripides [. . .], ivy, sparkling wine, bleating sheep, women walking in the fields, their dresses blowing in the breeze, even to the slave-girl who has fallen asleep on the ground with her overturned pitcher beside her – all brought before our eyes like a photograph of daily life taken from a bird's-eye view. The Athenians were happy to hear foreigners call their city violet-crowned and radiant.[65] It deserved this praise if only for its festivals, though Pericles in his oration says that they were intended to relieve the sadness of life. The most splendid ceremony of Athenian life was the annual feast of the Panathenaea, and its ideal image still exists in the frieze on the Parthenon. The holiest rites of Greece were the Eleusinia, and there were also the Dionysia with tragedies and comedies.

Greeks, as well as visitors, appreciated the significance of Athens as the cradle of culture. It was a matter of conviction that in Athens there existed the greatest freedom of speech, that is, that nowhere else was such frankness or so much receptive understanding possible. It was assumed that people who knew how to *speak* in the fullest sense were found only in Athens, while Elians and Boeotians, for instance, were regarded as unskilled in using words and in persuading youth. In no other city could a man like Antisthenes exult in his existence as he does in Xenophon's *Symposium* (4. 43) saying that he has plenty of leisure to look on at what was worth seeing, hear what was worth hearing, and – best of all for him – to be the friend of Socrates. In other places, apart from the creative artists, there seems to have been a lack of great personalities. History records scarcely anything of the cities of Asia Minor in the period; the great man of Ionia, Heraclitus of Ephesus, felt isolated among his fellow citizens and let them know of his distaste for them, and in the fifth century even Corinth had no citizens of note. Ionians of distinction, however, came to Athens; Thargelia and Aspasia were from Miletus, and Anaxagoras from Clazomenae. Athens was the only place in which gifted people from elsewhere would find an occupation or at least somewhere to live in safety, even if only as metics, and almost from the beginning the philosophers preferred it to any other, though they might sometimes be prosecuted for impiety and find restrictions placed on their studies. The best architecture and creative art was really only at home in Athens, where the foremost artists were born (though they created superb works in other places too); if they came from elsewhere, it was in Athens that they preferred to live.

For all this, we should not forget one Athenian of the age, who utterly rejected the whole life and activity of the city. This was Timon, known throughout Athens during the Peloponnesian War. He was originally a generous man, honourable and philosophically cultivated, who, because of the ingratitude of friends and protégés, came to loathe his native city; probably it is a later time which interpreted this as true misanthropy. They said of him that, typically, he felt warmly only towards Alcibiades, because he recognized in him the man destined to destroy Athens.[66]

In the Athenian theatre tragedy created the last and grandest realization of myth; writers now treated it with absolute freedom to attain a new psychological depth, while comedy delighted everyone with its grotesque transformation of daily concerns and its caricature of a richly varied world. Clearly Athens was the sole possessor of the two dramatic forms, and was to remain so. It was only here that the Greeks could grasp the perspective on Hellenic civilization that the theatre offered, though at the great agonal sites all the rest of poetic and musical art might be briefly presented in concentrated form. Till this time the only drama known to the ordinary Greek had been the sacred pantomime in which a priest or priestess acted single scenes from the myth of their own temple deity, or else the clowning, character imitations and farcical turns which probably developed impromptu from dialogue and horseplay. Now the Greek became aware that in one city in his country a living representation of the whole of myth had arisen out of the tumult of the Dionysian cult; he also learned that a huge structure was specially devoted to it, with a semicircular space where the audience felt as if it were in a second popular assembly, while, on a stage, the things that were elsewhere recited by bards or shown in pictures were magically enacted by real people and large choruses.[67] He also heard that on certain festive days, the image of the true Athens of real life was brought before its people in a colossal and grotesque transformation. Finally, the individual names of great writers rang throughout Greece as the inventors of all this, and of this new and unique kind of poetry. And this new thing was not some curiosity imported from Asia, but a Hellenic creation in the fullest sense, a deep and essential part of the national life.

Theatre had a darker side. As we have said, the compulsory *choregia* was often a burden on wealthy men. The personal insults usual in comedy were astonishingly coarse and crude, and what has always been reckoned filthy the world over was filth in Aristophanes too (as well as in the Iambic poets before him) – however hard some scholars try to make an exception for him. On one hand the tone of Athenian society must clearly have been conditioned by comedy, and on the other we cannot ignore the effect that this must have had on the victims. For a society and a social set accustomed to having comedy hanging over them all year round with all the other guillotines that menaced them, there was no doubt a strong incentive to affect indifference. In their heart of hearts nobody can really have been indifferent except those whom it robbed of all shame, and when, at every street-corner and at every banquet, people would meet the victims of the comic writers, or know that they themselves would be victims at the next Dionysia, it must have given rise to that form of consciousness in which the mind secretly closes one door after another, and finally the innermost door of all.

What is extremely characteristic of the Athenian temperament, as distinct, probably, from that of all other Greeks, but certainly from other nations, is the attitude of the old comedy to the political situation. No modern nation would tolerate this objective view of itself, and in a solemn, semiofficial context at that; least of all in emergencies and times of universal suffering or anxiety. The whole grotesque accompaniment to the Peloponnesian War which comedy provided would be condemned by any city in our day, and a writer like Aristophanes would be regarded as a heartless jester on the theme of public misery. Yet, as comedy shows, Athens then bred and tolerated not just one poet but a collection of poets of the same kind, writing in a mature, casual style and aloof from shared values in a way that has been unthinkable in later nations. Comedy was able to defy and mock not only the rulers of the day, but also universal common sentiment; Athens acknowledged the supremacy of the joke at her own expense.

As for other aspects of Athenian life, it was a time when intellect was honoured; a man might be poor and yet count for something. Lamachus, for instance, the brave and bold, was so modest and so far from wealthy that whenever he led out an army he was always allowed to charge the Athenians a small sum 'for clothing and soldier's boots'.[68] Since a simple way of life was prescribed, and especially because the pleasures of the mind were accessible to all, equality was far easier to achieve, and wealth made much less difference between people than it does now. Even so, its importance was often complained of in the saying 'Money, money makes the man!'; but broadly speaking it could not yet determine social status, though it was dangerous and becoming more so. One means to riches was leadership in politics. Themistocles for instance, who had inherited three talents from his parents, is reported to have had over one hundred at the time of the confiscation, and Cleon, who had started with nothing, left fifty talents. It was a rare politician who forgot his own interests as Aristides did. A few were rich by birth, such as Nicias and the dynasty in which the name Callias alternated with that of Hipponicus. Callias the Second, whose wealth was proverbial, is supposed to have had two hundred talents; his grandson of the same name, whose house is the scene of Plato's *Protagoras* and of Xenophon's *Symposium*, then squandered it all with harlots, parasites and sophists. But it seems that the preceding generation, about 500 B.C., flaunted their wealth in sumptuous possessions more than that of Pericles did. These old Athenians wore purple mantles and brightly coloured tunics, wore their hair in plaits fastened with golden cicadas, sported other gold jewellery and had their folding chairs carried behind them by servants.[69] In the time of Pericles, clothing became much simpler, a surprising development probably resulting from caution, as envy and greed might be aroused by display, but also, surely, from the awareness that simple dress suited a fine-looking person better and allowed more freedom of movement.[70] Various direct descriptions make clear that in practice there was considerable uniformity, and that a good appearance among rich and poor, men and women, depended on individual build and grace of movement. We know, for instance, that those who had no mantle of their own could hire one for half an obol a day from the tailor, and for economy men and women could wear the same kind.[71] The fabric was wool, and tradition says that spinning and weaving were the usual occupation of unmarried Greek women, apart from those of Sparta.[72] However, the comic poets record the names of many ornaments and other adornments, and vanity must always have found ways to distinguish itself;[73] but most depended on how each person wore the mantle.[74] In other ways too life was still simple. Everyone lived in houses with thin stone walls, quite easy for thieves to penetrate. There was some furniture, even among the poor,[75] but few people seem to have had any that was luxurious, and moderation was the rule in eating and drinking too. In all these matters a certain number of rich people must have been the exception; some of them already had their own gymnasia and baths.[76]

However, at the very same time when Sparta must have been generally under a cloud in the view of most Greeks, there was in Athens a party that persisted in Laconizing both in manners and in politics, and cultivated a still more austere way of life. They wore a short cloak and a leather belt, went in for strenuous physical exercise and had their ears disfigured by boxing, – as if the superiority of the Spartans over the Hellenes lay in these things.[77] This may have been partly bitter earnest, an expression of justified reproach against their native city, but partly only a fashion, and one not hard to keep up with, since many of these people were so poor; it seems likely, at a period when it had become rare to be able to afford an aristocratic life style, that some took to Spartan ways for thrift's sake.[78]

The opinion of a later time about the appearance of the old Athenians is given by the elder Philostratus, who says the notably shrewd and intelligent look of their eyes was typical, and also that the women of Athens made an impression of seriousness.[79] Aristophanes on the other hand speaks of Attic impertinence, shown in certain trenchant turns of phrase as well as in a specifically Attic expression of the eyes.[80] Slaves in Athens were especially bold and cheeky too.

Moral judgments about the Athenian character conflict. Much is said to their discredit; but Plato, generally an embittered witness, who knew and described the worst of them better than anyone else, is very fair to them in *Laws* where he makes his Spartan say that 'the good among them are very good indeed' as a popular opinion, based on their being 'good and truthful without compulsion, simply by nature, in accordance with divine fate.'[81] This unforced morality, linked with refined culture and self-reliance, was typical of the best in Athens. In general, too, they were the most impressionable of all the Greeks and the most inclined to tender feelings, but it was their weakness that, like Jean Jacques Rousseau's French readers, they took emotionalism and love of virtue to be a value in themselves, and yet persisted in all their faults none the less. The whole ethic of Socrates was preached at *them*, everybody wanted to make *them* better than they were, and the poets too aimed at this. The outcome of this perpetual edification was that the Athenians applauded goodness, because they had a taste for it, but remained what they were, like the hearers of a certain saint in legend. 'Most often you were unsuccessful because you did not want to do your duty, not because you did not recognize it,' says Demosthenes. The same truth is expressed in the charming story of the Spartan delegates in the theatre at Athens, who were given an ovation by the audience when they stood up to make room for an old man for whom nobody else would move. 'The Athenians know what is right but don't do it,' said one of them.[82]

An aspect of this was a habitual euphemism, a peculiar vice of the Athenians. They preferred to veil unpleasantness and, as Plutarch says, to give it the mildest names.[83] Solon was already practising this when he called his great expropriation 'shaking off burdens' (*seisachtheia*). Later on people called whores '*hetairai*' and instead of the tribute levied on allies (*phoroi*) would say 'contributions' (*syntaseis*) – but they groaned just the same. Military occupation (*phrourai*) became 'protection' (*phulakai*), prison was called 'dwelling' (*oikema*). Any disaster such as defeat, shipwreck, death and so forth was given the genteel circumlocution 'to have a misfortune' (*pathein ti*); Lysias expressed the opposite of prosperity in the state not as 'bad' but 'unskilful' or 'taking an undesirable direction'.[84] Traitors to their city were said to have been 'unlucky in regard to the city'[85] and in Aristotle's time robbers were even called 'breadwinners' (*poristai*).[86] All these might have seemed nuances with a certain charm, if it were not for the thing being given its full significance by Thucydides in Book Three (82). In his terrible portrayal, which applies to all Greece but surely most of all to Athens, the devaluation and abuse of language are arraigned and implicated in disintegration and decay.[87]

Passing on from the Athenians to consider the Greeks in general, the first thing that demands attention is the falling off from the true spirit of the agon. If there is one striking difference between the fifth and the previous century, it is this. Outwardly the prestige of athleticism remained, and Pindar, who was still celebrating the old Olympic glory, throws its reflection over his own time as if everything were still the same.[88] In small towns it was not yet suspected that the athlete might have ceased to be the ideal of humanity,[89] and an army like the Greeks of the *Anabasis*, as soon as they were more or less in safety, proceeded to hold an agon in the most uncomfortable conditions, including all forms of gymnastics and a horse race. But soon after Pindar, the *epinikion* seems to have died out, as though to let him know that he had been singing the praises of a power that already belonged to the past, and, living to be very old, he experienced the rather sudden outbreak of mocking attacks on the champion wrestlers. Philosophy had already protested, in an elegy of Xenophanes, that it was worth more than all the agonal victors, who could not bring wise laws or material prosperity to a city;[90] now similar gibes were heard on the Attic stage. 'It is not the broad-shouldered and broad-backed who can be relied on, but those with brains who are decisive' (Sophocles, *Ajax* 1250) and in the fragmentary *Autolycus* of Euripides the athletes are said to eat so much that they bring no wealth to their country, and never learn how to be poor: city idols in their youth, they go about later in life like worn-out cloaks. Why should the whole of Greece throng to see them? Which of these wrestlers, runners and so on who have been crowned victors has ever served the city afterwards? Do men go into battle armed with the discus? and so forth.[91] In daily life gymnastic exercise was kept going as a matter of course, if only for health's sake; but there was no longer much fuss about it, and even the Spartans seem to have grown weary of their everlasting physical jerks; the *ephoroi* in the garrison at Deceleia had to be ordered not to go strolling about when they should be exercising.

The explanation for this reaction is that since the time when the Greeks had treated exploits in the Persian War as an agon, quite different contests from those in the stadium at Olympia had come into being, with quite other prizes for distinction than the olive crown given there. Perhaps Herodotus is only telling a good story (8.123 f.) when he says that, after the battle of Salamis, the Greek generals on the Isthmus cast votes to decide which Hellene had deserved the most fame and which came second; of the two votes each general placed on the altar of Poseidon, the first was for himself and the second for Themistocles; then they thought better of it and dispersed without reaching a decision. But the anecdote is very important, showing a great change in Greek attitudes; each Greek wants to be foremost in serving Hellas and thinks the world will come to an end if he has not distinguished himself, but cannot refuse the palm for second place to Themistocles.[92]

With the increasing thrust of democracy, the social classes upon which the agon had chiefly depended lost their power and often their wealth too; the society Pindar celebrated was already in serious decline. Victories at Olympia and elsewhere no longer guaranteed the slightest influence in the *polis*, which was the general object. The *polis* preferred those who represented its own passions, and had lost all interest in noble excellence; in fact everything conspired to disgust thinking people with the idea of 'always trying to be the first'; indeed the whole practice of democracy gradually became a false agon, where scurrilous gossip, sycophancy etc. occupied the foreground. This *polis* continued to be immensely attached to spectacle, and exploited the last vestiges of competitiveness among the rich in supposedly voluntary *choregiae*; which is why the dramatic and choric agon remained alive (if only in Athens) till there too it fell victim to general dilettantism and no doubt also to the incompetence of the judges at the contests. Though for a long time in Athens the fiction was upheld that democracy was always bound up with it, 'noble excellence' served no further purpose, since the people controlled the majority, and that kind of excellence had its reasons for remaining inconspicuous; the display of wealth was slowly becoming risky everywhere, and money had been a precondition of the agonal tradition. The newly rich, though, at least in Theognis' Megara, probably spared themselves any attempt at *kalokagathia*.[93]

The rise of oratory, too, was damaging to gymnastic education. The Greeks had always been very good speakers and had prized oratory (both public and legal) as a splendid gift from the Muses, but in the fifth century this seemed outdated compared with the kind of thing they heard from the sophists of Greater Greece, and with what soon came to be thought indispensable in political and legal oratory. The earlier eloquence came from natural gifts of a high order, the modern kind was the result of training. The specific case or *causa* pleaded, from the time of the Sicilian trials, by this 'studied' speech was, indeed, a matter of indifference, and from the start, especially in the democratized courts, oratory served the most dubious moral ends. But in the larger cities an audience must soon have been found who admired this style and demanded more of it; an agon of orators must have arisen which now drew much more interest than that based on gymnastics. This is why Aristophanes is right to connect the deserted state of the Athenian gymnasia with sophistry; young men were spending their time in the lawcourts instead, and, while their elders went to war, making popular speeches, because talking brought fame; everyone else found the tone the young men used detestable, and Alcibiades was held to be the model for it; he was seen as 'the destroyer of the gymnasia'.

The power of personality no longer showed itself, therefore, in great examples of competitive achievement, that is by victories over another or a few similar contestants, but absolutely; and when Plutarch says of Themistocles that he wished to distinguish himself from others in every sphere, it is more or less true of all great men at that time (*Themistocles* 18). This did not prevent the foremost men of the individual states from wanting to make dazzling appearances at Olympia, and ingratiating themselves with all Hellas, even giving feasts for the visitors and outdoing the Spartans in this.

This brings us back to Alcibiades. Aristophanes had recently completely caricatured hippotrophy in *Clouds*, but the Greeks were still addicted to the excitement of horse racing. Alcibiades decided to exploit this passion to make himself the talk of all Greece. Having already squandered a great fortune, he now had plenty of money again through his marriage to the richest heiress in Greece, the daughter of Hipponicus. So he sent seven chariots to Olympia, as not even a king had ever done before, and won three prizes. Foreign cities, probably hoping to gain favour in Athens, contended for the honour of supporting him; Ephesus provided a magnificent tent for him, Chios gave fodder for his enormous stable and also animals for the sacrifice; Lesbos contributed wine and provisions for him to entertain countless Hellenes. It was a Panhellenic *choregia* on a huge scale, aiming at favourable publicity for Athens, but Alcibiades was looking beyond Athens too. It was plain that his extravagance would ruin the individual gymnastic champions on this occasion; he is said to have despised them because many came of humble families and from small towns, and had little education – perhaps also they were useless to him because they would have beaten him if they had had the chance; but he reckoned that the Greek onlookers were spoilt enough by now to prefer the tension of the chariot race to the sight of gymnastic excellence, and to be delighted with free banquets. He succeeded in getting himself and Athens talked about everywhere; but morally speaking the ground was cut away under the tradition by the fact that he had done the possibilities of chariot racing to death. A fellow Athenian, who had intended to compete for the honour of his family and for Athens, was simply forced to give up his chariot to Alcibiades, and this being known may have been decisive in frightening off the last honest idiots. In the democracies there was soon no-one rich or foolish enough to risk ranging himself beside such a man at the festivals.

At the same period, *kalokagathia*, formerly an idea simply based on the real aristocratic and agonal way of life, fell into the hands of the philosophers; while ostensibly preserving its old meaning they were really subjecting it to a complete purge in the name of ethics. Where *kalokagathia* had described a kind of existence, its place was now taken by a means of acting on others, in fact of 'improving people', and this became the yardstick applied to human beings and institutions; but Socrates, and those who spoke in his way, were using it to express a new ideal, and leaving reality to get along as well as it could. It was no longer the noble free individual they had in mind, but the citizen in general, and soon mankind as a whole.

Altogether the new distribution of people's values under democracy seems seriously to have shaken their belief in breeding. In Athens at least this must have been partly because of the strong dilution of the active population, the acceptance of metics and foreigners into citizenship, the growing prominence of seafarers since they won victory at Salamis as the hoplites did at Marathon, but in other places because of acts of violence at the fall of the oligarchs, and most especially because of the many mixed marriages, some voluntary and some, in catastrophes, forced. Theognis had lamented, long before, that because of money, noble blood had mixed with the base, and that breeding, so carefully preserved in sheep, donkeys and horses, was being spoilt in men, with noble men marrying women from low families and vice versa. In comedy the archetype of the mismatch is that of the countryman Strepsiades and his Megaclidion, the mother from whom their son has inherited his sublime passions (*Clouds* 41 ff.). Wealth, dangerous as it could be to its possessor, grew even more desirable as mockery of the rich became a commonplace, and this was for the good reason that though it no longer conferred respect, it had necessarily become the chief object with the disappearance of the higher distinction it had once been bound up with.

In this period the extension of the agon into a competition in every area of life brought individual personalities to a new prominence. Modesty became a thing of the past. The philosophers, sophists, poets, painters, engineers and those with any skills, who now took the place of the agonal victors as celebrities in Greece, had the ability and the will to claim their place without restraint, and public opinion expected it of them. All that *sophrosyne* dictated was that hubris should be avoided, not that worth should be concealed; the wise man was to acknowledge his wisdom, the fortunate had to admit his good fortune, if only as a form of gratitude to the gods;[94] there was no need to hide away and pretend to be the same as the ordinary little man; the fleeting nature of happiness might be put on one side for the time being. Splendid and stylish dress and appearance was part of all this, and must have been very conspicuous at a time when clothing in general was simple. The philosophers and sophists were now as finely dressed as the great musicians had formerly been at festivities. Empedocles, who among his Agrigentians and Selinuntians claimed to be a god descended to earth, wore purple,[95] as Gorgias and Hippias did, Gorgias with a golden diadem and Delphic crown as well, and we have already described the appearance of Parrhasius and Zeuxis.[96] Naïve self-glorification reached unbelievable extremes. Pindar is a well-known example; Simonides too coolly speaks in the epigrams of his unequalled memory and of the fame he acquired in old age by a choric victory.[97] The engineer Mandrocles, who built the bridge over the Bosphorus for Darius, used his reward from the king to commission a painting for the Heraeon at Samos; it showed the bridging of the sea with Darius enthroned and the army marching over it, and contained an inscription telling how he had won a crown for himself with his bridge and had brought fame to the people of Samos.[98] Parrhasius called his self-portrait 'Divine Hermes'; in his verses he said he was the offspring of Apollo, a prince of art or of the Hellenes, who had risen to the first rank and reached the highest goal – a judgment he might have left to be pronounced by posterity.[99] If Zeuxis gave away his paintings, the reason for this was most likely not that he considered them beyond price, but because he believed he might in this way rise above *banausia*, like Polygnotus;[100] but his pride speaks in the saying: 'It is easier to criticize me than to imitate me.'[101] Even a carpetmaker in Delphi wove into a carpet the boast that Pallas had endowed his hands with divine grace.[102] In general the use of signatures on works of art and handicraft begins very early, as we have seen; it would be interesting to know whether they were forbidden on dedications. Whole populations send up clouds of incense to themselves. 'Never, since Pontus divided Europe from Asia, and savage Ares ruled over the cities of mortals, was a finer deed done by earthdwellers than this, by land and by sea at once.' This is the inscription on the dedication set up by the Athenians to the Delphic Apollo after Cimon's land and sea victories in Cyprus.[103]

As in the heroic age, the nurses and tutors of famous persons were honoured and noted, showing the strength of the belief in education; in this way the names of some teachers who were slaves were preserved when those of mothers went unrecorded.[104] One famous example is Pericles' music teacher Damon, said to have taught him politics under the cover of music lessons, for which he was later exiled by the law of ostracism, and ridiculed by the comic writers, who called him Chiron (Plutarch, *Pericles* 4).

The picture that now presents itself is that of a majority of states, each in turn personified in prominent individuals, who also rise and fall in their turn; it is a phenomenon the world had never known before, certainly not even in the cities of Phoenicia or Carthage. It is in sharp contrast also to Rome, where, up to the sixth century of the city's history, all her great men, except for Coriolanus and a few other outlaws, are seen in one and the same aspect.[105] They existed purely for Rome, as warriors and servants of their state, and the liberated individual emerged only at a late stage with widespread education. Among the Greeks, individuals determined to stand out from all others were characteristic, and the concept of personal power became paramount; depending on circumstances, they ranged from the most devoted servants of the *polis* to those who committed the greatest crimes against it. This *polis* itself, with its mistrust and its narrow ideas of equality on one hand, and its high expectation of integrity (*arete*) from individuals on the other, drove gifted men to follow this course, which might lead them to reckless greed and possibly to megalomania. Even Sparta, which tried to contain potentially many-sided individuals within the strict bounds of their usefulness to the State, only succeeded in producing a breed of ruthless hypocrites; as early as the sixth century there is the terrible Cleomenes, then, in the fifth, Pausanias, and finally Lysander. It is debatable whether this development was beneficial for the *poleis*, and whether in any case it was avoidable; but as a result the Greek world makes the impression of an immense wealth of genius both for good and evil. The danger inherent in it was recognized later; Athens, the home of a brilliant succession from Themistocles to Critias, also gives utterance to an objective judgment in the words Aristophanes puts into the mouth of Aeschylus speaking of Alcibiades:

> It is folly to rear a lion cub in the city
> But once he's reared he has to be indulged.
> (*Frogs* 1431 f.)

Plato, however, in his *Gorgias*, supposed to be set in the time soon after the death of Pericles (§.483d ff.) gives Callicles a speech describing the vigorous personality and its claims, in opposition to false equality: 'It is the law of nature that the more gifted should rule over the insignificant. *Our* (Athenian) law of course is different; we catch the ablest and strongest when they are young, like lions, and tame them with magic lullabies and hocus-pocus, for we believe in equality and maintain it is the best and finest thing of all. But I think that when you get one with the right temperament, he throws all this off and tears it to pieces and breaks loose, trampling underfoot all your writings and spells and hymns and laws that contradict all that is human, and shows himself your master, so that nature's law shines out triumphant.'[106] In the fourth century, at least in Athens, things had changed. Personal power was no longer exerted in the *polis*, but confined to philosophy, oratory, art, private life and so forth.

Certain figures in tragedy demonstrate what constituted greatness; no matter that they are mythical and not fifth-century people. The Ajax of Sophocles is a prime example. His real guilt, in Calchas' definition which the messenger reports (758 ff.), is not defiance of the gods, only the awareness of extraordinary strength. When his father parts from him with the advice to try to conquer always with the help of a divinity, Ajax replies: 'With the gods, a weakling may prove strong, but I am confident of winning fame even without them.' He incurs the undying hatred of Pallas for having refused her help in battle because the enemy would be unable to overcome him. This shows a pride beyond what was allowed to mortals, and following the savage ancient myth to which the poet links his psychological study, he is blinded and driven mad by Athena so that he kills cattle and herdsmen. But it is important to note that even in his right mind he intended to murder the generals of the Achaean army treacherously by night, simply because they denied him Achilles' weapons. This would prevent a modern audience from considering him tragic, and cause modern public opinion to view him as 'lost' and 'degraded'. But for Sophocles and the Athenians he remains an ideal figure deserving complete sympathy, and the facts of his pathological condition, as he and Tecmessa relate them, are intended to create a sublime effect.[107] Medea too, with the motivation Euripides gives her, would be impossible on the stage today; and the Greeks could still feel sympathy and understanding for a dramatic character who roars out his lust for power as naïvely as Eteocles in *Phoenician Women*. What he wants, instead of reigning alternately with Polyneices according to law and previous agreement, is simply to retain power because he has it (504 ff.); to possess supremacy, 'the highest divinity', he would go to heaven or down to the underworld; to concede it to another and accept the lesser position, to serve voluntarily when he could rule, seems to him cowardice. He ends with the words:

> If sin must be, the best is after all
> To sin for power, and in all else be just.
>
> (*Phoenician Women* 524 f.)

This last proviso is thoroughly Athenian and reflects the attitude of a *polis* that can, with luck, rule for a while and perhaps pacify many other regions under its sway; if things go wrong and its power crumbles, the world may as well become a shambles.

As for the historical personalities of Athens, the temperament of the great men of the time, beginning with Themistocles, was the essence of Athens in its strongest form, which is why Cimon is said to have stood out so clearly as an exception.[108] The authentic representative of Athens was the man who steered the city towards progress at all costs, the astonishing Themistocles. The embodiment of personal power and recklessness, and ruled by the drive to be outstanding in everything, he attracted universal attention while still living through his wild youth; Alcibiades was later to show many traits in common with him.[109] To cut a dazzling figure in the democracy, Themistocles went through an enormous amount of money with no care for financial prudence; but as soon as he had acquired the influence he wanted, he achieved the extraordinary feat of persuading the citizens to give up an institution close to the heart of the democracy: the custom by which they all individually shared the proceeds of the silver mines of Laurium. His declared intention was to build triremes with this income for the war against the Aeginetans, though it is hinted that his secret purpose from the start was to use the ships for fighting the Persians, as was then done.

We may question whether this fifth-century Odysseus deserved the reputation he certainly had as a riproaring playboy. Much of the tradition about him goes back to the unreliable Stesimbrotus of Thasos, and even if its main outlines are already to be found in Herodotus, he was only reporting what he was told in Athens.[110] There can be no doubt that by the aid of his criminal tendencies Themistocles carried out amazingly bold acts in desperate circumstances and took terrible personal risks. The story of his bribing and outwitting the Spartans, his exile by ostracism and adventurous flight, the overwhelming impression he made on Artaxerxes and his death in Magnesia (though some of it may be invented, especially the last part) still keeps readers between suspense and admiration and draws them into its excitement.

Pericles, too, was a typical representative of Athenian ways; capable of self-control, and devoted to the service of the State, he identified its greatness with his own. It was his intention to present in himself the harmonious blending of contradictory qualities – those of the perfect citizen and of the gigantic personality; but in this, like Themistocles, he was not wholly successful. He too took immense risks, and must have looked forward, at the least, to the outbreak of the decisive war.

But it was *Alcibiades* who most fully personified Athens. We know him fairly thoroughly, not only from Plutarch's biography, but also from Thucydides, Andocides or pseudo-Andocides, and from Isocrates.[111] Yet it is not easy to speak about him. Plutarch shows us clearly enough how Athens nurtured the 'individuality' of the man by following him everywhere and noting all his doings; but what also becomes evident is the way the Athenian imagination worked on him, in the writings of Stesimbrotus or of others, and gave him credit for everything that had the faintest resemblance to his real actions; here it will never be possible to disentangle the historical from the typical. In his case the democratic equality of citizens confronts its true opposite, the deviation from all norms, the eccentric who will ultimately take over the powers of the State in an emergency. This eccentric was destined to begin life having and being everything it was possible to have and be in Greece.[112] Alcibiades was of noble birth and remained throughout his life strikingly handsome.[113] He also had a natural fluency in speech, and a gift of sympathy which won people's trust and love without effort or intention on his part. His friendship with Socrates suggests that as a young man he was intellectually gifted too. But we must be wary of believing all Plato says about this, for the *Symposium* does not set out to be a historical document; the author of a philosophical dialogue has the right to invent much of it. The relationship with Socrates may well have been briefer and less significant than in this account, and on Alcibiades' side perhaps only sought from caprice, or to vex his lovers; and, since he had such a tremendous power over his fellow citizens, Plato may have found it desirable to emphasize this element in his dialogue.[114] Whatever the truth about this, Alcibiades was certainly an astonishing compound of immense gifts and extreme showmanship, partly conscious and partly unconscious, in the exploitation of these gifts – the greatest demagogue of all, as Plutarch calls him.[115] Even his ability to adapt to the customs of other countries was a series of new aspects of his demagogy. The Athenians were totally bewitched by him, put up with his outrageous behaviour and were inclined to find everything about him interesting, even without his encouragement; the response he aroused was such that it would be a wonder if he had kept his head.[116] Later on, his appearance at Olympia showed all too clearly how he despised the Greeks as a people of gapers and gossips. On that occasion he was crude and flamboyant; in Athens his attitude soon led Timon to greet him as the man who would bring about the great disaster. As a young man he had believed that nobody could become outstanding unless he had been a hardened criminal in youth;[117] now, having eliminated the rest of the democrats by the power of his eloquence, he practised lying and deception in external affairs, and was chiefly responsible for the extermination of the people of Melos.[118] At the same time he infected the Athenians with the monstrous ambition that was peculiar to him, and showed his intention of fully exploiting their imagination for his own ends; although he knew perfectly well that the Melos affair was inhuman and the Sicilian adventure foolish, he pushed ahead with both, to pander to the Athenians' principal passion.

The consequence of the whole cult that had been devoted to Alcibiades was then inevitable. The ambition he had awakened or chiefly encouraged, not only to conquer Sicily but to rule far and wide, and to found a great empire in the West, led to the Sicilian expedition, the ultimate in presumptuous egoism. But, just then, having drawn the Athenians into this doomed project, he was incriminated in the affair of the mutilation of the herms, and his entire existence was suddenly threatened. Called home to face a charge, he escaped from the official ship sent to fetch him, and fled to Sparta; and then what Plato calls the dazzling law of Nature shone out. Hearing that the death sentence had been passed on him in Athens, he said: 'We will show them we are still alive.'[119] He not only became a perfect Spartan in his habits, but showed his true temperament by now becoming the wholehearted enemy of Athens, allowing himself no veiled regret or any other useful half-open door for retreat. Without hesitation he suggested the most effective measures for destroying Athens: he advised sending help to Syracuse and fortifying Deceleia, so that the Athenians would lose their income from agriculture as well as from the mines, and that their allies should desert them on seeing they were in trouble; then he brought about Ionia's break with Athens and the treaty between Sparta and Persia. Incidentally he also disgraced himself in the palace of Agis by seducing the King's wife Timaea, with the express purpose of leaving his own descendants to be kings of Sparta instead of the Heraclids.[120]

Forced to take refuge in Asia Minor when the Spartans became suspicious and plotted his death, he then cast his spell on Tissaphernes; for, as Plutarch says, no-one, whatever their nature or character, could have resisted the charm of his company, and even those who feared him delighted in his presence and his appearance. Then, after he had led a kind of floating existence for a while, the possibility arose for him to return to Athens, on which he had inflicted mortal harm. A report survives of an authentic-sounding incident from the negotiations on Samos about this. There, it seems, he 'wept' over his fate, because he had been forced by his enemies to use his own powers and distinction (*arete*) against his native city.[121] So this fine quality, quite divorced from devotion to the State, was exploited at all costs as the justification of his whole being, and his enemies provided the excuse for all his betrayals. The excuse was accepted, though his recall was, as Dionysus says in *Frogs*, 'a difficult birth';[122] still it was wonderfully well prepared by him, since he would not return empty-handed, but in splendour; and he was victorious again, and again successful in the service of Athens, when the curse hurled after him by the Eumolpidae was withdrawn, and his city gave him a magnificent welcome home. He really had no cause to complain that his genius was not recognized; he was given unconditional command by land and sea, and the mass of the people seem to have hoped that he would put an end to the constitution and the talking-shop which were ruining the State, and seize the reins of power himself. But at this point his legendary fame itself turned against him, because it was now believed that he could succeed in anything, and once this proved not to be the case he was blamed for lack of good will. When he failed to satisfy exaggerated hopes, and his deputy admiral had been defeated at Notion (trying, like a true Athenian, to win glory on his own account) complaints began to be heard again in the assembly; the *demos* elected ten generals and Alcibiades had to flee once more. In Thrace, where he had prepared a safe refuge for himself, he still had the opportunity to send an unheeded warning to the Attic generals about the exposed position they had taken up at Aegospotami; soon afterwards he was assassinated in Asia Minor.

Alcibiades' personality towered over all party allegiance in the popular assembly, the courts and the cliques, and was capable of ensnaring anybody. In Athens they said of him, as they did in Sparta of Lysander (who makes a far more repulsive impression): 'His homeland would be unable to survive another man like this.'[123] Yet later it survived much worse; *poleis* existed to produce tremendous exceptions. But in the fourth century, when many would gladly have resembled him, the old energies were no longer sufficient. Alcibiades must always give matter for reflection. The way in which his personal gifts allowed him to mislead Athens into the Sicilian expedition, how the city drove him to extremes, suffered terribly at his hands, welcomed him again and then finally rejected him, remains one of the most wretched series of events in Greek history.

The rise of great individuals was linked with the growing love of fame (*philotimia*), the effort each man made to give his life lustre by his actions. What they desired was fame in posterity, and this, even given quite extraordinary ambition, is rarely a strong motive in our own times; it is as if we were dimly aware that posterity may not amount to much. It was not so for the Greeks; Plato makes his Diotima say to Socrates: 'You see how human beings try as hard as they can to make a name for themselves and win undying fame for all time; all are willing to undergo danger for this purpose, more than for their children, to sacrifice their possessions and accept hardship and to die for it. Surely you cannot believe that Alcestis died because of Admetus, or Achilles for the sake of Patroclus, or that your Codrus would have sought fame so that his children should rule, if they had not known that the immortal memory of their virtues would live on, as it really does live on in us?' And Socrates replies: 'Far from it; everybody does what they do so that their merits shall be known for ever and their name glorious, and the better they are the more this is true.'[124] This longing for posthumous fame goes back to the heroic age, as we have seen;[125] then the agon takes on this highest role, while gradually notoriety begins to play a part besides celebrity, so that as well as famous individuals – beautiful women among them[126] – the most criminal and the ridiculous are also listed: stupidity, gluttony and drunkenness have their kind of fame too.[127]

The clearest evidence of the love of fame is given us by the increasing number of *monuments*. Among Eastern nations in antiquity, the only commemoration of individuals, apart from the kings, was the grave; and even this, with the exception of the Egyptian funerary steles, was hardly ever designed to bring the single individual and his doings closer to later generations. Despots had the exclusive right to notoriety in the future, so that in the Far East, in Persia and so on, only the graves of kings are known. In contrast, the Greeks accepted the glorification of the individual; this included the grave-inscription, which, in its poetic form, the grave-distichon, enjoyed an immense vogue in the fifth century with Simonides and his epitaphs on all and sundry. Dissociated from the grave, glorification then took the form of the statue in honour of a person, its earliest appearance being the athlete's statue as early as the sixth century; from the fifth century, statues were put up to every kind of celebrity – statesmen, generals, poets, musicians, orators and so forth – sometimes officially, sometimes by relatives, admirers or professional bodies.[128]

In time, municipal benevolence made citizens as eager to be voted a statue at public expense as to be rewarded with crowns, front-rank seats at festivals etc., and so it was that even in Pausanias' time the cities were full of statues of every kind, the later, awarded for very ordinary services or simply by party favour, outnumbering the earlier.[129] Besides the statues most commonly set up on the marketplace or the acropolis of each town, the great agonal sites each had its population of portrait-statues. Olympia and Delphi were particularly favourite places for the cult of fame to demonstrate itself; this was by no means limited to athletes but included notables of every kind. States honoured their fellow citizens there, even if they also had statues at home, and so there were collections of statesmen and military leaders (regardless of the hurt feelings of the defeated) peacemakers, historians such as Anaximenes of Lampsacus, orators such as Gorgias,[130] Spartan kings, *diadochoi* and so forth, all huddled together indiscriminately.[131]

Eventually, too, huge monumental propaganda groups were set up, Lysander for instance having himself represented at Delphi with several divinities round him and Poseidon in the act of crowning him, and accompanied by his priest, his steersman and twenty-seven figures of junior Spartan officers and some allied commanders, not otherwise known to fame.[132] However it is *à propos* a statue of Lysander commissioned for Olympia that Pausanias remarks on the way everybody used these symbols of honour to flatter the momentarily powerful. The Samians had once put up a bronze of Alcibiades as a dedication in their Heraion; after Aegospotami they sent the Lysander statue to Olympia, while the Ephesians put in their Artemision a Lysander, an Eteonicus, a Pharax and other quite obscure Spartans; but after Conon's victory at Cnidos the Ionians changed with the times, and a bronze Conon and Timotheus appeared in the Heraion as well as in the Artemision.[133]

As for Athenian celebrities, early portraits of them were painted rather than sculpted, and indeed the painted portrait became much more popular in the fifth century, in public frescoes and in pictures which might then be dedicated by the sitter's family in a shrine. Portraits such as these were later copied in large numbers and even reproduced in miniature in books.

Returning to the subject of graves, the *polyandria* or mass graves for the fallen should not be forgotten. At Plataea there was one each for the Spartans, the Tegeates, the Athenians, the Megarians and the Phliasians. The pride that was expressed in them can be imagined from the account of peoples who had not fought in the battle raising their own empty grave-mounds for the sake of their descendants. This story at least shows what cunning and blackmail seemed plausible in pursuit of glory, and is paralleled by the impudence of Pausanias inscribing the tripod at Delphi with his own name as the sole donor,[134] and the brash way in which different states, armies and leaders tried to claim the chief honours after the Persian Wars. As for the monuments at the mass graves, we know of the Lion of Chaeronea. There was no inscription on that figure, perhaps, as Pausanias thinks, because luck had been more important than valour (9.40.5), or else, more probably, because words were superfluous, or too dangerous given the continuing and increasing power of Macedonia.

Broader issues of social life demand our attention. On the subject of homosexual love we shall confine ourselves here to referring to the main document we have, Xenophon's *Symposium*, as evidence of the unquestioned assumptions made about it in general conversation. We will turn instead to the position of women. In comparison with the previous century this seems if anything still more reduced, and it sometimes appears that in Athens, the source of our information, the last vestige of tenderness for the sex had vanished. At the special festivals and mysteries for women they paraded all together in front of the whole people, a custom in strong contrast to the retiring life they normally led – this not only at the procession of the Panathenaea, but also in the celebration of fairly wild cults;[135] none of this suggests that women were accorded great respect. Slaves too had their particular cults. The best and highest things, all that belonged to the agon, poetry, literature and the whole of the drama, existed only for men.[136] Courtesans were the only women who counted for anything in social life; they could join in conversation at banquets; their company was valued for their wit, while the daughter of the house was admired for her silence and diffidence.[137]

This was equally true of the lady of the house, to whom Sophocles addressed the classic phrase: 'Silence, woman, is a woman's jewel' (*Ajax* 292). Not only was she to be reluctant to speak – the adornment also consisted in her not being spoken of. The conclusion of Pericles' funeral oration has a striking reference to this, and comes nearest to an official pronouncement on the position of women in Athens.[138] The orator first consoles the parents, then the brothers and sons of the fallen, and lastly the widows (it was something that they were allowed to be present); he says: 'I should not forget female virtue too, and to the widows I will say briefly all that needs to be said: your greatest honour will be that you remain true to your character, and that as little as possible is said of you whether in praise or blame.' This is the opinion of the man whose companion was Aspasia (he must have made an exception for her) and who surely had many other mistresses.[139]

Marriage was not thought much of. In the most serious discussions the same argument was always heard: the reason for its existence had nothing to do with love and certainly not with the satisfaction of sensual needs, but was only to produce children to care for their parents in old age,[140] and, as Antisthenes would usually add, it was on account of these future children that the woman chosen should be physically and mentally a good specimen.[141] We might be tempted to think that legal marriage would have disappeared in Athens altogether but for the regulation that only those whose parents both had the status of citizens were recognized as citizens themselves. In Xenophon's *Oeconomicus* Ischomachus gives an account of how he trained his young wife; his concluding words to her are morally the finest, and also the most genuinely respectful, that any husband seems to have risen to: 'If you prove better than I am myself, you will make me your servant'(42). But this is only an isolated phrase; the rest is all harshness. As a rule, while the wife was condemned to live in the women's quarters and made subservient in every way, the men enjoyed themselves with harlots and hetaerae; complaints of this are loudly voiced in Aristophanes' *Thesmophoriazusae* (785 ff.). Sophocles too pities the lot of women, pointing out how the girl who has lived happily in childhood is rejected by the domestic gods and her parents, and traded off, perhaps to strangers and barbarians, in any case to an unfamiliar house, and after her wedding night has to praise everything or seem to admire all she finds.[142] Courtship itself is often associated with repulsive customs. For example there is the unashamed jilting of brides as soon as their fathers are known to have died poor, as happened not only to the daughters of Lysander, but also (in one version) to those of Aristides the Just.[143] In his speech 'On the Mysteries', Andocides gives an account of the marriages of the spendthrift Callias III, who married, divorced and remarried entirely to suit his own convenience.[144] It may be said that Callias was only one man, and a depraved one; but the number of clear pronouncements on the subject leaves no doubt that even the most distinguished men held women in contempt. Whatever Xanthippe may have been like in other ways, Plato's account of her parting from Socrates is indirect evidence of the disrespect women had to endure. As Xanthippe sits weeping with the little boy near Socrates and cries out, as a woman would, 'Now you are speaking with your friends, and they with you, for the last time,' he glances at Criton and says, 'O

Criton, let someone take this woman home,' and she is led away loudly weeping and resisting. To Phaedo Socrates behaves quite differently, and there is a heartfelt warmth in the intimate detail of his ruffling Phaedo's hair in his familiar way.[145] Even though Plato was not present, the fiction he employs seems to us a perfectly acceptable version of what happened. Indirect light is shed on the position of women by the fact that of all the conversations recorded there are almost none with women; the speakers are almost exclusively men, and the women, even if some are present, are treated as if they were not there. The great exception is Diotima, to whom Socrates refers in the Platonic symposium; even if she is an entirely fictional figure, this would still be evidence of an unusual generosity on Plato's part.[146]

It was only here and there, on the fringes of the Greek world, that true political power and influence in affairs were exercised by women from the families of colonial tyrants or Persian vassals; as early as the sixth century there were Pheretime of Cyrene and Artemisia of Halicarnassus, already notorious for her treacherous nature; later, at Salamis, she rode down and sank a ship of her own fleet to save herself. Then there was the resolute Mania, widow of the Persian vassal Zenis ruler of Dardanos; she continued to rule in his stead by favour of Pharnabazus, and even commanded armies in battle, but was finally murdered by a son-in-law.[147] In Greece itself, warlike deeds by women are hardly heard of;[148] however the women of Sparta, with its peculiar traditions, may have been better able to make their voice heard than those elsewhere.

One typical consequence of the general contempt for women was the increasing sense of wonder at the Trojan War's having been caused by a woman's infidelity.[149] Not, however, that the adultery of women was taken lightly. In the *Andromache* of Euripides, in which Peleus among others (595 ff.) makes fun of the damaging effect of the Spartan women's gymnastics on feminine virtue, Hermione in her self-accusation is made to blame marital disasters on the wife's being constantly visited by other women (930 ff.). One from greed, another in order to have a companion in guilt, many out of coarse sensuality, all help to bring about the mischief; and indeed there must have been some danger, where a wife lived in other respects under such constraint, in allowing her to receive any woman she liked, including a random selection of neighbours. In any case, one great difference between then and now was that the unfaithful wife found no leniency in a public opinion that condoned love affairs – since women then had no share in forming public opinion – and that adultery was held to be equivalent to any other theft. The adulterous woman was not considered at all interesting and must have been a disgrace to her husband and to any children she already had, but there was none of the modern mockery of the husband, and he felt free to create a scandal in a way that would be unthinkable today.[150] Last but not least, the theatre was not concerned with the psychological interpretation and palliation of adultery. It is also interesting that, in myth, Hephaestus calls all the gods together to show them his wife caught in the net with Ares, and that they laugh not at him but at the trapped couple.

The depiction of women in poetry presents a problem; it is hard to decide how much to rely on Aristophanes in his three plays about women (*Thesmophoriazusae*, *Lysistrata* and *Ecclesiazusae*). We can have no idea what comedies might be like in our own day if the audience were entirely masculine, especially in the corrupt atmosphere of great cities. But the tragic writers must be taken seriously. Although one may argue that poetic documents can have little weight for the cultural historian if the poet is a devoted specialist and has turned his back on the world, the case is altered where, as in the antique epic, the poem is an expression of the popular consciousness, or where, as in tragedy, the people are being addressed or exhorted; then the testimony of poetry has great force and value. In such poetry the ideas conveyed can only be those that are generally approved.

Even Aeschylus' views are very harsh. In the *Eumenides* (657 ff.) Apollo maintains that only the father is the parent of the child, the mother simply a nurse, and that Athena had no mother; in her concluding speech (734 ff.) Athena sides *a priori* with the men. The unfeeling speech Eteocles addresses to the wailing, frantic crowd of Theban women (Aeschylus, *Seven against Thebes* 182 ff.) may be an exceptional case because of the terror of the moment; but in the *Suppliants* it makes an impression of extraordinary cruelty when King Pelasgus declares that he can scarcely justify the shedding of men's blood for women (476 f.). It is quite easy to believe the Euripides-figure in the *Frogs* of Aristophanes (1043 ff.) when he says that *this* poet (Aeschylus) never wrote a love scene.

We have said in connection with the *Tereus* fragment that Sophocles is capable of a note of melancholy sympathy in speaking of the fate of women [p. 252 n.142 above]. But it is questionable whether he would have created his Antigone and Electra if they were not imposed on him by the myth, which contains ideas so different from those of his own time; it seems as though such characters lived only on the stage, not in life.

Then Euripides. It is accepted that in his tragedies he prefers the motive forces to come from the women. In the great majority of his plays the principal interest centres on women, and the chorus consists almost always of women; it may be said that it is precisely his emphasis on women that makes him original and new. Was Euripides incapable of the ideal heroic vein? Or were the masculine characters perhaps exhausted, were the Ajax, Oedipus and Heracles of Sophocles the last possible appearances of these figures, and had the bloom quite gone off myth as a subject for further inspiration? If myth is altered and criticized as it often is in Euripides, perhaps it is inevitable that the men will mostly emerge as inferior. Thus his new ideal masculine character, to whom he devotes immense energy, is Hippolytus; Ion is far weaker. On the other hand his plays are full of female characters who are either awe-inspiring or else idealized, and this is so from the beginning down to what is probably his last play, the *Bacchae*, in which everyone is shown as in the wrong by contrast with the terrible and splendid raving of the women. The male characters, with their striking observations about women, have sometimes tended to encourage the idea that the poet is a misogynist, because these remarks have been taken to represent his own views. It would be more fitting to call him a misohero or heroomastix, for he treats many heroes appallingly badly (the Atreidae, for instance, almost always); generally they embody some fairly disreputable positive right or interest, while women represent self-sacrifice and passion – not very often, indeed, that of love, more usually revenge or something akin to it.[151]

In such plays as *Hippolytus* and *Orestes*, the risks of the marital relationship, and the nature of women as extraordinarily prone to evil and dreadful deeds, are denounced with a ruthless openness that is offensive.[152] A vital piece of evidence here is the great speech of Hippolytus (616 ff.); there is no need to suppose that all Greeks thought the same, but it suffices that Hippolytus can have these views and still be an ideal character, or certainly not one to be chased off the stage with derision or abhorrence.[153] He begins by lamenting that women are indispensable to the reproduction of the human race.[154] Now, he says, the father gives a dowry and marries his daughter off to be rid of his misfortune, but the husband takes the poisonous weed into his house with joy, and tends and adorns her, and in return for this he must live under constraint; either, when he has married into a worthy family, keeping his bad wife with (pretended) complacency, or, if he has a good wife and undesirable in-laws, taking the rough with the smooth. The husband who is best off is the one who has a hopelessly stupid wife sitting at home, useless though she may be: 'a clever one I hate. Let there be none in my household who thinks more than is good for a woman; for Cypris puts bad impulses and a capacity for boundless evil soonest into the clever woman, while the mindless one is guarded against folly by the very inadequacy of her wit.' In these words Hippolytus is certainly expressing a feeling widely shared in Athens at that time: the educated Athenian could not bear a clever woman unless she were a harlot. The following passage is just as truly Athenian, when he adds, in speaking of the Nurse, that no serving-woman should be allowed to go in and out of the women's apartments; rather, to prevent anyone coming in to gossip, dogs, which are both savage and speechless, should sit at their doors, so that the women in the house cannot occupy themselves with plotting evil, as they do at present, while the maids act as intermediaries. As long as the women had a connection with the outside world through the servants, the Athenians thought that shutting them up was useless.

Alongside Hippolytus stands the terrible figure of Phaedra. After Hippolytus has rejected the Nurse's offer in this tirade, Phaedra determines to satisfy Cypris by her own death, but also to ensure that it ruins Hippolytus rather than bringing him triumph. By deciding on suicide she retains her claim to good repute since her love has not been guilty in the physical sense.[155] The figure of the Nurse is very important. She is the go-between, and by making light of everything and insisting that all's well that ends well, she becomes the apologist of her mistress's sin.

In *Ion* (398 ff.) Creusa says that women are generally hated and ill-used by men. She too is one of the characters who can be understood only if we bear in mind that the will to dominate and to fulfil the passions is regarded as justifiable and allowed immense scope. It is a matter of course that a woman in Creusa's situation, who sees a stepson grow more powerful than she is in her own house, will believe she has the right to go to extremes; but here an extraordinary stroke is the motive urged on her by the Tutor for killing Xuthus and Ion when he says (843 ff.) that she ought to prove herself a woman. Euripides must have been particularly proud of this and of the long stichomythia (985 ff.) in which details of the murder are decided on, down to minute instructions for the poisoning. He succeeds in maintaining dramatic plausibility even in Creusa for all her terrible deeds.

Besides Creusa and Medea, the horrifying Electra of *Orestes* belongs in the list of dreadful women. In her case, again, we must beware of making the mistake of supposing that Euripides could not have meant to combine greatness or dramatic sublimity in a woman with the most sinister characteristics. The Ajax of Sophocles is just as terrible and yet sublime, and is considered worthy of total sympathy; the fearful energy of such female figures as these three is the counterpart of his violent temperament. On the other hand, this ideal is not incompatible with slyness and cunning, characteristic traits that Euripides admires, and presents, among other instances, in the long consultation between Helen and Menelaus in which an idea of the utmost craftiness, which they finally adopt, is expounded by her (*Helen* 1032 ff.).

Contrasting with all these are some figures of immensely noble self-sacrificing women; the two Iphigenias, Macaria, Polyxena, Theonoe and others. There is certainly a shade of difference between them and the Antigone of Sophocles, and yet they have a certain stilted quality.

To return from the imaginary figures of poetry to the Athenian reality, a further word must be said about the hetaerae of those times. In earlier days a few of them had risen to distinction by their wit and beauty, so that all Hellas knew of them, discussed them in the *leschê* and compared them. Now the hetaera-figure was moving very much into the foreground, and the type was being formed which, in the fourth century, was to produce Laïs. As we have already said, it was not for ordinary sexual relations that the Athenians sought out hetaerae; there were other women to cater for these (*pornai, pallachai*). The hetaera was rather the woman whose attraction was the grace of wit, and, as is well known, the outstanding example of this was Aspasia of Miletus, the friend of Pericles. How she came to Athens is not related; she is said to have followed as a rival in the footsteps of Thargelia, also a Milesian, and to have been, like her, not only very beautiful but clever too. Pericles lived with Aspasia in great style after separating from his legal wife, and had a son by her who bore his name. She was credited with the decisive influence in the outbreak of the Samian and even of the Peloponnesian Wars, and with having trained Pericles as an orator.[156] Yet she was firmly believed to keep girls for public prostitution,[157] and she was accused not only of *asebeia* but also of procuring free women, not slaves, for Pericles.[158] His tears saved her from judgment; but after his death she joined forces with Lysicles, a demagogue of low birth whom she made one of the principal men in Athens. The younger Cyrus named his Milto Aspasia in her honour.

It says much for Aspasia that Socrates could call himself her pupil, even if the tone is ironical,[159] and it is pleasing to believe that married men brought their wives to listen to her, as for instance, according to Cicero, Xenophon did his own, who must certainly have been an honourable woman;[160] they profited from the best thing Aspasia had to offer, her brilliant conversation. As for the very precise accusations made against her, there is no possibility of proving or disproving them. The whole society in which she existed was too shady and too disorderly, as is seen in every page of Aristophanes. Even if she was irreproachable, we are not in a position to prove it.[161]

In any case Pericles long remained the only Hellene in whose life a woman exercised an influence strong enough to affect all his actions. Other Greeks were at most temporarily entangled with some hetaera. It would have been quite foreign to Greek attitudes to think that a man might be judged according to the kind of woman who loved him, or that an ill-fated love affair could ruin his life. An unhappy marriage might cause great misery, but lasting happiness never depended, for a Greek, on love and marriage.[162] When passion was experienced it was transient, directed only to immediate enjoyment, and moreover regarded as an illness.[163] The wife was quite unable to make an exclusive claim on her husband materially, let alone emotionally; this kind of right over the individual was exercised only by the *polis*, which would imprison the man in such a case. The husband, however, insisted on his exclusive claim to his wife, and because of the children, who had to be legitimate, the *polis* supported him in this.

Another aspect of the question was that men were not educated or polished by love affairs with women. The woman was the guardian of morality in the home but did not determine the tone of a social 'set', and (although the women in Aristophanes rail at and complain of the men) she had no power over the reputation of her husband, still less of other men. Nor had she any say in matters of social standing, and least of all did she indicate her husband's rank by the way she dressed. There was no mixed society composed of families of a certain class; the symposium was something totally different. The daughters were married entirely by arrangement and had, like their mothers, no say in the matter. Although men certainly sought rich brides, or rather dowries, there was no blatant angling for rich young men, no flirtation, and least of all any training of the girls themselves for the chase. The whole concept of 'fashion' was not yet in existence. Styles of clothing scarcely changed, or only very slowly. Above all the women did not compete by showing off new clothes, and were never in a position to attract men by flaunting about in them. To compensate, they had their own special religious services like the Thesmophoria, when the finery was displayed in honour of the divinity.

This state of affairs is linked with the antibanausic attitude of mind. The idea of an obligation to earn in order first to create a home and then to live according to one's station would have been quite incomprehensible to the Greeks. The antibanausic attitude meant an unpretentious way of living, a simple upbringing for the sons, the limitation of journeys to those between the city and the farm.[164] A man of property was in any case so thoroughly bled by all kinds of *leitourgiai* and *choregiae* that he could not possibly afford any great expenditure on his household.

The later comedy gives a measure of what the love relationship had to offer: desire and, in case of its frustration, jealousy. Nowhere has it any spiritual depth; it seems to come to an end the moment the play is over.

As for social activity, as already observed [p. 203 above], the basis of it from early times was the symposium, which might be described as the principal outlet and relaxation of private life – and thus a natural requirement. Optional delights in the way of music and dancing, which were beginning to play a larger part in the symposium at this time, need be only briefly mentioned. There were girls playing the flute, the lyre and the cithar, and dancers and hetaerae might also be present; we need not dwell on the variety of jokes, riddles and forfeits, nor the dice-throwing and betting, except for the celebrated *kottabos* which gave endless amusement. This was a game in which wine had to be skilfully sprayed out of one vessel into another. The pattern in which it splashed up was supposed to be oracular, especially for questions concerning love, and by this teasing game a guest might be persuaded to confess to a love affair.[165] The increase in devices of luxury at the symposium is perhaps to be explained by the time and place. Costly dwellings and clothing were not customary, no-one owned more than the essential slaves, except for the tutor; there were no carriages, and horse breeding was in decline. In general, 'living according to one's rank' or 'in keeping with one's station' were notions not even formulated. Thus the symposium and the hetaerae were the only possible luxuries.[166]

All symposia took place in private houses; not even a self-respecting slave would have dared to eat in a tavern.[167] Unless the expense was borne by one individual, matters were so arranged that each guest paid his contribution (*symbole*), though there was always the chance of extra numbers since uninvited guests were often brought, and soon the parasites began to push in too. The normal course of events at a banquet of this period is fully documented. First the ritual prescribed the washing of hands, then the tables were carried in and the meal was eaten. Hands were again washed and the drink-offering was performed.[168] The presence of the flute-girl (perhaps more likely to have been an older woman than a pretty young one) was necessary for the purpose of this libation – in which, to honour the good spirit, undiluted wine was sipped by the now garlanded guests – and for the paean that was associated with it and sung by the whole assembly. Afterwards this flautist was probably sent away[169] and then the symposium itself began at the 'second tables', usually under the guidance of a presiding chairman chosen by some rota or by drawing lots with beans. Then the wine was mixed, with the addition of water in the proportion of two-thirds to one or three-quarters to one; these correct proportions are emphatically laid down in a poetic fragment as ensuring gaiety, since rowdiness would result if they were ignored, and even madness, if the quantity of water were cut by half.[170] The poets have many charming passages about wine and drinking,[171] but as it was usual to drink long and deep, there is often talk of drunkenness, and at the festivals of Dionysus this was even generally permitted.[172] The symposiarch could rule that pledges should be drunk (this was forbidden in Sparta) and there was also a system of fining by drinking; in fact there was a certain obligation to drink, which, according to a fragment of Sophocles (735 Radt), was no better than an obligation to be thirsty. One poet gives a character the wise remark: 'If the hangover came before the party no-one would drink too much' (Alexis in Athenaeus 9.34). The Greeks always showed the keenest interest in drinking vessels, with their variety of shapes and the wealth of symbolic figures and stories represented on them, from the horn of Nestor down to the unused wooden bowl in Theocritus. All the things connected with enjoyment were round, like the world, the sun and the moon – the table was round and so were cakes and drinking cups. This is very pleasingly put, and no doubt based on an older idea, by one of the speakers in Athenaeus (11.78). A later epigram runs: 'Give me the sweet goblet, made from earth, as I am; that earth in which I shall lie again when I am dead'; here the link between enjoyment and the thought of mortality is beautifully expressed.[173] We may reflect that the forms of these vessels were the same in the grave-vessels, never used, but given to the dead to take with them because of their beauty.

The liveliness of conversation was increased by song as well as by drinking. The singing was of three kinds; all the guests would sing together, then each in turn, and finally only those who could sing best, each from the place where he sat.[174] As this was done in no fixed order, but haphazard, this last form was called *scholion* (zigzag). For a long time the old familiar music was preferred, though even a poet of the old comedy complained that (evidently at the symposium) songs by the frivolous Gnesippus, who had composed serenades for adulterers, were heard instead of Stesichorus, Alcman and Simonides, who had gone out of fashion.[175] Much later, though, in the circle of Dionysius the Younger, paeans by Phrynichus, Stesichorus and Pindar were sung at table, and it was left to the flatterers to sing those composed by the tyrant.[176]

The main thing of course must have been the conversation. Nowhere else in the world, and at no time in history, has the banquet been so much the *repository of wit*. Because of the way in which the guests lay on their couches, facing towards the centre and each other, general conversation was not only possible but inevitable; it was not a matter of each talking as well as he could with his chance neighbour, and for this reason too, no doubt what was said was intended to be heard by all.[177] Just as there was no opportunity for quiet gossip between two people, so there was also complete protection from toasts, which always involve solemn eloquence being dragged in at dinner, with a single person forcing everyone to attend to him for a time. This conversation was also independent of wealth, position and rank; it had a candour and lack of affectation in the discussion of all aspects of life, as well as an absence of our modern humility, which are characteristic of the Greeks. Everyone's tongue was loosened, and what might still be wanting by way of 'learned' vocabulary was supplied by sophistry. We must imagine all this combined with a very marked politeness, with rules just as well defined as today's, but different; for tact has always been a grace given by the gods, and amiable conduct was certainly much prized by the Greeks. Athens, too, offered other themes than were available for the conversation of Asiatics or other Greeks. Here each felt a strong need to give his views on the course of the world in general, and no doubt many tirades in Euripides reflect this. This poet's popularity may well have arisen largely because he could express themes of general conviction in beautiful language which was yet free of rhetoric. Everyone was also in the mood for the discussion of all men and all things, and inclined to merriment and mockery; but it would be good to know, if it were possible, whether or not the symposium had its dangers in its close connection with political lobbying, which must have used it as its antechamber.

The easy social mix, at the symposium, of the distinguished and the famous must have been early observed and described. Plutarch, following Ion, gives a fairly detailed account (Plutarch, *Cimon* 9) of an Athenian symposium where Cimon was present and described his Persian campaign; Ion is also the source for the table talk of Sophocles on Chios, which begins with a boy pouring wine and continues into a literary discussion, until it ends at last with a kiss (Athenaeus 13.81). In the literature of the preceding period it is in the elegy (soon contracted to the epigram) that we find most of what is known about the symposium; in Plato's time philosophical dialogue assumes this role, and the very fact that the best writers used the symposium to such effect shows how high its value was as the receptacle of intellectual life.

Plato's *Symposium*, the foremost work of this kind, is probably a very free invention from beginning to end. The characters in it may in reality never have met, or not all on the same occasion, and what they say may be almost entirely Plato's invention. But even if it is not a strictly historical document, it is one of the greatest importance, since it shows what could be thought possible. Just to think of these people meeting together presupposes a unique moment in social life. What is also important is simply the assumption that at the moment of the highest intellectual flowering of Athens, but, equally, at a time of grave political crisis, there could be an incomparable level of conversation free from any private gossip, in which each participant could coherently express general views on a great theme, and often embody them in myth. That this was possible at such a time supports Renan's belief that the stormy periods of history are actually favourable to the life of the mind.

I need refer only briefly to the subtle detail of the Platonic *Symposium*, for example the exchange of compliments that occupies the interval separating the discourses of Pausanias, Eryximachus and Aristophanes from that of Agathon. But as to the broad outline, it must be remembered that this banquet is not entirely typical. When, after the paean, the drinking begins, there is no selection of a presiding speaker; and all the guests agree that each shall drink only as much as he likes (because they still have their hangover from the day before) and so they send the flute-girl away at once. And then this banquet has a second and a third act too. First Alcibiades bursts in on it in a high state of jollity, crowned with a dense garland of ivy and violets entwined with ribbons, and bringing a flautist and several merry companions, and then, after his most extraordinary discourses, there suddenly appear a party of roistering friends who find room for themselves – it is not clear if their right to do so results from Agathon's victory – whereupon things become very noisy, order turns topsy-turvy and everybody gets roaring drunk.

Plato's *Symposium*, then, gives a one-sided impression of the kind of parties that cultivated Athenians enjoyed. That of Xenophon tells us much more about the tone of sociability that was really possible, and is indeed by far its most important document, despite the fact that Socrates, who transcends all norms, is the very soul and focal point of it. Almost throughout this account the reader has the impression of authentic memories, even if they are those of half a lifetime concentrated into a single evening. Side by side with a refined sense of morality and courtesy, the striking features – in complete contrast to any modern social manners – are the open expression of intimate emotions and the discussion of other people's love affairs, and the glimpses into what seems astonishing indiscretion, which nevertheless has its limits. There is hardly a text that better demonstrates the possible composition of a society of the first rank, and how its elements were held in balance.[178] As this symposium takes place in a wealthy household, the author is free to make additions to the programme, among them the boy and girl belonging to a Syracusan (he performs with a flute-girl) who are permitted to interrupt the discussion in a very timely way with dances and mime.[179] The professional funny man turns up too, a contemptible person but – depending on the company – not invariably superfluous. He joins these people uninvited, smuggled in, and Callias allows him to stay because it would be unkind to send him away; when he sees that nobody laughs at his jokes, he becomes very sad and begins to cry, whereupon they all good-naturedly console him by promising to laugh again, and thus render him truly superfluous.[180]

The *Symposia* of Plato and Xenophon are the probable source of the established idea of the symposium as a literary form for the presentation of general attitudes and philosophical disputations, and ultimately of everything worth knowing.[181] This seems to be why Epicurus incorporated separate writings into this form. And even later, with Plutarch and Athenaeus, it developed into a framework for mere learned proceedings. Various successful poetic forms have, simply, to accommodate material that is alien to them. All this was only a reflection of the mythical glory of the banquet in the golden age.

But the symposium was not the only kind of social intercourse; strolling about in public places (*agorazein*) was another.[182] In bad weather, when the open square was uninviting, or when a smaller group was desired, people would lounge about and chat in the shops – in Athens, preferably those that were nearest the public square. Such a shop is kept by the invalid – a shoemaker perhaps, as he tells a shoemaker's joke – who in the twenty-fourth oration of Lysias argues his claim to State support. He defends himself against the accusation that evil plans are hatched in his shop by declaring that all traders who own shops also entertain visitors: 'For all of you, my lord judges, are frequenters of one or another – a perfumer's, a barber's, a cobbler's for instance, and for preference those that lie nearest the market.' Even in those days barbers had a reputation for talking too much, and were sometimes excused by their having the most talkative customers. When a barber asked King Archelaus, 'How shall I shave thee, O King?' he answered 'In silence.'

Thus sociability was inborn in the Greeks; everything encouraged them in that direction, even the conduct of the state, with its popular assembly and courts of justice; there was always a crowd going to the place where talk was in progress. The complete social being originates in this milieu, for instance Aristippus (his life spans the turn of the fifth century) who could wear the chlamys or dress in rags as the occasion demanded, and like Alcibiades adapt himself to any time, place or role; when he was asked what he had learned from philosophy, he replied that it was the ability to mix confidently with everybody (Diogenes Laertius 2.8.4). New focal points of society began to form, which were to be very important. One may be discerned at the court of that Archelaus of Macedonia just mentioned, who ruled from 413 to 399 B.C. Officially, indeed, Greeks trembled and blessed themselves at his very name; but at least, at his court, the talents of Euripides, Agathon, Choerilus of Samos and the painters Zeuxis and Timotheus were valued at their true worth; men may have been torn apart by dogs there, but not by sycophants. In Athens the Laconizers must have formed a separate group. A unique phenomenon is the great Athenian house described at the beginning of the *Protagoras* of Plato. A morning audience given there by the three great sophists brings out extraordinary refinements of politeness from the host – Callias once more – and from the others present.[183] Hippias acknowledges that this, the most fortunate house in the city which is the sacred hearth of Hellas, has the right to expect [of himself and his fellows] that their conversation will deserve the honour of this reception.

This brings us to *sophistry* as a social phenomenon.[184] In my view it is too often treated with a tragic seriousness that comes from paying too much attention to Plato's Socrates;[185] in the fifth century sophistry must really have been totally inevitable, and to judge from the openness of the sophists' behaviour it must have been looked upon as a matter of course.

So, then, the three men from Abdera, Ceos and Elis, and with them the great Leontinian [Gorgias], travelled through Greece, creating a tremendous sensation everywhere, and especially in Athens, won over the most important people,[186] often acted as ambassadors[187] and were rewarded, when they had made their personalities felt in every way, with high fees, statues in their honour, the freedom of cities and so on.[188] This powerful recognition and response is enough to show that the case went far beyond what Plato felt prepared to admit; the publicity campaign by itself – the aspect he selects to make the sophists ridiculous – would not explain it. True, the publicity was huge, as may be imagined from their appearances in splendid costume and the gilded statue Gorgias erected to himself at Delphi. But such things, in the context, must not be judged too harshly; in an age without newspapers each man had to be his own publicity agent, and it is not only sophists but some very great men (Alcibiades above all) who would certainly strike us at first as vulgar boasters, if we could see them behaving as they did. There is no point in thinking them better than others – these sophists were Greeks *too*; but they combined in their person or at least represented together, one more, another less, three things: namely thought (since their pursuit was *also* philosophy and indeed ethics), rich and various positive knowledge, and oratory, the technique of which they actually founded.

The chief charge against them is that through their doctrine of the 'two sides' they preached moral indifference in everything and thus encouraged decadence. But there is nothing intrinsically wrong with the principle that on every subject it is possible to sustain opposite views equally well and make them plausible by oratory; it is simply a statement of fact, and impresses on the student's conscience that he should argue only for what seems to him true and right. For the application of this principle to law and morals better sources are needed than Plato, who was their rival. The sophists' well-known claim to be able to make the weaker case prevail clearly involves only a mental exercise, and they expressly stated that right and wrong were left out of consideration; this was then interpreted as true moral indifference on their part, with no more justification than if they were the lawyer appointed by a court to defend a criminal. That the Greeks of all people should have been corrupted by this is completely incredible; it is rather that the nation had only itself to blame for having fallen in love with eloquence and constantly having to speak in public, and the Athenians in particular were good lawyers in daily conversation and long before Gorgias came on the scene; there is reason to suppose that in Athens there were always good talkers and good listeners. Tragedy provides the image of it, from circumstantial speech and reply (in which the violent inconsequentiality of excited dramatic expression is often very much subordinated to the rhetorically correct exposition of reasons and considerations) to the passionate succession of monostichs. Indeed it is tempting to trace one kind of eloquence in Euripides directly to the influence of sophistry, but most of this too must be of genuine Athenian origin;[189] which does not exclude our awareness that overrefined oratory is ruinous to countries and to peoples (cf. *Hippolytus* 486 f.).

The doctrine of the right of the stronger, too, was in Greece at that time neither more nor less than a statement of existing conditions, and is similarly expressed by Spinoza. The man who had won power in the state by force of arms or eloquence did in fact (as Thrasymachus and Callicles say in Plato's *Gorgias* and *Republic*) make laws of his own choice and to his own advantage; his commands were really law in that state, and what went against his will was called unlawful. In that sense the law was naturally only a matter of opinion and agreement; to draw attention to the facts is not however the same as praising them. If the sophists are reproached with having encouraged 'the pride of individualism against the generality of morals and the State', it is fair to ask if the most famous Athenians had not long ago risen up against that generality without the aid of sophism. Was there not a Themistocles, determined to stand out in all possible ways? Were not the most important people of all subjectivists? Are the Athenians thought of as children, who had waited for these newcomers to educate them in this revolutionary tendency? It is just the same with the sophists' sceptical attitude to popular religion. 'Of the gods I am unable to find out whether they are, or are not, for many things hinder my enquiry; the uncertainty of the thing and the brevity of human life' – these words, attributed to Protagoras, were spoken at a time when most of his Athenian clients shared this attitude to the gods and had arrived at it by themselves.

What the sophists did would have been done by others if they had not existed, because it was inherent in the age; they worked towards the formation of an *art* of speaking, capable of arguing for or against anything and everything, and thus brought the Athenians the gift they most wished for. At the same time they were masters of great extempore fluency, so that Hippias could boast of finding something new to say each time on any subject; like Gorgias – if the surviving report is reliable – he would guarantee to answer any question whatever on the spur of the moment.[190] This fluency was matched by that extraordinary elegance of delivery that Gorgias achieved by the symmetry of his constructions, by attention to precise expression (Prodicus was particularly known for this) and further by the exact knowledge of all the means of impressing judges and the popular assembly.[191] Soon, on the initiative of Gorgias, the zealous pursuit of the study of rhetoric developed.[192] Speaking contests were held; fictional cases were used as exercises and collections made of general maxims that could be woven in anywhere (*loci communes*); and the epideictic discourse was created, the greatest example of it, apart from the speeches of Gorgias, being 'Heracles at the parting of the ways' by Prodicus.[193] The first textbooks of eloquence also came into being in these circles. As we have seen [see p. 178 above] Gorgias and Antiphon appeared as speakers at the festivals of Delphi and Olympia, urging harmony among the Greeks and war against the barbarians; Hippias too 'put Hellas under his spell' at Olympia with varied and skilful addresses; the great agonal meeting places must have seen sophistry in all its lustre.

Virgil (*Aeneid* VI.847 ff.) names, as advantages the Greeks had over the Romans, the visual arts, eloquence (*orabunt causas melius*) and astronomy. Of these, astronomy is a practical benefit for the whole world, but not a national treasure. It is a great good fortune that works of art survive to testify to the Greek spirit; for, outside the sphere of art, eloquence was largely predominant among the general gifts of the Greeks from about 400 B.C. and tended to weaken spontaneity of expression. In public life, it became, like the press today, the instrument of very little good and three-quarters of everything bad; it coloured and enfeebled both poetry and historiography; even the philosophers were partly, in real life, really rhetoricians. And this was by and large the result of sophistry, which originated essentially as eloquence. The whole world of antiquity gave the sophists credit for this, and even their greatest opponents were influenced by them, including Plato, in spite of his dialogue form. Looked at in its broad outlines and from a distance, the phenomenon may be seen in the following way. In times of highly developed civilization, when gifts and energies are widely distributed, changes will occur if public circumstances do not hinder them, and all the more certainly if they do everything to further them.[194] An effective medium comes into being which develops a power of its own and becomes a weapon in the hands of the mediocre and of those whose talents and situation allow them to exploit it. Even the highly gifted and highly privileged are then obliged to make use of this medium to obtain a hearing of any kind; the strongest testimony in favour of Epicurus at a later time is that he gave up any recourse to eloquence. The transitional period, though, can be astonishing, when the new medium and the older power of the intellect, still intact, are working together, as in Thucydides and Euripides.

The Greeks were well aware that rhetoric should be regarded with suspicion.

> Brave are thy words; yet have I never known
> A worthy man speak brilliantly of all things

says the Oedipus of Sophocles to Creon (*Oedipus at Colonus* 806–7); and the Romans too learned in the course of history that victory is not always won by eloquence.

Sophistry, then, had many points of contact with philosophy. True, it was abhorred by real philosophers, and their resentment is readily understandable, for they saw themselves almost in a minority. Lucian (*Fugitives* 10) makes Philosophy say, 'I do not know how this species has grown up beside me, a hybrid like the centaurs, drifting somewhere between the condition of a windbag and that of philosophy.' But the philosophers could not help casting side-glances at the sophists, who were certainly familiar with the most important tenets of the different schools, indeed perfectly capable of giving their own systematic teaching in individual subjects. It is clear that, apart from all the arts of sophistry, Protagoras taught practical wisdom and virtue, and it is quite likely that he gave a serious course on ethics, just as many other sophists devoted themselves to education, of which they really possessed special knowledge.[195] Perhaps their dialectic was much like that of the philosophers and yet at the same time a form of mental gymnastics; even their ill-famed logical traps, which any intelligent Greek must have enjoyed solving in a moment, were no more than an excellent means of imparting logic, and in any case were also used by the Eleatic and the Megarian schools. Their alleged philosophical starting point, though, that there is no such thing as true and generally valid perception, no knowledge, only imagining, is in itself tenable, and they probably deserve a lot of credit as pioneers of the sceptical attitude to the proof of perception; though even in this doctrine of the subjectivity of perception the philosophy of Heraclitus had anticipated them.

It must be conceded, anyway, that in general the sophists made no pretence in their philosophy to turn the mind's attention to itself, to 'make people better'. Although Protagoras did touch upon this area, they placed more emphasis on specialized knowledge and accomplishments for practical application – which could be taught – than on claims to awaken convictions. In this aspect they were the wholly indispensable mediators of a kind of *training* suddenly much in demand, but as yet very little sustained by systematic study and adequate libraries, although contemporaries speak of it less as something universally known and unquestioningly accepted than as the strengthening of the weaker case.

What they were concerned with was the knowledge of many trades and crafts. When Hippias is said to be the wisest of men in most arts, and to have come to Olympia in a chariot he had constructed entirely with his own hands[196] (implying among other things that he had enough strength of mind not to fear the reproach of *banausia*), this conveys that striving for universality which is only conceivable in an age of relatively simple living, and it is in keeping with the spirit of an early but advanced civilization that he appears not only as widely enquiring (*polyhistor*) but also as having all-round competence. The same man in his 'Lectures' covered geometry, astronomy, music, and metrics, as well as poetry and sculpture;[197] in Lacedaemonia, because the Lacedaemonians with their will to power loved such themes, he spoke of systems of government, of colonies and of state enterprises; his knowledge is supposed to have included all that was understood by archaeology, and he is even said to have written on the names of peoples.[198] Plato tells us that Protagoras also offered to teach the art of good administration, both domestic and national, of which, given his experience of the world, he may have had much more interesting things to say than Plato puts into his mouth.[199] It is a pity that so little remains of this experience as it was possessed and communicated by the sophists, especially the comparative knowledge of the founding of cities, constitutions, institutions, and economic conditions. The fact that Thucydides probably studied these subjects under the sophists suggests the wealth of their ideas.[200] They practised grammatical and scientific research, explanations of the ancient poets, jurisprudence and military theory, and established the basis of formal logic. Since they were specialists in various fields of knowledge, their teaching was not only more useful, but much more entertaining than most of what the philosophers had to say, and so it is evident that the sophists provided exactly what was demanded by the current passion for education. It was wholly consistent with the idea of practical teaching that Hippias should work to produce a system of mnemonics, a method of consolidating what pupils had learnt. This mnemotechnic was an indispensable resource, given the relative rarity of books, as much for the travelling teacher himself as for anyone else, for he had to be one who carried his knowledge with him. Apart from the content, there was the additional attraction of a fine rhetorical form of communication which the hearer could study too – for instance in the lectures of Gorgias, held sometimes in public and sometimes in private. With all this, the success of the sophists, especially with rich and aristocratic youths,[201] is not for a moment to be wondered at, nor are the high fees they deservedly received, which were certainly not paid them for their logical traps and cunning tricks of rhetoric.[202] Not everyone maintained such an ironical and ascetic attitude to all knowledge as Socrates.

Now it was the peculiar fate of sophistry that it happened to suit the great joker Aristophanes, in his *Clouds*, to take the worst kind of hocus-pocus, together with Anaxagoras' discussion of celestial phenomena and his denial of the whole of old Olympus, hash them up with the Socratic dialectic, and set up the chief enemy of sophistry [Socrates] as the principal advocate of all this.[203] In this way every possible prejudice of the Athenian philistine, combining all the things he disliked (and moreover in this instance rather uninspired poetically) formed a composite caricature that fitted everything partly,[204] but nothing exactly. This caricature took account, admittedly, of the utilitarian knowledge professed by the sophists, in which there are certainly some elements that would strike us as dishonest. In any case they are not the actual teachers of lies they would appear to be from this representation; once again we see how cautious we must be in using the rapid, sketchy productions of Aristophanes with their cavalier approach to fact as a historical source. On the other hand the Athenians may well have been not only irritated by the arrogance of the young people who emerged from the sophists' schooling, but also felt threatened by really dangerous individuals, such as Critias, who frequented sophistic circles. It was hardly the fault of the sophists that in the Greek states, which were entirely based on equality of education, any raising of educational standards inevitably resulted in inequality between citizens; inequality that was immediately exploited to obtain greater political influence.

The subject of the sophists leads on to the widespread rejection of myth which began in their time; it must be said straight away that this was really no crime. By the fourth century myth appeared to be dead, except in the visual arts; epic and tragedy, which had nourished it, though still creative, had lost their former power, so that it was only in Alexandria that a renaissance of myth could occur. The causes of this were in part the impious attitude towards the gods found in old comedy, but also the lucid rationalistic way of thinking that predominated in the last generation of the fifth century, expressed by men like Thucydides and especially Pericles. And philosophy itself is essentially the demolition of myth; but for contemporary Athens the important thing was the loss of all *deisidaimonia* in daily life by means of natural explanations, particularly of celestial phenomena (all of course directed only at the relatively educated). This was associated less with Diagoras than with Anaxagoras, whose teaching expelled divinity from the whole of nature. Anaxagoras had the greatest influence on Pericles; as Plutarch says, he filled his mind with meteorology and lofty thought, influencing him to such an extent that his oratory was coloured with physiology as with a dye.[205] Demosthenes reminded the Athenians, when the Pythia took Philip's side, how Pericles had considered it a cowardly trick to depend on *chresmoi* and oracles, and had preferred to rely instead on reason and reflection (Plutarch, *Demosthenes* 20). And in this matter the poet joins the statesman; Euripides at times goes so far as actually to correct myth, and thus gives proof of the 'decay of mythical understanding'. This occurs for instance in the polemic against Aeschylus that he introduces into his *Electra* (508 ff.); and in the same play the chorus of Argive women are made to explain quite openly (737 ff.) that they themselves do not believe the story that Zeus, after the feast of Thyestes, altered the courses of the sun and stars – 'but these tales of terror are salutary, because they heighten the glory of the heavenly powers' – which is as much as to say that such beliefs were good enough for the common people. Thus too Aristophanes denounces his antagonist in one passage (*Thesmophoriazusae* 450 ff.) for denying the gods, and elsewhere makes fun of him and his Anaxagorean cosmogony; and in *Frogs* (893 ff.) before the beginning of the agon in Hades, he makes him call for aid, not from the gods, but from the air, his tongue, impertinence, and his own snuffling nose.

As for Socrates, Xenophon tells us (*Memorabilia* 4.7.6 ff.) that he warned against Anaxagoras' excessive longing for knowledge and tried to refute his theory about the sun, and in the Platonic apology too he protests against the charge of complicity with Anaxagoras. A most important passage about Socrates and myth is to be found in *Phaedrus* (229 ff.), where he and Phaedrus are discussing where it really was that Boreas carried off the nymph Oreithyia. 'Do you hold this myth to be true?' asks Phaedrus, and Socrates replies:

> If I doubted, as wise men do, it would not be contradictory. I would then (arguing unhomerically) say that the north wind snatched her from the nearby cliff, and when she had died thus, people said she had been carried off by Boreas . . . I consider such enquiries subtle, but as the work of an overzealous and not very fortunate man, if only because he is then faced with the necessity of providing a true explanation of the figure of the centaur, and after that the chimaera. And they will be followed by a great rush of gorgons and winged horses and others, too many to tell, and the strangest creatures of legend. If anyone who does not believe in them tries to explain each away according to the rules of probability he will need a great deal of time, since his understanding is not cultivated. But I lack the leisure for it, and for this reason: I cannot even know myself, as the Delphic oracle requires, and therefore it would be ridiculous to puzzle over strange things. So I let such questions be, and accept the popular view of them; I am more interested in contemplating myself, to know whether *I* am a wild animal, or a tame creature whose nature partakes of the divine . . .

It is not altogether easy to say whether at this time a general scepticism had taken hold. A general unscrupulousness, a preoccupation with selfish, greedy aims, a complete apathy as to gods or non-gods, was very probably widespread but not officially acknowledged.[206] But in weaker moments such defectors would relapse into *deisidaimonia*. The philosophical explanation of the world advanced by Diagoras, Anaxagoras and others, taking no account of divine rule, might venture into the open, but was regularly the subject of prosecutions for *asebeia*. These trials were consistent with a minimum of belief in the gods, and this minimum remained constant in antiquity even to the latest times. Euripides could dare to show the gods as not better but rather worse than they are in Homer, and the ancient and middle comedy could drag them through the mud – but to deny them was not permitted; for their envy and vengefulness remained formidable at least to the extent that in any calamity men 'could not be sure' whether some divine resentment was not its cause. Even with the slenderest thread of faith and the slightest reverence for the gods, it was still *safer* for the state and the individual to observe a certain degree of *eusebeia*; as soon as some responsibility is involved, everyone becomes prudent. Whatever religious feeling still existed at any period would combine with this prudence, and once more proclaim the rule of the gods. Again, the gods of the Greeks were not the models and original principles of ethics, but rather those of human passions, never holy, never more powerful than Moira (fate); thus belief in them did not trouble the ordinary conscience and was compatible with the love of pleasure. So why abolish them? In other respects, the immensely rich interweaving of the cult with the whole of public and private life, and in particular its close connection with festive occasions, were enough to safeguard it. And apart from all this, the preoccupation with what went on in Hades was if anything on the increase, despite the relaxing of religious faith; the *deisidaimonia* of the nether world was only just coming into flower. Among the philosophers in general, however, what took the place of faith was not atheism but something resembling monotheism.

In conclusion, we ought to review, with such evidence as exists, the inner transformation of all the Hellenic states in every aspect of civilization from 500 to 400 or 415 B.C. Necessarily the general picture would be the same everywhere: the horizon altered after the Persian Wars, the political structure predominantly democratic, individuals alert and fulfilled, but also a conflict between these individuals and their state, fought out everywhere, with reflection and reasoning prevailing over the simple fulfilment of duty. Philosophy had undertaken to explain the cosmos and humankind from its own resources; the social organization of life had undoubtedly reached its highest point. None the less, morality was shaken by the instability of the state, its most essential pillar; not only were morals relaxed, but culpable egoism was unbounded. In the fifth century there was a profusion of poetry; it was evolving the last of the great forms it was to find – the choric in its widest sense, tragedy, old comedy, the epigram – and was filling them with a truly vital content that makes the fourth century seem stale by comparison;

the new forms yet to come were only a few gleanings – the middle and later comedy – and what the fourth century produced in the old forms was lifeless. It was a different story in painting and sculpture, whose sublime achievements appeared no earlier than the fifth century, so that in the fourth there was still the opportunity to create enchanting loveliness, an art wholly inspired with spirituality.

It is strikingly obvious that Greek life fell into decay during the Peloponnesian War. What led up to it was the mood prevailing among the Greeks; since the Persian Wars they had been conscious of their own tremendous strength (in the individual *polis* or party, this bore little relation to whether they had fought in the wars, or even sided with the Persians) and in this consciousness they tended to live recklessly. It was then that the power struggle began, something formerly characteristic only of Sparta. The impulse for it came from democracy, which was now almost universal. Peoples who had conquered, or persuaded themselves that they had, were now consolidating their own states, but the unsettled condition of home affairs of course expressed itself externally too in violent acts. By the new criterion, which applied to everything, no-one felt they had enough power, just because they had felt so powerful in the Persian War. Ambition and vanity were no longer satisfied by the proclamations and applause for agonal victors; there was a need to direct self-assertion outwards, against other *poleis*, other groups who were very easily provoked, and in extreme cases might have to be destroyed if they were to be rendered harmless and incapable of revenge. In this situation, since all that had once been venerated was now worthless – myth, shrines, agonal fame in the cities – the power politicians had the last word. In Greece and in Sicily the whole of the fifth century from then on was nothing but the preparation for and prelude to the Peloponnesian War, that is to the grouping under two banners of the *poleis* who wielded power and those who submitted to it, and to establishing which were the stronger. While the *poleis* had hitherto been intent on independence, they were now forced to join alliances and hegemonies. Individually, but momentarily united, they had defeated Xerxes and Mardonius; now they were the victims of a general restlessness both within and without. But the war within the nation, to which this unrest was irresistibly tending, meant that the Persians, if they had any policy at all, could be sure of dominating Greece.

The terrible martial law that dated from mythical times was not simply still alive: it was only now methodically and hideously put into practice.

Extermination, selling prisoners into slavery, laying crops to waste, scorched earth and ravaging were commonplace. Ambition was not hindered by the weakening of energies: the proof of it is the Athenians' Sicilian venture while they were hourly under threat of war breaking out again. Athens well deserved total ruin as the reward of its cruelty and destructiveness.

Thucydides is our authority for the effect all this had on the national character. In a famous section of Book Three he links the description of pervasive rottenness with the horrors committed on Corcyra, because the revolution there was among the first, and so made a particularly terrible impression. Later 'the whole Hellenic nation was in turmoil', with the democrats all pro-Athenian and the oligarchs all pro-Spartan. It was now they learned how much more easily revolutions could be made in wartime than in peace, since during a war foreign help could be called in by those who wanted to overturn the constitution. In peacetime, the state as well as individuals had been inclined to mild behaviour as they were not suffering privation; war robs people of their earnings and their pleasures, and they turn vicious under this violent teacher (*biaios didaskalos*). But where the party split came later, it was all the more aggressive, hate-filled and retaliatory, as past atrocities were discovered and avenged. Thucydides speaks too of the changes in the meanings of words, and gives the whole political jargon as it developed, especially in the *hetaireia*, or cliques [cf. p. 204 above]. Here, incidentally, we get an insight into the ruinous effect of political cabals like these, not only on the state and morality, but on all social life. Apart from the dimming of the intellect caused by belonging to clubs, they make any intellectual exchange on a decently objective level impossible, and not only for one particular evening; all social relations are poisoned. Each is condemned to spending his whole existence in the worst company in the world, and bound to it by complicity.

Thucydides goes further in explaining the mutual reliance of partners in crime.[207] Men swore to stick together, but kept their word only when it was unavoidable and expedient; the diabolical development was that people found it not only safer, but more fun, to take revenge on their defenceless opponents by misusing their confidence (that is by having previously pretended to be their friends). Getting the upper hand by deceit demonstrated their cleverness; they preferred to be known as bad and cunning rather than as good and gullible, and in spite of their fine names the two factions would use any and every means in their contest (Thucydides does not betray his own allegiance by a single word). Having won power by an illegal vote or by force, they satisfied the current discontents by acting against their enemies. Special hatred was felt for citizens of moderate views: they were persecuted either because they would not take sides or out of envy of their honesty. Vicious ideas flourished, and the simplicity that is so much the mark of a noble nature was derided and despised. Enmity and bad faith abounded; no sacred word was safe, no sacred oath respected: self-interest was the sole preoccupation; the worst people of all, who had risen to the top, launched into action at once for fear they might be outwitted in argument or intrigue, and destroyed their more reasonable opponents while these were off their guard.

These imperishable chapters in Thucydides show us the fearful immorality common to all parties, both the horror of the conflict and the cold, inhuman calculation that informed it. Prudence was forgotten, for nothing could have been more favourable to the Persians, and Alcibiades encouraged them to let the two sides rage on; it was the simplest policy for the Persians to follow.[208] During the precarious peace of Nicias (in 421), when everything was in ferment, primitive minority peoples began to make opportunistic raids (a development which was to become a terrible threat a century and a half later in the shape of the Aetolian League): Dolopians, Aenians and Malians attacked Heraclea Trachinia, won a battle, besieged the city and were driven off only by a unit of Theban auxiliaries.[209] Both sides remained determined to fight to the last, and if we felt inclined to moderate what Thucydides says, his words are confirmed by the echoes we hear from Euripides' Eteocles in *Phoenician Women* and his Creusa in *Ion* [pp. 244 and 256 above]. Here too we learn what risks power seekers would run to retain the mastery.

The poets shed light on many things. For instance, though predatory communism first appeared in the time of Polybius, its very own arguments, pressing for universal equality of property, must already have been heard during the Peloponnesian War. We gather this from a tirade in Euripides, proclaiming that life would become impossible if there were only poor people, and that general wellbeing needs a mixture of rich and poor, since they depend on one another.[210] It is also characteristic of the time that the simple patriotism that still speaks so convincingly in Aeschylus' *Seven against Thebes* now sometimes rings false in Euripides. This is so in the long tirade of Erechtheus, when he is threatened by Eumolpus and the Thracians, and in his misguided noblemindedness proposes to sacrifice his daughter for his country.[211] In another fragment the same poet tells how people now began to perceive that custom was better than law, because no orator could distort it; law could be abused and damaged by oratory.[212]

For a guardian of morals, Aristophanes' tone perhaps seems strange; but in all literature there is no text to compare with the dialogue, in *Clouds*, (961 ff.) of the just Word and the unjust. Both speeches, to be understood, must have been recognized by a large number of Athenians as images of the older and the younger Athens; the audience must also have been in silent agreement on things the poet necessarily speaks aloud. In *Frogs* (1014 f.) Aristophanes makes Aeschylus say that the present generation are shirkers when it comes to civic duties, mean, dishonest, and shabby (remember that this is just before the battle of Aegospotami); from Euripides they have learned the love of talk that is emptying the *palaiestrai* and causing mutiny among the sailors of the ship of state; the city swarms with forgers and frivolous pretenders, but they take so little exercise that none has the strength to carry the torches at the procession. Here and there the authorities are accused of corruption;[213] or there is talk of the wickedness of men in general, backed up with mention of theft from public funds, desertion from the army or even kidnapping (*Thesmophoriazusae* 811 ff.) – though in this play it is the wretchedness and vice of women that are most harshly shown. Their infidelity, passing off their bastard children and so forth, are brought in as frequent occurrences, and there is talk of the increasing suspiciousness of husbands (perhaps not much exaggerated) with Euripides blamed as the cause of it.[214] In *Plutus* the good fortune of the wicked appears at the very beginning as a matter beyond doubt; Carion and his master Chremylus are each as bad as the other in their cold-blooded talk of dishonesty as the only way to get on in the world.

Old comedy itself is in reality part of the crisis of Greek life, and, as has been said [p. 230 above], is the proof that Athens was permanently charged with an electric force of scandal which was bound to break out like a thunderstorm, not only at the Dionysia, but throughout the year.[215] As a source for cultural history comedy is indispensable, and the digressions (*parabases*), where the poet speaks directly, are of particular documentary importance; Aristophanes may be totally slanderous where he is dealing with certain individuals, but, where he depicts general conduct, can *only* have said what everyone knew and felt to be recognizable.[216]

Aristotle says that Plato told a certain Archibius that it had become the fashion in Athens to be wicked (*poneros*).[217] This may remind us of the Italians in Machiavelli's time; in any case, in Plato's dialogues (supposed to take place in the late fifth century) some characters testify strikingly to the crisis in Greek life. At one point in his *Republic* (2.365), Plato confronts the old belief in divine rewards on earth with the notion of divine rewards as sensual pleasures in the afterlife. He starts from the common human tendency to evil, and from the sufferings of the good and the triumph on earth of the wicked, who, because they are rich, can outdo the just, even in religious observance, with sacrifices and votive offerings. What follows is a discussion of the effect on young people who are told that the gods send luck to the bad and misfortune to the good, and that they are influenced by formulae and incantations; a young man is then made to draw the conclusion 'Then I shall ape virtue but act slyly.' To avoid being unmasked, secret societies and clubs are useful. Then there are teachers of speechmaking for assemblies and lawcourts; by combining this kind of persuasion with force we shall be strong enough. The gods, we are told, can neither be tricked nor forced; if they exist at all, and care anything about life on earth, we know it only from legends and the genealogical poets; we also learn from them that the gods can be swayed by sacrifices, placatory vows and votive gifts. So we may as well sin and sacrifice; mere integrity will save us from divine punishment, but will deprive us of the benefits of dishonesty; if we are dishonest, we can make a profit and then escape punishment by imploring the gods for mercy. And if we and our descendants are threatened with punishment in Hades, the sacred rites and the gods of redemption can be of help, as we learn from the greatest *poleis* and from the sons of gods who have become poets and prophets.

A second passage (6.492) deals with demagogues. In all kinds of gatherings – the democratic assembly, lawcourts, theatres or military camps – the demagogues support or oppose what is said or done with the maximum noise and the wildest exaggeration, so that the stones and walls redouble the sounds of praise or blame. What are young people to make of this? What kind of education could possibly prepare them to resist this pressure, or keep them from being swept away with the current of partisan feeling until they assent and become like the others? Besides, the teachings of those mercenary men whom the demagogues call sophists, and regard as rivals, are fundamentally no different from these mass opinions that are propagated in the assemblies, and then called wisdom (*sophia*). It is as if they studied all the passions and urges of a great strong beast – how it is to be approached and handled, what makes it angry or gentle, and what tones of voice soothe or rouse it. The results are taught as a science (*techne*), and regardless of what is really fine or disgusting, good or bad, everything is classified according to the temperament of the great beast; what it likes is good, and what hurts it is bad.[218] A young, intelligent, energetic man, however, the hope of his family, especially if he is from an important city, rich, well-born, handsome and tall, is bound to be filled with Heaven knows what ambitions, and to think himself a gift to Hellenes and barbarians alike, becoming arrogant in his foolish shallow vanity.[219]

Further on (8.555 f.) comes the portrait of democracy, imagined in a future stage, when the poor have killed or driven out all the others, and shared out administrative posts among themselves. Freedom rules and there is no restraint on speech or action. All kinds of people have come to the top, and political offices are to be had for the choosing as if on a market stall. Everyone evades obligations and regulations as much as possible; crime arouses sympathy, so that those condemned to death or exile remain free and go about in public; education is neglected; a man is honoured merely for saying he loves the people. The frivolity of government is paralleled by that of the democratic citizen, who is as wild and capricious as the State; he lives for the desire of the moment, one day drunk and enjoying flute music, sober the next, now at the gymnasium, then idle and apathetic, sometimes philosophizing, but spending most of his time in political discussion, jumping up and saying or deciding on the first thing that comes into his head. He may be seized with envy of the military, and rush off to join them, then again attracted by speculation. His life has no order, no inner necessity, and yet he calls it pleasant, respectable, happy (no doubt most Athenians thought so). But this is the democracy that can occasionally produce tyranny. The democratic State, in its thirst for liberty, wanders into disreputable bars and gets drunk on too much undiluted wine. Unless the authorities are lenient in the extreme, they are accused of corruption and vilified, and those who still obey them are insulted as slavish nobodies. Popularity and honour are accorded to rulers who resemble subjects, and to subjects who resemble rulers. The same mood invades the family; the father is the equal of his son and afraid of him, while the son feels neither respect nor fear for his father. The metic is on a par with the citizen, and so is the foreigner; teachers fear and flatter their pupils, who despise their teachers and tutors; young and old compete in word and deed, the old men sit down with the young and try to make them laugh, so as to avoid seeming grumpy and superior. Even the bought slaves come to be as free as their masters, and there is complete freedom and equality between men and women. The very animals – bitches, horses and donkeys – go about more freely than elsewhere, and jostle whoever is in their way. People tend to become extremely irritable, and to resent written or unwritten laws, feeling that there should be no-one in authority over anyone else.

Another section of Plato's *Republic* (9.574) gives a wonderful description of the impoverished wastrel. When he has sacrificed everything to his love affairs and squandered the family fortune while forming endless bad habits, he will take to housebreaking or robbing strangers at night, then go on to loot a temple and soon think nothing of murder and other crimes.[220] In places where there are only a few men like this, they will go away to serve a tyrant, or else remain at home and commit many offences, though on a small scale (among which Plato reckons the evil doings of the sycophants); but where they become more numerous, a tyrant will emerge from among them by the help of popular folly, and this man (though here Plato is mistaken) will be the one who has the greatest tyrant in himself, by which he means the most vices. This would explain why none of the Attic conspirators of the type of Catiline could succeed in rising to be a tyrant.

In *Laws* (3.700) Plato links his account of decadence to the corrupting effects of music and to the mania for the theatre. Some features of this description, such as the disobedience towards parents and laws, read as in the *Republic*.[221] When the final collapse is near, oaths, loyalty and gods are all defied, in imitation of the so-called ancient titanic temperament; the ancient consequence then follows – a period of infinite misery.[222]

In *Gorgias* (471) the sophist Polus tells the story of the terrible family crimes by which Archelaus came to the throne of Macedonia, and Plato then puts into his mouth the question: 'Beginning with you, Socrates, is there a single Athenian who, if he had to be a Macedonian, would choose to be anyone except Archelaus?' Socrates replies: 'Almost all Athenians, and foreigners too, would admit that they would prefer to be Archelaus' – after which there is an ominous list of such Athenians.

Xenophon too describes the situation in the city which has forgotten *kalokagathia*. Its place is taken by disrespect for parents and contempt for gymnastic exercise; instead of helping others, people insult them and envy their neighbours more than anyone else; quarrels break out at public meetings and private gatherings, and fellow citizens are constantly going to law with each other; hostility and hatred are everywhere. Although rank is still observed at sea, and also (as Xenophon points out ironically) the judges at the gymnastic agon are still obeyed, like the conductors at choric performances, the hoplites and cavalrymen of Athens are the most undisciplined in the world.

These are some of the bitter complaints heard from various writers. They are based on facts; the existence of a man like Andocides is enough to assure us of this. Although himself, as a herald, descended from Hermes, he took part in the desecration of the herms and the mysteries, but was acquitted for having informed on the rest. He showed immense fervour in this, and denounced his own father Leogoras. 'The others he named were executed, but he saved his father, who was already in chains, by saying he could still be very useful to the *polis*. Leogoras then denounced many people for robbing the state and for other crimes, and was freed.[223]

Everyone in Athens came to congratulate Theramenes when a house collapsed just as he had stepped out of it, and he is said to have exclaimed: 'O Zeus, what fate have you in store for me!' This must have been an expression of real feeling, for they were all being carried onwards and expected a violent end, without knowing what it would be. Many must often have felt like saying: 'If only the earth would swallow me up in good time!'

V

The Fourth Century to
the Age of Alexander

AFTER THE PELOPONNESIAN WAR, Greek cultural history becomes, in essence, synonymous with Greek history. Before this, the Hellene was only to be understood as a living particle of his *polis*, which was the focal point of all his creativity, activity and morality. However, the darker aspects of the developing democracy, and the devastation brought down on the Greeks by the Peloponnesian War, had the effect – even in Sparta – of relaxing the moral and to some extent the practical ties that bound the ablest men to their *polis*. Some were only intent upon governing the state and exploiting the condition of Greece, without feeling themselves intimately bound to anything. Others lived for intellectual interests which no longer had any relation to the State; while the majority only sought enjoyment, and many would sell themselves as mercenaries to any powerful man who could pay enough.

This is the character of the fourth century. Yet in this process of transformation the nation still had enormous individual powers and a great future; in the next two centuries it was to provide the leaven for the whole of the Near East, and the source of intellectual training for the Romans. The meaning of Hellenism is that the whole world made use of and laid claim to the Greek world; it was to be the medium of spiritual continuity between antiquity, the Roman world and the Middle Ages.

We ought to jettison the habit of wishing that past times might have been different from what they were, if only because in our own time and our daily life we often wish for foolish things. But at least in relation to Hellenism it is out of the question to wish things had been otherwise. It would make no sense – and this is not merely a matter of the historian's quirky curiosity – to wish that instead of the Macedonian supremacy in Greece, and the conquest of Persia, Greece in its divided and weakened condition should have been overrun by some new barbaric elemental force from Asia or the Scythian North. The most likely consequence of this – that Rome should have remained deprived of Hellenic culture – is something impossible to wish for; for it is only the Philhellenism of Rome, the love of a Greece that was still alive, that was responsible for the survival of the whole culture of the ancient world. Hellenistic Rome was the indispensable basis for the spread of Christianity, and Christianity, apart from its role as a religion, was to be the single bridge destined to unite the old world with its Germanic conquerors. In this whole chain of cause and effect, Hellenism is the most important link.

A *change of geographical emphasis* occurs with the decline of Greater Greece. As early as 420, during the Peloponnesian War, Cumae, which had once fought bravely for its freedom, was taken by the Campanians, who killed or sold the inhabitants, and before long Naples was the last Greek city in the area. At the beginning of the fourth century the Lucanians renewed their attacks on the cities around the bay of Tarentum, which had joined in a defensive alliance (393) against the barbarians and their ally Dionysius the Elder, but which mostly fell to these two opponents after the devastating defeat of the Thurians at Laos in 390 B.C. Then came the invasions of the Samnites and the Bruttians, who at the time of Scylax's account of his travels (about 356) had conquered many Greek cities and were in control of the country from the Tyrrhenian to the Ionian Sea. Tarentum, which, in the first decades of the century, benefited from having as its citizen the distinguished statesman and general Archytas (also a Pythagorean philosopher, mathematician, engineer and musicologist) had alone remained in a condition to fight during the long conflict with the Messapians. Apart from the mercenaries, Tarentum is said to have been able to muster twenty thousand foot soldiers and two thousand cavalrymen from its own citizens; however the population must have been much Italianized, and its links with the peninsula must have been stronger than with the old homeland in Greece. But when the Lucanians turned the whole of their power against Tarentum, Metapontum and Heraclea, these cities periodically invited in foreign princes as condottieri. The first of these was Archidamus III of Sparta, said to have died on the same day the Greeks were defeated at Chaeronea; then Alexander of Epirus, the brother of Olympias, who liked to say that fate had granted his nephew victories over women, but himself hard fighting with men. After brilliant successes he quarrelled with the Tarentines themselves and was murdered in 332 after his luck turned at the battle of Pandosia. Last of all, in 330, the ruthless Spartan Cleonymus was called in to help against the Lucanians and the Romans; this was the same man who in his rage and vengefulness later led Pyrrhus against Argos. After initial successes Cleonymus too proved unreliable, and with the Lucanians and others he plundered Greek Metapontum and other places.

Despite these blows to the Greek presence in southern Italy, the larger Greek cities – Thurii, Metapontum, Heraclea, Rhegion and, as we have said, Naples – remained in being, though weakened and dependent. Even in the flatlands and in the smaller cities the Hellenes were tolerated, and among others Cyme, Poseidonia (Paestum), Laos and Hipponium continued to be Greek cities even under Samnite rule, as Scylax relates and as the coins also show.[1] Many however were destroyed, or resettled entirely by foreigners, and even where a small group of Greek citizens still held out, they were robbed of their land and had to huddle into the small space within their walls. The inhabitants of Poseidonia (Paestum) for instance, to judge by a fine passage from the music historian Aristoxenus, must have thought their fate was just the same as if they had fallen into the hands of the barbarians.[2] The Sabellic and Greek languages, too, were now widely spoken side by side. At the same time a peculiar quality of the Hellenic spirit ensured that both the language and the culture of Greece continued to flourish strongly even among the barbarians of southern Italy;[3] but it is undeniable that in this time and place the true Greek population suffered great losses.

In Sicily, where in earlier times even the better tyrants had enforced the mixture of the city populations by violent means, the failure of the Greek assault had the aftereffect that Egesta, which was half-Greek and in fear of the vengeance of all the Sicilians, called on Carthage for help. Hannibal was by nature opposed to the Hellenes and moreover set on avenging his grandfather Hamilcar's defeat at the river Himera. He appeared in 408 and took, one after the other, Selinuntium, Himera, Agrigentum, Gela and Camarina, and their inhabitants were either annihilated or expelled. After this gigantic blood-letting of Greek Sicily, the best that can be said of Dionysius the Elder (405 to 367) is that but for him the whole of Sicily would have fallen under Carthaginian domination for good, and have been lost to Greek culture;[4] but it soon became evident that he was only using the terror of Carthage in order to rule over the Greek cities, and had no interest in repelling the Carthaginians completely; indeed, he deliberately let them escape when he might have destroyed them. His methods, too, were hair-raising; against Greek cities he seems to have seen no alternatives except those of wiping out the Greek population or else transporting them to Syracuse. This city of a million inhabitants now swarmed with an astounding mixture of citizens, old settlers and new, including freed slaves and a great number of mercenaries. Whole areas of the city were reassigned to this varied mass of people, but in Ortygia, around the fortress, the ruler allowed only his special adherents and those in his pay, whom he also rewarded with the cities whose former inhabitants he had concentrated in Syracuse. It is obvious that this reign of terror, by which populations lost their own towns and lands, is the very negation of the *polis* and thus of true Hellenism. But what Dionysius did was what had to be done if the inhabitants of many different *poleis* were to be ruled as one, though his tyrannical effort to create a supreme state of Sicily – always with the pretext of the Carthaginian threat – inevitably gave rise in the suffering *poleis* to a violence of feeling otherwise seen only in the most terrible wars of religion. To be free of the Carthaginians *and* the tyrant was an ideal no longer to be attained, and so Syracuse at least remained submissive for the last two thirds of this reign.

The succeeding ruler was Dionysius the Younger, who was no more than a glutton and a frightful tyrant, and then came the useless so-called 'liberation' by Dion, which only exposed the helplessness of the Greeks. The outcome of all these confusions was that by the time the tyrant returned in 346, Syracuse was almost entirely laid waste, the rest of Sicily in a miserable condition because of the expulsions, and most of the *poleis* in the hands of wildly haphazard collections of barbarians, largely unpaid mercenaries whose leaders became tyrants.[5] Carthage was intervening again and again in Sicilian affairs, and the island would have been wholly lost had not the parent country made a supreme effort to preserve it. This was what brought Timoleon of Corinth to Sicily. His mission was valuable in two ways: first as a voluntary intervention on the part of Greece, and then because it was an indispensable link in the chain of events that retained Sicily for the Europeans. It was not the cure for the Sicilian misery, only a pause between two miseries. When he came, the unhappy cities at first distrusted him, because they had had enough of military leaders and feared it would all prove only a change of masters. Though Syracuse was relatively well off, long grass was growing in the agora, where horses grazed and their grooms were encamped; other cities were full of deer and wild boars, which were hunted through the outlying streets; the populations had therefore taken refuge in the citadels and forts, and none ventured down into the towns; the very idea of an agora, of political activity and the orator's rostrum, made them shudder, for their tyrants had mostly come to them as a result of these things.[6] Timoleon was the benefactor who changed all this. Syracuse was repopulated by the arrival of countless former exiles and other settlers, for the Corinthians proclaimed at the agon and at festivals, wherever Sicilian refugees were to be found, and as far away as Asia, that everyone who wished was invited to return. The total influx from Corinth, Greece and Italy amounted to sixty thousand people, and they were given free passage by Corinth. In the other cities too, Leontini, Apollonia and Entella, democracy was installed, Hellenic civilization established itself and Carthaginian power was undermined. After Timoleon defeated the Carthaginians on the Crimisus in 339, the local mercenary tyrants in the cities were soon overthrown too. The peace treaty left Carthage only the region west of the Halycus, and obliged her to allow the Greeks there freedom to leave at will, and to promise not to support any more tyrants.

Timoleon died in 336. He lived long enough to see the general influx from Greece, under threat from Philip of Macedon, and from the cities of Greater Greece under threat from the Lucanians. Sicily then experienced a true renewal; apart from Syracuse, the cities of Agrigentum, Gela, Camarina and others recovered to some extent, the last named thanks mainly to the help of Eleans and Chians, who brought the former citizens back with them. However it was a descendant of new settlers in Syracuse, Agathocles, the son of refugees from Rhegion, who re-established the tyranny after renewed factional struggles and ruled for twenty-eight years, from 317 to 289. He treated the Hellenic population essentially in the same way as Dionysius the Elder, only even worse. Yet his reign too must be regarded as having been the only possible salvation from Carthage. The cities which wanted to escape his authority had no choice but to kowtow to Carthage, like the earlier tyrants. But after his African campaign and many terrible battles, all that was achieved was a return to the division of the island of Sicily between the two powers; and thus, as under Dionysius, a period of recovery for the unhappy country occurred in the final years of Agathocles' rule.

At the same time that Greek power was in its death throes in the Sicilian *poleis*, various movements and changes in population were going on in other Greek regions. Mausolus of Caria (377 to 353) transplanted the inhabitants of six Lelegian towns to Halicarnassus and left only two in existence.[7] About the same time (366) the islanders of Cos founded their splendid capital and made it a flourishing city;[8] in the Peloponnese, after Leuctra, came the great foundations of Epaminondas – Megalopolis and the new city of Messene. The fact that Phocis was not wholly destroyed after the third Amphictyonic War was solely to the credit of Philip, who was content with rendering it completely defenceless, though its neighbours wanted it annihilated. Thus twenty-two Phocian towns were deprived of their walls, all their horses were sold and their weapons destroyed. As for the fringes of the Greek world, the Greeks of Pontus were probably much reduced in numbers. Cyrenaica must have remained entirely Greek, since some of the people from there could be spared for the reconstructed city of Messene. On the Ionian coast Greek life seems to have survived intact, even when the Persian tax collector[9] followed on the heels of the departing army of Agesilaus, and in their new condition as Persian ports, and perhaps centres of industry, the towns of Ionia may even have been less than enthusiastic about being 'liberated'.[10] Southern Thrace had once, in the fifth century, been capable of playing a part in Greek affairs both as ally and, under lawless chieftains, as enemy. Now, after the death of King Seuthes, the paymaster of what remained of Xerxes' Ten Thousand, it disintegrated into separate princedoms and became harmless. It was Philip of Macedon, not the Thracians, who destroyed the Chalcidian cities and robbed Greece of her strength on that coast. Epirus, because of its position on the Adriatic, was not well placed to intervene in Greek affairs and was considered merely a primitive power that had fallen into barbarism, which might be dangerous if it found unity under a leader.[11] Still it might be a blessing if these semibarbarians were strong enough to hold off the real barbarians from the Greeks; in 378 a mere famine had been enough to bring down the tribes of northern Thrace with 30,000 men to attack Abdera, almost wiping it out.[12]

Macedonia was soon to be Hellenic. It was a region which at least had some ancient Hellenic associations, for Herodotus tells us that the Dorians were originally Macedonians. The founder of the nation was called Pelasgus; their language only *seemed* barbarous to the Hellenes, as did that of the inhabitants of Achelous, and it belonged to the same linguistic family as Greek, related to it probably much as Swedish and Danish are to German, with no doubt some barbarian influence from the Illyrians.[13] The princely families were considered Hellenic on the grounds that at some period Corinthian Bacchiads and Argive Temenids, i.e. Heracleidae, had reached, respectively, the Lyncestis and the Orestis.[14] These Temenids had then conquered the coastal plain of Emathia with its population of Bottiaeans, supposed to have arrived there from Crete, bringing with them their cult of Apollo, and of Pierians, famous for their worship of Dionysus and the Muses; there were also Greek colonies on the Emathian coast, so this area was very open to Greek culture. The importance of Macedonia was mainly its being the northern Greek bulwark against the true barbarians, the Illyrians and no doubt, even at that time, the Celts too.[15] Another vital factor was that its kings, ever since that Alexander who warned the Greeks at Plataea of the impending attack, were all in some sense philhellenes, differing only in that one was more desirous of Hellenic culture, or fame, another rather more intent on getting possession of coastal towns. During the Peloponnesian War, the attitude of King Archelaus (413–399) resembled that of Philip of Burgundy during the chaos of the French wars, and we might also compare the way in which people flocked to Archelaus in his capital, Pella, with the procession of West Europeans to Russia in modern times.[16] *His* purpose was to acquire Greek culture with a view to future domination over the Greeks. The terrible disorders which followed the death of King Amyntas (390–369) brought the Thebans among others into the country as arbiters, and Ptolemaeus, who was protected by Pelopidas, was obliged to send his brother-in-law Philip to Thebes with thirty other high-born boys. This Philip was the genius in whose hands the insignificant state of Macedon was to become paramount in Greece.

While the Greek nation as a whole suffered a material decline, the disorder in the State inevitably brought a further disruption of morality. As we have seen, the whole moral and spiritual life of the Greeks was focused on the State; even the family was essentially a political institution, and the real strength of religion itself was in its local roots. As long as it was entire, that is being guided in a particular direction, this State had regarded itself as divine, and had given itself absolute licence in its omnipotence. Now that control was in the wrong hands and political animosities and persecutions began to poison the national life, everything, including religion, was bound to go to pieces.[17] And now, in reality as in myth, the Titans of the most terrible dissension tore this Zagreus asunder. When the process was over, and the god lay in fragments, the Greeks must have shuddered at themselves.[18] Some of them, as philosophers, could boldly resolve to choose *apolitia*; for the majority, their pride and their faith were in ruins with the *polis* which had been the highest aim of all their energies and the lofty image of their existence. For this reason and against all odds the *polis* was re-established, though as a poor shadow of itself. Again and again the anarchy of the Greek temperament gave rise to new conflicts, until the time of the definitive weakening which becomes apparent in the second century B.C.

Because divinity had vanished from the *polis* since the end of the Peloponnesian War, new gods arose; first the ruthless outlaws of whom Lysander was the chief, then tyrants of the later type, and finally Philip of Macedon. Amidst the toadying of idlers and the spiritless indifference of the better sort, personal power sought to emerge from the ruins of the old order now here, now there, occasionally making a direct claim on the veneration due to divinity. That 'better sort' of people, however, believed they would be better still if, as we have said, they turned their backs on the affairs of the state and belonged to it only passively or not at all. The only conceivable substitute, since the *poleis* were incapable of inspiring faith and hope in the new generations, would have been the formation of a great power, emerging from the miseries of many small states under one of the many gifted adventurers of the time as usurper, rather as in the unification of Italy, but this did not come about in the case of the Greeks. Such a power would have had to concentrate in itself all the criminal energy that was till then distributed among hundreds of thousands. But this was not to happen until the Romans came; for the Greek *polis*, as it was, could not die, nor was it possible for it to delegate power to a larger whole. Instead the outcome was, in succession, the temporary dominance of Sparta, then of Thebes, then of no-one, until Philip. Characteristically, even after the battle of Chaeronea, Macedon did not incorporate the various *poleis* but, except for Thebes, wisely left them 'independent', content to rule them only very partially and briefly.[19]

The fourth century, then, is above all the time of *political* decline, the point at which even some modern scholars abandon the edifying tone with which they usually treat Greek matters of earlier date, though they find it intolerable if it is transferred to the Christian era. Everywhere democracy nourished a tremendous degree of ill will. Private contempt for the real authorities in government and justice, and general mockery (also expressed in comedy) coexisted with banquets offered to the public and with riotous festivals; a true popular mob came into being, and the members of this now very volatile mob were capable of endangering the whole city by various excesses of behaviour.[20] The chief trouble was that through the collapse of any security the so-called democracy drove the more distinguished citizens to lawbreaking or to apoliticism, and was no longer accessible to informed criticism.[21] A characteristic of this time, resulting from the terrible mood to which Greece was then prey, was the *laudatio temporis acti* which appears in the perpetual inflated praise of virtuous ancestors, and piety towards parents, gods and temples, which became the stock-in-trade of orators.[22] Again, it was at this time that quite disproportionate efforts were made to enforce the solemnity of oaths;[23] Plato, for instance, found it necessary to confer priestly honours on his guardians to ensure their integrity, which ought to have been beyond question – rather as today we make use of monetary deposits as guarantees.[24] And so, as the century went on, anyone who remained incorruptible, like Phocion, was the subject of endless eulogies.[25] Even Conon in his day had felt able to advise Pharnabazus simply to buy over the demagogues of the Greek cities;[26] corruption was general and doubtless just as bad in Attica as in Sparta. Unfortunately we no longer have the section of the tenth book of Theopompus on the demagogues of Attica,[27] but the whole life of Demosthenes, his contests with the regents, with Meidias and with his later political enemies all leave the impression of a melancholy state of things, and of the brazen insolence of wickedness.

A particularly striking idea of how things really were in Greece can be obtained from one feature of life – the sons who turned out badly. Families may decline at any period and in all countries. But in Athens and in all Greece this stands out the more clearly because, first, the pride of reputation had previously been so boastful, and then because there had been an established faith in breeding, that is in inherited excellence, which now openly suffered the most crushing blows. True, the phenomenon is not first noted in the fourth century – which might well have seen itself as the unworthy offspring of the fifth – but much earlier in the sons of Aristides and the elder Thucydides.[28] It became so conspicuous as time went on that Aristotle derives a general observation from it; he considers that brilliantly gifted families turn out blighted by folly, while those of a steady and serious character run to simplicity and sloth. For the first kind he gives as examples the descendants of Alcibiades and Dionysius the Elder, and for the second the progeny of Cimon, Pericles and Socrates.[29]

I do not share Curtius's view that the degeneration of the Hellenic citizenry is to be traced to the practice of intermarriage between related families.[30] I believe that Athens herself ruined her own people by democratically conditioned freedom and its consequences, and that this was the cause of deterioration in sons. For the Athenian arrogance which had taken root even in old families, and was inherent in the 'new' families from the start, neither founded nor handed on any spiritual or moral conviction; the sons of gifted but arrogant fathers turned out merely arrogant, the grandsons hopeless; it is respect alone that sustains families and gives them traditions. It seems to us self-evident that the sons of the politically ambitious should be ne'er-do-wells. Socrates, whose sons were apparently stupid (Plutarch, *Cato the Elder* 20), is supposed to have maintained that the sons of politicians were no better than those of cobblers.[31] What Plutarch tells us of Pericles' family is wholly typical of a grand and intellectual household where many interesting people come and go, but where the children have not been brought up to respect their elders (*Pericles* 36). According to this, Xanthippus, the elder of the statesman's two legitimate sons, was a spendthrift by nature. Married to a young and extravagant wife, Tisandros' daughter, Xanthippus was impatient of his father's thrifty exactitude and with the small allowance he was given. So he sent to a family friend to ask for money as if on Pericles' behalf. When the friend later demanded the return of the loan, Pericles brought a charge against his son, and Xanthippus in his resentment made mock of his father by spreading accounts of the conversations Pericles had with the sophists. Moreover, he was responsible for spreading evil gossip 'about the lady' (Aspasia), and the consequent ill will between father and son lasted until the latter's death. This account is too essentially plausible to be dismissed as slander invented by Stesimbrotus, scandalmonger though he was, for our critical resources are inadequate to contradict him on every point. We have an insight here into circumstances which might reconcile a philosopher to celibacy.[32]

Another case of a son turning out badly is that of Alcibiades the Younger, attacked by Lysias in his orations 14 and 15. He gambled away his property, as many young Athenians did then – behaviour typical of a generation who no doubt inherited their fathers' temperamental need for excitement but not the strength that went with it. After this he took to piracy for a time. At a later date Ctesippus, the son of Chabrias, actually sold the stones of the monument erected to his father by the State at a cost of 1,000 drachmae; Phocion had tried to take him in hand but found him frivolous and ungovernable.[33] Phocion's own son Phocus, though once a victor at the Panathenaea, was a drunkard and led a life of excess. His father took him to Sparta and put him to school with the youths being brought up there. Despite this formal education he seems not to have improved; later he certainly took vengeance on his father's accusers, but never became a serious man [*aner spoudaios*] and married a girl whose freedom he bought from a brothel.[34]

For the rest we must not forget that all over Greece in those days democracy cost many 'oligarchs' their lives or their homes and families. Thus recurrent crises were leading to the disappearance of the upper class and with it any conception of lineage either good or bad. Later on of course we hear of one person or another claiming descent from the Ceryces or the Eumolpidai, but in general the famous old families vanish in the fourth century and by the time of Isocrates are only remembered by their sepulchres. Scarcely any contemporary of Demosthenes has a distinguished or well-known ancestry.[35]

Looking at the individual states, at the start of this period it is Lysander of Sparta who combines depravity with natural gifts in a way that was typically Spartan and yet generally Greek.[36] The Spartan system was frightful in itself, although Brasidas at an earlier time, and Callicratidas, as well as Lysander, knew how to present themselves in different colours. But after his victory Lysander entered into close complicity with the most disreputable men, frequenters of the oligarchic cliques; he tolerated all their crimes and did not hesitate to commit the most appalling massacres. Thus in Miletus he handed over, to be murdered by the oligarchs, eight hundred members of the popular party whom he had lured out of hiding with sworn promises;[37] the reward for his friends was licence and absolute power to rule over the cities (Plutarch, *Lysander* 19). Although he must secretly have obtained great sums to support his lavish expenditure,[38] he posed as the poor incorruptible Spartan of the old kind, while on the other hand, characteristically, he accepted, as the foremost of the Greeks, altars, offerings and paeans from the cities as though he were a god, playing up to the part and keeping the poet Choerilus as his eulogist constantly about him.[39] In the end it was not the complaints of the Hellenic cities but those of Pharnabazus that led to his being deposed. He then went on a journey to the Ammonium; and the notables of Sparta, to put an end to his continued exercise of power through the cliques he had left in his place, allowed the *demos* to make headway in the cities; but now the pendulum swung too far in this direction, and Lysander, on his return, was able to persuade the Spartans to help the oligarchs again. His last success was to install as king, instead of Leotychidas, his own candidate Agesilaus; but he then found that he had set an independent master over himself. He returned home in anger from accompanying Agesilaus to Asia, hating the whole Spartan State more than ever, and took up his earlier project to make the monarchy open to all the Heracleidae, even to all the Spartans; the king should no longer be the descendant of Heracles but 'the man who resembles him', so the choice would infallibly fall upon himself. With this aim he got Cleon of Heraclea to write him a speech addressed to his fellow citizens. Not content with this, he felt he must make sure of them through fear and superstition, so he tried bribing the oracles of Delphi and Dodona as well as the Ammonium, and produced a miraculous child trained for the purpose – in short he went in for a series of crude stunts which would not have deceived a real child. All these exploits had failed by the time this universally discredited man, half-mad with melancholy and rage, fell in battle at Haliartus in 395.

The direct cause of the decline of Sparta was the great power it won at Aegospotami and the resulting hubris. What came about in other places by defeat and factional fighting was achieved here by success – forced to rule over Greece with its fully developed individualism, this people too had to become individualized, and the Spartan spirit, already seriously undermined, was totally fragmented. King Agesilaus, whose campaigns in Asia Minor were unimportant, could not restore the dislocated pattern of thinking. To quote Isocrates (*Peace* 95 ff.):

> The community which had remained stable for seven hundred years was brought by its dominion [over others] into stormy times and nearly to dissolution; in some citizens, power was the cause of injustice, depravity, disrespect for the laws and greed for riches; in the State, of arrogance towards its allies, covetousness of property, contempt of oaths and treaties.

The orator knows it is erroneous to believe, as many do, that Leuctra was the cause of the problems:

> ... for the allies' hatred of Sparta did not originate then; Sparta declined because of the hubris it had shown earlier, and which began when it seized power over the seas.

After Leuctra, however, when the allies fell away, and Sparta had to part with everything that her old pride was based on, the symptoms of decay made their appearance – chiefly in the official abandonment of the traditional Spartan manner of treating deserters, and the Spartan form of *apolitia*, that is the absenteeism of her kings – among others Archidamus IV, the elder Acrotatus and the notorious Cleonymus[40] – who had begun to despise Sparta. Here too the *polis* of Sparta had to swallow all its former pride; Alexander dedicated the loot from his victory at the Granicus with the inscription 'Alexander and all the Hellenes except the Lacedaemonians', but his irony failed in its intention. The Spartans' vanity was not to be cured in this way, and they were just then planning a revolt against Alexander.

Unfortunately, all these things caused turmoil in the whole of the Greek world. Everywhere, before and particularly after Leuctra, the governments who had been kept in power by Sparta were done to death with the most terrible violence; in Argos this was the time of the scytalism [a system resembling the *lettres de cachet*] and of a series of dreadful crimes in Corinth, Phlius and Phigalia. About the middle of the century, Isocrates says that Argos is perpetually at war with stronger neighbours and annually sees its lands ravaged; just as regularly it proceeds to execute its richest and most respected citizens with a relish rarely shown at the killing of enemies; the orator believes this will cease when the war ends. It is instructive to see how in Diodorus these stories are intermingled with those of Dionysius' conduct in Sicily towards the Greeks. We would not maintain that the oligarchs who perished were one iota better than their opponents; but what is to become of a people that exterminates its prosperous and educated class in this way? Wealth vanished and with it went culture and also most of the splendour of the agon; in Greek intellectual life the annihilation of a higher class must have had even more strikingly visible effects. Even physical Nature showed hostility to Greece; in 373 an earthquake and the consequent flood wiped out the cities of Helice and Bura in Achaea, and their destruction was seen as the expression of divine wrath.

We must now turn to Athens once more. The city provides the clearest evidence of all, not because we have particularly good historical accounts of it – in fact political history has to be very largely divined by combining the evidence of Xenophon, Diodorus and others – but because we learn an abundance of moral facts from the orators and, as to the early period, from Aristophanes too. What we learn from them may be introduced by the remark of Isocrates (reported by Aelian) to the effect that the city of

Athens was pleasanter for a short stay than any other in Greece, but no longer safe for permanent residence because of the sycophants and the demagogues.[41]

How had Athens fared after Aegospotami? It is a fact that was well known, and expressed by Andocides as an unpleasant truth, that in that catastrophe the continued existence of Athens was made possible by Sparta, while, if her later allies the Thebans and Corinthians had had their way, her inhabitants would have been sold into slavery and the city laid waste.[42] Of course Sparta spared Athens only to prevent Thebes from becoming too powerful, just as after Leuctra it was not from generosity that the Athenians sent Iphicrates with 12,000 men to answer the Lacedaemonians' pleas for help, but from jealous anxiety about their near neighbour Thebes.[43] In any case Athens was saved, and after the brief rule of the Thirty Tyrants the state arose with its old forms newly reinstituted and democracy fully restored. However there was something doubtful from the start about the general amnesty then declared. The oligarchs had used the occasion of the defeat to deprive Athens of defences, ships and power, because they foresaw that any democracy in Athens would by infallible logic find itself on the old course towards the ruthless domination of ambition, and sycophancy. Despite the promise given, this occurred at once and inevitably. Retrospective accusations were made and proved on all sides, and because everything reminded people of that frightful time, the sycophants were able to fasten on their prey immediately after the restoration of normality.[44]

In external political affairs the tendency was to rest on memories of the time of Pericles. His aim had been to educate the Athenians through exclusively political and artistic occupations (or idleness) towards permanent hegemony over all the Greeks, but, as a result, democracy had matured with all its consequences. This had caused a ferment among the rest of the Greeks, who also had their vanity, and this led to the Peloponnesian War. At its conclusion the need for peace was pressing in all the states; but the lack of inner peace in men was so great that they could not keep the peace if they wanted to; their mental sickness caused new outbreaks like a devouring fever. So it was that the wastage of Greek humanity continued, first in the form of the war between Boeotia and Corinth, in which the battles were accompanied by city-revolutions on both sides.[45] Then, after the peace of Antalcidas in 387, many *poleis* which had gained 'autonomy' were torn by new dissension. Athens at least was able to recover with the removal of Spartan pressure, and after the liberation of Cadmeia in 378 it was even possible to form a new Athenian marine alliance. Spartan fleets were defeated in 376 by Chabrias off Naxos and in 375 by Timotheus at the Battle of Leucadia, and Athens still maintained its power over the islands of Lemnos, Imbros and Scyros as well as an area on the Chersonese in Thrace. But the new hegemony was very modest, the citizens' army on land was inadequate, and so any power-politics were out of the question; Athens no longer cast its spell, and although something of the old temperament remained, the Athenians were so far sobered as to recognize the impossibility of another Sicilian extravaganza; that rocket-like explosion of the national existence could only occur once and never again.

Since envy is even stronger than hatred, Athens allied itself with Sparta against Thebes after the battle of Leuctra, but could no longer act decisively, so that all the Athenian wars and alliances of this period remained fruitless. At the same time it must have been very humiliating that Pelopidas with his military fame should have more weight with the Great King than Athens with its rhetoric (Plutarch, *Pelopidas* 30); and worst of all was the daily spectacle of Aegina. This island had been laid under tribute in 457 and settled with cleruchs [Athenian citizens given land outside Attica] after the former inhabitants had been driven out. After Aegospotami, however, the cleruchs were dispossessed and the Aeginetans re-established, whereupon they forbade any Athenian to set foot on their island. This one fact is sufficient to suggest the Athenians' situation and their mood; for them it was almost as bad as the establishment of Messene had been for the Spartans, and like them the Athenians had to accept the reversal of one of their most glorious deeds.

Now that external power was lost while the pretension to it survived, the machinery of state continued to function relentlessly in its own territory of Attica. Notably there was a constant irrational fear that someone or other might overthrow the existing democratic constitution. By exploiting this superstitious dread the statesmen were able to resist a treaty with Sparta during the Boeotian-Corinthian War.[46] Aristophanes' *Ecclesiazusae*, possibly performed in 392, shows how strong the disgust with politics had become. Even scorn and spite seem enfeebled here; it is the first work by this writer in which no contemporaries appear, though he still occasionally quotes several to mock them, and hands down to posterity the most astonishing general principles.[47] In the fourth century, the jeering must gradually have lost much of its sting; the prohibition on recognizable masks no doubt resulted from the fact that it was now *possible* to forbid them. The state and public life no longer had celebrities such as Cleon, Euripides and Socrates; the best people lived out of contact with either, some in self-imposed poverty, and Athens was obliged to make do with lesser men to look after its affairs, whatever might be said against them, which was plenty. Women, the play suggests, ought to take over the State from men, because, as their leader Praxagora laments (176 ff.) the *polis* always chooses bad leaders: when one of them has behaved justly for a day he will be unjust for the next ten, and each one is worse than his predecessor, but the people too are only out for their own advantage. They attend the popular assembly as the labourers do, just for the sake of the three obols; it has come down to being a minimum daily wage. The Athenian bourgeois, according to his own wife, is typically a thief, sycophant and coward; only women know how to be silent, while men themselves admit that they can never keep their own counsel; only women do not deceive each other, as men do even in the presence of witnesses. In one passage (lines 473 ff.), as evidence of the lightheartedness which must have been a valued gift in that generation, we hear the old optimistic consolation: 'All our (Athenian) decisions that are unwise or stupid turn out well for us.' The Athenian love of what was new or extraordinary is neatly expressed (lines 455 ff.) when it is urged that the State should be handed over to women, because this is the only thing that has not yet happened to it.

In *Plutus*, too, produced on the stage in 388 in the version we possess, the prevailing mood is just as gloomy. The good are unlucky and the bad lucky; the orators get rich, and even a pretended friend will probably play a sycophant's trick on you (lines 377 ff.). At the same time, terrible poverty is shown as general; the theme of the wages of the ecclesiasts and the heliasts is used here too (377 f., 1166 f.), there are no good doctors left because the fees are so low (407 f.); shield and armour have been pawned for bread (450 f.), and times are hard even in the Asclepieion, for the priest is evidently dependent on the cakes and figs he can steal from the altar and 'consecrate' to his bag (676 ff.). A period of the deepest misery is indicated by poor people being in the habit of stealing the provisions placed each month on family graves by those who can afford it (595 ff.).

As we have already seen [pp. 230 ff. above], in this desolation certain orators took to idealizing the previous century immoderately. I may recall here how Isocrates, in the *Areopagiticus*, gives a picture of his own time, i.e. the administration of Eubulus, by praising the past. The orator's positive proposals aimed at restoring the power of the Areopagus were impracticable, since they would have depended on reviving ancient beliefs and ways of thinking.[48] Isocrates' ideas about the fifth and sixth centuries were also obviously fabulous, his historical and political learning shallow, and some things he simply made up. Clearly, if he could round off his phrases and put a fine speech together, the facts were a matter of indifference to him; but because the speech is a genuine resumé of all that was wrong in Attic democracy in the fourth century it remains instructive for us by virtue of its slashing attack on its own time.

Isocrates imagines an ancient Athens as it never was, one that was already democratic but still just and happy, and the ridiculously inflated praise of Attic democracy runs through the whole oration side by side with pitiful lamentation over the democracy that actually exists. He tells of patriotism in the good old days, in which the offices of State were not the object of ambition or intrigue; everyone, he says, minded his own business without expecting to improve it out of the public funds. Those who had leisure and means had to labour for the common cause; honesty was praised, dishonesty punished without respect of persons; in the observance of religion the traditional sacrifices had not yet been displaced by ostentatious new offerings. Such harmony existed between rich and poor that, without envy, the poor understood that their wellbeing depended on the wealth of others, while the rich perceived want and misery as shameful to themselves and assisted the poor by renting out parcels of land at low rates, by employing people in commercial affairs and by financial support, so much so that a borrower was made more welcome than a debtor coming to repay money. Thus there was peace at home, and foreign enemies were defeated. But in those days, of course, young men were not in the habit of spending their days in the gaming houses or with flute-girls; if they had to cross the agora they did so modestly. Contradicting or offending one's elders was judged more severely then than similar behaviour to one's parents is at present; not even a self-respecting slave would then go to eat in a tavern, and the jesters and mockers who now (with the fashion for satire) are considered talented, were then regarded as unfortunates. Things have changed for the worse; and the principal blame, according to Isocrates, rests with the generation immediately preceding his, which broke the power of the Areopagus. But evidently the mood of repentance had not yet set in; he describes the city as so well provided by the democracy with both religious and civic institutions that even now visitors consider it worthy to rule not only over the Greeks but over the whole world (66).

In any case, great changes had occurred in the composition of the citizen body. Even before and during the Peloponnesian War the workers had gained influence, but now, after the restoration, sheer 'manpower shortage' forced the admission of many of them as citizens. Large numbers of foreigners such as Thessalians and Andrians had thus acceded to full rights from 403 (no doubt through intermarriage).[49] In the Oration *Peace* (86 ff.), Isocrates explains that this had been made necessary by the deaths of many true Athenians in the Peloponnesian War; he calculates the enormous human losses that Athens suffered in the Egyptian expedition of 458, and then continues:

> Every year some communal tomb was erected to which our neighbours and other Greeks would make pilgrimage, not to mourn with us but to rejoice in our losses. It was not usually noticed that these tombs were filled with the bodies of citizens, while the *phratria* and citizenship rolls were made up of people unconnected with the city ... The families of the most distinguished men and the great houses that came down to us from before the tyranny and the Persian War have been wiped out. We should not call a city happy because it attracts masses of citizens from everywhere; a fortunate city is one in which the race of the original inhabitants is best preserved.

There were remarkable administrative contradictions in this *polis*. On the one hand there was the completely tyrannical government of the moment by the ecclesia and the autocrats; the State, unchallenged, saw enemies everywhere, imposed death sentences for trivial offences and relied on confiscation as a source of public finance. On the other hand the organs of State operated in the most disreputable way, and the whole of the Athenian State was powerless to control Nicomachus, the official in charge of drafting the laws, and his friends; they are the perfect illustration to *Ecclesiazusae*. Laws were being passed at such a rate that Isocrates, who sees the quantity and fussy detail of them as a proof of political rottenness, says (*Areopagiticus* 40 f.) that they fill the stoas with documents instead of filling men's minds with respect for law. Laws bearing *ad hoc* on a particular case, or with retroactive effect, were proliferating too. And this despite the most elaborate formal safeguards for the whole system, for example the requirement that when a law was amended the proposer had to exhibit the new draft and the existing law together on the marketplace, so that anyone could examine them and bring forward objections in the popular assembly, while the citizens could appoint advocates to defend the old law. Legislation and the courts simply could not alter the fact that the State had become a ragbag of laws and that individuals were malevolent and corrupt; the orators show how all safeguards were circumvented or openly flouted.

However the State postured and however tyrannically it intervened in particular cases, the immorality of personal behaviour, and the general determination to find loopholes in the laws, increased proportionately. People showed astonishing cunning (*panourgon*) in risking their lives for the sake of profit. I have mentioned how traders in grain would contravene laws that carried the death penalty. In its degenerate condition, and by its constant harassment of the citizens, the State had made itself odious to them, and they would circumvent the taxes it imposed as soon as they had the necessary influence to do so; the three hundred wealthiest, for instance, who from 357 formed the first category in the tax association for the equipment of triremes (*symmoriai*) and had to advance money to fit out naval expeditions, were bitterly reproached with unjustly distributing the burden among the less wealthy, so that the task of provisioning the ships was usually delayed and badly carried out.[50] Complaints of embezzlement were common. In a speech delivered during the Boeotian-Corinthian War, Lysias says: 'They steal what is yours and are safe from punishment. Either it is not noticed, and they enjoy their loot without fear, or if it is, they buy themselves out of danger with part of the proceeds, or else, if put on trial, by using their influence.' The subject of this oration is war-profiteers who started life poor; these men have enriched themselves by robbing and impoverishing the people, who are not even angry at the theft, but grateful for what little they still receive.[51] As for the officials, they were all more or less corrupt, and there was intense competition for these posts for the sake of the expected bribes. In many cases the motive was perhaps not only the wish to make money at whatever risk, but a kind of daredevilry, and pride in successfully cheating the system. All these circumstances give us the feeling that most contemporary Athenians must have had enough of public affairs, and longed for a private life of peaceful activity under the protection of the law.

In the midst of all this a financial charlatan came on the scene, offering the State splendid prospects of prosperity. This was the author of the treatise on *Revenues*, i.e. the aged Xenophon (if it was really he) who wrote his essay for the benefit of Eubulus during the Sacred War, after the Athenians had lifted his sentence of exile.[52]

Xenophon's plan was to increase state revenues by courting the metics, promising them building land and a new department of '*metoikophylakes*' devoted to their affairs; he also wished to exploit the silver mines more fully and greatly increase the numbers of slaves who worked them.[53] All this was in keeping with his patriarchal view that the citizens should and could exist solely for the State and its power. The time for this was long past. On the contrary, it was already the universal rule in Athenian life that people demanded rights, not duties, and pleasure instead of work; and it was now that the inevitable consequences of the antibanausic attitude became apparent. Since the pleasures of hard work had never been recognized, and everyone tried to avoid it, people had to find another way to the good life, and would use any means they could. Often they turned to criminality; perjury, false witness, common theft and murder for gain became commonplace, and with them the odious figure of the parasite. The State should of course have punished idleness and cured the mob of its passion for enjoyment, but the sad fact was that far from being able to do this, it could not even defend anyone against the vilest false accusations; in fact the attacker had the support of the full formal structure of State institutions.

The best account of the miserable condition of Athens at that period is that of the orator Isaeus, though as his speeches relate to civil actions they throw light on only one aspect of Greek depravity. In particular, they explain how every inheritance had to be guarded with great resolution from the threat of a crowd of greedy swindlers. In Oration 4, for instance, the case is that of a certain Nicostratus, who died abroad in the wars; the natural heirs to his fortune, which was worth only two talents, were the two sons of his father's brother. But a good many other people cut off their hair and wore mourning as if they were legal heirs. One claimed to be a nephew of the deceased, was proved a liar and withdrew; another maintained that the whole fortune was left to him, but also had to admit defeat; a third showed a three-year-old child as the son of the deceased, who had then been away from Athens for eleven years; a fourth declared that the bequest was dedicated to Athena, but also to himself; a fifth and a sixth first swore that the testator had lost a lawsuit against them for one talent and, when unable to prove this, said he was their freedman, but again failed to prove it. These were just the first to pounce on the inheritance; the sum they forfeited when their pleas were rejected was what they had deposited at the start of the case, fixed at only one tenth of the value of the sum claimed. The orator feels that this is far too little and that the claimant ought to forfeit to the State as much as he had hoped to gain; this would put an end to contempt of the law and prevent people from insulting the relatives and the memory of the deceased. It was only later that yet another person appeared with an alleged will made in his favour by Nicostratus, whom he also declared not to be the son of the heirs' uncle but a completely different man. Similarly, Oration 8 describes how Diocles, who had married into the family of a certain Ciron, told Ciron's daughter's sons, the sole heirs, that their mother was not Ciron's daughter at all. Incidentally it came out that the fortune this unscrupulous man already boasted of was not really his. He had acquired it dishonestly by pretending to be the adopted son of a father whose heirs were three daughters, though he was not mentioned in the will. The husbands of two of these daughters having demanded restitution, he kidnapped the elder daughter's husband, imprisoned and tortured him, for which he was charged with dishonourable treatment, but had remained thus far unpunished. He had the second daughter's husband assassinated by a slave, whom he sent abroad, accusing the wife, his pretended sister, of the murder. Intimidating her with horrible threats, he used his position as her son's guardian to seize his fortune too; he was now in possession of the son's country estate, for which he had given its rightful owners nothing but a few poor stony fields. From this terrible character sketch it is clear how violence could be used in Athens to get rich. There was no public prosecutor, and it seems that no sycophants would come forward against such a man as Diocles.

Cases like the one which gave rise to the Seventh Oration were probably of everyday occurrence. Here an uncle appointed as guardian turned out to be dishonest and grasping; he declared himself a coheir and appropriated the whole bequest. Or again, the misappropriation of an estate might be confirmed by a judicial decision until the rightful heirs, or their sons, were of an age to begin a new lawsuit for what was their own; this happened in the family of Demosthenes.[54]

A different area, that of the right to citizenship, is discussed in Demosthenes' speech against Eubulides. The issue concerns one of the census lists in the demes, in which all those who were not born of the marriage of two citizens were eliminated and degraded to the status of metics (in many cases correctly). Appeal to the people's court was allowed, but anyone who appealed and lost was sold into slavery. In proceedings of this kind, sycophancy was in its element, and in the *demos* of Halimus the disreputable Eubulides had made it his speciality. In the deme assembly, meeting in the town itself, he occupied the day with filibustering and trivial arguments against his victims, who included Euxitheus, the client of Demosthenes. He continued until darkness fell and most people went home; thirty remained, all in league with him, and a ballot was taken in which most voted more than once, so that over sixty votes against Euxitheus were found in the urn. The pretext upon which this man was robbed of his citizenship was that his father's speech and habits were foreign, a result, in fact, of a long period spent abroad as a prisoner of war. Also his mother, like many in that time of widespread poverty, had served as a wet nurse. The register of citizens held in the deme was said to have been lost in the troubles. Eubulides' motive was revenge, since Euxitheus had testified against him in one of his sycophancies; it was a great impudence as there were plenty of relatives of both parents and a crowd of other witnesses for Euxitheus; he and his kin had been recognized as citizens in his deme for decades, and they had let his name go forward in the drawing of lots for the priesthood of Heracles.[55]

Diabolical people have always existed, and our own standards of security cannot be applied to the violence of public affairs in Athens. The most repellent feature of Athens in the time of the orators is the way the popular assembly and the courts, with all their official apparatus, were the setting for the worst chicanery and persecutions, and provided the means for them. When we contemplate all the corrupt orators, the mass of decisions never put into practice, the claques and noisemakers to drown protests, the sycophants and false witnesses, the entanglement of the innocent in criminal proceedings, the silencing by murder of those who had right on their side, what amazes us is the immense arrogance of this unashamed parading of evil. It is reminiscent of conditions under the Terror of 1793–4 in France; but in Athens there must have been utterly depraved yet capable people in far greater numbers than could proportionately be found in any modern city.

All the same, the popular assembly and the courts were the institutions which allowed a Demosthenes to make himself heard and to succeed. It was only the political maturity and intellectual culture of Athens that ultimately made it possible for him to be appreciated. Here even the most objectionable elements testify to a very advanced culture.

At the time when the sole general interest was the pursuit of enjoyment, the State too made pleasure its business. The administration of Eubulus began in 354 and lasted fifteen years. Not only was there to be an end of wars – which would have been a wise decision at any date – but life was to be nothing but pleasure, with the festivals and associated distributions of money the main thing in Athenian life. The festival coffers became the most important in the state, and surpluses from all other funds were to go into them. 'Panathenaea and Dionysia,' says Demosthenes

> must always take place on the right date, while you put off the time for making war – and they cost you as much as any army; for the festivals everything is arranged promptly, and each of you knows long beforehand who is *choregos* and who gymnasiarch of each *phyle*, and when to apply, and to whom, for all that is needed, while nothing is properly organized for war.[56]

It is well known that the death penalty was imposed for using the money for any purpose other than entertainment, and it took Demosthenes a long time to tear this spider's web apart. This indicates what an abysmal condition the nation was in. However, it certainly put war out of the question, and the peace oration of Isocrates, shortly before Eubulus took office, expresses the deep longing for peace. Believing that the accursed ambition to rule others (*arche*) had ruined Athens as it ruined Sparta (94 f., 104 f.), Isocrates aimed to dissuade the Athenians from exercising any power abroad, from maritime ambitions and from making war, and to convince them that, in spite of all that had happened, this course would win them the love and respect of the rest of the world. Almost in the spirit of Eubulus himself, Isocrates paints a splendid future in which, freed from special taxes, trierarchies and the expense of war, they could safely live by agriculture, shipping and commerce; the city's income would be doubled and it would be full of merchants, foreigners and metics, and could send needy Athenians and other Greeks to settle on the Thracian coast.

For all the magnificence of the festivals, public works were in a pitiable state and had little to show but the whitewash on ramparts, roadsides and wellheads.[57] To make up for this, private owners and private luxury now became far more ostentatious; Demosthenes says that the wealthy lived much more splendidly than Miltiades and Aristides had done, and owned grander buildings than the State.[58] It must have been at this period that differences in fortune began to be more evident in the way people lived.

There was a general feeling, though, that the old glory was a thing of the past; the city seemed to have turned into a little old lady, sipping her barley soup and wearing slippers.[59] There would have been every reason to rise up and reject the life of ease and pleasure, for there were unpleasant reminders that these habits were unworthy. Offshore in the Saronic Sea piracy flourished; Diogenes, for instance, was captured on the trip from Athens to Aegina, and taken to Crete, by pirates whose leader, Captain Scirpalus, was apparently famous. One Alexander of Pherae boldly attacked Piraeus with his ships and stole all the money from the moneychangers' tables there.[60]

In fact the great Athens of old was gone beyond recall. In its total transformation from a political power into a cultural one, Hellenic civilization was to be the model for the whole of Greece; equally typical was the metamorphosis of the individual citizen of the *polis* into the man of learning, who was to be the bearer of Hellenic culture; philosophy set the example with its flight from the State. Intellectually, however, Athens was more than ever in the lead, for the cities of Ionia had lost their importance in the life of the mind, as Corinth, Thebes, Argos and Sparta had done. The single exception was, once more, pictorial art, which still existed everywhere. In philosophy, Athens took the first place as a matter of course, and such philosophers as there were in the rest of Greece all had to spend at least some time in Athens.[61] Oratory had such immense prestige that even on its own it would have ensured the primacy of Athens. Dionysius of Halicarnassus says of Isocrates that he had trained the most gifted men in Athens and the rest of Greece, some of them becoming orators in the lawcourts, others notable in the service of the State, others again historians of 'the doings of Hellenes and barbarians'. The city had to aim at remaining at least the chief home of oratory, because this soon became the most important source of power. It must not be forgotten that tragedy still held its own and inspired new plays, nor that Athens was the chief home of middle and new comedy; the continuing impression is of enormous intellectual energy; vital forces were at work in Athens which would not be found elsewhere.

Yet Athens was already in a very poor political and military situation by the year 350, when the Macedonian threat was increasing. The marine alliance was in complete decline after the defection of Chios, Rhodes, Cos and Byzantium and the unfortunate War of the Allies. Where the city still had allies or small subject settlements, the inhabitants lived in dread of a visit from the Athenian commanders with the fleet, because since Athens was to spend no more money on war, they were certain at best to have to pay large contributions, and at worst to be looted by hungry mercenaries with empty pockets. These troops and their commanders were the only army available.[62] However loud the complaints about villainous captains, it is fair to take their situation into account, for they had the politicians to contend with, intent on giving them instructions first and finding fault with them afterwards; and the Athenians were always ready to believe liars and make hasty decisions.[63] Demosthenes says that every military leader had to stand trial for his life two or three times; but as effective control over these mercenaries was impossible, the charge was never the one they should have faced, and the wrong one was pursued all the more energetically. Where Iphicrates had once brought armed men to intimidate the judges, Chares now left in Athens the funds meant for war to be distributed to those citizens who were orators, peddlers of honours and officials of the courts, after using what he needed to pay for his own debauches; and the *demos* never blamed him for it but loved him. 'For the people themselves lived in the same way,' says Athenaeus (532d); 'the young men idled in the taverns with the flute-girls or with courtesans, their elders passed the time in dicing and other games, and the *demos* spent more on banquets and distributions of meat than on the whole administration of the city.' In the speech *Against Aristocrates* Demosthenes says that Charidemus too had bribed the orators, and could therefore sometimes risk directly opposing Athenian interests. For example, he supported the pirates, who had gathered at Alopeconnesos on the west coast of the Chersonese, when the Athenians were intending to attack them; he also captured, by treachery, a Thracian chieftain and his son, who were friendly to Athens, and handed them over to the hostile Cardianians who he knew would show them no mercy, and who then drowned the father after killing the son before his eyes.[64] This too went unpunished, just as the city let itself be openly robbed, as long as the pleasures of Athens were taken care of. These political bosses, who were honoured in Athens with statues, and thanked for Athenian victories,[65] were securing safe havens for themselves in distant places because they knew that no Athenian could be trusted;[66] Conon in Cyprus, Timotheus on Lesbos, Iphicrates in Thrace, Chares in Sigeion, Chabrias in Egypt. They had no choice; but taken as a whole, the relationship between employer and employed has perhaps never sunk to greater depths of immorality.

Meanwhile the public conduct of the Athenian people was shameful. 'Things have reached the point when our citizens will no longer venture outside the walls to confront an enemy,' says Isocrates in his attack on the Athenians (*Peace* 77). And again: 'While we do not let a day go by without ill-using one another, we are unwilling even to turn up for a parade unless we are paid for it,' (*Areopagiticus* 82); or 'We want to rule, but not to take the field ourselves; we pick quarrels with half the world, but leave military preparations to homeless and unreliable mercenaries' (*Peace* 44). It was so bad that Phocion once allowed massive desertions of disaffected and undisciplined agitators, because they would only have been a liability in battle, and in this way could not vilify him in Athens with their own bad conscience, or use sycophancy to bring him down (Plutarch, *Phocion* 12). It did sometimes happen that citizens went as crewmen when the mercenaries were sent out in the guise of a hoplite army. When for once the citizens' army marched out in a 'splendid surge of feeling', what awaited them was Chaeronea.

We must now consider the means that were used by Eubulus and other leading statesmen to control the democratic assembly and the people's courts. This was done, as always, through the public orators (*rhetores*) who were generally known for their vices. Although corruption was liable to the death penalty, their speech, like their silence, could be purchased. 'When our professional optimists intend to urge war against another state, they have the audacity to say that we should behave like our ancestors, but they take money for saying it,' says Isocrates, for instance (*Peace* 36), and Demosthenes declares: 'If you were asked what kind of men you consider the worst in the *polis* you would not say the farmers or the merchants or those in the silver-mining business; everyone would agree in naming those who take money for their eloquence and for drawing up applications' (*Against Aristocrates* 146). They were notorious for handing out civic rights and other honours, even to enemies of Athens and to criminals, and for acting only when it was to their own advantage.[67] Fingers were pointed at some who had come from beggary to riches, or from obscurity to eminence, who built themselves splendid houses, and whose rise in the world kept pace with the decline of the state;[68] but even when they had committed the worst crimes and were publicly accused, they were acquitted in return for producing a couple of favours (*asteia*), and if one was found guilty, it was only for a trivial offence (*Against Aristocrates* 206). Athens still clung to these men though they had deceived her a thousand times; the explanation was that they always succeeded in posing as friends of the people (*demotikoi*), and the population, in constant terror of losing the democracy, was capable of deep hatred only for those who represented the old *kalokagathia* (Isocrates, *Peace* 133). This was why the *demos* would never allow disinterested men from noble families to act as mediators, for they were thought to favour oligarchy. As Isocrates puts it (*ibid.* 13), drunken men were credited with better judgment than the sober, because the *demos* saw that they pandered to its desires and sometimes helped it to satisfy its evil passions; for the Athenians were still given to cruelty.[69] Alongside those who had lost all shame, like Demades,[70] some were merely relatively bad: a certain Pytheas in Philip's time did not object when he was reproached with wickedness, but said that of the Attic politicians he had been wicked for the shortest time; he evidently prided himself on not having always been so, and thought he could not be doing wrong since he could not be reckoned among the worst of all (Aelian, *Varia Historia* 14.28). It hardly needs saying that sycophancy continued unabated; it was often not possible to distinguish between the sycophant and the orator, and this behaviour can be continuously traced onwards to the time at which the state of Attica with its last orator becomes indiscernible to us.[71]

In spite of all this, it goes without saying that whenever it suited the orators' purpose, their most forceful complaints of the condition of things were accompanied by the usual Athenian boasting. 'Not to flee dangers, but to shun what is dishonourable and shameful – that is your time-honoured practice,' says Isocrates, for instance (*Plataicus* 14.39), and in the speech *Against Aristocrates*, amidst all his plain speaking to the Athenians, Demosthenes also has to put in a flattering remark: 'You Athenians have never betrayed an ally, as the Thessalians have always betrayed every one' (112). A theme that was a particular favourite for boosting patriotic sentiment was the praise of tyrannicide, one that always delighted the hearers. Cotys, King of Thrace, who had been honoured with Athenian citizenship and with gold crowns, later turned against Athens; in 358 he was assassinated by one Python and the Heracleidae, who were then given citizens' rights and gold crowns in their turn, though this did not prevent Python from leaving all these honours and going over to Philip (*Against Aristocrates* 118 f., 127).

The empty State coffers were in stark contrast to the fine sentiments that were often paraded. It is true that total taxable property in Attica amounted to 6,000 talents, and Demosthenes can say that there is nearly as much money in the city as in all the others put together (*On the Taxation Groups* 19.25); but from the beginning of the century there are complaints of the fiscal situation, and quite early on Lysias gives the most shocking examples of the State's helping itself to the possessions of the innocent. Demosthenes tells his fellow citizens. 'You have not enough in the coffers to support an army for a single day.' There are also perpetual grumblings about the impoverishment of citizens. It is remarkable that a fortune of 90,000 drachmas should place Demosthenes' father in the highest tax category, while in Isocrates' *Areopagiticus* (54) we have the pitiful account of large numbers of people standing from early morning outside the lawcourts in the hope of drawing the lot to sit that day and earn half a drachma; he also says that the same people who appear in hired golden robes at festivals and processions are muffled in indescribable rags for the winter.

An important testimony to the general corruption of statesmen, orators and others, not only in Athens but in all Greece, is given in the Third Philippic of Demosthenes (36 ff.). First he paints contemporary Greek affairs in a way calculated to arouse indignation, and then says how different things were in the Persian Wars, when the worst disgrace was to be found out taking bribes; there was no such person, then, as a crooked orator or general who would sell information as to the right moment for making a deal, while now all this is available as if on the open market. Greece was sick now, he said, with a new trouble; envy of anyone who got any money, mockery if he admitted it, tolerance for wrongdoers, hatred for those who condemned them, and all the other ills corruption brings. It was the nation so described, and in this situation, that suddenly found its very existence in danger, with Philip of Macedon as its opponent.

We must first note the chief distinguishing feature of Athenian culture that was brought out by the war with Macedonia: in a way that is peculiar to Athens, the city was constantly being obliged through the mouths of its orators to sum up its own existence and balance its political accounts. We may compare the contemporary admonitions of the Jewish prophets with the Olynthiac and Philippic orations of Demosthenes; this alone serves to shed light on the whole of Greek life at that time, and no other Greek city offers anything resembling this self-awareness.[72] Demosthenes may be in error here and there, while Aeschines may lie and seek to confuse; none the less this was one place in which the truth of the situation was spoken aloud.

Certainly the Athenians heard plenty of home truths (Demosthenes

3.15). The great orator himself laid all the blame on them when he asked them to reflect that they had men who could give the right advice, and that they were themselves capable of weighing that advice, and also of acting on it if they roused themselves immediately; or when he cried out to them:

> If some Messenian or Peloponnesian behaves in a way contrary to their good sense, it is understandable; but you yourselves are well informed and have us to tell you of the threats and plots against you, yet you do nothing till the worst happens; the pleasure of the moment and your idleness are much dearer to you than any effort you might make to help yourselves.[73]

He often told them how easily they could bring about a change. 'Sparta is overthrown,' he says in the Third Olynthiac (27) 'and Thebes is occupied elsewhere; if we stood up for ourselves and for the rights of others we would be on our own, that is without rivals. As it is we have lost our own region and are 1500 talents poorer for no return.'

It may be uncertain whether Philip really intended, at the outset, to quarrel with Athens, but in any case he made the Athenians uneasy, and as he came nearer they separated at once into two parties. If Athens had had an absolute ruler, it is not unthinkable that she might have made common cause with Macedonia; but as there was no secret agenda, and everything had to be done through the democratic assembly, this was impossible; moreover, Philip was so daring and so much dreaded by the Greeks that it would not have been easy to persuade them into an alliance with him. Worse still, there was a pro-Macedonian party in Athens, headed by Aeschines, Demades and others, which became more and more notorious, until people said that the very schoolchildren knew which orators were in Macedonian pay, who were entertained by Macedonian visitors and who paid their respects to them on the streets.[74]

Demosthenes came out against them. It cost him much effort, as we know, to get a hearing; the people delighted in the eloquence of good orators and demanded it as a treat, evaluating and criticizing the points made by various speakers, but this did not mean they would be led by them.[75] It was only through the conflict with Philip that Demosthenes won political influence, and in the course of it he brought his best powers to bear in his outstanding eloquence and extraordinary persistence.[76] As for the question of his political morality, this was argued over even in antiquity, because no-one knew whether he had accepted gold from the Persians, or how much.[77] It is not for us to side against him in this. However it also seems too facile to base our judgment of this great orator on the aesthetic appeal of his work, to make him into a spotless model of patriotism, and to treat the criticisms of Hyperides, Theopompus and Demetrius of Phaleron as mere envious gossip; and so we cannot quite associate ourselves with his rehabilitation by modern scholarship.[78] We must admit that anyone who knows what Athens was like at the time will be extremely cautious in deciding such matters. Scandalmongering and malicious political rumour were everywhere and force us to conclude that even the best people were vulnerable – the same inescapable impression given by the Athens of Aristophanes [cf. p. 230 above and passim]; in such a period we can hardly expect to find a totally blameless personality.

In any case, Demosthenes deserves credit for having broken the power of Eubulus. A draught of fresh air seemed to blow through the city, so that decency could revive; Athens no doubt saw this as a welcome recovery of her reputation and self-respect, and took pride in having this fiery virtuoso speaker against Philip, even if with Aeschines and his party the opposite tendency was also at home in the city. As an orator Demosthenes was supreme, and it is impossible to read the Third Olynthiac Oration without admiration, nor indeed the Third Philippic, in which his tone of reproachful irony must have gone to the Athenians' hearts. The conclusion of this last-named speech is particularly effective, when he urges military preparations, alliances, and missions abroad to summon, unite, inform and warn the Hellenes, but then explains to his audience that they must lead by their own exemplary efforts, not wait for Chalcidians and Megarians to save Greece and think they themselves need do nothing; for *they* have inherited this glorious duty from their ancestors. No wonder the man who could deal such blows succeeded in getting Athens on to his own side and finally achieved the famous conversion of the previously hostile Thebans with their generals and Boeotarchs, so that the democratic assembly of Thebes, as well as that of Athens, was led by Demosthenes.[79]

Looking at matters more coolly, there are several question marks against his military policy. There is a strong possibility that Philip might have preferred to leave Greece unmolested south of Parnassus, in order to pursue his important plans against Persia. He had already offended the Corinthians, the Achaeans and the Thebans, but had not yet gone directly against Athens.[80] Despite this, the Third Philippic urges Athens to come forward as protectress for the whole Greek nation, because this is the sole argument by which Demosthenes can fire the Athenians. After a hundred years of wars in which the Greek cities had maltreated one another so cruelly, and called in foreign powers to intervene, it must have needed a strong faith to expect that Panhellenic patriotism would work a miracle at the last moment. Not only this, but the orator had to inform his Athenians that they were as yet too weak to wage a decisive war against Philip, and would face defeat; their enemy would not be like the Spartans they had fought in the Peloponnesian War; Philip's armies would be led in quite a different fashion.[81] In spite of all this, and though he knew exactly how feeble the citizens' army of Attica was, Demosthenes drove this spoilt and pleasure-loving nation into a war in which its very existence was certain to be at risk. Obviously he was hoping for something to happen in Macedonia itself, as he hints by saying they had only one man to deal with. But Philip was not yet to die or be assassinated. In any case this line of policy was rash in the extreme, and we must remember that not all Demosthenes' opponents were paid agents of Macedonia; Phocion in particular was against the whole campaign from the beginning.

It seems that when they were mustered for the decisive battle, all the young men eagerly set off as soon as possible for Boeotia (Diodorus 16.85) – the allies, however, bringing a strong force of mercenaries as well as their troops of citizens – and so they came to Chaeronea (in 338). It would have been a blessing for Demosthenes if he had been killed in this battle; instead, as recent historians say, he was 'caught up in the retreat', or, as Plutarch puts it less kindly, he deserted and fled like a coward, throwing his weapons away.[82] In the evening after the battle, Philip triumphantly recited the opening words of the Athenian declaration of war: 'Demosthenes son of Demosthenes of Paeania proposed this resolution.' This point marks a hiatus in the orator's life; later events did nothing to redeem his reputation.

When news of the defeat reached Athens, the first reaction was general panic. This is clear from the proposal Hyperides made to evacuate the women and children to Piraeus, give all the slaves their freedom and confer citizenship on all the metics, and to restore civil rights to those convicted of *atimia*.[83] This was immediately accepted, but fortunately not acted upon; it would have been giving way to the sheer terror of despair. The proposal in itself, on account of which Hyperides later had to stand trial, is enough to show the depths to which Athens had sunk, for earlier in the fourth century all whose parents were not married citizens had been deprived of the citizenship. Philip refrained from the attack on Athens they had feared, and behaved mercifully if with irony; he sent the dead home to Athens for burial, freed his two thousand Attic prisoners without demanding a ransom, and not only allowed the Athenians to keep Attica, but also gave them the border region of Oropus, which had belonged to their Theban allies and had always been quarrelled over. In return, they were of course obliged to make a treaty of alliance with him, but were permitted to keep their anti-Macedonian statesmen, and the *demos* continued to defend Demosthenes against all accusations. Since they were determined to show no remorse, it was to him that they entrusted the funeral oration for the fallen.

In Athens, once composure was restored, there was a positive epidemic of proceedings against the military leaders. Some were accused of having handed over ships, others of betraying allied cities, but the accused all fled, evidently because nobody expected fair dealing from the Athenian courts. The public informers must have worked themselves up into a fever of denunciation, and brought solemn state-complaints (*eisangelia*) on trivial grounds, one for instance against a man who had hired out flute-girls for more than the legal fees, or another who had registered in the wrong deme.[84]

Now the odious orator Lycurgus came on the scene. A patriot and an excellent financial administrator, innocent of the practice of stealing State funds,[85] he was also a completely blinkered fanatic.[86] It was on the basis of the charges he brought that the Athenians had to pass the death sentence on Lysicles, who had led the army at Chaeronea as well as he could, since Chares was no genius; in his speeches Lycurgus proved 'the harshest prosecutor'. A surviving extract from his address for the prosecution is in the style we recognize as that of the Terror of 1793–4.

'You were in command,' he says to Lysicles

> when a thousand citizens fell and two thousand were taken prisoner, where a memorial was erected to the defeat of Athens, and all Greece came under the yoke. After this outcome of your leadership, you *dare to live* and see the light of day and walk in the marketplace, a living reminder of the shame and humiliation of your country (Diodorus 16.88).

There is nothing on record to suggest that Lysicles had been at fault, and all the foregoing might have been used with equal force against

Demosthenes; but Lycurgus needed to unleash his sentiments or his affected patriotism, and Lysicles was his victim.

Philip was assassinated in 336 at his daughter's wedding party in Aegae. By then, when the allies assembled in Corinth, he had been appointed commander-in-chief of the Greek nation to make war on Persia. His death was celebrated with rejoicings in Athens. Thanksgiving sacrifices were offered, and Demosthenes appeared crowned and in bright clothing, although he had lost a daughter a few days earlier. The joy is understandable. What seems a high point of Athenian absurdity is the immediate award of a gold crown to the assassin – if they could catch him. Now it was Alexander they had to deal with. Demosthenes had made an astonishing error of judgment when he called him a mere boy and a *margites* (an imbecile); though he could hardly have known that this was to be one of the most powerful men of all times, he was wrong to speak in this way. Inexcusably, he now urged the Thebans to revolt and provided them with weapons, whereupon they murdered the Macedonian garrison. Demosthenes was in control as the leading orator; the Athenians armed, and were hoping for assistance from the Persian governors in Asia Minor; but when Alexander appeared in Boeotia the people's courage collapsed. Demosthenes 'went out like a light' as Plutarch puts it (*Demosthenes* 23) and Thebes, abandoned by Athens, was overrun; if they wanted an uprising in Thebes, much more should have been done for the city. A delegation went to Alexander with Demosthenes as a member, but he withdrew from it just in time, for fear of the king's anger; he was soon in great danger of being handed over to the conqueror, who was demanding ten anti-Macedonian politicians. Demades succeeded in placating the king, and his route was diverted to Asia.

Meanwhile the great feud between Demosthenes and Aeschines was developing in Athens. It had begun soon after Chaeronea, with Ctesiphon's application for the public crowning of Demosthenes, and the objection put in by Aeschines, and it lasted several years, ending with the triumphant acceptance speech of Demosthenes and voluntary exile for Aeschines. That this battle of words could grip everyone's attention in Greece, while Alexander was winning victory after victory in Asia, demonstrates how incurably the Greeks were addicted to eloquence. The speeches made by the two opponents on the subject, exposing a great deal of dirty linen in public, leave a painful impression and an unpleasant taste, even if the reader does not believe every word.

At this time, about 332, Lycurgus prosecuted Leocrates. The charge was that the accused had avoided military service, being out of the country at the time of the War of Chaeronea; and that the false reports he had spread, especially on Rhodes, that Athens was in Macedonian hands and Piraeus besieged, had caused the laden grain ships to remain in Rhodes harbour instead of sailing for Athens; later he lived for five years in Megara disguised as a metic. In prosecuting him, Lycurgus resorted to extremes of rabble-rousing to ruin this man who had returned to Athens in the certain knowledge that he would be put on trial. His main device was to load Leocrates with all the guilt of what would have happened to Athens if everyone had done as he did, and he carried this idea through relentlessly. Flattery of Athens was laid on as thick as possible; they were forced to listen straight-faced while he told them that of all nations they showed the most piety towards gods and parents, and the greatest patriotism, and that all this would seem to be neglected if Leocrates escaped their revenge. In the solemn tone of a funeral oration he presents it as a paradoxical truth that the dead at Chaeronea fell victorious, and that when they were carried to their graves the liberty of all Greece was buried with them; the Athenians alone knew how to honour valour, for in other cities the agora was full of the statues of athletes, while in their own they saw great generals and those who had murdered tyrants. The old refrain on the Persian War rings out again, about how once upon a time no barbarian warship dared enter Greek waters, and even the Greeks in Asia Minor were independent. He adds that it was the glory of Athens that her great deeds were the model for all the Greeks; just as Athens was the first in time, so their Attic forefathers had always been first of all others in courage; and then comes the story of how Codrus[87] sacrificed his life, told in detail with melodramatic passion.[88] There is a good deal of patriotic claptrap in this oration. At the very outset Lycurgus invokes the native gods and heroes as witnesses against the man who has stained their temples, holy places and ancient sacrifices by his treachery, and there are similar outbreaks of piety in later passages.[89] As Leocrates is accused of perjury, the oath of the ephebes is trotted out for a clerk to recite, and also an oath sworn by the Greeks before Plataea (oaths were not worth twopence at the time of this trial). Indirectly, and as far as one man could do so, Leocrates was said to have intended to do away with the traditional rites, to allow parents to fall into enemy hands and the dead to be robbed of the reverence due to them; accordingly there is much stress on the gods' concern with human actions and above all with proper behaviour to parents and the dead. In this connection Lycurgus narrates a legend of the stream of lava from Etna having parted to spare a son who was trying to rescue his father. Alongside these religious titbits, which were quite obviously ludicrous in the Athens of the time, the orator intrudes his personal delight in myth and antiquities.[90] Stern old Athenian decrees of punishment are dwelt on; but patriotic texts from the poets, such as Tyrtaeus, are also quoted – not long after this the Bacchic Hymn would be sung in Athens for Demetrius.

Athens remained the centre of all the counterplots against Alexander. It was now that the most extraordinary story of embezzlement ever known began to unfold, partly in the city. Alexander's treasurer, Harpalus, had absconded and arrived in Athens from Babylon with 700 talents left from the 5,000 he had stolen. The amount of the theft made the whole city uneasy, and in the course of the proceedings that were finally brought against the most influential demagogues for having first harboured the thief and then let him escape, Demosthenes too was involved. He had not wanted to take in Harpalus at the outset, and had only given way because, it was said, Harpalus had bribed him with twenty talents. The orator's guilt was asserted by Hyperides and the prosecutor, whose speech-writer was Deinarchus, as well as Theopompus the historian, whom Plutarch follows word for word.[91] Demosthenes was found guilty and condemned to a fine of fifty talents. Most modern scholars believe he was the victim of a plot, but conjecture about right and wrong is so inappropriate in such cases that we prefer not to give an opinion. In any case, Demosthenes was imprisoned, then succeeded in escaping and resigned himself to a long exile in Aegina and Troezen. This gave rise to one of the most important statements about Athens in general; Plutarch reports that when young men came to visit Demosthenes in exile he dissuaded them from a life in politics by telling them that if he had seen two ways open to him at the beginning, one to the orators' rostrum and the democratic assembly, the other straight to death, and if he had foreseen the evils, anxieties, envious persecutions, slanders and feuding of political life, he would rather have taken the short road to death.[92] In time all Athenian politicians probably came to feel the same.

Alexander's death in 323 gave new impetus to the idea of driving the Macedonians out of Greece, which was at least more practical than it had been before. Demosthenes was called home and given a splendid welcome; but after the first encouraging successes the *inner* weakness of the Greek cities became apparent in what was called the Lamian War; when the Macedonians were once more victorious, the orator fled again and in 322, as we know, met his death on Calauria.[93]

In our discussion of Athens we have often had to refer to the city's megalomania. But it must be said that not only Athens, but Greece as a whole, from the fifth century onwards, inherited immense expectations and a memory of past glory that allowed it no rest – a kind of heritage that has its advantages as well as its drawbacks. Each period in a nation's life may bring its special duty or task, which it is essential to recognize clearly without being dazzled by earlier triumphs. But this can apply only to cultural aims. Moral standards ought never to be lowered; but in moral terms Greece was palpably and obviously diminished since the fifth century, perhaps not so much in the private sphere as in everything that concerned the *polis*. The loftiest idea of Greek life had become blatantly bankrupt; it was openly recognized that the thinkers and the educated had turned their backs on the State and taken to *apolitia* and cosmopolitanism.

The only possible way this could be changed was by a huge exemplary effort on the part of individuals who were seen as influential. The shame of decline embittered the whole of Greece, and it should not be forgotten that things were probably not nearly so bad in Athens as elsewhere. Of the mental climate in most of the other cities our knowledge is scanty, incoherent and mostly negative. It is only in the creative arts that the cities of Ionia seem at least to have kept pace with Athens; in other respects they were totally insignificant, and lagged far behind communities such as Rhodes and Cos.

In the midst of general disillusionment with the *polis* for every kind of reason, that strenuous effort of individual idealism really did occur, if only in a few cases; it combined with the nation's now fully matured awareness of itself as compared with others, and so a new type emerged, whom for want of a better name we may call the 'virtuous Panhellene'. It was a type that had nothing in common with that of the famous Athenian statesmen – Conon, Timotheus, Chabrias, Iphicrates or Phocion – who, with the exception of Demosthenes, were *exclusively* Athenian;[94] this new type represented a cast of mind formed by reflection, and perhaps in essence the product of Pythagorean and Socratic ethics. While many preferred to ignore the State, their own as well as others, and to exist as philosophers, students or travellers, or else simply for pleasure, some few were led by this way of thinking to live for the nation in the wider sense, and above all to remain Greeks, that is political beings, in whatever region.

It would certainly not be correct to include, among these Panhellenes, men like Dionysius the Elder, although in the struggle with the barbarians he inevitably wished to pose as a representative of Hellenism. He was, though, its defender only so far as to serve his own ends, and, as we have seen, he deliberately avoided destroying the power of Carthage in Sicily to make sure he remained indispensable. Nor did the epideictic thinkers, from the fifth-century sophists to Isocrates, belong to this group, although their rhetoric made use of Panhellenic sentiment and they had begun to preach about Hellenic unity and making common cause against barbarians and tyrants. These appeals were facile; what was difficult was to live up to them. As it never came to that, their abuse of the idea was justly punished by the fact that the true Hellene, wherever he appeared, went unrecognized by these orators. For instance, Pelopidas and Epaminondas are never once mentioned by Isocrates, whose Greek patriotism is nothing but a melodious refrain.

Xenophon, on the other hand, really deserved to be placed among the Panhellenes. Taking command after the treachery of the generals, he naturally became the representative of Hellenism in his very heterogeneous army. Later, it is true, when he was exiled from Athens, probably for having served Cyrus, who was Sparta's ally, he displayed a narrow Spartanism and failed, like Isocrates, to recognize the national spirit when he saw it incarnate; but he may have believed that his Spartanism was the authentic Hellenism. Even in externals he apparently tried to live up to Panhellenism, and is described as armed with an Argive shield, an Attic breastplate, a helmet of Roman workmanship, his mount being a horse from Epidaurus.[95]

An extraordinary set of men, the Italian Pythagoreans, now became prominent. The sect founded by Pythagoras had not itself aimed at political power, and if it did exercise any practical influence after the crises in Croton and Metapontum, in which towns and their inhabitants were wiped out, some record of it would have come down from the fifth century. But after a long period when these people were perhaps living in seclusion, they began to be heard of again in the time of Socrates, and seem to have been active in politics. The line includes Philolaus of Tarentum (or of Croton) and Lysis of Tarentum, who both turned up in Thebes; and also Cleinias of Tarentum, who lived in the Lucanian city of Heraclea; and Eurytus, living in Metapontum, as well as, rather later, the great Archytas of Tarentum [cf. p. 283 above]. Whether there was really all the mumbo-jumbo of a secret society at any time is not important, and least of all in this later period;

even if there was, the essential bond was that of the intellect. They aimed at a moral and religious reform of Greek life, and could only hope to achieve it if they possessed political influence in the cities.[96] These were the people who continued to believe that an alliance based on philosophical aristocracy might help Sicily and restore its *poleis*. It was they who wrote urgent letters to Plato begging him to respond when Dionysius the Younger first invited him to Sicily, and, again on the entreaty of Dionysius, enabled him to make his last visit; when Plato had once more fallen out with his host, it was they who brought about his safe release by sending messengers with something approaching a threat. The man on whom their hopes were fixed was Dion, who was not only trained in the Pythagorean tradition but a close friend of Plato's. But Plato himself was steeped in Pythagoreanism, especially in his doctrine of the soul and the world beyond; for him it merged with the Socratic ethic. The intimate link between the two men was most defined during Dion's stay in Greece, when he provided Plato with the means for a splendid *choregia* and when Plato praised and commended him to the Greeks in every way.[97] The Greeks in any case tended to view the Sicilian project with sentimental and ineffectual admiration. There followed a completely hopeless plan to establish a constitution in Sicily on the lines of the ideal. After his success in expelling Dionysius from Syracuse, Dion fell victim to a conspiracy, an end which in the circumstances seems to have been inevitable for this model ruler.

The perfect example of the Panhellene was Epaminondas, and it is a great pity that Plutarch left no biography of him. We have already mentioned that Lysis, following Philolaus when he took refuge in Thebes, came to stay with Epaminondas' father, Polymnis, and lived as a member of the family. In daily contact with Lysis, the boy Epaminondas grew up to represent, for a highly specialized section of the population, the consciously Panhellenic ideal figure, with the dual characteristics of civic virtue and love of wisdom. What he aspired to is expressed in his remark that if the Thebans wished to be the leaders of Greece, they would have to set up the Athenian Propylaea on the ascent to the Cadmea.[98] With the help of some associates who shared his opinions or whom he educated in them, Pelopidas being personally the closest to him, Epaminondas succeeded in 379 in liberating Thebes from the Spartans, after which his party, the Young Boeotians, soon ruled all Boeotia and won over those who resisted. At the congress in Sparta in 371 he was the spokesman not only for Thebes, but for Greece as a whole, and after the victory of Leuctra he proved his

Hellenism by his actions. As well as restoring Messenia and uniting Arcadia as one state – achievements only possible for a Panhellene – he made up his mind to deal with hostile Sparta only by ensuring it was harmless, determined as always to avoid destroying Hellenic cities.[99]

Epaminondas' greatest influence, one he can hardly have expected, was on Timoleon of Corinth, who is described as his foremost emulator (Plutarch, *Timoleon* 36). When Timoleon arrived to save Sicily, the situation there offered no choice between Greeks and barbarians (that is the tyrants attached to Carthage): the Sicilians could accept rescue or say farewell to their nationality. Help now appeared in the person of this man straight from the misery of Corinth; from the start his plans included the establishment of Hellenism in Sicily.[100] We have already described [cf. pp. 285–6 above] how he succeeded in this by bringing a vast number of immigrants from all Hellas and Greater Greece. After the battle of the Crimisus he sent home as offerings such a wealth of objects that, in his city of Corinth, the finest temples were not, as elsewhere, adorned with spoils from fellow Greeks, but with those from barbarians (Plutarch, *Timoleon* 29). Timoleon was true to Panhellenism in his choice of a mixed population of all kinds of Greeks to settle in Sicily; he differed from Dion in not being aristocratically inclined, and installed democracy everywhere, which for better or worse was the only possible thing to do.

In memorable figures like Epaminondas and Timoleon there is a capacity for self-restraint, and for subduing the will to a higher cause, which is so uncharacteristic of the Greeks that we should not be too critical of the rarity of such men. It is useless to ask how many put these qualities into practice, but natural to want to know if they were ever put into practice at all; it is something we can be certain of in the case of these two leaders. The precedents they set gave Philip and Alexander every reason to present themselves as Panhellenes, and Isocrates explicitly tells Philip: 'Other descendants of Heracles may love their own city, but you, who are not a citizen of one *polis* only, can claim the whole of Greece as your place of origin, as once your ancestor (Heracles) did' (*Philip* 127). Light and shade are thrown on this by Diogenes' lantern as he goes in search of someone who is not a citizen, not even, perhaps, a Greek, but a human being.

Just as the *polis* was no longer enough to satisfy the ethical idealist, it also failed to fulfil the ambitions of the egoist. The case of Iphicrates gave Athens a bitter example of how little the customary civic honours now meant to some. 'As you know, Athenians,' says Demosthenes, 'we awarded

Iphicrates a bronze statue and dining rights in the Prytaneum, with gifts and other honours that made him proud and happy. And yet he had the audacity to fight your generals in the interests of Cotys, and thought the welfare of Cotys more important than the honours you have shown him' (*Against Aristocrates* 130). Perhaps what was most resented was that the man actually left his statue behind to go off on his own affairs.

To compensate, the *passion for fame* would still emerge in many ways, and men would try to gain nationwide attention, often by bizarre means. The great festivals offered opportunities. Dionysius the Elder, for instance, who must have lost his sense of the ridiculous along with his feeling for right and wrong, bombarded the Greeks, from Syracuse, with bad tragedies until at last the Athenians gave his *Liberation of Hector* the first prize at the Lenaea of 367. He was overjoyed, celebrated with a party and got so drunk that he died.[101] But the great way to fame was the publicity connected with funerals. As early as 364, when Pelopidas fell in battle, the grief-stricken Thessalians and other allies arranged an excess of commemorative honours ('outdoing all previous homage to human excellence' says Plutarch in *Pelopidas* 33 f.) with great processions from every city and district vying to join the cortège. This had not been entirely the expression of true emotion, but a kind of nervous contagion, a need to worship fame.[102] By 352, the funeral of the Carian ruler Mausolus was made into a public occasion not confined to his capital city of Halicarnassus but meant for all the Greeks. He himself had loved the monumental, and after rebuilding Halicarnassus he had drawn up the plans for his palace himself, with remarkable skill in his use of the site (cf. Vitruvius 2.8). Now that he was dead, his widow Artemisia, who was also his sister, turned the mourning into a national spectacle. This occasion, and her own rule, which was short (352–350), since grief seems to have led to her early death, occurred in the time just before Macedonia attracted the admiration of all gapers and spectators; thus grandiose publicity narrowly preceded real world-fame.[103] Not only did the Mausoleum outdo anything previously seen in the way of magnificent funeral monuments – as a structure it might well have been objected to in its unique ostentation – but at its completion, which Artemisia did not live to see, there was a gigantic celebration and a great agon with a tragedy contest, and also (as if one funeral oration were not enough) four leading orators competing in praise of Mausolus. The winner of this colossal epideictic extravaganza was the historian Theopompus.

Unregenerate individualism needed an outlet to compete with idealistic

Panhellenism; crime was also a way to fame, and the wicked wanted it as much as the good; they could no longer achieve it by devotion to the single *polis* (as in the saying *Spartam natus es; hanc orna* – you were born a Spartan; be worthy of her). Ambition, no longer fulfilled in true civic feeling, was now perverted not only into the abstractions of idealists, like the high-principled tyrannicides who killed Jason of Pherae, but sometimes into crazy destructiveness. Thus Herostratus, who in 356 set fire to the temple of Ephesus, confessed (if under torture) that he did it to become famous, and Theopompus in his histories gave away the arsonist's name, although the Ephesians had decided to keep it a secret (Valerius Maximus 8.14). Where once seven cities had quarrelled over which was the birthplace of Homer, disagreements now broke out as to whether the assassin of Epaminondas was a Mantinean, a Spartan, or the Athenian Gryllus (Pausanias 8.4). The Pausanias who murdered King Philip had asked the sophist Hermocrates how he could acquire the greatest fame, and got the answer: 'By killing the man who has done the greatest deeds'. In this way the murderer was embraced and borne up by the whole fame of his victim, and at the same time could satisfy his hatred of what was rare or unique.[104]

Others again, not content with conventional fame, might attempt *self-deification*. Respect for the gods and their power was at such a low ebb that this was not much of a compliment to pay oneself; but it was agreeable just the same to be promoted to divinity, as long as people believed in it, and so, where formerly *descent* from the gods had been a kind of letters patent, now in this time of universal rottenness any Tom, Dick or Harry declared *himself* a god.[105] Lysander, as we have seen [p. 292 above] was the first to throw himself into this kind of self-advertisement, accepting sacrifices and paeans, keeping his court poet at his side, and, when he had destroyed the democracy on Samos, holding a festival called Lysandreia there to replace that of Hera (Plutarch, *Lysander* 18). As time went on he had more and more imitators. The terrible Clearchus of Heraclea demanded the worship and the honours due to gods, took to wearing draperies like those on the statues of divinities, named himself, at his most modest, the son of Zeus, and his child Ceraunus, and had a golden eagle carried before him in the street.[106] Strangely enough, Heraclides Ponticus, also from Heraclea, seems to have behaved in much the same way, though he studied with Plato and Aristotle and was himself an author; he was somehow involved in freeing his native city from Clearchus' successors. This Heraclides wished for heroic honours. When ambassadors from Heraclea travelled to Delphi because of a famine, he bribed the Pythia to promise help on condition that he was awarded a gold crown in his lifetime, and honoured as a hero after his death. This turned out wretchedly for all concerned. During the coronation ceremony in the theatre, Heraclides suffered a stroke, and at the same moment the Pythia was bitten by a snake in the *adyton* at Delphi. On the point of death, Heraclides ordered that his corpse should be smuggled away and a snake laid in his bed, as if he had gone to join the gods. This trick too came to nothing, and Heraclides was proved to be not a hero but a fool.[107] After this story there is little cause for surprise in that told of the father-in-law of Iphicrates, the Thracian chieftain Cotys, a dangerous drunkard, who once arranged a banquet and a bridal chamber to celebrate his wedding with Athena. Two bodyguards, whom he sent to look out for her arrival, came back with a negative reply, and in his intoxicated state he shot them down one after the other; the third had the wit to say that the goddess had been awaiting him for some time. Nicostratus, a mercenary captain in the army of Artaxerxes Ochus, who about the year 350 proved himself both as a counsellor and a soldier in subduing the rebellious Persian province, is said to have shown a streak of folly for all his wisdom; a man of great physical strength, he went into battle with a lionskin and a club, in imitation of Heracles (Diodorus 16.44). Sufferers from similar delusions included the famous doctor Menecrates of Syracuse, who called himself Zeus because by his art he became the sole begetter of human life.[108] Patients he had cured of the falling sickness were forced to give him written acknowledgement that they were his slaves; they too had to dress up as gods, and walk behind him as his retinue – a Heracles, a Hermes with his chlamys, herald's staff and winged shoes, an Apollo and an Asclepius; with this chorus of divinities Menecrates paraded about in purple robes and jewelled shoes, gold-wreathed and carrying a sceptre. Writing a letter to King Philip he signed himself 'the giver of all life' and addressed it to 'the universal destroyer'; the king got his own back by sending him good wishes for the recovery of his senses. Philip is also supposed to have made fun of him at a grand banquet by giving him a seat of honour on a separate couch, and then putting nothing but incense before him while the rest feasted. Menecrates, at first pleased by this attention, then became hungry, like a mere mortal, and a silly one; in the end he went off in a rage saying he had been treated with hubris.[109] None of this should cause much surprise. People in this age were liable to such aberrations because, unless they settled for a run-of-the-mill political career, distinction could no longer be obtained in the *polis*, and because the simplest and best aims in life remained hidden from them. One last example of a reputation of this kind is worth mentioning – the figure of Phryne, whether she was historically one person or two. When she was accused of *asebeia* by Euthias, whom she had insulted, Hyperides was defending her and feared he would lose his case, so he tore open her dress and showed the judges her breasts; they were filled with sacred dread and decided they must not kill this priestess and messenger of Aphrodite. At the festivals of Eleusis and the Poseidonia she went down naked to bathe in the sea in the presence of all the Hellenes, which was all the more remarkable since she was usually modestly veiled, and never visited the public baths. Apelles took her as the model for his Anadyomene; what Praxiteles thought of her may be seen from the fact that in her native place, Thespiae, there stood not only his Eros, which he had given her, but her own statue side by side with an Aphrodite he had also made. When we add that in Delphi, too, a golden statue of Phryne stood with those of Archidamus and Philip, we have a strong impression that she was really confused with Aphrodite in people's minds, even if Praxiteles could still tell them apart; yet in the same period it was possible for Aristotle to be tried on a ridiculous charge of *asebeia* for having praised Hermeias of Atarneus as if he were a god (Athenaeus 696a).

Besides those who claimed or were given the status of gods, others contented themselves with appearing as idealized figures. Thus the comic writer and dithyrambist Anaxandrides would rehearse extracts from his dithyrambs aloud while riding about on a horse. He was a fine tall man with flowing hair and a purple robe, gold-bordered. If one of his compositions failed to win a prize, he would never rewrite it, but cut it up and put the fragments into the incense-burners to be consumed (Athenaeus 374b). People like him were fit victims for the Attic gift of sarcasm.

In discussing the subject of *private life* in this period we need to begin with a phenomenon that has already been mentioned from time to time – the *turning away from the State*. According to an old theory, it was 'inappropriate' to live elsewhere than in one's native place; the legislation and practice of tyrannical *poleis* were directed to making sure people remained where they were, and tried to present this obligation as a fine old custom.[110] In time, however, there were examples of distinguished men choosing to leave: Simonides, like Aeschylus, had left Greece for Sicily, Euripides had spent his last years in Macedonia, and Herodotus had lived in Thurii.[111] These were the facts, and there was no stopping people from fleeing the State, even though the dictatorial government, as long as it lasted, punished emigration as a crime, just as the French revolutionary government did in 1793–4. Presented as desertion from military service, attacked in savage speeches like that of Lycurgus prosecuting Leocrates, and liable to the death penalty, emigration was still not to be prevented; and things looked bad for the *polis* when the foremost citizens, even those who did remain at home, were so thoroughly shunning the patriotic sentiment that was thought to be vital to its existence.[112] To avoid being swallowed up by the *polis*, which was the fate of those who had opted for 'virtue' and decided to live within the State, shrewder people still stayed at home and put up with what could not be cured; but the *polis* no longer controlled their inner life, because of the very fact that it had increased its power beyond all reason; the imagination escaped its confines and took refuge in philosophy, the enjoyment of life or whatever it pleased.

Eloquence as a private occupation is personified in Isocrates. He was said to have won three claims to honour, one of them that of the highest *sophrosyne*, 'because he shunned the State and kept his resolution to have nothing to do with civic affairs'. His suicide at the news of Chaeronea therefore seemed the most convincing proof of his freedom of spirit.[113] The statements the *philosophers* make about the State are either negative criticisms or, in the Utopias, positive aspirations; these are the most striking testimonies of the turning away from the State. The free personality was itself partly defined by indifference to the *polis*; in the case of the poor man, the *polis* was indifferent to him in return. One after another the philosophers took this path. Plato spoke of the philosopher who did not know the road to the agora and the Pnyx, Antisthenes and Diogenes set up as completely cosmopolitan; Aristippus and the Hedonist sect are noteworthy here; in their vulgar philistine egoism they declare that the philosopher is a stranger wherever he goes. The same direction is taken by the scholars engaged in research, who necessarily relied on extensive travel. Democritus, Hippocrates and Eudoxus, and the historians Ephorus and Theopompus, agree on the subject; Aristotle cut himself off from the active life of Athens, but his political theorizing enabled him to recognize some honourable statesmen, so that he stood not only apart from the State but above it. Lastly, Epicurus, with his exhortation to live in obscurity, withdrew not only from the State but also from notoriety, so that he combined contempt for the State with contempt for human beings; perhaps his motive was also wariness of malice and of the general reluctance to make others happy – especially those more gifted – or even to tolerate their happiness.

The rejection of the State in democratic Athens took a particular form in the admiration of ancient institutions which had remained unchanged and remote from democratic development; above all this applied to Egypt, together with the enthusiasm of all oligarchs for Sparta, seen as modelled on Egypt. This high opinion of Egypt is expressed not only by Plato, who is famous for it, but occasionally by Isocrates too. When we find Busiris (15 f.) praising the caste system as the wise invention of an ancient founding father and lawgiver of the nation, and also read (*ibid.* 20) that life in Athens would be happiest if, as in Egypt, some were born to work and the others (the warrior caste) to guard wealth, we may recall that in the eighteenth century some Enlightenment thinkers admired China in much the same way; like Plato, Busiris devotes special praise to the Egyptians for their piety (*ibid.* 24).

The homeless (*planomenoi*) and mercenaries were excluded from the State by their peculiar situation; but those who still continued to live within it had only the choice between misfortune and ruthlessness.

Athens had also wearied of another ideal, that of the *agon*. Even in the fifth century a new agon had appeared, that of political competitiveness, and had set people against each other in a quite different way; but now other forces, too, began to weaken this attitude. Gymnastics certainly retained its fundamental position in the life of the freeborn,[114] and Aristotle even feels compelled here and there to protest at the sometimes excessive use of gymnastic exercise, which he thinks harmful to good looks and health,[115] or at least against its practice too early in life at the expense of general physical development.[116] There seems no good reason for the true agon not to have continued just as it was before, short of a catastrophe such as war. When the Olympic victor came home, the people, as always, crowded to see him from the rooftops; Polydamas, legendary for his size and strength, was famous as late as the turn of the century.[117] But it was no longer possible, as formerly, to win real fame by such feats, and hardly anyone can have been able to afford lyrical or choric competitions. Plato makes a direct contemptuous reference to chariot racing; when Anniceris of Cyrene (the same man who bought Plato out of slavery on Aegina), proud of his skill in this sport, showed it off to Plato by driving a faultless round in the Academy to general admiration, the philosopher said that a man who was so much in earnest about such small and trivial matters could never be serious about anything worthwhile (Aelian, *Varia Historia* 2.27). What was more important was that in most regions of Greece nobody wished, or had the means, to appear at the Olympics or elsewhere with the magnificent trappings of the past, if only because the rich were systematically persecuted in many places, and were lucky if they could still manage to provide for the *choregia* and all the rest at home. As things were, most of the four-in-hand driving was done by those from Greek lands overseas, which was why it occurred to Dionysius the Elder that he could now play at being Gelon or Theron. In 388 this evil tyrant sent his brother Thearides to the Olympics with several four-in-hand carriages, faster than all the others, and, for the festive meeting, tents of the most precious dyed materials decorated with gold. He also sent the most gifted reciters to perform his own compositions, and at first, because of their beautiful voices, everyone crowded to listen. Gradually, though, as they realized how feeble the poetry was, Dionysius was jeered; in fact derision turned to anger, and some stripped and looted his tents. The orator Lysias called on the crowds not to allow those sent by the godless tyrant to be present at the sacred agon at all, and when the agon took place nonetheless, some of Dionysius' chariots hurtled off the track, and the others collided and were smashed up.[118] Whether this story is true or not, the Greeks agreed in their verdict: 'Everyone enjoys seeing horses, chariots and tents; but we boo his bad verses off the stage.' We can gather from this that the proceedings in Olympia were still fairly democratic and in keeping with Attic theocracy.

As to the athletes, the discrediting of the whole Spartan system after Leuctra must have contributed to the decline of the gymnastic agon. True soldiers had ceased to think much of the athletes. Epaminondas insisted that the hoplite should exercise as a soldier rather than as an athlete (Plutarch *Kings: Epaminondas* 3). Nor had the philosophers anything to say in their favour. A direct refutation of the agonal principle is part of the Hedonist doctrine from Aristippus down to Epicurus; the slogan 'always to be the first' is incompatible with the good life. But Diogenes too was very critical of the musclemen. Although he provided a good gymnastic education for his pupils, the sons of Xeniades, he heaped sarcasm on the professional athletes. When he was asked why they were so insensitive, he replied that they consisted of pig and cattle flesh; and to an unsuccessful wrestler who had turned physician, he said, 'I suppose you want to finish off those who used to beat you?' (Diogenes Laertius 6.30, 49, 62). We doubt whether Plato was really a wrestling champion at the Isthmian games, as his biographers report (*ibid* 3.5, after Dicaearchus and the Anonymous). In any case, as time went on, the agon sank very low in Athenian opinion, as the following story shows. In 332 the city was fined because one Callippus had bought off his opponent in the Pentathlon; instead of simply settling the fine, the Athenians sent their chief prosecutor, Hyperides, to Elis, to plead for its remission, and when the Eleans refused, Athens still did not pay the fine but quietly submitted to being excluded from the Olympics. No doubt prompted by the Eleans, Delphi (to which the Athenians still wanted access) declared that until they paid up, the god would answer no more questions from the Athenians, and then they sent six figures of Zeus in atonement; Pausanias saw the inscriptions on them (Pausanias 5.21.3). Alexander, as a young man, had refused to race at Olympia because although he was a runner he despised athletes (Plutarch, *Alexander* 4). He offered prizes for the musical contests as well as those in hunting and fencing, but not for boxing or the *pankration*.

In the fifth century, the main agon had been competition for influence in the State, and this had become largely disreputable; the hunger for fame had found more terrible outlets, as we have seen; the most competitive area now was wit, and many individuals acquired a reputation for it. Otherwise there were people who became famous for such qualities as indolence – that is for what was most completely opposed to the agon, unless indolence can be competitive.[119] It was wealth, though, that was the chief criterion by which people were judged: a young Ionian arrived in Athens wearing a gold-bordered purple robe; asked where he came from, he replied, 'I am rich.'

From this we turn to the condition of intellectual life. Philosophy is certainly one of the dominating features of the fourth century. It was the moment for philosophy, in association with sophistry, rhetoric and learning in general, to seize on the vacant space in life left by the *polis*, which had lost its hold over thinking men, and by religion, the mythical basis of which was in ruins, and for which incipient monotheism was as yet a poor substitute. Democritus, Plato and Aristotle were all at work, and knowledge and thought were flourishing, since even the dangers and persecutions of Athenian life were not unfavourable to them.

Now that the philosophers were becoming the true celebrities of the age alongside the statesmen and military leaders, it was inevitable that their subject would be mediated and traduced by inferior poseurs. In this period, the process described five hundred years later by Lucian (e.g. in *Dependent*

Scholars) was just beginning to make itself felt, and is introduced to us by Isocrates in the short but important fragment which has been given the title 'Against the Sophists'. It shows that, perhaps as early as Plato's prime, a crowd of people flourished beside the true philosophers; they certainly figured as philosophers but were living all over the Greek world as teachers, orators and so on. Since they were not really competent either as philosophers or as orators, the disproportion between their pretensions and their knowledge threatened to bring the whole discipline into contempt with the laymen. Isocrates may have had a slight ulterior motive in attacking them, as he was describing his own rivals, and indeed to some extent his like; it is quite apparent that part of his deep disapproval came from their undercutting him.[120] Still, there must have been a generation of such men, presuming to give instruction in speaking in the widest sense by their own speech, shot through with philosophical and ethical pretension and offering the vain hope of improvement to their students. The whole blame for this must rest on Greece itself as it was at that time, with its inflated valuation of eloquence and its demand for the various tricks of oratory; this class of mediating communicators was bound to arise, whether they were popularizing something of value or only a debased imitation.

The different kinds of *poetry* all had their great achievements in the past, and the literature of ideas must have had to contend with contemporary incredulity, which prevented its becoming famous whatever its quality. The epic was finished; Lysander's Antimachus was, indeed, still alive, but to judge by the fragments that survive, his *Thebaïs* was no less a pedantic pastiche than the *Argonautica* of Apollonius Rhodius. The elegy too was dying out, or dwindling into epigram; great lyric poetry vanished with Pindar; of Attic tragedy, though it continued steadily throughout the century, almost nothing survives, and it brought fame only to individual actors. Poetry was simply being crowded out by politics and philosophy; anyone who could rattle on would put any poet in the shade, and at the same time those who could have been the new poets were intimidated and destroyed by the democracy. The old audience had gone too, the aristocratic Greece which had once filled the festival sites with brilliance, and for whom the epinician and hymeneal odes and threnodies had been composed; the symposium was the victim of social rottenness. There was as yet no private poetry, or else it remained in obscurity. Vitality was still to be found in the pleasurable, above all the middle and later comedy, the pursuit of music, with all its virtuosity, which had its place in the new dithyrambic, and the many performances for the cult, which were supported as before by the exploitation of the rich. The death of the state left a new science of politics, and correspondingly, as the practice of poetry declined at that period, theory took its place; Aristotle was composing his *Poetics*.

The only art-form which remained vigorous in fourth-century life was sculpture. Since by immense good fortune it was considered banausic, it attracted only the truly gifted. Rhetoric and philosophy were powerless to pull it to pieces with their chatter, and Plato's pious wish that there should be fewer works of art in the world, and more in the Egyptian style, was to be unfulfilled. This form of art, happily, succeeded in preserving the criteria and the direction formed in the fifth century, and in applying the same powers of execution while retaining spontaneity. It was not dependent, as the drama was, on a single success at a contest, confirmed by the judges, or, as in the theatre, on popular favour; it had no parody to haunt it as Euripides had in Aristophanes; it had not been dragged down in the general process of dissolution at the end of the fifth century. Art entered the new period with its energies completely intact, and only now began to develop the sweet fruit of its full Hellenic glory. As well as this, art was independent of political disaster, untouched by Leuctra, Mantinea and Chaeronea, and was encouraged by the early phase of the taste for private luxury.

These artists were also the last to see the gods with fresh eyes, and gave them their definitive forms in art. This age was more subjective in spirit, and aimed for a deeper feeling and a livelier expression of mood; this was the time of the gods of enthusiasm, longing and melancholy, the time for dream, and for the most exquisite charm and moulding of form illuminated by wonderful qualities of intimacy. Now Cephisodotus created what was perhaps the earliest cycle of the Muses, as well as the child-figure set beside the full-grown adult; Eirene with Plutus, Hermes with the young Dionysus. The work of the great sculptor Scopas had the effect of plunging the gods back into the melting pot to be recast; he was the first to represent Aphrodite naked, and to free the train of sea gods from all trace of the grotesque. His range of themes included the frenzied maenads and the three wonderful figures of Eros, Pothos and Himeros – Love, Longing, and Desire. The divine Praxiteles, somewhat younger than Scopas, continued on the same lines, adding to this last trio of figures those of Peitho and Paregoros (Persuasion and Consolation). The miraculous Aphrodite of Cnidos was by Praxiteles, also an Eros which must at least have equalled that of Scopas, and new conceptions of Dionysus and Hermes. In his Dionysian figures, such as the Satyrs, Praxiteles created a minor kind of beauty, the Sauroctonos, Apollino, Diadumenos and others. We should be unable to imagine what classical art could be but for the originality of works of this period such as the Vatican Hermes. Lysippus, who was amazingly productive, was at work as late as the time of Alexander; his innovation, in his bronzes, was the series of slenderer figures using the effects of nakedness in movement and action. Of his 1,500 works we may mention the Heracles and Alexander, and the Apoxyomenos. Parrhasius and Apelles were Praxiteles' contemporaries, and the supreme art of these masters did not die out with them, but survived, thanks to the contempt for *banausia*, into the third and second centuries. How fortunate it is that the writings of Aristotle contain nothing about sculpture or graphic art.

Social life in the fourth century was marked by the tone of wit and hilarity. The Greeks had always enjoyed these things, and some Greek peoples were well known for their uncontrollable laughter.[121] This now took on a nervous quality, and a new feature of the period was the *addiction* to merriment, the positive conspiracy against seriousness – which is far from implying an optimistic attitude to life.[122] Pleasure in laughter and mockery of every kind, with its parallels in the Hedonist doctrine of Aristippus and in the preference given to middle and later comedy over any other poetry, becomes particularly clear in the *Anthologies of Jokes* which now began to be compiled, and which we know from extracts in Athenaeus. Not all of this seems funny to us; people were evidently content with poor stuff, but we must not forget that for the Greeks anything crisply expressed counted as wit; the fact that they found it effective shows, perhaps, what a new phenomenon wit itself was.[123] In Athens there was a traditional site for the jokers of the temple of Heracles, in the deme of Diomeia near the Cynosarges. Sixty of these wits used to meet there, and when a good joke made the rounds the townspeople would say: 'The sixty said that.' Philip of Macedon sent the wits one talent as a gift, and commissioned some of his men to write down and send him what was said among them, rather as foreign princes in the eighteenth century kept correspondents in the Paris salons.[124] We do not know whether Philip also had *agents provocateurs* among the wits; in any case he wanted to know this aspect of the Greeks and to be Greek himself, as, in a different way and in the spirit of another time, his ancestor Alexander the Philhellene had been, through his political sympathies and his participation in the agon.[125]

What must have been an absolute plague at the symposium was the constant asking of riddles during dinner, with drinking-penalties imposed on those who could not find the answer (Athenaeus 10.69 ff.: 86.88). This was probably already a time-honoured custom, which became the fashion at this period; otherwise the poets of the middle comedy would hardly have made so much use of it (it did very little for the structure of their plays). People actually became famous for solving and making up these riddles, which are often very obscene. Other amusements were the recital of Homeric and other verses, or one person reeling off lists of Greek heroes to which another replied with the Trojans, and so forth (Athenaeus 10.86–7.) There were specialists in pantomime, like Eudicus, who was well known for his imitations of wrestlers and boxers in a parody of the agon (Athenaeus 1. 35). Of course the ordinary jester (*gelotopoios*) still existed, though he probably had severe competition from the parasite.[126] In the time of the *diadochoi* these jesters must have come back into favour as social life at the court coarsened with the introduction of semibarbarians and the military.[127]

At this time everything brought its own theories on its heels. An essay of Theophrastus 'On the Comic' must have been a collection of anecdotes, but probably philosophically treated, with definitions and reflections; another of Aristotle's pupils, Clearchus, wrote a book about riddles and proverbs which seems to have been well known.[128] In his *Orator* (2.54) Cicero spoke publicly on this theme in connection with wit, but thought it amounted to very little, and that the most laughable thing of all was the attempt at a theory of laughter. But he distinguished two different effects, one the humorous tone that pervades everything (*cavillatio*), and the other the brilliant single witticism (*dicacitas*). It must have been difficult for the philosophers to keep their own teaching clear of the mockery and ridicule so general in daily life.[129]

We must turn now to the *pleasures* of the period. In so far as people could afford them, sensual pleasures (*truphan*) had been dominant in Greek life from ancient times. The colonies with their abundance of splendid fruit and crops, where the Greeks controlled other inhabitants, or could heap up riches from trade, were bound to offer ease and luxury, especially where landowners (*chilioi*) formed the ruling class, and the Thessalian nobility must have been in the same situation. The tyrants had always been slaves to pleasure. In the fourth century, Dionysius the Younger gave himself up to appalling excesses; other great voluptuaries were the half-Greek rulers of the extreme margins of the Greek world, King Cotys of Thrace, King

Straton of Sidon, who were rivalled by Nicocles of Cyprus.[130] But in Athens, too, luxury had long been preferred to simplicity. Aristophanes has a good deal to say about this; he describes in comic detail the profound emotion of Dicaeopolis when, after six years of privation, he got possession of an eel from the Lake of Copaïs (*Acharnians* 885). The contemporary writers Telecleides and Pherecrates speak of a Land of Cockaigne devoted to gluttony (Athenaeus 6.95 f.). What is only to be explained by complete disillusionment with the *polis* and the agon is the new opportunity given to the uncultivated and grossly sensual private person to appear as a hedonist in a philosophical sect of his own, to develop his system, distinct from that of the Cynics, and to parade both in theory and in practice his adherence to a doctrine which still persists to the present day. A voluptuary like Polyarchus could now travel about to teach this new wisdom to people such as Archytas and his friends;[131] and equally new was the phenomenon of gluttony assuming an important place in poetry, and being used as an element in the whole of Attic comedy. In this respect the middle comedy took a lead from the Sicilian Epicharmus; three-quarters of the fragments of his work consist of stories about epicures and gourmets. The comedy itself gives the impression of constant lip-smacking, as if Athens were one huge kitchen; new comedy, too, overworks the theme of cooking and eating, while telling us extraordinarily little about the visual arts – our chief sources for this subject are the comments of the Romans. Theoretical and instructive information was provided by the food-poets with their poetic cookery books also originating in Sicily, which was proverbial for its cuisine.[132]

Another new feature of the time was that the symposium in private houses was no longer so important, and that the public tavern (*papeleion*) was no longer avoided; poorer people must have patronized taverns a good deal, perhaps because it was easier to cook well in a large kitchen than at home. Diogenes was breakfasting in a tavern and called Demosthenes, whom he saw passing, to join him, but he refused; Diogenes asked, 'Are you too proud? Your master (the *demos*) comes here every day' (Aelian, *Varia Historia* 9.19). Demosthenes seems to have had stricter views on this than Diogenes, and once used the word drunkards (*akratokothones*) of the young men of Attica in general (Hyperides, *Against Demosthenes, frag.* 14). Quite often a whole population is reproached with gourmandizing; Aristotle is speaking either of the Athenians or else the Byzantines when he says that they had read nothing at all except Philoxenus' *Banquet*, and not all of that (Athenaeus 1.10), and pickles (*taricos*) were supposed to have been so important in Athens that (on the evidence of a comic writer at least) the sons of a merchant who imported them were given citizens' rights for their father's merits (Athenaeus 2.90). As for the enjoyment of food, the crassest theory is only given (by Alexis) to a slave to express,[133] while other poets usually treat the subject with more humour;[134] but there is something very sad, however well put, about the conclusion a person in Antiphanes reaches after giving advice about the dangers to beware of in the *polis* and elsewhere: 'Nothing is certain,' he says, 'except what a man can secure for himself from day to day by way of enjoyment. Even then he may see the table snatched away from before his eyes while it stands ready for him; it is only when you have the morsel between your teeth that you can be sure of it' (Athenaeus 3.62). Anyone who could afford it did himself well, and this is shown by the poets' and other writers' giving catalogues of gluttons (*opsophagoi*); we should not assume they are lists of exceptions; in fact the naming of individuals could well express the envy of the hungry.[135] Athenaeus marshals whole galleries of big eaters from poets and collectors, with ponderous jokes about the appetites of entire peoples such as the Boeotians, the Pharsalians and so forth (beginning of Book 10). We learn of particular cases where people ate pitifully scanty food from heavy, precious silver plates, or those in real poverty who still used silver, but as thin as a leaf (Athenaeus 6.17), or that of the greedy miser who only ordered his dishes by diminutive names (*ibid* 8.58). Many delicacies are described and whole recipes for them are sometimes given in trimeters.[136] Complaints about fishmongers are scattered throughout many plays, making quite a melancholy effect.[137] Everyone rails at their outrageous prices, their bad temper, their refusal to answer a civil question; they are criminals, and pretend to have taken a vow to grow their hair long, when in fact its length conceals the mark of the brand. They also cheat when giving change, sell stale, rotten wares, charge ruinous prices; they are reckoned among the worst of all evils, and there is wailing at the existence of such wicked creatures who reduce their customers to beggary. Fishermen, too, acquired new status and grew prouder than the most distinguished generals.

The dangerous aspect of all this was stressed in warnings that the hungry poor might take to robbery or banditry. 'If a poor man has money to spend on good things to eat, you can depend upon it that he robs unarmed people he meets at night; that great strong beggarly youth you see buying eels from Mikion in the morning ought to be taken off to prison immediately,' says Alexis, and Diphilus praises a Corinthian law by which a poor man could be punished for eating well, and even handed over to the executioner, on the grounds that he must have committed some crime, either stealing clothes or housebreaking or sycophancy, or by selling himself as a false witness (Athenaeus 6.12).

A stock figure in comedy was the cook. In earlier times he was not generally a slave, but a hired servant, and in late comedy a hired cook, in addition to the kitchen slave, is indispensable for any important occasion. From fragments of the comedies we get a fair idea of him and his boorish self-esteem. Athenaeus (8.36) says: 'All cooks are boastful', and introduces one who brags that many of his employers have eaten themselves out of house and home for his cooking. The rogues are well read too; they like to pose as knowledgeable, are literary and philosophical in their boasting, and claim skill in sacrifices (Athenaeus 14.78). This went on into the time of the *diadochoi*, when a cook boasted of having served King Nicomedes with anchovies when he was twelve days' journey from the sea; he cut the shapes out of beetroots and prepared them in the correct sauce – for 'there's no difference between the cook and the poet, the art of both is in their genius' (Athenaeus 1.13). It is quite a relief when Athenaeus says: 'That's enough about cooks.'

Here and there we hear the diet of Attica described as frugal compared with that of Thessaly, and the Greek diet generally as less rich than that of the barbarians (Athenaeus 4.14–6). There was something ridiculous about the last of the Spartans insisting on their indifference to pastries and sweet things while eating enormous amounts of meat. Agesilaus for instance, as the guest of Tachos, liked wheaten bread, veal and goose, but ordered pastries, sweetmeats and creams for the helots; but by then he had sold himself and his reputation to Egypt as Sparta would no longer tolerate him. They had sunk very low.

A special figure of the time is the *parasite*, and Ribbeck gives a delightful picture of his many-faceted personality.[138] It was the Sicilians who had developed gastronomy a hundred years earlier, and from them that the perpetual smoke of offerings wafted over to Athens; so too we first encounter the parasite in Sicily, and his portrait accurately drawn by Epicharmus in his *Elpis*.[139] In Athens, too, such men existed even in the fifth century, but were then known as *kolakes* (flatterers). There was a play by Eupolis that bore this title, and which was based on the wealthy spendthrift Callias; in one passage the flatterers describe how they besiege a silly rich man with fulsome praise, so as to be invited to feast at his table, but have to continue making all sorts of pretty speeches (*charienta*) for fear of being turned out (Athenaeus 6.30). In this period of social refinement, three elements must have combined to form the type of the parasitic flatterer; a deep loathing of work, extreme flexibility and quick-wittedness, and an irresistible craving for good food. For the parasite, dishonour and the loss of self-respect were a small price to pay for sensual indulgence and the avoidance of work; he was an inevitable product of the antibanausic world, and his protector was essentially an even more repellent figure with his limitless need for company, timewasting and flattery, as well as for a whipping-boy when he was out of temper.

While the *polis* was strong, the true symposium would never have tolerated the rank weed of parasitism, which took root in the soil of a corrupt but still intelligent social life confined to the private sphere, and only when the symposium had degenerated into sensual pleasure-seeking; it could be said that as soon as parasites were considered normal, the symposium was doomed as a form of social intercourse.[140] First and foremost the parasite is an intimate; he ingratiates himself by assurances of love, willingly runs errands, never differs from his patron on matters of taste, and compulsively expresses his admiration for him in a way that would be inconceivable today. This is the host's reason for keeping him; no-one ever tires of praise and respect.[141] Depending on the circumstances, the parasite may be treated very unkindly, forced to put up with having the largest bones thrown at his head and show no resentment – 'You shouldn't be a parasite if you have feelings,' says Diphilus (Athenaeus 6.51). He is also made use of as the most insolent among the other insolent guests, or even as a lackey who has to throw out the drunks, and since he can show no pride he cannot refuse his master any service, lawful or not, including false witness or whatever is required.[142] All this sometimes depresses him, and he may complain of being enslaved by his belly,[143] but as he really is the slave of his senses he accepts everything without a murmur, even if today's fish reappears tomorrow and has gone off.[144] The best-known parasites had their nicknames (Athenaeus 6.41) and the comic writers, especially those of the middle comedy, ridiculed many of them personally on the stage; but the age was thick-skinned, people were quite used to much worse, and must hardly have felt such pinpricks. It was impossible to drive parasites away; the very phrase 'Come here!' brought them to mind: 'When I march out to war, and call upon Ares and Nike,

I call Chaerophon at the same time, because if I don't call him he comes just the same,' says a character in comedy. At weddings they mingle with the guests, even if they have to dress up and carry the birdcage;[145] gate-crashing might be excused by reference to the Zeus of Friendship (*Zeus philios*) or other mythical examples (Diodorus in Athenaeus 6.36). The jester in earlier times had really been far more respectable, with his special skills and traditions; he was employed for a fee, or could at least expect a present, while now it was merely a guest, tolerated rather than welcome, who had to see to the amusement of the company.

Still, it was possible to become famous as a parasite, like the Chaerophon just mentioned, and a certain Corydus whom Alexis names as envied by another, less successful; there were even memoirs written about Corydus.[146] Some of the jokes made by parasites are really humorous; but however much wit they displayed, they were poisoning social life, and what were the Greeks without this?

Inevitably, there were parasites at the various courts. At that of Alexander of Pherae there was a certain Melianthus who, when asked how the assassin had stabbed his master, replied reverently, 'Through his breast, straight into my stomach' (Plutarch, *On Flattery* 3). Dionysius the Younger also had his flatterers; he was short-sighted and they pretended to be so too, bumping into each other and overturning dishes; they learned his poems by heart and, because he liked it, put on a rather rough, free tone (Plutarch *ibid.* 27, Athenaeus 6.56). Similar stories are told about the famous Cleisophus at the court of King Philip of Macedon; when the King lost an eye, he put a patch over one of his own, and when Philip was wounded in the leg, he went limping along in his train (Athenaeus 6.54). There are also many notes on the parasites of the different *diadochoi*; at these courts they were a piece of Greek life determinedly perpetuated in a coarsened form, and even corrupted some Galatian princes.

Beside the ordinary dining-parasites, specialists in flattery also gradually crept in, evidently those who liked to use their gift for insinuating themselves. Plutarch speaks of them in *On Flattery* as if in connection with the Empire; but some of his examples show that flattery of the great and wealthy was typical at least of later Greece, if not of Greece in general. The flatterer not only imitates the myopia or deafness of his patron, but claims to suffer the same domestic misfortunes as his, for instance in the matter of bad wives, sons and relatives. Still later, courtiers around Mithridates let him cauterize or operate on them, because he liked to play the doctor.

Carneades said that the sons of rich men and of kings were taught nothing well except for riding; teachers flattered them, their wrestling partners fell down of their own accord, and only their horses knew nothing about compliments and distinctions of rank.[147]

Some of the most melancholy accounts of the period concern *family life*. Marriage, as always, was treated exclusively as a matter of law and politics, since all the State wanted from it was the production of accredited citizens [see p. 251–2 above]. Pericles' law, by which full citizens' rights could be claimed only by those whose parents were both citizens, was renewed as late as the end of the fifth century by the orator Aristophon, though he himself had some children by a courtesan. The reason for this law was itself purely political; it did not aim at upholding legal marriage on moral grounds, but at keeping the citizen-body intact. If the sons of hetaerae had been recognized as citizens and thus as qualified to inherit, everything would soon have fallen apart and legal marriage have become a thing of the past. But Demosthenes' second oration *Against Eubulides* gives an idea how this law could be a lever for the devices of sycophants – if 'the whole city rose up against these insolent intruders into the demes' [see pp. 302–3 above].

A woman, then, was no more than a thing, an instrument *ad hoc*; divorce was very easy; if men were disinclined to divorce it was mainly because it meant returning the dowry. The prime motive of getting heirs shows itself in the frequency of adoption. This was mostly resorted to when an only son had died, and a near relative was usually chosen; the law tried to regulate adoption, and it was only valid if the adoptive father was neither mentally ill nor senile, nor under the influence of magic spells or women's plotting; those who were adopted by living parents had a natural advantage over those named for adoption in a will. It may sometimes have been hard to prove that none of the exclusions applied, and in such circumstances the inhumanity of Athens at that time is explicable only by a rotten legal system and universal chicanery; it goes much further than any occasional present-day examples of people maliciously remarrying or adopting out of hatred for their own descendants. Because there was no public prosecutor, the state never intervened on legal grounds, so no proceedings could arise unless a charge was brought; here, as in much else, was a chance for greed and the conspiracies of sycophants. The result was the perpetual litigation between adoptive and blood relations for which Isaeus is our principal source. In his Third Oration, an illegitimate daughter is still, after twenty years, pursuing an adopted son, the heir, for the inheritance, alleging that her mother had been married; in the Second, a man is the plaintiff against his brother, who has adopted his wife's brother, and this because she had begged him to do so after he had divorced her on friendly terms after giving up hope of having children by her. The case of Diocles [p. 302 above] shows how a scoundrel could force his way into a family by actually forging an adoption.

An heiress could be the cause of many quarrels, since her nearest relative had the right either to marry her himself or to marry her to his son. In the case that gives rise to Isaeus' Tenth Oration, a paternal uncle marries off his niece to someone else but keeps her fortune; in the Sixth, a widow is claimed by a near relative as his bride, but then abandoned again when circumstances change. In Demosthenes' speech against Eubulides (40 f.) we learn of a poor man who simply leaves his wife, already the mother of his child, for a rich heiress. He, or rather her brother, hands over the wife to a close acquaintance, who then has more children with her, and all this is duly witnessed by the uncles on both sides.

Things were particularly bad in the matter of guardianship. Lysias tells of Diogeiton, uncle and grandfather of his wards, whom he shamefully robbed of their fortune. Demosthenes spent his early years in a fairly wealthy and aristocratic household. His father entrusted his estate of fourteen talents to three guardians: Aphobus, his sister's son; Demophon, his brother's son; and an old friend, Therippides. The conditions were that the first should marry the widow with a dowry of eighty *minae*, the second, on the same terms, the daughter (then five years old) when she was old enough, but with an interim present of two talents; the third guardian too was assigned the usufruct of seventy *minae* till the son, Demosthenes, came of age. Clearly the father wanted to secure the future of his wife and daughter by appointing two interested trustees, but it speaks volumes for the situation of women at the time that he was only able to do so by disposing of them as if they were objects. As is well known, the two nephews failed to keep their promises, and all three guardians spent the fortune at such a rate that when Demosthenes reached his majority only one twelfth of it remained.

As for *opinions of women*, in Aristophanes' *Ecclesiazusae* (214 ff.) Praxagora maliciously describes them as the more conservative element compared with male innovators; the usual slanders on them continue elsewhere in comedy.[148] To find a more agreeable picture, we may recall that Xenophon's *Oeconomicus*, though it presents a dialogue with Socrates, was written when the fourth century was well advanced, so that it is relevant to think of the words of Ischomachus already quoted [p. 252 above]. Certainly the degree of sensibility shown by this conventional landowner would seem absurdly frigid in a modern novel, but that splendid conclusion opens the reader's eyes to the nobility of the relationship between the husband and wife. It is pleasing to suppose that the same feeling existed in the couples fourth-century sculptors show on the wonderful funerary steles.

Women in Syracuse, which was mostly ruled by a monarchy and anyway of Dorian origin, had status and influence; even in the fifth century we may think of Demarete, the wife of Gelon I, and of the political and dynastic importance of the two wives of Dionysius the Elder; Dion's sister Aristomache and his wife Arete seem rather stronger personalities (Plutarch, *Dion* 51) and it is known that the women at the court of the younger Dionysius were very much interested in Plato (*ibid* 19). The younger Artemisia of Halicarnassus was a powerful woman, and so, later on, were some women at the courts of the *diadochoi*. The Spartan women were not very impressive. Some were very rich, and in time two-fifths of all the land was said to be in their hands; also, the heiresses had the right to bequeath their possessions as they pleased. But they seem to have been irresponsible and did not come well out of the shock of Leuctra. Not one of them had ever seen the smoke of enemy camp fires, and for centuries they had echoed the men in their patriotic boasting; so Epaminondas' invasion of Sparta caused them to panic, shrieking and running about wildly.[149]

In conclusion, the Pythagorean women should be remembered. In the collection of fragments Stobaeus preserved, those on Phintys and Perictione date from a later time,[150] but the attitudes they express may well be true to those of southern Italy in the fourth century and represent a parallel to that Pythagoreanism which was a source of Panhellenic virtue [see p. 317 above]. Phintys' essay on the moral dignity (*sophrosyne*) of woman gives an insight into a noble ideal of morality in women. These female followers of Pythagoras wanted not only to preserve the sacredness of marriage, but to make their husbands happy; they demanded a simple way of life, simple dress, religious festivals without frenzy but confined to popular offerings to the gods of the city, and, in general, domestic seclusion and purity; in fact they seem admirable women in every way.

The general *voluptuous tendency* of the period is in sharp contrast with these fine qualities. Homosexuality was gradually losing its ethical pretensions. In Sparta, it still retained its idealistic character in Agesilaus and in some late Spartans, but apart from this, the sacred band of Thebes whom Philip admired in their death at Chaeronea were probably the last in whom this could be found.[151] Alexander's relationship with Hephaestion was that of two equals, not of the lover and the beloved. For the rest, sensuality predominated in this aspect of life.

This is even truer of the *hetairai*. Of course this subject is as old as sensual enjoyment itself, but the immense public attention now paid to these women, and the huge importance of them in comedy, certainly exceeded what was common in the fifth century. General interest was evidently enormous, which suggests how little life offered in the way of noble aims. The poets devoted themselves to every fact connected with the hetaerae, whether they were slaves, hired or bought from a pimp after being suitably educated, or free women who kept a large house.[152] This attention is often unfavourable, as when a poet compares them for rapacity and exploitation with the monsters of myth;[153] indeed some writers advise steering clear of the dangers and expense of frequenting them (as also of affairs with married women) when it was so easy and uncomplicated to have ordinary girls (Athenaeus 13.24 f.) A poet of the middle comedy even composed an *Anti-Laïs*, in which he described the aging Laïs with derision (*ibid.* 26). Menander loved his Glycera, but when Philemon in a play had called a girl he loved 'good', he was still honest enough to reply that none of them was good (*ibid* 66). The hetaerae were often mocked, too, for using cosmetics and other adornments to help them hide physical defects.[154] Yet the same poets also have sweet and lovable things to tell of them;[155] they appear as charming and consoling when their lovers are out of humour, and really do honour to the name *hetaira* (a woman friend); in a fragment of Eubulus, when we read 'How prettily she ate', we are involuntarily reminded of the same touch in Goethe's Philine.[156]

This was the age of the great courtesans; in Greece at least they did not vanish into the bordello but remained on public view. Many of their names are known to us. Athenaeus (13.21) mentions five authors who had written books on the Athenian hetaerae, including the distinguished scholars Apollodorus and Aristophanes of Byzantium.[157] There are many anecdotes of the wit of courtesans from these sources (Athenaeus 13.46 ff.), some quite elegant, for there were well-educated women among the hetaerae.[158] One, Gnathaena, even wrote a book on table manners, a parody of philosophical works of the kind. There is no doubt that they had wit and grace, and that their conversation had a charm not found among married women. Biographical facts concerning the most celebrated, like Laïs, Thaïs, Phryne, or Glycera, are extraordinarily hard to assess. Given that they fascinated the Greek imagination so completely, it is not surprising that the reports about them lack exactitude and are often chronologically irreconcilable. Laïs in particular turned into a type, and it must be assumed there were at least two persons of that name; she was depicted as full of malice and greed.[159] The relationship of Praxiteles with Phryne was probably the one which had the greatest importance for art, as we have seen [p. 324 above].

According to a speech of Pseudo-Demosthenes, *hetairai* were for pleasure, slave-harlots (*pallachai*) for daily use, legal wives for begetting legitimate children and as reliable housekeepers (*Against Neaera* 122). The hetaera who had a child must often have exposed it, especially if it was a girl. In Lucian's Dialogues of courtesans, one who is expecting a child says to her lover, who is deserting her, that she will not expose it, especially if it is a boy, but, *hard though it is for a courtesan*, will bring it up to reproach the father in the future for his treatment of her. There must have been a great deal in real life to correspond to the deeply-felt judgement of Lysias (*fragment* 90): 'The day a woman abandons herself and leaves virtue behind, she strays from her destiny, considers her relatives as enemies and strangers as her friends, and thinks of good and evil in opposite terms from those she formerly believed in.' In the courtesans of comedy we find no traces of the spiritual, though there ought to be some if poetry wished to make use of such figures. The speech mentioned above, falsely ascribed to Demosthenes, gives a totally abhorrent picture of all the coarseness and wickedness of the real facts concerning go-betweens and whores.

Quite different aspects of *luxury* include some funeral monuments. It was the influence of Eastern splendour that brought about the increased magnificence in the *heroon*, and this not only in memory of men like Timoleon, who deserved it, but also of mediocre individuals who were merely rich. Disproportionate publicity and expense were devoted to this. On the grave of Isocrates there stood a column thirty ells high, with a seven-ell mermaid on top; nearby was a panel with figures, representing some poets and Isocrates' teachers (probably in relief), among others Gorgias gazing at an astronomical sphere, with Isocrates himself. At the grave of the tragic writer Theodectes, which was on the Sacred Way to Eleusis, he and other famous poets were shown, apparently in the form of statues, not merely in relief.[160] These men had of course achieved real fame. But the embezzler Harpalus joined in, setting up a monument in Babylon to his wife Pythionike, a former hetaera, and another on the Sacred Way, for which he paid in all 200 talents. This last was, in Pausanias' opinion, one of the two most striking of all pre-Roman monuments in Athens, the other being that of a Rhodian settled in Athens; from a distance, Pythionike's looked as if it must at least be for someone like Miltiades or Pericles.[161]

For the most part, private luxury in Athens, though loudly reproved in individual cases, was probably very primitive and only a minor symptom of decline. The only way to spend a great deal of money was in feasting and with hetaerae. It was dangerous to squander it on carriages and on building. A fine house could lead to a scandal, as we learn from Demosthenes [p. 307 above]. His own adversary Meidias was accused of having a palatial house at Eleusis as well his home in Athens; also of going to the mysteries and on other outings in a splendid white carriage ordered from Sicyon, riding like a woman on a silver-mounted Euboean saddle, and possessing numbers of servants, brilliantly-coloured clothing and fine plate. We must admit that if these were excesses, there was not much danger in the Attic luxury of the notoriously rich. But the people regarded private luxury as a theft from themselves, and this was why Demosthenes emphasized, in his speech for the prosecution, that Meidias had not given as much as he should for *leitourgiai*, while he himself, at the time of his quarrel with Meidias, had taken on the expensive *leitourgia* of a male chorus of flautists equipped with gold-embroidered garments and gold crowns (*Against Meidias* 153 ff.).

Things in other large cities were no doubt much the same as in Athens: money was very much the principal yardstick. However it was not the only one, and in many people the antibanausic sentiment was strong enough to make them prefer poverty to earning money. Work was still to some extent in disrepute, even though it could be very profitable, as it was for the moneychangers; and in addition there were such burdens and dangers attached to wealth as perhaps have not existed, at any civilized period, in countries outside Islam. Compared with our own age, one motive for getting rich was still lacking; social distinction depended not on wealth, but on the exercise of mental and physical powers; and women did not try to influence men to make money. There is a fine celebration of honourable and capable poverty in the self-defence of *Penia* (Necessity) in Aristophanes' *Plutus* (507 ff.), which is an important source for social conditions at the beginning of the century; Necessity demonstrates that she is the mother of all arts and progress, and clearly distinguished from mendicancy (*ptocheia*). If a person renounced pleasure, despite its many temptations, and parasitism too, he could cultivate his mind with very moderate means, and we know of a number of independent and high-minded personalities who were determined to remain poor. These were largely the philosophers, chiefly the Cynics and the Pythagoreans, but the musician Philoxenus is supposed to have abandoned his sumptuous house with the words: 'These possessions shall not be the end of me, but I will make an end of looking after them.' These people lived with the minimum, which was made easier for them by the climate, and had the will to achieve, rather as, in our own time – when to live in this way is so much more difficult – Count Bartolommeo Borghesi in San Marino existed on practically nothing and created works of the highest distinction.

There were a few others whose nature allowed them to refuse riches *offered* to them, as Aristides and Ephialtes did in the fifth century.[162] The two great Thebans are proverbial for this. Epaminondas, who, we may recall, followed the Pythagorean tradition, refused fifty gold pieces from Jason of Pherae, and borrowed fifty drachmae when he invaded the Peloponnese; when his shieldbearer accepted money from a prisoner of war, he said: 'Give me my shield and buy yourself a shop and live in it; you won't want to run any risks now you are a rich man.'[163] He himself is said to have sent back a gift of 30,000 drachmas from the Persian King. But for Athens the great example of such independence is *Phocion*. As Plutarch describes him, he is the living commentary on everything in his city and all that happened in his time. It may seem a somewhat forced reminiscence of Pericles when we read that no Athenian ever saw him laugh or weep, or bathe at a public bath, or use a gesture of the hand sufficient to disturb his cloak; but his inner independence of all Athenian tendencies and attitudes compels respect. As a private man he had the courage to refuse a contribution to the collection for a sacrifice, on the grounds that he owed money to creditors; and correspondingly in political affairs he would not be swayed by his fellow citizens. When they were about to attack the Boeotians over a border dispute, he told them to fight with words, which were their strong point, rather than weapons, where they would be at a disadvantage; aware of the poor military prospects before Chaeronea he advised against war, and later with as little success against the Lamian War; he declined to join a petition for the removal of the Macedonian garrison, probably because it seemed to him that Athens could very well live in the prevailing conditions. An oracle was interpreted as meaning that when Athens was unanimous, one man would be found to think differently from the whole city, and Phocion said: 'Don't puzzle over this, it means *me*.' It is a story that carries conviction. He returned Alexander's gift of a hundred talents, though the delegates told him he was the only man the King regarded as of noble character; Phocion replied: 'He will have to allow me to remain so.'[164] He also sternly rejected Harpalus when he arrived in Athens with his treasures, though Harpalus then succeeded in finding a haven with his son-in-law. Later Phocion again refused to take the second offer of Macedonian money either for himself or for his son. In the struggle between the rival Macedonian rulers, Polysperchon won, and established democracy, and then Phocion inevitably fell victim to the demagogues and sycophants who had regained power in the State; he was accused of oligarchic opinions and hatred of the *demos*. The proceedings were savagely vindictive; he barely escaped the torture, and even his corpse was exiled from Attica; it must have been the case that many Athenians could not stand him, precisely because he really was, as he was called in spite of his sharp tongue, 'the good man' (*chrestos*).[165]

VI

The Hellenistic Age

IN THIS PERIOD, the subject of *culture in the narrower sense* poses the question of how far the decline of the *poleis* and civic indifference can really be said to have liberated great talents for the intellectual life, and whether these developments encouraged outstanding ability or stifled it. Apart from what we learn about the *diadochoi*, the philosophers or other writers, and of scandals, the information we have is so scanty that it is impossible to give any satisfactory answer to these questions. Polybius clearly states that people turned away from the State and towards learning and scholarship, and students of philosophy, too, must have increased in number. It is very doubtful whether the arts benefited from new vigour in the same way. Those who were artists remained so, and it is obvious that the most superb work was still being done in sculpture and painting. But there is a sad gap in the tradition of that time; great artists ceased to be spoken of, and famous names were no longer recorded; the names of the sculptors of Rhodes and Pergamum are only known through some chance mention in connection with particular works, not as those of masters who were household words. The names of famous actors, for instance, practically cease to appear in literature, yet there may have been many still doing distinguished work who were not mentioned just *because* there were so many.

In other areas our insight is limited because only fragments have been preserved. Since, apart from theatres, we have no knowledge of a single building dating from the Asiatic and Egyptian realms of the *diadochoi*, we can make no judgments on the architecture of this period. Poetry too is preserved only in fragments, and, except for Theocritus, they do not represent the best of it.

Some kinds, choric lyrical poetry for instance, may well have dwindled away, but it is hard to see any reason for there being no good individual lyric poetry; perhaps there happened to be none in Alexandria.

The strongest surviving evidence for the Greek life of the intellect is in the three main directions of philosophy: Stoicism, Epicureanism and the Sceptics. Still, the energy of the Greek tradition is demonstrated by its having been able to Hellenize the Near East, not merely because the Macedonian governments brought political pressure to bear in its favour, but because it had an inner superiority and vitality. It would be important to know whether the average educated Greeks in general seemed particularly effeminate and soft in comparison with those of the past, but this is a matter we cannot decide.[1]

The earlier Hellenes had been inspired by shining *ideals*, especially that of *fame*; where were these ideals now? Even in the sad decline of the third century there were still some who sought fame. The few men who won fame in politics and war in so-called free Hellas, such as Aratus, Philopoemen and others, had serious flaws and defects, and in the case of the last Cleomenes it was not only after Sellasia that he showed himself incompetent as an individual; the whole of his reform had the flavour of the dissolution that was overtaking the Greeks. However, it was usual to speak of these men, and depict them, with the inflated sentiment of former times, and Cleomenes in particular must still have been surrounded by people who regarded him as a great man. His behaviour after the defeat in Sparta is, for instance, described in detail; refusing the help of a slave-woman, he neither drank nor sat down nor put off his armour, but only rested for a while, with his left arm leaning on a pillar and his head against his elbow, deep in thought, till finally he fled towards the sea (Plutarch, *Cleomenes* 29). Even if he was play-acting here, his death in Egypt was still a tragedy. It was a determined attempt to summon up an image of ancient Spartan fame.

Some *diadochoi* too had a feeling for glory. It may often have led them astray, and it may be thought that their real motives were vanity and megalomania; an exception was Cleomenes' opponent, Antigonus Doson, who showed mercy to Sparta and permitted it to keep all its institutions; already sick, he hurried home to Macedonia to find the joy of a genuine hero's death in battle with the invading Illyrians. According to a story probably embellished in the *leschai*, he died of a haemorrhage, still on horseback, in the moment of victory, saying 'What a wonderful day!' (Plutarch, *Cleomenes* 30).

Generally, though, the true pursuit of fame was in decline. *Fame in the agon* especially was dying out, as we know from a telling account in Plutarch's *Philopoemen* (3). From childhood, this great general had wanted to be a soldier, and learned everything he could about war. As he was also a natural wrestler, he was advised to become an athlete. When he asked whether the training would not conflict with his military studies, he was told, quite truthfully, that the athletic physique and regime were completely different from those of a soldier; the athlete needed plenty of sleep, great quantities of food and precisely ordered exercise alternating with rest, and would be put out by the slightest departure from these rules, while the soldier's life must be one of constant irregular moving about, with the habit of going without food and sleep. So Philopoemen rejected and despised athleticism and later forbade it among his troops as far as he could, by contempt and penalties, on the grounds that it made the healthiest body unfit for fighting; he strengthened his own physique by hunting and working in the field.[2]

Honour and reverence were now shown to the powerful and the despicable alike, so that a certain nervous excitement and expectation were generated. Even at the outset of this period, Harpalus was able to persuade the Greeks, in their native land, to allow him to commemorate his hetaera Pythionike as 'Pythionike Aphrodite' by the great monument he set up to her on the Sacred Way to Eleusis, with its grove and altar (see p. 341 above). Another example is Demetrius of Phaleron, who so enraptured the Athenians that they put up in his honour, all at once, three hundred statues, which of course met a sad fate on his fall from power, demonstrating how worthless such distinctions had become.[3] But immediately after this, Demetrius the besieger of cities was deified as it were to his face, and this led to the divine veneration of various *diadochoi*, not only in their own states, where the people had no choice, but in free Greece too. Statues came to be erected even to mere entertainers. In Athens there was one to the Carystian Aristonicus, who played ball with Alexander; he was granted citizenship at the same time 'for his art', which excludes the possibility that the statue was only intended to immortalize a graceful pose. Things went even further. The puppet-master Eurycleides was awarded a statue beside those of the great tragic writers, while his colleague Potheinus was permitted to use the same stage on which Euripides and his fellow poets had delighted the audience. In each case a certain nervousness was expressed in the decree: 'a statue is to be put up to such and such', yet the conjuror Theodorus was honoured in this way in the theatres at Hestiaea and Oreos, not to speak of performers like the lyre-player Archelaus at Miletus or the singer Cleon in Thebes (where there was no statue to Pindar).[4] The dearth of genuinely remarkable men makes it unsurprising that celebrity could now be gained by mere physical conspicuousness or by positively repellent characteristics, as can be seen from the lists in Aelian and Athenaeus of people who were thin, short, or fat, thick-headed, or gluttonous and drunken.[5]

One response to this chasing after cheap celebrity was straightforward condemnation, chiefly represented by Zoilus; his dates are not precisely known, but he probably lived in the time of Philadelphus. He was from Amphipolis, which was then in Macedonian territory, and wrote (as a Macedonian in his way) not only against Homer, but also against Plato and Isocrates, was given to ill-natured *railing*, since, as he said, he was not in a position to be an evil*doer*, and antagonized everyone by his carping at contemporaries as well as the dead. The name of this literary Thersites, or, as he was known, the rhetorical cynic, became proverbial as 'the scourge of Homer'.

Apart from the *diadochoi*, the foremost celebrities, then, were philosophers and hetaerae. The Athenians revered Zeno, and his fellow citizens of Cition, in Cyprus, dedicated a gilded statue to him for their own greater glory; when Carneades died, the moon was said to have gone into eclipse, while the sun clouded over. Scholars were also still discussed, but the records say nothing about artists. As for the hetaerae, those belonging to the *diadochoi* and to some philosophers, such as Epicurus, were evidently an important subject of conversation, and these women, formerly a distinct type, now became individual celebrities.[6] This is clear from the poem by Machon the Alexandrian, from the time of Philadelphus and Euergetes; it contains their witty ripostes and anecdotes of them, mostly threadbare and in bad taste, yet presented with elegant simplicity.[7] But as happened in the period of the *diadochoi* in general, individual energies seem to have been exhausted in the first hundred years; after 200 B.C. there were no more famous courtesans.

In this later Hellenistic period, really ambitious people must have experienced some frustration in their quest for fame. What final form could be taken by the competitive Hellenic will? Power and wealth were concentrated at the courts; the *polis*, where it survived, was like a bone with no meat left on it, and those who were still rich could achieve fame only locally, in the old way, by their contributions to popular entertainment (*euergesia*), especially later, in the peaceful Imperial age; public exhibition of skill (as a lyre-player, dancer, ball-player etc.) demanded special gifts not possessed by everyone. For the time being, the only way to shine was to practise oratory, since to some extent this could be learned; and this was now exclusively a matter of epideictic oratory, with any philosophical content depending on the individual. This necessarily entailed a wandering life; there was no such thing as writing entertaining books for money, and the most determined publicity-seeker had no newspapers to rely on, but had to make personal appearances everywhere. Thus, under the Emperors, when political activity was out of the question, and literary pursuits brought little reward for writers in Greek, one type of career was that of sophists like Philostratus, practising epideictic eloquence with only a slight political flavour. Those driven by the highest ambition could only hope to become occultists and prophets of new religions, like Apollonius of Tyana, and Alexander of Abonuteichus; even if he too were usually forced to live on the move, such a person might succeed in attracting followers wherever he was by introducing a new cult. We have already discussed the extreme case of hunger for notoriety in later times – Peregrinus Proteus, who burned himself to death at Olympia.[8]

A period is characterized by what it professes to look up to or in fact looks up to, but for the cultural historian some contemporary picture of its daily life is desirable as well. One source of this kind of information should be the new comedy, even though we know it almost exclusively from Roman imitations. However, its usefulness is not as great as we might expect; it shows us only a one-sided Athens in relatively few types that are very much generalized, so that for all the hints it gives about the customs of the time, they do not amount to a complete picture of life. A famous philosopher, Theophrastus, goes about the task quite differently, and his characters have a great deal more importance than the puppet-figures of comedy. The author of the *Characters* presents eternally flawed humanity, though mostly in the typical clothing of his nation and his age; the work dates from the third century and his twenty-ninth year, according to the preface, and its bold programme was to improve the younger generation. Theophrastus does not deal with virtuous people, and among the rest he chooses only the unmitigatedly, even excessively bad, and is not concerned with any halftones or mixtures of the good and the bad. Many stock characters are missing who might be expected to appear, such as the *miles gloriosus*, the sycophant, the usurer, the untalented poet; indeed it seems that Theophrastus is carefully avoiding the various professions or ranks and devoting himself strictly to the *ethical* nuances, which emerge as it were from *inner* dispositions. The purpose is philosophical and philological; basing himself in part on Aristotle's *Nicomachean Ethics*, he seeks to arrive at a judgment of the way in which each of a person's qualities determines the kind of life he has, and so he begins with a short definition of the features of different lives (though the commentators find this part unsatisfactory). Apparently he followed up, over time, some individuals he had recognized as types; for his best chapters can hardly have been based on gradual random observation. The actual result, apart from descriptions of a few fools and oafs, is nothing but a gallery of all the odious specimens to be found in Athens.

The overwhelming impression is that people in Athens were very much letting themselves go, chiefly in lying and deception, without caring for their good or bad name; there was an assumption of general barefaced impudence. Moreover, mass observation in the manner of Theophrastus was only possible in the total openness of Attic life. The Athenians were perpetually on show and consorting together, and the habitual attitude of 'hail-fellow-well-met' created a social atmosphere quite different from our own, so that the flatterer (*kolax*), for instance, could behave far more importunately than would nowadays be possible. At the same time we find the most varied specialization among these characters; some, who would strike us as single types, classified by subtler nuances. For instance Theophrastus distinguishes two kinds of flatterers; the silly, who make up to everybody for no reason but mannerism or temperament (*areskos*) and the sly, who ingratiates himself only with a single person for his own advantage (*kolax*). In the same way the loquacious are clearly divided into the trivially boring, who rattle thoughtlessly on all day and pour out stale news and indisputable facts (*adolesches*), and the unpleasant kind who stick like leeches (*lalos*).

We may draw attention here to the detailed description, in *Characters* 2, of the flatterer, whom Theophrastus has evidently studied from life. This is not the parasite who puts up with anything for the sake of his stomach, but another variety, intent on ingratiating himself at any price with a particular patron for what he can get out of him; the type had existed for a long time, alongside the parasite but separately, and was specifically a Greek one (see p. 333 above). This flatterer is keen above all to excite his patron's vanity. 'Look how all the heads turn as you pass! They don't notice anyone else.' 'Yesterday in the Stoa they were talking about you; thirty of them asked who was the noblest, and all agreed it was you.' He will pluck specks off the patron's clothing and bits of straw out of his hair, and then comment that for his age he still has a lot of black hair; when his patron speaks, he calls for silence and at the end he says, 'Hear! Hear!' If the patron is cracking jokes, he laughs himself sick; he buys apples and pears for the children of the house and makes sure he is seen distributing them, kissing the little ones with the words 'O offspring of a worthy father!' (The flattery of children recurs in the account of the *areskos* (5).) If his patron is buying sandals, he says, 'the foot is more elegant than the shoe', and when they go to see a friend he runs ahead to announce the visit, and runs back again to say he has done so. At table he is the first to praise the wine and then the food, in general and in detail. He is anxious that his patron should not take cold, wraps him up well and hangs over him while he is in conversation. At the theatre he takes the cushions from the servant and puts them under the patron. He admires the layout of the house, the well-cultivated land, and the striking resemblance of the master's portrait. In his introduction, Theophrastus implies that no Athenian was stupid enough not to recognize the flatterer as purely self-serving, yet these people existed and were well rewarded. The second half of chapter 5, on the *areskos*, is mixed up with chapter 1. It deals not with this type but with a zealous poseur and dandy, who goes to the theatre to sit near the military leaders, and buys things not for himself but for distant acquaintances; he may send purchases to Byzantium, Spartan hounds to Cyzicus, or honey from Hymettus to Rhodes, and insists on telling the whole city about it; he shows everyone his apes, baboons, Sicilian doves and so forth; he is really a harmless creature, taking exaggerated pleasure in his little possessions. A related type is the man who tries to distinguish himself by petty exploits (*microphilotimos*) (21). At banquets he has to be placed next to the host. When his son has his hair ceremoniously cut off on entering manhood, it is done, as among great families, in honour of Pythian Apollo; a special journey is made to Delphi, and the accompanying slave must be a black African. His pet dog is given a gravestone with the inscription Cladus, 'the Maltese'. When the *prytaneis* have sacrificed to the Divine Mother, he fights (evidently as one of their number) for the duty of making the public announcement of this, in festive costume and wearing a crown; then, at home, he tells his wife how happy he is.

In chapter 4 (*peri agroikias*), the independent landowner is portrayed as completely rustic and uneducated, drawing apparently on a real example Theophrastus studied. There is a masterly sketch (6) of the insolent fellow (*aponenoimenos*) and his impudence. He is not only a bold slanderer, but wants everybody to hear him and is never satisfied unless he can gather a crowd. He spends more time in prison than at home, will spread any dirty gossip and loves the task, shouting so he can be heard all over the agora. The 'shameless' man (*anaischuntos*) of chapter 9 confines his shamelessness to a probably widespread form of profiteering by procuring stolen goods or smuggling. Another shameless man (11) is the mischiefmaker (*bdeluros*), not for his own advantage but from inclination; his place is between the two just named. His scandalmongering is intentionally offensive; he is a plague to individuals and to whole crowds (e.g. in the theatre), and as sordid and greedy as the shameless. It would seem that this behaviour was often quite brazen. In democratic and irreligious Athens there can have been no-one to prevent the embittered from making themselves as hateful as they pleased. Gross incivility is represented too (24), in the passively arrogant boor (*huperephanos*), not one to seek out occasions to be insulting, but completely ruthless with any who are obliged to approach him.

The prolix talker (*lalos*) (7) makes one think that the Spartans knew what they were doing when they imposed their Laconism by force. They were aware of the effects of uncontrolled Greek garrulity, and had their own kind of malice. This chatterer is totally importunate, and so extremely inconsiderate that he breaks into any business, conversation or intimacy between others. He is apt to tell old stories he has read and to quote his own effective public speeches. He is perfectly aware of all this and finds it charming: 'I would not be silent, even if they said I twittered more than the swallows.' But even his own children mock him, and say, 'Tell us a story to put us to sleep.' The inventor of news items (8) is a self-important liar (*logopoios*). He is subject to a nervous compulsion, and his fantasies are made up in advance as facts to retail; as Theophrastus observes, it is done for no personal advantage. A thief may steal his cloak while he is speechifying at the baths, or, holding forth in the Stoa about victories on land or sea, he will lose his case in the courts. There are great numbers of people like this, lurking in every stoa, every workshop, every corner of the agora. Not very different from him is the boaster (23) or *alazson*, who swaggers mainly about his nonexistent wealth and possessions, but also about *choregiai* and trierarchies, or about having fought in Alexander's campaigns, or being in correspondence with Antipater; he is quite likely to pretend that the lodging house where he has a room is his family home, and that he intends to sell it because it is too small for his parties. The malicious gossip (*kakologos*) is here too (28), with something disreputable to tell about each of his friends and relations, living or dead.

We also meet the penny-pincher (*micrologos*) who, when he saves on small expenses, repeats his motto 'It all mounts up over the year', and who will never allow anyone to pick up a fallen fruit in his garden (a thing that must have been usual and tolerated in Athens); there is also the similar figure of the miser (*aneleutheros*). Then the disagreeable (19.20) comes in two variants: the *duscheres* is coarsely rude and might take more care of his person; the *aedes* is distasteful in his talk, and offends socially in many ways. The absent-minded man (*anaisthutos*) (14) is in part a comic subject, but the outstandingly tactless (*akairos*) (12) is an undesirable companion, forever choosing the wrong moment, for instance railing against the female sex at a wedding. (However it is Theophrastus who is in the wrong when he criticizes him for a tactless retort to someone who whips his slaves: 'One of my slaves who was whipped went and hanged himself.' Here the *akairos* may have been speaking as a human being.)

It is interesting that the superstitious person (*deisidaimon*) (16) is, to judge by his means, a man in comfortable circumstances, not of the lowest class. We are given a fairly detailed and striking list of superstitions as they affected daily life. Sometimes people gave up ordinary commonsense behaviour altogether; for instance when a mouse gnawed a hole in the floursack they went to the soothsayer (*exegetes*), and when he advised them to give the sack to the leatherworker to be patched, they were still not reassured and preferred to throw it away. Apart from the soothsayer there were also the interpreter of dreams, the *mantis*, the birdwatcher and, last but not least, the *orpheotelestes*, who performed a monthly rededication of the whole family; there was also a minor kind of priestess for purifications.

Even the most fortunate events could never be welcome to the carper (*mempsimoiros*) (17). Told that a son has been born to him, he replies: 'Why don't you add that now I've lost half of all I possess, then you'll be telling the truth.' Chapter 18 gives a most detailed sketch of the man who trusts nobody. He sets one slave to watch another, gets up at night to make the round of all the locks and bolts, and demands witnesses and guarantees for everything; the Athenians must have needed to keep their eyes open. Only a short, rather lacklustre chapter (26) is devoted to the believer in oligarchy, whose grumbling consists of a few timeworn refrains: the city is uninhabitable nowadays, and Theseus is to blame for all its ills. This suggests there was no longer any reason to fear this political faction. The brevity of this last chapter may indicate either omissions by the copyist, or that Theophrastus did not live to complete his account of these characters.

Those ruled by the *diadochoi* in Greater Greece had an advantage over the Athenians and others in Greece itself; however heavy the burden of taxation, they had at least escaped from the *polis*, which for the 'free Greeks' now existed only in the form of a murderous simulacrum. Of course, the cities of the *diadochoi* were still *poleis* to some extent; but they were well enough run, with some measure of civic officialdom and a degree of patronage, and the demands made on the citizens were no longer what they had been; the occasional unrest in cities like Seleucia, Antioch or Alexandria was very different from the civic crises in Greece.

It would be fair to say that the citizen (*polites*) of a former time had been a very different person from the subject of the *diadochoi*; but it was a time that was gone, and no power on earth could revive him. The 'unity of style', which had once made culture into a whole, whether it was expressed in politics or in art, had vanished for ever. In the place of the old citizenship, however, people could now fully enjoy private life, though this advantage had certainly cost them dear. Economic freedom meant that each individual was now genuinely free, and might pursue whatever activity appealed to him. So everyone could follow his personal inclinations, travelling, for instance, as much as his means allowed without being suspected of a capital offence, and use his energies as he pleased. Various callings were differentiated as they had never been before among the Greeks. Especially in the kingdom of the Ptolemies, a distinction was now made between the military and the official classes, while artists and scholars became specialists and were freed from their links with a particular state – a development which the *apolitia* of the philosophers had tended towards for a long time. What brought people together now was private activity instead of political interest; whether learned men gathered in the Museum of Alexandria, or actors in their professional groups, they were no less cosmopolitan than the mercenary armies of the time.[9]

All the same, what we call Hellenism, that is Greek tradition apart from the *polis*, remained centred on Greece, even in the East. Of the one hundred and thirty-one sayings (*proverbia*) which Pseudo-Plutarch quotes as current in Alexandria, we find that only one (97) refers to Egypt and one other

(119) to a place in Libya; all the rest are either drawn from the common stock of Greek proverbs, or are allusions to Greek mythology or anecdotes of Greek life. Many are of a kind which could hardly be handed down in conversation and must have been learnt from reading, so we can tell that Greek history must have been carefully cultivated in Alexandria; it becomes clear that attention was focused exclusively on the North.[10] So the Hellenic influence was preserved; but it seems that in contrast to the earlier colonies, where everyone knew exactly which Greek populations they were chiefly sprung from, and acknowledged them, here the old Greek *tribes* and strains were completely intermingled, and in general there was little interest in people's origins; at the courts, particularly, there must have been swarms of adventurers and parvenus from anywhere and everywhere.[11]

We are unable to settle the important question of how far, in the cities ruled by the *diadochoi*, the old education continued in the normal subjects (*enkuklios paideia*), including gymnastic training. It was no longer imposed as a requirement on the 'citizen'; and even the free cannot have had much leisure for it, least of all in the cities. We imagine the great mass of the population as a working proletariat, whose very cheap labour was already more sought after than that of slaves; over them, as now, was a class of wealthier men, bosses, merchants, the better educated and so on.[12] Education, then, must have been valued only in so far as the Greek heritage favoured it. Apart from this, there was now the distinct profession of learning, tending to collecting and classification, and directed by authority as a form of employment and protection, its individual disciplines 'cultivated by a wholly specialized and concentrated activity, which to the ancients would certainly have appeared banausic';[13] now at last it was permissible to be a specialist, that is a worker, to one's heart's content.

Religion, inevitably, was weak in the cities of the *diadochoi*, though there was some substitute for it in Oriental and Egyptian cults, as regards both gods and teachings; but here it lacked the ancient local cults which for the early Greeks had been its stronghold. Myth too, or any intimate faith in it, was almost abandoned in Greece, and even if here and there it was purposely and lovingly transplanted, it could hardly strike deep roots; what was seen of myth in the theatre did not inspire respect, and, besides, for many people, philosophy and its systems filled the place of religion.

In these circumstances it is surprising that the period shows so few signs of liberated poetic and artistic talents; they may well have been present in fact, or perhaps have been replaced to some extent by philosophical dilettantism and religious posturing. In any case, individuals and the external appearance they presented were now very widely differentiated. Formerly, because there were norms of education and training, the Greeks all had much in common with each other; now they separated into a mass of varied types, and the newer comedy, pastoral poetry and graphic art all do their best to illustrate these types in their particularity; it would be right to say that Greek humanity had gained in breadth.[14]

Turning our attention to *women*, we will speak first of the *last* living figures of Dorian women, as we encounter them in the quarrel of the Kings Agis and Cleomenes. A century earlier, after Leuctra, the Spartan women did nothing but lament, and, in the Holy War, Queen Deinicha joined in the looting. The rich heiresses who played a part in these later times were more dignified personalities. Agis was brought up in wealth and luxury by his mother Agesistrata and his grandmother Archidamia, who were the richest people in the land. Agis won them over to his own ideas, and after initial doubts they actually took to encouraging him to pursue them further, and propagated his views among the other women, though without success, since their friends did not wish to part with their possessions. Both his mother and his grandmother were murdered by cold-blooded treachery in prison immediately after the fall of Agis, Agesistrata having cut down her mother, who had been hanged, and laid her beside the corpse of Agis; her last words were 'If this can only be of help to Sparta'.[15] Leonidas, who had been expelled by Agis, had a daughter, Chilonis, married to his successor Cleombrotus; on Leonidas' return he was very angry with his son-in-law, but Chilonis persuaded him to let her husband escape, and took her children to share his exile, although she had disapproved of his behaviour to Leonidas.[16]

Agis' widow, Agiatis, heiress to great wealth and the most beautiful Greek of her day, was then forced by Leonidas to marry his youthful son Cleomenes. She converted her new husband to the ideas of the dead Agis, and Cleomenes' mother, Cratesiclea, went over completely to her son's way of thinking after the death of Leonidas, helped to convince eminent Spartans to adopt it, and married one of them to further Cleomenes' interests.[17] Agiatis died during the war with Antigonus, deeply mourned by her husband, who hurried back to Sparta at her death. Cratesiclea, and Cleomenes' children, were demanded by Ptolemy Euergetes as hostages for the assistance he promised them; when Cleomenes broke this news to her after long hesitation, she laughed aloud in her readiness to obey, hoping it would be to Sparta's advantage, and, taking leave of Cleomenes in the Temple of Poseidon on Tanaerum, begged him to bear up 'so that none shall see us weep or be unworthy of Sparta; this depends on ourselves alone, but our destiny is in the hands of our daimon'. Outwardly calm, she walked to the ship with her grandchildren. When already in Egypt, she learned that her son had the chance to join the Achaeans in defiance of Ptolemy; she sent him a message to say he should not continue to fear Ptolemy just for the sake of an old woman and little children.[18] Finally, in Egypt, she and the children, with her waiting-women, were implicated in the downfall of Cleomenes.[19] One of her ladies, the beautiful young wife of Panteus, behaved in her death as magnificently as her husband did in his; she had followed him in spite of terrible dangers. When the soldiers had seized Cratesiclea, she took her hand to lead her to the place of execution, where they saw Cleomenes' children murdered; their grandmother only cried out: 'O my children, where have you gone!' After Cratesiclea and the other women had received the deathblow, the wife of Panteus kilted up her cloak and went to soothe their last moments as well as she could. Then she modestly rearranged her dress, and carefully covered up her head and face so that she would not need this service from anyone else when she was dead; only the executioner was allowed to approach her, and she died a hero's death.

These Spartan women were an exception in the Greek world. It is explicitly stated that the men always deferred to them, and granted them a greater influence in public affairs than they themselves had in those of private life, and the women also controlled the greatest share of wealth.[20] But the time was not far off when, in his systematic extermination of Spartanism, Nabis would force them into marriage with his former helots. Other women prominent in life were the *hetairai*. Phryne and Glycera were still living at least at the beginning of the third century, and this was the age when such women became the focus of social pleasures for the younger generation. Well educated and witty as they appear in the letters of Alciphron – which were certainly written in imitation of Hellenistic models – they fascinated generals, statesmen, writers and artists, so that almost every well-known Hellenistic personality can be proved to have had connections with famous hetaerae. Those who belonged to the *diadochoi* were especially notable. Lamia and Leaena, the courtesans of Demetrius Poliorcetes, were honoured as Aphrodites with temples in Athens and Thebes, and some who belonged to the Ptolemies were so famous that the second Euergetes (Physcon) included them in his Commentaries. In the time of Polybius the finest houses in Alexandria were given the names of well-known flute-girls and hetaerae, and portrait-statues of others stood in temples and public buildings beside those of generals and statesmen.[21] On the vases of the period their lives are often represented. We have already said, however, that from the second century none became truly famous, and the simple reason for this is that the *diadachoi* were not men whose own fame could have made this possible; when the rulers had so degenerated, life at their courts was not likely to arouse much interest.

As for the rest of the feminine world, no change can be noted in the narrow confined circumstances of women's lives.[22] They had no share in dinner parties or social occasions such as visits to the theatre, so there was no flirtatious mingling of the sexes as there would later be in Rome; no respectable woman could yet venture into the streets, or to festivals in honour of the gods, unless accompanied by suspicious duennas; even if they were gaining more and more power over their husbands, they lived exclusively in the separate women's quarters, and above all the unmarried girl, 'cloistered' as one poet says, was not as yet free from the jealous imprisonment of her secluded life.[23] The tender, impassioned wooing that the poets wrote of at this time can scarcely have been taken from the life, for there was no betrothal, and the couple never met before the wedding.[24] All marriages were still decided by the father, who is sometimes blamed for choosing a bride who is a complete stranger. We cannot doubt that true love existed in the Greek world of that time, but it is impossible to find evidence of its having played any part in the institution of married life. Women were pitied for their lot; this is apparent in the ominous lines which survive of Poseidippus' *Hermaphrodite* (first half of the third century), where we learn that a male child will be brought up by his family, even if they are poor, while a girl is exposed at birth even by the rich.[25]

Still there were differences. In Greece itself, apart from the last of the Dorian women we have mentioned, there is scarcely a woman whose name has been handed down.[26] In the whole history of the Achaean League, for instance, not one appears even as a trouble-maker,[27] and the lack of characterization of women in the new comedy tends to prove the strict limitations of their condition; however, in the large cities under the *diadochoi*, they seem to move more freely, to be more developed as individuals, and more respected by the men. Culture and luxury were to be found at the courts of Alexandria, Antioch and Pergamum and the queens and their ladies had a share in this kind of life; this influence spread to other circles.

Theocritus sends a spindle to the wife of his friend Nicias in Miletus, and a poem to go with the gift; it is a pleasant attention that would have been impossible only a century earlier. The same poet's *Adoniazusae* (*Women at the festival of Adonis*) would have been quite unthinkable in Athens. It gives a most remarkable picture of life in the city of Alexandria; the festival of Adonis is celebrated in the halls of the royal palace, with a splendid picture of Adonis on a silver bed, surrounded by hovering cupids, with the mourning Aphrodite beside him in a bower of flowers. Among the great crowd of spectators are two friends of Dorian origin from Syracuse, the wives of Alexandrians of middle rank, who have daringly come there with a slave-woman, and who give a sharp answer to a man who mocks at their broad Doric; they slip in through the portico, admire the grand celebration and the singing of a girl from Argos, and go away again very delighted. This poem is like an account of events in a big modern city; no Athenian woman would have gone out into such a throng.[28] The queens in Alexandria and at some other courts of the *diadochoi* occasionally wielded political influence, but no woman of the period rivalled the terrible Olympias.

Both in life and in poetry, this period shows the first hints of *gallantry* in the men and of *coquetry* in the women.[29] Gallantry is expressed, at least towards princesses, in the epigrams on two pictures of Berenice, and in the astronomer Conon's flattery when he named a constellation Berenice's Hair; in Theocritus (XI.55) Polyphemus wants to kiss Galatea's hand, and Achilles, in another poet's work, kisses that of Deidamia. In Theocritus, again, Galatea behaves coquettishly towards Polyphemus; elsewhere in the idyll an affected city lady meets a lovesick cowherd, and on a decorated beaker a woman ogles two men who seem to be courting her; naturally it is the hetaerae who give the lead.[30] Generally the relations between the sexes now became the main subject of the three forms of poetry still existing – elegy, idyll and new comedy,[31] even if, in the last of these, the main interest is not so much love as intrigue and sly pursuit, and the plot centres on the young man's resistance to the arranged marriage, or the courtesan's determination to keep her hold on him or turn it into a marriage.[32] The Milesian legends now began to constitute a definite genre in literature. The Alexandrian scribblers were seeking out stories and legends of lovers, which hitherto had been handed on orally, and also improving on old myths by adding erotic motives; Duris of Samos (in the time of Philadelphus) tells of Achilles' love for Iphigenia; Atalanta, who in Euripides was completely opposed to marriage, now becomes the mistress of Meleager; later even

Galatea loves Polyphemus, though earlier she had disdained him, and, in Theocritus, had mockingly thrown apples at him. The myth of Daphne was probably tracked down among Arcadian peasants by Alexandrian poets, who added the attempt by Apollo to win the man-hating huntress with his music; in poetry as in pictorial art, the fashion for erotic dalliance gained ground, and on the vases (especially those of Southern Italy) there were more scenes showing men with decent women and girls.[33]

There is certainly a *vein of emotion* in the Alexandrian period which was lacking before. One example of this new tendency is the Ludovisi Juno, aware of her own majesty and yet mild. This can easily intensify and turn to sentimentality, which may or may not be thought a falling off from earlier times; Hellenism had a kind of precedent for it in Euripides. There is now much more indulgence in softer sentiments which in the past were usually restrained, much talk in the bucolic and elegiac poets of tears, unhappy love and despair, and descriptions of love sickness as a malady; anecdotes like that of Antiochus and Stratonice become popular. Apollonius of Rhodes recounts Jason's farewell to his mother with excessive sentimentality, and his treatment of Medea shows a deliberate avoidance of the terrifying personality of myth in favour of a deep study of the feminine temperament. In portraits of the *diadochoi*, and of Alexander himself, there is often a hint of melancholy; the same may be said of ideal types such as stylized heads of athletes, certain heads of Pallas, and the Giustiniani Apollo,[34] and a similar preference for suffering figures is found in painting too.[35]

The *refinement* of sensuality was the due complement of this sentimentality.[36] The prevailing tone was frivolous and smutty, as in the jokes about courtesans, still sometimes in the cheerful, hedonic form inherited from the fourth century, or again combined with a painful regret that people must fight each other when a peaceful life could be so pleasant.[37] For the rest, voluptuousness was on the increase in poetry and art. Poets dwelt on descriptions of female nakedness, and it was shown in pictorial art with a kind of intention that contrasts strongly with the treatment of the nude in the earlier period; in life too there was a vogue for lascivious partial or complete undress and for transparent garments.[38]

The practice of love between men and boys may have gone on much as before; but there was no longer a *polis* or any shared heroism in war, both of which had provided an element of cultivating or training the beloved, and so these relationships quite lost their former motivation in ethics, politics and love of education. The friendship of Cleomenes and Panteus was perhaps the last of its kind to lay claim to exalted feeling.[39] After that there were no famous pairs of male lovers, not even among the *diadochoi*, though Demetrius Poliorcetes might have provided an example; the boy who was loved no longer existed as a recognized feature of social life, but only as an instrument of pleasure, and sentimentality was forced to turn to relationships with women. Phanocles still made use of the motif, in learned poetry, for aetiological proofs, but otherwise it was only the subject of elegantly obscene jests, or of some epigrams which are in the nature of coded sighs; the last poet who was at home with it was Theocritus in his 'boy-poems' (*paidika*).

A further innovation in the mental scope of the Greeks was the intensified *feeling for natural landscape*.[40] In ancient Greece, too, there was an appreciation of the splendour of the world, as we know from Homer. But now a new element comes in; polytheism, yielding to philosophy, left the landscape bereft of its divinities, so that the woods and hills were no longer peopled by nymphs, satyrs and fauns; and nature, now impersonal, could begin to communicate *unmediated* with the human mind. This was just at the time when the new accessibility of the East was immensely increasing the knowledge of the world both in geography and natural history, bringing among other things a scientific and acquisitive approach to botany.

This heightened feeling for nature, and its very strong affinity with the sentimentality and melancholy we have been discussing, can be demonstrated by the great upswing in landscape painting, mainly known to us from Pompeian imitations. But there are other reasons to believe that the Greeks now began to enjoy fine views. Their forerunners in this were the Persians, whose love of nature is known not only from the tradition of their wonderful royal gardens (*paradeisoi*) and from the honour Xerxes paid to a beautiful plane tree,[41] but also through the information that King Darius had himself rowed over to the Cyaneae Islands for the sake of their view of the Bosphorus.[42] This was a new thing among the Greeks. The first we know of anyone climbing a mountain for the view is the ascent of Haemus by Philip the Younger of Macedon,[43] but some decades earlier Apollonius of Rhodes had used the idea as a poetic theme. In I, 1103 ff., when his Argonauts have landed in Cyzicus, he tells how they climb Dindymon for the purpose of sacrificing to Cybele, but it is obvious that the real object is the beautiful view. The same poet (III. 164) describes the panorama from Olympus; he is also unusually alert to light and meteorological effects.[44]

What was more, the landscape made its way into the large new cities which set the tone for others; as the city dweller felt the need for nature, his rulers responded by creating imitations of natural vistas. So Antioch on the Orontes had its splendid promenades with fountains, and in the neighbouring Daphne a wonderful park. In Alexandria the blocks of houses were interrupted by gardens and groves, and in the centre of the city rose the Paneion, an artificial hill which could be climbed, up an easy winding path, to where the panorama of the whole city lay visible; perhaps the idea was to show the old Egyptians how much prettier it was than a pyramid. The Palace of the Ptolemies was also surrounded by well-planned gardens, and at the Museum was an area for walking, shaded by trees, where the scholars took their exercise.

At the same time the first hanging promenade was constructed by Sostratus, the architect of the Pharos of Alexandria. Even in the planning of houses, attention was paid to the views they commanded; Vitruvius' *oecus Cyzicenus*, an apartment in the house of a great Hellenistic family, was designed to look out into the open landscape on three sides.

The Intellectual Necessity of Studying Ancient History

All human knowledge is accompanied by the history of the ancient world as music is by a base-chord heard again and again; the history, that is, of all those peoples whose life has flowed together into our own.

It is futile to assume that four hundred years of humanism have taught us everything, evaluated all experience and information and left us nothing more to discover, so that we can be content with the knowledge of modern times, or at best with the pitying or reluctant study of the Middle Ages, and devote the time saved to something more useful.

We can never cut ourselves off from antiquity unless we intend to revert to barbarism. The barbarian and the creature of exclusively modern civilization both live without history.

Our existence fills us with doubts and wonder, so that involuntarily we cling to our perception of human beings in themselves, to the empirical perception of humanity as we encounter it in life and as it is revealed in history. The contemplation of nature does not suffice, nor console, nor teach us enough.

Here we cannot afford to separate ourselves from the past, nor leave gaps in it unexplored, for only the whole can speak to us, in all the centuries that have left us records.

Are the three great ages of the world comparable to the ages of man in the riddle of the sphinx? It is better to think of them as a continual metempsychosis of acting and suffering humanity through all its countless outer forms. To perceive truly we need to recognise all these transformations and abandon any partisanship in favour of particular eras (though we may well have preferences as a matter of taste); we shall do so all the more readily, the greater our awareness of human limitations. As soon as we know that the blissful golden age of fantasy has never existed and never will, we are freed from the foolish tendency to over-praise some bygone age, from foolish despair of the present and from foolish hopes for the future, and can acknowledge that one of the noblest of all occupations is the study of times past, of the story of human life and human suffering as a whole.

Antiquity, however, should have a special importance for us: it gives rise to our concept of the State; it is the birthplace of our religions and of the most permanent elements of our culture. In the art and the writings of antiquity there is much that we aspire to but cannot equal. In our kinship with classical antiquity, as in our differences from it, we must endlessly be taking stock of what we owe to it.

It is perhaps enough to say that, for us, antiquity is only the first act of the human drama, and indeed, in our eyes, a tragedy complete in itself, one of incalculable efforts, transgressions and suffering. Though we are also the offspring of peoples who were still wrapped in the sleep of childhood at the time of the great civilizations of antiquity, it is from these that we feel we are truly descended, because they transmitted their soul to us, and their work, their path and their destiny live on in us.

NOTES

Introduction by Oswyn Murray

1. There is in fact an excellent general account of the contemporary culture of Basle in L. Gossman, 'Basle, Bachofen and the Critique of Modernity in the Second Half of the Nineteenth Century', *Journal of the Warburg and Courtauld Institutes* 48 (1984) pp. 136–85.

2. The standard biography of Burckhardt is that of W. Kaegi, *Jacob Burckhardt, Eine Biographie*, (Basle, 1947–82), in seven volumes. Burckhardt's letters are cited from Max Burckhardt, *Jacob Burckhardt, Briefe* (Basle, 1949–94) in eleven volumes; there is a good selection of these in *The Letters of Jacob Burckhardt*, translated by A. Dru (London, 1955); where possible I have used Dru's translation, which also contains an excellent brief discussion of his life in the introduction. The *Weltgeschichtliche Betrachtungen* (see below pp. xxii–xxiv) are cited in the edition of the Wissenschaftliche Buchgesellschaft (Darmstadt, 1962) as WB, and in the translation of MDH, *Reflections on History* (London, 1943).

3. p. 9; also 'we should maintain an attitude of reserve towards the present-day devastation of the mind by newspapers and novels': WB p. 13; *Reflections* p. 26.

4. Letter to H. Schauenburg, 28.2–5.3.1846: no. 174 (*Briefe* II p. 208); *Letters* p. 96–7.

5. Remarks quoted from Heinrich Wölfflin's diaries, cited in *Letters* p. 32; the original is not available to me, but see also on his personal relations with Burckhardt, H. Wölfflin, *Gedanken zur Kunstgeschichte* (2nd edn., 1941) pp. 135–63.

6. Letter to H. Schreiber, 2.10.1842: no. 69 (*Briefe* I p. 217); the letters of this period are full of plans for a new history: see also esp. nos. 59 and 61 (to G. Kinkel), 62 (to W. Beyschlag), and 63 (to K. Fresenius).

7. G. P. Gooch, *History and Historians in the Nineteenth Century* (2nd edn, London, 1952) p. 529; I have not been able to trace the source of this quotation.

8. *The Age of Constantine the Great*, trans. M. Hadas (London, 1949).

9. *Constantine* p. 229.

10. p. 242.

11. p. 214.

12. Quoted in Gooch op. cit. p. 532. The English translation of *The Renaissance* by S. G. C. Middlemore was first published in 1878; I have quoted from the Phaidon edition (London, 1950).

13. p. 81.

14. p. 104.

15. The idea of cultural history can be traced back to Voltaire's *Essai sur les Moeurs*. On the development of *Kulturgeschichte* and its relations to *Geistesgeschichte*, the best introduction in English is E. H. Gombrich, 'In Search of Cultural History', *Ideals and Idols* (Oxford, 1979) pp. 24–59.

16. *Letters* p. 28.

17. Letter to Bernhard Kugler, 5.10.1874: no. 653 (*Briefe* V p. 252); *Letters* p. 161.

18. *Historische Zeitschrift* 1 (1859) III–IV.

19. *Letters* p. 32.

20. See the classic work of Herbert

Butterfield, *The Whig Interpretation of History* (London, 1931).

21. The only 'complete' translation is G. W. F. Hegel, *The Philosophy of History* trans. J. Sibree (1857); on its inadequacies see Duncan Forbes' introduction to H. B. Nisbet's translation of the *Introduction to the Lectures on the Philosophy of World History* (Cambridge, 1975).

22. F. Nietzsche, *Unfashionable Observations*, trans. R. T. Gray (Stanford, 1995) p. 143.

23. See esp. A. D. Momigliano, 'New Paths of Classicism' in *Studies on Modern Scholarship* (California, 1994) pp. 223–85.

24. G. Walther, *Niebuhrs Forschung* (Frankfurt, 1993); and my chapter in *The History of the University of Oxford* vol. vi. 1 (Oxford 1997) pp. 520–42.

25. For the details of the development of the text of these lectures, and the role of Jacob Oeri, see now Peter Ganz's introduction to *Jacob Burckhardt, Über das Studium der Geschichte* (Munich, 1982). Since Ganz's edition does not offer a continuous text, I have continued to refer to the traditional German text (see above n. 2).

26. He promises to study it in the summer of 1842: letter to K. Fresenius, 10.6.1842: no. 631 (*Briefe* I p. 207).

27. Ganz p. 35f.; cf. 18f. On the general question see the lecture of E. Heftrich, *Hegel und Jacob Burckhardt* (Frankfurt, 1967).

28. *WB* p. 2; *Reflections* p. 15: derived from A. Schopenhauer, *The World as Will and Representation*, trans. E. F. J. Payne (New York, 1966) vol. II ch. xxxviii, p. 439.

29. *WB* p. 3; *Reflections* p. 17.

30. *WB* p. 20; *Reflections* p. 33.

31. See Ganz p. 23.

32. *WB* p. 180; *Reflections* p. 203. The final chapter of the traditional *WB* as published, on fortune and misfortune (or happiness and unhappiness) in history, in fact belongs originally to a separate lecture, which was later incorporated into the introduction of the series: see Ganz pp. 231–46.

33. *WB* p. 19; *Reflections* p. 32.

34. *WB* p. 20; *Reflections* p. 33.

35. The best account of the intellectual relations between Burckhardt and Nietzsche known to me is K. Löwith, *Jacob Burckhardt, Der Mensch inmitten der Geschichte* (Lucerne, 1936; Stuttgart, 1984) ch. 1; see also the polemical anti-Nazi book first published in 1940, A. von Martin, *Nietzsche und Burckhardt* (4th edition Munich, 1947); and the essay of Erich Heller, 'Burckhardt and Nietzsche', *The Disinherited Mind* (Cambridge, 1952).

36. Letter to C. von Geersdorff, 7.11.1870: no. 107 in *Nietzsche Briefwechsel*, ed. G. Colli, M. Montinari II.1 (Berlin, 1977) p. 155; also quoted in *Letters* of Burckhardt p. 23.

37. Letter to A. von Salis, 21.4.1872: no. 585 (*Briefe* V p. 158); *Letters* p. 150.

38. Letter to F. von Preen 27.9.1870: no. 554 (*Briefe* V p. 112); *Letters* p. 144.

39. The letters, which are printed in the respective collections of their authors, are conveniently gathered together in E. Salin, *Jacob Burckhardt und Nietzsche* (Basle, 1938) pp. 207–29.

40. F. Nietzsche, *Twilight of the Idols* (Harmondsworth, 1968) p. 63f.

41. Letter to L. von Pastor, 13.1.1896: no. 1598 (*Briefe* X p. 263); *Letters* p. 235.

42. F. Nietzsche, *Twilight of the Idols* p. 108.

43. There is however a clear reference to *The Birth of Tragedy* in a later version of the lectures on the study of history, where Burckhardt mentions 'the mysterious development of tragedy from the spirit of music', and the importance of Dionysus in this process. This must have been written not before the publication of the book in January 1872: see Ganz p. 289; Kaegi 6.1.119f; *WB* p. 55; *Reflections* p. 69. Nietzsche is also mentioned in a note, below p. 422 n. 122. See also Salin op. cit. pp. 96–106. I have not seen K. Joël, *Jacob Burckhardt als Geschichtsphilosoph* (Basle 1918).

44. I use the translation of R. T. Gray, *Unfashionable Observations* (Stanford, 1995); the reference to Burckhardt is on p. 103.
45. op. cit. pp. 116–8.
46. op. cit. p. 124.
47. Letter to Nietzsche 25.2.1874: no. 627 (*Briefe* V p. 222); *Letters* p. 158. Cf. 'our aim is not to train historians, let alone universal historians': *WB* p. 12; *Reflections* p. 26.
48. The German word is *Dilettantismus*: *WB* p. 16; *Reflections* p. 30.
49. A repeated phrase; e.g. to F. von Preen, 31.12.1870: no. 560 (*Briefe* V p. 120); *Letters* p. 146.
50. *Unfashionable Observations* p. 145.
51. Letter to F. von Preen, 31.12.1870: no. 560 (*Briefe* V p. 119); *Letters* p. 145.
52. Letter to Bernhard Kugler, 30.3.1870: no. 535 (*Briefe* V p. 76); *Letters* p. 136.
53. *Griechische Kulturgeschichte* I p. 5; below p. 5.
54. *WB* p. 3; *Reflections* p. 17.
55. The exact relation between the views of Burckhardt and Nietzsche on the agon is obscure, and would repay further investigation.
56. See most strongly A. W. H. Adkins, *Merit and Responsibility* (Oxford, 1962).
57. For an excellent general account of the genesis of the lectures on Greek culture, see W. Kaegi, *Jacob Burckhardt* vol. VII (Basel, 1982) ch. 1.
58. Letter to Otto Ribbeck, 10.7.1864: no. 406 (*Briefe* IV p. 155).
59. So described in a letter to Ribbeck, 16.10.1865: no. 431 (*Briefe* IV p. 197).
60. Letter to F. von Preen 3.7.1870: no. 546 (*Briefe* V p. 99); *Letters* p. 142.
61. Letter to F. von Preen 23.12.1871: no. 581 (*Briefe* V p. 150); *Letters* p. 149.
62. Letter to the publisher, E. A. Seemann 29.11.1889: no. 1283 (*Briefe* IX p. 224); these two sentences constitute the entire letter.
63. H. Gelzer, 'Jacob Burckhardt als Mensch und Lehrer', *Ausgewählte kleine Schriften* (Leipzig, 1907) p. 297.
64. The will is quoted by Ganz p. 13.
65. Wilamowitz, *Griechische Tragödie* (Berlin, 1899) vol II Vorwort, p. 7.
66. *The Complete Letters of Sigmund Freud to Wilhelm Fliess 1887–1904*, ed. and trans. by J. M. Masson (Harvard 1985) p. 342.
67. Albert Oeri, quoted by Kaegi p. 102; Albert was the son of Jacob Oeri, and compiled a plea to be used in a legal case arising from one of these attacks on his father as editor of Burckhardt.
68. *WB* p. 70; cf. p. 25; *Reflections* p. 86; cf. p. 38 (a quotation from Schlosser).
69. *WB* p. 64; *Reflections* p. 78. This passage about Greece occurs under the heading 'Culture determined by the State'; it reflects views expressed by Benjamin Constant in his famous lecture 'On the Liberty of the Ancient Greeks compared with that of the Moderns' (1819): see my essay, 'Liberty and the Ancient Greeks' in J. A. Koumoulides (ed.), *The Good Idea* (New York, 1995) pp. 33–55.
70. See the polemical work of W. Gawantka, *Die sogenannte Polis* (Stuttgart, 1985) ch. 1, arguing that Burckhardt was responsible for the invention of an illegitimate entity.
71. *WB* p. 82; cf. p. 100; *Reflections* p. 97; cf. p. 118.
72. *Griechische Kulturgeschichte* I p. 285.
73. *WB* p. 29; *Reflections* p. 42.
74. A. Schopenhauer, *The World as Will and Representation*, trans. E. F. J. Payne (New York, 1966) vol. II ch. XLVIII–IX; consistently Schopenhauer believed that modern tragedy was greatly superior to Greek tragedy: vol. I pp. 252–5, II pp. 433–8.
75. See M. S. Silk and J. P. Stern, *Nietzsche on Tragedy* (Cambridge 1981).
76. *WB* p. 33; *Reflections* p. 46.
77. Letter to Nietzsche, quoted above p. xxix.
78. *WB* p. 171; *Reflections* p. 193.
79. See my essay 'Cities of Reason' in O. Murray and S. Price (eds.), *The Greek City from Homer to Alexander* (Oxford, 1990) pp. 1–25.
80. Ganz op. cit. p. 54.
81. Letter to Emma Brenner-Kron denying that any of his lectures will

ever be published, 9.11.1866: no. 456
(*Briefe* IV p. 229).

82. I owe this information to Professor
Fritz Graf and Dr Leonhard
Burckhardt who are responsible for
the new edition. See also M. Seiber,
Studi storici 38 (1997) 91–105.

83. Cf. the remarks of H. R.
Trevor-Roper, *TLS* Oct. 8th 1982, pp.
1087–8.

84. Letter to Bernhard Kugler, 30.3.1870:
no. 535 (*Briefe* V p. 76); *Letters* p. 136.

85. *WB* p. 5; *Reflections* p. 19.

86. Letter to Heinrich von Geymüller,
6.4.1897: no. 1643 (Briefe X p. 316);
Letters p. 236.

THE GREEKS

I: Introduction

1. Later ninety hours, five hours a week.
2. *Hab' ich des Menschen Kern erst
untersucht/So weiß ich auch sein
Wollen und sein Handeln.* F. W.
Schiller, *Wallensteins Tod (The Death
of Wallenstein)*, Act II, scene 3.
3. E.g. in the Prophets, but literatures
much nearer to us in time and space
are sometimes full of difficulties.
4. Mere compilations have their own
special usefulness.
5. Mommsen, *Römische Geschichte*, V, p.
336.

II: The Greeks and their Mythology

1. Strabo 8.6.6 for the spread of the
names Hellenes, Pan-Hellenes etc.,
and for all that was known to a
greater or lesser extent as Argos and
Argives (instead of Pelasgians).
2. Outside the Greek world, however,
the name Ionians seems to have been
used as a collective one: Hebrew
Javanim – Persian *Jauna* – Egyptian
Uinin.
3. Hesiod *frag.* 296 Merkelbach-West.

4. F. Jacoby, *Fragmente der griechischen
Historiker* 1 F. 1.
5. A characteristic point is the
well-known Greek claim that even the
great names of the East stemmed
from Greek heroes – the Medes from
Medea, the Persians from Perseus, the
Achaemenids from a son of Perseus
whose name was derived from
Achaea.
6. Pausanias 8.1.2. Perhaps all the
legends of the great antiquity of the
people of Arcadia sprang only from
their very primitive condition, which
persisted until late times, so that
things which were merely
old-fashioned appeared by an optical
illusion to be really old.
7. Conon c. 47 in Jacoby, *FGH* 26 F. 1.
8. Antisthenes remarked that snails and
grasshoppers were autochthonous too:
Diogenes Laertius 6.1.
9. One of the longest and most
extraordinary lists of inventions and
origins is that of Pliny, *Natural
History* 7.57.
10. Others maintained that the
shield-grips, coat of arms and
helmet-plume were of Carian origin.
11. Apart from well-known statements by
Herodotus, see the Critias fragment,
B2 West.
12. Pausanias 10.16.1. The universal
inventor Palamedes first appears, as a
kind of afterthought, in the
post-Homeric myth, and gradually
comes to be credited with useful as
well as agreeable things: three or four
new letters of the alphabet, weights
and measures, board games, dice
etc.
13. Strabo 8.3.33.
14. This is explicit in Euripides, *Phrixos
frag.* 819 Nauck, and even in
Aeschylus, *Suppliants* 254. In
connection with the city names of
Boeotia Pausanias says the name of
the whole people is Boiotoi after
Boiotos (9.1.1.).
15. A river is called Asopos, and a
mountain Cithaeron, after two ancient
kings of Plataea who are said to have
given them their own names.

Pausanias adds his own reflection: 'I also believe that the Plataea for whom the town is named was the daughter of King Asopos and not of the River Asopos'. One of the simplest processes is that by which a town arises where a stream flows into the sea: Pausanias 9.38.6: the name of the place is Aspledon – he was the son of Poseidon and the nymph Mideia.

16. Plutarch *Moralia* 301a-c believes that it was the other way round, and that the people of myth had named rivers and springs after themselves.

17. Eudocia gives the following genealogy after Pherecydes: Poseidon was the father of Agenor who was married a) to Damno, daughter of Belus and b) to Argiope, daughter of the River Nile. The children of Damno were i) Phoenix, ii) Isaie (wife of Aegyptus) iii) Melia (wife of Danaus). The son of Argiope was Cadmus. A variant *ibid* § 950, where Kilix is the son of Phoenix.

18. Strabo 8.6. Orthos, the dog on Geryon's island of Hesperia, was the brother of Cerberus. Eudocia § 356.

19. Unfortunately the list of victors at the Olympics, regarded as chronologically reliable, was not really so, and may well have been arbitrarily put together at a late date by the sophist Hippias of Elis: Plutarch, *Numa* 1.

20. His older contemporary Heraclitus reckoned thirty-three years to a generation: Plutarch, *Moralia* 415e.

21. To say nothing of later chronologists who tried to establish synchrony between even the remotest mythical events and individual official lists, e.g. that of the priestesses of Hera at Argos.

22. Aristotle *On Marvellous Things Heard* 97 838a, in connection with traces of Heracles in Iapygia. The text also gives information about Hellenic influence in Italy in the mythical period. See too Strabo 5, Justin 20.1.2, Dionysius of Halicarnassus 1, etc. See Aeschylus, *frag.* 199 Nauck, for Heracles' traversal of the boulder-strewn landscape known as

La Crau [west of Salon de Provence] where he fought the Ligyans.

23. At Syracuse there was a beautiful garden called Mythos where King Hieron used to give audience.

24. Suetonius, *Tiberius* 70. The classic example of the well-meaning 'scientific' treatment of myth from that period is Diodorus of Sicily.

25. Cf. Westermann, *Mythographoi* – though the author himself has invented a good number of his myths.

26. Walz, *Rhetores Graeci*, Vol. 1. The examples quoted are from Nicolaus (fifth century A.D.) *ibid* for others, e.g. from Nicephoros (12th century) where similar speeches alternate with those supposedly spoken by Biblical and secular persons. There is no need to discuss here the importance of Greek myth in modern times, since the Renaissance.

27. Cf. Diodorus 4.69.

28. Cf. the old claims of the Heraclids to the western part of Sicily. Pausanias 3.16.4.

29. Plutarch, *Moralia* 826c-d.

30. Diodorus 12.45.49. On the occasions of their second invasion of Attica and the foundation of Heraclea Trachinia.

31. Plutarch *Moralia* 295a-b. This essay was composed mainly in order to link customs, costumes, ritual practices etc, which still existed, with the earliest times. The Spartan state-heralds of the family of the Talthybiads were descended from Agamemnon's herald (cf. Herodotus 7.134); on Ithaca the Koliads believed themselves descended from the divine swineherd Eumaeus, and the Bucolians claimed the cowherd Philoetius as their ancestor.

32. Herodotus 4.149. A famous case is the curse of the Alcmaeonids and its continued effects in later times.

33. Pausanias 1.28. Athens prided itself on being the oldest city in the world, Hyginus, *Fabulae* 164.

34. Cf. Isocrates, *Helen* 212–15 and *Panathenaicus* 259. And, earlier still, Euripides in *Suppliants* had mixed up

the reign of Theseus with the democracy in the strangest way.

35. Aristophanes, *Frogs* 142. A similar joke from Eupolis is in Athenaeus 1.30, naming the universal inventor Palamedes.

36. *Moralia* 558f.

37. 'The people of Troezen exalt their local monuments as highly as anyone else', Pausanias 2.30.6. He could have said the same of any other population.

38. The fact that Strabo, no great enthusiast for mythology, (10.3.23.) none the less reports locally current myths for countless places, is one more proof of the general preoccupation with them.

39. Pausanias 8.34.1f.

40. An extensive variant: Strabo 8.3.19.

41. This is how I would interpret what Strabo says, 10.2.9. A story that also belongs here is how King Cleomenes, when he wished to make the Arcadian chieftains swear an oath, summoned them to the Styx (the river by whose name the gods formerly swore their only binding oaths): Herodotus 6.74.

42. Plutarch, *Pelopidas* 16.

43. On a hill not far from Mantinea were the remains of the tent which sheltered Philip of Macedon when he rode out to win the Arcadians for himself: a spring nearby was called Philippion (Pausanias 8.7.4). The place from which the mortally wounded Epaminondas watched the battle after being carried off the field was later called Scopi.

44. However it is only weapons that are mentioned, e.g., in Plutarch's *Agesilaus* 19, the lance of Agesilaus.

45. Justin 20.1.2 (840a-b), Aristotle, *On Marvellous Things Heard* 106–10.

46. Pausanias has a list of ancient trees 8.23.3f.

47. [One of the names of the Queen of the underworld, the daughter of Poseidon and Demeter. Ed.]

48. Pausanias 8.10.4. There is a parallel story in Silius Italicus 13.115. In Epirus it was still believed much later that the snakes, living in the shrine of

Apollo there, were at least descendants of the Delphic serpent Python, Aelian, *On the Characteristics of Animals* 11.2.

49. A flood of light might be thrown on this matter if we could accept that in fairly early times the Homeric hymn to Aphrodite was composed for the court of a ruler of Ida descended from the family of Anchises and Aeneas.

50. The family tree of the Proclids from Heracles down to Lycurgus is given by Phlegon, in Jacoby, *FGH* 257 F.1.

51. Elsewhere (e.g. in Eudocia § 846) Dionysius too is brought in, on the grounds that Deianeira was his daughter, and the wife of Heracles from whom the Temenids were descended through Hyllos. This table was thus also valid for the Ptolemies, since Ptolemaus Lagi married a woman of the Temenid family.

52. Marcellinus, *Life of Thucydides* after Pherecydes.

53. According to Pausanias 1.3.1, Evagoras of Cyprus traced his descent from Teucrus and the daughter of Cinyras.

54. Cf. *Olympian Odes* VI.46, VIII.17.

55. The orator Andocides was descended from Odysseus by the marriage of Telemachus and Nausicaa, and according to Hellanicus (Plutarch, *Alcibiades* 21) the same Andocides, who was implicated in the mutilation of the herms, was, as a Keryx, descended from Hermes too (Plutarch, *Lives of Ten Orators*).

56. Ptolemy Hephaestus in Westermann's *Mythographoi*, § 183 = Photius, *Bibliotheca* 190.146b.17 ff.

57. Plutarch, *Moralia* 562e–563b.

58. Pseudo-Platonic *Axiochus* 371 d.

59. Several examples in Pausanias, e.g. that of Euthymus, 6.6.3, cf. 11. 2.

60. Among others by Speusippus, cf. Diogenes Laertius, *Life of Plato* 3.1.

61. Further east, Alexander became indifferent to his Libyan father, and on the Hydaspes he did not hesitate to boast of Heracles as his forefather since he was a Temenid: Arrian 6.3.2.

62. Plutarch, *Moralia* 182c.

63. Westermann, *Biographoi*, pp. 331–2 = *Suda* A735).
64. Herodotus 4.180: the festival procession beside the Lake of Tritonis, with a girl, dressed as Pallas, on a chariot.
65. I have collated the accounts from Polyaenus 8.59 and Plutarch, *Aratus* 32. The Mantineans declared that in their victorious battle against King Agis III (244–240 B.C.) their patron Poseidon had personally come to their aid.
66. Pausanias 9.22.6.
67. See the *Lives* of Pindar and Plutarch, *Numa* 4.
68. Herodotus 6.105, Pausanias 8.45.5.
69. Plutarch, *Moralia* 419c.
70. Plutarch, *Moralia* 543a.
71. *Life of Sophocles* 3. Plutarch, *Numa* 4. *Etymologium Magnum*.
72. Iamblichus, *Life of Pythagoras* 3, possibly from an old story.
73. Athenaeus 2.5 from Timaeus. In Tanagra they used to show a triton preserved in brine. Aelian, *Characteristics of Animals* 13.2.
74. Plutarch *Moralia* 502f.

III: *The* Polis

1. This is an inference from Herodotus, 5.69.
2. Apparent in Euripides, *Ion* 1580; also Herodotus 5.66.
3. Strabo 8.7.1 expressly differentiates between *phylai* and occupations; he says that Ion divided the population first into four *phylai* and only then into four occupations.
4. Elsewhere the expression was *kata demous*. Pausanias 8.45. 2. Cf. Aristotle, *Poetics*, 3.6.
5. Plutarch says it of the Megara region (*Moralia* 295b–c); this consisted of five communities, of which the Megarians were only one. Of the district about Tanagra *ibid.* 37.
6. The 'quadruple village' (*tetrakomia*) in Boeotia consisting of Heleon, Harma, Mycalessus and Pharae must

have been organized in common, we do not know how (Strabo 9.2.14.).
7. Diodorus 5.6.
8. Plutarch, *Moralia* 293f–294c, 297b–c.
9. The acquisition, by cunning, of a clod of earth as the claim to a whole region appears among other peoples in various forms. One example, where the later intense remorse is emphasized, in Plutarch, *Moralia* 296d–e. There is also the anecdote in *Corpus Paroemiographorum Graecorum* 1 p. 328: Aletes (the wanderer) driven out of Athens, begged a shepherd in the fields for something to eat, and the shepherd, obviously to make fun of him, gave him a clump of earth from his bag; he took it, thinking it a good omen, saying, 'Aletes accepts this piece of earth' – and it is easy to guess his secret thought.
10. In the third century B.C. the Aenianians were wiped out by the Aetolians in alliance with the Athamanians and Acarnanians, Strabo 9.4.11.
11. Herodotus 1.145, Strabo 8.7.4.
12. Strabo suggests that the people were more prosperous in the earlier period, e.g. in referring to Achaea, 8.7.5.
13. Despite all the pronouncements of Thucydides 2. 15. He emphasizes that from the earliest times, the Athenians lived in the countryside more than other Greeks.
14. Strabo 8.3.2.
15. Thucydides 3.2 f.
16. According to Diodorus 13.75 they really did make the move. Cf. Strabo 14.2.
17. Diodorus 12.34, Xenophon, *Hellenica* 5.2.12.
18. Diodorus 15.94. Cf. Pausanias 8.27.1–15, 9.14.2.
19. Strabo, 8.8.1. dates the beginning of Arcadia's barrenness from this.
20. *Myriandros polis.* As we shall see, a population of 10,000 men fit to bear arms, or of full citizens, was considered the ideal medium size for a city.
21. Strabo 13.1.59.

22. Strabo 13.1.52., in connection with the Scepsians. Strabo also notes many cases of towns displaced; formerly a town was here and now it is there. This probably mostly occurred when a better site was found, but also perhaps when a number of the citizens left because of discontent, as those of Cos did (14.2.19). If the group were strong enough they could take the name with them.
23. Cf. Jacobus de Aquis, *Imago Mundi*, in *Historiae patriae monum. scriptt* Vol. 3 Col. 1569, 1605, 1614, in part very disorganized chronologically.
24. Pausanias 9.14.2 and 10.3.2. After the battle of Leuctra, Mantinea was re-established as a city.
25. Aelian, *Varia Historia* 12.28. For Thebes, Pausanias 9.17.1, the grave of Antipoenus' daughters.
26. Iamblichus, *Life of Pythagoras* c. 9.
27. Plutarch, *Parallela Minora* 306e–f.
28. Plutarch, *Moralia* 163a–d.
29. If Pausanias Damascenus (*FGH* 854 F.10) is to be trusted.
30. Suda, *sv. Herodotus.*
31. In many cities and especially colonies the monument or at least the statue of the founder could be seen on the agora.
32. Talvj, *Serbian Folksongs* I. 78.
33. Herodotus' reference to the *theatron* in Sparta (6. 67) is to be understood as meaning a place for spectacle in general, not a theatre.
34. *Iliad* XI. 807. It was not far from the ships of Odysseus, which are said in line 5 f. to be in the middle of all the others.
35. Herodotus 4.153, which is informative in other ways too.
36. There are several statements which concur in this, including one in Lucian, *Enemies* 20, where Solon is the speaker.
37. Strabo, 14.5.19 mentions a city called Myriandros in Cilicia on the Gulf of Issicus. Perhaps it was founded with the intention that it should have 10,000 citizens.
38. Aristotle, *Politics* 2.5.
39. Much later, this attitude is seen in a

fine little essay of Lucian's, *Patriae encomium.*
40. Not always voluntarily; most early statutes include the death penalty for evading military service.
41. Aeschylus II in Page, *Epigrammata Graeca* p. 42. Cf. the words Aristophanes gives to Aeschylus, *Frogs* 1004 ff.
42. However, compare the very sensible answer Themistocles gave to a man from Seriphos who told him he owed his renown not to himself but to Athens: 'Yes indeed, but if I were a Seriphian I would not have become famous, and neither would you, if you had been an Athenian.'
43. K. F. Nägelsbach, *Nachhomerische Theologie* (1857) p. 293.
44. Opening of *Olympian* XII.
45. Pausanias 4.30.3 f.
46. Pausanias 3.11.8.
47. Herodotus 1.104.
48. Simpler peoples contented themselves with this ancient unwritten morality; e.g. the Lycians.
49. Aristotle, *Politics* 4.6.3.
50. Thucydides 6.18.7.
51. E.g. in Crete: cf. Aelian, *Varia Historia* 2.39. Yet the states of Crete were notoriously some of the most politically corrupt.
52. Herodotus 1.29.
53. 846, 1040 ff. Ion too has a harsh speech: 1334.
54. Isocrates, *Oration* 16 Chap. 26. When Phocion, about to drink the hemlock, sends his son his command not to seek revenge on the Athenians, this may not be a sign of his noble character, but of his wish to save his son from further persecution.
55. Lysias, *Oration* 13.72 (*Against Agoratus*).
56. Xenophon, *History of Greece* 2.4. 22.

IV: The General Characteristics of Greek Life

1. See above n. 43.
2. In section 3: 'Religion and Cult'.
3. There was no higher excellence than that displayed in relation to the State; this is Plutarch's meaning in his *Comparison of Aristides and Cato*, c. 3: 'It is generally agreed that men can achieve no higher perfection than political excellence.' How exactly this is to be understood becomes clear from his adding: 'Most think a very important part of this excellence is domestic virtue: for as a city is merely a collection of houses, the public virtue of the state must be increased if it contain many well-regulated households.' trs. Stewart and Long (George Bell 1906) p. 130.
4. The chief text is Plato, *Laws* 630 b ff., which also ranks these virtues in order of importance in relation to the fundamental good things of life.
5. Schopenhauer was not the first to criticize Plato's list of virtues: Menedemus did so (Plutarch, *Of Moral Virtue*, *Moralia* 440e–441b), also Ariston of Chios and King Agesilaus (Plutarch, *Anecdotes of Kings*, *Agesilaus*).
6. Compare Herodotus 1.32 with Plutarch, *Solon* 27.
7. *Iliad* IX.496 ff. A contrary example is that of a son's relentless denial of forgiveness to his father in the myth of Tennes and Cycnus. Conon (*FGH* 26) c. 28.
8. Though it is true this first occurs in Diogenes Laertius I.76. Pittacus, when he freed his son's murderer, had said that forgiveness was better than repentance.
9. Theognis 363. Cf. also 341 ff.
10. Herodotus 4.202–5.
11. Herodotus 8.105–6.
12. Lysias, *Oration* 13.4, 41–2 (*Against Agoratus*).
13. Antigone's speech to her father, Sophocles, *Oedipus at Colonus* 1189 ff.

14. Aelian, *Varia Historia* 12.49.
15. See *Rhetorica ad Alexandrum* 1.14–15 (attributed to Aristotle, probably the work of Anaximenes of Lampsacus).
16. Niobe boasted that she had more children than Leto, mother of Apollo and Artemis; these gods killed all her children, and Niobe became a rock on Mount Sipylus, running with perpetual tears.
17. Plato says (*Republic* 335 d) that the good just man should harm no-one; this is said by Socrates in the course of an extensive discussion.
18. Marcus Aurelius, 6.1: the best revenge is not to behave like him who offends you. Also 7.15: take care not to be as full of hatred for the cruel as they are to others, 7.22: we should love those who have done harm unknowingly or involuntarily, 7.26: we should ask ourselves what seems right or wrong to our enemies; then we shall be neither astonished nor angry at their offending us, only sorry for them. Besides, like them we have but a short time to live. (This in many variants.)
19. Aristophanes, *Frogs* 51.
20. Later writers are not to be unquestioningly believed when they claim that famous old historians tell lies, and even attribute these to unworthy motives. Cf. for instance in Marcellinus' *Life of Thucydides* some accusations of this kind against Herodotus, Timaeus, Philistus and Xenophon, and in the second *Life of Thucydides* against Thucydides himself.
21. Hesiod, *Works and Days* 801. Cf. 193 for how, in the real world, perjury flourished none the less.
22. The ritual is described by Plutarch in *Dion* 56.
23. Herodotus 6.68 f.
24. Pausanias 2.1.4.
25. Pausanias 5.24.2. Even the fathers, brothers and trainers of the competitors had to swear an oath over a sacrificed boar.
26. Babrius, *Fabulae* 2.

27. *Iliad* XIV.270 ff.
28. Lysias, *Oration* 12.10 ff. (*Against Eratosthenes*). See *Iliad* III.297 ff. for the curse pronounced on a man with his wife and children if he breaks his oath; this forms part of the preparations for a duel (between Paris and Menelaus) of which the gods are to decide the outcome, and which is then light-heartedly abandoned.
29. Herodotus 1.153. A variant of this is put into the mouth of Anacharsis; Diogenes Laertius 1.8.5.
30. Aristophanes, *Frogs* 101 f., probably referring to Euripides, *Hippolytus* 611.
31. *Pro Flacco*, especially 4 (9–10), 5 (11–12)
32. Polybius 6.56.
33. In connection with the campaign of L. Verus against the Parthians in 162 A.D.
34. Cf. especially Polyaenus 1.23.2, 1.39.4, 1.42.1, 1.45.1 and 4 (Lysander), 2.6, 2.19, 3.2, 3.9.40, 4.2 (Philip of Macedon), 4.6.1, 6.19 and 20, 7.23.2 etc.
35. In the speech of the Athenian ambassadors to Sparta 1.76.2.
36. Isocrates, *On the Antidosis* 217. See Diotima's speech in Plato, *Symposium*, 208 c. ff.
37. Plutarch, *On Busybodies*, *Moralia* 518a–c. Socrates, too, rather differently, cf. Xenophon, *Memorabilia* 3.9.8.
38. *Odyssey* IX.473, 501, 522.
39. Plutarch, *Pericles* 33. Cf. Pausanias 10.38.1–2 on the misfortune of belonging to a people whose name could sound ridiculous, à propos the Ozolian Locrians.
40. Lucian, *Dialogue of Prostitutes* 9.4.
41. Diogenes Laertius 1.91–2
42. Lucian, *Piscator* 25.
43. In the first *Bios* of Aristophanes, Westermann, *Biographoi* p. 155.
44. Like the famous Hyperbolus, Plutarch, *Alcibiades* 13.
45. *Knights* 128 ff.
46. The laws of Thurii, founded in 442 B.C., allowed comedy to make fun

only of adulterers and intriguers (*polupragmones*); probably the idea of exposing the adulterers to scorn was to safeguard legitimate birth among the citizens of the colony, which was as yet only loosely organized.
47. Pseudo-Xenophon, *Constitution of the Athenians* 2.18.
48. The testimony of Aelian (*Varia Historia* 2.13) runs counter to this. Reading *Clouds* 226, 247, 367 ff, 397 ff, 423, 830, and the whole last part of the play, we may ask how Aristophanes could possibly have done more, or done it more deliberately, to ensure that Socrates would come under suspicion of *asebeia*.
49. Plato is explicit on this, *Apology* 18–19.
50. Athenaeus 12.77.
51. Euripides, *Hippolytus* 998.
52. Aelian, *Varia Historia* 5.8.
53. Athenaeus 10.17.
54. Plutarch, *Timoleon* 32: 'words are more hurtful than deeds'.
55. Euripides, *Medea* 797, 1049, 1355, 1362.
56. Diogenes Laertius 2.21.
57. Plutarch, *On Flatterers* 32, gives other examples of such social vulnerability.
58. Plato, *Apology* 33 c.
59. Diogenes Laertius 6.88–9.
60. If Aeschines is to be believed, there was one case of fatal mutilation which was the result of courtroom speeches, *Against Timarchus* 172.
61. Lysias, *Oration* 10.2, *Against Theomnestes*.
62. Schopenhauer, *Parerga* Vol. 1, p. 399.
63. Musonius' important analysis, quoted by Schopenhauer, is in Stobaeus, in the collection *Peri anesikakias*, 3.19.16 (vol. 3 W-H). However Musonius was a later Stoic who lived at the beginning of the Empire.
64. Plutarch, *Themistocles* 11.
65. Alcibiades is said to have avenged himself on the poet Eupolis by having him thrown into the sea.
66. *Demosthenes vita quarta* in

Westermann, *Biographoi* § 305 f. – Demosthenes is supposed to have accepted 3,000 drachmae from Meidias, *ibid.* quoted from the *Suda.*

67. Compare e.g. the case of Demades.
68. Thucydides 3.37 ff.
69. Diodorus 12.12, 16–17, 20–21.
70. Diels-Kranz, *Fragmente der Vorsokratiker* B179.
71. Theognis 529. He himself had reason to complain of treacherous friends, cf. 575.
72. *Odyssey* III.380.
73. *Iliad* IX.713 and passim.
74. *Odyssey* XV.407. Cf. Penelope's wish, *Odyssey* XVIII.202.
75. Solon *frag.* 13 West. A more materialistic definition of *olbos* in *frag.* 23 West: *olbios* is one who has beloved sons, horses, hounds and a hospitable friend elsewhere. Cf. Herodotus 1.32, the distinction between *olbios* and the mere *eutuches* who has enjoyed superficial good fortune.
76. Euripides *Antiope, frag.* 198 Nauck.
77. So also in *Isthmian* V.16.
78. Cf. the beautiful passage on justice in Schopenhauer, *Die Welt als Wille und Vorstellung* 2.694.
79. Aristotle, *Eudemian Ethics* 1.1 and *Nicomachean Ethics* 1.8.
80. Sophocles, *frag.* 329 Nauck (*Creusa*).
81. In both the *Ethics* of Aristotle.
82. From a more idealistic viewpoint it was of course argued that fame could be dispensed with, Plutarch, *Agis* 2.
83. 'Health, most revered of the blessed ones among mortals, may I dwell with you for what is left of my life, and may you graciously keep company with me: for any joy in wealth or in children or in a king's godlike rule over men or in the desires which we hunt with the hidden nets of Aphrodite, any other delight or respite from toils that has been revealed by the gods to men, with you, blessed Health, it flourishes and shines in the converse of the Graces: and without you no

man is happy': Ariphron, Page *PMG frag.* 813.
84. Anaxandridas in Athenaeus 15.50.
85. In Lucian, *de lapsu in salutando*, c. 6.
86. The finest praise of it is in Solon's great elegy, *frag.* 13.7 ff. West.
87. Very emphatic at lines 173, 181: 'better dead than poor'.
88. Euripides *frag.* 326 Nauck, lines 173, 181: cf. *frag.* 327.
89. Euripides *frag.* 328 Nauck.
90. Athenaeus 2.12.
91. This consolation by reference to the insecurity and instability of wealth is of older date. Cf. Solon, *frag* 15 West. Theognis line 317 (very similarly expressed).
92. Bacchylides *frag.* 11 Snell-Maehler.
93. *Laws* 631 B ff., 661 A ff.
94. *Phaedrus* 248 d ff., referring to the uninhabited souls which are to embark on a new life.
95. Athenaeus 12.6.
96. Diogenes *Laertius* 2.136.
97. Aristotle, *Politics* 7.1.
98. Plutarch, *Moralia* 5C–6A.
99. Lucian, *The Ship*, especially c. 41 ff.
100. Aristotle, *Rhetoric* 1.6.
101. Hesiod, *Works and Days* 160.
102. Cf. Hesiod, in Pausanias 9.36.4.
103. Hyginus gives the first fully detailed account of the curse of the Atredae in all its ramifications, beginning with Pelops: Hyginus, *Fabulae* 84–8, 98, 117, 119, 120–3.
104. Apollodorus 3.15.8. Cf. the fate of Palamedes.
105. Hyginus, *Fabulae* 238–48.
106. *Iliad* XIX.274. For what follows cf. XVI.646, 788 ff., 848.
107. Euripides, *Orestes* 1639ff.
108. *Iliad* XVI.143.
109. Ptolemy Hephaestion 4. The variant has Iphigenea as a goddess on Leuce with Achilles, Antoninus Liberalis 27.
110. Simonides *frag.* 523 Page.
111. He is the enemy of all evil beings, *misoponeros.*
112. Augeas, too, refuses Heracles his due reward on the grounds that his famous task was not performed by physical exertion but by means of an

ingenious device (*sophia*); Pausanias 5.1.7.

113. *Odyssey* XI.121 in the words of Teresias.

114. Cf. the extracts from the *Telegonia*, Kinkel pp. 57f. Plutarch, *Moralia* 294 C-D; Hyginus, *Fabulae* 127; Parthenius 3; Ptolemy Hephaestion 4.

115. Diodorus 5.59 and Apollodorus 3.2.

116. Sophocles, *Oedipus at Colonus* 1399, the speech of Polynices.

117. *Iliad* VI.447.

118. The words of Apollo, *Iliad* XXIV.49.

119. Apollo to Poseidon, *Iliad* XXI.462.

120. *Iliad* XVII.446.

121. The horses have the power of speech, *Iliad* XIX.404 ff.

122. *Iliad* XXIV.527.

123. Pindar, *Pythian* III.81.

124. *Odyssey* VII.196.

125. *Homeric Hymn to Apollo* 186 ff.

126. Euripides, *Hippolytus* 45.

127. Thus in Athenaeus, 6.94–6 from comic poets.

128. *Works and Days* 106 ff., esp. 173 ff.

129. The Greek fantasies about the Hyperboreans are a sufficient example.

130. *Odyssey* II.97. Was it, in the earliest version of the legend, to be her bridal robe for a second marriage?

131. Pindar, *Olympian Odes* II.

132. Diogenes Laertius 7.6.

133. *Odyssey* VIII.578. Euripides gives the same words to the grief-stricken Hecuba, which is simply absurd; *Troades* 1243.

134. *Homeric Hymn to Hermes* 37. [The tortoise's shell was to be made into a lyre.]

135. Whole collections of statements on these matters are to be found in the *Anthology* of Johannes Stobaeus. The main chapter, *On Life*, concerning the brevity, triviality and heavy cares of life is chapter 34, book 4 (in vol.5 of W-H). The other relevant sections are: on unhappiness (4.40), on the insecurity of wellbeing (4.41), praise and complaint of age (4.50a-b), on death (4.51), praise and complaint of death (4.52), comparison of life and death (4.63), and finally a chapter of

consolation, *Paregorika* (4.56). Cf. Plutarch, *Consolation to Apollonius*, passim; and, among the *Consolations* of Seneca, especially that addressed to Marcia.

136. In Plutarch, *Solon 7*, there is a parenthetical polemic against the deliberate abandonment of intellectual possessions, occurring as an argument of Plutarch's own. This kind of renunciation may be connected not only with loss of hope for the future but also with the habit of trying to foresee that future.

137. Plutarch, *Moralia* 477c-f.

138. *Anthologia Graeca* 10.123.

139. Xenophon, *Memorabilia* 1.4.9 ff., 4.3.1 ff.

140. Aelian, *Varia Historia* 14.6.

141. Aeschylus, *Prometheus* 248 ff. To my knowledge, only Theognis, 1143 ff., seriously warns against a cult of hope – 'hopes which lead states into misfortune', Euripides, *Suppliants* 479.

142. Cf. e.g. Theognis 761 ff., 983 ff.

143. *Zethi* is a word which consists of the seventh to tenth letters of the Greek alphabet. Cf. the pun, *Anthologia Graeca* 10.43.

144. Athenaeus 9.9 from the *Tarentines* of Alexis.

145. *Suda*, in Westermann, *Biographoi* § 172.

146. Herodotus 2.78.

147. Sophocles, *Oedipus Rex*, 965 ff., spoken by Jocasta.

148. Euripides, *frag.* 34 Nauck (*Aiolos*). Euripides gives Theseus a long optimistic tirade in *Suppliants* 195 ff., but makes him speak quite differently at 549 ff.

149. The probably Hellenistic myth of the *Cura* in Hyginus, *Fabulae* 120.

150. Apuleius is the first to stress something of this, *On the god of Socrates* 4.3: Human beings live on the earth ... 'with fickle and agitated minds, crude and vulnerable bodies ... in wilful audacity, obstinate hope, vain labour, fragile fortune ... swift in passing, slow in wisdom, a life of complaints'.

151. Herodotus 3.40.
152. The great exception, very hard to interpret, is the creation of the first four generations of men by the gods, including Zeus.
153. Euripides, *frag.* 293 Nauck (*Bellerophon*).
154. *Odyssey* II. 276.
155. Diogenes Laertius 1.87.
156. Quoted by Plutarch, *Moralia* 481 f-482c.
157. *Aidos kai Nemesis, Works and Days* 196 ff.
158. *Medea* 439.
159. *Phainomena* 96–136.
160. *Metamorphoses* I.149. Virgil's renewed hope in Eclogue IV: *Iam redit et Virgo* etc. Marcus Manilius in the reign of Tiberius again takes a very sombre view, *Astronomica* II.592 ff.
161. Timon was alone in his 'insight' that shunning the rest of mankind was the only way to be happy. Pausanias 1.30.4.
162. In Stobaeus, 4.34.65.
163. In the pseudo-Platonic dialogue *Axiochus*, 366 a.
164. Sophocles, *frag.* 376 Nauck.
165. *Iliad* X. 70.
166. V. 42 ff. Cf. *Theogony* 569 ff, 591.
167. Stobaeus, 4.34.57.
168. *Axiochus*, 366 to 368. Cf. also the fragment of Teles in Stobaeus, 4.34.72.
169. Solon *frag.* 14 West.
170. Cf. e.g. the quotations in Stobaeus, 4.34. Even Alcidamas, a pupil of Gorgias, had composed a 'praise of death', a catalogue of the ills of human life. Cicero, *Tusculan Disputations* 1.48.
171. Stobaeus, 4.34.60.
172. Simonides *frag.* 520 Page. What survives of Pindar's threnodies contains nothing resembling this, but images of the heroic existence in bliss, and thoughts on metempsychosis.
173. Pindar, *Pythian* VIII. 95.
174. *Isthmian* VII.13.
175. Sophocles *frag.* 12 Nauck.
176. *Oedipus at Colonus* 1211.
177. Euripides, *frags.* 285, 491, 908 Nauck.
178. *Homeri et Hesiodi certamen* c. 6.
179. Cf. Eustathius' *Life of Pindar* in Westermann, *Biographoi* § 93. The same request was made at Delphi.
180. Thucydides 2.38.
181. Hyperides, *Funeral Speech* 43.
182. Stobaeus 4.50 (V.5 W-H).
183. Plutarch, *Moralia* 392a-e.
184. Aristotle, *Rhetoric* 2.14.
185. Aelian, *Varia Historia* 7.20.
186. *Ibid.* 11.4.
187. Mimnermus, *frag.* 2 West.
188. Semonides, *frag.* 1 West.
189. Euripides, *frag.* 332 Nauck.
190. Lucian, *On Mourning* 15–19.
191. Euripides, *Suppliants* 1108, the tirade of Iphis, which is also an important document of pessimism.
192. Aristotle, *Rhetoric* 2.12.13.
193. Eudocia 920. Cf. Aristophanes, *Clouds* 998.
194. Sophocles, *frag.* 863 Nauck.
195. Euripides, *frag.* 25 Nauck.
196. *Homeric Hymn to Aphrodite* 245.
197. Aelian, *Varia Historia* 2.34. Epicharmus died in his nineties.
198. Valerius Maximus 8.13.2.
199. Diogenes Laertius 1.26. Cf. Plutarch *Solon* 6.
200. Diels-Kranz B277. In Euripides one character argues against adoption, frag. 491 Nauck.
201. Cf. Hermann, *Privatalterhümer* § 11.
202. Hesiod describes rural customs (*Works and Days*, 374) which can be judged by each reader for himself.
203. Aelian, *Varia Historia* 2.7.
204. This is not intended to mean the lowest bidder.
205. Plutarch, *Commentary on Hesiod* frag. 69.
206. Cf. however the remarks of Polybius, 36.17, on the increasing numbers of people who had no relatives and no children.
207. Plutarch, *Moralia* 997c. Cf. impoverished Roman citizens as early as the time of the Gracchi, Plutarch, *Tiberius Gracchus* 8.
208. It is recorded of the ancient Persians that they refused to see their

children till they reached the age of seven.

209. Semonides, *frag.* 2 West.
210. Heraclides of Pontus mistakenly has 'Cos'.
211. Euripides, *frag.* 791 Nauck.
212. Plutarch, *Moralia* 254b-f. – Cf. Parthenius c. 9. We have not followed Plutarch precisely here.
213. Further information on the Thracians is given by Pomponius Mela, 2.2.
214. Strabo 11. 520.
215. Cicero, *Tusculan Disputations* I.39: 'When a little boy dies, they bear it calmly; a baby's death is not even mourned'. On the worthlessness and pain of existence, among others, Pliny, *Natural History* 7.41–4 (the fortunes of Sulla), 46 (the fortunes of Augustus), 51 the most important passages, 54 *mortes repentinae, hoc est: summa vitae felicitas*, 56 pointlessness of survival after death.
216. Babrius, *Fabulae* 25.
217. Stobaeus 4.34.65.
218. *Anthologia Graeca* 7. 339.
219. Quoted as early as Plato's *Gorgias*, 492 e. Cf. the Euripidean fragments s.v. *Polyidus* (634–46) and *Phrixus*, (819–38 Nauck).
220. Cf. also Euripides *frag.* 816 Nauck.
221. Nägelsbach, *Nachhomerische Theologie*, p. 394.
222. Hermann *Privatalterhümer* § 61.25 f.
223. Strabo 10.5.4–6. Heraclides Pontus (speaking of Cos, a mistake for Chios as already mentioned), Aelian, *Varia Historia* 3.37, Plutarch, *Moralia* 244d-e, Valerius Maximus 2.1.
224. Similar stories were believed of the Hyperboreans (Pomponius Mela 3. 5, evidently from an old source). They were said to throw themselves, garlanded, from a cliff into the sea.
225. *Odyssey* X.50. Elsewhere he asks about those who have 'stood the test' of suffering, *Odyssey* XIX.344. The exclamation 'endure!' in Theognis 1029 is impressive.
226. Aelian, *Varia Historia* 4.223.
227. *Phaedo* 68 a.
228. Eudocia 589. Cato was reading

Phaedo before he killed himself, Dio Cassius 63.11.
229. Plutarch, *Moralia* 249b-d.
230. Principal sources are Strabo 10.2.8–9 and Ptolemy Hephaestion 7 (in Westermann, *Mythographoi*).
231. There are numerous cases in myth of people dying voluntarily to save their native place because a god has spoken; they belong to quite another set of attitudes and are praised as great and genuine sacrifices. Besides, these were usually youths and maidens who probably still loved life.
232. *Republic* 407 d.
233. Quoted by Plutarch, *Consolation to Apollonius* 15 (*Moralia* 109F). From Roman times there are particularly striking passages in Pliny, *Letters* 1.12 and 22.
234. Cf. Euripides, *frag.* 816 Nauck, for the expectation that those who had gone blind would commit suicide.
235. Euripides, *frag.* 245 Nauck.
236. Plutarch, *Moralia* 244b-e. Pausanias 10.1.3. It is this *aponoia* that is notably lacking in the besieged Athenians after the battle of Aegospotami.
237. Diodorus 12.29.
238. *Ibid.* 18.22.
239. Polybius 16.29–34, Livy 31.17. Later events of the same kind are the self-immolation of the Xanthians when Brutus attacked them, Dio Cassius 47.34, and especially Plutarch, *Brutus* 31, which also refers to the earlier similar action of the Xanthians when they were at war with the Persians.
240. Diodorus 20.21. Polyaenus 7.
241. Strabo 14.5.6–7.
242. Dio Cassius 37.13.
243. Plutarch, *Antony* 71.
244. Aelian, *Varia Historia* 13.36.
245. Euripides, *Helen* 297.
246. Plutarch, *Moralia* 251a-253f. The whole anecdote is characteristic of these times.
247. Sophocles, *frag.* 866 Nauck.
248. For instance the watchman in *Antigone* 439.

249. Diodorus 20.34.
250. Plutarch, *Cleomenes* 31. Cf. 29 and 37.
251. Plutarch, *Aemilius* 34.
252. Polybius 30.7.8.
253. Polybius 40.3.
254. Cf. Euxitheos in Athenaeus 4.45.
255. Xenophon, *Apology*, especially 9, 14, 23. Plato *Crito* 45–46a.
256. Diogenes Laertius 6.18–19.
257. Though Aelian gives a contradictory account, *Varia Historia* 8.14. Metrocles strangled himself at an advanced age, Diogenes Laertius 6.95.
258. Diogenes Laertius 2.143–4.
259. According to the *Suda*, Zeno starved himself slowly by eating less and less each day, Westermann, *Biographoi* § 421.
260. Seneca, *De providentia* c.6, forcefully recommends suicide to his readers.
261. *Meditations*, 9.3. Cf. 10.8.
262. *Ibid.* 5.29.
263. *Suda* in Westermann, *Biographoi*, § 361.
264. *Ibid.* § 349.
265. Cf. Pausanias 6.8.3 the self-immolation of the athlete Timanthes.
266. Cf. among others Pausanias 8.2.2.

GREEK CIVILIZATION

I: *Introductory Remarks*

1. Adamantius Judaeus, *Physiognomica* 2.32, in R. Foerster [ed.], *Scriptores physiognomici Graeci et Latini*, vol. 1, Leipzig 1893. Cf. C. O. Müller, *Handbuch der Archäologie der Kunst*, Breslau 1830, p. 328 ff. Translation: J. Leitch, trans., *Ancient Art and its Remains*, London 1847, p. 333.
2. e.g. Lucian, *Imagines* 2.17, according to which it was Smyrna that had the most beautiful women of Ionia.
3. How old is the source for Aelian's description (*Varia Historia* 12.1) of the younger Aspasia, the mistress of Cyrus the Younger and of Artaxerxes Mnemon? Or is it Aelian's own?
4. Cicero, *On the Nature of the Gods* 1.28.79. Cf. also Dio Chrysostom, *Melancomas or of Beauty*, using the statues at Olympia as the criterion for the decline of masculine beauty; where beauty occurs it is said to go unappreciated or to be abused, and this leads to a discussion of barbarian attitudes to beauty.
5. Aristotle, *Rhetoric* 1.5.5. Ibid 6 of the qualities that make for attractiveness. He makes it clear that a certain stature is necessary for female beauty too. On the more rapid decay of women's beauty cf. Euripides, *frag.* 24 Nauck.
6. Compare e.g. Plato, *Republic* 474 d-e, where he speaks of lovers admiring various types of beauty.
7. Herodotus 6.61.
8. *Ibid.* 5.47.
9. *Ibid.* 9.25.
10. *Ibid.* 7.187.
11. Euripides, *frag.* 15 Nauck.
12. Some remarks on physiognomics, probably after Aristotle, are found in Antigonus 114.
13. Athenaeus 5.62. For the appearance of the Greek compared with the barbarian cf. Lucian, *Scytha* 3. The Greek differed principally in being clean-shaven.
14. *Iliad* X.79.
15. For complaints of old age see p. 117 above.
16. *Iliad* X.572 ff., XI.621 ff.
17. On the connection between physical health and beauty on one hand and the murder and exposure of weak and deformed children on the other, cf. Hellwald, *Kulturgeschichte* (below ch.II n. 1) p. 276.
18. For what life could be like for someone with a withered leg, see Plutarch, *Agesilaus* 1f.
19. Cf. Hermann, *Privatalterthümer* pp. 155–61.
20. The lack of surnames may sometimes have been felt, as we see from the use of names formed from the same root for a father and several sons. In

Lysias 17.3 a certain Eraton has sons called Erasiphon, Eraton and Erasistratos.

21. If the Greeks had formerly worshipped nameless gods, they made up for it handsomely later.

22. *Theogony* 243 ff. Some of these are simple, some beautiful compounds. Homer's catalogue of Nereids, apparently the earlier, differs from it. In this rich invention of names the various epic poets need not be supposed to have been unanimous.

23. *Theogony* 349 ff. Among these are famous names such as Dione, Metis, Calypso, Tyche, and Styx – 'the grandest of all'.

24. Welcker, *Die Komposition der polygnotischen Gemälde in der Lesche zu Delphi, Abhandlungen der Berliner Akademie* 1847, p. 116.

25. Herodotus 1.139. This presumably means there was a second name-giving, perhaps at the time of the ceremony of attaining manhood.

26. Artemidorus explains the predictive meaning of the names of those who appear in dreams (3.38).

27. Simple forms too are often beautiful. We learn from Lucian, *The Dream* 14, that the full derivative was considered more aristocratic than the root-form or the abbreviation; Simon, who has become rich, is addressed as Simon by Micyllus the cobbler and indignantly insists on being called Simonides. On names derived from those of gods, cf. Lucian, *Imagines* 27. There is an attempt to classify names by their meanings in Athenaeus 10.69.

28. Plutarch, *Themistocles* 32, *Cimon* 16.

29. Plutarch, *Dion* 6, Pausanias 6.12.2, Justinian 7.6.

30. Ptolemy Hephaestion knows of fourteen others besides the great Achilles (6).

31. Lysias, *Fragmenta*, in T. Thalheim, [ed.], *Lysiae Orationes*, 2nd edition, p. 354 lines 11f.

32. Cf. Hermann, *Privatalterthümer* pp. 56–9.

33. According to Strabo 7.3.13, § 304. Lucian, *Timon* 22 cites as common

slave-names Pyrrhios, Dromon, Tibios. A list of authentic names of Phrygian flautists is given by Athenaeus, 14.18.

34. Polyaenus (8.50) knows girls called Panariste, Mania and Gethosyne at the Seleucid court. The name Mania which also occurs elsewhere in Asia Minor (*ibid* 54) may be cognate with Manes, and is found in Aristophanes' *Thesmophoriazusae*.

35. Pausanias 6.10.2, 6.21.6, 8.25.5.

36. Tzetzes, *Lycophron* 344.

37. Eudocia 356.

38. Julius Pollux 5.47, following Aeschylus.

39. *Anth. Pal.* 7.304 (Pisander).

41. Strabo lists them, 9.5.19.

42. For the names of streams, with their often charming interpretations, cf. L. Preller, *Griechische Mythologie*, Leipzig 1854, Vol. I, p. 343.

II: The Heroic Age

1. [Friedrich von Hellwald, *Culturgeschichte in ihrer natürlichen Entwicklung bis zur Gegenwart*, p. 277. I am unable to find this actual form of words; Burckhardt is paraphrasing Ed.]

2. Hellwald offers as an example of primitive conditions (p. 236) the fact that salt was little known in Homer's time, and only in the form of sea-salt. It does not occur to him that Homer has another kind, since called 'Attic salt', beside which later civilizations tend to seem coarse and insipid.

3. This inspired the elaboration of the figure of Palamedes, who was supposed to have invented writing, arithmetic, measures, weights, board games, dice, music, money and signalling with fires, as well as the art of war (Alcidamas *Odysseus* 22). Cf. also Gorgias, *Defence of Palamedes* 30. According to Alcidamas, Odysseus then restored these inventions to other Greeks and foreign nations, and

left Palamedes those that were harmful and despised.

4. None the less it was a great moment when Schliemann uncovered the skeletons of twelve men, three women and, probably, two children in the Acropolis of Mycenae, and very comical to see the confusion of our modern scholars when these remains of real human beings from mythical times came to light. One school of thought argued that the graves were those of Mycenaean aristocrats dating from the siege [by Argos] of 468; that the gold was put in because otherwise the Argives would have seized it from the vanquished as they fled; that the Mycenaeans had looted the gold from the Persians, who had also no doubt brought a quantity of gold masks with them [when they invaded Greece] to cover the faces of their dead nobles who fell in battle. Others came to the conclusion that in the third century A.D. some barbarians of mysterious origin must have come to live at Mycenae and buried their leaders there as magnificently as possible. People are led into such absurdities by the fear of facing a simple truth. We no longer seek to know exactly who was buried there, but it was amusing that the nations should tremble for fear of the real Agamemnon rediscovered.

5. On the history of Thebes, with its many superimposed layers, cf. Diodorus 15.79 and 19.53.

6. Cf. the detailed explanation of why nothing is left of the defences of the Greek camp, *Iliad* XII. 3 ff. Later, people wondered at the smallness of the heroes' states in Homer. Cf. Isocrates, *Philip* 145.

7. On the cult of Apollo, cf. Preller, (p. 382 above, n. 42) 1. 161 and 2.54. On the Letoon near Xanthe, Strabo 14.665.

8. The Pamphylians, according to Herodotus (7.91), were descended from the men of mixed race who followed Calchas and Amphilochus

there from Troy. This migration must have occurred as part of the Doric one, and have been retrospectively assigned to heroic times, which were hardly separate from the *nostoi* in Greek consciousness. So too Salamis in Cyprus was founded by Teucrus, Olbe in Cilicia by his brother Ajax, Paphos in Cyprus by Agapenor, one of Helen's suitors and leader of the Arcadians at Troy. In Cilicia the chief connection comes about through Amphilochus. Tarsus is supposed to have been founded by Argives, who went with Triptolemus in search of Io. Strabo 14.5.12.

9. According to one story, in Eudocia 436, when Heracles, unarmed, was on the coast of Gaul, he was ambushed by the head of the Ligurian clan, and Zeus helped him by raining down from a cloud the stones which cover the plain of La Crau. A variant gives a location nearer home for the distant journeys: the Geryon whom Eurystheus sent Heracles to fight, lived not in Iberia but only Ambracia, and it was from there he fetched the cattle: Eustathius, *Commentarium in Dionysii periegetae orbis descriptionem*, in K. Müller [ed.], *Geographi Graeci Minores*, Paris 1861, vol. 2, § 558.

10. Livy 1.1, Mela 2.4.2.

11. Strabo 13.1.53 gives his whole route, via Egesta in Sicily, the Eryx and Lilybaeum, with his companion the Trojan Elymus.

12. On these, cf. Thucydides 6.2. A strange legend of the ancestry of Egestes, who founded Egesta, Eryx and Entella, is given by Tzetzes, *Lycophron* 471.

13. Strabo 5.1.9, Antoninus Liberalis 37.

14. Conon, *FGH* 26 F. 1, c.3.

15. Strabo books 5 and 6 passim.

16. Hesiod, *Theogony* 274 ff., 517 ff.

17. Hesiod, *Works and Days* 171. Pindar, *Olympian* II.77–79. Pindar thinks it inadvisable to venture westward from Cadiz: *Nemean* IV.69; cf. III.20–1.

18. For the probable earliest versions and subsequent filling out of the legends

of Heracles, Perseus, and the
Argonauts, until the whole later story
of Medea was attached to them, we
refer the reader to Preller's *Mythologie*
(p. 382 above, n. 42.)

19. We will make no attempt to deal with
the external life of the heroic period.
For its customs in eating, drinking,
and behaviour, cf. digressions in
Athenaeus 1.15 f., 44 f.

20. Both Glaucus and Achilles are sent to
war by their fathers with this
admonition, *Iliad* VI.208; XI.784.

21. *Personne ne se respecte* (there is no
false pride) would be a way of
describing this absence of posing.

22. The fear of blood guilt survived into
late times, especially when it was
expedient to threaten people with this
fear, as the Alcmaeonids were
threatened after betraying Cylon and
his adherents.

23. Pausanias 1.37.3 and 43.7. Pausanias
also gives a detailed account of
katharsis in telling of the purification
of Orestes by the Troezenians (2.31.11).

24. Zeus knows, though, that Achilles will
not kill Priam; as he is neither a fool
nor a criminal he will be kind and
spare the suppliant (XXIV.157 f.).

25. See for example how his nobility of
character early reveals itself (*Iliad*
I.334) in his reception of the
trembling heralds.

26. Apollodorus 2.6.4.

27. Solon obviously intended to improve
racial breeding by his prohibition of
dowries. Evidently it seemed to him
doubly desirable, in a city of
commerce and industry, to discourage
marrying for money.

28. Hesiod *frag.* 252 Merkelbach-West.
Xenophon gives a list of his pupils in
On Hunting 1. Theseus too had a
tutor, Connidas, Plutarch, *Theseus* 4.

29. Diomedes knows the gods and sees
them in their true likeness. Athena
herself leads him on to wound Ares
and Aphrodite.

30. Success is not worshipped until the
time of modern poetry.

31. *Iliad* IV.450–1, repeated in VIII.64–5.

32. *Iliad* VII.161 and VIII.261 list a group

of nine heroes, slightly varying their
names, who seem to represent a kind
of supreme aristocracy.

33. *Iliad* VII.87 f., X.212 f., XIII.326 f.

34. In *Iliad* VIII.164, Hector says to
Diomedes: 'Off with you, wretched
puppet', and in line 527 he calls the
Greeks 'Dogs dragged here to their
ruin by the Keres (Spirits of Death)'.
In this book even the gods abuse each
other in the same way. Iris, bringing
the angry message of Zeus to Athena,
adds of her own accord (line 423)
'You fearful shameless bitch'.

35. *Iliad* XVII.745–6. Cf the mockery of
Idomeneus, XIII.374–82.

36. *Iliad* III.58–75. This 'I am that I am'
is typically Greek.

37. *Odyssey* XX.59. In the *Helen* of
Euripides, 947–53, on the other hand,
Menelaus reserves the right to weep
but considers it nobler to refrain. An
exception to all rules is the grief of
Achilles at the news of Patroclus'
death, *Iliad* XVIII.22–34. Here, grief is
expressed symbolically and, for a long
time, in silence. The conversations
between Achilles, his mother and the
Myrmidons come later. At the death
of Patroclus, Achilles' horses weep
too, XVII.426 ff.

38. *Odyssey* IV.100–3, 190–5, 212–17. In
the recognition scene between
Odysseus and Telemachus, XVI.213–
24, night would have fallen while they
were still weeping together, had not
the son asked his father what ship
had brought him home.

39. *Odyssey* XI.355–61. Speaking to
Penelope before she recognizes him,
he repeats, in his invented story
(XIX.269–95), and with emphasis,
that Odysseus, while with the
Thesprotians, has asked for and been
given enough treasure to last him and
his heirs till the tenth generation; she
is informed that he does not come
empty-handed, but bringing enough
to replace what the suitors have
plundered.

40. For instance *Iliad* IX.312, where
Achilles is speaking.

41. For the bathing of heroes by kings' daughters, see Athenaeus 1.18.

42. Pausanias 1.35.3 ff., 6.5.1.

43. The character of Nauplius is described by Alcidamas, *Odysseus* 13 ff.: 'Only a poor fisherman, he has caused the disappearance of many Greeks, stolen much treasure from the ships, done endless harm to sailors and is a perfect scoundrel.'

44. Cf. *Odyssey* IV.628 ff. Antinous has 'beautiful feet' (XVII.410), and Odysseus himself tells him: 'You are like a god.' Similarly Odysseus distinguishes between the uncivil speech of Euryalus and his splendid appearance VII.176 ff.

45. Cf. also the detailed description of the life of the ruler, in the speech of Sarpedon to Glaucus, *Iliad* XII.310–28, explaining the relation between his wealth and his duty as hero and prince. When the life of luxury is to be described, the tone used even in later times is still mythical, as we learn from the paean of Bacchylides, *frag.* 4.61 ff. Snell-Maehler.

46. On the subject of *olbos* see p. 81 above.

47. Details of these, with the correct procedures, in Athenaeus 1 and 5.

48. *Odyssey* II.341 ff. and IX.196 ff. Cf also the comfort of Nestor's tent, *Iliad* XIV.5 ff., where Machaon is invited to sit and drink the sparkling wine, until Hecamede with the curly hair has heated the water for his bath and washed off the bloodstains.

49. Cf. *Odyssey* IX.5 ff.

50. In Hesiod, *frag.* 1 the gods appear to all the heroes and mingle freely with them.

51. On the Phaeacians cf. especially *Odyssey* VI.203 ff., VIII.241 ff., VIII.117 ff., 84 ff., VI.305 ff., VII.34 ff., VIII.557 ff., XII.113 ff. (where the ship vanishes after Odysseus is marooned).

52. *Odyssey* XV.407 ff.

53. cf. *Odyssey* VII.237 ff., VIII.28 ff., 548 ff., IX.19.

54. See above note 12.

55. Philostratus, *Imagines* 2.15.

56. Tzetzes, *Lycophron* 93 and 97.

57. Strabo 9.5.18. Tzetzes, *Lycophron* 344.

58. The heroes' weapons were of bronze, and Pausanias confirms this from Homer, with the lance of Achilles in the temple of Phaselis and the sword of Memnon in the temple of Asclepius at Nicomedia. Iron was no doubt first used by the terrible fifth generation of men. Cf. too Hesiod, *Works and Days* 150 f.

59. While the Telchines and the Dactyles are craftworkers in metal, the savage *getwerge* of northern myth are guardians of treasure, and should possibly be thought of as miners. The (Tyrolean) King Laurin is a treasure-king and master of a subterranean realm.

60. Like the other pupils of Cheron, who was a teacher of music and of medicine. Plutarch, *On Music* 40. Achilles' lyre, to which he sang of the famous deeds of the old heroes, came from the booty of Eetion (Iliad IX.186 ff.).

61. Euripides, later, is critical of heralds, who only have to do with the powerful and the fortunate, *Orestes* 889 and 895.

62. For instance Myrtilus, Pausanias 8.14.7. Eurymedon was buried at Mycenae near the grave of Agamemnon, *ibid* 2.16.5.

63. The charming alternative ending, in which Nausicaa later marries Telemachus, goes back to Hellanicus and to Aristotle: Eustathius, *Commentarii ad Homeri Odysseam*, (ed. G. Stallbaum), Leipzig 1825–6, vol. 2, p. 117. In Telemachus, Odysseus as it were lives again, this time in youth.

64. The duties of housekeeper and those of the nurse may well have been combined in one person. Thus in the *Homeric Hymn* (101 ff.) Demeter introduces herself to Cleos as an old woman, childless 'as the children's nurses in royal houses are, and the housekeepers in the echoing rooms' – and later she wishes to work in a house as older women do: 'to carry a child in her arms and tend it well, to

supervise the house, to prepare the
bed of the lord and lady and teach
the maids the skills of women' (138
ff.).

65. Pausanias (2.22.7) has a very different
variant of the traditional legend;
Helen is abducted by Theseus and
reclaimed by the Dioscuri, later giving
birth to Iphigenia, whom she hands
over to Clytemnestra. From this
starting-point, Lucian worked out
that Helen was at least middle-aged
by the time of the Trojan War.
Earlier writers had allowed her to
remain young.

66. *Iliad* XIX.175 ff. and 258 ff. Achilles
has Diomede in his tent, Patroclus
has Iphis, and both have been won as
booty (*Iliad* IX.664 ff.); Nestor too
has Hecamede in his tent (*Iliad*
XIV.6).

67. In *Hippolytus* (407 ff.) Euripides
represents what is probably the view
generally taken by tragedy, according
to which princesses have set the
example of faithlessness, and noble
families are to blame for the ruin of
women; for if great ladies choose to
behave scandalously, such conduct
will seem splendid to those of bad
character. The woman who falls in
love with her stepson, and then
makes a false accusation against him
to her husband, resulting in the son's
death, is found not only in the story
of Phaedra, but also in that of
Phylonome. Tzetzes, *Lycophron* 232.

68. A characteristic view we may note
here is one naively expressed in the
Iliad, that because the wife has been
won for a bride-price of one hundred
cattle, with the promise of a thousand
sheep and goats, she will recompense
her husband with gratitude (*charis*);
the young Iphidamas does not live to
put this to the test, since he is killed
by Agamemnon (XI.241 ff.). Among
the touching examples of marital
loyalty is that of Evadne, who leaps
into the flames of the funeral pyre of
her husband, Capaneus. It was
generally assumed in mythical times
that widows did not remarry;

Pausanias says that Gorgophone, the
daughter of Perseus, was the first to
break with the custom of remaining a
widow. Marriages between brother
and sister in mythical times occur
among the children of Aeolus, and in
the story of Byblis and Caunus, and
also, according to Polyaenus (8.44) in
the case of Thessalus' parents. In
Homer there is as yet no trace of
special feminine homage to the gods,
or of women's festivals. But they
must certainly have originated in the
remote past.

69. There are of course heroic women of
more restricted fame in the
semi-historical and historical periods,
as Plutarch tells us in *Of Female
Virtue*; but none who succeeds in
saving the whole of her nation.

70. Pausanias 1.27.9. But this does not
lead to any thought of the power of
nature in the sense put forward by
Ludwig Preller.

71. Ps.-Lucian says that some believe
Homer lived in the heroic age, others
place him in the Ionian period (i.e.
after the Dorian migration); which
shows that a clear distinction was
made (*Demosthenis encomium*. 9).

72. See pp. 150–1 ff. above.

73. *Iliad* XI.385. 'You little archer,
showing off with your bow, watching
out for the girls . . .' Cf. later,
Euripides *Madness of Heracles* 159 ff.,
188 ff.

74. *Iliad* X.257 ff., 261 ff. The
'otter-helmet' of the Trojan Dolon
(*ibid*. 335) too, was no doubt
originally thought of as making its
wearer invisible.

75. Other images from hunting and
animal life, mostly from books X to
XII and from XVI, include: the two
hounds and the deer or hare (X.360
ff.), the hunter urging on his hounds
after boar and lions (XI.292 f.), the
two hunted boars destroying the
woodland as they hurtle through it
(XII.146 ff.), the lion craving meat
(*ibid*. 299 ff.), the lion in the doe's
den (XI.113 ff.), the one which carries
off a cow (XVII.61 ff.), and the other

which is scared away from the flock (*ibid.* 657 ff.), the eagle watching for its prey (*ibid.* 674 ff.), the ass which continues to graze in the meadow in spite of blows (XI.558 ff.), the flies round the milk-churn (XVI.641 ff.). Natural phenomena include the star appearing between the clouds and hiding itself again (XI.62 f.), the storm that whips up the sea (*ibid.* 297 f.), the great snowfall as the metaphor for the stones that rain down while the armies fight (XII.278 ff.), the landscape that is suddenly lit up as the clouds part (XVI.297 ff.). There are magnificent pictures from nature such as: the storm in the forest (XVI.765 ff.), the forest fire (XI.155 ff. and XX, 490 ff.), the mountain torrent carrying away whole woods (XI.492 ff.), the great oaks standing firm (XII.132 ff.) and the olive tree felled by the storm (XVII.53).

76. This people's court has some extremely odd features. The case concerns a typically Greek quarrel; the *gerontes* can hardly have remained uninfluenced by the noisy interventions of the two contesting parties. A fee of two talents is lying ready for the judge who gives the fairest opinion. Whose money is this?

77. Is this in the right place?

78. The scene of the battle is all the more vivid since the goddesses of death (Kerai and Moirai?) are quarrelling violently over one of the fallen warriors (261). Beside them stands the precisely detailed figure of Achlys (the darkness of death).

79. Compare the passage about Horcus and Dike (219 ff), the complaint Dike makes to Zeus (256 ff.), the thirty thousand immortal guards, shrouded in mist, who patrol in order to protect justice (252 ff.), although Aidos and Nemesis have already been abandoned, since they are to vanish from the Earth.

80. Hesiod's brother Perses was not a model brother.

III: The Agonal Age

1. A sixth-century elegiac poet quoted by Plato (*Republic* 407a) as saying that one should look after one's livelihood first and virtue afterwards.

2. Diogenes Laertius 2.56. Xenophon, who intended to embody all the essential features of *kalokagathia* in his own person, was in this a true old knightly warrior with a strong admixture of Spartan values. His equipment comprised an Argive shield, Attic armour, a Boeotian helmet and a charger from Epidaurus.

3. The origin of the agonal contest was no doubt the same the world over – two men competing for some prize, a title or perhaps a bride, then, later, for the honour of victory. Among ancient peoples the higher stage developed in this contest was the duel, regarded as an arbitration or divine judgment, fought out before witnesses chosen by both parties and according to certain rules. The Greeks preferred the wrestling or boxing match using no weapons.

4. Hand-to-hand spear-fighting was later abandoned as too dangerous.

5. If we had to come to an agreement on a new way of reckoning time, what proposals could we expect to hear? First the French would suggest the 14th July 1789 (the fall of the Bastille) or want to count by republican years starting in 1792, since many in France consider these things universally valid. Other proposals might be the date of the first railway – or even the first steam-engine or cotton-gin, on the grounds that 'we' made money from them. Perhaps, though, it would simply be impossible for such ancient and intelligent nations as we are to come to an agreement, and we might consent with much grumbling to a date already unilaterally adopted by a particularly powerful trading nation, as we did for the metric system.

6. Herodotus 6.103. However when Cimon won at Olympia for the third time with the same horses, the Peisistratids had him murdered at night by a gang near the Prytaneion. The Olympic champion was not a favourite with tyrants.

7. Although Pindar does not write of any Spartiate games.

8. As Pausanias reports (6.9.3) the Hellanodikai merely deprived Cleomedes of the victory because of this infringement, upon which, mad with resentment, he went home and committed terrible crimes. Damoxenus too, who had killed his opponent Creugas in a famous match at the Nemean games, got no worse punishment than to be sent away, though he had broken all the rules of the contest; cf. Pausanias 8.40.2 f., where the death of Arrachion is also related; both corpses were crowned. For what was allowed and not allowed cf. Philostratus the Elder, *Imagines* 2.6, where the technicalities of the pankration are detailed. In Sparta, they permitted biting and forcing the fists into the opponent's ribs, which were forbidden everywhere else. Biting became very common among the athletes of Roman times. Lucian's Demonax (c.49) thought that 'lions' was a good name for them.

9. *Olympian* VIII. 91 and *Pythian* VIII. 120 f.

10. For the successive introduction of the various types of competition see Pausanias, 5.8.3 ff.

11. This is why, in Aelian (14.18), a Chian threatens his lazy slave with being taken to Olympia; Lucian (*Herodotus* 8) stresses the sultry heat.

12. In the *Electra* of Sophocles (680 ff.) there is an account of Orestes' supposed death in the chariot race at the Pythian games. From it we receive a vivid impression of the enthusiasm and the connoisseurship, not only of a great poet but of a whole people, in the matter of chariot racing, and see how Sophocles could rouse the Athenians to wild excitement by simply telling the story.

13. Pausanias 6.24.3. Were the Nomophylakes the Hellanodikai of the previous Games?

14. Cf. Pausanias 6.20.6. For the hurling of offenders over the cliff of Typaion 5.6.5; *ibid.* the account of the exception made for Callipateira. According to Aelian (*Varia Historia* 10.1) a certain Pherenice was permitted to watch the Olympics because her father and three brothers had been Olympic victors and her son was to take part. Given the fact that the menfolk of Olympia talked of nothing but the agon the whole year round and that the Spartan girls' gymnasium was in the neighbourhood, it was however inevitable that a mild form of contest for women should develop at Olympia. This was a girls' race divided into three age groups and held there every four years at the festival of Hera, and the organisers were the sixteen women of Elis who wove the *peplos* for Hera. (The description of these runners, given in Pausanias 5.16.2 ff., corresponds to the female runner in the Vatican Museum, who, though usually identified as a Spartan girl, is thus more likely to be one from Elis.)

15. Publicity-seeking victors would feast the whole gathering, as did Anaxilaus the tyrant of Rhegion (497–476) after winning with his mules, a victory also celebrated by Simonides in a song in which he praised the mules with great eloquence: Simonides *frag.* 10 Page. Empedocles, who had won with his horses, but as a Pythagorean ate no meat, had a bull made out of sweetmeats and shared it among the multitude (Athenaeus 1.5.). Alcibiades will be discussed later.

16. Plutarch, *Lives of Ten Orators, Lysias* (conclusion).

17. Lucian, *Demonax* 57.

18. Here and there portrait-statues already existed, e.g. according to Plutarch, *Aratus* 3 the features and physique of Periander were faithfully reproduced. One consequence of the representation of athletes was the creation of the Ganymede-type. A Ganymede by Dionysius is among the votive offerings of Micythus as early as the 75th Olympiad (Pausanias 5.26.2); and the group of Zeus and Ganymede by Aristocles is somewhat later (*ibid.* 24.1).

19. At Miletus for instance there were many statues of Olympic and Pythian victors, which seems to argue against the assumption that Ionia rarely participated in the Panhellenic games. Cf. Plutarch, *Moralia* 180a.

20. This is apparently alluded to by Pausanias (5.21.1) in his curious distinction between *andriantes* and *anathemata* in Olympia.

21. Cf. p. 175 above, the fate of Astylus.

22. Pausanias 6.3.3. Or the name of the wrestling instructor might also be inscribed on the statue with the victor's (Pausanias 6.2.4).

23. Aelian, *De Natura animalium* 12.40. On the grave of Cimon's horses cf. p. 174 above.

24. It may have struck people as odd at first when victors put up their statues without even having been present at Olympia; but they got used to it and even let the Spartan princess Cynisca do so.

25. Pausanias (9.9.1) gives up counting the individual athletes and winners of poetic contests depicted at Delphi but otherwise unknown to fame.

26. The emphasis is on the statues, as though the barbarians might be expected to have gymnasia and palaistrai as a matter of course.

27. Cf p. 165 above. Herodotus 5.67 too calls their recitation of Homer a contest.

28. According to Plutarch, *Against Ignorance* 9, one man who boasted of his skill on the lyre, and failed miserably, was condemned by the *agonothetai* to be ruthlessly scourged and expelled from the sanctuary.

29. In Catholic districts of our own day, villages compete to carry the biggest banner or candle on a pilgrimage – a modest rivalry by comparison.

30. An example in Plutarch, *Lives of Ten Orators* 2: the orator Andocides was in charge of the *choregia* for his *phyle* with a cyclic choir in the dithyrambic agon, and set the tripod he won as the prize on a high pedestal. It is a curious symptom of decline (noted at 7 in the same text) that at the agon of Poseidon in Piraeus, under the administration of Lycurgus, money-prizes of 10, 8, and 6 *minae* were offered for the three best cyclic choirs. It may be inferred that the zeal of the *choregoi* had slackened so far that it was no longer possible to exact the *choregia* without this recompense.

31. Plutarch, *Cimon* 8 shows how in the Attic theatre too the partisan feelings of the audience could make the judges' task very difficult.

32. No doubt another performer on the lyre had rival supporters.

33. The joker Stratonicus (4th century), after his success at Sicyon, went so far as to put up a *tropaion* in the temple of Asclepius there, with the inscription 'To Stratonicus from the inferior citharists', Athenaeus 8.45.

34. Cf. C. F. Hermann, *Lehrbuch der gottesdienstlichen Alterthümer der Griechen*, Heidelberg 1846, §29 for the ease with which the agonal takes over of itself, on all occasions at which there are singing, dancing, exercises, celebrations or games.

35. Istrus says of Sophocles in the biography: 'He worked hard as a boy in the *palaistra* and at music, for both of which he won crowns.' On the weakling Demosthenes as the exception cf. Westermann, *Biographoi* p. 294.

36. As in Cyzicus. Cf. Westermann, *Biographoi* p. 225, Teucrus.

37. The connection of the agonal system with the all-pervading agon of Greek

life as a *meizon agon* is stressed in the words of Solon according to Lucian, *Anacharsis* 15 f. There too (36) we find the sentence: 'If the longing for fame were to be banished from life, what would be left to us worth having?'

38. Plutarch, *Agesilaus* 26 and *Spartan Anecdotes* 72 tells a story about Agesilaus which has the ring of characteristic truth: when the allies once complained that many more of them than of the Spartans were obliged to go to war, the king separated the two parties and his herald called out: 'Let the potters stand up.' Quite a number of the allies did so, and the same order was given to the smiths, then to the carpenters and so on through all the crafts, and at each summons more of the allies stood up, but not a single Spartan, for they were forbidden to engage in any branch of trade. In this way the allies were made to admit that the Spartans had contributed more soldiers than they had (that is real soldiers, not merely conscripts).

39. Aristotle, *Politics* 6.1., 8.2 f.

40. In this context he was forced to condemn training for victory in the agon as well, since the exclusive pursuit of gymnastics equally makes a man banausic. The Hippocrates of the Platonic *Protagoras* (312a and b) shows how people are held to be banausic even if the career they profess is concerned with noble ambitions; here the grammarian, the citharist and the gymnastic instructor, all indispensable to Attic education, are said to be only *demiourgoi*, that is equivalent to *banausoi*. Their pupils do not study with them to become what *they* are. (All scholars of today would therefore have been regarded as *banausoi*, particularly our modern specialists.)

41. Though later they took pride in gymnastic excellence. Pausanias (6.2.4) speaks of a votive inscription

at Olympia, part of which reads: 'The Samians are the best in athletics and naval warfare.'

42. According to Herodotus 4.152 the Samians gave a tithe of the immense gains they made from their Tartessos expedition to the temple of Hera, in the form of the famous crater resting on three colossal statues.

43. Women in their society seem to have been less free. Instead of the songs of heroes, there were now only hired girls playing the stringed instruments and the flute at the symposia; they wore long robes, sometimes of patterned material or deep-dyed purple, and their hair was elaborately dressed (Athenaeus 12.28 ff.). Most of the information given here about the luxury of Abydos, Ephesus, Samos, Colophon and so on concerns dress and adornment. There is a charming account, in a fragment of Asius (30), of the Samians going in procession to the Heraeon.

44. Plutarch, *Moralia* 297f-298a.

45. Plutarch, *Solon* 2. In 25 too, Solon gives the sea voyage as the pretext for his later journey.

46. 'The laws declare it to be slander to reproach any citizen, male or female, for engaging in work in the marketplace', Demosthenes, *Oration* 57, 30. So it seems it was still necessary to protect traders (here the ribbon sellers on the agora) from contemptuous insult and abuse.

47. Pericles in the funeral oration, Thucydides 2.40.

48. Plutarch, *Moralia* 807d-e.

49. Cf. the poetic listing of all the things that could be obtained, in Antiphanes, Hermippus and especially in the *Elegy* of Critias, Athenaeus 1.28b-c = Critias *frag.* B2 West.

50. *Orestes* 920. On the other hand in the same poet's *Suppliants*, 420, the Theban herald says: 'A poor man who tills the soil, even if he is not born to ignorance, is prevented by

his work from paying attention to the common weal.'

51. Heraclides, *On Politics* (conclusion). Possibly landowners with paid labourers are meant; they seem to have become impoverished and to have been heavily in debt to the Thebans.

52. Xenophon, *Oeconomicus* 4 f.

53. *Politics* 6.4; the plebs include the farmers, workers, traders and labourers. Cf also 7.8.11.

54. *Ibid* 8.2.

55. *Ibid* 6.2.

56. Herodotus (2.167) says in speaking of the hereditary Egyptian warrior caste, who engaged in no manual work, but passed on their military status from father to son: 'Whether the Hellenes learned this from the Egyptians I dare not decide, since I see that the Thracians, Scythians, Persians, Lydians and almost all the barbarians have a low opinion of craftsmen and their progeny (who are judged entirely as if of lower caste) and on the other hand consider noble those who are freed from the necessity of work, especially the warriors. All Hellenes have taken over this view, especially the Spartans. It is the Corinthians who show the least contempt for craftsmen.'

57. The word originally means work at the anvil.

58. E.g. *Knights* 738 ff.

59. Xenophon, *Apology* 29.

60. Xenophon, *Oeconomicus* 4.

61. In another very typical passage (5.12.) we learn how and why Plato considers his class of guardians fortunate. Poverty was not yet respectable at the time.

62. In this matter (*Politics* 1.4.11) a further distinction is made between *banausoi* who have learned a particular skill and those who are using only muscular strength. The first he grades, beginning with those whose products are the most elaborate and the least subject to chance, and then progressively

declining, the more their physique is damaged in the mere servile use of strength, till the point is reached at which there is the least need for excellence in the service of the State.

63. *Politics* 1.5. According to 3.2 f. there are several categories of slaves; one of them is that of the manual workers who live by the work of their hands, and the banausic *technites* belong to this class. The difference is only that the true slave serves an individual, the *banausos* the public. The last is disqualified from citizenship in aristocracies, but in oligarchies (plutocracies) not altogether, as he may become rich; in democracies he can easily become a citizen.

64. *Gorgias* 512 b-c.

65. Plutarch, *Marcellus* 17.

66. For instance, on Aegina, with its multitude of slaves, manufacture must have been carried on entirely by slaves for contractors and capitalists, and this industry may have relied on an elaborate financial basis; the founding fortune could have been a great trading company, possibly even dealing in shares. Pausanias (8.5.5) leaves us in no doubt that their products, especially in weapons and other metalwork, were indispensable even in poor and remote hinterlands; in the time of the old Arcadian ruler Pompus, trading Aeginetans landed at Cyllene and conveyed their wares on pack animals (was there a road made on purpose?) up to Arcadia. Pompus honoured the Aeginetans for this reason and named one of his sons Aeginetes because of this friendly relationship.

67. Cf. the Life of Sophilus in Westermann, p. 126, that of Demosthenes of Libanius in Westermann, p. 293, and Plutarch's *Demosthenes* 4. For the father of Isocrates see Dionysius of Halicarnassus, *Isocrates* 1, Plutarch, *Lives of the Ten Orators, Moralia*

836e and Philostratus, *Lives of the Sophists*, 1.17.

68. According to *Rhetorica ad Alexandrum c.* 2.16 the speaker argues, on the occasion of new military expenditure, that the poor should sacrifice their bodies to the perils of war, the rich provide the money and the traders the weapons. Lysias and his family, before the time of the Thirty, were an example of wealthy metics; they ran a shield-making business.

69. The patriarchal Xenophon, in what is perhaps his last work, *Revenues* (c. 2), is keen to preserve the metics as a separate and even a favoured class of tradesmen.

70. Xenophon, *Symposium* 4.40.

71. *Axiochus* 368 b.

72. So Curtius says, *Griechische Geschichte* vol. 2, p. 345 f. Cf. too the important passage in Aristophanes' *Frogs* 727 ff. The story of Apollodorus of Cassandrea, who enlisted the support of men from the workshops along with slaves to found his tyranny, is proof that in industrial towns the free workman might also become dangerous. Polyaenus 6.7.

73. *Iliad* XVIII. 410 ff. Even the fact that Pallas herself had taught so many accomplishments to 'skilful people' and gentle girls was no longer enough to ennoble these things.

74. Note that no tragic writer is named with these poets.

75. *Moralia* 802a.

76. It was just the same with architects; the father of the philosopher Menedemus, says Diogenes Laertius, was of noble birth *but* an architect and poor (2.18.1).

77. Here we should mention one of the first orators, Alcidamas in the fifth century, for the disapproving and disdainful tone in which he treats works of sculpture and painting.

78. Plutarch, *Agesilaus* 2.

79. Strabo 8.6. 'painters and sculptors and other *demiourgoi*'.

80. Plutarch, *Pericles* 31.

81. Pausanias, 9.16.1. Pindar had commissioned two Theban masters for his statue of Dindymene; but even then the material was Pentelic marble, *ibid* 9.25.3.

82. Attic workmanship and Pentelic marble must often have been combined when funds permitted, Attic artists being called in when the native artists were inadequate or non-existent. According to Pausanias 10.33.4, the temple of Apollo and Artemis at Lilaea in Phocis had statues of Attic workmanship made from Pentelic marble.

83. Pausanias 9.37.3.

84. Thus there are anecdotes of painters but scarcely any about the sculptors. Writings concerning painters are common; Diogenes Laertius 2.8.19 names among others two painters called Theodorus; Menodotus writes of one and the other is mentioned by Theophanes in his work on painting. In the *Suda* too (Westermann p. 433) a philosopher Pamphilus is mentioned, one of whose writings concerns painters and their inspiration.

85. Yet no-one dared remove these figures, and later a superstition arose to the effect that the likeness of Pheidias was incorporated in the group by a secret device, so that if it were taken out the whole thing would fall apart and collapse. No place was ever found for a statue of Pheidias, though Pericles at least, in the next generation, was accorded one, the work of Cresilas. This was not decreed by the State and not set up on the agora or the Ceramicus, but placed by relatives or admirers on the Acropolis, as a dedication.

86. The painter Nicias spurned the sixty talents offered him by one of the successor-kings (Attalus, in one account, but, according to Plutarch in *Moralia* 10.93e, a Ptolemy) as payment for his 'Sacrifice to the Dead' (no doubt based on Book XI of the *Odyssey*), and later presented the painting to Athens, his native

city. Characteristically, competition between painters is spoken of as an agon; and painters could aspire to marry well; for instance, a Hellanodicus gave Aetion his daughter's hand because of his admiration for a painting showing the wedding of Alexander and Roxana, Lucian, *Herodotus* 4.

87. In Teles (Stobaeus, 3.1.98), we are later told as a matter of course that the young boy visits instructors in gymnastics, grammar, music *and painting.*

88. In Theophrastus, *Characters* 6 there is a sweeping statement about these despicable persons: whoever has fallen prey to desperation is ripe to become a publican, a brothel-keeper or a tax-collector.

89. See the interesting suggestion (7.11) for an *agora eleuthera* (a market for freemen), as distinct from the ordinary market, and on which no *banausos* and no peasant should show himself unless summoned by authority. The idea derives from Thessaly, where it was perhaps really possible to put such a rule into practice. On the other hand, what is said (3.3) about the Theban law, allowing nobody to hold office unless he had kept away from the agora for ten years, is an expression of the extreme contempt for buying, selling and barter.

90. Cf. Lysias 10.18. In Plato's *Symposium* 173 c a pupil of Socrates says to a financier: 'When I hear philosophy discussed or speak of it myself, I feel the better for it and am happy; but if I hear other kinds of talk, especially yours, the conversation of the rich and money-minded, I am melancholy and feel sorry for you, because you think you are achieving something when you are not.'

91. On the subject of idle pleasures, the various kinds of fishing should not be forgotten; with nets, poles, baskets and the line, as described by Aelian, *De Natura animalium* 12.43.

The last was the most refined. Bird-trapping comes in the same category. Aristophanes, in *Birds*, displays such intimate acquaintance with the subject that he must have been an adept himself.

92. Though there were supposed to be mythical precedents, such as the rape of Chrysippus by Laius, whose age it would be interesting to know. Ganymede may have been thought of only as Zeus's cupbearer. For the myths cf. Athenaeus 13.77–9.

93. Cf. the main passage in Aelian, *Varia Historia* 3.9. Spartans and Cretans sacrificed to Eros before battle (Preller, *Griechische Mythologie* Vol. I, 239). According to Athenaeus 13.12, the sacred Theban host consisted of pairs of lovers, who manifested the dignity of the god by welcoming a sublime death in place of an ignoble life.

94. Cf. especially Plato, *Symposium* 182, Xenophon, *Constitution of the Lacedaemonians* 2.13 ff.; the important passage in Xenophon, *Anabasis* 7.4, 5f. and the detailed analysis of this relationship in Crete given in Strabo 10.4.21 after Ephorus. In the original there was evidently a particular link with the Dorian superiority in war; elsewhere the aim of avoiding overpopulation is cited. According to Aelian, *Varia Historia* 3.10, the practice appears elevated to the status of a law in Sparta; here, we learn, the lover was held responsible for the boy's misdeeds.

95. Athenaeus 13.78, also giving instances of lovers conspiring against tyrants. Polycrates, who is said to have destroyed the *palaistrai* for this reason, none the less retained his own male harem.

96. For Solon's legislation for the protection of the gymnasia and of youth in general, and to prevent any pretensions to citizenship by male prostitutes, cf. the examples in Aeschines, *Against Timarchus* 12.16.21 and Demosthenes, *Against Androtion* 30. Solon is supposed to have feared

393

that if their numbers grew these men might overthrow the constitution. In *Against Timarchus* 137 we hear particularly explicit language about the scandal: 'I believe uncorrupted love is noble, but to prostitute yourself for the sake of money is shameful.'

97. On the one-sided legal and political importance of marriage cf. Hermann, *Privatalterthümer* § 29 f. In contrast to the practice in Homeric times, there has been an innovation, and the bride has to be provided with a dowry, while formerly a bride-price was exacted from the bridegroom.

98. The assumption made here is that Theognis 590–612 and *Works and Days* 47–89 are of later origin; Weigel identifies the first passage as an interpolation, and Bernhardy the second.

99. Phocylides, *frag.* 2 Diehl.

100. After the version by Propertius IV.4, in which Tarpeia betrays the fortress for love, not, as in the usual legend, for gold.

101. The principal motif of this story occurs too in the legend of Scylla betraying her father Nisus to her beloved, Minos. A variant is that of the fall of the city of Pedasos. Here a lovelorn girl throws Achilles an apple with a message written on it telling him the defenders have run out of water and he has only to wait for their surrender: Kinkel, *Epicorum Graecorum Fragmenta* p. 120. According to Parthenius 22, even the capitulation of Sardis to Cyrus was brought about by the king's daughter Nanis, who asked Cyrus to marry her formally, a promise he did not keep. In Herodotus 6.134 f. it is Timon, the assistant priestess of the chthonic goddesses, who tries to betray Paros to Miltiades. The opposite occurs in Parthenius 9, where Polycrite persuades an enemy captain to treason and becomes the saviour of Naxos.

102. Athenaeus 13.90. We would like to know who played Paris to these goddesses.

103. *Ibid.* after Theophrastus, but he gives no place or date. The participation of southern Italian women in Pythagoreanism seems to me to have more to do with the Pythagorean doctrine of the soul than with the fact that these women belonged to the Dorian race.

104. The Athenian poetess Hedyle, who composed an elegy for Scylla, lived about 300 B.C.; in the old days a woman poet would have been quite unthinkable in Attica.

105. 2.134 f.

106. 13.69.

107. Were these spits intended for great festival offerings, or is this perhaps some joke, the symbolism of which must escape us in our absolute modern distaste for symbolism? The gift of Rhodopis might be thought of as rather like those ladders offered by Pittacus to various temples in Mytilene (according to Aelian, *Varia Historia* 2.29) which symbolized the ups and downs of fortune.

108. The *leschai* [clubs] were the places where people came together to talk; much idle chatter must have gone on there, yet it is because of them that the Greeks appear to us as the nation of conversation. It would have been difficult anywhere else in the world to create an adjective such as the one Herodotus presumably coined for the case – *perilescheneutos*.

109. The *eranos* in *Odyssey* I. 226 and the Hesiodic feast *ek koinou* in *Works and Days* 722 f. are one and the same thing.

110. The first *apo symbolon*, the second *apo spuridos deipnein*. For this and much else see Athenaeus, 8.64, where his pedantic talkers list all the traditions of Greek social gatherings of all periods.

111. Plutarch, *Moralia* 147e. The story was told of the Sybarites that their ladies were invited a whole year in advance, to give them time to prepare

appropriate robes and gold ornaments.

112. They were called *akletoi, epikletoi* and only in Roman times *skiai* (shadows). Naturally this was not permitted everywhere or without question; Chilon in Plutarch, *Moralia* 148a, did not accept till he had been informed of each guest's identity. 'For,' he said 'a fellow traveller on board ship and a fellow soldier sharing your tent must be tolerated even if you have not been introduced, but no sensible man will mix with any old random drinking companions.'

113. The libation of unmixed wine was usually offered to the good daimon, and a later one of mixed wine to Zeus the Preserver. Cf. Diodorus 4.3.

114. Aelian, *Varia Historia* 12.31, reckons up nine famous kinds and also records that the wine could be mixed with a variety of fragrant substances. *Ibid.* 13.6 for the wild stories the Greeks were apt to tell about their wines. In Heraea in Arcadia there was one which made men mad and women fertile, on Thasos one that brought deep sleep and another that caused insomnia, etc.

115. Alcidamas in *Odyssey* 4 makes it plain that quarrels easily arose at the symposium; Odysseus says he has never quarrelled with Palamedes, not even in the *palaistra* or at the symposium, where most disagreements occur. The proverb 'I hate a fellow-drinker who remembers' (*miso mnemona sympoten*) must also be very early.

116. Later writers such as Athenaeus (15.17) were of a different opinion; they thought the garlanding was invented because of the discovery that binding the head was good for headache. In Diodorus 4.4 Dionysus himself wears his crown because heavy drinkers get headaches.

117. Athenaeus 8.65, and he also believes that at that time they did not drink to the point of drunkenness.

118. Only women sat, and they were present only on family occasions; boys too, but these withdrew at the start of the symposium proper; hetaerae reclined.

119. Plutarch, *Moralia* 147f, gives the opinion that the wise man comes to dine not just to fill himself like a vessel, but to talk both seriously and in jest, and to hear and speak what the moment suggests to the company for its pleasure. In his account the conversation unfortunately soon deteriorates into pedantic themes, the wise men showing off with definitions and solving riddles. For fantastic stories of sybaritic symposia see Aelian, *De natura animalium* 16.23.

120. Athenaeus 2.44.

121. Sometimes the political talk was rather fanciful. At a banquet given by a pupil of the philosopher Xanthus, someone proposed the question as to what might cause the greatest upset in the world, to which Aesop, who was standing in attendance at the back, replied: 'If the dead were resurrected and all demanded to have their belongings returned.' Maximus Planudes, *Life of Aesop* p. 49.

122. Of the *thuterion* (the sacrificial offering for serious oaths) see Pseudo-Eratosthenes, *Catast.* 39: 'Which men bring into the symposium and sacrifice, encouraging each other to swear an oath of loyalty, and which they touch with their right hand, regarding this as pledge of good faith.'

123. Theognis 467 ff. At riotous feasts a man who could not stay awake might have a mixture of the lees of wine poured over him. Plutarch, *Moralia* 147e.

124. Amasis is described by Herodotus (2.174) as 'loving jokes and full of teasing mockery at banquets'.

125. Cf. the quotation in Plutarch, *Moralia* 1104e from an unknown but certainly early poet.

126. Cf.p. 205 above. Where did Herodotus have it from? Athens, one would think, but for the objective view of Athenian frivolity it provides.

127. Lucian too, in *Scytha* 5, makes his Toxaris say to Anacharsis: 'This city will not lightly let you go; it has many charms for the stranger.'

128. Plutarch, *Solon* 12 ff., with the story of the crime against the Cylonians and its expiation through Epimenides, then the rise of the well-known three parties and the economic sufferings of the people, Solon's archonship and legislation and the complication of events by the tyranny of Peisistratus.

129. Note his view of the world in his elegies in contrast to that of e.g. Hesiod.

130. Yet we may ask how much credit Solon deserves compared with the countless earlier colonial lawgivers; the whole Greek nation was already acquainted with many innovations of a utilitarian kind. In Plutarch's account (14) it seems a very ridiculous Athenian trait to have tried to make Solon out as an Athenian playboy, exploiting both the main interests against each other. Later Themistocles and others were similarly treated.

131. Aelian, *Varia Historia* 4.22, lists their ornaments one by one, and adds: 'In spite of this finery they were victorious at Marathon'. As for their love of good living, Diodorus (9. *frag.* 3) speaks of Solon having transformed this into *arete*.

132. Aulus Gellius 6.17: *Libros Athenis disciplinarum liberalium publice ad legendum praebendos primus posuisse dicitur Pisistratus tyrannus.*

133. Diogenes Laertius (1.1.1) says of Thales: 'He was the first to be called wise, in the year that Damasias was chief magistrate at Athens, and after him the seven wise men were also named.'

134. Hipponax speaks in this way of the Malian Myson, whom Plato later puts in the place of Periander in *Protagoras*: Diogenes Laertius 1.9.2. Who would be named in modern Europe or in Germany if seven had to be singled out?

135. Diogenes Laertius 1.4.6, 1.5.4–6 on Pittacus and Bias. In Cleobulus (1.6.5) at least the grave-inscription is mentioned in which the 'mourning native town of Lindos' is heard to speak.

136. *Greek Anthology* 11.12.

137. The Cercopes, a prefiguring of the picaresque genre, also belong to this time, and were also believed to be Homeric. In the verses from the *Suda* (*s. v. Kerkopes*) they appear as vagabonds. Since they were shown parading on a metope at Selinus they must have been a novelty.

138. According to the principal text, Plato's *Protagoras* 342 d-f., an insignificant Spartan seems at first insignificant in conversation too; but at the earliest opportunity he hurls a brief, lapidary remark into the talk like an accomplished spear-thrower, so that the other speaker stands abashed like a mere boy.

139. The original form of the well-known joke about the Cretans is told by Demodocus (West, *Iambi et Elegi Graeci*, vol. 2, p. 57) and is made to refer to the Chians; another joke of his, at the expense of the Milesians, is also preserved.

140. His fables, only forty-one altogether, are all found among Aesop's. If not really a contemporary of Solomon he is at least mentioned in the Koran.

141. See Walz I, p. 10, 59, 172f.

142. Besides Aesop, the other fabulists (*mythopoioi*) known to Theon are Connis the Cilician, Cybissus the Libyan and Thurus the Sybarite. Babrius, in the prooemium to book M, emphatically describes the 'Syrians' of Nineveh and Babylon as 'inventors'.

143. A charming myth of the origin of the animal-fable occurs in Philostratus, *Life of Apollonius of Tyana* 15.

144. In the fable of Themistocles told in Plutarch's *Themistocles* 18 there is a quarrel between the feast-day and the 'morning after'.

145. Aristophanes' *Birds* (471, 651) shows

that in his day it was a mark of
ignorance not to know Aesop, whose
works could already be referred to as
a collection.

146. Philostratus in *Imagines* 1.3 writes of
the animal-stories: 'by which
children learn about the ways of the
world'.

147. In Plutarch, *Moralia* 157a-f.

148. Think, for instance, of our own
mediaeval art and its inability to
represent the dynamism of the body
at the time when it was creating
superbly expressive heads;
Renaissance art had to rely on
antiquity and on the influence of a
southerly climate for its hard-won
success in lifelike representation
before it could develop its full beauty
and charm.

149. Herodotus gives an important
example in 4.161, where the god is
asked about the complex affairs of
Cyrene, but a human reformer,
Demonax of Mantinea, is appointed,
who then reorganizes the state.

150. One such date, however, might be
approximately 600 B.C., when,
under Cleisthenes, the cult of
Adrastus in Sicyon gave way to that
of Dionysus. It is possible too that
Spartan restrictions on music after
the eighth century should be
considered indirect evidence.

151. There is unfortunately no way of
knowing when this occurred. The
Hymn to Demeter still makes no
mention of Iacchus and he is not
named in imitations elsewhere.

152. The story of his two departures from
Samos because of tyranny there is no
doubt fictional and of interest only
as coinciding in date with Polycrates
(Strabo 14.1.16). According to
Aristoxenus (in Porphyrius 22) he
was joined in Croton by Lucanians,
Messapians, Peucetians and Romans,
and it was not for nothing that the
Romans put up a statue to him in
the forum. Though these
semi-barbarians probably learned
little from him, he was none the less

capable of inspiring religious feelings
in them.

153. In the *Life* by Iamblichus, where the
tradition of Pythagoras is most
obscured by all kinds of inventions
and late-Roman tendentiousness, the
reader still cannot fail to be
impressed by the apparent
genuineness of the anecdotes about
his life and the cohesion of the sect.
The political aspect is the most
dubious, yet it is hard to imagine
that it has no basis in fact. As given
by Porphyrius and Iamblichus it is
indeed quite unbelievable. What is
known of politics in southern Italy at
that time is very scanty, but can
scarcely be reconciled with the
existence of a group exercising
political power. All the same, from
the group we may draw a conclusion
about its master; if we had absolutely
no contemporary evidence about
St Francis of Assisi, and only relied
on the oral accounts current in the
fifteenth century, the great institution
of his order would still prove to us
that he lived and had his influence.

154. Diodorus 10.3.5.

155. Iamblichus 5. f.

156. An idea of the effect he had may be
gained from the fragment of
Empedocles (Porphyrius 31) which
runs: 'By concentrating his whole
mind, he could see everything there
is in ten or even twenty generations.'
As well as this he could hear the
harmony of the spheres.

157. Porphyrius 31.

158. Diodorus 10.4. According to
Porphyrius 60, the tyrant himself,
when exiled in Corinth, told the
story to Aristoxenus.

IV: The Fifth Century

1. We may think of Cambyses lusting
after the 'table of the sun' of the
long-lived Ethiopians, Herodotus
3.17–23.

2. For instance Plutarch, *Aristides* 19,

gives small, but in this case authentic, figures for the Greeks who fell at Plataea; they point to the conclusion that the opposing army of Mardonius numbered far less than 300,000.

3. As against this immense multitude Herodotus can name every one of Leonidas's 300 men (7.224).

4. Cf. Diodorus 11.1.

5. Even Roman religion is nothing to this; the nearest comparison is with the vanity of Louis XIV.

6. Thucydides in the epitaph for Euripides, *Greek Anthology* 7.45.

7. Euripides, *frag.* 981 Nauck.

8. *Medea* 824 ff. Xenophon (*Revenues* 1) praises the climate, produce and situation of Attica in a closely argued passage. Cf. also Aelius Aristides for an account of the geography of Attica, about which the islands cluster like the propylaea before kings' palaces or like stars round the moon, and of the beauty of the landscape, with its splendid harmony of sea and land, plain and mountains. *Panathenaicus* 155, 158, 162.

9. Cf. the quotation from Antiphanes given by Athenaeus (3.6); following Istros, Athenaeus mentions too an old law forbidding the export of figs, to ensure that only the inhabitants should enjoy them. The honey must have been very special to earn praise, since it was the only sweetener and used for all offerings etc. The best kind seems to have come from the district of the silver mines, the next best from Hymettus: Strabo 9.1.23., where he also speaks of the mines. An important fragment from the *Horae* of Aristophanes (Athenaeus 9.14) describes how the fruit and flowers of every season could be had in Athens all year round, and complains of the constant temptation to spend money on them.

10. Plato, *Alcibiades* 122 d.

11. If the speech is correctly dated to

397–6, the property had, in fourteen years, at least four owners, the last of whom, Lysias himself, leased it from 404 to four tenants in succession, two of whom rented it for only one year each; in the end he farmed it himself.

12. Even Solon in his day urged the Athenians to take possession of the Thracian Chersonese (Diogenes Laertius 1.2.2). Sigeion on the opposite shore was intermittently in Athenian hands in the sixth century.

13. Boeckh, *Staatshaushaltung* I.9.

14. Lysias 6.49.

15. Argument to Demosthenes' *Against Theocrinus*.

16. Lysias 22.14 assumes that the judges readily condemn the plaintiffs as sycophants.

17. Lysias 22.21, accusing the *sitopoloi* of conspiring against the foreigners, says: 'You will dispose them in your favour if you punish the dealers, and if you do not, what will they think of you?'

18. *Oedipus at Colonus* 1125 ff. Earlier, 1006 f., he says: 'If any country knows how to honour the gods, this one knows it best.'

19. Plutarch, *Aristides* 27, *Pelopidas* 6.

20. Plutarch, *Cimon* 10.

21. Aelian, *Varia Historia* 3.38. According to Philochorus in Athenaeus 2.7 and 5.8, the mixing of wine with water was first understood in Attica, and then human beings learned how to walk upright. Dionysus taught King Amphictyon this.

22. This comes from the speech of Nicolaus in Diodorus 13.22 ff., and is followed, it is true, by the catalogue of Athenian shortcomings spoken by Gylippus. In Pausanias 1.17.1 there is another boast of Athenian piety, which also starts with the altar of mercy.

23. Athenaeus 5.12.

24. The Theban myths are given by Pausanias (9.5) from the autochthonous Ogygus down to the descendants of Thersandrus and the abolition of the monarchy. This is

evidently merely a conflation of different stories and mythical persons needing to be fitted together. The gaps are filled in with family connections and regencies.

25. The chief sources are: Apollodorus 3.14 ff, Strabo 8.7, 1.9.1 *passim*, Pausanias 1 *passim*, Justin 2.6.

26. Pausanias 1.3.2 says of the historically ignorant Athenians that they believed in what they had heard from childhood in choruses and tragedies.

27. Pausanias 1.14.7 reports from the *deme* of Athmon the story of Porphyrion, who put up a shrine to Urania. He is obviously the Phoenician murex-fisherman.

28. One of these is the catalogue of ships (*Iliad* II.546) where the Athenian contribution is described in detail. It was also said (Strabo 9.1.10, Diogenes Laertius 1.2.2) that Solon or Peisistratus, wishing to prove that Salamis had always belonged to Athens, had smuggled in, after line 557: 'Ajax led twelve ships from Salamis', another which runs: 'and moored them where the Athenians were drawn up'. Strabo (13.3.5) says that Elaia, the later site of an Attalid port, was founded by Menestheus – the Athenians thus found time to set up colonies while engaged in the Trojan War. Another attempt to muscle in on it is the Trojan Horse in bronze on the Acropolis, with the figures of Menestheus and Teucrus, as well as the sons of Theseus, leaning out of it, Pausanias 1.23.10.

29. *Suda s.v. Daphidas.* (Westermann p. 363.)

30. Diogenes Laertius 2.5.23. (A fine for the *Menesthai*!).

31. The Attic hero Phaleros was supposed to have gone with Jason to Colchis (Pausanias 1.1.4).

32. General sources for this in Strabo 14.1.3, Pausanias 7.2–5.

33. Thucydides 1.2. Similarly Xenophon, *Memorabilia* 3.5.12. Praise of autochthony also in the Euripides

fragments given in Plutarch, *Moralia* 604d.

34. Isocrates for instance stresses that only Athens is autochthonous, like a fortress; he praises the hospitality she has offered from early times to Messenians, Plataeans etc, and insists on her philanthropy in helping the oppressed to emigrate to the Cyclades and the coast of Asia Minor, and on the assistance she gave other cities by actually luring away their rebellious elements.

35. On the locality of the battle with the Amazons see Plutarch, *Theseus* 27.

36. Pausanias 1.32.5.

37. According to Euripides' *Suppliants*. As Pausanias 1.39.2 has it, the Thebans said they had voluntarily handed over the corpses, and no battle took place.

38. This is not the only court of law said to date from mythical times; the mythical origin of several Athenian tribunals is boasted of by Demosthenes (*Against Aristocrates* 23.64 ff.), that is at a time when they could only have been staffed by fourth-century Athenians.

39. Pausanias 4.5.1. It was in the second of these wars that the Athenian Tyrtaeus was called to Sparta at the command of Dephi. Thus in the seventh century Athens must have represented a kind of intellectual tribunal for Delphi. Prayers to the gods could have been commanded by Delphi itself; Tyrtaeus brought neither cult nor offerings. What was the true reputation of Athens in Delphi, and who was the go-between in this affair?

40. *Suppliants* 349 ff., 403 ff., 429 ff.

41. Diodorus (12.1 f.) sums up the general later argument in his account of the fifty-year prosperity of Hellas after the Persian Wars, and its wealth of art and great men. He claims that the Athenians were outstanding in reputation and valour, and famous almost throughout the world.

42. Diodorus 19.106. Perhaps the Carthaginians were the wiser.
43. Lycurgus, *Against Leocrates* 46 ff.
44. On the *euteleia* of Pericles himself cf. Isocrates, *Peace* 184 d, where he is said to have left less wealth than he inherited, but to have deposited 8000 talents on the Acropolis.
45. It was the view of the Spartans too (Thucydides 4.55) that, when they had missed an opportunity for action, the Athenians always believed they had fallen short of what they could have achieved.
46. According to Diodorus (11.71) Inarus promised the Athenians royal power in Egypt. It must have been quite out of the question for this distant land to be ruled from Athens.
47. R. Meiggs, D.M. Lewis, *Greek Historical Inscriptions* no. 33.
48. Diodorus 11.70.
49. Diodorus 11.85.
50. Incidentally, it was here that Pericles first used siege-machines (*krioi* and *chelonai*), the work of Artemon of Clazomenae; thus artillery is an Athenian invention: Diodorus 12.28.
51. Alcibiades is blamed for this in Pseudo-Andocides, *Against Alcibiades* 12.
52. The balance sheet for the second half of the fifth century is drawn up by Plutarch (*Cimon* 19) in one sentence: 'From the time of Cimon's death no great campaigns were mounted against the barbarians; instead, urged on by demagogues and warmongers, the Hellenes fought each other, with no-one to mediate between them, giving the Persians a useful breathing space but bringing untold ruin on themselves.'
53. On the cost of a *choregia* cf. Antiphon 6.11–13. In Lysias (21) a man accused of taking bribes begins his defence by saying that it is absurd to bring this charge against one so open-handed as himself. He then gives (21.1–15) this enormous list of his contributions:
'After I had qualified for public office under the Archon

Theopompus (in the year 411) I spent 30 *minae* as *choregos* for tragedies, and a further two thousand *drachmae* when I won at the Thargelia in the third month with a male choir. Under Glaukippos (410) I gave 800 *drachmae* for Pyrrhic dancing at the Great Panathenaea. In the same year I was victor as *choregos* at the Dionysia and spent 5,000 *drachmae* inclusive of the dedication of the tripod. Under Diocles (409) I gave 300 *drachmae* at the Little Panathenaea for a cyclic choir. Meanwhile I was trierarch for seven years and contributed six talents. Besides these expenses, and while I was daily endangering myself and absent from home on your affairs, I paid two taxes on my income, one of 30 *minae* and the other of 4,000 *drachmae*. On returning home by sea during the archonship of Alexias (405) I at once took on the gymnasiarchy for the Promethean Games and won there at a cost of twelve *minae*. Later I became *choregos* for a boys' choir and spent fifteen *minae*. Under Eucleides (403) I was victor as *choregos* for comedies and spent sixteen *minae*, and at the Little Panathenaea the *choregia* for beardless Pyrrhic dancers cost me seven *minae*. I won the race for triremes off Sunion and spent fifteen *minae*. Besides this I have spent more than thirty *minae* on *architheoriai* and *arrephoriai* and so forth. If I had given only what the law decrees for all this it would not have come to a quarter of the amount.' Later (21.12 f.) the speaker declares that a just decision will be in the interest of the judges themselves. As the city's income has diminished, and what remains is plundered by the officials, the safest funds are those belonging to those who give voluntarily; if the judges are wise, they will look after his money as if it were their own, since they can use it in just the same way;

it is known to all that he is a much better guardian of his wealth than those who administer the State treasury; if he is impoverished, they themselves are the losers, and others will share out his confiscated property as they do everything else. In Oration 19 the speaker tells how he often heard his father calculate that in the course of his life he had contributed twice as much to the state as he was leaving to his sons.

54. *Dikazesthai* (litigation) appears as the specific trait of the Athenians in Lucian's *Icaromenippus* (c.16) when, looking down from the Moon, Icaromenippus watches the activities of the various nations on Earth.

55. For example the case on which Antiphon's oration *On the choreuteai* is based: a boy at choir-practice drank some water and died immediately afterwards, and the *choregos* was accused of murder; the accusers had been suborned by his enemies, not until some days after the event.

56. This story, retailed by Antiphon (5.69 ff.) is a parallel to the trial of the generals at Arginusae. But it must have taken place about the middle of the century, for the orator, speaking around 415, adds: 'The older among you will, I think, remember this; the younger have heard tell of it, like me.'

57. Andocides, *On the Mysteries* 36.43 ff. 20. Cf. also Thucydides book 6 for his incomparable account of the period of the attacks on the herms. According to Plutarch (*Alcibiades* 18) some believed the Corinthians had organized these crimes so that the bad omen should deter Athens from attacking their colony in Syracuse.

58. In Aristophanes' *Frogs* (83 ff.) he goes 'to the banquets of the blest'.

59. Honours, according to Plutarch (*Cimon* 8) were given in moderation until well into the fifth century. When Miltiades demanded a crown (probably of olive) someone stood

up in the popular assembly and shouted: 'Yes, one day when you have won a battle all on your own you shall be honoured alone.'

60. Plutarch, *Dion* 58 (referring to Callippus).

61. *Rhetoric* 2.6.24. Cydias in fact said this in the time of Demosthenes. Similarly Isocrates, *Panegyricus* 46: 'What *we* have resolved becomes so well known that it is respected by all men everywhere.'

62. Pseudo-Xenophon, *Constitution of Athens* 2.8.

63. P. 205 above.

64. Antiphon, in Athenaeus 397c.

65. Aristophanes, *Acharnians* 637 ff.

66. The main source is Plutarch's *Antony* 70, where the anecdote occurs about Timon's announcing in the popular assembly that, on the site where he was intending to build, there grew a fig tree which had already been used by several citizens to hang themselves, and that anyone who still wished to do so had better hurry up about it. Contemporary references to Timon are in Aristophanes' *Birds* (1549) and *Lysistrata* (809 ff.). Lucian (with a few sombre digs at the Roman period) makes the figure of Timon loom larger as a hater of gods and men.

67. In Plato's *Symposium* 175 e, the great theatre is said to have room for more than thirty thousand spectators when Agathon's plays were performed in 416. This figure may well have corresponded to the number of Athenian citizens.

68. Plutarch, *Nicias* 15.

69. Aelian, *Varia Historia* 1.18, also considers the women's dress of earlier times excessively showy; they wore high diadems, sandals and long pendant earrings; the sleeves of the chiton were not seamed, but held together by a row of gold and silver hoops. Cf. also, on the dress of the Ionians of Colophon, Xenophanes, *frag.* 3.

70. The Parthenon frieze is not a sure

guide here. Renan concludes, from the simplicity of the clothes it shows worn at the highest festival, that everyday wear must have been even simpler. He fails to recognize that whatever people really looked like, the artist depicting costume has a definite interest in 1) restraint in favour of the naked figure, and 2) keeping it free of elaborate ornament. Still, it must be said that a nation in love with finery would have insisted, as in Assyria, on having it displayed on public monuments.

71. Athenaeus 5.62. It is true Xanthippe refused, as Aelian records (*Varia Historia* 7.10) to put on Socrates' *himation* to go out and see a procession, and Socrates told her: 'You go out not to see, but to be seen.' Phocion's wife, however (*ibid* 9) wore his *himation* and needed no other adornment (though finery was the custom at the time, among those less famous for virtue, and is listed in detail).

72. Xenophon, *The Constitution of Sparta* 1.3.

73. For instance Cinesias, the poet and later sycophant, referred to by Aristophanes (*Birds* 1377) as 'the lime-wood man'. This is explained by Athenaeus (12.76) who says he was a tall thin man who wore a corset of lime-wood. The Greeks feared aging so much that about the time of the Peloponnesian War hair-dyeing came in. A Chian, vain and ashamed of his age, drew the attention of King Archidamus II by doing this, and incurred a royal sneer: 'Not content with lying in his heart, this man carries a lie about with him on his head.' Aelian, *Varia Historia* 7.20.

74. Cf. Lucian, *Anacharsis* 16, for evidence that everyone went bare-headed even in the heat of the sun. The *pilos* was apparently worn only when travelling. Possibly the aim was to preserve the beauty of the hair.

75. Compare, in Aristophanes' *Plutus* 535 ff., Chremylus' portrayal of Poverty, to which Poverty replies: 'The life you describe is not mine, but the beggar's.'

76. Pseudo-Xenophon, *Constitution of Athens*.

77. Plato, *Protagoras* 342 c. The conversation is supposed to be taking place in Pericles' time.

78. 'Clever people spent their time criticizing their city and praising the institutions of Sparta' (Renan).

79. *Imagines* 16.29.

80. *Clouds* 1171 ff.

81. *Laws* 642 c.

82. Andocides reproaches the Athenians with the contradiction between their responsiveness to tragedy and their indifference in real life: 'When you see these things in the theatre (Alcibiades begetting a son with a woman of Melos sold into slavery, and the son being destined to bring ruin on Athens) you find it terrible; when it actually happens in the city, you think nothing of it. What you see in the play may be true, or invented by the poet, but when you know it has happened you take no notice.'

83. *Alcibiades* 16. (The *à propos* is worth looking up!) Cf. also *Solon* 15.

84. Lysias, *Against Philocrates* 10.

85. Lysias, *Against Alcibiades* 41. Cf. the similar use in Italian of *disgrazia* and the Swiss *Ung'fell*.

86. *Rhetoric* 3.2.10.

87. Plutarch (*On Flattery* 12) refers to Thucydides in discussing the devaluation of words in flattery.

88. E.g. *Olympian* I, 158.

89. Cf. p. 174 above for Thucydides' description of the welcome given to Brasidas in Scione.

90. *Frag.* 2.

91. Euripides, *frag.* 282 Nauck.

92. Diogenes Laertius I.2.8 speaks of Solon having reduced the prizes given by the Athenians to the agonal victors (probably Polyzelus, Cynaegeirus, Callimachus and all the marathon runners) on the grounds

that those who fell in battle were more deserving; for now the aim was to win noble distinction *in war*; some sarcasms at the athletes' expense follow. It may well be that immediately after Marathon and Salamis there was a relative devaluation of athleticism. Cf. Plato, *Symposium* 220 e, on the honours distributed by the generals among troops in action.

93. A most important text on the relationship between democracy and the agonal spirit is in Pseudo-Xenophon, *Constitution of Athens* I.13, which goes so far as to say: 'Those in Athens who practised gymnastics or music have been deprived of power by the people, not because they do not think these things beautiful, but because they recognize that it is not possible for them (the people) to cultivate them. So they oblige the rich to support the *choregia* and exact payment for their participation in the performances.'

94. Cf. the fragment from Alexis in Athenaeus 2.12.

95. Aelian, *Varia Historia* 12.32.

96. See p. 196 above.

97. Simonides, *frag.* 89 West.

98. Herodotus 4.88.

99. Athenaeus 12.62. The word *habrodiaitos*, which he used of himself, was not surprisingly converted into *rabdodiaitos* (living by the paint-brush, i.e. a manual worker).

100. See p. 197 above. This attitude does not conflict with his having charged an entrance fee to those coming to see his 'Helena'.

101. Compared with him, the later artist Apelles was modest; he recognized talent in others and only corrected the incompetent.

102. Athenaeus 2.30.

103. Diodorus 11.62.

104. Plutarch, in *Alcibiades*, states that there is no record of the names of the mothers of Nicias, Lamachus, Demosthenes, Thrasybulus and Phormion, all well-known contemporaries of Alcibiades, and contrasts this with the fact that we have the names of Alcibiades' own Laconian nurse, Amycla, and his tutor Zopyrus. This slave was entrusted with his education by his guardian, Pericles (according to Plato, *Alcibiades* 122 a-f.).

105. For a list of these, cf. Cicero, *De Domo Sua* c. 38.

106. Note that Plato is using the same image as Aristophanes.

107. The last great monologue (815 ff.) is of moving beauty and expresses the depths of bitterness. Ajax has plunged the sword Hector gave him upright in the earth and then prays first to Zeus that Teucrus may come to save his corpse from enemies, from dogs and from birds, then to Hermes, to be given a good resting-place, to the Erinyes, asking them to come and see how he is dying because of the Atreidae and to be unsparing in their vengeance on the whole army and to Helios, to give his parents the sad news. Then comes the final invocation to the sunlight and to his home in Salamis, to Athens and the springs, rivers and meadows of the Trojan land: 'This is the last word Ajax speaks to you; all the rest is for Hades and the underworld.' The transfiguration of the dead hero begins even in the mourning outcry of Tecmessa, whose hearth and home he once destroyed, and whose one desire is yet to live through him and for his sake. His greatness is exalted as the drama proceeds, and the towering shade dominates all the sayings and doings of the others. The *peripeteia* begins only now; even as a corpse he arouses the utmost tension through his effect on Teucrus, Menelaus, Agamemnon and the chorus of warriors. Bargaining and threats result, and the solemn guarding of the dead man; accusations of bad blood and of family horrors are exchanged, till at last Odysseus

intervenes, as the *deus ex machina* and the bearer of higher wisdom and moderation, to settle the quarrel and ensure the burial.

108. Plutarch, *Cimon* 4.
109. Cf. the stories in Plutarch, *Themistocles* 5.
110. It is not too difficult to believe the story of the Greek admirals being bribed with Euboean gold (Herodotus 8.5); but we cannot swallow the legend of the inscriptions carved into the cliffs of Euboea, by which Themistocles lured or compromised the Ionians in the Persian fleet after the battle of Artemisium (*ibid.* 22). It would seem that the Athenians soon persuaded themselves into the firm belief that, when the Greeks were ready to flee, it was Themistocles who sent the secret warning to Xerxes not to allow them to escape – using his children's tutor Sicinnos as the messenger! (*ibid.* 75). This impish ruthlessness in a high patriotic cause is very Athenian, and the rumour fed the Athenians' scorn for the allies; but the huge manoeuvre of the Persian fleet and army at Salamis could certainly not have been influenced at this point by any such secret intelligence. The whole reconciliation with Aristides too (*ibid.* 79) is as suspect as the peculiar victory won by Aristides on Psyttaleia (*ibid.* 95). Athenian inventiveness wanted to preserve both the legend of the admirable man and that of the gifted rogue. (In Plutarch's account, this double fiction about Themistocles and Aristides is enriched by their conflicting opinions as to whether the bridge on the Hellespont should be destroyed, and also over the burning of the Greek fleet at Pagasae, an anecdote no doubt inspired by Athenian malice.) Sicinnos' second errand (*ibid.* 110) seems obviously invented, like the still more implausible parallel story in Plutarch's *Themistocles*, 16.
111. The text Plutarch used (whether by Andocides or someone else) is not a speech that was actually delivered, but an accusatory essay on a fictional theme. It pretends to be composed some time after the invasion of Melos and before the Sicilian expedition, but probably dates from the last period of Alcibiades' life; the sufferings he caused the Athenians are presented as if predicted. The author is unable to consider it a mere scholastic address from a later time, though there are some, known as *loidoriai Alkibiadou*.
112. There was an exceptional quality in him. Plutarch: *Alcibiades* 16.
113. According to Lysias 14.39, however, his ancestors were a brood of criminals.
114. It may well be true that, as he says of himself (*Alcibiades* 216 b), nobody would have accused him of being afraid of anyone. What follows – that he made an exception for Socrates – is perhaps invented. Still, there is a notable passage in Plato's *Alcibiades* I. 132a, where Socrates says to him: 'What I fear most is that you will become the darling of the *demos*, and be lost to *us*, like many gifted Athenians; for the *demos* of haughty Erechtheus has a beautiful face – but it's another thing to see him without his clothes!'
115. Plutarch, *Moralia* 52e.
116. For his setting the fashion cf. Athenaeus 12.47 ff. A particular kind of sandal was known much later as 'the Alcibiades'. Even in Athens some things did arouse the disapproval of respectable people. For instance his having an Eros put on his shield, hurling thunderbolts, and Aristophon's painting of Nemea with Alcibiades in her arms.
117. Lysias 14.25.
118. He took an unfortunate Melian woman to live with him, and had a child by her. Athenaeus (12.48) tells of another mistress from Abydos.
119. Aelian, *Varia Historia* 13.38.
120. Plutarch, *Agesilaus* 3. This turned out

badly for Leotychides, the son born to Timaea.

121. Diodorus 13.41.

122. *Frogs* 1425. Euripides then votes against him, because he was slow to help the city and quick to harm her, found plenty of resources for himself and little for Athens; after which Aeschylus speaks the lines quoted on p. 243 above.

123. Aelian, *Varia Historia* 11.7.

124. *Symposium* 208 c. ff.

125. See p. 144 above.

126. Athenaeus lists them, 13.89.

127. Aelian and Athenaeus, the chief sources, give an endless series of persons well known for some quality or other, and Athenaeus (12.72) descends into a list of the fat and the thin. For the individual names they could resort to the Old, Middle and New Comedy.

128. Statues of orators and philosophers began with Gorgias and became common only from the fourth century.

129. In the theatre at Athens, where Plutarch says (*Moralia* 821 f.) that bronze statues of the three great tragic writers were not put up till the fourth century, it was evidently thought imprudent to deny the 'minor deities' the same honour, but in Pausanias' time the more famous were no longer there. He found (1.21.1) 'mostly statues of the less important tragic and comic writers'; the only famous comic writer was Menander, which suggests Aristophanes was absent. It may be that Roman thefts of art-objects were to blame. Pausanias also mentions (9.30.2) the statues of poets and musicians on Mount Helicon. Some were of historical figures, e.g. Hesiod, Arion and Sacadas, some mythical: Thamyris, and Orpheus with the mysteries and the animals turned to stone.

130. A statue of Gorgias was set up by his great-nephew at Olympia, where he had once appeared; he himself ordered the gilded statue at Delphi.

According to Valerius Maximus (8.16) the whole of Greece contributed to a solid gold statue of him at Delphi. See Pausanias 6.17.5, 10.18.7.

131. At Delphi the amphictyony officially erected statues to defenders of the country, Pausanias 9.19.1. Soldiers commemorated their recruiting officer Pythes at Olympia with two statues by Lysippus, Pausanias 6.14.4. The one of Aristotle also at Olympia may have been put up by a disciple, or, since he was much respected by Alexander and Antipater, by a military man, Pausanias 6.4.5.

132. Pausanias 10.9.4. The Aetolians too later put up statues of generals with gods at Delphi to honour great deeds against the Gauls, Pausanias 10.15.1. He speaks of one Aetolian general who defeated the Gauls, 10.16.2.

133. Pausanias 6.3.6. The supplanted figures seem not to have been thrown out, however, and may even simply have been given new heads.

134. Thucydides 1.132. The Spartans immediately had the inscription corrected.

135. Cf. the beginning of Aristophanes' *Lysistrata* and then (387 ff.) the question the Proboulos asks, recalling the day four years earlier, when the speech Demostratus was making in favour of the Sicilian expedition at the popular assembly was interrupted by loud cries from all the rooftops as the women celebrated and danced in honour of Adonis, shouting: '*aiai Adonin*' and 'Adonis is dead'. In the same play we learn details (641 ff.) of the solemn procession of women, some in costume, at certain rites. One, who seems to be an ordinary Athenian woman telling of common experiences, says: 'When I was just seven, I carried a relic for Pallas; in my tenth year I became a mill-girl (*aletris*) serving Pallas Archegetes; then I was disguised in saffron robes as a she-bear at the Brauronia, and when I grew to be a pretty girl I was

one of the basket-carriers and had a net of figs to hold.'

136. In *Medea* 1081 Euripides expresses women's claim to the life of the mind and to poetry: the chorus of Corinthian women say: 'often my mind has sought what is hidden, and I have tried to win the prize of truth less modestly than befits our sex; but we too have our muse [does this refer more to poetry or rather to sharing the world of the mind?] and she dwells with us; not with all, and you might find only a few of us among many; yet the world of women is not without its muse.' We may remember the Boeotian women-poets.

137. Cf. Sophocles, *frag.* 61 Nauck.

138. Thucydides 2.45.

139. It is hard to credit Plutarch's *Pericles* 28, where Pericles gives a funeral oration on the Athenians who have died fighting at Samos, and is then crowned by the women like a victorious athlete, with garlands and ribbons; only Elpinice, Cimon's sister, reproaches him bitterly, and he replies very uncivilly and scornfully.

140. Xenophon, *Memorabilia* 2.2.4, *Oeconomicus* 7.11 and 19.

141. Diogenes Laertius 6.1.5.

142. Sophocles, *frag.* 524 Nauck.

143. Aelian, *Varia Historia* 10.15. Others say that the Athenian State provided dowries for his daughters.

144. Callias first married Glaucon's daughter, who bore him a son, Hipponicus the Fourth, and after her death a daughter of Ischomachus. Less than a year later, when his father-in-law died, he began a liaison with her mother, who drove her daughter out of the house (it is true this was considered shocking). Soon tiring of his new mistress, he turned her out and tried to marry a relative of Andocides, but Andocides forbade it, and Callias made efforts to set his wishes aside by cunning. The last wife, after her rejection, then bore a son, whom Callias refused at first to

recognize; later he fell in love with her again and accepted the child. Incidentally, the marriage of siblings was avoided only when they were born of the same mother; Plutarch, in *Themistocles* 32, states that Archeptolis, the son of Themistocles, married Mnesiptolema, his sister by a different mother. As long as the number and quality of citizens did not suffer, nobody in antiquity had any objection to such unions.

145. The women who come in, bringing their children, after Socrates has bathed, and before he takes the poison, and with whom he talks for a while until he sends them away too, are probably relatives, perhaps his sisters. When his pupils then also break down in tears, he says he has sent the women away on purpose to avoid such foolishness.

146. Aspasia is also introduced, though indirectly, in the pseudo-Platonic *Menexenus.*

147. Polyaenus 8.54.

148. The heroic deed of Telesilla of Argos at the invasion of Cleomenes, recounted in Pausanias, 2.20.7, occurs at the turn of the sixth to the fifth century; we cannot know how much is true and how much is myth.

149. Cf. also Herodotus 1, on the abduction of Io, and the parody about the origin of the Peloponnesian War in Aristophanes' *Acharnians* 529 ff.

150. In Lysias 1, *On the Murder of Eratosthenes,* Euphiletus tells a court of heliasts how he caught his wife's seducer, Eratosthenes, *in flagrante* and killed him. It was the peculiarity of Eratosthenes to seduce only married women. Because he knows that the judges take such cases seriously, Euphiletus goes into the detail of having been deceived by a slave-woman in the seducer's pay, and, warned by a woman Eratosthenes had abandoned, having forced this slave to help in unmasking his wife. At the decisive moment, when Eratosthenes was in

the house, Euphiletus went out, collected neighbours and friends as witnesses, and returned with torches to find the lovers together. In spite of his pleas and offers of money the seducer was killed by Euphiletus, with the melodramatic words: 'It is not I who kill you, but the law of the State.'

151. The love affair was not a motive used as a matter of course by these dramatists, as is clearly shown by *Orestes*. Electra has long been engaged to Pylades, but this betrothal has no dramatic force in the play. Not only is there no mention of it in the first scene between Orestes and Pylades, so that we only hear of it quite late (line 1079), but also, in the great scene with the three together, where Electra and Pylades first meet, they take no notice of each other for a long time. It is Orestes who remarks that he has betrothed his sister to Pylades, who confirms this (1092) and announces his intention of dying with them both; this does not prevent the ungallant bridegroom from saying just afterwards, when he refers to his fear that the chorus may babble about their plans for revenge, 'I do not trust these women.'

152. For instance *Orestes* 602, naively repeated by the female chorus.

153. A retort is given by the chorus in *Thesmophoriazusae* 785 ff.

154. His opinion is, more or less, that it ought to be possible to shake children down off the trees; compare Milton, *Paradise Lost* 858. Old Susarion, in the line quoted by Aristophanes in *Lysistrata* (1038) seems to have drawn the conclusion of the specifically Athenian view that woman was a necessary evil: 'neither with the deadly pests nor without the deadly pests'. [Susarion is reputed to be the father of Attic comedy.]

155. Cf. 771. It is also of interest that when she thinks of suicide earlier in the play (419 ff.) she justifies her intention by the need to avoid bringing scandal on her husband and sons, conforming to what was always the chief concern in Athens – the importance of a blamelessly respectable marriage; the mother's later infidelity would harm the legitimate sons. There is supposed to be a fifth-century parallel to Phaedra's vengeance on Hippolytus. According to Ptolemy Hephaestus, the elder Artemisia loved Dardanus, a young man from Abydos; her love was not returned, and she put out his eyes while he slept; when the pangs of love only grew worse, she consulted an oracle and leapt from the Leucadian Rock (Westermann, *Mythographoi* p. 198).

156. Thargelia, who was married fourteen times, also had political influence. Plutarch (*Pericles* 24) says she had won over all her lovers to Persia, so that the Persian party flourished in all the places where these men were respected citizens.

157. Athenaeus (13.25) says she brought numbers of beautiful women into Greece, and that her hetaerae were everywhere.

158. It was a preliminary accusation.

159. In the pseudo-Platonic *Menexenus*, 235 e.

160. *De inventione* 1.31.

161. A determined attempt at a complete whitewash is made by Adolf Schmidt in *Perikleischer Zeitalter*, vol. I, p. 89 and p. 288. According to Schmidt, Aspasia was neither a harlot nor at any time resident in a brothel; she did not marry Lysicles but merely accepted his protection after the death of Pericles, whom she outlived by only a year; Aspasia, further, probably ended her days peacefully in Athens and long enjoyed the society of Socrates and Xenophon. Though it is admitted that Cratinus in *Chirones* (about 440 B.C.) refers to her as *pallaché* and Eupolis in *Demes* (about 413 B.C.) as *porné* these, says Schmidt, are pejoratives commonly used by the comic writers. The fact that the whole period (that of the ancient comedy) offers

absolutely no basis for historical criticism is ignored by this worthy scholar, in whose work (p. 113) the social circle of Pericles and Aspasia comes over as just like that of a liberally inclined professor or Cabinet Minister of our own day.

162. As so little interest was devoted to these relationships in comparison with the rest of life, it was a long time before the development of the novel of love, which could only come into being when the Greeks were reduced to the horizons of private life.

163. Cf. the fragment from Plutarch's *On Love*, partly based on Plato and the tragic writers, which stresses the pathological aspect of passion.

164. There were no special health-resorts; the really ill went on pilgrimages to temples of Asclepius. Visiting places away from home for pleasure would have been unthinkable, and Aristippus, who travelled for enjoyment, was marvelled at.

165. On the *kottabos*, cf. Pauly-Wissowa.

166. In *Protagoras* 347 cf. it is explained that in the houses of humble people, who were unable through lack of education to entertain each other over their wine by their personal gifts and conversation, flute-players were necessary and musical originality was well rewarded; but where cultivated people met together there was no need of them, nor of dancing-girls of lyre-players.

167. Isocrates, *Areopagiticus* 49.

168. This is the order given in Aristophanes' *Wasps* (1216 f.)

169. Plato, *Symposium* 176 e.

170. Mnesitheus in Athenaeus 2.2. It was probably a different Mnesitheus, a doctor, who prescribed hard drinking as a purge. He recommended that only good wine, not undiluted, should be used, and nothing eaten with it, also that the patient should not go to sleep without having vomited.

171. For instance in the *Bacchae* of Euripides, 278 ff.

172. Plato, *Laws* 637 b.

173. *Greek Anthology* 11.43.

174. Athenaeus 15.49.

175. Athenaeus 14.43.

176. Athenaeus 6.56.

177. In the foregoing period a change had been introduced from sitting to reclining, though we have no exact record of it. This may well have been to make conversation more general.

178. The figure of the rich man, Callias, is worth noting. He is rejoicing in the success of his beloved Autolycus, who has been a victor at the Panathenaea, and whose father, Lycon, is present, which seems to cause no embarrassment. Critobulus, vain of his beauty, is openly in love with Clinias and this too is accepted as a matter of course; Critobulus is already married and Clinias (4.23) is somewhat his senior. Here we have, in Antisthenes, perhaps the earliest portrait of the cynic, very carefully drawn. Envied even by Callias himself (4.44), he is allowed some keen thrusts of wit, and asks Socrates, who has said that women in general are a civilizing influence, why he has the worst wife in the world. He replies that it is because if he can put up with Xanthippe he can get on with anybody and everybody. Finally (8) everyone present turns out to be in love, and Socrates makes fun of Antisthenes' declaration of love. He praises the sublimity of Callias's love for Autolycus (which is the talk of the town) and Hermogenes replies: 'I admire the way you have managed to flatter Callias and at the same time to teach him (the host) how he ought to behave.' Then comes Socrates' great description of the evils of the kind of love between men which has no spiritual element and does not aim at virtue; he solemnly addresses Callias again and claims his virtue as an example for the city. Then Autolycus and his father take their leave, and there follows the mime by the two dancers

(as Ariadne and Dionysus) and the general goodbyes, with the single men swearing to marry and the husbands hurrying home to their wives. Socrates, Callias and the rest go to catch up with Autolycus and his father.

179. This man from Syracuse, who speaks surprisingly freely (4.52 ff.), also accosts Socrates rather uncivilly and repeats some of the vulgar Athenian criticisms of him (i.e. the paid entertainer criticises the guest). Socrates then asks for the usual acrobatics to be replaced by a charming pantomime, representing Charites, Horai and Nymphs.

180. Cf. Athenaeus 613d f. for the suggestion that this type, perhaps traditional in good society from an earlier time, might be detestable. Here the author finds him useful as a relief from the guests' admiration and wonder at the beauty of Autolycus. A harsher kind of joker, playing tricks on everyone including his own sons, was the illusionist (*planos*), Athenaeus 615e.

181. Athenaeus discusses both *Symposia* (504c ff. and 186e, Plato's in particular in 192a–f).

182. Conversations in the open air often took place in the semi-circular spaces, or seats (*hêmikuklion*); there, according to Plutarch, *Alcibiades* 17, the amateur politicians sat before the Sicilian expedition, and drew Sicily and Africa in outline on the ground.

183. Protagoras is strolling in the *prostoon* (portico), flanked on the left by Callias, Paralus and Charmides, on the right by Xanthippus, Philippides and his most distinguished pupil, Antimoerus of Mende. Listeners follow them, most of them strangers, drawn by Protagoras from cities everywhere, but some Athenians too. All take great care not to walk ahead of him; each time he turns, they divide neatly left and right and fall in again behind him and his six companions. In the portico opposite, Hippias is found seated, also surrounded by many Athenians and foreigners on the benches; Prodicus has been given a special little room (*oikema*) where he is resting on cushions and wrapped in rugs, with, again, many listeners round him on couches. Freedom of speech is remarkable here too (320 a); though Alcibiades is present, Socrates talks of how Pericles (Alcibiades' guardian, here supposed to be still alive) sent his brother Clinias to a different tutor for fear Alcibiades would corrupt him.

184. For this we refer the reader to Schwegler, *Geschichte der griechischen Philosophie* p. 90 ff. and Curtius, *Griechische Geschichte* vol. 3, 97 ff. As for the name, Protagoras was the first to call himself *sophistes*. Plato however makes him explain that the more prudent sophists avoided the name, and pretended that their art was part of gymnastics, music and so forth (*Protagoras* 316.d. f).

185. For instance, Plato represents Gorgias and his companion Polus as falling into all kinds of traps laid by Socrates, and as incapable of keeping their bad intentions secret. He also of course makes them lose their tempers, while Socrates asserts that it gives him as much pleasure to be defeated in an argument as to win it; he would rather suffer injustice than act unjustly. A source in Athenaeus (504e ff.) takes the side of Gorgias against Plato, when Gorgias, after reading Plato's dialogue, is supposed to have said that he had neither said nor heard what was recorded there. Aristotle (*Rhetoric* 3.18) says Gorgias had a special method with opponents, answering their serious remarks with sarcasm and their sarcasm with seriousness. When he was asked how he remained healthy in his old age, he said he had never done anything 'for pleasure's sake'. In any case, the fact that Plato wrote a *Protagoras*, a *Hippias* and a *Gorgias*, and felt obliged to mention Prodicus, as well as the attack in the last

quarter of *Phaedrus*, all shows how maddeningly important they were to him.

186. Protagoras is said by Plutarch (*Pericles* 36) to have been close to Pericles, who had him sent to Thurii in 443, to revise the city's laws. There is no mistaking the influence of Gorgias on Thucydides; Philostratus says that he and Pericles were older men, Alcibiades and Critias still young, when Gorgias attached them to himself; and Isocrates too was considered a pupil of his.

187. Especially Hippias, according to Philostratus, *Lives of the Sophists* 1.11.

188. In the reign of Septimius Severus, Philostratus says (*ibid.* 1.10) that taking fees was a business without dishonour, because people appreciate what they pay for more than what they get free. Is it thought that they received high fees because the Athenians were stupid?

189. In a fragment of his *Antiope* Euripides says plainly that given any degree of eloquence it is possible to derive a *pro* and a *contra* from every subject (*frag.* 189 Nauck).

190. Cf. Xenophon, *Memorabilia* 4.4.6. Plato, *Hippias* 363 c. f., *Gorgias* 456. This was an implicit but open admission that in the case in point they made no factual claim, but argued the case as an exercise; Plato twists this as if Gorgias were saying that each time they spoke on a specialized subject the orator could seriously defeat the expert.

191. For Philostratus, what distinguished the sophists was, first, speaking impromptu, and then this power of eloquence; not what Plato calls sophistry. Because they possessed this gift, Eudoxus of Cnidos, a pupil of Plato's, and also Leon of Byzantium, were counted among the sophists, like all the philosophers of outstanding fluency (*Lives of the Sophists* 1.1 and 1.2).

192. In Plato's *Symposium* 198 c, after Agathon has finished the brilliant description of Eros, Socrates says (referring to *Odyssey* XI.633 ff.): 'I felt like Odysseus in Homer. I was afraid Agathon would end by sending me the head of Gorgias (the Gorgon's head) and turn me to stone in speechless astonishment.'

193. Did Prodicus really recite it by way of an entrance fee, as Philostratus says in the Introduction to *Lives of the Sophists*? We should also mention here the consolatory lectures of the sophist Antiphon, who promised to drive out the heaviest grief from the mind. Another epideictic feat must have been the defence of Busiris by a sophist living in Cyprus, who is attacked by Isocrates in his *Busiris*. This poor devil, who had also composed an accusation against Socrates, no doubt put together the crudest paradoxical subject-matter for the sake of effect.

194. This shows the opposite, the Spartan conciseness in speech (brachylogy) in its true light.

195. Altogether the sophists may well have been rather refreshing beside the ethical chatter of the philosophers.

196. Plato, *Hippias Minor* 368 b.

197. Philostratus, *Lives of the Sophists* 1.11.

198. Plato, *Hippias Major* 285 d.

199. *Protagoras* 318 e.

200. He may have owed his leaning towards statistics and economics to their influence.

201. Philostratus tells us that Prodicus got together young noblemen and the sons of the rich, and that he had a network of assistants to hunt for them.

202. Protagoras asked 100 *minae* for his course, and earned more than Pheidias.

203. The 'holy word' (*Clouds* 1036 ff.), entirely given over to conjuring tricks, conveys some idea of the worst sophists.

204. It may be questioned, for instance, whether the sophists even once chose the theme of arguing away financial obligations; perhaps

Aristophanes is merely anticipating such a case, as if to say: 'Sophistry would end up making this or that possible.' On the subject of Pheidippides, who was transformed into a brilliant talker by the teachings of Socrates, Aristophanes says (*Clouds* 1173 ff.) that all this was a native growth; so it could not be blamed on foreign sophists.

205. Plutarch, *Pericles* 5.8, where following Plato in *Phaedrus* 270a it is explained that apart from his own fortunate gifts, Pericles owed Anaxagoras his idealistic purpose in all he did. We cannot tell how far Plutarch is a reliable source for the things that Thucydides does not report.

206. It was not long afterwards that a certain Dionysius dared to commit a temple-robbery.

207. A sinister illustration of this is given in Polyaenus' story (1. 40) of how Alcibiades tested his friends by showing them, in a dark corner, a dummy made to look like a man who had been murdered, and asking each of them for his support in the affair. Everyone retreated except Callias, who fell in with the thing and became his best friend.

208. Diodorus 13.37.

209. Diodorus 12.77.

210. Euripides, *frag.* 21 Nauck.

211. For this extravagant legend cf. Preller, *Griechische Mythologie* 2. p. 100 f. The fragment of *Erechtheus* preserved in the Leocrates speech of Lycurgus ends with the cry: 'O my country, if all who dwell here loved you as I do! Then we would live here in peace and no harm would come to you.'

212. Euripides, *frag.* 597 Nauck.

213. The 'hollow hand' of the *prytaneis* is spoken of in *Peace* (907 ff.) and *Thesmophoriazusae* (936), and in *Birds* (1111 ff.) the judges at the games are offered the chance of getting a nice little post and making something on the side.

214. *Thesmophoriazusae* 395 ff. Also the speech of Mnesilochus while

disguised as a woman (466 ff.) cannot be entirely rejected as historical evidence. He speaks of adultery with serving-men and mule-drivers, and gives details of the deceptions practised on the husband to arrange the lover's visits, and to have a baby accepted as legitimate. Later, at line 555 ff., there are accounts of wine-drinking, paying the go-between with gifts of meat, plotting to claim the husband is mad, exchanging children, when the wife has borne a girl and her slave a boy, and so on. The parabasis (785 ff.) can only offer meagre excuses, first, that men desire women in spite of all, and secondly, that men are just as bad.

215. Late antiquity never idealized this comedy as modern classical scholarship often does; in imperial times Aristophanes was considered a vulgar joker, and Plutarch (*On Flattery* c. 27) takes the view that the malice and filth that burdened the poets outweighs any possible achievement. Besides, amidst all this, what can the Athenians have made of a figure such as the Hippolytus of Euripides? Were there any parallels in real life for this orphic and abstinent youth?

216. This was the reason for Plato sending the comedies of Aristophanes to Dionysius the Elder, who wished to learn about the Athenian *politeia*. Cf also W. Vischer, 'Über die Benutzung der alten Komödie als geschichtlicher Quelle' ('On the use of the old comedy as a historical source'), *Kleine Schriften* I, pp. 459–85.

217. *Rhetoric* I. 15.15. Was it a generally admitted thing: 'Yes, none of us are good'? Or did people proudly say of themselves in particular: 'I am bad'? The word *poneros* means not exactly a good-for-nothing, rather the sinner who is clever enough to know better.

218. Rather more flatteringly, Athens is compared in *Apology* 30 e with a noble great horse, whose only fault is

that its sheer size makes it rather lazy so it needs the spur. As for rhetoric, Aristotle and Anaximenes treat their listeners just like the 'great beast'.

219. The rest of the argument, aimed of course at Alcibiades, shows how men like this are lost to philosophy.

220. During the reign of terror under the Thirty, as in the French Revolution, freebooters appeared, preying on defenceless country people and taking the little they had (Lysias 31.18).

221. It often happened at this time that fathers took their sons to law for not supporting them. Cf. Aelian, *frag.* 4. Socrates blamed the fathers who failed to educate their sons and then, when in want, sued them in the courts and accused them of ingratitude.

222. *Laws* 872 d emphasises the large number of domestic murders in cities where order had broken down.

223. Plutarch, *Moralia* 834 e ff.

v: The Fourth Century to the Age of Alexander

1. Mommsen, *History of Rome* book II ch. V.

2. 'They have changed their language and their former aims, but to this day they still celebrate one of the Hellenic festivals, when they all assemble to remember the old names and customs; then they mourn and weep together and go their ways.' Quoted by Athenaeus, 633c; Aristoxenus, writing before the end of the fourth century, believed, probably wrongly, that the conquerors were Etruscans. The city yielded between 438–424 B.C.

3. Mommsen, *History of Rome*.

4. We must note, though, that there are still in existence some Sicilian coins of beautiful Greek design with Punic inscriptions.

5. Plutarch, *Timoleon* 1.

6. *Ibid* 22.

7. Strabo 13.1.59.

8. Diodorus 15.76.

9. Cf. Plutarch, *Cimon* 19.

10. Plutarch says (*Alexander* 3) that when the Artemision at Ephesus caught fire (356 B.C.) 'all the magicians to be found in Ephesus' were beside themselves – just as though there were a great many. This is the only testimony of its kind.

11. According to what was probably the official geography, in Plutarch, *Phocion* 29, Epirus would still have been part of Greece, which reached from Taenaron to the foothills of the Ceraunian range.

12. Diodorus 15.36.

13. Cf., on Macedonia, Curtius, *Griechische Geschichte*, vol. 3, 394 ff.

14. Cf. the principal source, Herodotus 8.137 ff., for the genealogical table of the Temenids down to Alexander Philhellene.

15. The Celts were considered by Aristotle, *Nicomachean Ethics* 3.10, as the most recklessly brave of all races, fearing nothing, not even earthquakes or the sea.

16. Strabo says (7. *frag.* 20) that Pella was the commercial centre of Macedonia. Philip, who was born in this old administrative city, later enlarged it.

17. Philosophy helped to tear it apart. For an account of how civic crises could lead to the outbreak of private quarrels cf. Plutarch, *Moralia* 479a, where the intriguing slave, the insinuating flatterer and the envious scandalmonger are listed as those accused in the line: 'in civil war even the criminal finds honour'.

18. It was clear at a later date to Pausanias, for instance (3.7.10), that the Peloponnesian War 'split the foundations of Hellas'. In the surviving fragment of his *Olympiacus* (33.) where Lysias advises the honoured guests at his banquet to free Sicily by driving out Dionysius, and to make a start at once by

looting the splendid tent this tyrant had sent to Olympia – much use that would have been – the wretched condition of Hellas (which here means the whole of Greece) is outlined as follows:

'Much of Hellas is in the hands of the barbarians, many cities have been laid waste by tyrants. If this had come about through weakness, we would have had to accept the inevitable; but since it is the result of dissension and vindictiveness, why not put a stop to all this? . . . All about us we see great dangers; you know that power belongs to those who control the sea, and now the Persian King possesses great wealth, and thanks to this an army of Greek mercenaries and a fleet of ships, and so does the tyrant of Sicily. What we must do is lay aside our differences, work to save ourselves and repent of the past . . .'

Finally the speaker expresses his astonishment at the attitude of the Spartans, who are letting Hellas burn, that is tolerating the oppression of Greater Greece and Greek Asia by tyrants – to which Sparta might have replied: 'We were making excellent progress against the Persians in Asia Minor under our Agesilaus until Athens, Thebes, and the rest, bribed by the Great King, rose against us and forced us to recall our leader.'

19. Isocrates in his *Philip* develops the foolish fantasy of Greek cities, each free and able to 'consult' the Macedonian court by means of delegates, all reconciled with each other by Philip and at the same time ready to be his trusted allies and auxiliaries against Persia. The orator says (68) that if Philip as the benign ruler of the Hellenes could not bring this about, he would yet win the love of the Hellenes, and this would be a far greater achievement than taking many Greek cities by force. In reality, if this national parliament had come into being at Pella, the delegates would have been plotted against in the different cities, and any whose requests were refused by Philip would have faced State trials at home. The delegates would also have arrived with the set purpose of evading the king and making a fool of him by getting their hands on the sums of money that flowed in from the Persian court, which had its paid agents everywhere.

20. We need only think of the way the Tarentines behaved to the Roman ambassadors. It was this element that was to blame for the disaster of the Sicilian expedition.

21. Plutarch in *Phocion* 2 gives this general description of the political mood and behaviour in the degenerate *polis*: it might be thought the *demos* would be most insubordinate to good rulers when things were going well, and they enjoy a feeling of activity and power; but the opposite happens too – misfortune makes people plaintive and quick to anger; the slightest emphatic word causes offence. Anyone who is blamed for a mistake feels his troubles are being thrown in his face; to speak freely is to seem contemptuous . . . A city in unexpected difficulties is full of protests, feeble, and cannot stand frankness, just when most in need of it; the situation makes it impossible to put right what has gone wrong.

22. Cf. p. 230 above. This manner is represented chiefly by Isocrates in the fourth century, and later it became even more common.

23. Cf. p. 68 above. The Zeus of oaths in the *bouleuterion* at Olympia may well have been given his bolts of lightning in both hands at this time. Certainly it was now that the practice of buying and selling agonal victory either began or spread. At the 98th Olympics in the boxing contests a Thessalian bribed three opponents to be beaten. A deception of another kind occurred in Alexander's time, when Anaximenes

of Lampsacus used his facility in
pastiche to forge a libel in the style
of Theopompus on several Greek
states, and made Theopompus very
unpopular (Pausanias 6.18.3).
24. *Laws* 947.
25. Cf. e.g. Aelian, *Varia Historia* 1.25.
26. Polyaenus 1.48.3.
27. Athenaeus 166e ff. quotes some of it
on Eubulus and Callistratus.
28. In Plato *Laches* 179 c these sons
blame their inadequacy on the fact
that their fathers let them do as they
liked in youth. A younger
descendant of Aristides earned his
living by interpreting dreams.
29. *Rhetoric* 2.15.3.
30. *Griechische Geschichte* vol. 3. p. 549
ff.
31. Pseudo-Plato, *Theages* 126 d.
32. The famous story of how Sophocles
in old age was brought to trial is
also one of bitter disagreement
between father and son. In
Aristophanes (*Birds* 1337 ff.) the
patraloias, who means to murder his
father for his inheritance, is a
sinister figure. It is true the poet
does not show him as a
representative Athenian, but in
modern times the situation in the
play would never suggest the
thought of parricide.
33. See Plutarch, *Phocion* 7, and
Athenaeus 165e. f. Cf. Schäfer,
Demosthenes vol. 1. p. 373 f.
34. See Plutarch, *ibid* 20, 30, 38.
Athenaeus (168e) says he was
universally hated and made fun of as
a spendthrift and a flatterer of the
Macedonian commander of
Munychia.
35. When a descendant of Harmodius
reproached Iphicrates with his
humble birth, the reply was 'My
family begins with me, yours will die
out with you.' Plutarch, *Moralia*
187b. Iphicrates was perhaps
over-optimistic.
36. Besides Plutarch, the main source is
Diodorus 13. It is mentioned here
that Lysander's father was on visiting
terms with the king, who ruled the

region about the Ammonium, and
that his brother was named Libys in
honour of this friendship, an odd
one for a Spartan.
37. Though in his way he was a kind of
rescuer; we should not forget what
these same oligarchs had suffered
from their *demos* everywhere.
38. Diodorus says that on his last
journey to the Ammonium he took
a great treasure with him, which
must have been the loot from his
conquests. However he died poor,
and his daughters' suitors deserted
them because of this and were
punished: Plutarch, *Lysander* 30.
39. Plutarch, *Lysander* 18. He filled
another eulogist's hat with silver,
and crowned a third.
40. The fact that Agesilaus left to go to
King Tachos might perhaps be
favourably interpreted on political
grounds, though Plutarch (*Agesilaus*
36) admits that he could no longer
bear to be in Sparta and sold
himself and his fame to the
Egyptian; in Athenaeus 536 he is
said to have gone away to live
'abroad and in comfort' because he
could not stand life at home; this
was in 338, certainly a time when
Sparta needed all the men she had.
In 314, Acrotatus became the
military leader of the Agrigentines
against Agathocles; he was expelled
from their service because of
scandalous behaviour.
41. Aelian, *Varia Historia* 12.52. He
compares the city with the harlots,
whom men want to be with only
once, and would never think of
living with, unless they were mad.
42. *Peace* 21. Earlier (19) he stresses the
helpfulness the Lacedaemonians
showed in spite of their victory, and
asks: what kind of peace treaty
would they have obtained from us,
if they had been defeated in a single
battle?
43. Diodorus (15.63) attributes the help
Athens gave Sparta on this occasion
to generosity.
44. Compare the passage in *On the*

Mysteries 103 ff. where Andocides warns the Athenians not to invalidate the amnesty by individual exceptions, thus depriving many people of their security; and also the case dealt with by Lysias in his Oration 18. Eucrates, the brother of General Nicias, and his son Niceratus, had been executed under the Thirty because they refused to cooperate. Despite this, a plea was brought immediately after the restoration of the democracy for confiscation of Eucrates' estate on the grounds of a crime he was alleged to have committed. It was unsuccessful at first; but it seems that in 397 a certain Poliuchus renewed the charge, and the sons of Eucrates defended themselves (8) by asking: 'Who else would suffer as we shall if this is done? Under the oligarchy members of our family were killed for being on the side of the people, and under the democracy we are to lose our possessions for being against the people.' The orator then tells the judges to their face that they usually give decisions from which the orators hope for personal gain, and that the confiscations might be justified if the State got some benefit from them; but as things are, part of the confiscated property disappears, part is sold at a loss, and the State would anyway be better off if the owners kept the money and paid their *leitourgia*. The conclusion is very eloquent: 'I am unable to call anyone as witness in our favour; for some of our relatives fell in war as brave men and defenders of the State, while the others have drunk the hemlock under the Thirty for the democracy and for your liberty; the virtue of our house and the city's misfortune are to blame for our isolation.' (It would be a good thing if some of the scholars who still praise fourth-century Athens could be forced to live in it for a year or so.) According to the

important hypothesis in Lysias 34, it was already feared, when the Thirty fell from power, that the masses might once more rise against the propertied class, and one Phormisius proposed that the active citizenship should be restricted to the landowners, which would have excluded five thousand citizens from it. Naturally Lysias, or his client, is against the proposal, but the fear was well founded.

45. The speech of Andocides *On the Peace* was an argument for an end to this war. The orator lists the times in the fifth century when a peace treaty was followed by new glory for Athens, and confutes the fools who want to continue the war till the Spartans are destroyed by asking what could then be expected from the barbarians (that is from the Great King, who will not tolerate one predominant power in Greece). He points out the complete lack of the necessary resources for a war, emphasizes that despite their victories the Spartans have offered reconciliation while Athens has always continued hostile, shows the worthlessness of an alliance with Argos (linking this with the usual disastrous consequences for Athens of befriending the weak instead of the strong, and making war for others' interests instead of keeping peace in her own) and declares that persuasion, cunning, bribery and force, not war, were the means by which Athens won her past greatness.

46. Andocides, *On the Peace* 1 ff.

47. Cf. what he says (112 f.) of young men making the best orators.

48. On the ridiculous shrine with the old tribunals dating from the mythical past – and staffed by contemporary Athenians! – cf. also Demosthenes, *Against Aristocrates*, 23.65–79, where they are all mentioned (the Areopagus, Palladium, Delphinium, Prytaneum

and the one in Phreattys) with their antiquities.

49. Andocides, *On the Mysteries* 149.

50. Cf. Rauchenstein on Demosthenes *On the Crown*, 18.103. Demosthenes goes on to boast (107) of having improved things in every way by his law. Isaeus' Oration 5 deals with the case of Dicaeogenes, which is typical of the impudence with which the burdens of State taxes were evaded. 'Do not pity him, o judges,' says the orator (35 ff.) 'as if he were poor and miserable, nor show him favour as one who has benefited the city. I shall prove him a rich man and a great scoundrel in his dealings with the city, his relatives and his friends. He could not evade the *choregia* but performed it as cheaply as he could. When so many offered themselves as trierarchs, he did not, nor did he share a trierarchy with others, though some became trierarchs whose whole fortune was less than his income from rents. And when all the citizens contributed so much in taxes on possessions (*eisphorai*) for the Corinthian War and to save the city, he paid nothing, not even the three hundred drachmas he had promised when he was challenged in the popular assembly. For this his name was put on the list of shame in front of the statues of the national heroes, with the inscription: "the following have failed in their promise to give money voluntarily to the *demos* to save the city".' The remaining details of Dicaeogenes' deceptions and mean actions to his family, his friends and the temple are of a kind often reported but rarely in such an accumulation. This man was descended from Harmodius, though he had no dining rights in the Prytaneum. It is sad to think that such a person could boldly face a court of law.

51. *Against Epicrates*, 27.6. The next speech too, *Against Ergocles*, begins with a powerful diatribe on those who are making a fortune by theft from the State and bribe-taking at a time when everyone is heavily taxed.

52. This is Boeckh's assumption in *Staatshaushaltung* vol.1, p. 777.

53. The same purpose was supposed to be served by making trade with Attica attractive to foreign merchants and shipowners, not only by an efficient system of commercial law, but also by entertainments and banquets, offered in return merely for 'liberal decisions and courtesies'.

54. Cf. Lysias, *frag.* 43 Thalheim (22 Gernet) for evidence that an honest guardian was sometimes falsely accused by officials appointed by the court.

55. From various sources it appears that things were worse in Halimus than in any other deme. Sons of the same father and mother would be given different status, one being turned down and the other accepted. The census jury had omitted from the lists the sons of old people with no money, and put in foreigners as citizens instead, sharing the bribes among themselves (five drachmas per head), and generally saved or ruined many persons according to what they could pay. Eubulides' father, too, had once, when he was *demarchos*, rejected ten people, nine of whom were reinstated by the court; on that occasion too the list of citizens had conveniently disappeared. During the persecution of Euxitheus, the weapons he had dedicated to Athena were stolen and the decree with which the *demos* had honoured him was mutilated; he was then said to have done this himself in the hope of incriminating his enemies; there was also a robbery at an isolated house he owned.

56. *Philippic* 1.35. In Isocrates' *Areopagiticus*, 53 f. too, the passion for festivals is seen as a disease. Another important testimony is that of Plutarch in *Moralia* 348d f., probably from an orator. The total spent on the tragic drama is calculated, with the apt comment of

a Spartan, who saw the reckoning,
that the Athenians took play in
earnest, wasting on the theatre sums
fit for great expeditions and armies.
Adding up the cost of all drama till
then, the demos would be found to
have spent more on Bacchae,
Phoenician Women and Medeas etc
than on wars for hegemony and
freedom. The *choregoi* also had to
supply the actors with delicacies for
their long periods of rehearsal, while
the seamen ate raw flour, onions
and cheese. Justin (6.9) has a
passage on the slackening of Attic
valour after Epaminondas' death,
with special mention of festivals and
drama. He remarks that this gave
Macedonia her chance of greatness.

57. Demosthenes 3.29.

58. *Ibid.* and *Against Aristocrates*, 13.206.

59. As Demades put it, Curtius,
Griechische Geschichte Vol. 3. p. 730.

60. Polyaenus 6.2.2. Andocides (*On the
Mysteries* 138) describes the terrible
fate that often awaited those
kidnapped and sold.

61. Plutarch (*de prof.* 10) says: 'By far
the greatest number of them were
attached to the Athenian schools.'
Cf. also Plutarch, *Moralia* 605a.

62. Diodorus says of Chares (15.95) that
he always took care to avoid the
enemy and attack the allies, and in
Phocion 11 Plutarch tells how when
an Athenian fleet arrived, the allies
and islanders would usually set up
palisades on the walls and barriers
round the harbours, while the slaves,
women and children were taken into
the towns for protection; but when
Phocion came they sailed out to
greet him with garlands twined
round their spears. Cf. also *ibid.* 14
on Chares.

63. E.g. Isocrates, *On the Peace* 50: 'It is
true the death penalty is imposed for
corruption, but we appoint known
bribe-takers as generals.' And 55:
'We send out, as generals, men we
would never consult in our private
affairs nor even in matters of state.'

64. 23. 166 ff. The Thracian,

Cersobleptes, would have pardoned
him, as it was not the Thracians'
custom to kill each other (Philip too
preferred to spare human lives); a
Greek city was the right place for
the purpose.

65. Cf. Demosthenes' complaint, 23. 196
ff, that people now said Timotheus
took Corcyra, Iphicrates destroyed
the Spartan regiment, and Chabrias
won the battle of Naxos, while
famous deeds of the past such as
Marathon were attributed to the
polis. But in reality it was no longer
the Attic *polis* that won victories, but
mercenaries led by capable officers.

66. Athenaeus 532b.

67. 23.196 ff. At 185 we find:
'Charidemus might be well rewarded
by you if no proceedings were taken
against him. But this will not satisfy
the orators; they insist on
proclaiming him a citizen! A
benefactor! Let him be given crowns
and gifts! And for this he bribes
them in secret, and you sit there
duped and wonder what is going
on.'

68. Demosthenes 3.29, and similarly
23.207 ff.

69. After a victory on Euboea, Phocion
once released all the Greeks he had
taken prisoner for fear the Athenian
orators would whip up the people to
maltreat them, Plutarch, *Phocion* 13.

70. He seems to have been the type of
the demagogue who took bribes
because of his gluttony. According
to Plutarch (*Moralia* 525c. f.)
Demades was astonished, when once
he saw Phocion at breakfast, to
think that this statesman could be
satisfied with so little; he himself
was a demagogue for the sake of his
stomach. Antipatrus, who saw him
in old age, said that he was like an
animal that had been sacrificed —
there was nothing left of him but his
tongue and his belly.

71. Hyperides in his *Defence of
Euxenippus* (33), attacks the
scandalous sycophancy of Polyeuctus
against the innocent Euxenippus:

'There is no state in the world, nor any monarch, nor any people, more magnanimous than the demos of Athens, for we do not allow those who are persecuted by the sycophants, whether singly or as a group, to be ruined, but come to their aid.' And there follows a catalogue of confiscations from innocent people by which the sycophants had tried in vain to bribe the *demos*. A certain Tisis tried to confiscate the fortune (60 talents) of Euthycrates; then he proposed that of Philippus and Nausicles, who had made money from mining; but here he made his mistake, and was convicted of *atimia*. Another, Lysandrus, brought information against Epicrates of Pallene, the owner of a mine in which the wealthiest citizens were shareholders; he promised that confiscating the profits would enrich the city by 300 talents, but the judges stuck to the law and confirmed the owners' title. After some further arguments about the damage done by such confiscations, the orator asks: 'If making and saving money is harmful, who is going to accept any risks at all?' But a fair question is also how *much more* often, on other occasions, did the *demos* consent to the confiscation? Perhaps the cases Hyperides lists were in fact exceptions.

72. If anything of the kind existed the Alexandrian scholars would mention it. As things were, when Philip came to the Peloponnese, the Spartans had nothing to oppose to him except their hard-bitten Laconicism, and from Thebes we have no direct testimony in the time of his hegemony. It is a pity that Plutarch left no Life of Epaminondas.

73. *Philippic* 2.27. A similar appeal to Athenian vanity occurs in 23.107, where the Olynthians are held up as an example to the Athenians.

74. Hyperides, *Defence of Euxenippus* 33 f. Though by the time this was delivered Alexander was already in Asia.

75. Plutarch tells in *Demosthenes* 7 how the actor Satyrus helped Demosthenes to improve his delivery when he was in despair at not getting a hearing, while coarse, drunken men dominated the rostrum; but we doubt whether the best utterance in the world would have had much effect against this crew. But Demosthenes himself (8) believed that attention to fluency was the mark of the democrat, while indifference as to the reception of a speech was typical of the oligarch, who would rely more on force than persuasion. Later on, when he had grown popular with the masses, the connoisseurs (*charientes*) considered his speech-making vulgar, commonplace and cheap (11). Phocion was rated the speaker who conveyed the most meaning in the briefest form. For a long time the worst orators had the most success, independently of eloquence.

76. Plutarch (*Demosthenes* 12) says that the choice of Demosthenes to represent Greek rights against Philip gave him a fine subject for his political activity; he put up a splendid fight, and his courageous speeches made him admired throughout Greece, while he won high praise from the King of Persia and even the good opinion of Philip himself.

77. Cf., on the Persian payments, the texts quoted from Westermann in Pauly's *Realencyclopädie* vol. 2. p. 970.

78. A. Schäfer makes out a reasoned critical defence of him.

79. Cf. Plutarch, *Demosthenes* 14, for his having been given power to execute traitors.

80. It is sometimes said that originally Philip sincerely wanted an agreement with Athens as the foremost naval power, but that Athens could not abandon her secure hold on the Chersonese,

while Philip needed it for his projects of conquest in Asia; the main point this proves is the artificiality of the Attic state. It must always be an error to depend for existence on such remote and precarious positions.

81. It would not be hard to put together a counter-argument in favour of peace and friendship with Philip, even using particular facts Demosthenes himself cites, like the Oreos affair, to the opposite effect. A retrospective account of the War of Chaeronea, assembling what can be said in its favour, and how it might have turned out much worse for Athens, is given in *On the Crown* (Oration 18).

82. Plutarch, *Demosthenes* 20. The rest of the story traditionally accepted in Athens is no doubt as given by Lucian, *Parasites* 42, where he describes the behaviour of the great men of Athens as follows: 'Isocrates never went into a court of law, let alone to war, either from timidity or because he hadn't the voice for it. Demades, Aeschines and Philocrates betrayed the city and themselves to Philip, and were his agents in Athens ... Hyperides, Demosthenes and Lycurgus had pretended to be so brave and roared so loud against Philip in the democratic assembly, and what did they do in the war? Hyperides and Lycurgus never left the city gates, but stayed within the walls hammering out little motions and little resolutions for the Council; while the chief orator, who had so often ranted in the assembly about "that coward from Macedonia, where you cannot even buy a decent slave", got as far as Boeotia and then threw away his shield before the hand-to-hand fighting began; all this is known to the whole world.' Cf. Plutarch, *Demosthenes* 8, on his 'cowardice in the field', because of which he made no spontaneous reply when Demades accused him of

it. *Ibid* 3 for his 'cowardice in danger and war'.

83. Plutarch, *Lives of the Ten Orators* on Hyperides, *Moralia* 848d ff. This proposal would defy belief, if it did not also appear in the dramatic, almost tragicomic description of the situation after Chaeronea by Lycurgus, *Against Leocrates* 41.

84. Hyperides, *Defence of Euxenippus* 18 ff., which also lists cases protected by the law from *eisangelia*. It is openly stated here that since the orators enjoyed honours and privileges because of their political activities, it was unjust to make the non-orators (*idiotas*) responsible for the dangers that the orators had caused.

85. The decree of honour awarded to him states that while he was in charge of the finances (twelve years, from 338 to 326) he increased the annual revenues of the state to 1,200 talents. Pausanias' view of him reads like a tribute to a second Pericles. 'The revenues he secured exceeded those of Pericles by more than 6,500 talents; he installed [new and more magnificent?] equipment (*pompeia*) for the festival of the goddess, and golden Nikes and ornaments for 100 maidens, as well as weapons, siege-engines and 400 triremes for use in war; his building work included the completion of the theatre others had begun, and also the arsenals in Piraeus and the gymnasium at the Lyceum.' One thing he could not change: the citizens' army was still defeated as at Chaeronea, and, soon after his death, was again beaten in the Lamian War.

86. For all his wealth he wore the same cloak summer and winter, and put on sandals only when absolutely necessary. He also imposed a fine of 6,000 drachmas to prevent women from using carriages to go out to Eleusis, so that the poor would not feel humbled by the rich; when his own wife disobeyed the regulation,

he paid the talent, but gave it to the sycophants. In personality he seems to have resembled a virtuous Jacobin.

87. [Codrus was the legendary King of Athens when it was threatened by the Dorians who had conquered the Peloponnese. They were told by an oracle that they would succeed if they spared the king, so Codrus went disguised to the Dorian camp, provoked a quarrel and was killed, whereupon the Dorians withdrew. Ed.]

88. The Athenians in their incorrigible vanity later really believed a story that, after conquering Thebes, Alexander sent a message to the heavily compromised Athenians that they should deal with Hellenic affairs because if he died they would rule Greece, Plutarch, *Alexander* 13.

89. Cf. 17, 25, 26, 59.

90. Cf. p. 389, note 30 above for the fact that money-prizes had to be introduced at the musical agon that Lycurgus himself founded; without them there was no longer sufficient enthusiasm.

91. From the surviving fragments of Hyperides' speech for the prosecution we quote the tenth for the insight it gives into the orators' circumstances: 'You reward the generals and the orators, in the kindness of your hearts, much more generously than the law prescribes, but with the one reservation that what they receive comes to them *through* you and not against your interests. Demosthenes and Demades (i.e. the former adversaries) have each earned more than seventy talents, not counting the money from the Persian Court and what they had from Alexander. But none of this satisfies them, and they have accepted presents that could have cost the State its very existence.'

92. Plutarch, *Demosthenes* 26. Of course people who talk like this are never quite in earnest, but only preaching

to others. Demosthenes went back to politics as soon as he could.

93. The last days of Demosthenes are recounted by Plutarch, *Demosthenes* 27 ff., evidently with much anecdotal embroidery.

94. Demosthenes of course wanted to make his city of Athens greater by all possible means, and only then to ensure its place as the leading power in the struggle for Greek freedom. Cf. B.G. Niebuhr, *Kleine Philologische Schriften*, Vol. 1, 480.

95. Aelian, *Varia Historia* 3.24.

96. Cf. Curtius, *Griechische Geschichte* vol. 3. p. 258: 'This Pythagorean doctrine was reformist. It laid claim to the whole human being, not just to the mind. It was an ideal of Hellenism, intended to be realized in life, and those who embraced it were impelled to spread its teaching.'

97. For the way in which the good Dion was taken to task by his moral tutors, cf. Plutarch, *On Flattery* 29 (*Mor.* 69f). This tells how, as Dion's striking personality and behaviour made him everyone's favourite, Plato warned him against pride over being singled out in this way (*authadeia*), and Speusippus in a letter told him not to become conceited at being so much talked of by women and young men, but to do honour to the Academy by giving Sicily piety, justice and good laws.

98. To some extent the outlook of these philosophical circles becomes clear in *The Sign of Socrates*, where Plutarch attempts a kind of historical novel in conversations, using documents which are mostly adequate, if fragmentary, and observing the background of time and place as well as he can. The story is that of a nobly-born Crotoniate, the wise Theanor, arriving in Thebes to take home to Italy the bones of Lysis; the news of his death has been brought by his daimon. He also wishes to repay Polymnis, the father of Epaminondas, for the hospitality he

has shown to Lysis. He learns, though, that all the special rites the sect prescribes have been performed for the dead man by his Theban friends, and that they will not accept his money, because Lysis has inspired them with the ideal of voluntary poverty – 'best nurse and beloved companion of man' – and taught them the duties of the Pythagorean ascetic. Lysis had left a lasting influence there. Cf. Curtius (n. 96) on the education of Epaminondas.

99. Polyaenus (2.3.5) however says his reason for not destroying Sparta was that otherwise Thebes would have joined his Peloponnesian allies in a war which could only have served to humiliate Sparta, not to increase the power of Thebes.

100. Plutarch (*Timoleon* 20) tells how Timoleon's people reproached the Greek mercenaries serving in the Carthaginian army.

101. According to Olympiodorus in his *Life of Plato* 4, Dionysius, who had already committed terrible crimes, was very proud of his abilities as a judge and boasted of them to Plato.

102. Rites in honour of the dead were generally very lavish among these Panhellenes. Timoleon's funeral procession was a splendid festival too (Plutarch, *Timoleon* 39).

103. We will not discuss whether Artemisia really consumed her husband's ashes a little at a time in drinks, as we are told by Gellius (10.18) and Valerius Maximus (4.6). It appears from Vitruvius, among others, that as a widow she was not wholly occupied by her mourning. She showed strength, cunning and tenacity in the war with the Rhodians. She is said to have conquered Rhodes completely, and to have put up a monument there to her victory, representing the city of Rhodes branded (with the iron) by herself. The Rhodians did not dare to remove it even later, but simply built a watchtower over it which they

called *abaton* – 'not to be approached'.

104. Diodorus 16.94. Compare the argument Dio Cassius attributes (42.32) to the unruly Dolabella when he despairs of obtaining Caesar's pardon: 'He desired to do something really wicked before dying, hoping thus to gain eternal fame.' Plutarch's accounts of the liberation of Thebes, in his *Life* of Pelopidas and in *The Sign of Socrates*, show a characteristic delight in the detail of a conspiracy and a crisis. Here Plutarch brings to mind the Italian writers of the Renaissance.

105. Cf. p. 31 ff. above.

106. Justin 16.5, Aelian, *frag.* 86.

107. Diogenes Laertius 5.6.6 and a variant in the *Suda, s.v. Heraclides*.

108. Athenaeus 7.33 f. A pun may be involved here, on *zen* as resembling Zeus, Zenos.

109. Plutarch in his *Agesilaus*, 21, says the letter was sent to Agesilaus. The story of the banquet is also told by Aelian, *Varia Historia* 12.51. There was a Carthaginian, Anno, who was not content with mortal status. He bought some birds, secretly trained them to say 'Anno is a god' and let them fly. Once free they sang their own melodies and forgot about Anno. Aelian, *ibid* 14.30.

110. Plutarch, *Moralia* 602b certainly used an old source for his maxim that it was neither noble nor just to leave one's home country and live in another; for instance a Spartan should honour his country even if it were in a shamefully bad condition and politically disrupted!

111. *Moralia* 604d f. Euripides expresses the idea of *ubi bene, ibi patria* – my home is where I feel at home – in the fragment (Nauck 1047) 'The eagle soars in flight through every sky, and to the good man every land is home.'

112. As early as Lysias (*Oration* 31.6) there is condemnation of those who could feel settled anywhere that offered them tolerable conditions; it was not

the city, he says, that they regarded as home, but their money-bags.

113. Pausanias 1.18.8. On the death of Demosthenes, too, Pausanias is surely expressing the accepted Greek view: 'It seems to me true to say that no man ever came to a good end if he gave himself up wholly to politics and relied entirely on the *demos*' (*ibid* 1.8.4).

114. Cf. Plutarch's important text *Mor.* 793 on physical exercise for old men, as well as young, even in imperial times.

115. *Politics* 8.3; he says of the cities which take most care of education that they aim at making all their children into athletes, while the Spartans, who avoid this, turn them into fighting animals (which is of no greater use to them).

116. *Politics* 8.4. He calculates that only two or three of the Olympic victors were successful both as boys and as grown men.

117. Pausanias 6.5.3. Polydamas was a victor at the 93rd Olympics.

118. Diodorus 14.109. Dionysius' ship on its way home to Sicily was driven into Tarentum by storms. The tyrant was consoled by his flatterers, who told him his talents had aroused envy, and he went on industriously writing, calling in famous poets to help revise his poetry. These collaborators praised him so much that he became much vainer of his poetic achievements than of his military successes; only Philoxenus, according to a well-known anecdote, refused to hold his tongue, Diodorus 15.6. Cf. p. 321 above for the story of the prize-winning tragedy Dionysius sent to Athens, and p. 175 for his sometimes successful attempts to persuade foreign boxers to pass themselves off as Syracusans.

119. Cf. the lists of various tendencies in Athenaeus, book 9.

120. For instance he complains that their teaching fees were three or four *minae* (he himself charged ten) and yet they pretended to despise gold

and silver; that they were alert to illogicalities in theory but not in life; claimed to know the future, but had nothing sensible to say of the present, and were thus inferior to ordinary people who only followed their own opinions but behaved more consistently and justly than these men who flaunted their learning. Those who set up as political teachers are attacked in much the same way. Of these bunglers Isocrates says that they could write no better than ordinary people could speak impromptu, and yet promised to make rhetors of their pupils. It is, he says, well known that many studied philosophy (in the hope of getting on as politicians or orators) and had no success, while others who had nothing to do with these sophists became famous speakers and politicians by their natural energy and with practice.

121. Cf. Athenaeus' story (261d) about the Tirynthians, and *ibid* the tradition of the outstanding wit of the inhabitants of Phaestus in Crete.

122. On this merriment cf. Nietszche, *Birth of Tragedy* § 9 ed. Karl Schlechta. [The main part of this runs: 'When by an effort we look straight at the sun, and turn away dazzled, we find dark, coloured flecks before our eyes as a kind of remedy: the contrary is the case with that bright clarity (*lit.* 'photographic effects') of the Sophoclean hero that is the Apolline mask; it is the necessary product of our glance into the inner terror of nature, like bright flecks to heal the sight after it has been seared by terrible darkness. It is only thus that the serious meaning of "Greek laughter" is to be understood; of course at the present time we are always meeting at every turn the mistaken idea of this merriment as a sign of undisturbed peace of mind.' Tr.]

123. For instance Athenaeus quotes (338a) the *geloia apomnemoneumata* of a

certain Aristodemus, and 348d f., the jokes of the celebrated fourth-century lyre-player Stratonicus, retold by Machon of Alexandria in leisurely iambics; this is all of very uneven interest and some of it sober to the point of dullness. Stratonicus' collection of jokes from prose writers (*ibid* 350ff.) might be used to give a fairly thorough account of Greek humour. (According to Ephorus, Stratonicus modelled his wit on that of the great Simonides.) Athenaeus also gives (98c) a good many epithets invented by Dionysius the Elder, by the orator Demades and others as more or less witty new descriptions of various things. When the real poets went in for this, they were often bold, but trenchant and appropriate. But in the fourth century this was an occupation for the idle moments of wits and pedants. Thus Dionysius has '*menandros*' for '*parthenos*' because a virgin is 'waiting for a man', '*menecrates*' for '*stylos*' because a pillar is strong and enduring; for '*muon diekdoseis*' (mouse-holes) '*mysteria, hoti tous mus terei*'. He intended to be witty; Demades' efforts were more in the nature of hackneyed phrases when he called Aegina 'rheum in the eye of Piraeus', Samos a piece torn off from Athens, the ephebes the springtime of the people, the city walls the garment of the city, the trumpeter the cockerel of the Athenians. For this he was known as 'the name-hunter'. A number of circumlocutions like these, intended as poetic, and some very amusing, are quoted by Athenaeus (10.70) from a fragment of Antiphanes. Flowers of speech no doubt were aimed at, though they are presented as riddles. Laconisms were similarly collected.

124. Athenaeus 260a, 614e. Cicero says that the Athenians, Siceliots, Rhodians and Byzantines were considered the wittiest of all (*Orator*

2. 54. 217). Argos, Corinth and Thebes get no mention.

125. Cf. Athenaeus 10.46 on the *bomolochoi* Philip was surrounded by.

126. See p. 332.

127. Cf. Athenaeus 14.3 on the *plethos tes sophias tautes* in Athens, including the sixty wits. This remained a recognized genre (*eidos*) which might recruit the occasional lyre-player, probably because there was no longer a demand for lyre-players, or jesting was better paid.

128. Clearchus is said by Athenaeus (10.86) to have preferred the older ways of asking riddles, and been critical of the new fashion for smutty jokes, questions about food, and the kisses now awarded as prizes, while drinking undiluted wine was the prescribed penalty.

129. Aelian (*Varia Historia* 3.35) reports that in earlier times laughter was not allowed in the Academy; the place was meant to be preserved from all boisterousness and frivolity.

130. Athenaeus 12.42.41 quoting Theopompus, cf. Aelian, *Varia Historia* 7.2.

131. Athenaeus 12.64 f. The logical conclusion of his address is that the happiest person on earth at that moment was the King of Persia; compared with him, Dionysius the Younger (whose ambassador in Tarentum Polyarchus then was) could make only a poor showing.

132. Lucian, *Dialogues of the Dead* 9.2. Philoxenus, the friend of Dionysius the Elder, wished he had the maw of a crane; in the new comedy a cook still gratefully mentions Labdacus the Sicilian as an innovator, Athenaeus 9.68.

133. From *Asotodidascalos* in Athenaeus 8.15.

134. Examples in Athenaeus 7.12 f.: 8.14.

135. Cf. Athenaeus 8.28 f., where even Aristotle is included; in Athenaeus the whole of this subject is dense with names.

136. E.g. on the Lydian speciality

'candaulos' Athenaeus 12.12. Goose-liver occurs as a delicacy in Eubulus, Athenaeus 9.32.

137. Athenaeus 6.4–11. Archippus even wrote a play entitled *Ichthyes*.

138. O. Ribbeck, *Kolax* (Leipzig 1883).

139. Athenaeus 6.28. His parasite says: 'I dine with anyone I please; he only has to send for me, and anyone who doesn't want me need not send for me, I'll be there anyway. I behave charmingly and make everyone laugh and praise the host. If someone contradicts him, I shout back and rebuke them. Then I have plenty to eat and drink, and go away. No slave goes before me carrying a torch. I slip along through the muddy puddles alone in the dark . . .'

140. The parasite of course felt a deep dislike of picnics. 'Whoever invented the custom of eating other people's food was a true friend of the masses, but as for the man who first thought of inviting guests to bring their own contributions – let him go penniless into exile' says a character in Eubulus: Athenaeus 6.35.

141. The real motive for inviting him was to make sure that someone, at least, would laugh at the host's own jokes, cf. Machon in Athenaeus 12.42.

142. Antiphanes in Athenaeus 6.35.

143. Alexis and Diphilus in Athenaeus 10.19.

144. Axionicus in Athenaeus 6.37. Occasionally a parasite was admired for his gluttony, like one mentioned by Athenaeus (10.18, quoting Alexis) who silently ate on, snuffling, and only nodded in answer to questions.

145. Apollodorus of Carystos in Athenaeus 6.43. The number of guests at one wedding was limited to thirty; the officials counting them found a parasite as the thirty-first and tried to turn him out, so he said: 'Count us again, and this time start with me' (Athenaeus 6.45).

146. Athenaeus 6.39. Aelian also gives a list of famous *kolakes* and information about them (*frag.* 107 f.).

147. Plutarch, *On Flattery* 14.16. The parasites of the *diadochoi* brought the art of flattery to a rare perfection; it can be judged from Plutarch's description (*ibid* 17) of the courtly group around Ptolemy Philopator with their parade of a critical attitude to his verses and textual readings, combined with their total silence about his crimes and Bacchanalian excesses.

148. Cf. Athenaeus 13.6 ff. Alexis for instance (7) makes someone say: 'We men know how to forgive a wrong, but [women] complain when they themselves have wronged others. They go about what they ought not to do, and leave undone what they should do, and swear untruths as well.' Amphis says that the hetaera's fortune is her aimiability, while the housewife stands on her rights; he concludes that the first is to be preferred (*ibid*).

149. Aristotle, *Politics* 2.6. Plutarch, *Agesilaus* 31.

150. Erwin Rohde, writing on the Greek novel, places them no earlier than the first century B.C. and assumes that they originated in Alexandria, but admits the influence of old Pythagorean concepts (*Der griechische Roman* p. 67).

151. Plutarch, *Pelopidas* 18.

152. Athenaeus (13.21) cites seven comedies whose titles were the names of hetaerae.

153. Cf. Anaxilas in Athenaeus 13.6.

154. E.g. Eubulus in Athenaeus 13.6 and Alexis *ibid* 23.

155. Cf. Athenaeus 13.29.

156. In *Wilhelm Meisters Lehrjahre*.

157. The poet Philaenis of Leucas was defended in her epitaph, composed by Aeschrion, from the charge that she had written *to peri aphrodision akolaston syngramma*, really the work of the Athenian Polycrates.

158. Glycera said to the philosopher Stilpon, referring to the epilogue of the *diaphtheirein tous neous*: 'To the unhappy it makes little difference

whether they live with a courtesan or a philosopher.'

159. Aelian, *Varia Historia* 12.5, 14.35.

160. Plutarch, *Lives of Ten Orators*, on the life of Isocrates.

161. Pausanias 1.37.4.; Athenaeus 13.67; Plutarch, *Phocion* 22.

162. Aelian, *Varia Historia* 2.34, 11.9.

163. Plutarch, *Kings, Epaminondas* 21. Still, the rich men of the sixth and the fifth centuries had not been afraid of danger. The account of the poverty of Epaminondas seems padded out with anecdotes in Aelian, *Varia Historia* 5.5.

164. Plutarch, *Phocion* 18. When the messengers then went to his home, it seems they found his wife kneading bread, and Phocion himself drawing water from the well to wash his feet; he probably had no slave. Aelian (*Varia Historia* 1.25) gives more detail, but it seems partly invented.

165. Just before his death Phocion said to a man condemned with him, who was weeping: 'Why? Are you not happy to die with Phocion?'

VI: *The Hellenistic Age*

1. The passage from Clearchus on perfume and cosmetics seems to suggest this (Athenaeus 15.35).

2. Though Lucian was writing much later, under the Empire, he gives Anacharsis, in the dialogue of the same name, a bantering tone about the athletes which is relevant here. He boasts that with his short sword he can chase off all the bronzed gymnasts howling through the arcades, and declares that the whole practice of gymnastics is the opposite of serious preparation for war. Lucian again, in *Demonax* 16, reports that the Olympic victors were still occasionally full of insolent pride even under the Romans. When Demonax mocked one for wearing a flower-patterned tunic, the athlete

threw a stone and wounded him in the head.

3. Incidentally, in its determination to be always in the right, Athens made no distinction between lost wars and victories when it came to glorifying her heroes on monuments. In the temple of Athena at Piraeus was the portrait of Leosthenes, the general in the Lamian War, with his sons, painted by Arcesilaus, Pausanias 1.1.3.

4. Athenaeus 1.34 f.

5. Athenaeus 10.6: 13.15 (from comic writers). Aelian, *Varia Historia* 1.27, 2.41 (Among the drunkards are several Seleucids).

6. Lists, and detailed accounts, in, among others, Athenaeus 13.37.39 f. 42. *Ibid* 53 on the courtesans of Epicurus and his pupil Leontion.

7. Long extracts from it are given by Athenaeus, 13.39.41 ff.

8. See p. 124 above. Lucian's loathing of Peregrinus is probably not only a matter of his enlightened views, but in any case he dreaded any symptoms that might lead to a new religion.

9. This partly from W. Helbig, *Über die campanische Vasenmalerei* (*Campanian Vase-paintings*) p. 185.

10. It is on record, for instance, that when Aristagoras was in Sparta his rich Ionian dress drew the comment that Milesian customs belonged at home. Empty promises were called the promises of Chares (the well-known Attic mercenary leader). A Taenarian crime was the description given to a very serious offence, because of the murder of the helots by the Spartans at Taenaros. A bold aggressive answer was 'the Scythian word' because the Scythians had told Darius he would come to a bad end. When a judge habitually deferred decisions, people said 'Bulias is sitting' from an old story of a quarrel between Elis and Callione. One who preferred to destroy something himself rather than let an enemy have it would say,

like the Athenians in Xerxes' time, 'The Mede shall not have this in his care.' An oath never to return home was 'a Phocian oath'. Terpander was famous for having pacified the disagreements of the Spartans by his song, and when there was talk of a reconciliation the Spartan expression was 'like the singer from Lesbos'. Even minor insults from the old Attic comedy were current in Alexandria: 'The thigh of Perdix' was a reference to a lame shopkeeper in Attica, who must have been dead for a hundred years. The old Samian metalworker Glaucus was cited when some piece of ironmongery turned out unsatisfactory: 'This is not up to Glaucus' standard.' See Plutarch in *Paroemiographi Graeci*

Elsewhere there are allusions to the sharp eyes and sharp tongues of the Alexandrians. Some of their proverbial expressions referred to: the meanness of offerings made in Phaselis and Caria, the shabbiness of the people of Chalcis in Euboea and of Myconos, the behaviour of the harlots of Corinth, luxury in Massalia and Samos, the simple-mindedness of the inhabitants of Arbelae in Sicily. If people were making business deals in secret, the expression was 'Attic citizens are holding their Eleusinia.' If someone was depressed and cross, he was said to have asked Trophonius for an oracle. Of hospitable people they said: 'There are always guests at Cydon's house' (he was a proverbially generous Corinthian). If you wanted to warn someone of probable ingratitude, a very old event was referred to in the saying 'You may be bringing an oracle to the Boeotians.'

11. Helbig *op. cit.* p. 189 f.
12. We are quite in the dark as to the increase or decrease in slavery. There were still house-slaves as before; but in Egypt, instead of the manufacturing slave, there must now have been Egyptians, whose work in former times (though this was no longer so) had been a matter of caste, but never of slavery. On the great commercial activity which the Emperor Hadrian found in Alexandria, cf. *Historia Augusta, Saturninus* 8.
13. To quote Erwin Rohde, *Der griechische Roman* p. 17.
14. Helbig p. 186; he comments that in the earlier age it would have been impossible to find contemporary types showing such variety as there is between the fiery head of Alexander the Great with its expression of tempestuous energy, the chiselled scholarly features of Aristotle, and the face of Menander with his characteristic glance of ironic observation. Later historical accounts, too, give much more attention to the appearance of the persons involved, the effect they produced and so on, all of which is taken to excess in the later Roman Empire.
15. Plutarch, *Agis* 4.6.20.
16. *Ibid* 17 f. Chilonis, embracing her husband, threatens her father with her immediate suicide if Cleombrotus is condemned to death; it is a pity that the scene is conceived in the style of a post-Euripidean tragic writer.
17. Plutarch, *Cleomenes* 1.6.
18. *Ibid* 22. Though the phrase about the daimon sounds like a bit of interpolated philosophy.
19. *Ibid* 38. Cf. p. 121 above.
20. Plutarch *Agis* 7.
21. Helbig, p. 195 f. is the source for most of this.
22. According to Rohde, *op. cit.* p. 68 ff., from which most of what follows is quoted verbatim.
23. Cornelius Nepos explains in his preface (*Vitae*) that every Roman took his wife with him to the banquet, 'which was very different from the custom in Greece; there the women took no part in banquets unless with close relatives, nor did they sit anywhere except in the inner

part of the house called the women's quarters, where nobody was allowed but members of their family.' That marriage was nothing but a convenient legal arrangement without the slightest emotional content is shown, for example, by Diogenes Laertius, 2.8.14. The philosopher Menedemus and his old friend Asclepiades married a mother and daughter. When the daughter died, Asclepiades married the mother, handed over to him by Menedemus, who himself, now the ruler of the state, took a wealthy wife; but, as he continued to live with Asclepiades, still entrusted the management of the household to his first wife. All this was about the year 300 or later.

24. Diodorus (19.33) protests against young people marrying for love; he is certainly repeating an argument from the time of the *diadochoi*. When the Indian custom of suttee became known, the Greeks of the later period deduced that there must have been many troubled marriages which frequently led to poisonings, and that the marriages had come to grief because they were not arranged by the parents, but agreed on by the couples themselves, so that they were bound to fail when they repented of their choice.

25. In Stobaeus, *Anthology* (ed. Hense) vol. IV, pp. 613–5, where there is much else about the immense advantage of having sons rather than daughters. Cf. also pp. 110–11 above.

26. The many learned women, philosophers, poets and painters (e.g. Crates' Hipparchia from Thebes, Hedyle of Samos, the painter Anaxandra of Sicyon etc.) are such isolated cases as to prove

nothing in general. What follows here is again largely verbatim from Helbig, p. 191 ff.

27. 'Stauffacherin' – the reference is to Gertrud Stauffacher, a fiery-tempered character in Schiller's *Wilhelm Tell*.

28. Rohde points out, though, that the free behaviour of the Adoniazusae can be considered informative only about Alexandria and only about Dorian women (*op. cit.* p. 63 note 1).

29. Helbig p. 194 f.

30. In Pompeian mural paintings of Hellenistic inspiration we can also see how attentively Perseus guides Andromeda down from the rock, and how Aphrodite flirts with Paris at the Judgment: Helbig, p. 201.

31. From Helbig, p. 196 f.

32. Cf. Preller in Pauly's *Realencyclopädie*, vol. 3 p. 1287.

33. Cf. Helbig, pp. 223, 237, 242.

34. Is it possible the Vatican Hermes also dates from this late period?

35. This follows Helbig, p. 244 ff. Rohde, *op. cit.* p. 68, assumes that the learned poetry can only have appealed to educated courtesans. As books then cost so much, it would be good to know more of the kind of men and women who really read this literature.

36. Cf. Helbig on this, p. 249.

37. Cf. Athenaeus 7. 13, where he quotes from Apollodorus of Carystos.

38. Compare, for the earlier period, the account of Phryne, p. 324 above.

39. Cf. p. 121 above.

40. This section too is mostly taken from Helbig, p. 269 ff.

41. Herodotus 7.31. Semiramis' hanging gardens, too, were famous long before.

42. Herodotus 4.85.

43. Livy 40.22.

44. Cf. Helbig, p. 213 f.

Corresponding page numbers of
the German edition and
the English translation

The German text used for this translation is that of Jacob Oeri, revised by F. Staehelin (1930); the pagination is that of the reprint published by the Wissenschaftliche Buchgesellschaft (Darmstadt 1956).

BIBLIOGRAPHY

Ancient sources

References to ancient authors have been revised to standard modern editions, and to the following collections or special editions. Abbreviations are given in square brackets:

Alcidamas, *Odysseus*: L. Radermacher, *Artium Scriptores* (Vienna 1951) pp. 141–7
Bacchylides, ed. B. Snell and L. Maehler, 10th edn. (Leipzig 1970. [Snell-Maehler]
E. Diehl, *Anthologia Lyrica Graeca* I, 3rd edn. (Leipzig 1949) [Diehl]
H. Diels, W. Kranz, *Fragmente der Vorsokratiker*, 6th edn. (Zurich 1951–2) [Diels-Kranz]
Eudocia: *Eudociae Augustae Violarium* ed. I. Flach (Leipzig 1880)
Eustathius, *Commentarii ad Homeri Odysseam*, ed. G. Stallbaum (Leipzig 1825–6)
R. Foerster, *Scriptores Physiognomici Graeci et Latini* I (Leipzig 1893)
Hesiod fragmenta: *Fragmenta Hesiodea*, ed. R. Merkelbach and M. L. West (Oxford 1967) [Merkelbach-West]
Jacobus de Aquis: ed. G. Avogadro in *Historia Patriae Monumenta 3: Scriptorum Tomus* I (Turin 1839)
F. Jacoby, *Die Fragmente der griechischen Historiker* (Berlin-Leiden 1923–58) [*FGH*]
G. Kinkel, *Epicorum Graecorum Fragmenta* I (Leipzig 1877)
E. L. von Leutsch, *Corpus Paroemiographorum Graecorum* (Göttingen 1851)
Lysias fragmenta: *Lysiae Orationes*, ed. T. Thalheim, 2nd edn (Leipzig 1913)
Maximus Planudes, *Life of Aesop*: A. Eberhard, *Fabulae romanenses Graece conscriptae* I (Leipzig 1872) pp. 226–305
R. Meiggs, D. M. Lewis, *Greek Historical Inscriptions* (Oxford 1969)
K. Müller, *Geographi Graeci Minores* (Paris 1855–61)
A. Nauck, *Tragicorum Graecorum Fragmenta* 2nd edn. (Leipzig 1889) [Nauck]
D. L. Page, *Poetae Melici Graeci* (Oxford 1962) [Page]
D. L. Page, *Epigrammata Graeca* (Oxford 1975)
Paroemiographi Graeci: ed. E. L. Leutsch and F. G. Schneidewin (Göttingen 1839–51)
Stobaeus: *Ioanis Stobaei Anthologium* ed. C. Wachsmuth and O. Hense (Berlin 1884–1912)
Suda: Suidae Lexicon, ed. A. Adler (Stuttgart 1928–71)
C. Walz, *Rhetores Graeci* (Stuttgart 1832–6)
M. L. West, *Elegi et Iambi Graeci* (2nd edn. Oxford 1989–92) [West]
A. Westermann, *Biographoi, Vitarum Scriptores Graeci* (Brunswick 1845)
A. Westermann, *Mythographoi, Scriptores Poeticae Historiae Graeci* (Brunswick 1843)

The Greeks and Greek Civilization

Contemporary works cited by Burckhardt:

A. Boeckh, *Die Staatshaushaltung der Athener* 2nd edn (Berlin 1851)

E. Curtius, *Griechische Geschichte* (Berlin 1858–67)

W. Helbig, *Untersuchungen über die campanische Vasenmalerei* (Leipzig 1873)

F. von Hellwald, *Culturgeschichte in ihrer natürlichen Entwicklung bis zur Gegenwart* (Augsburg 1875)

K. F. Hermann, *Lehrbuch der griechischen Privatalterthümer* (Heidelberg 1852)

K. F. Hermann, *Lehrbuch der gottesdienstlichen Alterthümer der Griechen* (Heidelberg 1846)

K. O. Müller, *Handbuch der Archäologie der Kunst* (Breslau 1830)

K. F. Nagelsbach, *Die nachhomerische Theologie des griechischen Volksglaubens* (Nuremberg 1857)

B. G. Niebuhr, *Kleine historische und philologische Schriften* (Bonn 1828)

A. F. von Pauly, *Realencyclopädie der classischen Alterthumswissenschaft* 1st edn. (Frankfurt 1839)

L. Preller, *Griechische Mythologie* (Leipzig 1854)

O. Ribbeck, *Kolax, eine ethologische Studie* (Leipzig 1883)

E. Rohde, *Der griechische Roman und seine Vorläufer* (Leipzig 1876)

A. D. Schäfer, *Demosthenes und seine Zeit* (Leipzig 1856)

Adolf Schmidt, *Das Perikleischer Zeitalter* (Jena 1877)

A. Schwegler, *Geschichte der griechischen Philosophie* (Tübingen 1859)

W. Vischer, 'Über die Benutzung der alten Komödie als geschichtliche Quelle', *Kleine Schriften* (Leipzig 1877) pp. 459–85

F. G. Welcker, 'Die Komposition der polygnotische Gemälde in der Lesche zu Delphi', *Abhandlungen der Preussischen Akademie der Wissenschaften zu Berlin 1847, Philol.-hist. Abtheilung* pp. 81–151

INDEX

abortion, 54

abuse: verbal (*loidoria*), 72, 144–5, 207, 208, 233–4; of language, 237

Achaean League, the, 31, 34, 121, 359

Achaeans, the, 14, 43–4, 44, 174, 180, 358

Achaemenids, the, 216

Achilles, 22, 23, 24, 30, 32, 33, 88, 89, 90, 90–1, 93, 95–6, 141ff., 149ff., 156, 164, 200, 201, 244, 249, 360

actors, 346, 355

adoption, 38, 209, 338–9

adultery, 37, 200, 252, 253–4, 258

Aegina, 16, 32, 227, 296, 305, 316, 326

Aegospotami, battle of, 218, 250, 277, 293, 295, 296

Aeolians, the, 14, 201

Aeschines, 78, 309, 310, 311, 314

Aeschylus, 10, 19, 22, 56, 65, 144, 166, 254, 271, 277, 324

Aesop, 202, 208–9

Aetolian League, 276

Aetolians, the, 14, 18, 34, 168

afterlife, the, xxxix, 27, 33, 101, 113–14, 278; *see also* 'Hades'

Agamemnon, 24, 26, 32, 67, 101, 141, 145, 150, 153, 154, 164, 200

Agathocles, 107, 121, 286

Agathon, 230, 262, 263, 264

Agesilaus, 25, 171, 194, 287, 293, 335, 341

agon (contest), agonal competition, xxxii, xli, 71, 79, 96, 149, 155, 157, 160, 161, 162–6, 167ff., 174ff., 179, 181, 182, 184, 185, 188, 196, 199, 201, 205, 206, 207, 212, 219, 225, 237ff., 249, 251, 286, 294, 321, 326–8, 331, 332, 333, 348; false, 238; *see also* 'first and best', 'judges', 'number and variety', 'Panhellenic agon', 'prizes', 'success', 'victors'

agora, the, 49, 50–2, 51–3, 73, 183, 198, 204, 264, 286, 298, 315, 325, 353

agorazein, 52, 264

agriculture, 16–17, 21, 45, 47, 51, 156, 157, 188–90, 217, 218, 219, 222, 304; *see also* 'farming', 'field work', 'peasants', 'rural life', 'shepherds', 'slaves', 'viticulture'

aidos, 79, 79–80

Alcibiades, 33, 60, 171, 230, 231, 233, 239–40, 243, 245, 245–8, 250, 262–3, 264, 265, 276, 290

Alexander the Great, xxxvii, xl, xli, 26, 33, 118, 172, 193, 214, 283, 294, 314, 316, 320, 328, 331, 341, 345, 349, 353, 359

Alexandria, Alexandrian, 119, 126, 271, 347, 355, 356, 359, 360, 361, 363

alliances, allies, 44, 57, 225ff., 231, 274, 283, 287, 293ff., 305–6, 308, 310ff.

alphabet, source of Greek, 17

Amazons, the, 22, 26, 31, 131, 154, 197, 220, 221, 223

ambition, 58, 78, 175, 212, 225, 247, 274, 275, 279, 295, 298, 304, 320, 322, 349–50; *see also* 'self-display'

amiable conduct, and the Greeks, 261

amphictyoniai (temple leagues), 44

amusement, as the aim of life, in Athens, 205; *see also* 'pleasure'

amusements, 259, 298, 306, 332; *see also* 'symposium'

Anaxagoras, 111, 225, 232, 270, 271, 272

ancestry, importance of, 33, 37, 42, 104, 290, 356; *see also* 'breeding and birth', 'heredity'

ancient institutions, admiration of, as rejection of the state, 326

anger, and the hero, 66, 145

animals: mythological, 19–20, 154; fabulous, and the value of life, 112; and naming, 132; *see also* 'fables'

anointing, of the whole body, 129

Antigonus Gonatas of Macedon, 32, 33–4, 123

Antioch, 50, 355, 359, 363

antiquarians, xix, xx, xxx, 3–4, 4–5, 6, 9, 21, 30

antiquities, 316

Antisthenes, 123, 192, 193, 325

Apelles, 324, 331

Aphrodite, 81, 142, 145, 151, 153, 154, (Pandemos) 202, 210, 324, 330, 360

apolitia, 289, 290, 294, 317, 355; *see also* 'cosmopolitanism', 'indifference', 'turning away'

Apollo, 29ff., 43, 81, 83, 88, 89, 117, 141, 143, 148, 156, 163, 168, 181, 183, 191, 196, 204, 207, 211, 219, 220, 242, 254, 288, 328, 361

Apollodorus, 131, 341

Apollonian and Dionysian, the, xxvii, xxxviii, 211

creativity, and the Greeks, 133, 135

crime, criminality, 301, 322, 334–5

crisis in Greek life, 277, 278

Critias, 243, 271

Croesus, 65, 102, 171, 206, 209

Croton, 49, 83, 169, 175, 211, 212, 318

cruelty, Athenian, 308

cuckoldry, 74, 254

cult, cults, xxxvii, 22, 24, 29, 37, 38, 42, 46, 48, 50, 57, 58, 58–9, 64, 133, 138, 167, 168, 174, 176, 182, 206, 207, 211, 212, 233, 250, 251, 273, 288, 330, 350, 356

cultural history, xvi–xvii, xxiii–xxiv, xxx– xxxii, xxxii–xli, 3ff., 12, 63, 85, 254, 277, 282, 350

cunning, 144, 257, 275, 300

cupidity, (for significant objects, not treasure), and the heroic world, 150

curses, 26, 27, 141, 152, 174, 200, 248

Cynicism, the Cynics, 77, 98, 123, 198, 333, 344

Cyrus the Elder, 52, 69, 214

Cyrus the Younger, 257, 318

dances, dancing, 27, 148, 156, 157, 161, 162, 169, 205, 231, 259, 263

Darius, 214, 215, 242, 362

death, attitude to and evaluation of, 81, 85, 90–1, 94–5, 98, 99, 103ff., 111ff., 121ff., 141, 146, 172, 173, 206, 260, 316; *see also* 'departure from mankind', 'exposure', 'suicide'

decadence (decline, disintegration, decay), 56, 81, 162, 230, 237, 264, 274ff., 280, 283–4, 288, 289–90, 291, 293, 294, 304, 307, 316–17, 317, 322, 329, 330, 336, 343, 346, 347, 348, 359 359–60; *see also* 'degeneration', 'theorizing'

deceitfulness, dishonesty, xxxviii, 5, 68–71, 80, 144, 247, 250–1, 275, 277, 278, 297, 300, 301, 302, 351; *see also* 'lawcourts', 'truth'

defeat in war, consequences of, 96 117ff., 215, 247, 274–5, 282ff., 293, 295, 312–13, 330

defence, of the *polis*, and divided counsels of *banausoi*, 190

deformity, and the Greeks, 54, 74, 110, 130, 190, 193

degeneration, 100, 142, 155, 290–1; *see also* 'breeding and birth', 'heredity'

deisidaimonia, 271, 272, 273, 354; *see also* 'fear of the gods', 'religion'

delicacy of feeling, of the Homeric world, 65, (*aidos*) 79–80, 135, 146

Delphi, Delphic oracle (the Pythia), xxxvii, 17, 29, 49, 49–50, 82, 89, 92, 102, 141, 174, 176, 178–9, 180, 197, 202, 207, 209, 210–11, 213, 220, 223, 250, 265, 267, 271, 272, 293, 323, 325, 328, 352; *see also* 'Pythian games'

demagogues, demagogy, xxxvi, 27, 74, 246, 257, 278, 290, 295, 316, 345

Demeter, 17, 21, 33, (Chamyne) 177, (Eleusinian) 201, 207

Demetrius Poliorcetes, 358, 362

democracy, democracies, democrats, the democratic, xxxvi, 59, 59, 60, 73, 96, 131, 162, 170, 185, 186, 189, 191, 215, 216, 222, 227, 228, 229, 231, 238, 239, 240, 240–1, 245, 246, 247, 273, 274, 275, 278, 279, 282, 286, 289ff., 295, 296, 298, 307ff., 316, 320, 322, 326, 327, 329, 345, 353

Democritus, 109, 113, 122–3, 325, 328

demos, the, xxxvi, 47, 74, 75, 189, 229, 292–3, 306, 308, 313, 333, 345; *see also* 'people'

Demosthenes, xxxvii, 30, 56, 78, 80, 111, 191, 223, 224, 230, 271, 290, 292, 302, 303, 304, 308ff., 310–12, 313, 314, 316, 316–17, 317, 333, 339, 342, 343

denunciation (public accusation), 73, 96, 196, 218, 219, 281, 301, 307, 313, 345; *see also* '*asebeia*', 'lawcourts'

departure from mankind, mysterious, 33, 176, 184

descent, from gods or heroes, 16, 20, 32–4, 142, 176, 242, 278, 322

destiny, 65, 93, 99, 102, 358; *see also* 'fate'

devotion to the state (*polis*), 186, 243, 245, 248, 322

diadochoi, the, 33, 40, 48, 50, 100, 132, 181, 250, 332, 335, 337, 340, 346ff., 355, 356, 358, 359, 361

Diagoras of Melos, 176, 271, 272

dialectic, 268; *see also* 'Socratic dialectic'

dialogue, the philosophical, 182, 246, 262, 268

dignity, and the hero, 140

dilettantism, the dilettante, 183, 195, 239, 357

Diodorus, 19, 131, 294

Diogenes, 77, 123, 305, 320, 325, 327, 333

dioikizein (to send to separate districts), 49; *see also* 'synoecism'

Diomedes, 22, 31, 91–2, 129, 137, 138, 141, 143, 145, 155, 164

Dion, 285, 319, 320, 340

Dionysian, the, *see* 'Apollonian and Dionysian'

Dionysian: festivals (Dionysiae), 61, 73, 207, 211, 232, 233, 234, 260, 277, 304; mysteries, 211; excess, 212

Dionysius the Elder, 30, 132, 175, 178, 283, 284–5, 286, 290, 294, 318, 321, 328, 340

Dionysius the Younger, 261, 285, 319, 332, 337, 340

Dionysus, (Kissos) 17, 20, 29, 35, 131, 211, 288, 330; *see also* 'Dionysian'

disaster, its ideal purpose in Greek mythology, 95, 150

discus- and javelin-throwing, 163, 167

dishonour, and suicide, 120–2

Index

prime of life, the, 91, 107, 128

private: life, 224, 231, 244, 259, 273, 280, 300, 324ff., 336, 355, 358; luxury, 304, 330, 343, *see also* 'luxury'

prizes, agonal, 164, 165, 170ff., 174, 178, 181, 183, 238, 328

Prodicus of Ceos, 265, 267

profit, 71, 300

'progress', and the Greeks, 135–6; progress, and Athens, 226, 245

proletariat, urban, 52, 356

Prometheus, 16, 87, 101, 136, 200

property: rights of, 37, 37–8, 38; common, 38; personal, and the *polis*, 58; in Hesiod's world, 158; income from, 185; universal equality of, 276; loss of, by son, 280, 291; *see also* 'ownership'

prophecy, prophets, 92–3, 176, 278; prophets of new religions, 250; *see also* '*mantis*', 'seers'

prosperity, as a blessing of life, 81, 82; *see also* '*olbos*', 'wealth'

prostitution, prostitutes, 200, 201, 202, 257; *see also* 'harlots', 'hetaerae', 'whores'

Protagoras of Abdera, 265, 266, 268, 269

prudence (imprudence), 99, 245, 273, 276, 280

prytaneion, 45, 51, 73, 220

psephismata (popular decrees), 60

Ptolemies, the, 355, 358, 363

Ptolemy (III) Euergetes, 349, 357, 358

public: speaking, 229, 239, 266; opinion, 241, 253–4; finance, 299, 301, 308–9; works, 304; *see also* 'oratory', 'political life', 'taxes and tithes'

publicity, 178–9, 239, 240, 250, 265, 321, 342, 350

punishment: (penalties) in the *polis*, 46, 57, 61, 67, 78, 79, 114, 196, 203, 218, 229, 242, 247, 258, 279, 294, 299, 300, 301, 304, 307, 313, 316, 325, 335, 345; after death, 101, 113, 114, 278, 345

purification (*katharsis*), 141, 354

purity, of the Homeric world, 65, 146

Pythagoras, 35, 56, 68, 77, 97, 211–12, 318

Pythagoreanism, the (Italian) Pythagoreans, 101, 114, 122, 212, 317, 318–19, 319, 340, 344

Pythian games, the, 164, 169, 171, 178, 181–2, 183

races, fabulous or half-fabulous, 25, 139, 148

rape, (the threat of) 120, 200

reading, 356; *see also* 'learning', 'libraries'

realism, and Homer, 143–4, 156

reason, 205, 271, 273

recklessness, rashness, 226, 228, 243, 245, 274, 312

recognition (*anagnorisis*), of offspring, 110, 200

reflection, (and sensibility) 65, 205, 222, 271, 273, 317; philosophical, 210

refuge, refugees, 215, 219, 221, 230, 286, 319, 325

religion, xxxvii–xxxviii, 37, 57–8, 58, 60, 64, 101, 161, 182, 204, 206, 210–12, 214, 266, 273, 278, 288, 298, 319, 328, 349, 354, 356, 357; the *polis* as itself a, 58, 288; *see also* '*deisidaimonia*', 'cult', 'gods', 'monotheism', 'oracles', 'pollution', 'polytheism', 'prophecy', 'purification', 'ritual', 'sacrifice', 'soothsayer', 'temples'

renunciation: of pleasure, 344; of political life, *see* 'turning away'

repentance, 101, 298; and the hero, 140

reputation: a noble or high, as a blessing of life, 82, 82–3; pride of, 290

resentment, and the gods, 66

resignation, and the Greeks, 95

respect, 83, 251, 252, 291, 299, 322, 359; *see also* 'disrespect'

restlessness, general, 274

revenge, vengeance, xxxviii, 61, 66–8, 72–3, 87, 88, 141, 229, 275, 303, 315; *see also* 'divine wrath'

reverence, due to parents and the dead, 315–16

revolutions, 275; city-, 295

rewards: in the *polis* (civic honours), 57, 61, 94, 174, 196, 249–50, 265, 306, 308, 314, 320–21, 322–3; in the afterworld, 113, 278; divine, on earth, 278; *see also* 'honours', 'prizes'

rhapsodes, 15, 178, 181, 327

rhetoric, rhetoricians, 24, 167, 223, 224, 267, 268, 270, 328, 330; *see also* 'eloquence', 'oratory', 'sophists'

riches: and ostentatious display, 84, 198, 235, 239, 241, 304; (with intelligence), as a blessing of life, 85; and political leadership, 235; new, 239; refusal of proffered, 244–5; *see also* 'wealth'

riddles, 259, 332

ridicule, and philosophy, 77; *see also* 'mockery'

right of the stronger, doctrine of the, 266

rights: discussion of, 213; demand for, not duties, 301

ritual, rites, 35, 140, 177, 207, 225, 278, 315, 340; *see also* 'purification'

Rome, Empire, the Romans, 12, 23–4, 31, 32, 34, 36, 40, 58, 70, 96, 109, 110, 110–11, 112, 121, 123, 130, 163, 193, 223, 242–3, 267, 268, 282, 283, 284, 289, 333, 337, 350, 359

rule of law, the, 59

rulers and ruled, in the *polis*, 55, 60–61, 66, 96, 185, 187, 188, 189, 279, 282, 285, 292, 297; *see also* 'political life'